WINNING WAYS

WINNING WAYS

for your mathematical plays

VOLUME 2: GAMES IN PARTICULAR

Elwyn R. Berlekamp
John H. Conway
Richard K. Guy

1982

ACADEMIC PRESS

London   New York
Paris   San Diego   San Francisco
São Paulo   Sydney   Tokyo   Toronto

A Subsidiary of Harcourt Brace Jovanovich, Publishers

ACADEMIC PRESS INC. (LONDON) LTD
24/28 Oval Road,
London NW1 7DX

United States Edition published by
ACADEMIC PRESS INC.
111 Fifth Avenue,
New York, New York 10003

British Library Cataloguing in Publication Data

Berlekamp, E. R.
　Winning Ways, Vol. 2
　1. Mathematical recreations
　I. Title　II. Conway, J. H.　III. Guy, R. K.
　793.7′4　　QA95　　LCCCN 81-66678
ISBN 0-12-091152-3

Text set in 10/12pt Times, printed
in Great Britain by Page Bros (Norwich) Ltd.
Mile Cross Lane, Norwich

To Martin Gardner

who has brought more mathematics
to more millions than anyone else

Elwyn Berlekamp was born in Dover, Ohio, on September 6, 1940. After spending two years as Assistant Professor at the University of California, Berkeley, and five years at the Bell Telephone Laboratories, in 1971 he became Professor of Mathematics and Electrical Engineering–Computer Science at Berkeley.

His book *Algebraic Coding Theory* received the best research paper award of the IEEE Information Theory Group. Eta Kappa Nu named him the "Outstanding Young Electrical Engineer" of 1971 in the US, and he has been President of the IEEE Information Theory Society. In 1977 he was elected to membership of the US National Academy of Engineering.

John Conway was born in Liverpool, England, on December 26, 1937. He is a Fellow of Gonville and Caius College and a former Fellow of Sidney Sussex College, Cambridge, and is Reader in Pure Mathematics at the University of Cambridge. He has held visiting professorships at several universities and has made original contributions to many branches of mathematics, notably transfinite arithmetic, the theory of knots, many-dimensional geometry and the theory of symmetry (group theory).

He has published two previous books, *Regular Algebra and Finite Machines* and *On Numbers and Games*. He has recently been made a Fellow of the Royal Society.

Richard Guy was born in Nuneaton, England, on September 30, 1916. He has taught mathematics at many levels and in many places—England, Singapore, India, Canada. Since 1965 he has been Professor of Mathematics at the University of Calgary and he is a member of the Board of Governors of the Mathematical Association of America.

He edits the Unsolved Problems section of American Mathematical Monthly; he wrote the volume on Number Theory for the series *Unsolved Problems in Intuitive Mathematics* and is preparing another on Combinatorics, Graph Theory and Game Theory. He is a keen member of the Alpine Club of Canada.

Preface

Does a book need a Preface? What more, after fifteen years of toil, do three talented authors have to add.

We can reassure the bookstore browser, "Yes, this is just the book you want!"

We can direct you, if you want to know quickly what's in the book, to the last page of this preliminary material. This in turn directs you to pages 1, 255, 427 and 695.

We can supply the reviewer, faced with the task of ploughing through nearly a thousand information-packed pages, with some pithy criticisms by indicating the horns of the polylemma the book finds itself on. It is not an encyclopedia. It is encyclopedic, but there are still too many games missing for it to claim to be complete. It is not a book on recreational mathematics because there's too much serious mathematics in it. On the other hand, for us, as for our predecessors Rouse Ball, Dudeney, Martin Gardner, Kraitchik, Sam Loyd, Lucas, Tom O'Beirne and Fred. Schuh, mathematics itself is a recreation. It is not an undergraduate text, since the exercises are not set out in an orderly fashion, with the easy ones at the beginning. They are there though, and with the hundred and sixty-three mistakes we've left in, provide plenty of opportunity for reader participation. So don't just stand back and admire it, work of art though it is. It is not a graduate text, since it's too expensive and contains far more than any graduate student can be expected to learn. But it does carry you to the frontiers of research in combinatorial game theory and the many unsolved problems will stimulate further discoveries.

We thank Patrick Browne for our title. This exercised us for quite a time. One morning, while walking to the university, John and Richard came up with "Whose game?" but realized they couldn't spell it (there are three tooze in English) so it became a one-line joke on line one of the text. There isn't room to explain all the jokes, not even the fifty-nine private ones (each of our birthdays appears more than once in the book).

Omar started as a joke, but soon materialized as Kimberley King. Louise Guy also helped with proof-reading, but her greater contribution was the hospitality which enabled the three of us to work together on several occasions. Louise also did technical typing after many drafts had been made by Karen McDermid and Betty Teare.

Our thanks for many contributions to content may be measured by the number of names in the index. To do real justice would take too much space. Here's an abridged list of helpers: Richard Austin, Clive Bach, John Beasley, Aviezri Fraenkel, David Fremlin, Solomon Golomb, Steve Grantham, Mike Guy, Dean Hickerson, Hendrick Lenstra, Richard Nowakowski, Anne Scott, David Seal, John Selfridge, Cedric Smith and Steve Tschantz.

No small part of the reason for the assured success of the book is owed to the well-informed and sympathetic guidance of Len Cegielka and the willingness of the staff of Academic Press and of Page Bros. to adapt to the idiosyncrasies of the authors, who grasped every opportunity to modify grammar, strain semantics, pervert punctuation, alter orthography, tamper with traditional typography and commit outrageous puns and inside jokes.

Thanks also the the Isaak Walton Killam Foundation for Richard's Resident Fellowship at The University of Calgary during the compilation of a critical draft, and to the National (Science & Engineering) Research Council of Canada for a grant which enabled Elwyn and John to visit him more frequently than our widely scattered habitats would normally allow.

And thank you, Simon!

University of California, Berkeley, CA 94720   *Elwyn Berlekamp*
University of Cambridge, England, CB2 1SB   *John Conway*
University of Calgary, Canada, T2N 1N4   *Richard Guy*

Contents

Biography   ix

Preface   xi

Contents of Volume 1   xxiii

♣

GAMES IN CLUBS!

Chapter 14   **Turn and Turn About**   **429**

TURNING TURTLES 429
MOCK TURTLES 431
ODIOUS AND EVIL NUMBERS 431
MOEBIUS, MOGUL AND GOLD MOIDORES 432
THE MOCK TURTLE THEOREM 432
WHY MOEBIUS? 434
MOGUL 435
MOTLEY 437
TWINS, TRIPLETS, ETC. 437
THE RULER GAME 437
CIRCUMSCRIBED GAMES 438
TURNIPS (OR TERNUPS) 438
GRUNT 440
SYM 441
TWO-DIMENSIONAL TURNING GAMES 441
ACROSTIC TWINS 441
TURNING CORNERS 441
NIM-MULTIPLICATION 443
SWIRLING TARTANS 444
THE TARTAN THEOREM 445
RUGS, CARPETS, WINDOWS AND DOORS 446
ACROSTIC GAMES 450
STRIPPING AND STREAKING 451
UGLIFICATION AND DERISION 451

Extras
UNLOCKING DOORS 456
SPARRING, BOXING AND FENCING 456
COINS (OR HEAPS) WITH INFINITELY
MANY (OR 2^{2^N}) "SIDES" 456
REFERENCES AND FURTHER READING 456

Chapter 15 **Chips and Strips**   **457**

THE SILVER DOLLAR GAME 457
PROFIT FROM GAMING TABLES 458
ANTONIM 459
SYNONIM 460
SIMONIM 462
STAIRCASE FIVES 465
TWOPINS 466
CRAM 468
WELTER'S GAME 472
FOUR-COIN WELTER IS JUST NIM 473
AND SO'S THREE-COIN WELTER! 473
THE CONGRUENCE MODULO 16 473
FRIEZE PATTERNS 475
INVERTING THE WELTER FUNCTION 477
THE ABACUS POSITIONS 478
THE ABACUS STRATEGY 479
THE MISÈRE FORM OF WELTER'S GAME 480
KOTZIG'S NIM 481
FIBONACCI NIM 483
MORE GENERALLY BOUNDED NIM 483
EPSTEIN'S PUT-OR-TAKE-A-SQUARE GAME 484
TRIBULATIONS AND FIBULATIONS 486
THIRD ONE LUCKY 486
HICKORY, DICKORY, DOCK 487
D.U.D.E.N.E.Y. 487
STRINGS OF PEARLS 488
SCHUHSTRINGS 489
THE PRINCESS AND THE ROSES 490
ONE-STEP, TWO-STEP 495
MORE ON SUBTRACTION GAMES 495
MOORE'S NIM_k 498
THE MORE THE MERRIER 499
MOORE AND MORE 499
NOT WITH BANG BUT A WHIM 500

Extras
DID YOU WIN THE SILVER DOLLAR? 501
HOW WAS YOUR ARITHMETIC? 501
IN PUT-OR-TAKE-A-SQUARE, 92 IS AN $\mathcal{N}$-POSITION 501
TRIBULATIONS AND FIBULATIONS 501
OUR CODE OF BEHAVIOR FOR PRINCES 503
REFERENCES AND FURTHER READING 505

Chapter 16 **Dots-and-Boxes**   **507**

DOUBLE-DEALING LEADS TO DOUBLE-CROSSES 509
HOW LONG IS "LONG"? 512
THE 4-BOX GAME 513
THE 9-BOX GAME 515
THE 16-BOX GAME 515

OTHER SHAPES OF BOARD 516
DOTS-AND-BOXES AND STRINGS-AND-COINS 516
NIMSTRING 518
WHY LONG IS LONG 520
TO TAKE OR NOT TO TAKE A COIN IN NIMSTRING 521
SPRAGUE-GRUNDY THEORY FOR NIMSTRING GRAPHS 522
ALL LONG CHAINS ARE THE SAME 527
WHICH MUTATIONS ARE HARMLESS? 528
CHOPPING AND CHANGING 530
VINES 530

Extras
DOTS + DOUBLECROSSES = TURNS 537
HOW DODIE CAN WIN THE 4-BOX GAME 538
WHEN IS IT BEST TO LOSE CONTROL? 540
COMPUTING THE VALUES OF VINES 541
LOONY ENDGAMES ARE NP-HARD 543
SOLUTIONS TO DOT-AND-BOXES PROBLEMS 544
SOME MORE NIMSTRING VALUES 546
NIMBERS FOR NIMSTRING ARRAYS 548
REFERENCES AND FURTHER READING 550

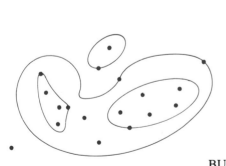

Chapter 17 **Spots and Sprouts** **551**

RIMS 551
RAILS 552
LOOPS-AND-BRANCHES 552
CONTOURS 553
LUCASTA 554
A CHILD'S GUIDE TO NORMAL LUCASTA 555
THE MISÈRE FORM OF LUCASTA 556
THE POSITIONS (7, 3, 1) AND (11, 1, 1) 560
CABBAGES; OR BUGS, CATERPILLARS
AND COCOONS 563
JOCASTA 563
SPROUTS 564
BRUSSELS SPROUTS 569
STARS-AND-STRIPES 569
BUSHENHACK 570
GENETIC CODES FOR NIM 571
BUSHENHACK POSITIONS HAVE GENETIC CODES! 572
VON NEUMANN HACKENBUSH 572

Extras
THE JOKE IN JOCASTA 573
THE WORM IN BRUSSELS SPROUTS 573
BUSHENHACK 573
REFERENCES AND FURTHER READING 573

Chapter 18 **The Emperor and His Money**   575

{16}, {18}, {24}, {27}, {32}, {36}, . . .?

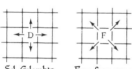

SYLVER COINAGE 576
HOW LONG WILL IT LAST? 576
SOME OPENINGS ARE BAD 577
ARE ALL OPENINGS BAD? 579
NOT ALL OPENINGS ARE BAD 581
STRATEGY STEALING 582
QUIET ENDS 583
DOUBLING AND TRIPLING? 586
HALVING AND THIRDING? 586
FINDING THE RIGHT COMBINATIONS 587
WHAT SHALL I DO WHEN g IS TWO? 592
THE GREAT UNKNOWN 595
ARE OUTCOMES COMPUTABLE? 596
THE ETIQUETTE OF SYLVER COINAGE 597

Extras
CHOMP 598
ZIG-ZAG 598
MORE CLIQUES FOR SYLVER COINAGE 602
5-PAIRS 602
POSITIONS CONTAINING 6 602
SYLVER COINAGE HAS INFINITE NIM-VALUES 606
A FEW FINAL QUESTIONS 606
REFERENCES AND FURTHER READING 606

Chapter 19 **The King and the Consumer**   607

CHESSGO, KINGGO AND DUKEGO 607
QUADRAPHAGE 608
THE ANGEL AND THE SQUARE-EATER 609
STRATEGY AND TACTICS 609
DUKEGO 610
THE GAME OF KINGGO 611
THE EDGE ATTACK 611
THE EDGE DEFENCE 613
A MEMORYLESS EDGE DEFENCE 613
THE EDGE-CORNER ATTACK 617
STRATEGIC AND TACTICAL STONES 618
CORNER TACTICS 618
DEFENCE ON LARGE SQUARE BOARDS 622
THE 33 × 33 BOARD 623
THE CENTRED KING 624
LEAVING THE CENTRAL REGION 624
THE CORNERED KING 627
THE SIDELINED KING 627
HOW CHAS. CAN WIN ON A 34 × 34 BOARD 629
RECTANGULAR BOARDS 630

Extras
MANY-DIMENSIONAL ANGELS 631

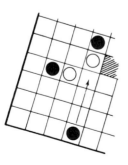

Sol Golomb's
Duke

Ferz, forerunner
of Chess Queen

GAMES OF ENCIRCLEMENT 631
WOLVES-AND-SHEEP 631
TABLUT 632
SAXON HNEFATAFL 632
KING AND ROOK VERSUS KING 633
REFERENCES AND FURTHER READING 634

Chapter 20   Fox and Geese   635

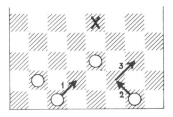

SOME PROPERTIES OF OUR STRATEGY 638
THE SIZE OF THE GEESE'S ADVANTAGE 639
THE PARADOX 642
PUNCHING THE CLOCK 644

Extras
MAHARAJAH AND SEPOYS 646
REFERENCES AND FURTHER READING 646

Chapter 21   Hare and Hounds   647

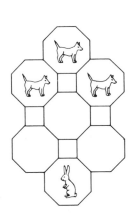

THE FRENCH MILITARY HUNT 647
TWO TRIAL GAMES 649
HISTORY 649
THE DIFFERENT KINDS OF PLACE 649
THE OPPOSITION 650
WHEN HAS THE HARE ESCAPED? 651
LOSING THE OPPOSITION 652
A STRATEGY FOR THE HARE 654
ON THE SMALL BOARD 657
ON THE MEDIUM AND LARGER BOARDS 658

Extras
ANSWERS TO QUESTIONS 661
A SOUND BOUND FOR A HOUND? 661
ALL IS FOUND FOR THE SMALL BOARD HOUND 661
PROOF OF THE THIRTY-ONE THEOREM 665
REFERENCES AND FURTHER READING 665

Chapter 22   Lines and Squares   667

TIT-TAT-TOE, MY FIRST GO, THREE JOLLY
BUTCHER BOYS ALL IN A ROW 667
MAGIC FIFTEEN 668
SPIT NOT SO, FAT FOP, AS IF IN PAN! 668

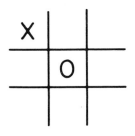

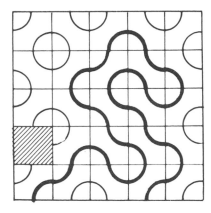

JAM 668
HOW LONG CAN YOU FOOL YOUR FRIENDS? 669
ANALYSIS OF TIC-TAC-TOE 669
OVID'S GAME, HOPSCOTCH, LES PENDUS 672
SIX MEN'S MORRIS 673
NINE MEN'S MORRIS 673
THREE UP 673
FOUR-IN-A-ROW 673
FIVE-IN-A-ROW 674
GO-MOKU 676
SIX, SEVEN, EIGHT, NINE, . . ., IN A ROW 676
n-DIMENSIONAL k-IN-A-ROW 678
STRATEGY STEALING IN TIC-TAC-TOE GAMES 679
HEX 680
BRIDGIT 680
HOW DOES THE FIRST PLAYER WIN? 680
THE SHANNON SWITCHING GAME 680
THE BLACK PATH GAME 682
LEWTHWAITE'S GAME 683
MEANDER 683
WINNERS AND LOSERS 684
DODGEM 685
DODGERYDOO 687
PHILOSOPHER'S FOOTBALL 688

Extras
REFERENCES AND FURTHER READING 692

SOLITAIRE DIAMONDS!

Chapter 23 **Purging Pegs Properly**   **697**

CENTRAL SOLITAIRE 698
DUDENEY, BERGHOLT AND BEASLEY 699
PACKAGES AND PURGES 701
PACKAGES PROVIDE PERFECT PANACEA 703
THE RULE OF TWO AND THE RULE OF THREE 705
SOME PEGS ARE MORE EQUAL THAN OTHERS 706
REISS'S 16 SOLITAIRE POSITION CLASSES 708
THE CONTINENTAL BOARD 711
PLAYING BACKWARDS AND FORWARDS 711
PAGODA FUNCTIONS 712
THE SOLITAIRE ARMY 715
MANAGING YOUR RESOURCES 717
UNPRODUCTIVITY AND THE PRODIGAL SON 719
DEFICIT ACCOUNTING AND THE G.N.P. 720
ACCOUNTING FOR TWO-PEG REVERSAL PROBLEMS 720
FORGETTING THE ORDER CAN BE USEFUL 721
BEASLEY'S EXIT THEOREMS 723

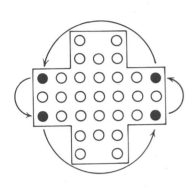

A STOLID SURVIVOR PROBLEM 723
ANOTHER HARD PROBLEM 725
THE SPINNER 727

Extras
OUR FINE FINALIST 728
DOING THE SPLITS 728
ALL SOLUBLE ONE-PEG PROBLEMS ON THE
CONTINENTAL BOARD 729
THE LAST TWO MOVES 729
A 20-MAN SOLITAIRE ARMY 729
FOOL'S SOLITAIRE, ETC. 729
BEASLEY PROVES BERGHOLT IS BEST 731
THE CLASSICAL PROBLEMS 733
REFERENCES AND FURTHER READING 734

Chapter 24 **Pursuing Puzzles Purposefully**   **735**

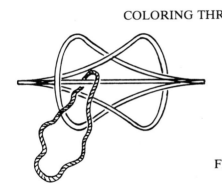

SOMA 735
BLOCKS-IN-A-BOX 736
HIDDEN SECRETS 736
THE HIDDEN SECRETS OF SOMA 737
HOFFMAN'S ARITHMETICO-GEOMETRIC PUZZLE 739
COLORING THREE-BY-THREE-BY-THREE BY THREE, BAR THREE 740
WIRE AND STRING PUZZLES 741
THE MAGIC MIRROR METHOD 741
BARMY BRAID 745
THE ARTFUL ARROW 746
THE MAGIC MOVIE METHOD 746
PARTY TRICKS AND CHINESE RINGS 748
CHINESE RINGS AND THE GRAY CODE 750
THE TOWER OF HANOÏ 753
A SOLITAIRE-LIKE PUZZLE AND SOME COIN-
SLIDING PROBLEMS 755
FIFTEEN PUZZLE AND THE LUCKY SEVEN PUZZLE 756
ALL OTHER COURSES FOR POINT-TO-POINT 759
THE HUNGARIAN CUBE—BÜVÖS KOCKA 760
JUST HOW CHAOTIC CAN THE CUBE GET? 761
CHIEF COLORS AND CHIEF FACES 761
CURING THE CUBE 763
A: ALOFT, AROUND (ADJUST) AND ABOUT 764
B: BOTTOM LAYER CORNER CUBELETS 764
C: CENTRAL LAYER EDGE CUBELETS 764
D: DOMICILING THE TOP EDGE CUBELETS 764
E: EXCHANGING PAIRS OF TOP CORNERS 766
F: FINISHING FLIPS AND FIDDLES 766
EXPLANATIONS 766
IMPROVEMENTS 767
ELENA'S ELEMENTS 768
ARE YOU PARTIAL TO PARTIAL PUZZLES? 768
OTHER "HUNGARIAN" OBJECTS 768
A TRIO OF SLIDING BLOCK PUZZLES 769
TACTICS FOR SOLVING SUCH PUZZLES 770

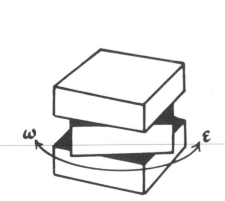

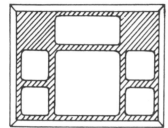

COUNTING YOUR MOVES 777
PARADOXICAL PENNIES 777
PARADOXICAL DICE 778
MORE ON MAGIC SQUARES 778
THE MAGIC TESSERACT 783
ADAMS'S AMAZING MAGIC HEXAGON 784
THE GREAT TANTALIZER 784
POLYOMINOES, POLYIAMONDS AND SEARCHING POLICY 786
ALAN SCHOEN'S CYCLOTOME 789
MACMAHON'S SUPERDOMINOES 791
QUINTOMINAL DODECAHEDRA 792
THE DOOMSDAY RULE 795
. . . AND EASTER EASILY 797
HOW OLD IS THE MOON? 799
JEWISH NEW YEAR (ROSH HASHANA) 800

Extras
BLOCKS-IN-A-BOX 801
THE SOMAP 801
SOLUTIONS TO THE ARITHMETICO-GEOMETRIC
PUZZLE 804
. . . AND ONE FOR "THREE" TOO! 807
HARES AND TORTOISES 807
THE LUCKY SEVEN PUZZLE 807
TOP FACE ALTERATIONS FOR THE HUNGARIAN CUBE 808
THE CENTURY PUZZLE 810
ADAMS'S AMAZING MAGIC HEXAGON 810
FLAGS OF THE ALLIES SOLUTION 811
ANSWER TO EXERCISE FOR EXPERTS 811
WHERE DO THE BLACK EDGES OF MACMAHON
SQUARES GO? 812
THE THREE QUINTOMINAL DODECAHEDRA 813
DOOMSDAY ANSWERS 813
REFERENCES AND FURTHER READING 813

Chapter 25 **What is Life?** **817**

STILL LIFE 819
LIFE CYCLES 820
THE GLIDER AND OTHER SPACE SHIPS 821
THE UNPREDICTABILITY OF LIFE 824
GARDENS OF EDEN 828
LIFE'S PROBLEMS ARE HARD! 829
MAKING A LIFE COMPUTER 830
WHEN GLIDER MEETS GLIDER 831
HOW TO MAKE A NOT GATE 832
THE EATER 833
GLIDERS CAN BUILD THEIR OWN GUNS! 837
THE KICKBACK REACTION 837
THINNING A GLIDER STREAM 837

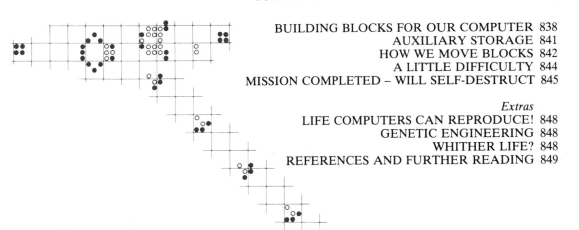

BUILDING BLOCKS FOR OUR COMPUTER 838
AUXILIARY STORAGE 841
HOW WE MOVE BLOCKS 842
A LITTLE DIFFICULTY 844
MISSION COMPLETED – WILL SELF-DESTRUCT 845

Extras
LIFE COMPUTERS CAN REPRODUCE! 848
GENETIC ENGINEERING 848
WHITHER LIFE? 848
REFERENCES AND FURTHER READING 849

Index

I

Contents of Volume 1

Biography ix

Preface xi

Contents of Volume 2 xxiii

♠

SPADE WORK!

Chapter 1 **Whose Game?** 3

BLUE-RED HACKENBUSH 4
THE TWEEDLEDUM AND TWEEDLEDEE ARGUMENT 5
HOW CAN YOU HAVE HALF A MOVE? 6
. . . AND QUARTER MOVES? 8
SKI-JUMPS FOR BEGINNERS 10
DON'T JUST TAKE THE AVERAGE! 12
WHAT IS A JUMP WORTH? 13
TOADS-AND-FROGS 14
DO OUR METHODS WORK? 15

Extras
WHAT IS A GAME? 16
WHEN IS A MOVE GOOD? 17
FIGURE 8(d) IS WORTH $\frac{3}{4}$ 18
REFERENCES AND FURTHER READING 19

Chapter 2 **Finding the Correct Number is Simplicity Itself** 21

WHICH NUMBERS ARE WHICH? 21
SIMPLICITY'S THE ANSWER! 23
SIMPLEST FORMS FOR NUMBERS 24
CUTCAKE 26
MAUNDY CAKE 28
A FEW MORE APPLICATIONS OF THE SIMPLICITY RULE 29
POSITIVE, NEGATIVE, ZERO AND FUZZY POSITIONS 30
HACKENBUSH HOTCHPOTCH 31
SUMS OF ARBITRARY GAMES 32
THE OUTCOME OF A SUM 33
THE NEGATIVE OF A GAME 35
CANCELLING A GAME WITH ITS NEGATIVE 36
COMPARING TWO GAMES 37
COMPARING HACKENBUSH POSITIONS 38

THE GAME OF COL   39
A STAR IS BORN!   40
COL CONTAINS SUCH VALUES   41
GAME TREES   42
GREEN HACKENBUSH, THE GAME OF NIM, AND NIMBERS   42
GET NIMBLE WITH NIMBERS!   44
CHILDISH HACKENBUSH   45
SEATING COUPLES   46

Extras
WINNING STRATEGIES   48
THE SUM OF TWO FINITE GAMES CAN LAST
FOREVER   48
A THEOREM ABOUT COL   49
COL-LECTIONS AND COL-LAPSINGS   50
MAUNDY CAKE   53
ANOTHER CUTCAKE VARIANT   53
HOW CHILDISH CAN YOU GET?   54
REFERENCES AND FURTHER READING   54

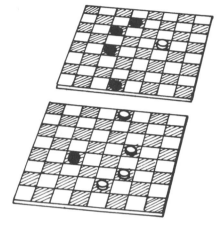

Chapter 3   Some Hard Games and How to Make Them Easier   55

POKER-NIM   55
NORTHCOTT'S GAME   56
BOGUS NIM-HEAPS AND THE MEX RULE   57
THE SPRAGUE-GRUNDY THEORY FOR IMPARTIAL GAMES   58
THE WHITE KNIGHT   59
ADDING NIMBERS   60
WYT QUEENS   61
REVERSIBLE MOVES IN GENERAL GAMES   62
DELETING DOMINATED OPTIONS   64
TOADS-AND-FROGS WITH UPS AND DOWNS   65
GAME TRACKING AND IDENTIFICATION   67
WHAT ARE FLOWERS WORTH?   68
A GALLIMAUFRY OF GAMES   69
WHO WINS SUMS OF UPS, DOWNS, STARS AND NUMBERS?   70
A CLOSER LOOK AT THE STARS   71
THE VALUES $\{\uparrow \mid \uparrow\}$ and $\{0 \mid \uparrow\}$ 71
THE UPSTART EQUALITY   73
GIFT HORSES   74

Extras
THE NIM-ADDITION RULE IN SEVERAL VARIATIONS   75
WYT QUEENS AND WYTHOFF'S GAME   76
ANSWERS TO FIGS. 8, 9 AND 11   77
TOAD VERSUS FROG   77
TWO THEOREMS ON SIMPLIFYING GAMES   78
BERLEKAMP'S RULE FOR HACKENBUSH STRINGS   79
REFERENCES AND FURTHER READING   80

Chapter 4 **Taking and Breaking** 81

KAYLES 82
GAMES WITH HEAPS 82
$\mathcal{P}$-POSITIONS AND $\mathcal{N}$-POSITIONS 83
SUBTRACTION GAMES 83
FERGUSON'S PAIRING PROPERTY 86
GRUNDY SCALES 87
OTHER TAKE-AWAY GAMES 87
DAWSON'S CHESS 88
THE PERIODICITY OF KAYLES 90
OTHER TAKE-AND-BREAK GAMES 91
DAWSON'S KAYLES 92
VARIATIONS 93
GUILES 93
TREBLECROSS 93
OFFICERS 94
GRUNDY'S GAME 96
PRIM AND DIM 97
REPLICATION OF NIM-VALUES 97
DOUBLE AND QUADRUPLE KAYLES 98
LASKER'S NIM 99

Extras
SOME REMARKS ON PERIODICITY 100
STANDARD FORM 100
A COMPENDIUM OF OCTAL GAMES 101
ADDITIONAL REMARKS 101
SPARSE SPACES AND COMMON COSETS 109
WILL GRUNDY'S GAME BE ULTIMATELY PERIODIC? 111
SPARSE SPACE SPELLS SPEED 111
GAMES DISPLAYING ARITHMETIC PERIODICITY 112
A NON-ARITHMETIC-PERIODICITY THEOREM 114
SOME HEXADECIMAL GAMES 116
REFERENCES AND FURTHER READING 116

Chapter 5 **Numbers, Nimbers and Numberless Wonders** 117

DOMINEERING 117
SWITCH GAMES 119
CASHING CHEQUES 120
SOME SIMPLE HOT GAMES 123
THE TINIEST GAMES 123
MODERN MANAGEMENT OF CASH FLOW 124
TINY TOADS-AND-FROGS 125
THE OPENING DISSECTION OF TOADS-AND-FROGS 126
SEATING BOYS AND GIRLS 130

Extras
TOADS-AND-FROGS COMPLETELY DISSECTED 132
TOADS-AND-FROGS WITH TWO SPACES 135
MORE DOMINEERING VALUES 137
REFERENCES AND FURTHER READING 140

Chapter 6   The Heat of Battle   141

SNORT 141
A GRAPHIC PICTURE OF FARM LIFE 142
DON'T MOVE IN A NUMBER UNLESS THERE'S
NOTHING ELSE TO DO! 144
WHAT'S IN IT FOR ME? 144
THE LEFT AND RIGHT STOPS 146
COOLING—AND THE THERMOGRAPH 147
COOLING SETTLES THE MEAN VALUE 148
HOW TO DRAW THERMOGRAPHS 149
WHEN A PLAYER HAS SEVERAL OPTIONS 150
FOUNDATIONS FOR THERMOGRAPHS 151
EXAMPLES OF THERMOGRAPHS 152
WHO IS TO MOVE FROM THE FINAL STOP? 154
A FOUR-STOP EXAMPLE 154
THE CHEQUE-MARKET EXCHANGE 155
EQUITABLE GAMES 156
EXCITABLE GAMES 156
THE EXTENDED THERMOGRAPH 157
GETTING THE RIGHT SLANT 159
THE THERMOSTATIC STRATEGY 159
THERMOSTRAT'S NOT OFTEN WRONG! 162
HEATING 163
DOES THE EXCITEMENT SHOW? 166
HOW TO SELL INFINITESIMAL VALUES TO YOUR
PROFIT-CONSCIOUS FRIENDS 167
NIM, REMOTENESS AND SUSPENSE IN HOT GAMES 169
OVERHEATING 170
COOLING THE CHILDREN'S PARTY 174
BUT HOW DO YOU COOL A PARTY BY ONE DEGREE? 175

Extras
THREE SNORT LEMMAS 176
A SNORT DICTIONARY 179
PROOF OF THE NUMBER AVOIDANCE THEOREM 179
WHY THERMOSTRAT WORKS 179
REFERENCES 182

Chapter 7   Hackenbush   183

GREEN HACKENBUSH 184
GREEN TREES 184

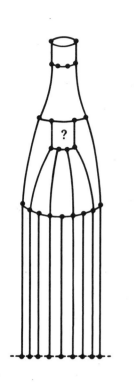

FUSION 186
PROVING THE FUSION PRINCIPLE 187
A MORE COMPLICATED PICTURE 189
IMPARTIAL MAUNDY CAKE 190
BLUE-RED HACKENBUSH 191
HACKENBUSH HOTCHPOTCH 191
FLOWER GARDENS 192
THE BLUE FLOWER PLOY 193
ATOMIC WEIGHTS 194
ATOMIC WEIGHT OF JUNGLES 196
MAKING TRACKS IN THE JUNGLE 199
TRACKING DOWN AN ANIMAL 200
AMAZING JUNGLE 203
SMART GAME IN THE JUNGLE 204
UNPARTED JUNGLES 205
BLUE-RED HACKENBUSH CAN BE HARD, TOO! 206
REDWOOD FURNITURE 206
REDWOOD BEDS 210
HOW BIG IS A REDWOOD BED? 211
WHAT'S THE BOTTLE? 213

Extras
ORDINAL ADDITION, THE COLON PRINCIPLE, AND
NORTON'S LEMMA 214
BOTH WAYS OF ADDING IMPARTIAL GAMES 214
MANY-WAY MAUNDY CAKE 215
SOLUTION TO FIGURE 15 215
TRACKS CLEARED THROUGH THE AMAZING JUNGLE 216
HOW HARD WAS THE BED? 216
NP-HARDNESS 218
THE BOTTLE AT THE END OF CHAPTER SEVEN 220
REFERENCES AND FURTHER READING 220

Chapter 8   **It's a Small, Small, Small, Small World**   **221**

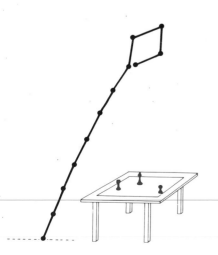

UPPITINESS AND UNCERTAINTY 222
COMPUTING ATOMIC WEIGHTS 223
EATCAKE 225
SPLITTING THE ATOM 226
TURN-AND-EATCAKE 227
ALL YOU NEED TO KNOW ABOUT ATOMIC
WEIGHTS BUT WERE AFRAID TO ASK 228
CHILDISH HACKENBUSH HOTCHPOTCH 229
ATOMIC WEIGHTS OF LOLLIPOPS 230
PROVING THINGS ABOUT ATOMIC WEIGHTS 232
PLAYING AMONG THE FLOWERS 232
WHEN IS g AS UPPITY AS h? 233
GO FLY A KITE! 234
ALL REMOTE STARS AGREE 235
LARGE AND SMALL FLOWERBEDS 236
PLAYING UNDER A LUCKY STAR 237
GENERAL MULTIPLES OF UP 238
PROOF OF THE REMOTE STAR RULES 239

PROOF THAT ATOMIC WEIGHT = UPPITINESS 240
THE WHOLENESS OF HACKENBUSH HOTCHPOTCH 242
PROPER CARE OF THE ECCENTRIC 242
GALVINIZED GAMES 243
TRADING TRIANGLES 244

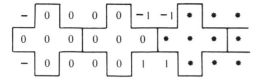

Extras
MULTIPLES OF POSITIVE GAMES 246
MULTIPLES WORK! 246
FIRST FOR THE "WITH" RULE: 247
NOW FOR THE "WITHOUT" RULE: 248
SHIFTING MULTIPLES OF UP BY STARS 249
A THEOREM ON INCENTIVES 249
SEATING FAMILIES OF FIVE 251
REFERENCE 253

CHANGE OF HEART!

Chapter 9   If You Can't Beat 'Em, Join 'Em!   **257**

ALL THE KING'S HORSES 257
WE CAN JOIN ANY GAMES 258
HOW REMOTE IS A HORSE? 258
WHAT IF THE FIRST HORSE TO GET STUCK WINS? 261
A SLIGHTLY SLOWER JOIN 263
MOVING HORSES IMPARTIALLY 263
CUTTING EVERY CAKE 264
EATCAKES 266
WHEN TO PUT YOUR MONEY ON THE LAST HORSE 266
SLOW HORSES JOIN THE ALSO-RANS 266
LET THEM EAT CAKE! 269

Extras
ALL THE KING'S HORSES ON A QUARTER-INFINITE BOARD 272
CUTTING YOUR CAKES AND EATING THEM 272
REFERENCES AND FURTHER READING 278

Chapter 10   Hot Battles Followed by Cold Wars   **279**

HOTCAKES 279
UNIONS OF GAMES 280
COLD GAMES—NUMBERS ARE STILL NUMBERS 280
HOT GAMES—THE BATTLE IS JOINED! 280
TOLLS, TIMERS AND TALLIES 280
WHICH IS THE BEST OPTION? 283

HOT POSITIONS 284
COLD POSITIONS 284
TEPID POSITIONS 286
TALLY TRUTHS TOTALLY TOLD 288
A TEPID GAME 288
SELECT BOYS AND GIRLS 290
MRS. GRUNDY 290
HOW TO PLAY MISÈRE UNIONS OF PARTIZAN GAMES 292
URGENT UNIONS (SHOTGUN WEDDINGS?) 292
PREDECIDERS—OVERRIDERS AND SUICIDERS 292
FALADA 292
ONE FOR YOU, TWO FOR ME, NOTHING FOR BOTH OF US 299
TWO MORE FALADA GAMES 300
BAKED ALASKA 301

Extras
A FELICITOUS FALADA FIELD 304
THE RULES FOR TALLIES ON INFINITE TOLLS 305
TIME MAY BE SHORTER THAN YOU THINK 306

Chapter 11 **Games Infinite and Indefinite**   **307**

INFINITE HACKENBUSH 307
INFINITE ENDERS 309
THE INFINITE ORDINAL NUMBERS 309
OTHER NUMBERS 310
INFINITE NIM 310
THE INFINITE SPRAGUE–GRUNDY AND SMITH THEORIES 313
SOME SUPERHEAVY ATOMS 313
LOOPY GAMES 314
FIXED, MIXED AND FREE 315
ONSIDES AND OFFSIDES, UPSUMS AND DOWNSUMS 316
STOPPERS 317
on, off AND dud 317
HOW BIG IS on? 318
IT'S BIGGER THAN ALL OF THEM! 318
SIDLING TOWARDS A GAME 318
SIDLING PICKS SIDES 320
STOPPERS HAVE ONLY ONE SIDE 320
'TIS! – 'TISN' – 'TIS! – 'TISN'! – . . . 322
LOOPY HACKENBUSH 323
DISENTANGLING LOOPY HACKENBUSH 323
LOOPILY INFINITE HACKENBUSH 324
SISYPHUS 326
LIVING WITH LOOPS 328
COMPARING LOOPY GAMES 328
THE SWIVEL CHAIR STRATEGY 329
STOPPERS ARE NICE 330
PLUMTREES ARE NICER! 332
TAKING CARE OF PLUMTREES 334

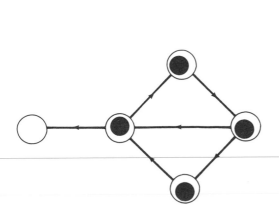

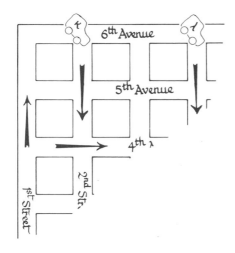

WORKING WITH UPSUMS AND DOWNSUMS 335
on, off AND **hot** 336
A SUMMARY OF SOME SUM PROPERTIES 337
THE HOUSE OF CARDS 337
THE DEGREE OF LOOPINESS 341
CLASSES AND VARIETIES 342
NO HIGHWAY 344
BACKSLIDING TOADS-AND-FROGS 347

Extras
BACH'S CAROUSEL 349
PROOF OF THE SIDLING THEOREM 351
ANSWER TO EXERCISE ONE 354
tis AND **tisn** 354
upon 355
BACKSLIDING TOADS-AND-FROGS 355
REFERENCES AND FURTHER READING 357

Chapter 12 **Games Eternal—Games Entailed**   359

FAIR SHARES AND VARIED PAIRS 359
HOW SOON CAN YOU WIN? 361
THERE MAY BE OPEN POSITIONS (0-POSITIONS) 362
DE BONO'S *L*-GAME 364
ADDERS-AND-LADDERS 366
JUST HOW LOOPY CAN YOU GET? 371
CORRALL AUTOMOTIVE BETTERMENT SCHEME 371
SHARING OUT OTHER KINDS OF NUT 373
FAIR SHARES AND UNEQUAL PARTNERS 374
SWEETS AND NUTS, AND MAYBE A DATE? 374
THE ADDITIONAL SUBTRACTION GAMES 375
HORSEFLY 375
SELECTIVE AND SUBSELECTIVE COMPOUNDS OF
IMPARTIAL GAMES 376
ENTAILING MOVES 376
SUNNY AND LOONY POSITIONS 377
CALCULATING WITH ENTAILED VALUES 378
NIM WITH ENTAILING MOVES 380
GOLDBACH'S NIM 381
WYT QUEENS WITH TRAINS 382
ADDING TAILS TO PRIM AND DIM 384
COMPLIMENTING MOVES 385
ON-THE-RAILS 387

Extras
DE BONO'S *L*-GAME 388
PROVING THE OUTCOME RULES FOR LOOPY POSITIONS 388
FAIR SHARES AND UNEQUAL PARTNERS 390
WERE YOUR WAYS WINNING ENOUGH? 390
DID YOU MOVE FIRST IN HORSEFLY? 391
REFERENCES AND FURTHER READING 392

Chapter 13 **Survival in the Lost World** **393**

MISÈRE NIM 393
REVERSIBLE MOVES 395
THE ENDGAME PROVISO 396
THE AWFUL TRUTH 396
WHAT'S LEFT OF THE OLD RULES? 398
AS EASY AS TWO AND TWO? 399
THE MISÈRE FORM OF GRUNDY'S GAME 399
ANIMALS AND THEIR GENUS 402
WHAT CAN WE DO WITH THE GENUS? 403
FIRM, FICKLE AND TAME 403
WHICH ANIMALS ARE TAME . . . 405
. . . AND WHICH ARE RESTIVE? 405
SOME TAME ANIMALS IN THE GOOD CHILD'S ZOO 407
MISÈRE WYT QUEENS 407
JELLY BEANS AND LEMON DROPS 408
STALKING ADDERS AND TAKING SQUARES 409
"BUT WHAT IF THEY'RE WILD?" ASKS THE BAD CHILD 410
MISERE KAYLES 411
THE NOAH'S ARK THEOREM 412
THE HALF-TAME THEOREM 415
GUILES 416
DIVIDING RULERS 416
DAWSON, OFFICERS, GRUNDY 418

Extras
ALL SUBTRACTION GAMES REDUCE TO NIM 422
PRIM AND DIM 422
PROOF OF THE NOAH'S ARK THEOREM 423
MISÈRE OCTAL GAMES 423
STOP PRESS: EVEN MORE GAMES ARE TAMEABLE 426
REFERENCES AND FURTHER READING 426

Index I

You are
now here

If you want to know roughly what's elsewhere,
turn to the little notes about our four main themes:

Adding Games... ... ... ♠ page 1
Bending the Rules ... ... ♡ page 255
Case Studies ... ... ♣ page 427
Doing It Yourself ... ... ◇ page 695

There are a number of other connexions between various chapters of the book:

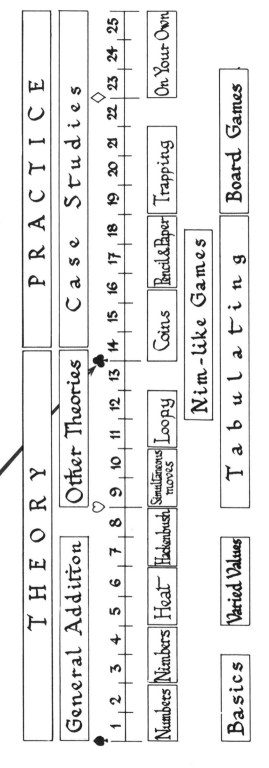

However, you should be able to pick any chapter and read almost all of it
without reference to anything earlier, except perhaps the basic ideas at the start of the book.

GAMES IN CLUBS!

To be an Englishman is to belong to the most exclusive
club there is.
        Ogden Nash, *England Expects.*

There are lots of games for which the theories we've now developed are useful, and even more for which they're not, and we've grouped them into clubs according to how you play them.

First some games you can play with coins, either by turning them over (Chapter 14) or moving them along strips or about in heaps (Chapter 15).

Then games for which you'll need pencil and paper, perhaps to draw straight lines (Chapter 16), or curved ones (Chapter 17) or merely to do the calculations in Chapter 18.

And for board games we have three case studies in which one player wins by trapping his opponent (Chapters 19, 20, 21) and finally many more which are usually won by the first player to establish some kind of winning configuration (Chapter 22).

Chapter 14

Turn and Turn About

Because I do not hope to turn again
Because I do not hope
Because I do not hope to turn.
        T.S. Eliot, *Ash Wednesday*, I.

Open not thine heart to every man, lest he requite thee
with a shrewd turn.
        Ecclesiasticus, 8:19.

These games, based on an idea of H.W. Lenstra, are similar in that they all involve turning things over, but we shall see that they call for a variety of strategies.

TURNING TURTLES

Figure 1. Playing Turning Turtles.

In Fig. 1 the Walrus and the Carpenter are playing a rather cruel game. At each move a player must put one turtle on its back and may also turn over any single turtle to the left of it. This second turtle, unlike the first, may be turned either onto its feet or onto its back. The player wins who turns the last turtle upside-down. Which turtles should the Walrus (*l.*) turn?

Like most readers of this book, he wearily suspects another disguise for Nim. Here only turtles 3, 4, 6, 8 and 10 are on their feet, and since the nim-sum of 3, 4 and 6 is 1, he may turn 10 onto its back and 9 onto its feet, producing 3, 4, 6, 8, 9, a $\mathscr{P}$-position since $8 \neq 9 = 1$. The Carpenter (*r.*) responds by turning 8 and 5 producing the position 3, 4, 5, 6, 9 as in Fig. 2. In Nim

Figure 2. After the Carpenter's Reply.

there is only one good move from this position—reduce 9 to 4, so as to produce 3, 4, 4, 5, 6, which, since two equal Nim heaps may be cancelled, is much the same as 3, 5, 6, which the Walrus reaches by turning both 9 and 4 on their backs (Fig. 3).

Figure 3. How The Walrus Won.

Nim moves become turtle turns as follows. We reduce a heap to a size not already present by turning one turtle on its back and putting another on its feet, as in the Walrus's opening move. If a heap of the reduced size is already present we turn two turtles on their backs as in the Walrus's response to the Carpenter's move (cancelling two equal heaps). To eliminate a heap entirely we merely turn the appropriate turtle. So since 4, 6, 8, 10 is a $\mathscr{P}$-position, the Walrus could have won from Fig. 1 by just turning turtle 3.

Since all our turning games are impartial they are solved by computing the nim-values, and often may be thought of as heap games in disguise; but many games with interesting theories are more naturally suggested by the turning version.

MOCK TURTLES

Figure 4. The Mock Turtle Joins in.

Let the players turn up to three turtles subject only to the condition that the rightmost of these must be turned from his feet onto his back. We may think of this as a game with numbers in which any number may be replaced by 0, 1 or 2 smaller ones. So $\mathcal{G}(n)$ is the least number not of any form

$$0, \ \mathcal{G}(a), \ \mathcal{G}(a) \overset{*}{+} \mathcal{G}(b),$$

in which a and b are any numbers less than n.

If we number the positions from 0 we find the nim-values shown in Table 1.

$n =$	0	1	2	3	4	5	6	7	8	9	10	11	12	13	14	15	16	17	18	...
$\mathcal{G}(n) =$	1	2	4	7	8	11	13	14	16	19	21	22	25	26	28	31	32	35	37	...

Table 1. Nim-values for Mock Turtles.

We see that $\mathcal{G}(n)$ is always $2n$ or $2n+1$, so that its binary expansion is obtained by adjoining a digit 0 or 1 to that of n. Which shall it be?

$n =$	0	1	10	11	100	101	110	111	1000	1001	1010	...
$\mathcal{G}(n) =$	1	10	100	111	1000	1011	1101	1110	10000	10011	10101	...

Table 2. The Odious Numbers Revealed.

Table 2 suggests we choose whichever makes the total number of 1-digits *odd*.

ODIOUS AND EVIL NUMBERS

Every number is **odious** or **evil** according to the number of 1's in its binary expansion (odious for odd, evil for even). These behave under Nim addition like odd and even numbers under ordinary addition:

$$\text{EVIL} \overset{*}{+} \text{EVIL} \ = \ \text{EVIL} \ = \text{ODIOUS} \overset{*}{+} \text{ODIOUS},$$

$$\text{EVIL} \overset{*}{+} \text{ODIOUS} = \text{ODIOUS} = \text{ODIOUS} \overset{*}{+} \text{EVIL}.$$

When we compute $\mathscr{G}(n)$ in Mock Turtles, the next odious number is *never* excluded, because the nim-sum of two odious numbers is evil, but smaller evil numbers always *are* excluded.

If $a_1, a_2, \ldots, a_n$ is a $\mathscr{P}$-position in Nim, so that

$$a_1 \overset{*}{+} a_2 \overset{*}{+} \ldots \overset{*}{+} a_n = 0,$$

then for the corresponding odious numbers $\mathscr{G}(a_i)$ in Mock Turtles we shall have

$$\mathscr{G}(a_1) \overset{*}{+} \mathscr{G}(a_2) \overset{*}{+} \ldots \overset{*}{+} \mathscr{G}(a_n) = 0 \text{ or } 1.$$

But if n is even, this nim-sum is evil, and so 0; while if n is odd it is odious, and so 1. The $\mathscr{P}$-positions in Mock Turtles are therefore just those $\mathscr{P}$-positions in Nim for which n is even.

Note that in Mock Turtles we number the turtles from 0. The turtle numbered 0, called the Mock Turtle, must take his turn with the rest and cannot be neglected in the conversion to Nim. To obtain a $\mathscr{P}$-position in Mock Turtles from the Turning Turtles position of Fig. 3, the Mock Turtle must be brought into the game with his four feet on the ground. In Mock Turtles, 3, 5, 6, is *not* a $\mathscr{P}$-position, but 0, 3, 5, 6 is (Fig. 4).

MOEBIUS, MOGUL AND GOLD MOIDORES

Table 3 shows the nim-values, kindly checked for us on the computer by M.J.T. Guy, for similar games in which we may turn over up to t objects for $t = 1, 2, \ldots$. Because the numbers get much larger than the other nim-values in this book, we have written them in base 8 (octal) notation. Nim-sums of octal numbers may be computed digit by digit thus:

$$
\begin{array}{c}
1\ 2\ 3\ 4\ 5\ 6\ 7\ 0 \\
1\ 3\ 5\ 7\ 0\ 2\ 4\ 6 \\
\hline
1\ 6\ 3\ 5\ 4\ 3\ 6.
\end{array}
$$

In the table we have only named the most interesting cases: $t = 3, 5, 7$ and 9. Note that C, E, G and I are the 3rd, 5th, 7th and 9th letters of the alphabet. For convenience, and to avoid cruelty to turtles, the reader may play these games with coins. The coins will show heads or tails according as the turtle is on his feet or on his back, and the rightmost coin that is turned must change from heads to tails.

THE MOCK TURTLE THEOREM

Take a $\mathscr{P}$-position in the game for an even value of t, $t = 2m$, and place an extra coin (the Mock Turtle) at the left, whichever way up will ensure an even number of heads. Positions obtained in this way will be called "good" positions for the next odd value of t, $t = 2m + 1$. We assert that the good positions are precisely the $\mathscr{P}$-positions for the game $t = 2m + 1$.

n	t = 1	2	MOCK TURTLES 3	4	MOEBIUS 5	6	MOGUL 7	8	MOIDORES 9
THE MOCK TURTLE	1		1		1		1		1
1	1	1	2	1	2	1	2	1	2
2	1	2	4	2	4	2	4	2	4
3	1	3	7	4	10	4	10	4	10
4	1	4	10	10	20	10	20	10	20
5	1	5	13	17	37	20	40	20	40
6	1	6	15	20	40	40	100	40	100
7	1	7	16	40	100	77	177	100	200
8	1	10	20	63	147	100	200	200	400
9	1	11	23	100	200	200	400	377	777
10	1	12	25	125	253	400	1000	400	1000
11	1	13	26	152	325	707	1617	1000	2000
12	1	14	31	200	400	1000	2000	2000	4000
13	1	15	32	226	455	1331	2663	4000	10000
14	1	16	34	253	526	1552	3325	7417	17037
15	1	17	37	333	667	1664	3551	10000	20000
16	1	20	40	355	733	2000	4000	20000	40000
17	1	21	43	367	756	2353	4726	31463	63147
18	1	22	45	400	1000	2561	5343	40000	100000
19	1	23	46	427	1056	2635	5472	52525	125253
20	1	24	51	451	1123	3174	6370	65252	152525
21	1	25	52	707	1617	3216	6435	100000	200000
22	1	26	54	1000	2000	3447	7116	113152	226325
23	1	27	57	1031	2063	3722	7644	200000	400000
24	1	30	61	1055	2132	4000	10000	213630	427461
25	1	31	62	1122	2245	10000	20000	263723	547646
26	1	32	64	1203	2407	20000	40000	306136	614274
27	1	33	67	1443	3106	34007	70017	400000	1000000
28	1	34	70	1537	3277	40000	100000	416246	1034515
29	1	35	73	1746	3714	54031	130063	521055	1242133
30	1	36	75	2000	4000	64052	150125	724616	1651435
31	1	37	76	2033	4066	70064	160151	1000000	2000000
32	1	40	100	2056	4134	100000	200000	1023305	2046613
33	1	41	103	2130	4261	114053	230126	1347214	2716431
34	1	42	105	2221	4443	124061	250143	2000000	4000000
35	1	43	106	2465	5153	130035	260072	2027151	4056322
36	1	44	111	2501	5203	144074	310170	2457261	5136542
37	1	45	112	3124	6250	150016	320035	3166444	6355111
38	1	46	114	3512	7225	160047	340116	4000000	10000000
39	1	47	117	4000	10000	174022	370044	4055666	10133554
40	1	50	121	4034	10071	200000	400000	4632577	11465377
41	1	51	122	4045	10113	214301	430603	5251417	12523036
42	1	52	124	4211	10423	224502	451205	7514712	17231625
43	1	53	127	4504	11211	230604	461411	10000000	20000000

Table 3. These Nim-values are in Octal (base 8), *not* Decimal.

We show first that there is no way of changing from one good position to another by turning at most $2m+1$ coins. If there were, the number of coins turned would necessarily be even, since the good positions have evenly many heads, and so would actually be at most $2m$. But this would entail a move between two $\mathscr{P}$-positions in the $2m$ game.

It remains to show that from any bad position in the $2m+1$ game there is a move to some good position. If the position is bad because it corresponds to an $\mathscr{N}$-position in the $2m$ game, there is a move in that game to some $\mathscr{P}$-position, and, by turning the Mock Turtle if necessary, we obtain a move to a good position in the $2m+1$ game. The other bad positions correspond to $\mathscr{P}$-positions in the $2m$ game, but have an odd number of heads. In this case, by turning over the rightmost head, we obtain a position that gives an $\mathscr{N}$-position in the $2m$ game. We can now turn over at most $2m$ further coins to make this a $\mathscr{P}$-position and then, if necessary to obtain a good position, also turn the Mock Turtle. We have turned at most $2m+2$ coins in all, but since we started with an odd number of heads and finished with an even number, we have in fact turned over at most $2m+1$ coins, and so have made a legal move in the $2m+1$ game.

This result is equivalent to the statement:

> Every nim-value for the $2m+1$ game
> is an odious number,
> and the corresponding value for the $2m$ game
> is obtained by dropping the final binary digit.

THE MOCK TURTLE THEOREM

WHY MOEBIUS?

$$\infty \quad 1 \quad 4 \quad 0 \quad -4 \quad -1 \quad 5 \quad 6 \quad -8 \quad 2 \quad -3 \quad -5 \quad 8 \quad 3 \quad -7 \quad 7 \quad -6 \quad -2$$

Ⓗ Ⓗ ⓣ Ⓗ ⓣ ⓣ Ⓗ ⓣ ⓣ Ⓗ Ⓗ ⓣ ⓣ ⓣ ⓣ ⓣ ⓣ ⓣ

Figure 5. Moebius Labels Make $\mathscr{P}$-positions Easy to Find.

When restricted to 18 coins, the $\mathscr{P}$-positions of the game with $t=5$ possess a remarkable symmetry. To see this, name the heads of a position by the numbers shown in Fig. 5. For example, the $\mathscr{P}$-position with heads in just the first 6 places is $\infty, 0, \pm 1, \pm 4$. In this notation $\mathscr{P}$-positions remain $\mathscr{P}$-positions when their numbers are increased by any fixed amount, modulo 17, leaving ∞ unchanged. Adding 1 to the numbers $\infty, 0, \pm 1, \pm 4$ we find $\infty, 1, 2, 0, 5, -3$, so that the position displayed in Fig. 5 is another $\mathscr{P}$-position. The 15 positions shown in Table 4 yield a total of $15 \times 17 = 255$ $\mathscr{P}$-positions in this way. It is also true that a $\mathscr{P}$-position remains a $\mathscr{P}$-position if we interchange heads and tails in every place. The positions with all tails or all heads are therefore both $\mathscr{P}$-positions, giving $2 \times 255 + 2 = 512$ $\mathscr{P}$-positions in all, distributed as follows:

Number of heads	0	6	8	10	12	18
Number of $\mathscr{P}$-positions	1	102	153	153	102	1.

6 *heads*

∞, 0,	±1,	±4
∞, 0,	±2,	±8
±1,	±3,	±6
±2,	±5,	±6
±4,	±5,	±7
±3,	±7,	±8

8 *heads*

∞, 0,	±1,	±5,	±7
∞, 0,	±2,	±3,	±7
∞, 0,	±3,	±4,	±6
∞, 0,	±5,	±6,	±8
±1,	±2,	±4,	±8
±1,	±2,	±3,	±5
±2,	±4,	±6,	±7
±3,	±4,	±5,	±8
±1,	±6,	±7,	±8

Table 4. The $\mathscr{P}$-positions for Moebius.

Dropping the Mock Turtle (at ∞) we find that the $\mathscr{P}$-positions for the game $t=4$ on 17 coins are distributed:

Number of heads	0	5	6	7	8	9	10	11	12	17
Number of $\mathscr{P}$-positions	1	34	68	68	85	85	68	68	34	1.

We can also double the numbers (modulo 17) of any $\mathscr{P}$-position to give another. Thus ∞, $0, 1, 2, -3, 5$ of Fig. 5 becomes $\infty, 0, 2, 4, -6, -7$. We can invert them modulo 17; since $1/2 = -8$, $1/3 = 6$ and $1/5 = 7$, Fig. 5 inverts into $0, \infty, 1, -8, -6, 7$. In fact we can make any transformation (modulo 17)

$$x \to \frac{ax + b}{cx + d}, \qquad ad - bc = 1.$$

Since these are known as the Möbius transformations, we have named our game after that distinguished mathematician.

MOGUL

On 24 coins the game for $t=7$ displays even more symmetries. The $\mathscr{P}$-positions among the first 24 places are distributed as follows:

Number of heads	0	8	12	16	24
Number of $\mathscr{P}$-positions	1	759	2576	759	1.

Figure 6 enables us to find the 759 $\mathscr{P}$-positions with just 8 heads, or equally those with 8 tails. In either case the set of 8 places involved is called an **octad**. In Fig. 6 there are 35 **pictures** and each picture shows the 24 places colored in six sets of four (the 6 colors used are black, white, star, circle, plus and dot). Any two sets of 4 (any two colors) in the same picture make an octad: in particular this gives every octad with just 4 places in the last pair of (black and white) rows,

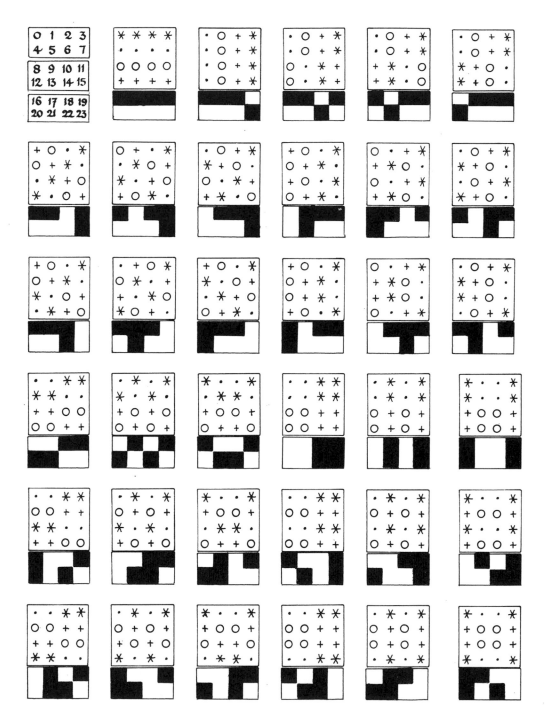

Figure 6. Curtis's Miracle Octad Generator.

and this pair of rows themselves form an octad. By interchanging this last pair of rows with the first pair, or the middle pair, of the same picture, we can now find all the octads, since it can be shown that these pairs of rows form octads and that every other octad meets at least one of them in just 4 places.

This Miracle Octad Generator, or MOG, is due to R.T. Curtis, but we have modified it slightly for the Mogul player's convenience. Various regular features of its arrangement make it easy for the practised user to locate the unique octad containing any five given places. It seems to be the case that the winner in 24-place Mogul need never play into a 12-head $\mathscr{P}$-position.

MOTLEY

This is the game in which any number of coins may be turned. When well played it lasts at most one move, since we can turn all the heads to tails instantly! The nim-values are the powers of 2:

$$1, 2, 4, 8, 16, 32, 64, 128, 256, 512, \ldots$$

so, when played with several rows, Motley is yet another disguise for Nim; the heads in a row are binary digits 1 in the number of beans in the corresponding Nim-heap.

TWINS, TRIPLETS, ETC.

We can also play the game **Twins**, in which we must turn *exactly* two coins, or **Triplets**, in which we turn exactly three, etc. The nim-value sequence for the game in which we turn exactly t coins consists of $t - 1$ zeros followed by the nim-value sequence for the game in which we turn *at most* t coins. Thus the nim-values for Triplets are

$$0, 0, 1, 2, 4, 7, 8, 11, 13, 14, 16, 19, 21, 22, 25, \ldots .$$

We may think of the first $t - 1$ coins as $t - 1$ Mock Turtles which may be used to fill out our move to its proper complement of turns.

THE RULER GAME

If the coins we turn must be *consecutive* but are otherwise unrestricted (except that the rightmost coin must be turned from heads to tails), then the nim-values are computed by the rule:

$$\mathscr{G}(n) = \text{mex} \begin{cases} 0 \\ \mathscr{G}(n-1) \\ \mathscr{G}(n-1) \overset{*}{+} \mathscr{G}(n-2) \\ \mathscr{G}(n-1) \overset{*}{+} \mathscr{G}(n-2) \overset{*}{+} \mathscr{G}(n-3) \\ \cdots\cdots\cdots\cdots\cdots\cdots\cdots\cdots\cdots \end{cases},$$

and are found to be reminiscent of Dividing Rulers (Fig. 7 of Chapter 13).

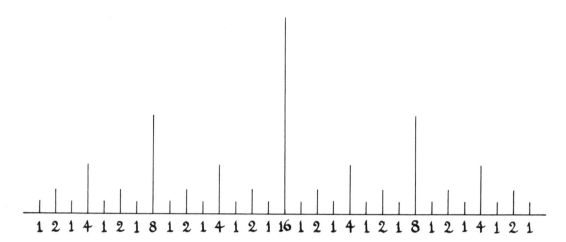

1 2 1 4 1 2 1 8 1 2 1 4 1 2 1 16 1 2 1 4 1 2 1 8 1 2 1 4 1 2 1

Figure 7. Nim-values for the Ruler Game.

If the coins are numbered starting from 1. $\mathcal{G}(n)$ is just the highest power of 2 dividing n.

CIRCUMSCRIBED GAMES

We can play any of these games under the additional restriction that the coins to be turned may not be too far apart. Thus in **Mock Turtle Fives** we may turn *up to three* of five consecutive coins. In **Triplet Fives** we turn *exactly three* out of five consecutive coins. In **Ruler Fives** we may turn 1, 2, 3, 4 or 5 consecutive coins. The nim-values for these three games are:

Mock Turtle Fives: 1 2 4 7 8 1 2 4 7 8 1 2 4 7 8 1 2 4 7 8 ...

Triplet Fives: 0 0 1 2 4 0 0 1 2 4 0 0 1 2 4 0 0 1 2 4 ...

Ruler Fives: 1 2 1 4 1 2 1 4 1 2 1 4 1 2 1 4 1 2 1 4 ....

These are parts of general patterns. Thus, **Moebius Nineteens**, for example, would have the first 19 values of Moebius repeated indefinitely. This happens for all the above games except the Ruler game; Ruler Fours, Sixes and Sevens have the same values as Ruler Fives, while Ruler Eights to Fifteens all have nim-values:

1 2 1 4 1 2 1 8 1 2 1 4 1 2 1 8 1 2 1 4 1 2 1 8 1 2 1 4 1 2 1 8 1 ....

TURNIPS (or TERNUPS)

This game has a richer theory, but it is a great pity that the full theory is only needed by people wealthy enough to play with a very large number of coins. The move is to turn over any three equally spaced coins, the rightmost going from heads to tails as usual. Numbering from 0 we find that the nim-values for 0 to 100 are:

0– 8	0	0	1	0	0	1	2	2	1		
9–17	0	0	1	0	0	1	2	2	1		
18–26	4	4	1	4	4	1	2	2	1		
27–35	0	0	1	0	0	1	2	2	1		
36–44	0	0	1	0	0	1	2	2	1		
45–53	4	4	1	4	4	1	2	2	1		
54–62	7	7	1	7	7	1	2	2	1		
63–71	7	7	1	7	7	1	2	2	1		
72–80	4	4	1	4	4	1	2	2	1		
81–89	0	0	1	0	0	1	2	2	1		
90–100	0	0	1	0	0	1	2	2	1	4	4 ...

Table 5. The Nim-values for Turnips.

To find $\mathscr{G}(n)$ in general, we expand n in base 3:

	n in ternary	$\mathscr{G}(n)$	
$\phi = 0$ or 1	... $\phi\ \phi\ \phi\ \phi\ \phi\ \phi\ \phi$	0	
$? = 0, 1$ or 2	... $?\ ?\ ?\ ?\ ?\ ?\ 2$	1	the
	... $?\ ?\ ?\ ?\ ?\ 2\ \phi$	2	odious
	... $?\ ?\ ?\ ?\ 2\ \phi\ \phi$	4	numbers
	... $?\ ?\ ?\ 2\ \phi\ \phi\ \phi$	7	in
	... $?\ ?\ 2\ \phi\ \phi\ \phi\ \phi$	8	order
	... $?\ 2\ \phi\ \phi\ \phi\ \phi\ \phi$	11	
	....	...	...

In words, $\mathscr{G}(n) = 0$ if the ternary expansion of n has no 2-digit, but is the kth odious number if the last 2-digit is in the kth place from the right, when we call n a k-**number**. The numbers n whose ternary expansions have no 2-digit will be called **empty numbers**.

To see all this, note that $\mathscr{G}(n)$ is the mex of all the numbers

$$\mathscr{G}(n-\delta) \overset{*}{+} \mathscr{G}(n-2\delta) \qquad \text{for } \delta = 1,2,\dots .$$

We show first that the putative value for $\mathscr{G}(n)$ is not one of these numbers, or equivalently that

$$\mathscr{G}(n) \overset{*}{+} \mathscr{G}(n-\delta) \overset{*}{+} \mathscr{G}(n-2\delta) \neq 0.$$

Since the nim-sum of three odious numbers is odious, this will be true unless one of

$$\mathscr{G}(n), \ \mathscr{G}(n-\delta), \ \mathscr{G}(n-2\delta)$$

is zero and the other two coincide. But if the last non-zero ternary digit ($x = 1$ or 2) of δ is in the kth place, the expansions of n, $n-\delta$, $n-2\delta$ look like:

$$
\begin{array}{ccc}
 & \overset{k \quad\quad j}{} & \\
\delta: & \text{? ? ? x 0 0 0 0 0 0} & \\
\end{array}
\qquad\qquad
\begin{array}{cc}
 & \overset{k}{} \\
\delta: & \text{? ? ? x 0 0 0 0 0} \\
\end{array}
$$

$$
\left.\begin{array}{r}
n \\
n-\delta \\
n-2\delta
\end{array}\right\} :
\left\{\begin{array}{l}
\text{? ? ? 0 ? ? ? ? 2 } \phi\ \phi \\
\text{? ? ? 1 ? ? ? ? 2 } \phi\ \phi \\
\text{? ? ? 2 ? ? ? ? 2 } \phi\ \phi
\end{array}\right.
\quad\text{or}\quad
\left.\begin{array}{r}
n \\
n-\delta \\
n-2\delta
\end{array}\right\} :
\left\{\begin{array}{l}
\text{? ? ? 0 } \phi\ \phi\ \phi\ \phi\ \phi \\
\text{? ? ? 1 } \phi\ \phi\ \phi\ \phi\ \phi \\
\text{? ? ? 2 } \phi\ \phi\ \phi\ \phi\ \phi
\end{array}\right.
$$

according as n has or has not a 2-digit in some j place, $j < k$. In the first case the three putative nim-values are all the jth odious number, and in the second exactly one of them is the kth odious number, so they cannot have zero nim-sum.

Now we know from our analysis of Mock Turtles that each odious number is the first number not the nim-sum of two or fewer earlier ones. It suffices to show that if n is a k-number, we can choose δ so as to make $n-\delta$ and $n-2\delta$ i- and j-numbers or empty, for any i and j less than k. The subtraction sums in Table 6 show how to do this.

$$
\begin{array}{ll}
 & \overset{k\quad j\quad i}{} \\
\delta\ : & \text{2 0 0 1 0 0} \\
n\ : & \text{... ? ? 2 } \phi\ \phi\ \text{1 } \phi\ \phi\ \text{1 } \phi\ \phi \\
n-\delta\ : & \text{... ? ? ? ? ? 2 } \phi\ \phi\ \text{0 } \phi\ \phi \\
n-2\delta : & \text{... ? ? ? ? ? ? ? ? 2 } \phi\ \phi
\end{array}
\qquad
\begin{array}{ll}
 & \overset{\quad\quad\quad\quad\quad\quad\quad\quad k}{} \\
\delta & \text{1 0 0 0 1 0 1 0 0 1 0 0} \\
n\ : & \phi\ \text{2 } \phi\ \phi\ \text{2 } \phi\ \text{2 } \phi\ \phi\ \text{2 } \phi\ \phi \\
n-\delta\ : & \phi\ \text{1 } \phi\ \phi\ \text{1 } \phi\ \text{1 } \phi\ \phi\ \text{1 } \phi\ \phi \\
n-2\delta : & \phi\ \text{0 } \phi\ \phi\ \text{0 } \phi\ \text{0 } \phi\ \phi\ \text{0 } \phi\ \phi
\end{array}
$$

$$
\begin{array}{ll}
\delta\ : & \text{1 0 0 1 0 0} \\
n\ : & \text{... ? ? 2 } \phi\ \phi\ \text{0 } \phi\ \phi\ \text{1 } \phi\ \phi \\
n-\delta\ : & \text{... ? ? ? ? ? 2 } \phi\ \phi\ \text{0 } \phi\ \phi \\
n-2\delta : & \text{... ? ? ? ? ? ? ? ? 2 } \phi\ \phi
\end{array}
\qquad
\begin{array}{ll}
 & \overset{\quad\quad\quad\quad\quad\quad\quad k\quad\quad i}{} \\
n\ : & \phi\ \text{2 } \phi\ \phi\ \text{2 } \phi\ \text{2 } \phi\ \phi\ \text{1 } \phi\ \phi \\
n-\delta\ : & \text{? ? ? ? ? ? ? ? ? ? 2 } \phi\ \phi \\
n-2\delta : & \text{0 0 0 0 0 0 } \phi\ \text{0 0 0 } \phi\ \phi
\end{array}
$$

$$
\begin{array}{ll}
\delta\ : & \text{1 2 2 2 0 0} \\
n\ : & \text{... ? ? 2 } \phi\ \phi\ \text{1 } \phi\ \phi\ \text{0 } \phi\ \phi \\
n-\delta\ : & \text{... ? ? ? ? ? 2 } \phi\ \phi\ \text{1 } \phi\ \phi \\
n-2\delta : & \text{... ? ? ? ? ? ? ? ? 2 } \phi\ \phi
\end{array}
\qquad
\begin{array}{ll}
n\ : & \phi\ \text{2 } \phi\ \phi\ \text{2 } \phi\ \text{2 } \phi\ \phi\ \text{0 } \phi\ \phi \\
n-\delta\ : & \text{? ? ? ? ? ? ? ? ? ? 2 } \phi\ \phi \\
n-2\delta : & \text{0 0 0 0 0 0 } \phi\ \text{0 0 1 } \phi\ \phi
\end{array}
$$

$$
\begin{array}{ll}
\delta\ : & \text{0 2 2 2 0 0} \\
n\ : & \text{... ? ? 2 } \phi\ \phi\ \text{0 } \phi\ \phi\ \text{0 } \phi\ \phi \\
n-\delta\ : & \text{... ? ? ? ? ? 2 } \phi\ \phi\ \text{1 } \phi\ \phi \\
n-2\delta : & \text{... ? ? ? ? ? ? ? ? 2 } \phi\ \phi
\end{array}
$$

In the last two cases above, the first ϕ of the last line is whichever of 0 or 1 makes $n-2\delta$ have the same parity as n. Then δ can be found from n and $n-2\delta$.

Table 6. How to Make $n-\delta$, $n-2\delta$ into i- and j-numbers, or Empty.

GRUNT

In a move of this game one must turn over four symmetrically arranged coins of which the first must be the leftmost coin of the game and the last must be turned from heads to tails. Numbering from 0 the restriction is that we turn numbers

$$
0,\ a,\ n-a\ \text{and}\ n, \qquad 0 < a < \tfrac{1}{2}n,
$$

and we find the nim-values:

n	0	1	2	3	4	5	6	7	8	9	10	11	12	13	14	15	16	17	18	19	20	21	22	...
$\mathcal{G}(n)$	0	0	0	1	0	2	1	0	2	1	0	2	1	3	2	1	3	2	4	3	0	4	3	....

Figure 8. A Winning Move in Grunt.

Since $\mathscr{G}(0)=0$, $\mathscr{G}(n)$ can more easily be computed as the mex of all numbers of the form

$$\mathscr{G}(a) \stackrel{*}{+} \mathscr{G}(n-a), \qquad 0 < a < \tfrac{1}{2}n,$$

and so the game is a disguise for Grundy's Game (see Chapter 4) in which any heap may be split into two smaller heaps of different sizes.

SYM

As an example where the nim-values display no recognizable pattern, let us turn over any symmetrically arranged set of coins, not necessarily including the leftmost coin, number 0. We find

$$n = 0\ 1\ 2\ 3\ 4\ 5\ 6\quad 7\quad 8\quad 9\ 10\ 11\ 12\ 13\quad 14\ 15\quad 16\ \ldots$$
$$\mathscr{G}(n) = 1\ 2\ 4\ 3\ 6\ 7\ 8\ 16\ 18\ 25\ 32\ 11\ 64\ 31\ 128\ 10\ 256\ \ldots.$$

The reader can also try to solve the game **Sympler** in which the leftmost coin *is* to be included in the symmetrical set of coins turned.

TWO-DIMENSIONAL TURNING GAMES

All our one-dimensional games were played with the restriction that the rightmost coin to be turned was to be changed from heads to tails. In the two-dimensional games the corresponding requirement is that the most "south-easterly" coin which is turned must go from heads to tails. In such games we'll write $\mathscr{G}(a,b)$ for the value of a coin in row a and column b.

ACROSTIC TWINS

We start with a very simple game. The move is to turn two coins which must either be in the same row or in the same column. The typical entry in the nim-value table is therefore the least number not appearing earlier in the same row or column, and we find Table 7. So we see that Acrostic Twins defines nim-addition:

$$\mathscr{G}(a,b) = a \stackrel{*}{+} b.$$

TURNING CORNERS

This is a much more interesting game. The move is to turn over the four corners of any rectangle with horizontal and vertical sides. The nim-values can be computed using

$$\mathscr{G}(a,b) = \operatorname{mex}\{\mathscr{G}(a',b) \stackrel{*}{+} \mathscr{G}(a,b') \stackrel{*}{+} \mathscr{G}(a',b')\},$$

where a' and b' are any numbers respectively less than a and b (see Fig. 9). Table 8 gives values for a and b less than 16.

0	1	2	3	4	5	6	7	8	9	10	11	12	13	14	15
1	0	3	2	5	4	7	6	9	8	11	10	13	12	15	14
2	3	0	1	6	7	4	5	10	11	8	9	14	15	12	13
3	2	1	0	7	6	5	4	11	10	9	8	15	14	13	12
4	5	6	7	0	1	2	3	12	13	14	15	8	9	10	11
5	4	7	6	1	0	3	2	13	12	15	14	9	8	11	10
6	7	4	5	2	3	0	1	14	15	12	13	10	11	8	9
7	6	5	4	3	2	1	0	15	14	13	12	11	10	9	8
8	9	10	11	12	13	14	15	0	1	2	3	4	5	6	7
9	8	11	10	13	12	15	14	1	0	3	2	5	4	7	6
10	11	8	9	14	15	12	13	2	3	0	1	6	7	4	5
11	10	9	8	15	14	13	12	3	2	1	0	7	6	5	4
12	13	14	15	8	9	10	11	4	5	6	7	0	1	2	3
13	12	15	14	9	8	11	10	5	4	7	6	1	0	3	2
14	15	12	13	10	11	8	9	6	7	4	5	2	3	0	1
15	14	13	12	11	10	9	8	7	6	5	4	3	2	1	0

Table 7. How to Play Acrostic Twins.

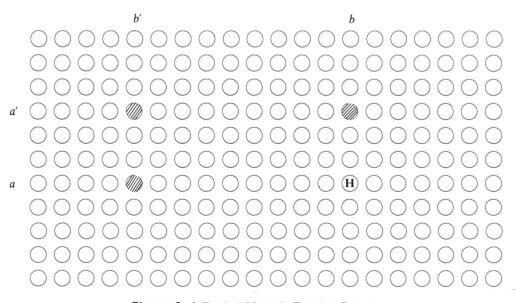

Figure 9. A Typical Move in Turning Corners.

0	0	0	0	0	0	0	0	0	0	0	0	0	0	0	0
0	1	2	3	4	5	6	7	8	9	10	11	12	13	14	15
0	2	3	1	8	10	11	9	12	14	15	13	4	6	7	5
0	3	1	2	12	15	13	14	4	7	5	6	8	11	9	10
0	4	8	12	6	2	14	10	11	15	3	7	13	9	5	1
0	5	10	15	2	7	8	13	3	6	9	12	1	4	11	14
0	6	11	13	14	8	5	3	7	1	12	10	9	15	2	4
0	7	9	14	10	13	3	4	15	8	6	1	5	2	12	11
0	8	12	4	11	3	7	15	13	5	1	9	6	14	10	2
0	9	14	7	15	6	1	8	5	12	11	2	10	3	4	13
0	10	15	5	3	9	12	6	1	11	14	4	2	8	13	7
0	11	13	6	7	12	10	1	9	2	4	15	14	5	3	8
0	12	4	8	13	1	9	5	6	10	2	14	11	7	15	3
0	13	6	11	9	4	15	2	14	3	8	5	7	10	1	12
0	14	7	9	5	11	2	12	10	4	13	3	15	1	8	6
0	15	5	10	1	14	4	11	2	13	7	8	3	12	6	9

Table 8. Have You Learnt Your Tims Table?

NIM-MULTIPLICATION

Observing that the nim-value $\mathscr{G}(0,n)=0$, while $\mathscr{G}(1,n)=n$, we guess that this might be a kind of multiplication, so we shall write

$$a \overset{*}{\times} b$$

(and you will read "a **tims** b") for the nim-value $\mathscr{G}(a,b)$ of the general coin in Turning Corners. We shall call this the **nim-product** of a and b.

It is shown in ONAG (Chapter 6) that this remarkable operation has all the usual algebraic properties of multiplication, and in particular obeys the distributive law

$$a \overset{*}{\times} (b \overset{*}{+} c) = a \overset{*}{\times} b \overset{*}{+} a \overset{*}{\times} c$$

with nim-addition. For example

$$7 \overset{*}{\times} (5 \overset{*}{+} 6) = 7 \overset{*}{\times} 3 = 14,$$

$$7 \overset{*}{\times} 5 \overset{*}{+} 7 \overset{*}{\times} 6 = 13 \overset{*}{+} 3 = 14.$$

But note, for example, that the nim-sum of 6 and 6 is not two sixes but no sixes, since $1 \overset{*}{+} 1$ is not 2, but 0.

In computing nim-products of larger numbers, the **Fermat powers** of 2,

$$2, \ 4, \ 16, \ 256, \ 65536, \ 4294967296, \ ..., \ 2^{2^n}, \ ...$$

play a role similar to that played by *all* the powers of 2 in nim-addition. Recall that in nim-addition if N is any power of 2 we have:

$$
\begin{aligned}
N \overset{*}{+} n &= N + n \quad \text{for } n < N, \\
N \overset{*}{+} N &= 0.
\end{aligned}
$$

For nim-multiplication, if N is any *Fermat* power of 2 we have:

$$
\begin{aligned}
N \overset{*}{\times} n &= N \times n \quad \text{for } n < N, \\
N \overset{*}{\times} N &= \tfrac{3}{2} N.
\end{aligned}
$$

For example, $16 \overset{*}{\times} 5 = 80$, as usual, but $16 \overset{*}{\times} 16 = 24$. Table 9 gives products of powers of 2.

1	2	4	8	16	32	64	128	256 ...
2	3	8	12	32	48	128	192	512 ...
4	8	6	11	64	128	96	176	1024 ...
8	12	11	13	128	192	176	208	2048 ...
16	32	64	128	24	44	75	141	4096 ...
32	48	128	192	44	52	141	198	8192 ...
64	128	96	176	75	141	103	185	16384 ...
128	192	176	208	141	198	185	222	32768 ...
256	512	1024	2048	4096	8192	16384	32768	384 ...

Table 9. Nim-products of Powers of 2.

SWIRLING TARTANS

Figure 10 indicates the coins which may be turned in a typical move of this game. The boxed places form what we call a **tartan**. In general we select a certain number of rows and a certain number of columns and the places of the tartan are where our chosen rows meet our chosen columns. In **Swirling Tartans** we may turn the coins of *any* tartan, but in other games there will be restrictions on the rows and columns we may choose. Table 9 is actually a table of nim-values for Swirling Tartans. This is a particular case of the following theory.

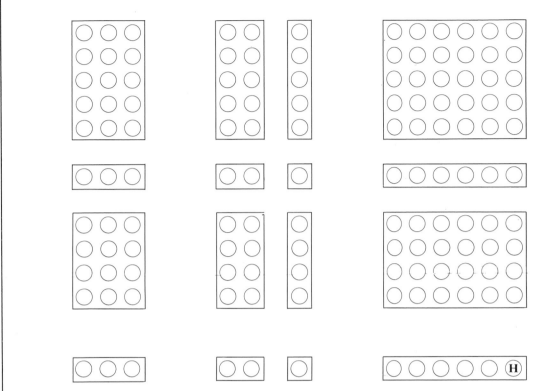

Figure 10. A Tartan.

THE TARTAN THEOREM

We can build a **tartan game**, $A \times B$, from two one-dimensional turning games, A and B, by specifying that the rows of the tartan shall correspond to the coins which may be turned in a move of game A and the columns to the coins which may be turned in a move of game B. Taking both A and B to be the game of Motley, in which *any* sets of coins may be turned, we see that

$$\text{MOTLEY} \times \text{MOTLEY} = \text{SWIRLING TARTANS}.$$

It follows from the Tartan Theorem that the nim-values for Swirling Tartans are the nim-products of those for two games of Motley—since the latter nim-values are just the powers of 2; this justifies our assertion about Table 9. More generally:

> the nim-values for the tartan game $A \times B$ are the nim-products of those for A and B:
>
> $$\mathscr{G}_{A \times B}(a,b) = \mathscr{G}_A(a) \overset{*}{\times} \mathscr{G}_B(b).$$

THE TARTAN THEOREM

The proof, which we do not give, depends on the following characterizing property of the nim-product $a \overset{*}{\times} b$.

> If $x_1, x_2, \ldots$ are numbers for which
> $$a = \mathrm{mex}(a \overset{*}{+} x_i)$$
> and $y_1, y_2, \ldots$ are numbers for which
> $$b = \mathrm{mex}(b \overset{*}{+} y_j)$$
> then we have
> $$a \overset{*}{\times} b = \mathrm{mex}(a \overset{*}{\times} b \overset{*}{+} x_i \overset{*}{\times} y_j).$$

This can be deduced from a result on p. 55 of ONAG.

RUGS, CARPETS, WINDOWS AND DOORS

In Turning Corners we turned over the corners of a rectangle, so that

$$\text{TURNING CORNERS} = \text{TWINS} \times \text{TWINS}.$$

In **Rugs** we turn over *all* the coins in some solid rectangle, in other words the tartan must be defined by a block of consecutive rows and a block of consecutive columns. Since in the Ruler Game a move was to turn over a block of consecutive coins, we have

$$\text{RULER} \times \text{RULER} = \text{RUGS},$$

and so the nim-values are those of Table 10.

A **carpet** is a tartan in which both rows and columns form symmetrical sets, as in Fig. 11, and the corresponding game, **Carpets**, has therefore the nim-values of Table 11:

$$\text{CARPETS} = \text{SYM} \times \text{SYM}.$$

1	2	1	4	1	2	1	8	1	2	1	4	1	2	1	16
2	3	2	8	2	3	2	12	2	3	2	8	2	3	2	32
1	2	1	4	1	2	1	8	1	2	1	4	1	2	1	16
4	8	4	6	4	8	4	11	4	8	4	6	4	8	4	64
1	2	1	4	1	2	1	8	1	2	1	4	1	2	1	16
2	3	2	8	2	3	2	12	2	3	2	8	2	3	2	32
1	2	1	4	1	2	1	8	1	2	1	4	1	2	1	16
8	12	8	11	8	12	8	13	8	12	8	11	8	12	8	128

Table 10. A Rug with a Table on it.

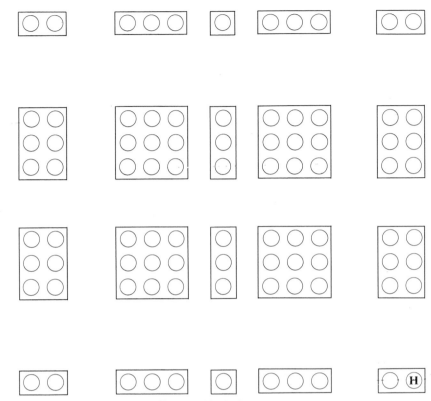

Figure 11. A Carpet.

In **Fitted Carpets** one is only allowed to turn carpets which fit snugly into the corner of the room, so

$$\text{FITTED CARPETS} = \text{SYMPLER} \times \text{SYMPLER}$$

whose analysis is left to the reader.

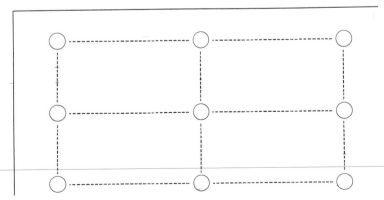

Figure 12. A Move in Windows.

1	2	4	3	6	7	8	16	18	25	32	11	64	31	128	10	256
2	3	8	1	11	9	12	32	35	46	48	13	128	37	192	15	512
4	8	6	12	14	10	11	64	72	79	128	7	96	65	176	3	1024
3	1	12	2	13	14	4	16	49	55	16	6	192	58	64	5	768
6	11	14	13	5	3	7	96	107	97	176	10	224	100	112	12	1536
7	9	10	14	3	4	15	112	121	120	144	1	160	123	240	6	1792
8	12	11	4	7	15	13	128	140	133	192	9	176	130	208	1	2048
16	32	64	48	96	112	128	24	56	136	44	176	75	232	141	160	4096
18	35	72	79	107	121	140	56	27	166	28	189	203	205	77	175	4608
25	46	79	55	97	120	133	136	166	20	204	178	187	117	221	171	6400
32	48	128	16	176	144	192	44	28	204	52	208	141	124	198	240	8192
11	13	7	6	10	1	9	176	189	178	208	15	112	184	144	4	2816
64	128	96	192	224	160	176	75	203	187	141	112	103	91	185	48	16384
31	37	65	58	100	123	130	232	205	117	124	184	91	17	173	167	7936
128	192	176	64	112	240	208	141	77	221	198	144	185	173	222	16	32768
10	15	3	5	12	6	1	160	175	171	240	4	48	167	16	14	2560
256	512	1024	768	1536	1792	2048	4096	4608	6400	8192	2816	16384	7936	32768	2560	384

Table 11. A Greatly-Valued Carpet.

In the game **Windows** we turn the nine coins where three equally spaced rows meet three equally spaced columns, as in Fig. 12, so that

$$\text{WINDOWS} = \text{TURNIPS} \times \text{TURNIPS}.$$

The nim-values form the most complex system we have yet discovered. To calculate the outcome of a given position we must perform no fewer than four successive operations:

1. Expand the two coordinates of a head in base 3 and find the last 2-digit (if any) in each.
2. Replace the coordinates by the corresponding odious numbers (or zero). This involves a further expansion, in base 2.
3. For each head find the *nim-product* of the two numbers so obtained.
4. Find the *nim-sum* of the numbers so found for all the heads.

In all these games there has been the condition that the coin most to the South-East in any move be turned from heads to tails. So that our next game deserves its name we will play it "upside-down" and impose the condition on the most North-East coin. The move in **Doors** is to turn over the twelve coins where any three equally spaced columns meet four symmetrically arranged rows, which must include the bottom row, as in Fig. 13. This shows that

$$\text{DOORS} = \text{TURNIPS} \times \text{GRUNT}$$

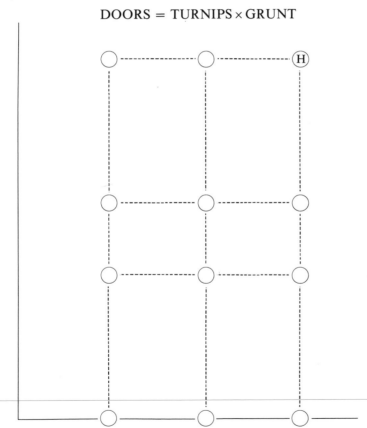

Figure 13. A Typical Move in Doors.

so you should soon be able to find the nim-value of the Doors position in which there is a single head in the 100th row and 100th column. (Beware: the first row is row number 0.)

ACROSTIC GAMES

There is another way to build a two-dimensional game out of two one-dimensional turning games, A and B. In the **acrostic product** $A \cup B$, the coins we turn must either all be in the same

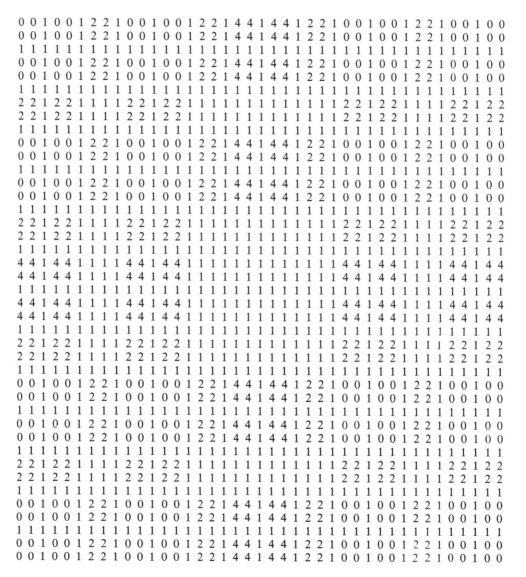

Table 12. A Field of Turnips.

column or all be in the same row. If the coins are all in a column, they must correspond to a move of game A; if all in a row, to a move of game B. We have already met one game of this type:

$$\text{ACROSTIC TWINS} = \text{TWINS} \cup \text{TWINS}.$$

In **Acrostic Turnips** we must, of course, upturn three turnips which are equally spaced and either in the same row or in the same column, the furthest from the corner of the field being turned from top to tail.

$$\text{ACROSTIC TURNIPS} = \text{TURNIPS} \cup \text{TURNIPS}.$$

The first 1681 nim-values are displayed in Table 12. It is not hard to prove that a row or column that begins with zero repeats the nim-sequence for Turnips itself, while the values not in such a row or column are 1.

STRIPPING AND STREAKING

We have no idea how to play the general acrostic product $A \cup B$, even when the one-dimensional games A and B are fully understood. But if it just should happen, as sometimes it does, that every nim-value of a place in each of your games is either 7 or a power of 2, we can offer you some help. We first discuss two easy games of this kind.

In **Streaking** we turn over any collection (**streak**) of coins all in the same row or column, so that

$$\text{STREAKING} = \text{MOTLEY} \cup \text{MOTLEY}.$$

Since the nim-values for Motley are exactly the powers of 2, and each nim-value for Streaking is the mex of all numbers that are sums of earlier nim-values from the same row or earlier nim-values from the same column, we find Table 13.

In **Stripping**, the coins we turn must be consecutive (form a **strip**) in either a row or a column. The entries in Table 14, of nim-values for

$$\text{STRIPPING} = \text{RULER} \cup \text{RULER},$$

can apparently be obtained from entries in Table 13. How do we explain this?

UGLIFICATION AND DERISION

We introduce an ambitious distraction. We shall call an entry in Table 13 (or 14) the **ugly product** of the two powers of 2 that head its row and column, and write

$$4 \mathbin{\overset{*}{\cup}} 8 = 10 \quad (\text{"four } \textbf{uggles} \text{ eight is ten"})$$

for example. Ugly products of other numbers can then be found using the distributive law:

$$4 \mathbin{\overset{*}{\cup}} 11 = 4 \mathbin{\overset{*}{\cup}} (8 \mathbin{\overset{*}{+}} 2 \mathbin{\overset{*}{+}} 1) = 10 \mathbin{\overset{*}{+}} 5 \mathbin{\overset{*}{+}} 4 = 11,$$
$$5 \mathbin{\overset{*}{\cup}} 11 = (4 \mathbin{\overset{*}{+}} 1) \mathbin{\overset{*}{\cup}} 11 = 11 \mathbin{\overset{*}{+}} 11 = 0.$$

The latter equation shows that 5 and 11 are **deriders of zero**. An uglification table up to 16 is given in Table 15.

```
  1    2    4    8   16   32   64  128  256 ...
  2    1    5    9   17   33   65  129  257 ...
  4    5    2   10   18   34   66  130  258 ...
  8    9   10    4   20   36   68  132  260 ...
 16   17   18   20    8   40   72  136  264 ...
 32   33   34   36   40   16   80  144  272 ...
 64   65   66   68   72   80   32  160  288 ...
128  129  130  132  136  144  160   64  320 ...
256  257  258  260  264  272  288  320  128 ...
.........................................................
```

Table 13. Streaking Values.

```
 1   2   1   4   1   2   1   8   1   2   1   4   1   2   1  16
 2   1   2   5   2   1   2   9   2   1   2   5   2   1   2  17
 1   2   1   4   1   2   1   8   1   2   1   4   1   2   1  16
 4   5   4   2   4   5   4  10   4   5   4   2   4   5   4  18
 1   2   1   4   1   2   1   8   1   2   1   4   1   2   1  16
 2   1   2   5   2   1   2   9   2   1   2   5   2   1   2  17
 1   2   1   4   1   2   1   8   1   2   1   4   1   2   1  16
 8   9   8  10   8   9   8   4   8   9   8  10   8   9   8  20
 1   2   1   4   1   2   1   8   1   2   1   4   1   2   1  16
 2   1   2   5   2   1   2   9   2   1   2   5   2   1   2  17
 1   2   1   4   1   2   1   8   1   2   1   4   1   2   1  16
 4   5   4   2   4   5   4  10   4   5   4   2   4   5   4  18
 1   2   1   4   1   2   1   8   1   2   1   4   1   2   1  16
 2   1   2   5   2   1   2   9   2   1   2   5   2   1   2  17
 1   2   1   4   1   2   1   8   1   2   1   4   1   2   1  16
16  17  16  18  16  17  16  20  16  17  16  18  16  17  16   8
```

Table 14. Stripping Values.

0	0	0	0	0	0	0	0	0	0	0	0	0	0	0	0	0
0	1	2	3	4	5	6	7	8	9	10	11	12	13	14	15	16
0	2	1	3	5	7	4	6	9	11	8	10	12	14	13	15	17
0	3	3	0	1	2	2	1	1	2	2	1	0	3	3	0	1
0	4	5	1	2	6	7	3	10	14	15	11	8	12	13	9	18
0	5	7	2	6	3	1	4	2	7	5	0	4	1	3	6	2
0	6	4	2	7	1	3	5	3	5	7	1	4	2	0	6	3
0	7	6	1	3	4	5	2	11	12	13	10	8	15	14	9	19
0	8	9	1	10	2	3	11	4	12	13	5	14	6	7	15	20
0	9	11	2	14	7	5	12	12	5	7	14	2	11	9	0	4
0	10	8	2	15	5	7	13	13	7	5	15	2	8	10	0	5
0	11	10	1	11	0	1	10	5	14	15	4	14	5	4	15	21
0	12	12	0	8	4	4	8	14	2	2	14	6	10	10	6	6
0	13	14	3	12	1	1	15	6	11	8	5	10	7	4	9	22
0	14	13	3	13	3	0	14	7	9	10	4	10	4	7	9	23
0	15	15	0	9	6	6	9	15	0	0	15	6	9	9	6	7
0	16	17	1	18	2	3	19	20	4	5	21	6	22	23	7	8

Table 15. The Uglification Table up to 16s.

For larger numbers we may use the following rules:

$$
\begin{aligned}
&\text{If } N \text{ is any power of 2 and } n < N, \\
&\text{we have} \\
&N \overset{*}{\circ} n =
\begin{cases}
N + \lfloor \tfrac{1}{2}n \rfloor & \text{if } n \text{ is odious} \\
\lfloor \tfrac{1}{2}n \rfloor & \text{if } n \text{ is evil,}
\end{cases} \\
&N \overset{*}{\circ} N = \lceil \tfrac{1}{2}N \rceil.
\end{aligned}
$$

The rows and columns of Table 15 which correspond to 7 and powers of 2 have been printed in bold type and their intersections have been boxed. We shall use the following properties of these rows.

1. The entries in any **bold** row are distinct. In symbols, if a is 7 or a power of 2, and $b \neq \bar{b}$, then

$$a \overset{*}{\cup} b \neq a \overset{*}{\cup} \bar{b}.$$

2. Each boxed entry is the mex of all previous entries in its row and column. That is, if both a and b are 7 or powers of 2, then $a \overset{*}{\cup} b$ is the mex of all numbers of the form

$$a' \overset{*}{\cup} b \text{ or } a \overset{*}{\cup} b', \qquad a' < a, \quad b' < b.$$

These are used in proving the following theorem.

If every nim-value of a place in each of A and B
is 7 or a power of 2, then the nim-values of the acrostic game $A \cup B$
are obtained by uglification of those for A and B:

$$\mathscr{G}_{A \cup B}(a,b) = \mathscr{G}_A(a) \overset{*}{\cup} \mathscr{G}_B(b).$$

THE UGLIFICATION THEOREM

To see this, let the typical move in game A or B turn the coins in places

$$a_1 < a_2 < \ldots < a$$

or

$$b_1 < b_2 < \ldots < b$$

respectively. We will denote the nim-values of these places by

$$\alpha_1, \alpha_2, \ldots, \alpha$$

and

$$\beta_1, \beta_2, \ldots, \beta$$

respectively. Then the nim-value $\mathscr{G}(a,b)$ in the acrostic product $A \cup B$ is the mex of all numbers of the form

$$\alpha_1 \overset{*}{\cup} \beta \overset{*}{+} \alpha_2 \overset{*}{\cup} \beta \overset{*}{+} \ldots$$

or

$$\alpha \overset{*}{\cup} \beta_1 \overset{*}{+} \alpha \overset{*}{\cup} \beta_2 \overset{*}{+} \ldots,$$

that is to say the mex of all numbers of the form

$$\bar{\alpha} \overset{*}{\cup} \beta \quad \text{or} \quad \alpha \overset{*}{\cup} \bar{\beta},$$

where

$$\bar{\alpha} = \alpha_1 \overset{*}{+} \alpha_2 \overset{*}{+} \ldots$$
$$\bar{\beta} = \beta_1 \overset{*}{+} \beta_2 \overset{*}{+} \ldots.$$

Now α is the mex of all numbers $\bar{\alpha}$ which arise in this way, and β is the mex of all numbers $\bar{\beta}$, so that every $\alpha' < \alpha$ is one of the numbers $\bar{\alpha}$ and every $\beta' < \beta$ is a $\bar{\beta}$. But each of α and β is either 7 or a power of 2 by assumption, so that certainly $\alpha \overset{*}{\cup} \beta$ is the mex of all numbers of the form

$$\alpha' \overset{*}{\cup} \beta \quad \text{or} \quad \alpha \overset{*}{\cup} \beta'.$$

Also, α is distinct from all the numbers $\bar{\alpha}$, and so $\alpha \overset{*}{\cup} \beta$ is distinct from all the numbers $\bar{\alpha} \overset{*}{\cup} \beta$, and similarly from $\alpha \overset{*}{\cup} \bar{\beta}$, and so $\alpha \overset{*}{\cup} \beta$ is *their* mex also.

This explains the values we found for Stripping and enables us to discuss a few similar games. For instance, in **Strip and Streak**, where we may turn coins in a horizontal strip or a vertical streak, the first few nim-values are as in Table 16.

1	2	1	4	1	2	1	8	1	2	1	4	1	2	1	16	1	2	...
2	1	2	5	2	1	2	9	2	1	2	5	2	1	2	17	2	1	...
4	5	4	2	4	5	4	10	4	5	4	2	4	5	4	18	4	5	...
8	9	8	10	8	9	8	4	8	9	8	10	8	9	8	20	8	9	...
16	17	16	18	16	17	16	20	16	17	16	18	16	17	16	8	16	17	...

Table 16. Strip and Streak.

Table 17 gives the nim-values for **Acrostic Mock Turtle Fives** in which we turn *up to three* coins provided that these are all contained in some horizontal or vertical strip of *five*.

1	2	4	7	8	1	2	4	7	8	1	2	4	7	8	...
2	1	5	6	9	2	1	5	6	9	2	1	5	6	9	...
4	5	2	3	10	4	5	2	3	10	4	5	2	3	10	...
7	6	3	2	11	7	6	3	2	11	7	6	3	2	11	...
8	9	10	11	4	8	9	10	11	4	8	9	10	11	4	...
1	2	4	7	8	1	2	4	7	8	1	2	4	7	8	...
2	1	5	6	9	2	1	5	6	9	2	1	5	6	9	...

Table 17. Acrostic Mock Turtle Fives.

EXTRAS

UNLOCKING DOORS

For Turnips, Table 5 shows that $\mathcal{G}(99) = 4$, while for Grunt, the discussion of Grundy's Game in Chapter 4 shows that $\mathcal{G}(99) = 5$; so a coin in the 100th row and 100th column of Doors has value

$$4 \text{ tims } 5 = 2.$$

SPARRING, BOXING AND FENCING

Turning games can be played in any number of dimensions. We mention just three 3-dimensional games. In **Sparring** we turn over any two coins in the same row, column or vertical, that is to say the two ends of a "spar". The typical entry in the nim-value table is the mex of previous entries in its row, column or vertical, so we have

$$\mathcal{G}(a,b,c) = a \overset{*}{+} b \overset{*}{+} c.$$

In **Boxing** we turn the eight corners of a rectangular "box". This is the 3-dimensional version of Turning Corners and its nim-values are three-term nim-products

$$\mathcal{G}(a,b,c) = a \overset{*}{\times} b \overset{*}{\times} c.$$

In **Fencing** we turn the four corners of a rectangular "fence" whose edges are parallel to any two of the three coordinate axes. It can be shown that

$$\mathcal{G}(a,b,c) = b \overset{*}{\times} c \overset{*}{+} c \overset{*}{\times} a \overset{*}{+} a \overset{*}{\times} b.$$

In each case the furthest turned coin from the origin must go from heads to tails.

"COINS" (OR HEAPS) WITH INFINITELY MANY (OR 2^{2^N}) "SIDES"

may be used to give lots of new "turning" games whose theory also involves Nim-multiplication. Thus if the move is to alter at most two of the heaps $H_{-1}, H_0, H_1, \ldots$ of which the rightmost one must be reduced, the $\mathcal{P}$-positions are those with

$$H_0 \overset{*}{+} H_1 \overset{*}{+} H_2 \overset{*}{+} \ldots = 0 \quad \text{and} \quad 0 \overset{*}{\times} H_0 \overset{*}{+} 1 \overset{*}{\times} H_1 \overset{*}{+} 2 \overset{*}{\times} H_2 \overset{*}{+} \ldots = H_{-1}$$

REFERENCES AND FURTHER READING

J.H. Conway, "On Numbers and Games", Academic Press, London and New York, 1976, Chapter 6.

Richard K. Guy, She loves me, she loves me not; relatives of two games of Lenstra, Een Pak met een Korte Broek, Papers presented to H.W. Lenstra, 77:05:18, Mathematisch Centrum, Amsterdam.

H.W. Lenstra, Nim multiplication, Séminaire de Théorie des Nombres, 1977–78 exposé No. 11, Université de Bordeaux.

Chapter 15

Chips and Strips

Many of the games in this chapter are derived in some way from Nim. Although Nim is usually played with heaps of chips it can also be played with coins on a strip, the move being to shift any coin leftwards any number of squares. Figure 1 shows the same Nim position in both versions. Moving a coin leftwards corresponds to reducing a heap.

We obtain many generalizations of Nim by varying the conditions under which heaps can be reduced, or coins moved.

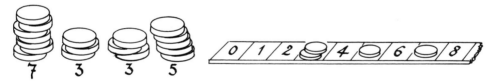

Figure 1. Two Forms of Nim.

THE SILVER DOLLAR GAME

In our first variant we allow at most one coin per square and do *not* allow one coin to jump over another. It can take quite a long time to discover that this is a cunning disguise for Nim, related to the game of Poker-Nim in Chapter 3. The sizes of the Nim-heaps are the lengths of *alternate* gaps between the coins starting from the rightmost coin (Fig. 2).

Observe that any *decrease* of one of these numbers is possible (by moving the coin at the *right* end of the gap) and that some *increases* are also possible (by moving the coin at the *left* end of a gap). We've indicated sample moves of both types in the figure. But just as in the theory of Poker-Nim, the increasing moves are mere reversible delaying moves and the winner wins by playing Nim.

457

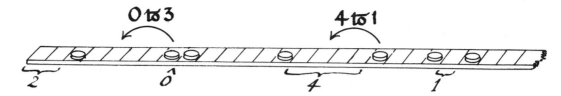

Figure 2. The Silver Dollar Game Without the Dollar.

N.G. de Bruijn has made the game more interesting by turning the leftmost square into a moneybag capable of holding any number of coins and making one of the coins a Silver Dollar, more valuable than all the others put together. Now the leftmost coin not already in the moneybag, may be put into the moneybag, as a move. The person who bags the dollar loses the game, because we also allow another move—pocket the moneybag!

Figure 3. De Bruijn's Silver Dollar Game.

In this version the moneybag counts as a *full* square when the first coin to the right of it is the Silver Dollar; otherwise as an *empty* one (it's because we don't want to put the dollar into the bag that we think of it as full when the dollar is the nearest coin to it!) If we win the Nim game we won't be forced to put the dollar into the bag.

If we allow whoever bags the dollar to pocket the bag all in one move, we count the bag as *full* only when there's just one other coin between it and the dollar. (We don't want to put *this* coin in the bag because our opponent will make sure it is immediately followed by the dollar!)

Find the winning moves in Fig. 3 in both versions.

PROFIT FROM GAMING TABLES

What do you do when you meet a game that's *not* analyzed in *Winning Ways*? You might be very lucky and get the hang of it after your first few games, but if you can't quite see what's going on and our theories don't seem to provide much of a clue, the best thing to do is to compile a **gaming table**. To do this profitably can take some skill in organizing the information. There'll be some varied examples in this chapter.

ANTONIM

Antipathetic Nim is Nim in which no two heaps are allowed to have the same number of chips. Of course, we don't notice empty heaps, so if you want to play it with coins on a strip the condition is that no two coins may be on the same square unless this square is the moneybag (square 0).

We can analyze 3-coin Antonim in a single table (Table 1). The headings are the sizes of two of the heaps and the entry is the unique size of heap that completes these to a $\mathscr{P}$-position. The typical entry is filled in as the least number not coinciding with any earlier entry in the same row or column, nor coinciding with either the row or column heading. An X denotes an illegal position. There is an obvious pattern showing that:

> (a, b, c) is a $\mathscr{P}$-position in Antonim just when
> $(a+1, b+1, c+1)$ is a $\mathscr{P}$-position in Nim.

	0	1	2	3	4	5	6	7	8	9	10	11	12	13	14
0	0	2	1	4	3	6	5	8	7	10	9	12	11	14	13
1	2	X	0	5	6	3	4	9	10	7	8	13	14	11	12
2	1	0	X	6	5	4	3	10	9	8	7	14	13	12	11
3	4	5	6	X	0	1	2	11	12	13	14	7	8	9	10
4	3	6	5	0	X	2	1	12	11	14	13	8	7	10	9
5	6	3	4	1	2	X	0	13	14	11	12	9	10	7	8
6	5	4	3	2	1	0	X	14	13	12	11	10	9	8	7
7	8	9	10	11	12	13	14	X	0	1	2	3	4	5	6
8	7	10	9	12	11	14	13	0	X	2	1	4	3	6	5
9	10	7	8	13	14	11	12	1	2	X	0	5	6	3	4
10	9	8	7	14	13	12	11	2	1	0	X	6	5	4	3
11	12	13	14	7	8	9	10	3	4	5	6	X	0	1	2
12	11	14	13	8	7	10	9	4	3	6	5	0	X	2	1
13	14	11	12	9	10	7	8	5	6	3	4	1	2	X	0
14	13	12	11	10	9	8	7	6	5	4	3	2	1	0	X·

Table 1. $\mathscr{P}$-positions for Three-Coin Antonim.

For Antonim with 4 coins we need a 3-D table, which we can build in layers. The next layer (Table 2) suggests that there is unlikely to be a simple rule, even for positions

$$(1, a, b, c),$$

so we have cut short the further layers (Table 3).

0	X	1	2	3	4	5	6	7	8	9	10	11	12	13	14
X	2	X	0	5	6	3	4	9	10	7	8	13	14	11	12
1	X	X	X	X	X	X	X	X	X	X	X	X	X	X	X
2	0	X	X	4	3	6	5	8	7	10	9	12	11	14	13
3	5	X	4	X	2	0	7	6	9	8	11	10	13	12	15
4	6	X	3	2	X	7	0	5	12	11	14	9	8	15	10
5	3	X	6	0	7	X	2	4	11	12	13	8	9	10	16
6	4	X	5	7	0	2	X	3	14	13	12	15	10	9	8
7	9	X	8	6	5	4	3	X	2	0	15	14	16	17	11
8	10	X	7	9	12	11	14	2	X	3	0	5	4	16	6
9	7	X	10	8	11	12	13	0	3	X	2	4	5	6	17
10	8	X	9	11	14	13	12	15	0	2	X	3	6	5	4
11	13	X	12	10	9	8	15	14	5	4	3	X	2	0	7
12	14	X	11	13	8	9	10	16	4	5	6	2	X	3	0
13	11	X	14	12	15	10	9	17	16	6	5	0	3	X	2
14	12	X	13	15	10	16	8	11	6	17	4	7	0	2	X

Table 2. $\mathscr{P}$-positions $(1,a,b,c)$ for Antonim.

It's not hard to show that the $\mathscr{P}$-positions with numbers $\leqslant 7$ are just

$$(0)12, \quad (0)34, \quad (0)56, \quad 135, \quad 146, \quad 236, \quad 245,$$
$$1234, \quad 1256, \quad 1367, \quad 1457, \quad 2357, \quad 2467, \quad 3456$$
$$(0)123456.$$

The 3-heap $\mathscr{P}$-positions are the lines of Fig. 4, counting the top node as 0; the 4-heap ones are the complements of lines, counting it as 7.

SYNONIM

In **Sympathetic Nim** all heaps of the same size must be treated alike—if you reduce one heap of a given size you must reduce all heaps of that size and by the same amount (no move may affect heaps of different sizes). In the strip version the move is to take *all* the coins from some square and put them on to any earlier square.

Table 2

0	X	1	2	3	4	5	6	7
X	1	0	X	6	5	4	3	10
1	0	X	X	4	3	6	5	8
2	X	X	X	X	X	X	X	X
3	6	4	X	X	1	7	0	5
4	5	3	X	1	X	0	7	6
5	4	6	X	7	0	X	1	3
6	3	5	X	0	7	1	X	4
7	10	8	X	5	6	3	4	X

Table 3

0	X	1	2	3	4	5	6	7
X	4	5	6	X	0	1	2	11
1	5	X	4	X	2	0	7	6
2	6	4	X	X	1	7	0	5
3	X	X	X	X	X	X	X	X
4	0	2	1	X	X	6	5	8
5	1	0	7	X	6	X	4	2
6	2	7	0	X	5	4	X	1
7	11	6	5	X	8	2	1	X

Table 4

0	X	1	2	3	4	5	6	7
X	3	6	5	0	X	2	1	12
1	6	X	3	2	X	7	0	5
2	5	3	X	1	X	0	7	6
3	0	2	1	X	X	6	5	8
4	X	X	X	X	X	X	X	X
5	2	7	0	6	X	X	3	1
6	1	0	7	5	X	3	X	2
7	12	5	6	8	X	1	2	X

Table 5

0	X	1	2	3	4	5	6	7
X	6	3	4	1	2	X	0	13
1	3	X	6	0	7	X	2	4
2	4	6	X	7	0	X	1	3
3	1	0	7	X	6	X	4	2
4	2	7	0	6	X	X	3	1
5	X	X	X	X	X	X	X	X
6	0	2	1	4	3	X	X	8
7	13	4	3	2	1	X	8	X

Table 3. $\mathscr{P}$-positions (k,a,b,c) for Antonim, $2 \leqslant k \leqslant 5$.

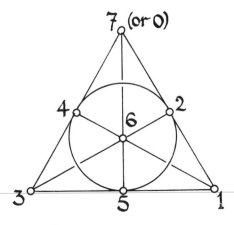

Figure 4. Fano's Fancy Antonim Finder.

This game need not detain us long. Since all the heaps of a given size must be treated in the same way they may be regarded as a single heap. A move reducing this heap to the size of an already existing heap has the same effect as removing the heap entirely. We might as well say that the heaps must always be of different sizes, so

> SYNONIM is
> just a synonym
> for ANTONIM!

SIMONIM

SImilar MOve NIM, or **Simonim**, was rediscovered by Simon Norton. It is just Nim with the additional feature that a player may make any number of moves provided that these are all exactly similar, i.e. that they all reduce some number a to another number b. It differs from Synonim in that we are *not* required to reduce *all* the heaps of a given size. If we play it with coins on a strip the rule becomes that any number of coins may be moved from any square to any earlier square, occupied or not. Table 4 is a bit harder to compute.

	0	1	2	3	4	5	6	7	8	9	10	11	12	13
0	→↓0	2	1	4	3	6	5	8	7	10	9	12	11	14
1	2	3	0	↓1	→4	7	8	5	6	11	12	9	10	15
2	1	0	4	→3	↓2	8	7	6	5	12	11	10	9	16
3	4	→1	↓3	2	0	9	10	11	12	5	6	7	8	17
4	3	↓4	→2	0	1	10	9	12	11	6	5	8	7	18
5	6	7	8	9	10	11	0	1	2	3	4	↓5	→12	19
6	5	8	7	10	9	0	12	2	1	4	3	→11	↓6	20
7	8	5	6	11	12	1	2	9	0	↓7	→10	3	4	21
8	7	6	5	12	11	2	1	0	10	→9	↓8	4	3	22
9	10	11	12	5	6	3	4	→7	↓9	8	0	1	2	23
10	9	12	11	6	5	4	3	↓10	→8	0	7	2	1	24
11	12	9	10	7	8	→5	↓11	3	4	1	2	6	0	25
12	11	10	9	8	7	↓12	→6	4	3	2	1	0	5	26
13	14	15	16	17	18	19	20	21	22	23	24	25	26	27

Table 4. $\mathscr{P}$-positions for Three-Coin Simonim.

As usual we try to fill in the least number not seen earlier in the row or column (or diagonal, if the entry is on the diagonal). But at most one entry n (written $\vec{n}$) in a row may equal its column label, at most one entry m (written $\downarrow m$) in a column may equal its row label and only the diagonal entry 0 may coincide with its row *and* column label.

When you've stared at Table 4 for an hour or two you'll notice various patterns which make the structure crystal clear. The solid dividing lines mark the closing up of the leading

$$1 \times 1, 5 \times 5, 13 \times 13,$$

and, in general

$$2^n - 3 \quad \text{by} \quad 2^n - 3$$

portions, which form Latin squares. The arrowed entries fall into 2×2 boxes. Various portions of the table resemble the nim-addition table.

After we'd extended the table into three dimensions and enlarged it in two, we were able to work out a general rule for 4-heap Simonim. With Simon's help we were even able to prove it!

Partition the positive integers into **ranges**

$$1, \quad 2\text{--}3, \quad 4\text{--}7, \quad 8\text{--}15, \quad 16\text{--}31, \quad \dots.$$

Then transform the Simonim position as follows:
Replace the first occurrence of a number n by n',
a second occurrence by n'', and a third by n''', where

$$n' = \begin{cases} n+3, & \text{if this is in the largest range} \\ & \text{that is represented in the} \\ & \text{transformed position,} \\ n+1, & \text{if this is in the next largest range} \\ & \text{that is represented in the} \\ & \text{transformed position,} \\ n, & \text{otherwise.} \end{cases}$$

$$n'' = \begin{cases} \text{the largest number in the range before } n', \text{ or} \\ \text{the next-to-largest number in this range,} \\ \quad \text{if } n \text{ is the next-to-largest number} \\ \quad \text{in the original position.} \end{cases}$$

$$n''' = \text{the largest number from the range before } n''$$

The original position will be a $\mathcal{P}$-position in
SIMONIM just if the transformed position
is a $\mathcal{P}$-position in NIM.

RULE FOR 4-HEAP SIMONIM

In applying the rule it's best to write the numbers in descending order. What should we do from

$$n \quad 16 \quad 9 \quad 4 \quad 1\,?$$

We find

$$n' \quad 19 \quad 10 \quad 4 \quad 1$$

whose nim-sum involves 16, so it can't be a $\mathscr{P}$-position. We must therefore decrease 16 to some value x for which $x+3$ won't be in the 16–31 range. Then

$$
\begin{array}{ccccc}
n & x & 9 & 4 & 1 \\
\hline
n' & ? & 12 & 5 & 1
\end{array}
$$

so ? must be $12 \overset{*}{+} 5 \overset{*}{+} 1 = 8$. Since this is in the largest range to appear in the transformed position,

$$x \text{ must be } 8 - 3 = 5.$$

Let's do

$$n \quad 9 \quad 9 \quad 7 \quad 2$$

Here we find $\left\{\begin{array}{ccccc} n' & 12 & & 10 & 2 \\ n'' & & 7 & & \end{array}\right\}$ nim-sum 3.

We can change the nim-sum to 0 by changing 2 into 1, 10 into 9 or 7 into 4, yielding the positions

$$
\begin{array}{cccc|cccc|cccc}
n & 9 & 9 & 7 & 1 & 9 & 9 & 6 & 2 & 9 & 3 & 7 & 2 \\
\hline
n' & 12 & & 10 & 1 & 12 & & 9 & 2 & 12 & 4 & 10 & 2 \\
n'' & & 7 & & & & 7 & & & & & &
\end{array}
$$

A really tricky example is

$$
\begin{array}{ccccc}
n & 44 & 33 & 22 & 11 \\
\hline
n' & 47 & 36 & 23 & 11 & \text{nim-sum } 23
\end{array}
$$

There's no hope of changing any of the nim-values 47, 36, or 11 by 23, while if we *remove* the 22 heap:

$$
\begin{array}{ccccc}
n & 44 & 33 & 0 & 11 \\
\hline
n' & 47 & 36 & 0 & 12 & \text{nim-sum } 7
\end{array}
$$

we don't arrive at a $\mathscr{P}$-position. The trick is to equalize the two small heaps:

$$
\begin{array}{cccc}
n & 44 & 33 & 11 & 11 \\
\hline
n' & 47 & 36 & 12 & \\
n'' & & & & 7
\end{array}\Big\} \text{ nim-sum 0.}
$$

STAIRCASE FIVES

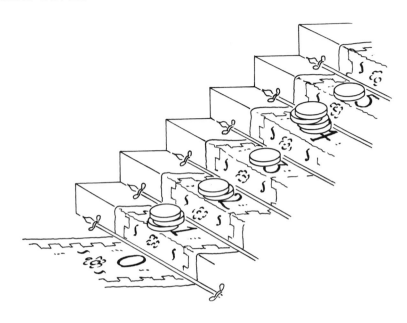

Figure 5. Stacks on Stairs.

You play this with coins on a staircase (Fig. 5). The move is to take any number, *less than five*, of coins from one step and put them on any lower step, *less than five* stairs away. The winner is the one who puts the last coin on the bottommost step.

If there are only 4 coins and 5 steps, the "five" restrictions don't matter and the game reduces to Antonim. A study of the upper 5×5 portion of Tables 1–3 provides an unexpectedly simple rule:

> Mentally interchange the coins on steps 2 and 4.
> Then the position is a $\mathscr{P}$-position just if the sum
> of the heights of all the coins is a multiple of 5.

Thus you should arrange that after your move, if there are

$$a \text{ coins on } 0, \quad b \text{ on } 1, \quad c \text{ on } 2, \quad d \text{ on } 3 \quad \text{and } e \text{ on } 4,$$

then

$$0 \cdot a + 1 \cdot b + 4 \cdot c + 3 \cdot d + 2 \cdot e$$

is divisible by 5.

The rule continues to apply with more coins and more steps provided we interchange steps $5n+2$ and $5n+4$.

TWOPINS (pronounced "Tuppins")

is a bowling game which generalizes Kayles ($\cdot$77) and Dawson's Kayles ($\cdot$07) in Chapter 4. This time the pins are set up in columns of 1 or 2 and the condition is that, as in Kayles, a legal shot must remove just 1 or 2 adjacent columns. But there is the additional rule that it is illegal to remove just a single pin.

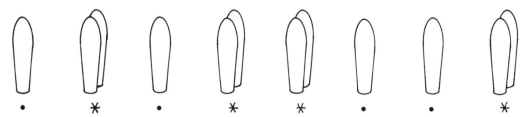

Figure 6. A Game of Twopins.

In discussing Twopins configurations we'll use

> $\cdot$ for a column of one,
> $*$ for a column of two,

so that the 2^n possible configurations of n non-empty Twopins columns are represented by the 2^n sequences of n $*$'s and $\cdot$'s. For instance we find

$$\cdot = 0, \qquad \cdot\,\cdot = \cdot\,\cdot\,\cdot = \cdot\,* \;\; = \cdot\,*\,\cdot = *, \qquad *\,\cdot\,* = *\,+\,* = 0,$$

and happily $*$, $**$, $***$ have values $*$, $*2$, $*3$; however, $**** = *$. Fortunately we don't need to list all possible sequences separately because there are several useful equivalences. For example it's easy to see that

$$\sim\!\sim\!\sim *\,\cdot\,. \qquad \sim\!\sim\!\sim \cdot\,\cdot \quad \text{and} \quad \sim\!\sim\!\sim *$$

all behave the same in play, while

$$\sim\!\sim\!\sim *\,\cdot\,\cdot\,* \sim\!\sim\!\sim \quad \text{behaves like} \quad \sim\!\sim\!\sim *\,*\,* \sim\!\sim\!\sim$$

There is also a useful **Twopins Decomposition Theorem**:

$$\sim\!\sim\!\sim *\,\cdot\,* \sim\!\sim\!\sim \;=\; \sim\!\sim\!\sim *\,+\,* \sim\!\sim\!\sim$$

After these theorems you can suppose that all strings have stars at each end and that dots come in internal blocks of three or more. Also the sequence $(*)^n$ of n stars behaves like the Kayles position K_n, while the sequences $(\cdot)^n$ and $*(\cdot)^{n-4}*$ behave like D_n in Dawson's Kayles, so you can read off their values from Chapter 4. Our Twopins-Wheel (Fig. 7) gives the nim-values of all other Twopins sequences of length 9 or less, except

$$*\,\cdot\,\cdot\,\cdot\,*\,\cdot\,\cdot\,*, \quad \text{nim-value 1}$$

Figure 7. A Twopins-Wheel.

All our equivalences remain valid in misère play, but the entries in the Twopins-Wheel should be replaced according to the scheme

For	read	genus	For	read	genus
0	0	0^1	**0**	$2+2$	0^0
1	1	1^0	**1**	$3+2$	1^1
2	2	2^2	**2**	$k_1 k 3_2 2_2 30$	2^2
3	3	3^3	**3**	$2_2 21 = d$	3^{1431}
4	$2_2 321 = k$	4^{146}	**4**	$3_2 320$	4^{046}
5	$k+1$	5^{057}	**5**	$kd3_2 210$	5^{3146}

Twopins has applications to Dots-and-Boxes (Chapter 16) and to

CRAM

which is Martin Gardner's name for impartial Domineering. It has also been called Plugg and Dots-and-Pairs, and is associated with the names of Geoffrey Mott-Smith, Sol Golomb and John Conway. You play it just like ordinary Domineering (Chapter 5; Martin Gardner called it Crosscram) except that *either* player may place his dominoes in *either* direction. You just cram them in however you can.

If you start with a rectangle with an even number of squares, then there's a simple symmetry strategy for the second player if the aim is to be the last to move, so it's a good idea to declare that the last one is the *loser*, i.e. to play Misère Cram.

It helps to see what's going on if you replace the available regions by graphs with nodes for squares, joined by edges when they're adjacent, as we did for Col (Chapter 2) and Snort (Chapter 6).

In this form the move is to delete two adjacent nodes and all edges running up to them, and you can play the game on arbitrary graphs. Only the abstract structure of the graph matters, so that many differently shaped regions can have the same graph, e.g.

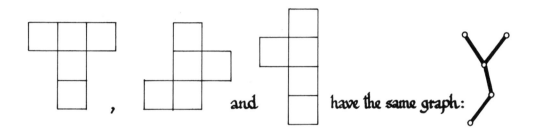

This graph, like many others, is a caterpillar. Formally, a **caterpillar** is a graph whose **body**

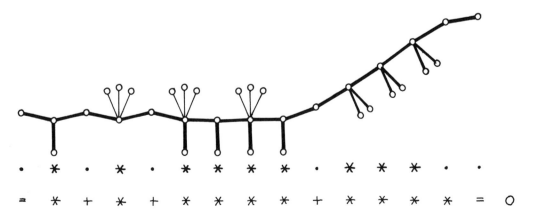

Figure 8. Even a Complicated Cram Caterpillar is a Twopins Position.

consists of a chain of nodes, some of which may have **tufts** (or legs) i.e. 1 or more edges leading to otherwise isolated nodes. Luckily, even the most complicated caterpillar (Fig. 8) is equivalent to a Twopins configuration, by letting

- · replace each untufted body node, and
- * represent any tufted one.

In this notation our Twopins equivalences become

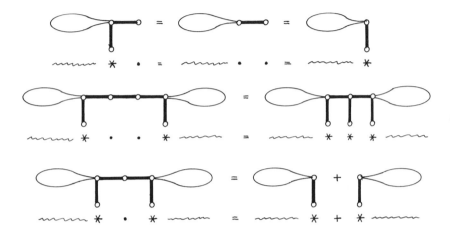

the last of which we might indicate in a single picture, using thin lines for edges which can all be omitted without affecting its value.

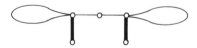

The balloons in our pictures need not be caterpillar-shaped and can even be allowed to meet, so our last identity becomes

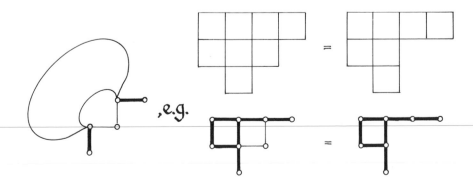

The diagrams in Fig. 9 have similar properties for example, the deletion of *all* thin edges in a diagram will not affect its value.

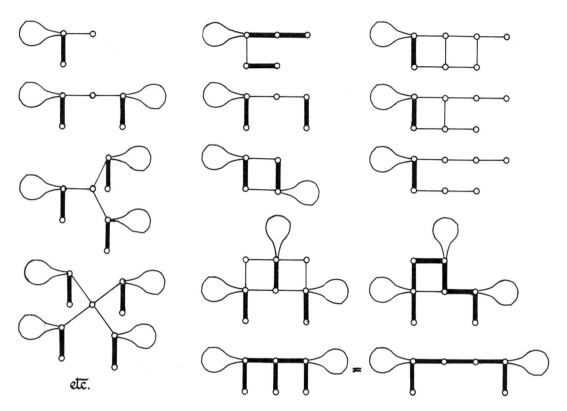

Figure 9. A Packet of Cram Crackers.

Table 5 gives values of a number of Cram positions. The dotted line indicates a chain of n edges where n is at the head of the table. We've given the full genus so that you can play Misère Cram. We use the letters

k for 2_2321 (position K_5 in Kayles),
d for 2_121 (position D_{10} in Dawson's Kayles),
e for 2_231 (arises in the *Ex*-Officer's Game, $\cdot 06$), and
f for 2_21 (arises in Flanigan's Game, $\cdot 34$)

in the last column, to list the games which are not Nim-heaps.

Some other values appear in Fig. 10. The ladder values in particular are easy to remember and the remark about tufts makes them extremely useful.

	0	1	2	3	4	5	6	non-Nim-heaps
number of edges in the dotted line								
	1	1	2	0	3	1	1	–
	2	2	3	3	1	2	4^{146}	k
	3	3	1	2	4^{146}	3	3	k
	1	1	4^{146}	0	3	5^{057}	2^2	$k, k+1, k_1k3_22_230$
	3	3	2	2	0	3	5^{057}	$kd3_2320$
	1	1	2	0	3	1	2^{0520}	$k3_230$
	0	0	1	1	2	2^{1420}	3	f
	0	3	1	2	2^{1420}	3	5^{3146}	$e, ked3_210$
	3	1	2	0	3^{1431}	3	2^{0520}	$d, d+1$
	1	1	2	0	3	1	2^{0520}	$kd3_230$
		3	1	0^0	4^{146}	1^1	3	$2_2, k, 3_2$
		1	2	2	3	3^{31}	5^{057}	$kf3_2210, k+1$
		2	2^{1420}	0	1	1	2	f

Table 5. The Genus of Various Cram Positions.

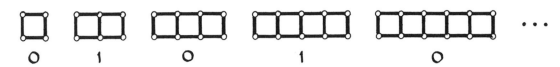

(The values of these ladders alternate and are unaffected by the addition of up to two tufts.)

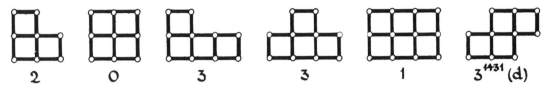

Figure 10. A Few More Cram Values.

WELTER'S GAME

This is the coin-on-strip game in which at most one coin may be on a square, and any leftwards move of a coin onto an empty square is permitted, even if it passes over other coins. Although the simplest cases were investigated by Roland Sprague, C.P. Welter discovered many remarkable properties of the general case. A simplified version of the theory is given in ONAG. Here we'll just tell you the answers and describe some new discoveries.

We'll write

$$[a|b|c|\ldots]_k \qquad (\text{"}a\text{ welt }b\text{ welt }c\text{ welt }\ldots\text{"})$$

for the nim-value of the Welter's Game position with coins on the k different squares

$$a, b, c, \ldots,$$

and will often omit k when the number of terms is clear. The easiest way to compute this **Welter function** is the **Mating Method**.

Mate those two of the k numbers that are congruent modulo the highest power of 2. Then select a pair of mates from the remaining $k-2$ numbers by the same rule, and so on. Eventually we have mated all except possibly one of the numbers (the **spinster**, s), say as

$$(a, b), (c, d), \ldots, \text{and possibly } s.$$

Then

$$[a|b|c|\ldots]_k = [a|b] \overset{*}{+} [c|d] \overset{*}{+} \ldots \qquad (\overset{*}{+} s \text{ if } k \text{ is odd}).$$

The two-term Welter function can be evaluated using the formula

$$[x|y] = (x \overset{*}{+} y) - 1.$$

For example,

$$[2|3|5|7|11|13|17|19]_8$$
$$= [3|19] \overset{*}{+} [5|13] \overset{*}{+} [7|11] \overset{*}{+} [2|17]$$
$$= \quad 15 \quad \overset{*}{+} \quad 7 \quad \overset{*}{+} \quad 11 \quad \overset{*}{+} \quad 18 \quad = 17,$$

there being no spinster in this case, while in

$$[0|1|4|9|16|25|36]$$
$$= [4|36] \overset{*}{+} [0|16] \overset{*}{+} [9|25] \overset{*}{+} 1$$
$$= \quad 31 \quad \overset{*}{+} \quad 15 \quad \overset{*}{+} \quad 15 \quad \overset{*}{+} 1 = 30$$

we see that 1 is the spinster. In this example there were two equally well mated pairs, (0, 16), (9, 25). In such cases it doesn't matter which pair we mate first.

FOUR-COIN WELTER IS JUST NIM

When you play a few games you'll soon notice, like many other people, that a Nim-like strategy suffices for Welter's Game with four coins, so that

$$[a|b|c|d] = 0 \quad \text{just if} \quad a \overset{*}{+} b \overset{*}{+} c \overset{*}{+} d = 0.$$

Welter's theory explains this by noting that if a, b and c, d are the mates, these equalities reduce to

$$[a|b] = [c|d] \quad \text{and} \quad a \overset{*}{+} b = c \overset{*}{+} d$$

which are equivalent since $[x|y] = (x \overset{*}{+} y) - 1$.

AND SO'S THREE-COIN WELTER!

If one of your four coins is on 0, you're really just playing three-coin Welter with the others, but shifted one place. In symbols

$$[0|a|b|c] = [a-1 \,|\, b-1 \,|\, c-1]$$

or

$$[a|b|c] = [0 \,|\, a+1 \,|\, b+1 \,|\, c+1].$$

Thus the Welter position with coins on 2, 5, 7 is equivalent to the Welter or Nim position with coins on 0,3,6,8, which is cured by moving 8 to 5, so in the three-coin position we should move 7 to 4.

THE CONGRUENCE MODULO 16

Although the Mating Method makes it very easy to work out nim-values, it's not so easy to find which move you should make to restore the nim-value to 0. But if the number of coins is a multiple of 4, there is a remarkable connexion with Nim:

$$\boxed{\begin{array}{c} [a|b|c|\ldots]_{4k} \equiv 0, \bmod 16 \\ \text{exactly when} \\ a \overset{*}{+} b \overset{*}{+} c \overset{*}{+} \ldots \equiv 0, \bmod 16. \end{array}}$$

This ensures in particular that when the $4k$ coins are among the first 16 places the Welter's game $\mathscr{P}$-positions are exactly the $\mathscr{P}$-positions in Nim that have distinct numbers. What are the good moves from

$$(0,1,2,3,5,7,11,13)?$$

The numbers	0	1	2	3	5	7	11	13	nim-add to 4,
and we get	4	5	6	7	1	3	15	9	by nim-adding 4 to them.
But the marks	×	×	×	×	×	×	×	√	

show that only the last of these is legal (the rest involve increases or moves to occupied squares) so the only good move is from 13 to 9.

Now let's look at

	2	3	5	7	11	13	17	19,	nim-sum 7,
giving	5	4	2	0	12	10	22	20,	on nim-adding 7,
which reduce to	5	4	2	0	12	10	6	4,	modulo 16.
	×	×	×		×				

So the only hopeful moves are

$$7 \text{ to } 0, \qquad 13 \text{ to } 10, \qquad 17 \text{ to } 6 \quad \text{and} \quad 19 \text{ to } 4.$$

But of the Welter functions

$$[2|3|5|0|11|13|17|19], \qquad [2|3|5|7|11|10|17|19], \qquad [2|3|5|7|11|13|6|19], \qquad [2|3|5|7|11|13|17|4]$$

only the third can be zero (glance at the mate of 17 to see that the binary expansion of the others must have a 16-digit). So the unique good move is from 17 to 6.

What happens when the number of coins *isn't* a multiple of 4? If there are 6 coins, say, on positions

$$1, 2, 3, 5, 8, 13$$

you can pretend that there are really 8 coins on places

$$-2, -1, 1, 2, 3, 5, 8, 13$$

on a strip you've perversely numbered starting from -2. Renumbering from 0 we see the position

	0	1	3	4	5	7	10	15	nim-sum 1
yielding	1	0	2	5	4	6	11	14	
	×	×		×	×		×		

so this time there are three good moves, from

$$3 \text{ to } 2, \quad 7 \text{ to } 6, \quad 15 \text{ to } 14, \quad \text{in the new notation,}$$
$$\text{or} \quad 1 \text{ to } 0, \quad 5 \text{ to } 4, \quad 13 \text{ to } 12, \quad \text{in the old.}$$

If there are 5 coins, say on

			2	3	5	7	11	
we increase by 3:	0	1	2	5	6	8	10	14	nim-sum 12
yielding				9	10	4	6	2	
				×	×		×	×	
decreasing again:						1			

showing that the only good move is from 5 to 1.

FRIEZE PATTERNS

Patterns of numbers such as

```
1    1    1    1    1    1    1    1    1    1    1    1    1   ...
   1    2    2    3    1    2    4    1    2    2    3    1   ...
      1    3    5    2    1    7    3    1    3    5    2   ...
         1    7    3    1    3    5    2    1    7    3   ...
      1    2    4    1    2    2    3    1    2    4   ...
   1    1    1    1    1    1    1    1    1    1   ...
```

(in which each diamond of numbers

$$\begin{matrix} & b & \\ a & & d \\ & c & \end{matrix} \quad \text{satisfies} \quad ad = bc + 1 \quad \text{so that} \quad d = \frac{bc + 1}{a}),$$

have many wonderful properties. For example, if you start with two horizontal rows of 1's connected by any zigzag of intermediate 1's, say

```
1    1    1    1    1    1    1    1    1    1    1
   1    ?    ?    ?    ?    !    ?    ?    !    .    .
      1    ?    ?    ?    !    ?    ?    ?    !    .
   1    ?    ?    ?    !    ?    ?    ?    !    .    .
      1    ?    ?    ?    !    ?    ?    ?    !    .
         1    ?    ?    !    ?    ?    ?    ?    !    .
      1    1    1    1    1    1    1    1    1
```

you'll find that all the entries are whole numbers and that each ! is 1 so that the pattern repeats itself alternately one way up then the other. These self-checking properties mean that your children can have fun while practising their arithmetic. If you want to check your own arithmetic on the above example, see the Extras.

G.C. Shephard has observed that we can replace multiplication by addition, making each diamond

$$\begin{matrix} & b & \\ a & & d \\ & c & \end{matrix} \quad \text{satisfy} \quad (a+d) = (b+c) + 1 \quad \text{so that} \quad d = b + c + 1 - a.$$

If we replace the starting 1's by 0's the resulting pattern

0	0	0	0	0	0	0	0	0	0	0	0	0	...
	0	1	2	4	3	0	1	2	4	3	0	1	...
		0	2	5	6	2	0	2	5	6	2	0	2	...
			0	4	6	4	1	0	4	6	4	1	0	...
		0	1	4	3	2	0	1	4	3	2	0	1	...
0	0	0	0	0	0	0	0	0	0	0	0	...

has similar properties, but this time it repeats itself the same way up.

We thought it might be a good idea to take the basic operation as nim-addition rather than ordinary multiplication or addition, and to our great surprise found that we had discovered a new way of calculating the Welter function!

You start with a row of zeros above the Welter position you want to evaluate, and work downwards making each diamond

$$\begin{array}{c} b \\ a \quad d \end{array} \quad \text{satisfy} \quad (a \overset{*}{+} d) = (b \overset{*}{+} c) + 1 \quad \text{so that} \quad c = ((a \overset{*}{+} d) - 1) \overset{*}{+} b,$$

(with c at the bottom)

and, in the unlikely event that you make no mistakes, you'll find the Welter function at the bottom of the triangle; e.g.

$$
\begin{array}{ccccccccc}
0 & & 0 & & 0 & & 0 & & 0 & & 0 & & 0 & & 0 & & 0 \\
& 2 & & 3 & & 5 & & 7 & & 11 & & 13 & & 17 & & 19 \\
& & 0 & & 5 & & 1 & & 11 & & 5 & & 27 & & 1 \\
& & & 7 & & 6 & & 14 & & 6 & & 16 & & 8 \\
& & & & 5 & & 6 & & 12 & & 16 & & 12 \\
& & & & & 4 & & 7 & & 29 & & 11 \\
& & & & & & 4 & & 21 & & 5 \\
& & & & & & & 23 & & 18 \\
& & & & & & & & 17
\end{array}
$$

yields the same answer as before, so *we* probably haven't made any mistakes! This rule is equivalent to the identity

$$[a|b|\ldots|y|z]_{k+1} = [[a|b|\ldots|y]_k \mid [b|\ldots|y|z]_k] \overset{*}{+} [b|\ldots|y]_{k-1}$$

which you can find in ONAG (p. 159).

Although by hand this calculation seems much longer, it's quite a good technique to use if you want to teach your computer to play Welter's Game.

INVERTING THE WELTER FUNCTION

Suppose that you've evaluated

$$[a|b|c|\ldots] = n$$

and have in mind a number $n' \neq n$. Then there are unique numbers

$$a' \neq a, \quad b' \neq b, \quad c' \neq c, \quad \ldots$$

for which

$$[a'|b|c|\ldots] = n',$$
$$[a|b'|c|\ldots] = n',$$
$$[a|b|c'|\ldots] = n',$$
$$\ldots\ldots\ldots\ldots\ldots$$

Moreover it can be shown that the equation

$$[a|b|c|\ldots] = n$$

remains true if any *even* number of the letters $a, b, c, \ldots, n$ are replaced by the corresponding primed letters. We express this happy state of affairs by the single "equation"

$$\begin{bmatrix} a & b & c & \ldots \\ a' & b' & c' & \ldots \end{bmatrix} = \begin{matrix} n \\ n' \end{matrix}$$

Using this Even Alteration Theorem and the properties of frieze patterns your computer can invert the Welter function.

For example, if you have five numbers with Welter function

$$[a|b|c|d|e] = n,$$

and want to find the numbers

$$a', b', c', d', e'$$

for which

$$\begin{bmatrix} a & b & c & d & e \\ a' & b' & c' & d' & e' \end{bmatrix} = \begin{matrix} n \\ n' \end{matrix}$$

you should complete the frieze pattern

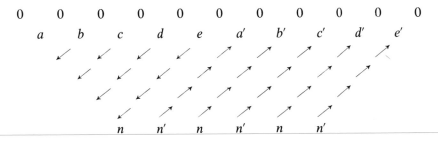

in which n and n' alternate along the bottom row, by working in the directions shown by the arrows.

Thus to find the good moves from

$$1 \quad 4 \quad 9 \quad 16 \quad 25$$

we must change one number to make the Welter function 0. The calculation

```
0    0    0    0    0    0  / 0    0    0    0    0  / 0    0
   1    4    9   16   25 / 36   33   12   13   28 / 1    4
      4   12   24    8 / 60    4   44    0   16 / 28    4
         3   26   31 / 42   19    6   39    2 / 23   22
           20   28 / 60    4   16   12   36 / 4   28
              29 / 0   29    0   29    0 / 29    0
```

(in which the rightmost two diagonals are only for checking) shows that

$$\begin{bmatrix} 1 & 4 & 9 & 16 & 25 \\ 36 & 33 & 12 & 13 & 28 \end{bmatrix} = \begin{matrix} 29 \\ 0 \end{matrix}$$

and so the only good move is from 16 to 13.

THE ABACUS POSITIONS

One day we idly wrote down the infinite frieze pattern

```
...  0   0   0   0   0   0   0   0 / 0 \ 0   0   0   0   0   0   0   0 ...
... 14  12  10   8   6   4   2 / 0   1 \ 3   5   7   9  11  13  15 ...
...  1   5   1  13   1   5 / 1   0   1 \ 5   1  13   1   5   1 ...
... 15   9   3  13   7 / 1   0   1   0 \ 6  12   2   8  14 ...
...  0   8   0   8 / 0   1   0   1   0 \ 8   0   8   0 ...
... 14   4  10 / 0   1   0   1   0   1 \ 11   5  15 ...
...  1  13 / 1   0   1   0   1   0   1 \ 13   1 ...
... 15 / 1   0   1   0   1   0   1   0 \ 14 ...
... / 0   1   0   1   0   1   0   1   0 \ ...
 ...  ...  ...  ...  ...  ...  ...  ...
```

which suggested to us the sequence of equations

$$\begin{bmatrix} 0 \\ 1 \end{bmatrix} = \begin{matrix} 0 \\ 1 \end{matrix} \qquad \begin{bmatrix} 2 & 0 \\ 1 & 3 \end{bmatrix} = \begin{matrix} 1 \\ 0 \end{matrix} \qquad \begin{bmatrix} 4 & 2 & 0 \\ 1 & 3 & 5 \end{bmatrix} = \begin{matrix} 1 \\ 0 \end{matrix} \quad \begin{bmatrix} 6 & 4 & 2 & 0 \\ 1 & 3 & 5 & 7 \end{bmatrix} = \begin{matrix} 0 \\ 1 \end{matrix} \cdots$$

$$\cdots \begin{bmatrix} 14 & 12 & 10 & 8 & 6 & 4 & 2 & 0 \\ 1 & 3 & 5 & 7 & 9 & 11 & 13 & 15 \end{bmatrix} = \begin{matrix} 0 \\ 1 \end{matrix} \cdots$$

Since we can interchange any even number of the pairs

$$(a,a'), (b,b'), (c, c'), \ldots , (n,n'),$$

we can reorder these equations to say

$$\begin{bmatrix} 0 \\ 1 \end{bmatrix} = \begin{bmatrix} 0 & 1 \\ 3 & 2 \end{bmatrix} = \begin{bmatrix} 0 & 1 & 2 \\ 5 & 4 & 3 \end{bmatrix} = \begin{bmatrix} 0 & 1 & 2 & 3 \\ 7 & 6 & 5 & 4 \end{bmatrix} = \begin{bmatrix} 0 & 1 & 2 & 3 & 4 \\ 9 & 8 & 7 & 6 & 5 \end{bmatrix} = \cdots = \begin{matrix} 0 \\ 1 \end{matrix}$$

For some reason the particular equation

$$\begin{bmatrix} 0 & 1 & 2 & 3 & 4 \\ 9 & 8 & 7 & 6 & 5 \end{bmatrix} = \frac{0}{1}$$

made us think of our abacus (Fig. 11) so we call the positions evaluated in the equation

$$\begin{bmatrix} 0 & 1 & 2 & \dots & k-3 & k-2 & k-1 \\ 2k-1 & 2k-2 & 2k-3 & \dots & k+2 & k+1 & k \end{bmatrix}_k = \frac{0}{1}$$

the k-coin **Abacus Positions**. Thus the equation

$$[9|1|2|6|5]_5 = 1$$

shows a 5-coin Abacus Position with its Welter function (or nim-value) 1.

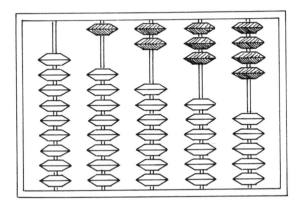

Figure 11. Swanpan.

THE ABACUS STRATEGY

We can give an explicit strategy for the Abacus Positions. Let the putative equation

$$[a|b|c|\dots]_k = 0$$

represent one of the Abacus Positions which we believe has Welter function 0. Define

$$a' = 2k - 1 - a, \qquad b' = 2k - 1 - b, \qquad c' = 2k - 1 - c, \qquad \dots$$

and note that we have an even number of

$$a > a', \quad b > b', \quad c > c', \quad \dots.$$

Now suppose your opponent makes the move which replaces a by x. Then since every number $\leqslant 2k - 1$ appears in the list

$$a, a', b, b', c, c', \dots,$$

x must be one of

$$a', b', c', \dots,$$

say b' or a'. If $x = b'$ we must have

$$a > b', \quad \text{and so} \quad b > a'$$

and we can respond with the move from b to a' since

$$[b'|a'|c\ldots]_k = 0$$

represents a simpler Abacus Position. If $x = a'$, then we have $a > a'$ and therefore an *odd* number of

$$b > b', \quad c > c', \quad \ldots$$

so that we can respond with one of the moves

$$b \text{ to } b', \quad c \text{ to } c', \quad \ldots.$$

A similar strategy shows that if

$$[a|b|c|\ldots]_k = 1$$

represents one of the Abacus Positions asserted to have Welter function 1, then for every move our opponent makes except the very last move of the game, we can reply with a move to another such position.

THE MISÈRE FORM OF WELTER'S GAME

The remarks we've just made show not only that the Abacus Positions really do have the asserted nim-values 0 and 1, but actually that they are equivalent to nim-heaps of sizes 0 and 1 even in the misère form of Welter's Game, for it is easy to see that there is a move from any non-terminal Abacus Position to an Abacus Position of the other value. In the language of Chapter 13,

> every Abacus Position is *fickle*,

because nim-heaps of sizes 0 and 1 swap outcomes when we change from normal to misère play. On the other hand,

> every *non*-Abacus Position is *firm*,

a result which establishes that

> Welter's Game
> is really tame!

It suffices to show that if we can move from some *non*-Abacus Position

$$(x, b, c, \ldots)\ldots$$

to some Abacus Position

$$(a, b, c, \ldots)$$

then we could also have moved to an Abacus Position of the opposite value. But in our previous notation, if $x > a'$ we can move to

$$(a', b, c, \ldots).$$

Otherwise we must have $x < a'$, since

$$(a', b, c, \ldots)$$

is an Abacus Position. Since all numbers $\leqslant 2k - 1$ appear among

$$a, a', b, b', c, c', \ldots$$

we can suppose that $x = b'$, say, whence

$$b' < a' \quad \text{and so} \quad a < b$$

so that we could have moved to

$$(b', a, c, \ldots).$$

> If you intend to *lose* Welter's Game,
> play as if you meant to win, until
> this would make you move into an
> Abacus Position, and then move instead to
> an Abacus Position of the opposite kind.

T.H. O'Beirne considered the misère form of Welter's Game. However our complete analysis, which independently reaches the same conclusions as that of Yamasaki, shows that his simple rule only works for very small numbers.

KOTZIG'S NIM

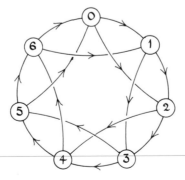

Figure 12. Kotzig's Nim on a 7-Place Strip with Move Set {1,2}.

You play this by placing coins on a circular strip. Start by placing a coin on any square—after that each player in turn puts a coin just m places further round the strip in a clockwise direction from the last coin placed. You must choose m from a previously decided **move set**. You lose if all the places where you might put coins are already occupied—you're only allowed to put one coin in any one place. Figure 12 is the directed graph (that's the way Anton Kotzig originally described his game) showing the successive places which may be occupied when the move set is $\{1, 2\}$ and you play on a 7-place strip. What happens?

By symmetry we can assume that the first player plays on 0, and then he can win as follows:

2nd	1st	2nd	1st	2nd	1st
1?	3!	~	6!		
2?	4!	5?	6	1	3.
		6?	1	3	5.

The sign $\sim$ means "any legal move". Where there's a choice of moves, we've put ! or ? to indicate winning or losing; other moves are forced.

If the move set contains only one move, m, the game is just She-Loves-Me, She-Loves-Me-Not. For if there are n places on the strip, there will be just n/d moves made, where d is the g.c.d. of m and n. If n/d is even, the second player wins; if odd, the first.

If the move set is $\{1, 2\}$, all values of n are $\mathscr{P}$-positions, except for $n = 1, 3$ and 7. We've already seen that $n=7$ is an $\mathscr{N}$-position, and it's easy to check that $n=1$ and 3 are, too. Here's a strategy for the second player in all other cases:

	1st	2nd	1st	2nd	1st	2nd	2nd	1st	2nd	1st	2nd
$n = 3k+2\ (k \geqslant 0)$	0?	1!	~	4!	~	7! ~ ... ~	$(3k+1)!$				
$n = 3k(k \geqslant 2)$	0?	2!	3?	4!	~	7! ~ ... ~	$(3k-2)!$	$3k-1$	1		
			4?	5!	~	8! ~ ... ~	$(3k-1)!$	1	3		
$n = 3k+1\ (k=1, k \geqslant 3)$	0?	2!	3?	5!	~	8! ~ ... ~	$(3k-1)!$	$3k$	1		
			4?	6!	7?	8! ~ ... ~	$(3k-1)!$	$3k$	1	3	5
					8?	9! ~ ... ~	$(3k)!$	1	3	5	7

(in the last case, if $k=1$, the move 4 is illegal, so play goes 0? 2! 3 1).

We've got quite used to games which behave regularly after a while, with a few exceptions near the beginning. If the move set is $\{1, 3\}$ the game is *exactly* periodic with period 6. The $\mathscr{N}$-positions are just those with $n \equiv 1$ or 3, mod 6. Here's Richard Nowakowski's explanation.

If n is even the first player always plays on even places, so the second player wins, since the move $m=1$ is always available to him.

If n is odd, then on the first tour of the strip, if a player A responds to a coin placed on p, say, with a coin on $p+1$, then the other player wins by putting a coin on $p+2$ (so long as $p+2 < n$) and A will find himself blocked the next time round. So each player uses the move $n=3$ as long as he can.

So if $n \equiv 3$, mod 6, the first player will arrive on $n-3$, forcing the second player to $n-2$, leaving $n-1$ to the first player, who wins next time round.

If $n \equiv 1$, mod 6, the first player arrives on $n-1$. The second time round both players are forced to play on places $p \equiv 2$, mod 3, and the last time round on places $p \equiv 1$, mod 3. Since n is odd, the first player wins.

If $n \equiv 5$, mod 6, the second player wins since first time round he arrives at $n-2$. The first player now plays on $n-1$ or on 1, and the corresponding winning replies are 2 and 4.

For the move set $\{2, 3\}$ we leave the reader to verify that

$$n \equiv 0, 1 \text{ and } 4, \quad \text{mod } 5 \text{ are } \mathscr{P}\text{-positions, } except \text{ for } n = 1, 5 \text{ and } 11, \text{ and}$$

$$n \equiv 2 \text{ and } 3, \quad \text{mod } 5 \text{ are } \mathscr{N}\text{-positions, } except \text{ for } n = 2.$$

Omar will also confirm that if the move set is $\{1, 2, 3\}$, then

the $\mathscr{P}$-positions are $n \equiv 0, 1, 2$, mod 4, except for $n = 1$ and 5, and
the $\mathscr{N}$-positions are $n \equiv 3$, mod 4,   except for $n = 7$,

and will go on to examine more complicated move sets.

FIBONACCI NIM

Suppose you play with just one heap of chips, and let the first player take away any number he likes, but not the whole heap. After that each player may take at most twice as many as the previous player took. Who wins?

The $\mathscr{P}$-positions turn out to be heaps with a Fibonacci number

$$u_1 = u_2 = 1, \quad u_3 = 2, \quad u_4 = 3, \quad u_5 = 5, \quad 8, \quad 13, \quad 21, \quad 24, \quad 55, \quad 89, \quad \ldots$$

of chips. Zeckendorf has a remarkable theorem which says that any whole number has a *unique* expression as the sum of *non-neighboring* Fibonacci numbers, for instance

$$54 = 34 + 13 + 5 + 2.$$

If the heap has a *non*-Fibonacci number of chips, the next player can win by taking any number of small terms from such an expansion, provided their total is *less than half* the next largest term. E.g. from a heap of 54 take 2, but not $2 + 5 = 7$ in case your opponent then takes 13.

MORE GENERALLY BOUNDED NIM

Suppose the rules are changed very slightly to read

"may take less than twice as many as"

instead of

"may take at most twice as many as";

does it make much difference? Curiously enough we get the same result as if we had changed the rules to read

"may take no more than".

If the number of chips is a power of 2 it's a $\mathscr{P}$-position in either case; otherwise the next player can win by taking the highest power of 2 which divides the number of chips.

Of course, if the rules say

"may take less than",

then, provided there's more than one chip, you win immediately by taking one, since your opponent then has no legal move. It's a disguise for She-Loves-Me-Constantly.

There are two whole series of such games, in which the rules read

"may take less than k times as many as"

or

"may take at most k times as many as".

For the "less than" games the sequence of $\mathscr{P}$-positions $\{a_n\}$ satisfies the recurrence relation

$$a_{n+1} = a_n + a_{n-l} \qquad \text{for } n \geqslant n_l,$$

and for the "at most" games the relation is

$$a_{n+1} = a_n + a_{n-m} \qquad \text{for } n \geqslant n_m,$$

where l, m, n_l and n_m are given in the table:

$k =$	1	2	3	4	5	6	7	...
$l =$	–	0	2	5	7	10	13	...
$m =$	0	1	3	5	7	10	13	...
$n_l =$	–	2	5	13	14	23	28	...
$n_m =$	2	3	6	9	11	19	24	...

To be consistent with the usual labelling of the Fibonacci numbers we start each sequence with $a_2 = 1$. The "less than" sequences continue with

$$a_i = i - 1 \quad (2 \leqslant i \leqslant k+1), \qquad a_i = 2i - k - 2 \ (k+1 \leqslant i \leqslant (3k+2)/2), \qquad \ldots$$

and the "at most" ones with

$$a_i = i - 1 \quad (2 \leqslant i \leqslant k+2), \qquad a_i = 2i - k - 3 \quad (k+2 \leqslant i \leqslant (3k+5)/2), \qquad \ldots$$

but as k increases, it takes longer and longer before the sequences settle down. Omar, having stayed with us so far, will doubtless find the exact way in which these sequences and the above table continue.

EPSTEIN'S PUT-OR-TAKE-A-SQUARE GAME

This is also played with just one heap of chips. At each turn there are just two options: to add or take away the largest perfect square number of chips that there is in the heap. For example, if the number in the heap *is* a perfect square other than 0, the next player can win by taking the whole heap.

This is a loopy game! If we start from a heap of 2, the legal moves are to add or subtract 1. The first player won't take 1, leaving a perfect square, so he adds 1 to make 3. For the same reason his opponent doesn't *add* 1, so he takes 1 and the game is drawn.

But 5 is a $\mathscr{P}$-position since 5 ± 4 are both squares! And $4 \times 5 = 20$, $9 \times 5 = 45$, $16 \times 5 = 80$ are also $\mathscr{P}$-positions; why not 125? A slightly more interesting $\mathscr{P}$-position is 29. The next player won't *subtract* 25, but when he adds it to make 54, his opponent can go to 5 and win.

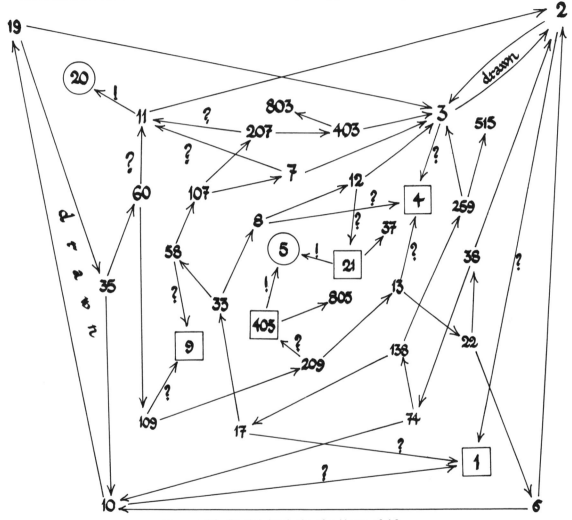

Figure 13. Partial Analysis of a Heap of 10.

Figure 13 shows part of the analysis of games starting from 10. If you continue the figure you'll soon realize why we don't give a complete analysis of Epstein's game. Squares and other $\mathscr{N}$-positions are in square boxes, $\mathscr{P}$-positions are circled.

Here is a list which includes all $\mathscr{P}$-positions of remoteness $\leqslant 14$ below 5000, and a few of the more interesting $\mathscr{N}$-positions.

$\mathscr{P}$-positions	$\mathscr{N}$-positions
Remoteness 0 : 0	
	Remoteness 1 : all squares
Remoteness 2 : 5, 20, 45, 80, 145, 580, 949, 1305, 1649, 2320, 3625, 4901, 5220, …	
	Remoteness 3 : 11, 14, 21, 30, 41, 44, 54, 69, 86, 105, 120, 126, 141, 149, 164, 174, 189, 216, 291, …
Remoteness 4 : 29, 101, 116, 135, 165, 236, 404, 445, 540, 565, 585, 845, 885, 909, 944, 954, 975, 1125, 1310, 1350, 1380, 1445, 1616, 1654, 1669, 2325, 2340, 2405, 2541, 2586, 2705, 3079, 3150, 3185, 3365, 3380, 3405, 3601, 3630, 3705, 4239, 4921, 4981, 5225, 5265, …	
	Remoteness 5: 52, 71, 84, 208, 254, 284, 296, 444, …
Remoteness 6 : 257, 397, 629, 836, 1177, 1440, 1818, 1833, 1901, 1937, 1988, 2210, 2263, 2280, 2501, 2516, 2612, 2845, 2861, 3039, 3188, 3389, 3621, 3654, 3860, 4053, 4105, 4541, 4693, 4708, 4813, 4930, …	
	Remoteness 7 : 136, 436, 1291, …
Remoteness 8 : 477, 666, 5036, …	
	Remoteness 9 : 252, 342, …
Remoteness 10 : 173, …	
	Remoteness 11 : 92, …
Remoteness 12 : 3341, 3573, 3898, 4177, 4229, 4581, …	
	Remoteness 13 : 1809, 1962, …
Remoteness 14 : 1918, …	

If you want to know how to win from a heap of 92, look in the Extras.

The misère form of the game is uninteresting, because the increasing move is always available.

TRIBULATIONS AND FIBULATIONS

What happens if we use another system of numbers instead of squares? An easy case is $2^k - 1$, but more interesting ones have been suggested to us, namely the triangular numbers 1, 3, 6, 10, 15, 21, … (Simon Norton) and the Fibonacci numbers plus one, 1, 2, 3, 4, 6, 9, 14, 22, 35, … (Mike Guy). See the Extras.

THIRD ONE LUCKY

Ordinary Nim ends when a player takes the last stick. Misère Nim may be thought of as over when only one stick remains. What happens if we say the game's over when exactly two sticks remain, the winner being the player who takes the third last stick? Even the three-heap version of this game is quite hard.

If there are m sticks in the first heap, and n in the second, there is a unique size for the third heap to make a $\mathcal{P}$-position. For fixed m, this size is eventually arithmetico-periodic in n. The periods for

$$m = 1\ 2\ 3\ 4\quad 5\quad 6\quad 7\ 8\ 9\ 10\ 11\ 12\ 13\ 14\ 15\ 16\ 17\ 18\quad 19\ \ldots$$
$$\text{are}\quad 1\ 2\ 4\ 2\ 12\ 12\ 12\ 8\ 8\ 10\ 60\ 60\ 84\ 84\ 84\ 16\ 18\ 180\ 20\ \ldots$$

HICKORY, DICKORY, DOCK

Dean Hickerson suggested this game in which a move replaces a heap of n by *three* heaps of sizes

$$k, n-k, n-2k \qquad \text{where} \qquad 1 \leqslant k \leqslant \tfrac{1}{2}n.$$

It looks rather like Turnips in the last chapter, but in fact the nim-values for $n = 1, 2, 3, \ldots$ are the exponents, 0, 1, 0, 2, 0, 1, 0, 3, 0, ... of the nim-values (Fig. 7 of Chapter 14) for the Ruler Game.

D.U.D.E.N.E.Y

is a game,

Deductions Unfailing, Disallowing Echoes, Not Exceeding Y;

a particular case of which was described by Dudeney as "The 37 Puzzle Game".

From a single heap either player may subtract a number from 1 to Y:

"Not Exceeding Y"

except that the immediately previous deduction may not be repeated:

"Disallowing Echoes"

and you win if you can always move:

"Deductions Unfailing",

but at some stage your opponent cannot.

If echoes were *not* disallowed, the $\mathcal{P}$-positions would be the multiples of $Y+1$ and the winner would always follow a deduction of X by one of $Y+1-X$. This strategy still works for D.U.D.E.N.E.Y when Y is even because it is impossible for $Y+1-X$ to equal X. So we'll suppose from now on that Y is odd.

Here are the good moves from N when $Y = 3$:

from N =	0	1	2	3	4	5	6	7	8	9	10	11	...
deduct	?	1	1, 2	3	?	1	1, 2, 3	3	?	1	1, 2, 3	3	...

and here they are for $Y = 5$:

from N =	0	1	2	3	4	5	6	7	8	9	10	11	12	
deduct		?	1	1, 2	3	4	5	3	?	1, 4	2, 3	3, 5	4	5

from N =	13	14	15	16	17	18	19	20	21	22	23	24	25	...
deduct		?	1	1, 2, 4	3	4, 5	5	3	?	1	1, 2, 3	3, 5	4	5 ...

For $Y = 3$ there is an ultimate period of 4; for $Y = 5$ a period of 13. The easiest way to win is to move to one of those **pearls** among numbers, which have a ? entry, indicating that the next player has no good move at all. Pearls are $\mathscr{P}$-positions no matter what the previous move, but there are other $\mathscr{P}$-positions in which the only winning move is disallowed by the echo rule.

In general the pearls are spaced at intervals of either

$$E = Y + 1, \quad \text{the next even number after Y, or}$$
$$D = Y + 2, \quad \text{the next odd one.}$$

For, if P is a pearl then after most moves from $P + E$ or $P + D$ we can go immediately to P. The only exceptions are the moves from

$$P + E \text{ to } P + \tfrac{1}{2}E \quad \text{and} \quad P + D \text{ to } P + E.$$

If the first of these is a bad move, $P + E$ is a pearl, and if it's a good one, $P + D$ is a pearl.

From a given position there's usually only one move which will prevent your opponent from reducing to an earlier pearl, though sometimes there can be two. So it's fairly easy to determine the status of the critical move

$$P + E \text{ to } P + \tfrac{1}{2}E$$

by searching back along one or two alleys. In the case $Y = 5$, the critical moves from

$$13 \text{ to } 10 \quad \text{and} \quad 26 \text{ to } 23$$

are bad, because they can be answered by

$$10 \text{ to } 5 \quad \text{and} \quad 23 \text{ to } 18$$

but those from

$$6 \text{ to } 3 \quad \text{and} \quad 19 \text{ to } 16$$

are good, and are indicated by bold **3**'s.

STRINGS OF PEARLS

Knowing the pearls helps you to win the game: move directly to a pearl if you can, and otherwise prevent your opponent from doing so. So all we need tell you is the sequence of D's and E's separating the pearls. These are (ultimately—see entries 55 and 95) periodic. In Table 6 the periods are in parentheses, and $r \geqslant 0$. Much of the work was done by John Selfridge and Roger Eggleton.

In his chapter on subtraction games, Schuh discusses this game, together with its misère form, and the two variants in which the outcome is changed if play terminates at 1.

Y	Pearl-string	Y	Pearl-string
3 or $8r+3$	(E)EEE ...	41	(DDDEDE) ...
5 or $8r+5$	(DE)DEDE ...	55	DD(EDE)EDE ...
7	(DEE)DEE ...	63 or $128r+63$	(E)EE ...
9	(DDE)DDE ...	65 or $128r+65$	(DDDE)DDDE ...
15 or $32r+15$	(E)EE ...	71 or $64r+71$	(DE)DEDE ...
17 or $32r+17$	(DDE)DDE ...	73 or $128r+73$	(DDEDE)DDEDE ...
23	(DDEDDDEE) ...	87 or $128r+87$	(DDE)DDE ...
25 or $32r+25$	(DE)DE ...	95	DDEE(DDE)DDE ...
31 or $128r+31$	(DEE)DEE ...	97	(DDEDDDE) ...
33	(DDDEDDE) ...	103	(DE)DEDE ...
39 or $128r+39$	(DEE)DEE ...	105 or $128r+105$	(DE)DEDE ...

Table 6. Strings of Pearls for D.U.D.E.N.E.Y for $\frac{53}{64}$ of the odd Values of Y.

SCHUHSTRINGS

Prof. Schuh also discusses the variation in which 0 is a permissible deduction, but the person who first gets to 0 wins.

Starting from any positive number n you'll always have at least one good move, because if no positive deduction wins for you, you can deduct 0 and present your opponent with a similar situation, except that 0 is now illegal. How can a positive deduction

$$n \text{ to } n-g$$

possibly be a good move? The only move it prohibits from $n-g$ is

$$n-g \text{ to } n-2g$$

and so this must be the unique good move from $n-g$. But then similarly

$$n-2g \text{ to } n-3g,$$
$$n-3g \text{ to } n-4g,$$
$$\dotsb$$

must be good moves, the last of which must be from

$$g \text{ to } 0.$$

A positive deduction g can therefore only be good at a **string**,

$$g, 2g, 3g, \dots, kg, \dots,$$

of multiples of g. It will be good from $(k+1)g$ if and only if it was the *unique* good move from kg. The first multiple of g from which there's another good move will terminate the g-string.

Thus, when the permissible deductions are 0, 1, 2, 3, 4, 5, we find that the good moves are:

from $n = 1$ 2 3 4 5 6 7 8 9 10 11 12 13 14 15 16 17 18 19 20 ...

deduct   1 1,2] 3 4 5 3 0 4 3 5 0 3,4] 0 0 5 0 0 0 0 5 ...

The 1- and 2-strings terminate at 2 and the 3- and 4-strings at 12, but the 5-string continues indefinitely.

In general, if there are two or more numbers

$$a, b, \ldots$$

whose strings have not yet terminated, then the first number to occur in two or more strings will terminate those strings. At most one string continues forever. In Table 7 an entry (a, b) means that the a- and b-strings terminate at their l.c.m., while an entry $g\infty$ corresponds to an infinite g-string, and is only relevant when the largest deduction is odd. It is not known whether there is any Schuhstring game in which three or more strings terminate simultaneously.

2 or 3	4 or 5	6 or 7	8 or 9	10 or 11	12 or 13	14 or 15
(1,2)	(1,2)	(1,2)	(1,2)	(1,2)	(1,2)	(1,2)
3∞	(3,4)	(3,6)	(3,6)	(3,6)	(3,6)	(3,6)
	5∞	(4,5)	(4,8)	(4,8)	(4,8)	(4,8)
(1,2)		7∞	(5,7)	(5,10)	(5,10)	(5,10)
(3,6)		(1,2)	9∞	(7,9)	(9,12)	(7,14)
(4,8)		(3,6)	(1,2)	11∞	(7,11)	(9,12)
(5,10)		(4,8)	(3,6)	(1,2)	13∞	(11,13)
(7,14)		(5,10)	(4,8)	(3,6)	(1,2)	15∞
(9,18)		(7,14)	(5,10)	(4,8)	(3,6)	(1,2)
(11,22)		(9,18)	(7,14)	(5,10)	(4,8)	(3,6)
(12,24)		(11,22)	(9,18)	(7,14)	(5,10)	(4,8)
(13,26)		(12,24)	(11,22)	(9,18)	(7,14)	(5,10)
(15,20)		(15,20)	(12,16)	(12,16)	(9,18)	(7,14)
(21,27)	(16,17)	(13,16)	(15,20)	(15,20)	(12,16)	(9,12)
(16,17)	(19,21)	(17,19)	(13,17)	(11,13)	(11,13)	(11,13)
(19,23)	(23,25)	(21,23)	(19,21)	(17,19)	(15,17)	(15,16)
25∞		25∞	23∞	21∞	19∞	17∞
27	26	25 or 24	23 or 22	21 or 20	19 or 18	17 or 16

Table 7. Schuhstrings Corresponding to Various Maximum Deductions.

THE PRINCESS AND THE ROSES

When we originally planned *Winning Ways*, the Princess was to have had a chapter all to herself, but as with other beautiful and intriguing women, we probably dallied too long in her company and it now seems more discreet to limit our memoirs to a brief résumé of our rencontres.

Perhaps our narrative will steer a course between the original bare account of Prof. Schuh and the later flights of fancy of Monsieur Filet de Carteblanche.

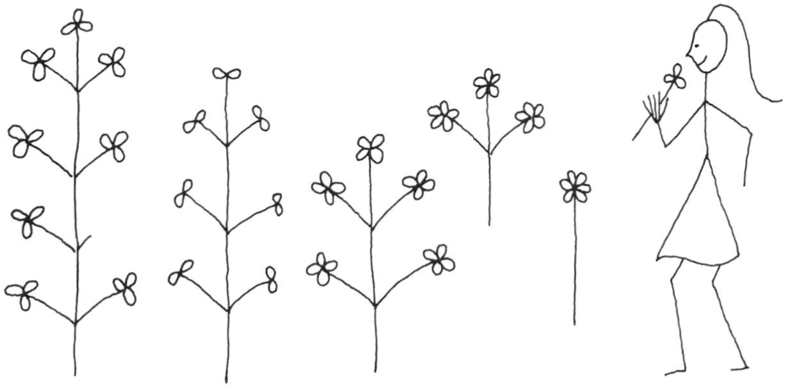

Figure 14. Princess Romantica Smells Charming Charles's Rose.

The Princess Romantica is known to have had two princely suitors, Handsome Hans and Charming Charles. Each suitor went in turn to the rose-garden and would bring back a rose, or two roses from different bushes. In Fig. 14 you can see the Princess smelling the beautiful rose that Charming Charles has just brought from the largest bush. Eventually one suitor, finding himself unable to bring her a rose because none was left in the garden, crept despondently away, and left the other to claim her hand as in Fig. 15. Which was the lucky Prince?

Figure 15. Who Won the Hand of the Princess?

Of course, you can play the game as a heap game in which the legal move is to take any one chip, or any two, one from each of two distinct heaps. Prof. Schuh showed that a worldly prince in a 5-bush garden should always arrange that when the numbers are put in descending order, they form one of the patterns

$$\text{even–even–even–even–even,}$$
$$\text{even–odd –odd –odd –odd,}$$
$$\text{odd –even–even–odd –odd,}$$
$$\text{odd –odd –odd –even–even.}$$

Obviously Charles knew what he was doing and Prof. Schuh's researches leave little doubt that he must be the man depicted in Fig. 15.

You can see from Prof. Schuh's rule that when there's only a small number of bushes (which may contain a large number of roses).

$$\boxed{\text{parity considerations are paramount.}}$$

However, when there are many few-rose bushes then

$$\boxed{\text{it is triality that triumphs}}$$

because the $\mathscr{P}$-positions ultimately are just those in which the total number of roses is a multiple of three.

This reveals itself by the final subscript 3's in Tables 8, 9 and 10 which respectively list all $\mathscr{P}$-positions of the forms

$$3^x 2^y 1^z \qquad \text{or} \qquad a.2^y 1^z \qquad \text{or} \qquad a.b.1^z,$$

i.e.

$$
\left.
\begin{array}{l}
x\ \text{3-rose bushes,} \\
y\ \text{2-rose bushes,} \\
z\ \text{1-rose bushes}
\end{array}
\right\}
\quad \text{or} \quad
\left.
\begin{array}{l}
1\ a\text{-rose bush,} \\
y\ \text{2-rose bushes,} \\
z\ \text{1-rose bushes}
\end{array}
\right\}
\quad \text{or} \quad
\begin{array}{l}
1\ a\text{-rose bush,} \\
1\ b\text{-rose bush,} \\
z\ \text{1-rose bushes.}
\end{array}
$$

In these tables an entry n_3 represents all numbers of the infinite arithmetic progression

$$n, n+3, n+6, n+9, \ldots$$

while $m_d n$ represents the finite progression

$$m, m+d, m+2d, \ldots, n,$$

and so on; for example, the entry $_6 7_5 17_3$ represents 1, 7, 12, 17, 20, 23, 26, 29, ...

x \ y	0	1	2	3	4	5	6	7	8	9	10	11
0	0_3	$_44_3$	$_55_3$	0_3	$_44_3$	$_55_3$	0_3	$_44_3$	$_55_3$	0_3	$_44_3$	$_55_3$
1	$_46_3$	4_3	2_3	3_3	4_3	2_3	3_3	4_3	2_3	3_3	4_3	2_3
2	$_56_3$	4_3	2_3	3_3	1_3	2_3	3_3	1_3	2_3	3_3	1_3	2_3
3	0_3	$_44_3$	$_55_3$	0_3	1_3	2_3	0_3	1_3	2_3	0_3	1_3	2_3
4	3_3	4_3	2_3	0_3	1_3	2_3	0_3	1_3	2_3	0_3	1_3	2_3
5	$_56_3$	4_3	2_3	0_3	1_3	2_3	0_3	1_3	2_3	0_3	1_3	2_3
6	0_3	1_3	2_3	0_3	1_3	2_3	0_3	1_3	2_3	0_3	1_3	2_3
7	0_3	1_3	2_3	0_3	1_3	2_3	0_3	1_3	2_3	0_3	1_3	2_3

Table 8. $\mathscr{P}$-positions of Type $3^x 2^y 1^z$. Entries Are Sets of Values of z.

y \ a	0	1	2	3	4	5	6	7	8	9	10	11
0	0_3	2_3	$_44_3$	$_46_3$	$_48_3$	$_410_3$	$_412_3$	$_414_3$	$_416_3$	$_418_3$	$_420_3$	$_422_3$
1	$_44_3$	3_3	$_55_3$	4_3	$_66_3$	4_48_3	$_66_410_3$	4_412_3	$_66_414_3$	4_416_3	$_66_418_3$	4_420_3
2	$_55_3$	4_3	0_3	2_3	$_44_3$	$_46_3$	$_48_3$	$_410_3$	$_412_3$	$_414_3$	$_416_3$	$_418_3$
3	0_3	2_3	$_44_3$	3_3	$_55_3$	4_3	$_66_3$	4_48_3	$_66_410_3$	4_412_3	$_66_414_3$	4_416_3
4	$_44_3$	3_3	$_55_3$	4_3	0_3	2_3	$_44_3$	$_46_3$	$_48_3$	$_410_3$	$_412_3$	$_414_3$
5	$_55_3$	4_3	0_3	2_3	$_44_3$	3_3	$_55_3$	4_3	$_66_3$	4_48_3	$_66_410_3$	4_412_3
6	0_3	2_3	$_44_3$	3_3	$_55_3$	4_3	0_3	2_3	$_44_3$	$_46_3$	$_48_3$	$_410_3$
7	$_44_3$	3_3	$_55_3$	4_3	0_3	2_3	$_44_3$	3_3	$_55_3$	4_3	$_66_3$	4_48_3

Table 9. $\mathscr{P}$-positions of Type $a \cdot 2^y 1^z$. Entries Are Sets of Values of z.

b \ a	0	1	2	3	4	5	6	7	8	9	10	11
0	0_3	2_3	$_44_3$	$_46_3$	$_48_3$	$_410_3$	$_412_3$	$_414_3$	$_416_3$	$_418_3$	$_420_3$	$_422_3$
1	2_3	1_3	3_3	$_45_3$	$_47_3$	$_49_3$	$_411_3$	$_413_3$	$_415_3$	$_417_3$	$_419_3$	$_421_3$
2	$_44_3$	3_3	$_55_3$	4_3	6_3	$_48_3$	$_610_3$	$_412_3$	$_614_3$	$_416_3$	$_618_3$	$_420_3$
3	$_46_3$	$_45_3$	4_3	$_56_3$	$_58_3$	$_67_3$	$_69_3$	$_67_411_3$	$_69_413_3$	$_67_415_3$	$_69_417_3$	$_67_419_3$
4	$_48_3$	$_47_3$	6_3	$_58_3$	$_510_3$	$_59_3$	$_6{}_511_3$	$_610_3$	$_612_3$	$_610_414_3$	$_612_416_3$	$_610_418_3$
5	$_410_3$	$_49_3$	$_48_3$	$_67_3$	$_59_3$	$_511_3$	$_513_3$	$_67_512_3$	$_69_514_3$	$_613_3$	$_615_3$	$_613_417_3$
6	$_412_3$	$_411_3$	$_610_3$	$_69_3$	$_6{}_511_3$	$_513_3$	$_515_3$	$_514_3$	$_6{}_616_3$	$_610_515_3$	$_612_517_3$	$_616_3$
7	$_414_3$	$_413_3$	$_412_3$	$_67_411_3$	$_610_3$	$_67_512_3$	$_514_3$	$_516_3$	3_518_3	$_67_517_3$	$_69_519_3$	$_613_518_3$
8.	$_416_3$	$_415_3$	$_614_3$	$_69_413_3$	$_612_3$	$_69_514_3$	$_6{}_616_3$	3_518_3	$_520_3$	$_519_3$	$_66_521_3$	$_610_520_3$
9	$_418_3$	$_417_3$	$_416_3$	$_67_415_3$	$_610_414_3$	$_613_3$	$_610_515_3$	$_67_517_3$	$_519_3$	$_521_3$	$_523_3$	$_67_522_3$
10	$_420_3$	$_419_3$	$_618_3$	$_69_417_3$	$_612_416_3$	$_615_3$	$_612_517_3$	$_69_519_3$	$_66_521_3$	$_523_3$	$_525_3$	$_524_3$
11	$_422_3$	$_421_3$	$_420_3$	$_67_419_3$	$_610_418_3$	$_613_417_3$	$_616_3$	$_613_518_3$	$_610_520_3$	$_67_522_3$	$_524_3$	$_526_3$

Table 10. $\mathscr{P}$-positions of Type $a \cdot b \cdot 1^z$. Entries Are Sets of Values of z.

The tables also illustrate that there are places between the parity and triality regions in which the outcome depends on considerations mod 4 and 5, so that

> quaternity's a quality,

> quinticity can be quintessential,

and there are even hints that

> sex may be significant;

but we have explored other regions in which it sadly seems that

> randomness reigns.

In his first paper on this subject *M*. de Carteblanche asks for a code of behavior for princes in a 6-bush garden wherein there's a bush with only 1 rose. You'll find one in the Extras. In a second paper he further describes how the princes, after their weddings to Romantica and her even more beautiful younger sister Belladonna, transformed the rose game into a different one with chocolates and discovered some more interesting games to play.

ONE-STEP, TWO-STEP

This is the strip game in which arbitrarily many coins are allowed on a square, and the legal move is to make either one step or two steps, a **step** being to move a single coin just one space leftwards. The coins moved in the two steps of a 2-step move may be the same or different.

Letting a_n be the number of coins on square n, we can ask when

$$a_0 a_1 a_2 \ldots$$

represents a $\mathscr{P}$-position. The answer certainly won't depend on a_0 since coins on square 0 will never be moved again.

There's a surprising connexion between this game and our previous one. In fact the position described above behaves exactly like

$$a_1 + a_2 + a_3 + \ldots + a_n, \quad a_2 + a_3 + \ldots + a_n, \quad a_3 + \ldots + a_n, \quad \ldots, a_{n-1} + a_n, \quad a_n$$

in the Princess-and-Roses game! We leave it to Omar to work out why.

So when your coins are all in the first 6 places, you can translate Prof. Schuh's rules to give the $\mathscr{P}$-positions, which are

$$?eeeee, \quad ?deeed, \quad ?deded, \quad ?eedee,$$

where e means even, d means odd and ? means anything.

MORE ON SUBTRACTION GAMES

Since $\mathscr{G}(n)$ for a heap of n beans in the subtraction game (see Chapter 4)

$$S(s_1, s_2, \ldots, s_k)$$

depends only on k earlier values, namely

$$\mathscr{G}(n-s_1), \mathscr{G}(n-s_2), \ldots, \mathscr{G}(n-s_k),$$

we see that $\mathscr{G}(n) \leqslant k$. Moreover this sequence of k values must eventually repeat so the nim-sequences of all subtraction games are (ultimately) periodic. But the bound on the length of the period given by this argument seems astronomical when compared with the facts. Can you find something nearer the truth?

We have seen that if the g.c.d. $(s_1, s_2, \ldots, s_k)$ is $d > 1$, then the game is just the d-plicate of a simpler game. Thus $S(s_1)$ is the s_1-plicate of $S(1)$, She-Loves-Me, She-Loves-Me-Not, and so has period $2s_1$ and nim-sequence $\dot{0}.00\ldots0111\ldots\dot{1}$.

We can also analyse $S(s_1, s_2)$ and $S(s_1, s_2, s_1 + s_2)$ completely. Write

$$s_1 = a, \quad s_2 = b = 2ha \pm r \quad \text{for } 0 \leqslant r \leqslant a$$

and suitable h. After the g.c.d. remark we needn't consider $r = 0$ or a unless $a = 1$.

$S(1, 2h)$ has period $2h+1$ and nim-sequence $\dot{0}.10101\ldots01\dot{2}$, and $S(1, 2h+1) = S(1)$. (In fact $s_1 = 1$ and all s_i odd gives She-Loves-Me, She-Loves-Me-Not.)

For $a>1$ the period of $S(a, b)$ contains $a+b$ digits, alternating blocks of a 0's and a 1's, except that the last $a-r$ 0's are replaced by 2's, where r is as above. For example: $a=3$, $r=1$; the nim-sequences for $S(3, 11)$ and $S(3, 13)$ are

$$\dot{0}.0011100011122\dot{2} \quad \text{and} \quad \dot{0}.001110001110022\dot{1}.$$

Here is a general method for analyzing $S(s_1, s_2, \ldots, s_k)$. Write the numbers in $k+1$ columns. The first row is

$$0, \quad s_1, \quad s_2, \quad \ldots \quad s_k.$$

Each later row is of the form

$$l, \quad l+s_1, \quad l+s_2, \quad \ldots \quad l+s_k,$$

where l is the least whole number which hasn't appeared in earlier rows. The table will eventually become periodic in that a block of c consecutive rows can be obtained from the preceding block of c by adding p to all the entries, for a suitable c and p.

The first column contains all numbers n for which $\mathscr{G}(n)=0$, and the second, by Ferguson's pairing property, just those for which $\mathscr{G}(n)=1$. Later columns contain numbers for which $\mathscr{G}(n)\geqslant 2$, apart from repetitions of entries in the second column. We illustrate with $S(1, b, b+1)$. If b is even (Fig. 16(a)) there are no such repetitions, the period is $2b$ and the nim-sequence is

$$\dot{0}.101\ldots012323\ldots2\dot{3}.$$

$\mathscr{G}(n) =$	0	1	2	3		$\mathscr{G}(n) =$	0	1	3	2	except that
$n =$	0	1	10	11		$n =$	0	1	9	10	$\mathscr{G}(9) = 1$
	2	3	12	13			2	3	11	12	
	4	5	14	15			4	5	13	14	
	6	7	16	17			6	7	15	16	
	8	9	18	19			8	9	17	18	
	20	21	30	31			19	20	28	29	$\mathscr{G}(28) = 1$
	22	23	32	33			21	22	30	31	
	24	25	34	35			23	24	32	33	
	26	27	36	37			25	26	34	35	
	28	29	38	39			27	28	36	37	
	40	41	50	51			38	39	47	48	$\mathscr{G}(47) = 1$
	42	...					40	...			
		(a)						(b)			

Figure 16. The Subtraction Games $S(1,10,11)$ and $S(1,9,10)$.

If b is odd (Fig. 16b) there is one repetition $(9, 28, 47, \ldots)$ in each period, whose length is $2b+1$. The nim-sequence is as before, but with the final 3 omitted:

$$\dot{0}.101\ldots012323\ldots\dot{2}.$$

To complete the analysis of $S(a, b, a+b)$ note that the case $a>1$, $b=2ha-r$, $0<r<a$ is fairly straightforward. It is illustrated by a period of ha rows in Fig. 17; there are r repetitions (boxed in the figure) so the period is $4ha-r=2b+r$. The period comprises h blocks of a 0's and a 1's followed by $h-1$ blocks of a 2's and a 3's, then a 2's and $a-r$ 3's.

$G(n) =$	0	1		
$n =$	0	a	$2ha - r$	$(2h+1)a - r$
	1	$a+1$	$2ha - r + 1$	$(2h+1)a - r + 1$
	2	$a+2$	$2ha - r + 2$	$(2h+1)a - r + 2$
	. . . .	. . . .	. . . .	. . . .
	$r-1$	$a+r-1$	$2ha - 1$	$(2h+1)a - 1$
	r	$a+r$	$2ha$	$(2h+1)a$
	. . . .	. . . .	. . . .	. . . .
	$a-1$	$2a-1$	$(2h+1)a - r - 1$	$(2h+2)a - r - 1$
	$2a$	$3a$	$(2h+2)a - r$	$(2h+3)a - r$
	$2a+1$	$3a+1$	$(2h+2)a - r + 1$	$(2h+3)a - r + 1$
	. . . .	. . . .	. . . .	. . . .
	$3a-1$	$4a-1$	$(2h+3)a - r - 1$	$(2h+4)a - r - 1$
	$4a$	$5a$	$(2h+4)a - r$	$(2h+5)a - r$
	$4a+1$	$5a+1$	$(2h+4)a - r + 1$	$(2h+5)a - r + 1$
	. . . .	. . . .	. . . .	. . . .
	$5a-1$	$6a-1$	$(2h+5)a - r - 1$	$(2h+6)a - r - 1$
	. . . .	. . . .	. . . .	. . . .
	$(2h-2)a$	$(2h-1)a$	$(4h-2)a - r$	$(4h-1)a - r$
	$(2h-2)a+1$	$(2h-1)a+1$	$(4h-2)a - r + 1$	$(4h-1)a - r + 1$
	. . . .	. . . .	. . . .	. . . .
	$(2h-1)a - r - 1$	$2ha - r - 1$	$(4h-1)a - 2r - 1$	$4ha - 2r - 1$
	$(2h-1)a - r$	$2ha - r$	$(4h-1)a - 2r$	$4ha - 2r$
	. . . .	. . . .	. . . .	. . . .
	$(2h-1)a - 1$	$2ha - 1$	$(4h-1)a - r - 1$	$4ha - r - 1$

(The entries $2ha-r$ through $2ha-1$ in the $G(n)=0$ column near the top, and $2ha-r$ through $2ha-1$ in the lower portion, are shown boxed.)

Figure 17. Analysis of $S(a,b,a+b)$, $b = 2ha-r$, $0 < r < a$, $(a,b) = 1$.

The case $b = 2ha + r$, $0 < r < a$, is more complicated. The period is a times as long, $(2b+r)a$. We illustrate it with the particular case $a = 5$, $b = 43$, $h = 4$, $r = 3$ in Fig. 18. The $ar\ (=15)$ repetitions are shown boxed.

In either of the cases $b = 2ha \pm r$, the ith value of n for which $\mathcal{G}(n) = 0$ is

$$n_i = i + \left\lfloor \frac{i}{a} \right\rfloor a + \left\lfloor \frac{2i}{b+r} \right\rfloor b$$

and the ith value for which $\mathcal{G}(n) = 1$ is $a + n_i$ by Ferguson's pairing property.

```
 0   5  43  48     93  98 136 141                      269 274 312 317
 1   6  44  49     94  99 137 142                      270 275 313 318
 2   7 [45] 50     95 100[138]143                      271 276[314]319
 3   8 [46] 51     96 101 139 144                      272 277[315]320
 4   9 [47] 52     97 102 140 145                      273 278 316 321

10  15  53  58    103 108 146 151   186 191 229 234    279 284 322 327    362 367 405 410
11  16  54  59    104 109 147 152   187 192 230 235    280 285 323 328    363 368 406 411
12  17  55  60    105 110 148 153   188 193 231 236    281 286 324 329    364 369 407 412
13  18  56  61    106 111 149 154   189 194 232 237    282 287 325 330    365 370 408 413
14  19  57  62    107 112 150 155   190 195 233 238    283 288 326 331    366 371 409 414

20  25  63  68    113 118 156 161   196 201 239 244    289 294 332 337    372 377 415 420
21  26  64  69    114 119 157 162   197 202 240 245    290 295 333 338    373 378 416 421
22  27  65  70    115 120 158 163   198 203 241 246    291 296 334 339    374 379 417 422
23  28  66  71    116 121 159 164   199 204 242 247    292 297 335 340    375 380 418 423
24  29  67  72    117 122 160 165   200 205 243 248    293 298 336 341    376 381 419 424

30  35  73  78    123 128 166 171   206 211 249 254    299 304 342 347    382 387 425 430
31  36  74  79    124[129]167 172   207 212 250 255    300 305 343 348    383 388 426 431
32  37  75  80    125[130]168 173   208 213 251 256    301[306]344 349    384 389 427 432
33  38  76  81    126 131 169 174   209 214 252 257    302 307 345 350    385 390 428 433
34  39  77  82    127 132 170 175   210 215 253 258    303 308 346 351    386 391 429 434

40 [45] 83  88    133[138]176 181   216[221]259 264    309[314]352 357    392[397]435 440
41 [46] 84  89                      217 222 260 265    310[315]353 358    393 398 436 441
42 [47] 85  90    177 182 220 225   218[223]261 266                       394 399 437 442
                  178 183[221]226   219 224 262 267    354 359[397]402    395 400 438 443
86  91[129]134    179 184[222]227                      355 360[398]403    396 401 439 444
87  92[130]135    180 185[223]228   263 268[306]311    356 361[399]404
```

Figure 18. Analysis of $S(5,43,48)$.

MOORE'S NIM$_k$

E.H. Moore suggested the heap game in which the legal move is to reduce the size of any positive number, up to k, of heaps. Thus Nim$_1$ is ordinary Nim, and Nim$_2$ is the game in which you can reduce just *one* or *two* heaps. The theory rather surprisingly involves calculations in base two and in base $k+1$. You

> *Expand* the numbers in base 2, and
> *Add* them in base $k+1$, without carrying.

You should move to positions in which this "sum" is zero.

For example, if $k = 2$, and you are confronted with

5 =	101		5 =	101
6 =	110		6 =	110
9 =	1001		3 =	11
10 =	1010		7 =	111
	——			——
	2222			000

you must reduce the 9 and 10 heaps, replacing them by 3 and 7.

Smith's analysis of Subselective Compounds (Chapter 12) is similar. Nim-values for Moore's game have been found by Jenkyns and Mayberry. Yamasaki has shown that it is tame, and that a position is fickle only if its nonzero heaps are all of size 1, and the number of them is 0 or 1 modulo $k + 1$.

THE MORE THE MERRIER

Bob Li has suggested that ordinary Nim can be adapted for n players. They take turns in a fixed cyclic order and there are different grades of winner.

> *First prize* goes to the player who makes the last move,
> *Second prize* to the immediately previous player, and so on, until the
> *Booby prize*, which goes to the player who was first unable to move.

Sharing of prizes is not permitted: as soon as the game ends each player must take his prize and set off for his home town without any under-the-table payoffs for help he might have received from some of the other players.

Li was surprised to find that his game was very similar to Moore's. Take the position you're faced with and add the binary expansions of your numbers in base n without carrying. You're the Booby only when the sum is 0.

MOORE AND MORE

If we allow each of the n players to reduce any number up to k of the heaps at his move, the theory, also due to Li, is similar. The Booby this time is the player who sees 0 when he adds the binary expansions of the numbers modulo $k(n-1) + 1$, without carrying.

We have not discussed games for more than 2 players elsewhere in this book because the stipulations to prevent coalitions are somewhat artificial, and lead to paradoxes of the "surprise exam" type. See the article by Paul Hudson in the References.

There are so many generalizations of Nim with interesting theories that we certainly haven't said the last word on the subject, and so

> This is the way the chapter ends,
> This is the way the chapter ends,
> This is the way the chapter ends,

NOT WITH A BANG BUT A WHIM

Perhaps you might like to play Nim, but on just one occasion one of the two players is allowed, instead of his usual Nim move, to exercise his **Whim** to decide whether the outcome will be decided by normal or by misère play. If we use

> 0-nim to mean normal Nim
> 1-nim to mean misère Nim, and
> 2-nim to mean Whim,

then we can continue the sequence with

> 3-nim = **Trim**,
> 4-nim = **Quam**, etc.

The move in d-nim ("**Denim**"), $d \geqslant 2$, is

> *either*   to move as in Nim
> *or*   to reduce d (but not both).

This is easy to analyze if you introduce a **quiddity heap**, to keep account of just which game you're playing. Then each of these games becomes like Nim with an extra heap. If $2^k \leqslant d < 2^{k+1}$, the quiddity heap behaves like a heap of size d when all other heaps are of size less than 2^{k+1}, but like a heap of size $d-1$ when they're not.

DID YOU WIN THE SILVER DOLLAR?

You did if you moved the coin behind the $ just 2 squares or 1, leaving (3, 2, 1) or (2, 3, 1), depending on which version you're playing. Notice that, in the latter case, there's only one coin between the $ and the bag.

HOW WAS YOUR ARITHMETIC?

When you filled in the frieze pattern it should have looked like

```
1     1     1     1     1     1     1     1     1     1     1     1     ...
   1     2     3     2     2     1     4     3     1     2     3     ...
      1     5     5     3     1     3    11     2     1     5     5     ...
   1     2     8     7     1     2     8     7     1     2     8     ...
      1     3    11     2     1     5     5     3     1     3    11     ...
         1     4     3     1     2     3     2     2     1     4     3     ...
            1     1     1     1     1     1     1     1     1     1     1     ...
```

IN PUT-OR-TAKE-A-SQUARE, 92 IS AN $\mathcal{N}$-POSITION

In Fig. 19 the $\mathcal{P}$-positions are in the centre column, squares on the right and other $\mathcal{N}$-positions on the left.

TRIBULATIONS AND FIBULATIONS

Norton conjectures that in his game of **Tribulations** no position is drawn and $\mathcal{N}$-positions are more numerous than $\mathcal{P}$-positions in golden ratio. Richard Parker has verified these assertions for numbers <5000 (for which the calculations sometimes run into the millions). The remoteness and suspense numbers (which are probably always finite) are shown in Table 11. Play from 51, 52 and 56 is especially interesting; draw diagrams like Fig. 19.

For Mike Guy's game of **Fibulations** we have proved the corresponding assertions and can in fact give a complete analysis. It is well known that any number can be economically expressed as the sum of Fibonacci numbers by the **Zeckendorf algorithm**: always subtract the largest Fibonacci number you can. Less economically we can use the **Secondoff algorithm**: always take off the *second* largest Fibonacci number you can, e.g.

$$100 = 89 + 8 + 3 \text{ (Zeckendorf)} \quad \text{or} \quad 55 + 21 + 13 + 5 + 3 + 2 + 1 \text{ (Secondoff)}$$

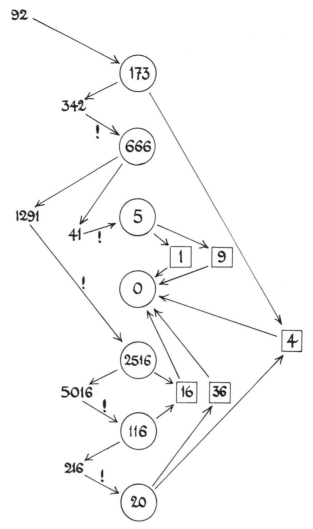

Figure 19. How to Win Epstein's Game starting from 92.

n	1	2	3	4	5	6	7	8	9	10	11	12	13	14	15	16	17	18	19	20	21	22	23	24	25
R	1	2	1	6	3	1	5	3	2	1	2	3	4	3	1	9	3	6	7	8	1	10	3	2	3
S	3	2	1	4	3	1	3	3	2	5	4	5	2	5	1	3	3	2	5	4	3	4	5	2	5

n	26	27	28	29	30	31	32	33	34	35	36	37	38	39	40	41	42	43	44	45	46	47	48	49	50
R	4	5	1	4	3	8	7	5	9	7	1	14	3	4	7	4	2	9	4	1	2	3	4	7	8
S	4	3	5	4	3	2	5	3	5	5	3	4	5	2	5	4	2	5	4	7	2	5	2	5	4

n	51	52	53	54	55	56	57	58	59	60	61	62	63	64	65	66	67	68	69	70	71	72	73	74	75
R	12	16	9	3	1	12	3	14	7	6	4	8	6	3	2	1	6	3	5	7	11	4	13	8	3
S	2	4	5	3	5	4	5	2	5	4	2	4	4	7	2	1	4	3	3	5	5	2	3	4	5

Table 11. emoteness and Suspense Numbers for Tribulations.

A number is a $\mathscr{P}$-position in Fibulations if and only if

> *either* its Secondoff expansion ends $3 + 1 + 1$ or $5 + 2 + 1$
> *or* it is 3 more than a Fibonacci number which is at least 8.

The numbers	0, 11, 5, 8, 13, 21, 34, 55, 89, 144, ...
have remotenesses	0, 8, 2, 2, 2, 4, 6, 8, 10, 12, ...

The remoteness of any other $\mathscr{P}$-position is found by adding twice the number of Secondoff steps you take to get to one of these and the remoteness of an $\mathscr{N}$-position is one more than the smallest remoteness of its $\mathscr{P}$-options. E.g. from 1000 we get to 34 (remoteness 6) after 4 subtractions (of 610, 233, 89 and 34) so 1000 has remoteness $6 + (4 \times 2) = 14$. On the other hand, 1001 has remoteness 3 (move to 13). We believe, and Omar might confirm, that the suspense numbers (which are all finite) and nim-values (which are all 0, 1, 2 or ∞_0) have similar patterns.

OUR CODE OF BEHAVIOR FOR PRINCES

in that 6-bush rose-garden with a 1-rose bush is best described by translating it into the One-Step, Two-Step game. It can be checked that all the resulting positions except

?*edede*1	?*eddde*1	?*ddede*1	?*dddde*1
?*ededd*1	?*eddd d*1	?*ddedd*1	?*ddddd*1
?0*eeee*1	?0*edee*1	?*ed0ed*1	?*dd0ee*1

can be moved to one of Schuh's $\mathscr{P}$-positions, and that these 12 classes of position, when joined by possible moves, form the graph of Fig. 20. In the figure a boxed position is $\mathscr{P}$, an unboxed one is $\mathscr{N}$, and

e	means any even number, including 0,
d	means any odd number,
E	means any even number $\geqslant 2$,
D	means any odd number $\geqslant 3$, and
?	means any number,

and the dotted arrow indicates that moves can only be made in that direction. The positions of form ?00*dee*1 and ?00*eee*1 have been omitted from the figure because they cannot be reached from the other ones. To complete the figure, adjoin

?00*dee*1	?00*eee*1
except	except
?00*dEE*1	?00*EEE*1
?001021	?000*E*01
?001041	?002021.

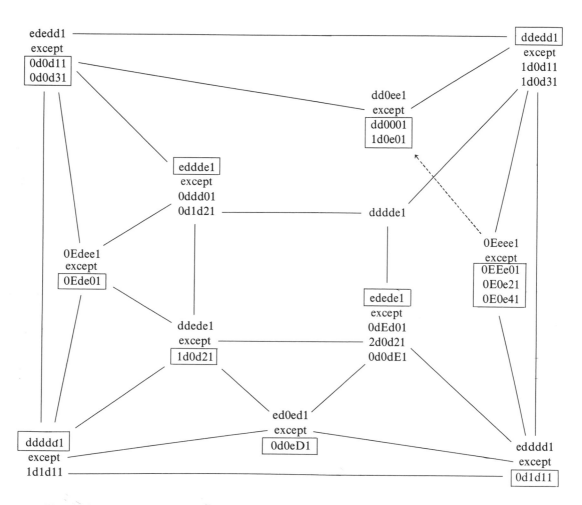

Figure 20. Our Code of Behavior for Princes in 6-bush Rose-gardens with a 1-rose Bush.

REFERENCES AND FURTHER READING

Richard Austin, Impartial and Partisan Games, M.Sc. thesis, University of Calgary, 1976.

W.W. Rouse Ball and H.S.M. Coxeter, "Mathematical Recreations & Essays", 12th edn., University of Toronto Press, 1974 (esp. pp. 38–39).

E.R. Berlekamp, Unsolved problem #4, in W.T. Tutte (ed.) "Recent Progress in Combinatorics", Academic Press, New York and London, 1969, pp. 342–343.

E.R. Berlekamp, Some recent results on the combinatorial game called Welter's Nim, Proc. 6th Conf. Information Sci. and Systems, Princeton, 1972, 203–204.

F. de Carteblanche, The princess and the roses, J. Recreational Math. 3 (1970) 238–239.

F. de Carte Blanche, The roses and the princes, ibid. 7 (1974) 295–298.

J.H. Conway, "On Numbers and Games", Academic Press, London and New York, 1976, Chapters 11 and 13, and p. 181.

J.H. Conway and H.S.M. Coxeter, Triangulated polygons and frieze patterns, Math. Gaz. 57 (1973) 87–94, 175–183; MR 57 #1254–5.

H.E. Dudeney, "536 Puzzles and Curious Problems" (ed. Martin Gardner) Chas. Scribner's Sons, N.Y., 1969; #475 The 37 Puzzle Game, 186–187, 392–393.

Robert J. Epp and Thomas S. Ferguson, Remarks on take-away games and Dawson's Game, Abstract 742–90–3, Notices Amer. Math. Soc. 24 (1977) A-179.

Jim Flanigan, Generalized two-pile Fibonacci Nim, Fibonacci Quart, 16 (1978) 459–469.

Richard K. Guy, Anyone for Twopins?, in David Klarner (ed.) "The Mathematical Gardner", Prindle Weber and Schmidt, 1980.

Paul D.C. Hudson, The logic of social conflict: a game-theoretic approach in one lesson, Bull. Inst. Math. Appl. 14 (1978) 54–66.

Thomas A. Jenkyns and John P. Mayberry, The skeleton of an impartial game and the nim-function of Moore's Nim$_k$, Internat. J. Game Theory 9 (1980) 51–63.

S.-Y.R. Li, N-person Nim and N-person Moore's games, Internat. J. Game Theory, 7 (1978) 31–36; MR 58 #4367.

Eliakim H. Moore, A generalization of the game called Nim, Ann. of Math. Princeton (2) 11 (1910) 93–94.

J. von Neumann and O. Morganstern, "Theory of Games and Economic Behavior", Princeton, 1944.

T.H. O'Beirne, "Puzzles and Paradoxes", Oxford University Press, London, 1965, Chapter 9.

I.C. Pond and D.F. Howells, More on Fibonacci Nim, Fibonacci Quart. 3 (1965) 61.

Fred. Schuh, "The Master Book of Mathematical Recreations", (transl. F. Göbel, from "Wonderlijke Problemen; Leerzaam Tijdverdrijf Door Puzzle en Spel", W.J. Thieme, Zutphen, 1943; ed. T. H. O'Beirne) Dover, London, 1968. Chapter VI, 131–154; Chapter XII, 263–280.

Allen J. Schwenk, Take-away games, Fibonacci Quart. 8 (1970) 225–234, 241; MR 44 #1446.

G.C. Shephard, Additive frieze patterns and multiplication tables, Math. Gaz. 60 (1976) 178–184; MR 58 #16353.

Roland Sprague, "Recreations in Mathematics" (trans. T.H. O'Beirne) Blackie, 1963; #14: Pieces to be moved, pp. 12–14, 41–42.

R. Sprague, Bemerkungen über eine spezielle Abelsche Gruppe, Math. Z. 51 (1947) 82–84; MR 9, 330–331.

C.P. Welter, The advancing operation in a special abelian group, Nederl. Akad. Wetensch. Proc. Ser. A 55 = Indagationes Math. 14 (1952) 304–314; MR 14, 132.

C.P. Welter, The theory of a class of games on a sequence of squares, in terms of the advancing operation in a special group, ibid. 57 = 16 (1954) 194–200; MR 15, 682; 17, 1436.

Michael J. Whinihan, Fibonacci Nim, Fibonacci Quart. 1 (1963) 9–13.

Yōhei Yamasaki, On misère Nim-type games, J. Math. Soc. Japan, 32 (1980) 461–475.

Chapter 16

Dots-and-Boxes

Come, children, let us shut up the box.
        William Makepeace Thackeray, *Vanity Fair*, Ch. 67.

I could never make out what those damned dots meant.
        Lord Randolph Churchill.

Dots-and-Boxes is a familiar paper and pencil game for two players and has other names in various parts of the world. Two players start from a rectangular array of dots and take turns to join two horizontally or vertically adjacent dots. If a player completes the fourth side of a unit square (**box**) he initials that box and must then draw another line (so that completing a box is a complimenting move). When all the boxes have been completed the game ends and whoever has initialled more boxes is declared the winner.

A player who *can* complete a box is not obliged to do so if he has something else he prefers to do. Play would become significantly simpler were this obligation imposed; see the article by Holladay mentioned in the references.

Figure 1 shows Arthur's and Bertha's first game, in which Arthur started. Nothing was given away in the fairly typical opening until Arthur was forced to make the unlucky thirteenth move, releasing 2 boxes for Bertha. Her last bonus move enabled Arthur to take the bottom 3 boxes, but he then had to surrender the last 4.

This is how most children play, but Bertha is brighter than most. She started the return match with the opening that Arthur had used. He was happy to copy Bertha's replies from that game. and was delighted to see her follow it even as far as that unlucky thirteenth move, which had proved his undoing (Fig. 2). He grabbed those 2 boxes and happily surrendered the bottom 3, expecting 4 in return. But Bertha astounded him by giving him back 2. He pounced on these, but when he came to make his bonus move, realized he was doubled-crossed!

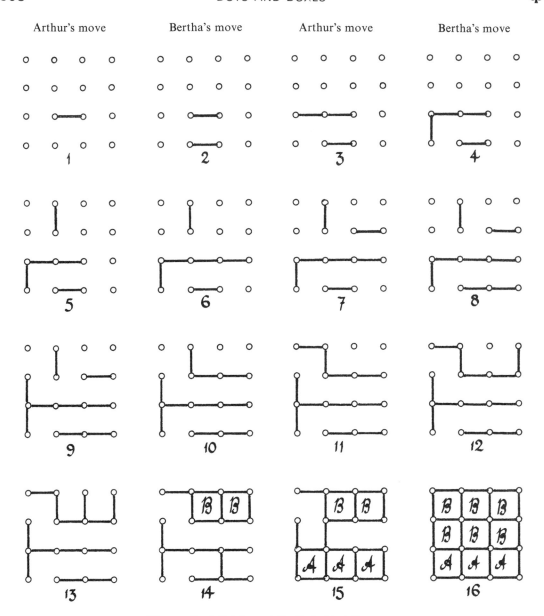

Figure 1. Arthur's and Bertha's First Game.

Bertha beats all her friends in this double-dealing way. Most children play at random unless they've looked quite hard and found that every move opens up some chain of boxes. Then they give the shortest chain away and get back the next shortest in return, and so on.

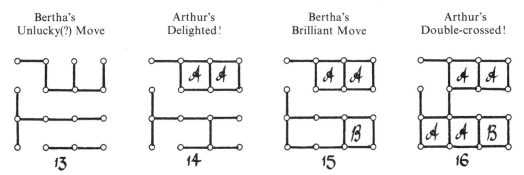

Figure 2. Bertha's Brilliance Astounds Arthur.

But when you open a long chain for Bertha, she may close it off with a double-dealing move which gives you the last 2 boxes but forces you to open the next chain for her (Fig. 3). In this way *she* keeps control right to the end of the game.

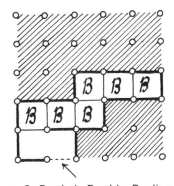

Figure 3. Bertha's Double-Dealing Move.

You can see in Fig. 4 just how effective this strategy can be. By politely rejecting two cakes on every plate but the last you offer her, Bertha helps herself to a resounding 19 to 6 victory. In the same position you'd have defeated the ordinary child 14 to 11.

DOUBLE-DEALING LEADS TO DOUBLE-CROSSES

Each double-dealing move is followed, usually immediately, by a move in which two boxes are completed with a single stroke of the pen (Fig. 5). These moves are very important in the theory. We'll call them **doublecrossed** moves, because whoever makes them usually has been!

You to Move   Bertha (*B*) beats you (*y*)   You (*Y*) beat the
                                                            ordinary child (*c*)

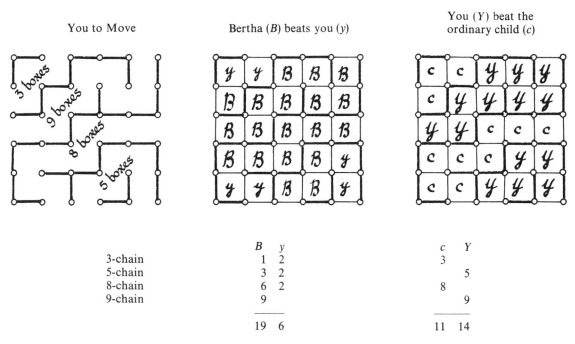

	B	*y*		*c*	*Y*
3-chain	1	2		3	
5-chain	3	2			5
8-chain	6	2		8	
9-chain	9				9
	19	6		11	14

Figure 4. Double-Dealing Pays Off!

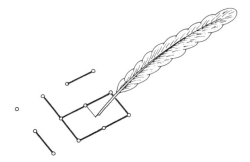

Figure 5. A Doublecross—Two Boxes at a Single Stroke.

Now Bertha's strategy suggests the following policy:

> Make sure there are long chains about
> and try to force your opponent to be
> the first to open one.

Try To Get Control ...

We'll say that whoever can force her opponent to open a long chain has **control** of the game. Then:

> When you have control, make sure you
> keep it by politely declining 2 boxes
> of every long chain except the last.

… And Then Keep It.

The player who has control usually wins decisively when there are several long chains.

So the fight is really about control. How can you make sure of acquiring this valuable commodity? It depends on whether you're playing the odd- or even-numbered turns … .

Figure 6. Which is Dodie and Which is Evie?

Arthur and Bertha live next to the Parr family, in which there are two little sisters called Dodie and Evie (Bertha often teases them by calling them the Parrotty Girls!). You can see them playing the 4-box game in Fig. 6. Dodie's a year younger than Evie and so always has first turn in any game they play. They've got so used to playing like this that even when they're playing somebody else, Dodie always insists on taking the odd-numbered moves while Evie will only take the even-numbered ones:

> Dodie Parr: odd parity,
> Evie Parr: even parity.

The rule that helps them take control is:

> *Dodie*
> tries to make the number of
> initial dots + doublecrossed moves
> *odd.*
> *Evie*
> tries to make this number
> *even.*

Be SELFish about Dots + Doublecrosses!

In simple games the number of doublecrosses will be one less than the number of long chains and this rule becomes:

THE LONG CHAIN RULE

> Try to make the number of
> initial dots + eventual long chains
> *even* if your opponent is *Evie*,
> *odd* if your opponent is *Dodie*.

The OPPOsite for Dots + Long Chains!

The reason for these rules is that whatever shape board you have on your paper, you'll find that:

Number of dots you start with

+ Number of doublecrosses

———————————————

= Total number of turns in the game.

We'll show this in the Extras.

HOW LONG IS "LONG"?

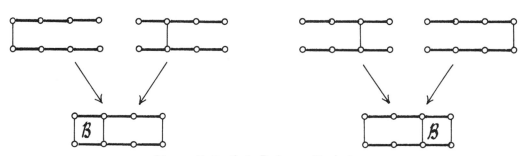

Figure 7. Bertha's Endgame Technique.

We can find the proper definition of long by thinking about Bertha's endgame technique. A **long chain** is one which contains 3 or more squares. This is because whichever edge Arthur draws in such a chain, Bertha can take all but 2 of the boxes in it, and complete her turn by drawing an edge which does not complete a box. Figure 7 shows this for the 3-square chain. A chain of 2 squares is *short* because our opponent might insert the *middle* edge, leaving us with no way of finishing our turn in the same chain. This is called (Fig. 8(a)) the **hard-hearted handout**.

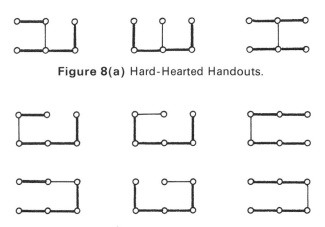

Figure 8(a) Hard-Hearted Handouts.

Figure 8(b). Half-Hearted Handouts.

When you think you are winning, but are forced to give away a pair of boxes, you should always make a hard-hearted handout, so that your opponent has no option but to accept. If you use a **half-hearted** one (Fig. 8(b)) he might reply with a double-dealing move and regain control. But if you're losing, you might try a half-hearted handout on the Enough Rope Principle (Chapter 1 Extras). Officially this is a bad move, since your opponent, if he has any sense, will grab both squares. But boys by billions, being bemused by Bertha's brilliance, blindly blunder both boxes back.

THE 4-BOX GAME

When Dodie was *very* young, the girls often played the 4-box game and offset Dodie's first move advantage by calling it a win for Evie (the second player) when they each got 2 boxes:

> TWO TWOS IS A WIN TO TWO

At first Dodie would never give away a box if she could see something else to do, and Evie, who you can see is a very symmetrical player, would always win by copying Dodie's moves on the opposite side of the board. But after watching Bertha playing Evie, Dodie found how to counter this strategy by making a Greek gift on her 7th move. Evie can still win if Dodie dares to stray from the Path of Righteousness but must resist her temptation to make *every* move a symmetrical one (Fig. 9).

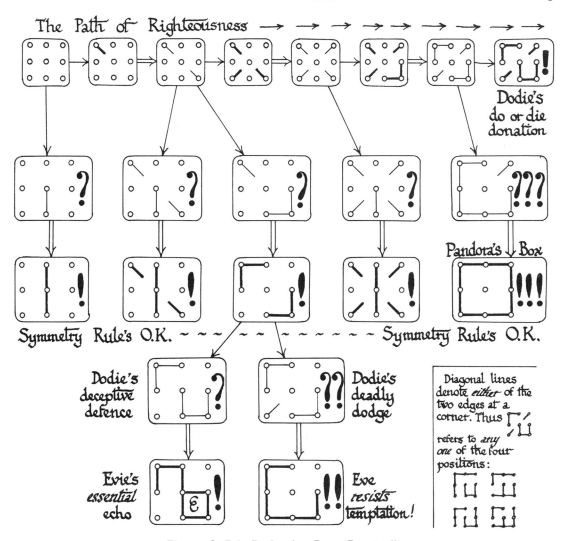

Figure 9. Evie Envisaging Every Eventuality.

Even though Dodie has the win, it's much harder to write out in full her best plays against sufficiently cunning opponents. In Fig. 34 of the Extras we give an adequate strategy for Dodie and in Fig. 35 a complete list of $\mathscr{P}$-positions for both players. This little game is full of traps for the unwary, and those of you who have written to us for advice on becoming Professional Boxers will find these tables very useful in the bruising preliminary contests on the 4-box board.

If the chain lengths are

		loop of 4
4	or	2 + 2
3 + 1		1 + 1 + 1 + 1

the winner will usually be

| Dodie | or | Evie |

in agreement with the Long Chain Rule, but on this small board, Dodie should often defy the rule and win by splitting the chains as $2+1+1$.

THE 9-BOX GAME

Surprisingly, the Long Chain Rule makes the 9-box game seem easier than the 4-box one. This time Evie wins, and her basic strategy is to draw 4 spokes as in Fig. 10, forcing every long chain to go through the centre. Against most children this wins for Evie by at least 6–3, but Dodie can hold her down to 5–4, perhaps by sacrificing the centre square, after which Evie should abandon her spoke strategy. Of course, Evie's real aim is to arrange that there's just one long chain, and she often improves her score by forming this chain in some other way.

Figure 10. Lucky Charms Ward Off More Than One Long Chain; Evie Puts Spokes in Dodie's Wheel.

Evie usually prefers to put her spokes in squares where another side is already drawn, and she's careful to draw spokes in only *one* of the two swastika patterns of Fig. 10. There usually aren't any double-crossed moves, so that Evie wins at the $(16+0=)$ 16th turn.

Dodie tries to arrange *her* moves so that some spoke can only be inserted as a sacrifice, and *either* cuts up the chains as much as possible (maybe with a centre sacrifice) *or* forms *two* long chains when Evie isn't thinking. Every now and then a half-hearted handout has saved the game for her just when she thought that all was lost.

THE 16-BOX GAME

We don't know who wins on the 4×4 box board, which makes a very interesting game to play. Evie tries to make the number of long chains 2, while Dodie tries to cut it down to 1 or force

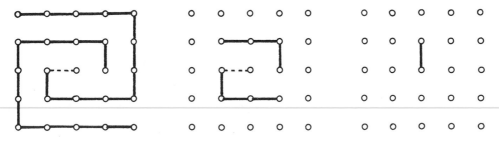

Figure 11. "Come into my symmetrical parlor!"

it up to 3. Evie beats many children with her symmetry strategy, but Dodie remembers her trick from the 4-box game. If she thinks her opponent will mimic her every move, she can lure him into the spider's web of Fig. 11(a), but when he's less predictable she finds it safer just to use the middle of the web (Fig. 11(b)). Dodie doesn't usually open with Fig. 11(c), because she finds the symmetry strategy very hard to beat.

OTHER SHAPES OF BOARD

To beat all your friends on larger square and rectangular boards you'll really need the Long Chain Rule. Remember to count a closed loop of 4 or more cells as *two* long chains and that each doublecross, no matter who makes it, changes the number of long chains you want. (Think of a doublecross as a long chain that's already been filled in.) It's good tactics to make the long chains as long as possible and avoid closed loops when you can, because you forfeit *four* boxes when declining a loop. These rules work for all large boards and even for triangular Dots-and-Boxes boards, like that in Fig. 12.

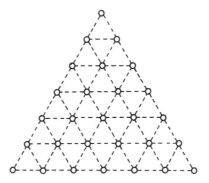

Figure 12. A Board with 28 Dots and 36 Triangular Cells.

Of course, if your opponent is also using the Long Chain Rule, the fight for control might be quite hard. The game of Nimstring, discussed in the rest of this chapter, is what control is all about. There's a piece in the Extras that describes some of the rare occasions when you might find it wise to lose control.

DOTS-AND-BOXES AND STRINGS-AND-COINS

You can play a dual form of Dots-and-Boxes, called **Strings-and-Coins**, with strings, coins and scissors. The ends of each piece of string are glued to two different coins or to a coin and the ground (each string has at most one end glued to the ground) and each player in turn cuts a new string. If your cut completely detaches a coin, you pocket it and must then cut another string (if there's one still uncut). The game ends when all coins are detached and the player who pockets the greater number is the winner.

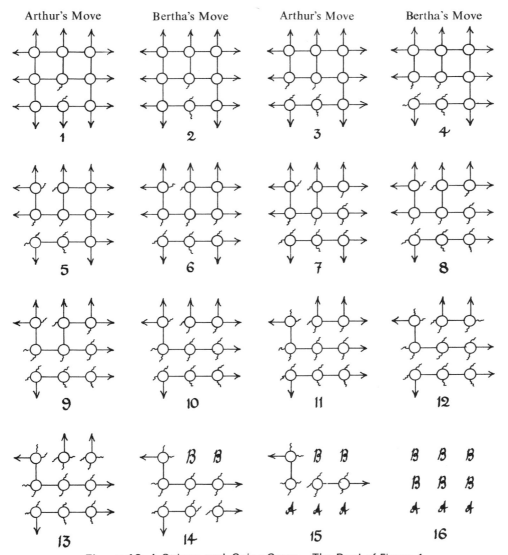

Figure 13. A Strings-and-Coins Game—The Dual of Figure 1.

Figure 13 shows the dual of Arthur's and Bertha's first game (compare it with Fig. 1). It started with 9 coins connected by 24 strings, 12 of them between coins and coins, the other 12 between coins and the ground. We use little arrows for strings that run to the ground. The coins and strings form the nodes and edges of a **graph**. It's easy to make a graph to correspond to any Dots-and-Boxes position. However, there are lots of graphs which *don't* correspond to such positions; for example the graph may have cycles of odd length or nodes with more than 4 edges, or the graph may be *non-planar*. In fact Strings-and-Coins is a generalization of Dots-and-Boxes.

NIMSTRING

The game of **Nimstring** is played on exactly the same kind of graphs as Strings-and-Coins, and you make exactly the same move by cutting a string (which is a *complimenting* move whenever you detach a coin). In Strings-and-Coins the winner is the player who detaches the larger number of coins, but Nimstring is played instead according to the Normal Play Rule. So, for ordinary Nimstring positions you *lose* when you detach the last coin, for then the rules require you to make a further move when it is impossible to do so. (But a Nimstring graph *may* have a string joining the ground to itself, and if the last move cuts *this* it doesn't detach a coin, and so *wins*.)

Nimstring looks quite different from Strings-and-Coins, but closer investigation shows that Nimstring is in fact a special case of Strings-and-Coins.

> You can't know all about Strings-and-Coins
> unless you know all about Nimstring!

Figure 14(a). A Hard Nimstring Problem.

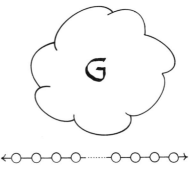

Figure 14(b). This Strings-and-Coins Problem is Just as Hard.

Figure 14 shows the construction which proves this. If *G* represents an arbitrary Nimstring problem, we add a long chain to it and consider the resulting Strings-and-Coins game—the long chain should have more coins than *G*. Because the chain is so long and whoever first cuts a string of it allows his opponent to capture all the coins of the chain on his next turn, both players will try to avoid cutting any string of the chain. Neither player can force his opponent to move on the chain until all the strings of *G* have been cut. In other words, the only way to win the Strings-and-Coins game of Fig. 14(b) is to play a winning game of Nimstring on the graph *G*.

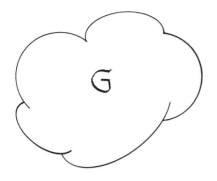

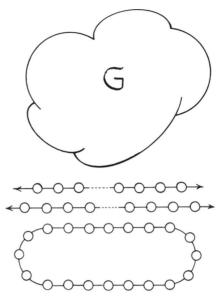

Figure 15(a). Another Nimstring Game.

Figure 15(b). A Corresponding Strings-and-Coins Game.

Figure 15 shows another construction. This time we get the Strings-and-Coins game by adding several long chains and cycles to the Nimstring game *G*. If these are long enough the winning strategy for the Strings-and-Coins game is then:

> *If your opponent moves in G,*
> reply in *G* with a move from
> the winning Nimstring strategy.
> *If he moves in a long chain,*
> take *all but two* coins of that
> chain, leaving just the string
> which joins them.
> *If he moves in a long cycle,*
> take *all but four* coins of the
> cycle, leaving them as *two pairs*
> each joined by a string.

This strategy gives you all but 2 coins of each long chain and all but 4 of each long cycle, so it will win for you if the total number of nodes in the added chains and cycles exceeds

$$\begin{aligned} &\text{(the number of nodes in } G) \\ &+ 4 \times \text{(the number of added long chains)} \\ &+ 8 \times \text{(the number of added long cycles).} \end{aligned}$$

In practice the Nimstring position will often contain (potential) long chains of its own, so that the strategy is of wider application. Recall that the "all but 2" principle was used by Bertha in her second game with Arthur (Fig. 2). Well-played games of Dots-and-Boxes are usually played like the corresponding Nimstring games, except at the very end. The last long chain in a Nimstring game is treated like any other; the winner takes all but the last 2 coins, which he gives to the loser by a hard-hearted handout. For the last chain in Dots-and-Boxes, of course, winner takes all!

WHY LONG IS LONG

The argument explains why "long" must be defined precisely as follows. We should call a chain **long** if it contains 3 or more coins, because no matter which string of such a chain our opponent might cut, we may take all but 2 of its coins and finish by cutting another string of the chain. We must call a chain of 2 coins **short**, because he might cut the middle string and prevent us from declining those 2 vital coins (the hard-hearted handout). For a similar reason a closed loop of 2 or 3 coins would be called **short** (short loops don't arise in rectangular Dots-and-Boxes). However, a loop with at least 4 coins is called **long**, because we can politely decline the last 4 coins no matter which string our opponent cuts. Figure 16(a) shows how to do this on a 6-loop. When your opponent has cut the first string as shown, you only take 2 of the coins and then cut the string in the middle of the remaining 4. Figure 16(b) shows how this corresponds with Bertha's way of playing Dots-and-Boxes.

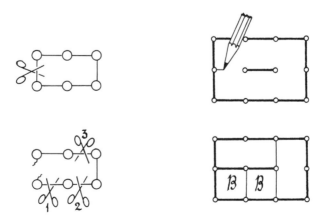

Figure 16. Bertha Politely Declines a Long Loop.

Well-played games of Dots-and-Boxes frequently lead to the duals of positions like those in Fig. 15(b). Most of the coins are in the long chains and loops, and the winner is whoever can force his opponent to cut the first string in one of these. It seems to be almost always the case that the winning strategy for Nimstring also gives the winning strategy for Strings-and-Coins. There are many other graphs than those satisfying the conditions of Fig. 15(b) for which this can be proved to happen. To win a game of Dots-and-Boxes or Strings-and-Coins, you should try to win the corresponding game of Nimstring and at the same time arrange that there are some fairly long chains about. In the rest of this chapter we'll teach you how to become an expert at Nimstring.

TO TAKE OR NOT TO TAKE A COIN IN NIMSTRING

A coin which has only a single string attached is **capturable**. Whenever there's a capturable coin the next player has the option of removing the corresponding branch, thereby detaching the coin and getting another (complimentary) move. For some graphs this is the best move; for others, including one of those encountered by Bertha in the game of Fig. 2, the winning strategy is to refuse to detach the coin. As you might guess, the decision as to whether it's better to take a coin or decline it often depends on the entire graph. However a great deal can be deduced by examining only local properties of the graph near the capturable coin.

Any capturable coin must look like one of the six possibilities in Fig. 17. The string from the capturable coin goes either to the ground (Fig. 17(a)) or to another coin. If to another coin, the

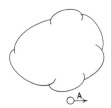

Figure 17(a). TAKE!
A free coin.

Figure 17(b). TAKE!
Two free coins and a
doublecross.

Figure 17(c). TAKE!
Three free coins and a
doublecross.

Figure 17(d). TAKE!
A free coin.

Figure 17(e). WIN!

Figure 17(f). WIN!

Half-hearted handouts.

number of strings there is either one (Fig. 17(b)), two (Figs. 17(c), (e) and (f)) or three or more (Fig. 17(d)). If there are two strings, the second goes either to another capturable coin (Fig. 17(c)), or to the ground (Fig. 17(e)), or to a coin with two more or strings (Fig. 17(f)). In each of the six cases the cloud contains all the coins and strings not regarded as near enough to the capturable coin. The dotted lines in Figs. 17(d) and (f) are possible additional strings which may or may not be present.

We claim that in the first four cases (Figs. 17(a)–(d)) the player to move might as well cut string A and capture the coin, and in Fig. 17(c), he might as well continue by cutting string B, taking two more coins. For suppose you have a winning strategy starting from one of these graphs. If this tells you to complete your first turn by cutting only certain *un*lettered strings, then your opponent has the option of beginning *his* turn by cutting the lettered ones. But the same position will be reached if instead you first cut all the lettered strings and then cut the same unlettered ones as before. If there's any winning strategy at all, starting from these four cases, there's one which begins by cutting the lettered strings. So there's no loss in generality in supposing that a good player will TAKE a capturable coin of one of the four types in Figs. 17(a)–(d).

The other two positions (Figs. 17(e) and (f)) are much more interesting. If it's your turn to move in one of these two cases, you can either *detach* the capturable coin by cutting string A, or *decline* to take it by cutting string B. No matter what the rest of the graph might be, *one or other* of these two moves will WIN. But you might need to look at the whole graph to decide whether your winning strategy begins by cutting string A or string B!

This somewhat surprising result is proved by a cunning use of Strategy Stealing (Fig. 18). We ask, for the games of Figs. 17(e) and (f):

> who wins the smaller game G consisting of just the unlettered strings (Figs. 18(e) and 18(f))?

This is either the player who has to move from G or the player who doesn't. Whoever this fortunate player is, you should arrange to steal his strategy. If the player to move from G can win, then when playing from Fig. 17(e) or (f) you should start by cutting string A (which detaches a coin, so you continue), then cut string B (detaching another coin, so you continue again) and then begin the game on G, which of course you will play according to the winning strategy for the first player. On the other hand, if there's no winning move for the first player from G then, starting from Fig. 17(e) or (f), you should finish your turn immediately by cutting string B and so force your opponent to start the game G (he might as well start by cutting string A; if he doesn't, you will later).

The fact that the declining move forfeits 2 coins to your opponent makes no difference in Nimstring, where the winner is determined by the last move. In Strings-and-Coins (and Dots-and-Boxes) it *might* matter, but is unlikely to when there are long chains about.

SPRAGUE–GRUNDY THEORY FOR NIMSTRING GRAPHS

We now try to define values for arbitrary Nimstring graphs. We'd like these values to be nimbers so that we can use the ordinary Mex and Nim Addition Rules. The only trouble is that there are positions like that shown in Fig. 19.

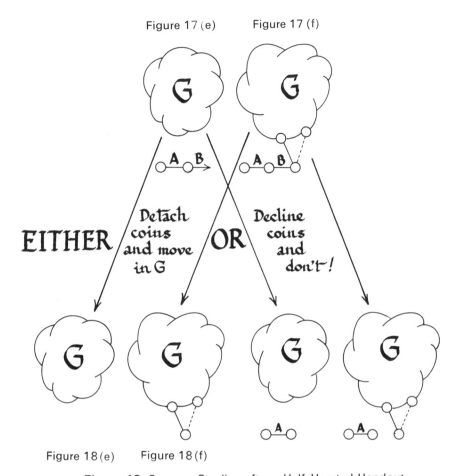

Figure 17 (e)   Figure 17 (f)

Figure 18 (e)   Figure 18 (f)

Figure 18. Strategy Stealing after a Half-Hearted Handout.

Figure 19. A Loony Nimstring (or Dots-and-Boxes) Position.

Our discussion of Fig. 17(e) shows that no matter what graph G is added to this, the result is a win for the first player. The supposed value, $*x$, for Fig. 19 must therefore have the property that

$$*x + *y \neq 0$$

for every nimber $*y$, including even $*x$ itself, so that in particular

$$*x + *x \neq 0.$$

Those of you who have read Chapter 12 will see at once how to resolve this paradox. Figure 19 is what we call a **loony** position, whose value is 𝒟. The theory of complimenting and complimentary moves in that chapter applies to Nimstring (where the complimenting moves are those that capture coins) and shows that every position has either an ordinary nimber value or the special value 𝒟. But don't reread Chapter 12 now, because we can easily summarize the rules for finding values at Nimstring:

The value of a graph without strings is 0.

The value of a graph with a capturable coin of one of the four types in Figs. 17(a)–(d) is equal to that of the subgraph obtained by removing the capturable coin(s) and its string(s).

The value of a graph with a capturable coin of one of the two types in Figs. 17(e) and (f) is 𝒟.

The value of a graph with no capturable coins is found from the values of the graphs left after cutting single strings by using the Mex Rule (Chapter 4).

VALUES FOR NIMSTRING

When adding these values, remember that

$$\mathcal{D} + 0 = \mathcal{D} + *1 = \mathcal{D} + *2 = \ldots = \mathcal{D} + \mathcal{D} = \mathcal{D},$$

as well as the ordinary nim-addition rules.

We show the calculation for some graphs in Fig. 20. When there are no capturable coins we write against each string the nim-value of the sub-graph obtained by cutting that string. Thus the last picture has options of nim-values 0, 1, 3, i.e. values *0, *1, *3, and so its own value is *2, because 2 = mex(0, 1, 3). Strings marked 𝒟 are loony options for the first player—if he cuts such a string he will LOSE against proper play even if some other graphs are added to the position. The nim-value of each graph is found from the mex of the numbers against its strings—in this you should ignore the 𝒟 values, which correspond to suiciding moves.

Although Dodie wins the 4-box game of Dots-and-Boxes, we can deduce from Fig. 20 that Evie wins the corresponding Nimstring position:

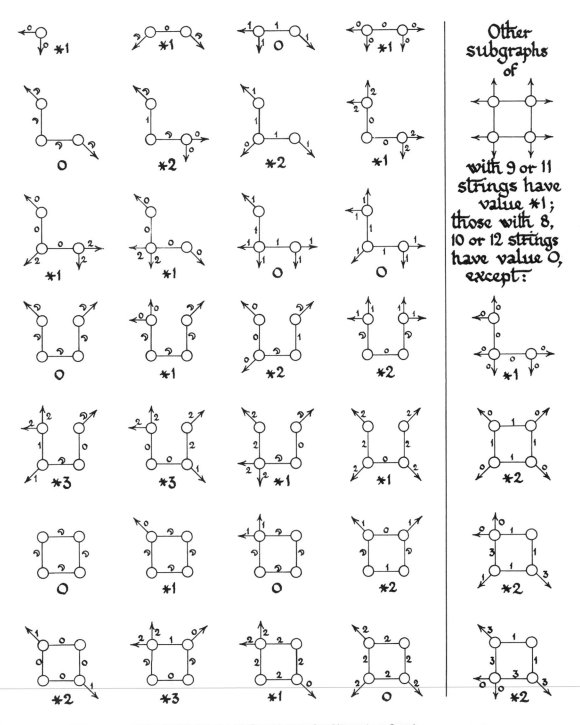

Figure 20. Working Out Values for Nimstring Graphs.

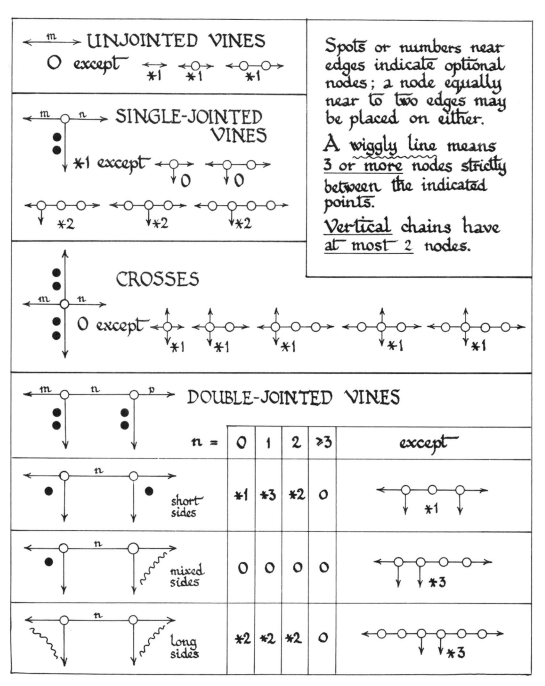

Figure 21. Noteworthy Nimstring Nimbers.

This means that even in Dots-and-Boxes she should win

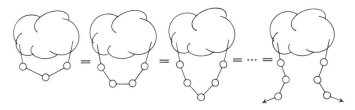

Figure 21 assembles answers for all graphs with at most 4 ends and no internal circuit. You'll find an extended table in the Extras that covers tree-like graphs with 5 ends.

ALL LONG CHAINS ARE THE SAME

Look at the various positions of Fig. 22, in which the clouds all conceal exactly the same thing, and the necklaces that hang from them all have at least three beads. The graphs all behave the same way in Nimstring because all the visible edges will always be loony moves.

Figure 22. Three or More's a Crowd.

> Provided a chain has
> 3 or more nodes along it,
> the exact number
> doesn't make any difference
> to the value.

This makes it handy to have a special notation for long chains:

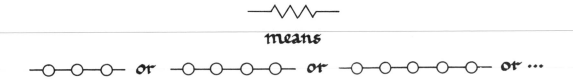

WHICH MUTATIONS ARE HARMLESS?

More generally we can put in or take out some beads on any Nimstring graph G to obtain **mutations** of the graph (a **bead**, of course, is a node with just 2 edges). Figure 23 shows a graph G and two mutations, H and K.

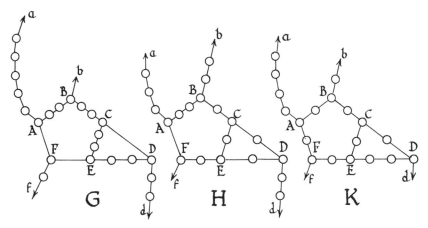

Figure 23. A Graph, a Harmless Mutation and a Killing One.

We'll use the word **stop** to mean *either* an arrowhead where the graph goes to ground (an **end**) *or* any of the nodes which have 3 or more edges (the **joints**). A path between two stops is **long** if it passes through 3 or more intermediate nodes, **short** otherwise. Mutation usually affects the value, but there are a lot of **harmless** mutations that don't:

> A mutation between two graphs
> will certainly be harmless if
> every short path between stops
> in either graph corresponds to a
> short path in the other.

THE HARMLESS MUTATION THEOREM

In Fig. 23, H is a harmless mutation of G, since the only short paths are AE, Af, Ef, and the ones other than Aa that don't pass through a stop. But AE is long in K, and Cd is short, so this mutation is not covered by our theorem. In fact G and H have value $*2$, while K has value 0.

When G and H are related by a harmless mutation you just play H like G. A non-loony move must cut some string of a short chain between two points A and B that were stops at least until the move was made. A and B must have been stops in the original graph and we can find a similar non-loony move in the mutated graph because the distance between A and B will be short. (Fig. 24).

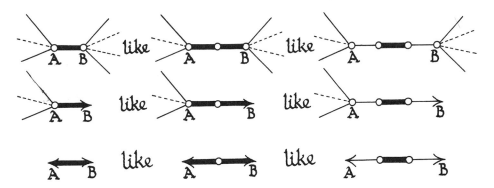

Figure 24. Like Moves in Harmless Mutations.

We can strengthen our Mutation Theorem a little:

> If the path between two stops
> passes through one end of a
> long chain, you needn't worry
> about the length of the path.

(For in a graph like Fig. 25—in which *A* or *B* might have been ends—*AB* won't become a chain unless someone makes a loony move cutting the long chain ending at *C*.)

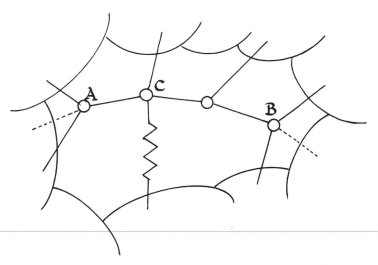

Figure 25. The Path *AB* Passes a Long Chain at *C*.

CHOPPING AND CHANGING

There are lots of more drastic changes we can make to Nimstring graphs without affecting their values; for instance:

> Long chains snap!

This was hinted at in Fig. 22, and Fig. 26(a) shows how it's written in our long chain notation.

The remaining equivalences of Fig. 26 are more interesting. The middle equivalence of Fig. 26(b) is particularly useful (the left equivalence is a long chain that snaps). It asserts that when an edge runs to a node from which two long chains emanate, then this edge may be replaced by an edge running directly to the ground. More generally, when two long chains are attached to a node, all other edges ending at this node may be replaced by edges running to the ground (Fig. 26(c)).

The idea of the proof is that a node at the end of two long chains can't be captured until after someone concedes the game by making a loony move. We can apply the equality between the first and last parts of Fig. 26(b) to every branch that runs to the ground, so as to eliminate ground branches from every graph. But usually it's more convenient to use it in the other direction, eliminating many branches and nodes by introducing new ends. Sometimes, as in Fig. 26(d), this gives rise to a branch joining the ground to itself (a 0 by 1 game of Dots-and-Boxes!); such a branch contributes ∗1 to the value.

The equality between the first three parts of Fig. 26(e) follows from the Harmless Mutation Theorem, but that between these and the last three doesn't, because some short chains have become long. The letters label corresponding moves, and the ꙃ's show moves which we should ignore. Figures 26(b), (d), (f) and (g) show that we can sometimes eliminate circuits from our graphs—the last diagram of Fig. 26(f) is our shorthand notation for any of the previous three, which are harmless mutations of each other. Figure 26(h) has many variants, abbreviated in Fig. 26(i) (using the notation of Fig. 21).

VINES

A **vine** is a Nimstring graph without circuits or capturable nodes in which all the joints lie on a single long path (the **stem**) and each joint belongs to just 3 edges. The chain joining an end to its nearest joint is called a **tendril**, so a single-jointed vine has 3 tendrils (Fig. 21). Vines with more joints have 2 tendrils at their endmost joints and just 1 at intermediate ones. If the distance between two neighboring joints is long, the vine decomposes into two smaller ones because long chains snap, so we can suppose such distances *short*, if we like.

A **Twopins-vine** is one whose every distance between *non*-neighboring stops (which may be either ends or joints) is *long*. It is a remarkable fact that the value of any Twopins-vine is equal to that of a corresponding configuration in the game of Twopins (Chapter 15). Each joint with a *short* tendril becomes a column of *two* pins (even if it has also a long tendril); each other joint becomes a column of *one*; and two neighboring joints a long distance apart correspond to an *empty* Twopins column (Fig. 27). A bowling shot which removes a *single* column at Twopins corresponds to a *tendril* move at Nimstring; one which removes a *pair* of columns corresponds to a move on the *stem* of the vine.

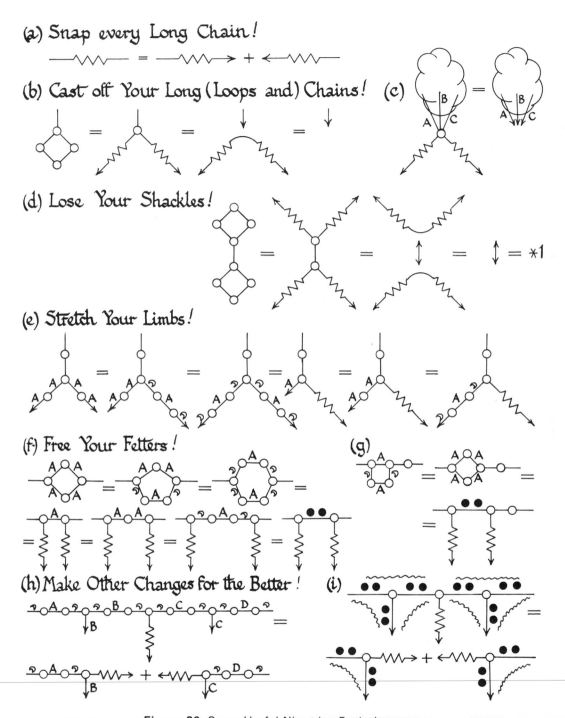

(a) Snap every Long Chain!

(b) Cast off Your Long (Loops and) Chains! (c)

(d) Lose Your Shackles!

(e) Stretch Your Limbs!

(f) Free Your Fetters!   (g)

(h) Make Other Changes for the Better!   (i)

Figure 26. Some Useful Nimstring Equivalences.

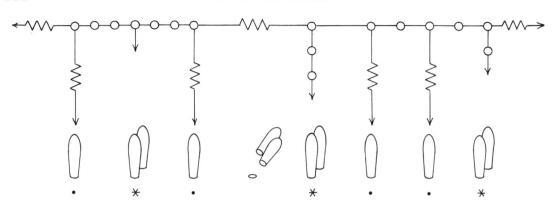

Figure 27. A Twopins-vine and a Game of Twopins.

Our remarks about vines show that:

> You can't know all about Nimstring
> without knowing all about Twopins!

If you've read Chapter 15 you'll know that Kayles and Dawson's Kayles are just special cases of Twopins, so, combining several slogans of this chapter:

> You can't know all about
> Dots-and-Boxes
> unless you know all about
> Kayles and Dawson's Kayles!

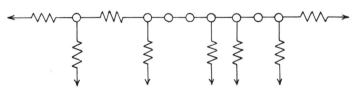

Figure 28. A Snappable Dawson's-vine, $D_1 + D_4$, value $0 + *2 = *2$.

A **Dawson's-vine** (*Parthenocissus dawsonia*) is a Twopins-vine all of whose tendrils are long. Of course if any distance between neighboring joints is *long* the Dawson's-vine will snap, like the one in Fig. 28. If all these distances are *short*, the nim-values, D_n, of n-jointed Dawson's-vines are (Chapter 4):

n	0	1	2	3	4	5	6	7	8	9	11	13	15	17	19	21	23	25	27	29	31	33
D_n	**0**	**0**	1	1	2	0	3	1	1	0	3 3	2 2	4 **0**	5 **2**	**2** 3	3 0	1 1	3 0	2 1	1 0	4 5	**2** 7
D_{n+34}	4	**0**	1	1	2	0	3	1	1	0	3 3	2 2	4 4	5 5	**2** 3	3 0	1 1	3 0	2 1	1 0	4 5	3 7
D_{n+68}	4	8	1	1	2	0	3	1	1	0	3 3	2 2	4 4	5 5	9 3	3 0	1 1	3 0	2 ...			

A *Kayles* position corresponds to a Twopins-vine with a *short* tendril at every joint. However, we can extend this class by observing that we don't need to worry about some of the distances between joints and ends:

> A vine is a **Kayles-vine** if
> (i) every joint has a *short* tendril, and
> (ii) every distance between two ends or two non-neighboring joints is *long*.

Again, if any distance between neighboring joints of your Kayles-vine is *long*, it snaps (Fig. 29). From Chapter 4, the nim-values, K_n, of unsnappable n-jointed Kayles-vines are:

n	0	1	2	3	4	5	6	7	8	9	10	11	12	13	14	15	16	17	18	19	20	21	22	23
K_n	0	1	2	**3**	1	4	**3**	2	1	**4**	2	**6**	4	1	2	**7**	1	4	**3**	2	1	**4**	**6**	7
K_{n+24}	4	1	2	8	**5**	4	7	2	1	8	**6**	7	4	1	2	**3**	1	4	7	2	1	8	2	7
K_{n+48}	4	1	2	8	1	4	7	2	1	**4**	2	7	4	1	2	8	1	4	7	2	1	8	**6**	7
K_{n+72}	4	1	2	8	1	4	7	2	1	8	2	7	4	1	2	8	1	4	7	2	1	8	2	7

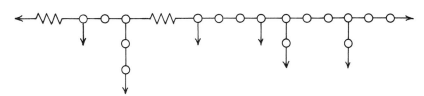

Figure 29. A Snappable Kayles-vine, $K_2 + K_4$, value $*2 + *1 = *3$.

The correspondence between the Twopins-vines and the game of Twopins enables us to interpret the Decomposition Theorem of Figs. 26(h) and (i) as a generalization of the Decomposition Theorem for Twopins. There are Nimstring generalizations for all the Twopins equivalences:

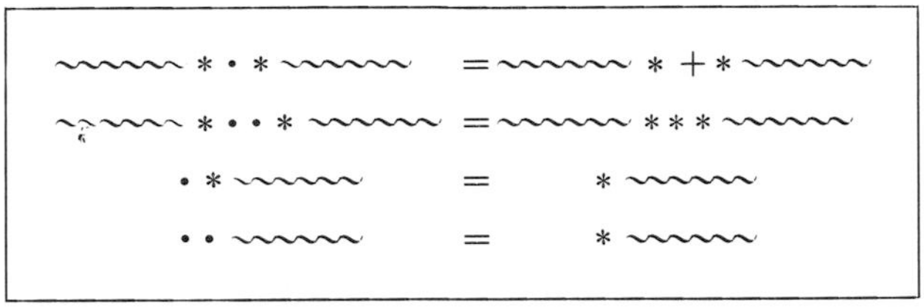

```
~~~~ * · * ~~~~   = ~~~~ * + * ~~~~
~~~~ * · · * ~~~~ = ~~~~ * * * ~~~~
     · * ~~~~     =      * ~~~~
     · · ~~~~     =      * ~~~~
```

The last two enable us to suppose that the endmost joints of a Twopins-vine have short tendrils (they correspond to uses of Fig. 26(b)). Collectively the Twopins equivalences allow us to suppose that the joints with no short tendrils come in strictly internal blocks of 3 or more and so all the simplest Twopins-vines reduce to compounds of Kayles-vines. Figure 30 is a small Twopins dictionary culled from Chapters 4 and 15. The equivalences of Fig. 26 enable us to show that many graphs that don't look like vines are really equivalent to them; for instance Fig. 31(a) is equivalent to D_8.

Kayles-vines, K_n		n	Dawson's-vines, D_n			Other Twopins-vines	
*	= *1	1	·	=		* * · · · · *	0
* *	= *2	2	· ·	= *		* * * · · · *	= *3
* * *	= *3	3	· · ·	= * ·	= *1	* * · · · * *	= *1
* * * *	= *1	4	· · · ·	= * *	= *2	* * · · · · *	= *4
* * * * *	= *4	5	· · · · ·	= * + *	= 0	* * * * · · · *	= *5
* * * * * *	= *3	6	· · · · · ·	= * * *	= *3	* · * * · · · * *	= *4
* * * * * * *	= *2	7	· · · · · · ·	= * · · · *	= *1	* * * · · · · *	= *3
* * * * * * * *	= *1	8	· · · · · · · ·	= * · · · · *	= *1	* * · · · · · * *	= *3
* * * * * * * * *	= *4	9	· · · · · · · · ·	= * · · · · · *	= 0	* * · · · · · *	= *3
* * * * * * * * * *	= *2	10	· · · · · · · · · ·	= * · · · · · · *	= *3	* · · · * · · · *	= *1

Figure 30. Various Vines Values.

Twopins-vines are **decomposing** in the sense that when any branch of the vine is removed the new vine decomposes—often by snapping a chain—into two smaller ones. Some other vines, including that of Fig. 31(b), are decomposing in the same sense. It is rather straightforward to compute the value of a decomposing vine from the values of those of its subvines which include all of a consecutive sequence of the original tendrils. Since the number of such subvines is proportional only to the square of the number of tendrils this idea is feasible for quite long decomposing vines, and can easily be implemented on a computer.

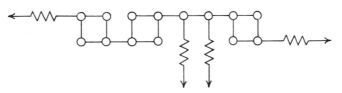

(a) A graph equivalent to the Dawson's-vine D_8.

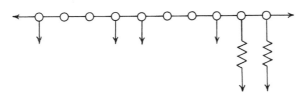

(b) A decomposing vine.

Figure 31. Two Uses of Figure 26.

Dots-and-Boxes is, like other good games, remarkable in that it can be played on several different levels of sophistication.

● First, there's Arthur's way: you just don't open up any boxes unless you have to and then you open as few as possible. This seems to be the only level that many players reach.

● Then there's Bertha's double-dealing endgame technique which gets the winner a lot of boxes at the finish and makes it seem likely that Nimstring will be useful.

● Next comes the Parrotty girls' parity rule for long chains.

● Then we realize that to get the right parity is an exercise in Sprague–Grundy theory, so we need tables of nim-values.

● The unwieldiness of these tables forces us to use equivalence theorems whenever we can, and to look for interesting classes of analyzable graphs.

● We can use Twopins theory to reduce many games to positions in the well-known games of Kayles and Dawson's Kayles.

● Finally, experts will need to know something about the rare occasions when the Nimstring theory does not give the correct Dots-and-Boxes winner.

What moves would you recommend for the positions in Fig. 32? We give our own recommendations in the Extras.

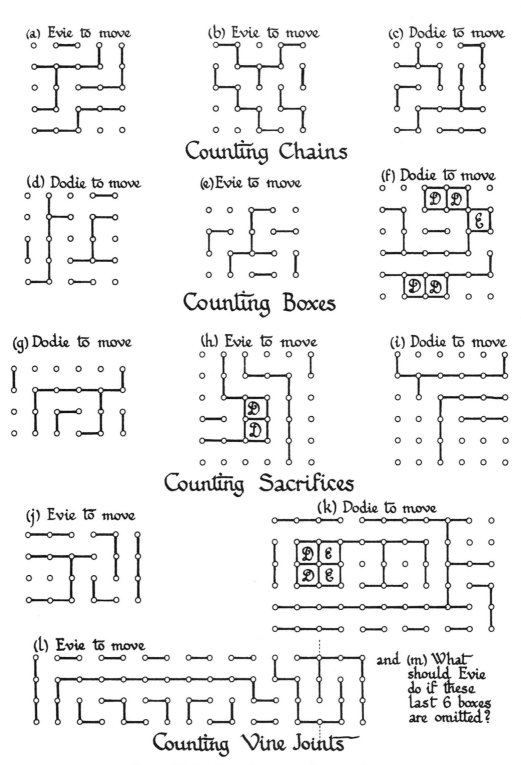

(a) Evie to move

(b) Evie to move

(c) Dodie to move

Counting Chains

(d) Dodie to move

(e) Evie to move

(f) Dodie to move

Counting Boxes

(g) Dodie to move

(h) Evie to move

(i) Dodie to move

Counting Sacrifices

(j) Evie to move

(k) Dodie to move

(l) Evie to move

and (m) What should Evie do if these last 6 boxes are omitted?

Counting Vine Joints

Figure 32. Try These Dots-and-Boxes Problems.

EXTRAS

DOTS + DOUBLECROSSES = TURNS

Suppose we play a Dots-and-Boxes game, starting with D dots, that takes T turns to draw L lines and finish with B boxes. Then if there are no doublecrosses, each line except the last either creates just one box or hands the turn to the next player, so

$$L = B + T - 1.$$

However Fig. 33 shows that

$$L = B + D - 1,$$

so a game with no doublecrosses lasts for exactly the same number of turns as the initial number of dots. But each doublecross creates 2 boxes instead of 1, so in general the number of turns will be the number of dots we started with plus the number of doublecrosses.

When we've broken
B edges to flood
the B boxes ...

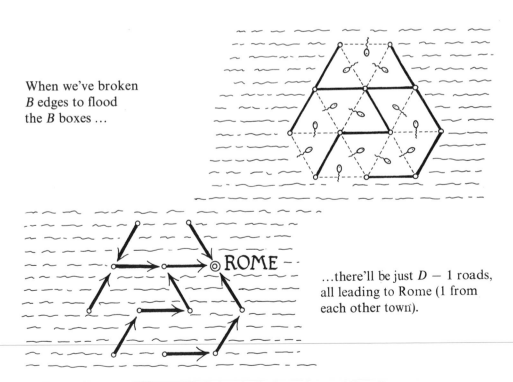

…there'll be just $D - 1$ roads,
all leading to Rome (1 from
each other town).

Figure 33. Euler via Rademacher and Toeplitz.

537

HOW DODIE CAN WIN THE 4-BOX GAME

Figure 34 shows a sufficient set of $\mathscr{P}$-positions to enable Dodie to win the 4-box game. Figure 35 shows *all* $\mathscr{P}$-positions except those in which a player has already signed enough boxes to win, classified according to the number of moves made. Figure 36 shows the three $\mathscr{N}$-positions in which a sacrifice wins but a non-sacrifice *loses*. In these figures broken lines indicate boxes with three sides already drawn.

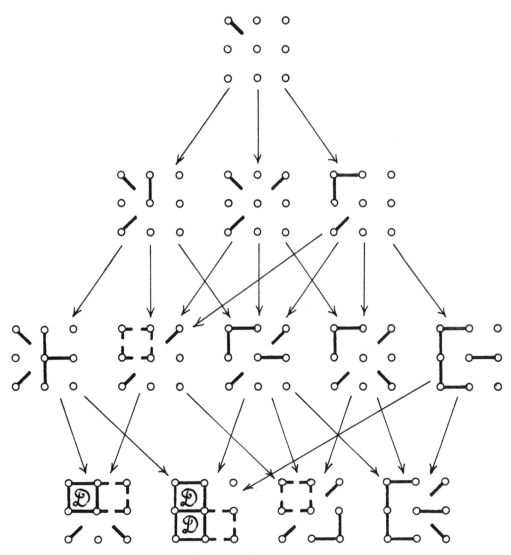

Figure 34. A Winning Strategy for Dodie.

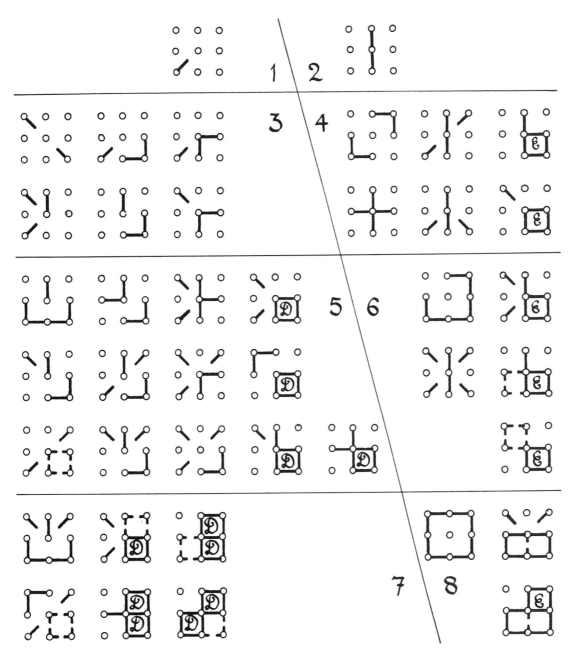

Figure 35. All $\mathscr{P}$-positions in the 4-box Game.

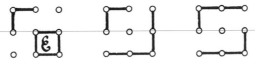

Figure 36. Three Tricky $\mathscr{N}$-positions.

WHEN IS IT BEST TO LOSE CONTROL?

It is clearly not *always* a good idea to keep control. For suppose all that's left of a game is 1001 chains, all of length 3, and your opponent has just opened the first of these. If you slavishly insist on keeping control to the very end, you'll have to give away 2 boxes in each chain but the last and so you'll only get 1003 to your opponent's 2000.

What the question really boils down to is this: when your opponent has just opened a long chain or made a half-hearted handout, should you, like Bertha, decline the last 2 boxes, or, like Arthur, grab them all and be forced to move elsewhere? Suppose for a moment that you use Bertha's tactic and give up 2 boxes in order to force your opponent to move first in the rest of the position, in which, by playing perfectly, you get D more boxes than your opponent. Then Arthur's strategy would take those 2 boxes and give you D less of the rest than your opponent. Comparing:

Bertha's technique	Arthur's technique
$-2 + D$	$2 - D$

shows you should

> adopt Bertha's technique unless
> D is less than 2.
> (Either will do, if D is just 2.)

That's all very well, but you still won't know which is best if you don't know the value of D. We can't say much about this in general, but we have a rule which gives D when the position is made up entirely of long chains of lengths

$$a, b, c, \dots .$$

For such a position

$$D = (a-4) + (b-4) + (c-4) + \dots + 4$$

provided the right side is positive; otherwise $D = 1$ or 2.

Using this rule we can answer our question for positions made entirely of chains:

> You should keep or gain control, *unless*
> there are *evenly* many short chains, *and*
> *either* there are no long chains
> *or* the long chains can be partitioned
> into two sets, each of average
> length strictly less than 4.

The A.B.C. of Control when Long Chains are Short.

Of course, for such positions, keeping or gaining control involves making Bertha's move if this would leave an even number of unopened short chains, and Arthur's move otherwise.

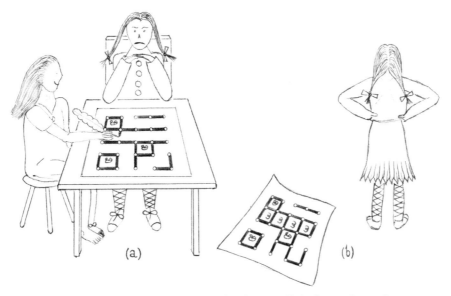

Figure 37. Dodie's Drawing the Game—Evie Loses Control.

Figure 37(a) shows a position where Evie, who's not feeling very well, has only managed to keep control so far by sacrificing 3 boxes. Dodie's now foolishly opening a chain of length 4 with the move shown. Since the remaining long chains satisfy the exceptional condition in our A.B.C., Evie's best move (Fig. 37(b)) is to *lose* control and take all 4 squares of the chain as Arthur would. The boxes are then divided:

		4-chain	three 3-chains			
to Evie		4	2	2		an $\frac{8}{8}$ tie,
to Dodie	3 already +	1	1	3		

where Bertha's response would give

		4-chain	three 3-chains			
to Evie		2	1	1	3	a $\frac{7}{9}$ loss.
to Dodie	3 already +	2	2	2		

COMPUTING THE VALUES OF VINES

On most graphs made of Twopins-vines and long chains a winning Nimstring strategy really does win at Dots-and-Boxes. For let V be the number of separate vines, counting long chains as unjointed vines. *Don't* use Fig. 26(a) to decompose vines with long stems—*instead* let I denote the number of these internal long stems. Let J be the total number of joints and L the Nimstring loser's present score. We study the quantities

$$f = L + 2J + 2V, \qquad g = I + 2L + 3J + 4V$$

during any double turn, consisting of the loser's move and the winner's reply, assigning any boxes given away by a move to that move rather than to the next one. First for the Nimstring winner's move:

Move on	Change in					
	I	L	J	V	f	g
Stem	0	$\leqslant 2$	-2	1	$\leqslant 0$	$\leqslant 2$
Inner tendril	$\leqslant 1$	$\leqslant 2$	-1	0	$\leqslant 0$	$\leqslant 2$
End tendril	$\leqslant 0$	$\leqslant 2$	-1	0	$\leqslant 0$	$\leqslant 1$

And now for the Nimstring loser's move:

Move on	Change in						and including winner's reply	
	I	L	J	V	f	g	f	g
Stem	0	0	-2	1	-2	-2	$\leqslant -2$	$\leqslant 0$
Inner tendril	$\leqslant 1$	0	-1	0	-2	$\leqslant -2$		
End tendril	$\leqslant 0$	0	-1	0	-2	$\leqslant -3$		
Loony stem move that winner must accept	$\leqslant 0$	0	-2	1	-2	$\leqslant -2$	$\leqslant -2$	$\leqslant 0$
Loony tendril move that winner must accept	$\leqslant 1$	0	-1	0	-2	$\leqslant -2$	$\leqslant -2$	$\leqslant 0$
Loony chain move (declined by winner)	0	2	0	-1	0	0	0	0
Loony stem move (declined by winner)	$\leqslant 0$	2	-2	1	0	$\leqslant 2$	0	$\leqslant 2^\dagger$
Loony tendril move (declined by winner)	$\leqslant 1$	2	-1	0	0	$\leqslant 2$	0	$\leqslant 2^\dagger$

(No loony chain move makes the winner *accept*, because by *declining* he leaves the value unchanged.) The next to last column shows that f *never* increases and so:

> If the number of nodes, N, in the game exceeds
>
> $$4(J + V)$$
>
> then the Nimstring winner wins the Dots-and-Boxes game.

(For the loser's score at the end of the game will be less than $N/2$.)

Since all Dawson's-vines and many Twopins-vines have more than four nodes per joint, they satisfy this condition. *If g* never increased, we could similarly assert that the Nimstring strategy works for Twopins-vines with

$$N > I + 3J + 4V,$$

but since the daggered entries can be positive a skilful Nimstring loser might win the occasional Dots-and-Boxes game.

Such cases are very rare. The Nimstring loser can increase g only by choosing a loony stem or tendril move that the Nimstring winner must decline (*most* loony moves can be accepted). Usually the winner has other opportunities to decrease g by playing on an end tendril or making a move conceding fewer than two boxes.

Even though we have been able to construct some examples (Fig. 32(m)), the difficulties of composing them and the closeness of their scores reinforce our opinion that:

> Your best chances at
> Dots-and-Boxes
> are likely to be found
> by the Nimstring strategy.

LOONY ENDGAMES ARE NP-HARD

If you're faced with a position in which all the edges are on long chains you'll lose at Nimstring because only loony moves are possible. But if you've already got lots of boxes you might still manage to win the Dots-and-Boxes game. How do you find *which* loony move to make to stop your opponent from catching up?

To simplify the argument we'll suppose that the last move will take place on a chain (between ground and ground) that's long enough to ensure that your opponent's best strategy for the remaining boxes is the Nimstring strategy, which requires that he conclude each turn, except the last, with a double-dealing move. Any of the m moves you make on isolated cycles will give you 4 boxes, while any of the other n moves on chains (except the last) will give you 2 boxes each, so your score will be

$$4m + 2n - 2.$$

Suppose the graph has j joints with total valence v, counting grounded ends as having valence 1 each. A move on an isolated cycle doesn't change the valence, but a move on a chain decreases the valence by 1 at each end, except that whenever the valence of a joint changes from 3 to 2 that joint disappears. This happens just once for each joint, so

$$v = 2n + 2j$$

and your score will be

$$4m + v - 2j - 2.$$

Since v and j are fixed, we want to make as many moves on isolated cycles as possible. These isolated cycles are disjoint, and any disjoint set of cycles can be isolated just by playing all chain moves first.

> You can't know all about (possibly
> generalized) Dots-and-Boxes unless
> you know all about how to find
> a largest set of node-disjoint cycles
> in an arbitrary (possibly non-planar)
> graph.

Finding a largest set of node-disjoint cycles in arbitrary graphs is known to be NP-hard (cf. the Extras to Chapter 7).

SOLUTIONS TO DOTS-AND-BOXES PROBLEMS

Here are *our* answers to the problems in Fig. 32.

(a) Evie wants an even number of long chains. She immediately establishes just two by drawing either edge at the top left-hand corner.

(b) This time Evie establishes two long chains by sacrificing the box whose lower left corner is the central dot. An additional sacrifice in the lower left-hand corner will be needed if Dodie tries to make a third long chain there.

(c) Dodie wants an odd number of long chains. She should sacrifice two boxes by a hard-hearted handout drawn rightwards from the central dot, and will win 9–7.

(d) Neither player can afford to sacrifice four boxes of the central loop, so the long chain theory doesn't really apply. Either player can force a tie (making no sacrifices). A well-played endgame will have chains of length 3 at top and bottom and a loop of 4 in the centre. The left side may be a single chain of length 4 or a pair of chains of lengths 1 and 3; either position is a tie.

(e) A little trap for Nimstring players! The *dotted* move is the only good Nimstring move, but involves too much sacrifice and will lose the Dots-and-Boxes game 5–7 against an extremely skilful opponent. The *dashed* move loses at Nimstring, but only if the opponent sacrifices two boxes on the next turn, and with the board then broken into many small pieces we get a tie.

(f) The Nimstring game is essentially over, but at Dots-and-Boxes what matters is whether the top left-hand corner becomes a chain of length 2 or two chains of length 1. Dodie should force the former by drawing the second edge on the top row and will win 13–12 rather than losing 12–13.

(g) Dodie forces a treble sacrifice! She wants an even number of long chains but can see only one. Her dotted opening move threatens to create a second long chain at EFG on the next move. Since Evie can be prevented from making a third long chain, she must cut between F and G, sacrificing two boxes. Accepting these, Dodie repeats her threat by the dashed move, which threatens a long chain at CDE, forcing Evie to sacrifice D and E. Dodie accepts these and repeats

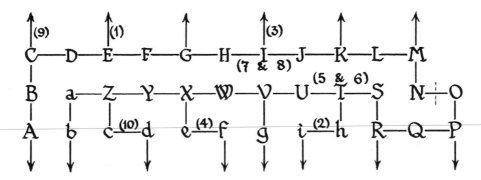

the threat yet again, drawing the left edge of *B*. Although Evie wins the Nimstring game by sacrificing *B* and *C*, Dodie will have 8 boxes: *F, G*; *D, E*; *B, C*; *N, O*; enough to win the Dots-and-Boxes game.

(h) Evie does likewise! Starting with the next to last of the top edges she repeatedly threatens to construct a third long chain at the right. Dodie can stop this only by three 2-box sacrifices. Evie then makes a loony move conceding the chain of length 3 to the left of the 2 captured boxes, acquiring 2 boxes after the resulting doublecross. Since she has now changed sides, she threatens to build another long chain in the top left-hand corner, forcing a further sacrifice from Dodie. She then stops further growth of the length 7 chain and awaits her last 3 boxes to win 13–12.

(i) A very complicated position! Dodie *must* prevent a third long chain from forming in the top row. She first sacrifices one of the top corner boxes (and will probably need more sacrifices) and strives vigilantly to chew up as much of the empty space as she can by extending her long chains. If Evie sacrifices either long chain too soon, Dodie accepts.

(j) An easy one! There is a treble-jointed Kayles-vine, value ∗3, and four boxes at the lower left, value ∗2 from Fig. 20. Evie wins by drawing the middle top edge or rightmost bottom one, which reduces K_3 to K_2. (There are other moves that do this, but they sacrifice too much.)

(k) There's a 4-jointed Kayles-vine, value ∗1, at the bottom, and four boxes at top right, worth ∗3 from Fig. 20. The rest of the figure is a 5-jointed Kayles-vine, value ∗4, under a disguise you can strip off by looking at Figs. 26(a) and (b). Dodie's Nimstring move must therefore replace K_5 by $K_3 + K_1$, which she can do only by drawing the vertical edge at the top left-hand corner or by isolating the loop just to the right of the captured boxes. In this problem it's only if Dodie plays carefully that her Nimstring strategy will also win at Dots-and-Boxes. When she has a choice of several Nimstring moves, she should select whichever scores more boxes. On the Kayles-vines any stem move (by either player) leads ultimately to another long chain, which will give two more boxes to Evie. So Dodie prefers to make tendril moves whenever possible, while Evie selects stem moves which make Dodie respond with more stem moves.

(l) A unique winning move! Cut the 12-jointed Kayles-vine into two 5-jointed ones by separating *N* from *O*. The rest is easy!

(m) In the modified problem, if Evie really respected Dodie's skill, she would resign! If she opened as before by sacrificing N, O, Dodie could unground E. Evie is then faced with $K_3 + K_1 + K_5$, and the Nimstring replies give Dodie two more boxes, e, f or h, i, say the latter (2). Dodie then (3) ungrounds I, leaving $4K_1 + K_3$, and Evie can't do better than (4) giving Dodie e and f (say) too. Evie now has $6K_1$ and has won the Nimstring game, but Dodie makes a loony move (5) on STU, which Evie's sadly forced to decline (6), conceding two more boxes. Dodie can make another loony move (7) on HIJ and collect two of those as well (8). Finally (9), Dodie can reduce $2K_1$ to K_1 by ungrounding C, which makes Evie (10) sacrifice c, d (or a, b). The resulting position

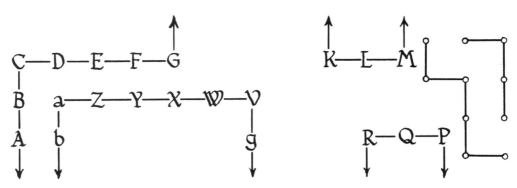

has five chains, lengths 3, 3, 4, 7, 8, but Evie has only 2 boxes to Dodie's 12. Although of the remaining chains Evie collects 17 boxes to Dodie's 8, Dodie wins 20 to 19! Rather than risk this disgrace, we recommend to Evie a timid opening such as ungrounding E; it's just conceivable that Dodie doesn't remember the first nine Kayles values!

SOME MORE NIMSTRING VALUES

As in Fig. 21, dots near edges are optional additional nodes and a dot equally near two edges may be placed on either. A wiggly line means 3 or more nodes strictly between the indicated points. The symbol

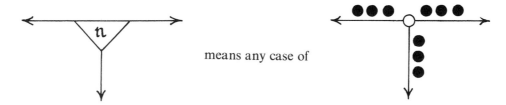

means any case of

that has value $*n$ (see Fig. 21).

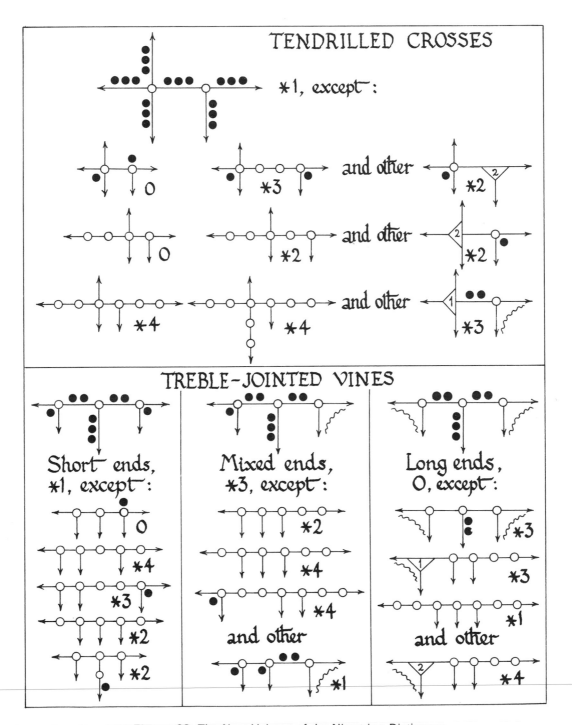

Figure 38. The Next Volume of the Nimstring Dictionary.

NIMBERS FOR NIMSTRING ARRAYS

To show the sides on which rectangular arrays are grounded we give their dimensions with primes (or double primes), for example:

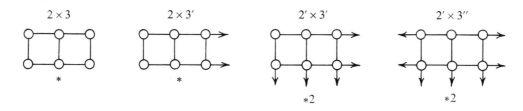

Tables 1 and 2 give values for such rectangular arrays:

	1′	2	2′	3	3′	4	4′	5	5′	6	6′	7	7′	8
2	*	0	*2	*	*	0	*2	*	*3	0	*2	*	*3	0
3	*2	*	*2	*	*2	*	*2	*						

Table 1. Nimstring Values for Ungrounded Rectangular Arrays or Arrays Grounded along One Edge.

n	2	3	4	5	6	7	8	9	10	11
$1′ \times n$	*	*2	*	*2	*3	0	*3	0	*	*2
$1′ \times n′$	0	*	0	*3	*2	*3	*2	*5	*4	*5
$1′ \times n″$	*	0	*	0	*	*2	*3	*	*3	
$2′ \times n$	*2	*2	*	*	*					
$2′ \times n′$	*2	*2	*	*						
$2′ \times n″$	0	*2	*5	*						

Table 2. Nimstring Values for Arrays Grounded at 1, 2 or 3 Edges.

Figure 39 shows Nimstring values for some less regular arrays.

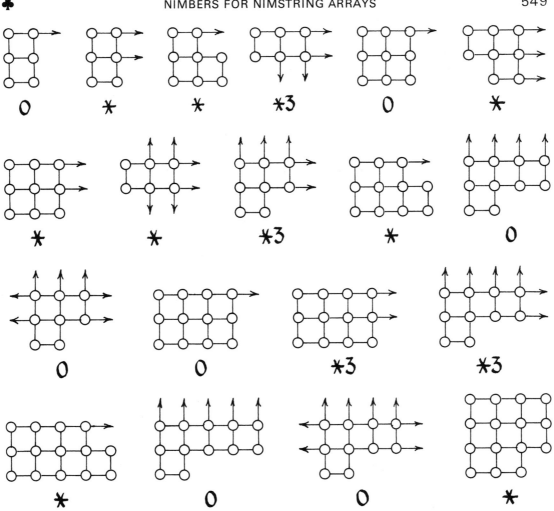

Figure 39. Nimbers for Various Arrays.

We have seen that we can play Nimstring on any graphs; here are the nim-values of small complete graphs, K_n and complete bipartite graphs, $K_{m,n}$:

n	2	3	4	5	6	7	8	9	10
K_n	0	*	0	*	*				
$K_{2,n}$	0	*	0	*	0	*	0	*	0
$K_{3,n}$	*	*	*	*	*	*			
$K_{4,n}$	0	*	0	*					

Does the value of $K_{m,n}$ depend only on the parity of $(m-1)(n-1)$?

REFERENCES AND FURTHER READING

John C. Holladay, A note on the game of dots, Amer. Math. Monthly, **73** (1966) 717–720; M.R.

Hans Rademacher and Otto Toeplitz, "The Enjoyment of Mathematics", Princeton University Press, 1957.
   Pages 75–76 give the proof of Euler's theorem.

Chapter 17

Spots and Sprouts

He shall not live, with a spot I damn him.
William Shakespeare, Julius Caesar IV, i, 6.

The games we treat here are played with spots (or crosses) on a piece of paper, the move being to join two spots by a curve satisfying various conditions specified in the rules of the game. *We shall always demand that no curve crosses itself or another curve.* We have just devoted a whole chapter to such a game, but here we shall consider games whose theories, while not all trivial (or even all complete) will occupy only a few pages each. We had to make an exception for Lucasta, with whom we fell in love.

RIMS

Here the move is simply to draw a loop passing through at least one and arbitrarily many of the spots. The only further condition is that no two loops may cross. A typical Rims position is shown in Fig. 1. What should be our next move, supposing normal play?

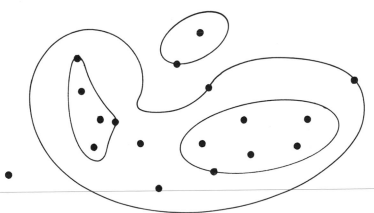

Figure 1. A Game of Rims. (or Rails).

On examining the position, we see that the loops divide the plane into regions containing respectively 5, 2, 3, 1, 1 spots (and sometimes other regions with internal spots). When we make a move in a region with n spots, we automatically divide it into two regions with a and b spots, where $a+b$ is less than n, but a and b are otherwise arbitrary. It follows that Rims is merely a disguised form of Nim with the additional possibility of dividing the heap we've just reduced into two smaller ones. This is the game $0 \cdot \dot{7}$ in the octal notation of Chapter 4, where we saw that the extra possibility doesn't affect the strategy, so the only good move in Fig. 1 is to draw a loop through just 4 of the spots in the 5-spot region. The theory of Misère Nim tells us that exactly the same move should be made in Misère Rims. In general we move so that the nim-sum of the spot counts is zero, except that in the misère form we must make the nim-sum 1 if every spot count is 0 or 1.

RAILS

Let us require that the loop must pass through just *one* or *two* spots, the rules otherwise being as in Rims. What should now be our move in Fig. 1? The legitimate moves in an n-spot region produce regions of a and b spots, where we require that $a+b = n-1$ or $n-2$. Since these moves correspond exactly to the legal moves in Kayles, our moves can be deduced from the theory of that game. For the Rails position of Fig. 1, this tells us to draw a loop through just one of the spots in the 5-spot region, in either normal or misère play.

Many other octal games can be reformulated very nicely as spot and loop games, and we find by observation that more people can be persuaded to play them this way. Often the geometrical form suggests particular rules very naturally, and sometimes the rules suggested do not quite correspond to natural games with heaps. Here are two further examples.

LOOPS-AND-BRANCHES

The move is to join two spots together, *or* join a single spot to itself so as to form a loop. No spot may be involved in two different moves. The game is isomorphic to the octal game $\cdot 73$, for which we computed the nim-values in Chapter 4 (Table 6) and the reduced forms in Chapter 13 (Extras, Table 5, Notes A and T, Adders). The patterns in Table 1 continue indefinitely.

n	0	1	2	3	4	5	6	7	8	9	...
nim-value	0	1	2	3	0	1	2	3	0	1	...
reduced form	0	1	2	3	2+2	3+2	2+2+2	3+2+2	2+2+2+2	3+2+2+2	...

Table 1. Nim-values and Reduced Forms for Loops-and-Branches.

So we have complete strategies in both normal and misère play. In both cases we move so that the nim-sum of the nim-values is zero, *except* that in misère play we must make the nim-sum one if every region has at most one spot.

CONTOURS

This game is rather more interesting. The move is to draw a closed loop (or *contour*) through just one spot, with the side condition that every loop must have at least one spot strictly inside (possibly internal to some further contours). In other words, when we view the position as a system of contours drawn on a map, every hill must have its peak marked (and every valley its bottom).

In this game, we must distinguish a region containing n spots and nothing else (type n) from one which, in addition to n free spots, contains a contour or contours with their internal spots (type $\hat{n}$). But the number or structure of the contours within a region of type $\hat{n}$ is immaterial, and the spots inside them do not count in computing n. So Fig. 2 has five regions, of types $\hat{5}$, 5, $\hat{3}$, 3, 2. What should be our move here?

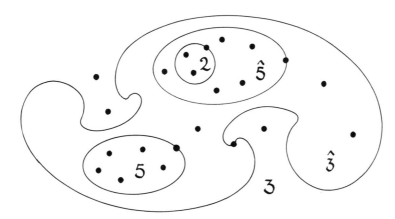

Figure 2. A Game of Contours.

The moves available from the general position are:

$$n \text{ or } \hat{n} \text{ to } a + \hat{b} \quad (a > 0)$$
$$\hat{n} \text{ to } \hat{a} + \hat{b}$$

where in each case $a + b = n - 1$. So we can draw up a table of nim-values, as in Table 2.

n:	0	1	2	3	4	5	6	7	8	9	10	11	12	13	14	15	16	17	18	19	20	...
$\mathcal{G}(n)$:		0	1	0	1	0	3	2	0	5	2	0	1	4	3	2	0	5	2	3	1	...
$\mathcal{G}(\hat{n})$:	0	1	2	3	1	4	3	2	0	5	2	3	1	4	3	2	0	5	2	3	1	...

Table 2. Nim-values for Contours.

We see that for $n \geqslant 12$ the two nim-sequences coincide and have period 8. So the starting position with n spots is a $\mathcal{P}$-position in normal play only if n is 1, 3, 5, 11, or a multiple of 8. We have not found a complete misère analysis, but Table 3 gives the start of a genus analysis (Chapter 13).

n	0	1	2	3	4	5	6	7	8	9	10	11	12	13	14	15	16
genus of n		0	1	0	1	0	3	2	0	$5^{057}_{A_1}$	2^2_C	0^3	1^0	4^{146}	3^3	2^{20}	0^1
genus of $\hat{n}$	0	1	2	3	1	4^{146}_A	3	2	0^1_B	$5^{057}_{A_1}$	2^2_D	3^3	1^0	4^{146}	3^3	2^{20}	0^1

Table 3. The Genus of Contours Positions.

$A = 2_2321$, $B = A_2A_1321$. For every position with all numbers $\leqslant 10$, the genus is correctly computed by pretending that $A + A = B = 0$, $C = D = 2$.

In the position of Fig. 2, the nim-values are 4, 0, 3, 0, 1, and so we must make a move changing nim-value 4 to 2. This can only be done by converting the region of type $\hat{5}$ into two of types $\hat{3}$ and $\hat{1}$, so we must draw a loop surrounding the inner contour of this region and just 1 or 3 more points, at least in normal play. It turns out that we have exactly the same good moves in misère play also.

LUCASTA

This is an old game first described by Lucas, and since it does not seem previously to have had a proper name, we have named it for him. It is quite remarkable that we can give complete strategies for both normal and misère play from the starting position, although the general theory is very complicated. Our strategy for normal play is easily proved when once found, but the misère play strategy is very tricky indeed.

The move is to draw a curve having as endpoints two distinct spots. These may *not* be the two endpoints of a single previously drawn curve (though they *may* be linked together by a chain of curves through intermediate spots). No two curves may cross, and no spot may be an endpoint of more than two curves, so that the curves can only build up into chains or into closed loops which must go through three or more spots.

The loops separate the plane into connected regions, as in the previous games, but now the situation within one of these regions needs a triple (a, b, c) of three numbers to describe it adequately. Here a is the number of *atoms*, or isolated spots, b the number of *branches* joining two otherwise isolated spots, and c is the number of *chains* consisting of three or more spots joined by a sequence of edges. It turns out that the number of spots in a chain is immaterial, except that chains (3 or more spots) must be distinguished from atoms and branches (1 and 2 spots).

The possible moves are classified as follows:

> aa: join two atoms to form a branch,
> ab: join an atom to a branch, making a chain,
> bb: connect two branches, forming a chain,
> ac: lengthen a chain by adjoining some atom,
> bc: extend a chain by attaching a branch,
> $c!$: *pull* a chain by joining its ends together.

Since pulling a chain divides a region into two, the result may depend on how it separates the remaining atoms, branches and chains from each other. We denote this by (for example) $c!(a^3)$ or $c!(ab)$, which mean that we separate 3 atoms or an atom and a branch into a region of their own. It is also possible to make a move cc: joining two chains to form a longer one: but the same effect could be achieved by *sharply* ($c!!$) pulling one of the chains, that is, with no separation.

A CHILD'S GUIDE TO NORMAL LUCASTA

We were fortunate that the nim-values we computed for Lucasta suggested a pattern for the outcomes of all positions with at most one chain. This pattern is displayed in Table 4 in which the entry (a, b) is

P if $(a, b, 0)$ is a $\mathscr{P}$-position, so $(a, b, 1)$ is an $\mathscr{N}$-position
+ if $(a, b, 1)$ is a $\mathscr{P}$-position, so $(a, b, 0)$ is an $\mathscr{N}$-position
− if $(a, b, 0)$ and $(a, b, 1)$ are both $\mathscr{N}$-positions.

Notice that the columns repeat with period 4, after the first four, while the rows alternate.

$a=$	0	1	2	3	4	5	6	7	8	9	10	11	12	13	14	15
$b=0$	P	P	−	+	P	P	P	−	P	P	P	−	P	P	P	−
1	P	P	−	−	−	P	−	−	−	P	−	−	−	P	−	−
2	P	P	−	+	P	P	P	−	P	P	P	−	P	P	P	−
3	P	P	−	−	−	P	−	−	−	P	−	−	−	P	−	−
4	P	P	−	+	P	P	P	−	P	P	P	−	P	P	P	−
5	P	P	−	−	−	P	−	−	−	P	−	−	−	P	−	−
6	P	P	−	+	P	P	P	−	P	P	P	−	P	P	P	−
7	P	P	−	−	−	P	−	−	−	P	−	−	−	P	−	−

Table 4. Lucasta With At Most One Chain.

A complete analysis may be difficult, though a machine attack will probably show that the nim-values have period 2 in b and c. However we can give a strategy which enables you to win all the positions you deserve to, when the number of chains is small. This strategy also proves that the pattern of Table 4 persists indefinitely. It uses the *special $\mathscr{P}$-positions*

$$(0, b, 0), \quad (1+4k, b, 0), \quad (3, 2m, 1), \quad (4+2k, 2m, 0) \quad \text{and} \quad (0, 2m, 2), \qquad b, k, m \geqslant 0.$$

It is almost always bad to leave chains in a position because they can be pulled in a number of different ways.

Our opponent can move from one of the special positions so as to leave two or more chains in only a few ways. If he joins two branches to form a chain we pull it smartly; if he joins a branch to a chain we join another. In either case the total effect is to remove two branches. The only other case is the ab move from $(3, 2m, 1)$ to $(2, 2m-1, 2)$ after which we join the two atoms to get the position $(0, 2m, 2)$. Our responses to positions with at most one chain are given in Table 5. Observe that we have completely justified Table 4. The nim-values on which we based our strategy are shown in Table 6. The entry (a, b) gives the sequence of nim-values for $c = 0, 1, 2, \ldots$; the last pair of values always repeats indefinitely, so that 13145 abbreviates 131454545.... Each unprinted row in the first five columns has the same entries as that with b decreased by 2. We have shown that all $\mathscr{N}$-positions $(a, b, 0)$ except $(2, 2m+2, 0)$ and $(6, 1, 0)$, have nim-value 1 and all $\mathscr{N}$-positions $(a, b, 1)$, except $(0, 2m, 1)$, $(1, 2m+1, 1)$ and $(5, 0, 1)$ have nim-value at least 2.

	$a = 0, 1, 5, ..., 1+4k$	$a = 2$	$a = 3$	$a = 4, 6, ..., 4+2k$	$a = 7, 11, ..., 7+4k$
$c = 0$	$\mathscr{P}$-positions; bad luck! Hope for a blunder	aa gives $(0, b+1, 0)$	aa gives $(1, b+1, 0)$	b even: bad luck! b odd: ab gives $(3, 2m, 1)$ if $k=0$. aa gives $(2+2k, 2m+2, 0)$ otherwise	aa gives $(5+4k, b+1, 0)$
$c = 1$	$c!!$ smartly gives $(0, b, 0)$ or $(1+4k, b, 0)$	$c!(a)$ round a solitary atom: $(1, 0, 0) +$ $(1, b, 0)$	b even: bad luck! b odd: bc gives $(3, 2m, 1)$	$c!$ separating atoms from branches, $(0, b, 0) + (4+2k, 0, 0)$	$c!$ separating all but one of the atoms from the branches: $(1, b, 0) + (6+4k, 0, 0)$

Table 5. How to Win at Lucasta.

	$a = 0$	1	2	3	4	5	6	7
$b = 0$	01	023	13145	10201	0351732	01023245	0245713101	13169498
1	023	01	124567	13132	1464601	02518189	230645	154578Xx
2	01	023	2356745	10401	0258589	046262Tt	06798	1316XTFf
3	023	01	15478967	13132	1567Xx	020101tFf		
4	01	023	2376945	10401	0278549t98	046292TfTt		
5	023	01	15498X67	13132	15696x6xX	020101fF		
6	01	023	2376X45	10401	027854Tt98	0462X2tSs		
7	023	01	15498x67	13132	15696T6xSxX			
8	01	023	2376X45	10401	027854F89			
9	023	01	15498x67	13132	15696T6xSxX			

$$X = 10$$
$$x = 11$$
$$T = 12$$
$$t = 13$$
$$F = 14$$
$$f = 15$$
$$S = 16$$
$$s = 17$$

Table 6. Nim-values for Positions (a, b, c) in Lucasta.

THE MISÈRE FORM OF LUCASTA

It is remarkable that we can still give a strategy for misère Lucasta from any starting position $(a, 0, 0)$. This is largely because the player who wins can do so without allowing the creation of too many chains, for of course positions with many chains are very difficult to analyze. For fairly small values of a, b, c we can of course compute the genus, as in Table 9, given later, which show that the complete theory is very complicated. In fact, Table 9 was first used in constructing our other tables and figures, and it then suggested our general strategy. This strategy is described in Table 7, Fig. 3, Table 8 and the explanatory notes to these. In Table 7 the notation is as in Table 4, and the patterns continue.

$a=$	0	1	2	3	4	5	6	7	8	9	10	11	12	13	14	15	16	17	18	19
$b=0$	+	−	P	P	−	P	−	P	−	P	−	−	P	P	−	−	−	P	−	−
1	−	+	P	−	P	−	P	−	P	P	−	+	P	P	P	−	P	P	P	−
2	+	P	−	P	−	P	−	−	P	P	−	−	−	P	−	−	−	P	−	−
3	P	−	P	−	P	P	−	+	P	P	P	−	P	P	P	−	P	P	P	−
4	−	P	−	−	P	P	−	−	−	P	−	−	−	P	−	−	−	P	−	−
5	P	P	−	+	P	P	P	−	P	P	P	−	P	P	P	−	P	P	P	−
6	P	P	−	−	−	P	−	−	−	P	−	−	−	P	−	−	−	P	−	−
7	P	P	−	+	P	P	P	−	P	P	P	−	P	P	P	−	P	P	P	−
8	P	P	−	−	−	P	−	−	−	P	−	−	−	P	−	−	−	P	−	−
9	P	P	−	+	P	P	P	−	P	P	P	−	P	P	P	−	P	P	P	−

Table 7. Outcomes of Some Misère Lucasta Positions.

Table 7 gives the outcome of positions of form $(a, b, 0)$ or $(a, b, 1)$, and is the skeleton of our strategy. Most of the rest of our discussion is concerned only with the justification of the + entries. First we show how the remaining entries can be deduced from these. We use three principles.

(1) The entry (a, b) is P if and only if it is non-terminal and there is no entry of form

P	in	$(a-2, b+1)$	the only	aa	to	$(a-2, b+1, 0)$
+	in	$(a, b-2)$	moves from	bb	to	$(a, b-2, 1)$
or +	in	$(a-1, b-1)$	$(a, b, 0)$ being	ab	to	$(a-1, b-1, 1)$.

(2) The entry (a, b) cannot be + if there is any entry of form

P	in	$(a, b-2)$	because	$c!(bb)$	from $(a, b, 1)$	$(a, b-2, 0) + (0, 2, 0)$
P	in	$(a-1, b-1)$	there are	$c!(ab)$	to each	$(a-1, b-1, 0) + (1, 1, 0)$
P or +	in	$(a-1, b)$	moves	$c!(a)$ or ac	of the	$(a-1, b, 0) + (1, 0, 0)$ or $(a-1, b, 1)$
P or +	in	$(a, b-1)$		$c!(b)$ or bc	positions	$(a, b-1, 0) + (0, 1, 0)$ or $(a, b-1, 1)$

and the positions $(0, 2, 0)$, $(1, 1, 0)$, $(1, 0, 0)$, $(0, 1, 0)$ can be neglected, since they necessarily last for exactly 0 or 2 moves.

(3) The entry $(a, 0)$ cannot be + if there is a P entry in $(a-4, 1)$ or $(a-6, 0)$. (For from the position $(a, 0, 1)$ we can move to $(a-2, 0, 0) + (2, 0, 0)$, and whatever our opponent does to this, we can move to the sum $(a-4, 1, 0) + (0, 1, 0)$ on our next move, in which $(0, 1, 0)$ can be neglected. We can also move to $(a-6, 0, 0) + (6, 0, 0)$ and we shall show later that $(6, 0, 0)$ can be neglected, being equivalent to 0.)

The reader should now check that all the entries in Table 7 follow from the + entries using only these three principles, and the obvious fact that each entry *is* P or + or −, since $(a, b, 0)$ and $(a, b, 1)$ cannot both be P.

It is not such a routine matter to justify the + entries themselves, the main difficulty being that our opponent might try to create two or more chains, and we cannot allow this to persist, or the position will become too complicated for words (or pictures). The backbone of our strategy (supporting the skeleton of Table 7) is illustrated in Fig. 3, which illustrates winning strategies for the second player from each of the positions

$$(0, 0, 1), (1, 1, 1) = (0, 2, 1), (3, 5, 1), (3, 7, 1), (3, 9, 1), \dots .$$

which are all but two of the $\mathscr{P}$-positions corresponding to the + entries in Table 7. We write $(1, 1, 1) = (0, 2, 1)$ because a single atom has exactly the same effect on the game as another branch. For the same reason, we have systematically replaced any position $(1, b, c)$ which should appear in Fig. 3 by the equivalent position $(0, b+1, c)$.

Some further remarks need to be made about Fig. 3. The positions surrounded by double boxes represent $\mathscr{P}$-positions which will be dealt with shortly. All other $\mathscr{P}$-positions are surrounded by single boxes, and all their options also appear on the Figure. Every unboxed position on the diagram represents an $\mathscr{N}$-position, for which a $\mathscr{P}$-option is always given. The symbol $abcD$ denotes the sum of the position (a, b, c) with another position (like $(0, 0, 1)$) which necessarily lasts an *odd* number of moves (usually *one* move), however played, while $abcE$ denotes the sum of (a, b, c) with a position (like $(0, 2, 0)$ or $(1, 1, 0)$) which necessarily lasts an *even* number of moves (usually *two*). In any later analysis, we have always supposed that these odd and even numbers were *one* and *zero*, respectively. Finally, $*abc$ denotes the sum of any two positions (x, y, z) and $(a-x, b-y, c-z)$. To continue the figure downwards increase b by 2.

The two $\mathscr{P}$-positions $(7, 3, 1)$ and $(11, 1, 1)$ corresponding to the only + entries in Table 7 not yet verified, are discussed in Table 8.

It remains to discuss the double-boxed positions of Fig. 3.

Theorem. The sum of any number of positions of the form $(0, b, 0)$ together with a game which necessarily lasts for exactly n moves, is a $\mathscr{P}$-position if and only if:

> *either* n is odd, and all the numbers b are 0, 1, 2, or 4
>
> *or* $\quad$ n is even, and at least one of the numbers b is *not* 0, 1, 2, or 4.

Proof. The positions $(0, 0, 0)$ and $(0, 1, 0)$ are ended, while $(0, 2, 0)$ lasts exactly two moves, so all of these positions can be neglected. In fact positions $(0, 4, 0)$ can be neglected as well, since we can always arrange that they last an even number of moves. The only line of play from $(0, 4, 0)$ lasting an odd number of moves is

$$(0, 4, 0) \text{ to } (0, 2, 1) \text{ to } (0, 1, 1) \text{ to } (0, 1, 0).$$

We need never make the move from $(0, 2, 1)$ to $(0, 1, 1)$, and if our opponent does so, we can immediately reply with a move from $(0, 1, 1)$ to $(0, 0, 1)$ which makes the game last an extra move.

Neglecting $(0, 4, 0)$ and positions which always last an even number of moves, the only real assertion is that a sum of positions $(0, b, 0)$, with each b either $=3$ or $\geqslant 5$, is a $\mathscr{P}$-position. The only move from $(0, b, 0)$ is to $(0, b-2, 1)$ from which we can move to any position $(0, x, 0) + (0, y, 0)$ with $x+y = b-2$. However our opponent moves, we can use this to restore the position to another one covered by the theorem, *unless* it is just the single position $(0, 3, 0)$, from which our opponent can only move to $(0, 1, 1)$, and we then move to $(0, 0, 1)$, leaving him to make the last (losing) move.

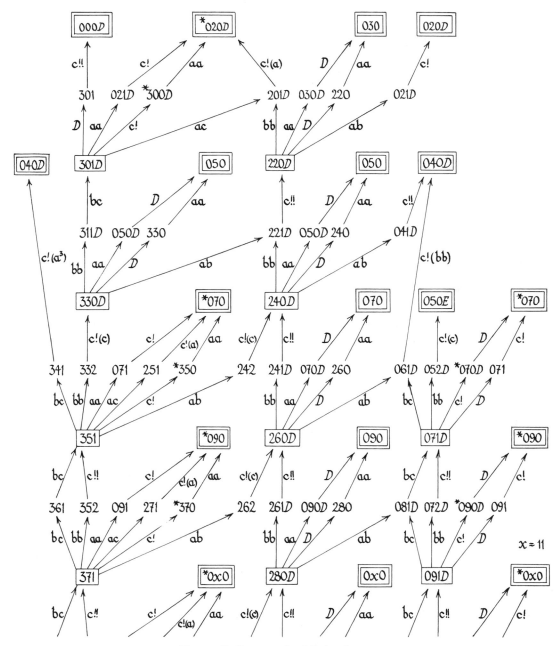

Figure 3. Strategy for Misère Lucasta.

THE POSITIONS (7, 3, 1) AND (11, 1, 1)

In Table 8, to each option of either of these positions, we give a response, which is in every case expressed as the sum of a $\mathscr{P}$-position from Table 7 and some position which can be verified to be equivalent to 0 from Fig. 4. In fact the + entries in Table 7 corresponding to (7, 3, 1) and (11, 1, 1) are not needed to verify any other entry, and so are not used in our strategy from any initial position, so that Table 8 is not really necessary for the strategy.

The options of (7, 3, 1)	have good replies	The options of (11, 1, 1)	have good replies
aa (5, 4, 1)	(5, 2, 0) + (0, 2, 0)	(9, 2, 1)	(9, 0, 0) + (0, 2, 0)
ab (6, 2, 2)	(3, 2, 0) + (3, 0, 1)	(10, 0, 2)	(7, 0, 0) + (3, 0, 1)
bb (7, 1, 2)	(1, 1, 1) + (6, 0, 0)		
ac (6, 3, 1)	(5, 3, 0) + (1, 0, 0)	(10, 1, 1)	(9, 1, 0) + (1, 0, 0)
bc (7, 2, 1)	(7, 0, 0) + (0, 2, 0)	(11, 0, 1)	(7, 0, 0) + (4, 0, 0)

The other options are all sums of two positions $(a, b, 0)$, and in every case we move in the region which has just 2, 3, 6, 7, 10, or 11 atoms, and join two of these atoms together.

Table 8. (7, 3, 1) and (11, 1, 1) are $\mathscr{P}$-positions.

It is interesting to note that the positions

$$000, \ 010 = 100, \ 020 = 110, \ 040 = 130,$$
$$400, \ 420, \ 510, \ 600, \ 800,$$
$$301, \ 022 = 112, \ 002, \ 004, \ 006, \ldots$$

are equivalent to 0 in the misère sense. (This remark can be useful in play from more complicated positions than those which need arise if our strategy is followed.) To prove that a position is misère-equivalent to 0 it is necessary and sufficient to show, first, that it is an $\mathscr{N}$-position and second, that each of its options has itself an option misère-equivalent to 0. This is done for the above positions in Fig. 4, in which the subscript

P denotes a $\mathscr{P}$-position
N denotes an $\mathscr{N}$-position *not* misère-equivalent to 0
O denotes an $\mathscr{N}$-position misère-equivalent to 0.

In a strategically fought game of Misère Lucasta, we find three phases. In the first phase, both players join pairs of atoms together to form branches. If either player dares to form a chain, his opponent can certainly win by closing the chain around some small number of atoms and branches (which can be neglected), and converting the rest of the position to a $\mathscr{P}$-position. When the number of atoms is reduced to just above three, the winner is the player able to convert the position to $(3, 2n+1, 1)$, and the game enters its second phase, in which play follows the lines of Fig. 3. The third phase is reached when the position becomes a sum of positions $(0, b, 0)$ in which only branches (with isolated atoms) remain, together possibly with some rather trivial game. From then on, the winner always restores the position to a similar form, except that near the end of the game he is careful to restore the position $(0, 3, 0)$ to a single chain $(0, 0, 1)$.

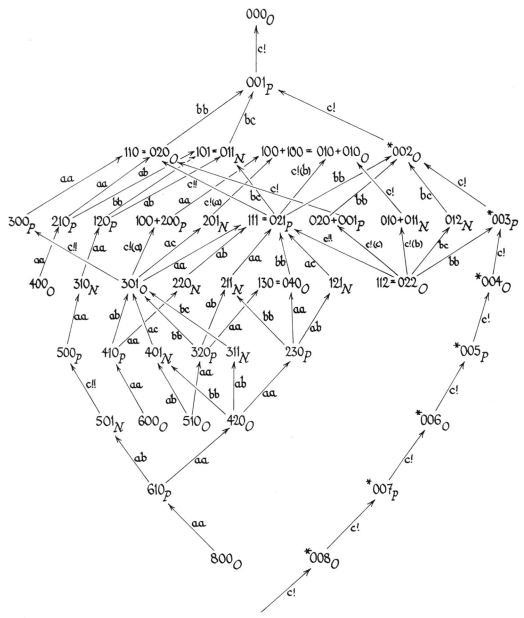

Figure 4. Proof of Misère-equivalence to Zero.

Table 9. The Genus of Lucasta Positions.

$a = 0$

$b \backslash c$	0	1	2	3	4	5	6	7	8
0	0	1	0	1	0	1	0	1	0
1	0	2	3	2	3	2	3	2	3
2	0	1	0	a	a_1	a	a_1	a	a_1
3	2_+	2	3	b	c	d	d_1	d	d_1
4	0	e	f	g	h	i	j	k	k_1
5	2_+	l	3^{04}						
6	e_+	1^3	0^{52}						
7	l_+	2^1							
8	0^0	1^2							
9	0^0								
10	0^0								

$a = 1$

$b \backslash c$	0	1	2	3	4	5	6	7	8
0	0	2	3	2	3	2	3	2	3
1	0	1	0	a	a_1	a	a_1	a	a_1
2	2_+	2	3	b	c	d	d_1	d	d_1
3	0	e	f	g	h	i	j	k	k_1
4	2_+	l	3^{04}						
5	e_+	1^3	0^{52}						
6	l_+	2^1							
7	0^0	1^2							
8	0^0								
9	0^0								

$a = 2$

$b \backslash c$	0	1	2	3	4	5	6
0	1	3	1	p	p_1	p	p_1
1	1	2	4	q	r	s	s_1
2	t	u	v	6^{686}			
3	1	w	4^{04}				
4	K	3^3	5^{16}				
5	1^1	5^4					
6	2^1	3^{203}					
7	1^2						
8	2^1						

genus	name	structure
1^{4313}	a	2_2320
2^{2020}	b	$a2_+30$
3^{0431}	c	$ba_1a2_{+1}2$
2^{1520}	d	$cb_1a_2a_1a2_+3$
1^{3131}	e	2_+20
0^{1202}	f	$ea2_{+2}321$
1^{4313}	g	$fe_1ba_12_{+3}2_230$
0^{5202}	h	$gf_1ecba2_{+2}3_21$
1^{4313}	i	$hg_1fe_1dcb_2a_12_{+3}2_20$
0^{5202}	j	$ih_1gf_1ed_1dc_2b_3a2_{+2}3_21$
1^{4313}	k	$ji_1hg_1fe_1d_2d_1dc_3b_2a_aa_12_{+3}2_20$
0^{0202}	a_a	$a_{22}a_3a_2a$
2^{2020}	l	$e2_+30$
4^{1464}	p	2_2321
5^{5757}	q	$pa3_243210$
6^{6846}	r	$qp_1pa_1a2_25320$
7^{7957}	s	$rq_1p_2p_1pa_2a_1a3_24321$
2^{1420}	t	2_+31
3^{3131}	u	$t2_+210$
5^{5757}	v	$ut_1pa2_{+2}43210$
5^{2057}	w	$ute2_{+1}2_+4310$

genus	name	structure
0^{3131}	A	$pa3_221$
1^{2020}	B	$Ap_1pa_12_230$
0^{3131}	C	$BA_1p_2p_1pa3_221$
1^{5313}	D	$p2_+4320$
3^{6464}	E	$DAqp_1b2_{+1}2_2421$
1^{1313}	F	$2_+3 = 2_{+1}$
1^{2020}	H	F_+30
2^{0313}	I	$H0$
1^{1313}	J	$u2_+3$
2^{1313}	K	$ue2_+$
0^{0202}		$2_+, e_+, l_+, F_+$

	$a = 3$	$a = 4$	$a = 5$	$a = 6$	7	8	9
$c =$	0 1 2 3 4 5 6	0 1	0 1	0 1	0	0	0
$b = 0$	1 0 2 A B C C_1	0 3	F_+ H	0 2^3	1	0	0^0
1	F 3 D E	1 4^4	0	I	1^1		
2	1	0	0^0				
3	J						

Note: If $c \geqslant 2b + 2a$, then
(a, b, c) has value x_1, where $(a, b, c-1)$ has value x.

To save space in Table 9 the abbreviating conventions are *not* the same as those of Chapter 13. In the table

$$g^{a \cdots x} \quad \text{means} \quad g^{a \cdots xyxy \cdots} \quad \text{where} \quad y = x \ast 2$$

and no assertions about tameness or restiveness are intended. In the notes opposite, the genus is given to four superscripts even when the period starts earlier, and now the last two superscripts repeat indefinitely.

CABBAGES; OR BUGS, CATERPILLARS AND COCOONS

If we modify Lucasta by allowing the move which completes a closed loop passing through only two spots and consisting of two curves joining them, we get a simpler game. Here, we call the isolated spots *bugs*, chains of two or more spots *caterpillars*, and closed loops *cocoons*. The cocoons separate the plane into regions, so that the general position is a sum of positions (b, c), where these numbers specify the numbers of bugs and caterpillars per region.

It turns out that the position (b, c) in this game behaves just like the position $(0, b, c)$ in Lucasta, so we have the analysis already. (Using our nim-value table for Lucasta we can in fact analyze arbitrary positions in normal play.) In particular, we have:

The initial position $(n, 0)$ is a $\mathscr{P}$-position in normal play for all n,
and   in misère play for all n except 0, 1, 2, 4.

JOCASTA

We obtain an even simpler game by allowing in addition the move which joins an isolated spot to itself to form a closed loop passing only through that spot.

SPROUTS

This game (introduced by M.S. Paterson and J.H. Conway some time ago) has a novel feature which complicates the analysis to such an extent that the normal outcome of the 7-spot game is still unknown. Even the 2-spot game is remarkably complicated.

The move in Sprouts is to join two spots, or a single spot to itself (Fig. 5) by a curve which does not meet any previously drawn curve or spot. But when this curve is drawn, a new spot must be placed upon it. No spot may have more than three parts of curves ending at it.

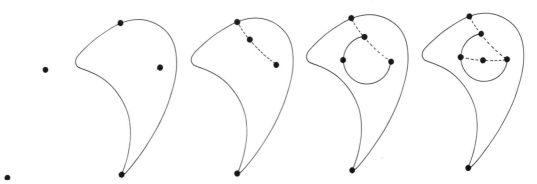

Figure 5. A Short Game of Sprouts.

A typical game is shown in Fig. 5, with the second player's moves drawn as dotted lines. Since the new spots can still be used in later moves, a Sprouts game will last longer than a Cabbages game from the same initial position, and it is perhaps not even obvious that it need ever end. But there is a simple argument which shows that in fact a Sprouts game starting from n spots can last at most $3n - 1$ moves. We take the 3-spot game as an example. Each spot has potentially 3 ends of curves available to it, which we shall call its three *lives*, so initially the 3-spot game has 9 lives. But each move takes one life away from the two spots it joins (or two lives away from a spot joined to itself), and adds a new spot which has just one life. Therefore each move reduces the total number of lives by one. Since the very last spot to be created is still alive at the end of the game, the total number of moves is at most $9 - 1 = 8$. But Fig. 6 shows just how complicated even the 2-spot game really is.

One of the most interesting theorems about Sprouts (due to D. Mollison and J.H. Conway) is the Fundamental Theorem of Zeroth Order Moribundity (FTOZOM). We shall not prove it here, but will at least state it. The FTOZOM asserts that the n-spot Sprouts game must last at least $2n$ moves, and that if it lasts exactly this amount, the final configuration is made up of the insects shown in Fig. 7.

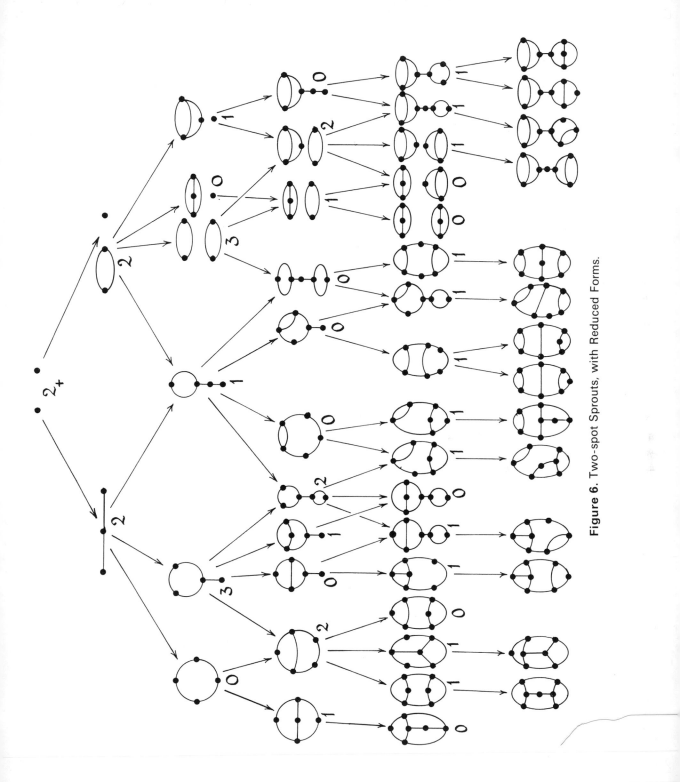

Figure 6. Two-spot Sprouts, with Reduced Forms.

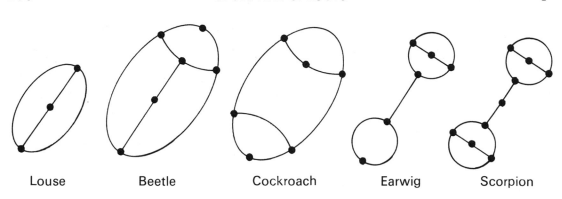

Figure 7. The Five Fundamental Insects.

To be more precise, the final configuration must consist of just one of these insects (which might perhaps be turned inside out in some way) infected by an arbitrarily large number of lice (some of which might infect others). One of the possible configurations is shown as Fig. 8—it consists of an inside-out scorpion inside an inside-out louse, liberally infected with other lice!

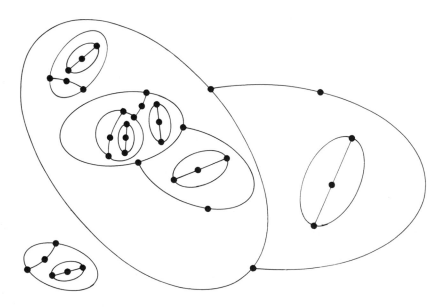

Figure 8. The Lousy End of a Short Sprouts Game.

How should we play if we wish to win a Sprouts game? It is clear that whether the play is normal or misère, the outcome only depends on whether the total number of moves in the game is odd or even, so in some sense winning is controlling the number of moves. Now the 3-spot game necessarily lasts for 6, 7, or 8 moves, and it is very difficult to make it last 8 moves, so that really the fight is between 6 and 7 moves. Apparently the same thing happens in larger games—essentially one player tries to make the game last m moves, while the other tries to drag it out to $m+1$, all other numbers being very unlikely.

To see how to control the number of moves, we examine the situation at the end of the game, which we suppose to have started with n spots and lasted for m moves. The final number of spots is $n+m$, and the total life at the end of the game is $l = 3n-m$, since we started with $3n$ lives, and subtracted one per move. Each of the live spots at the end of the game has two dead spots as its two nearest neighbors, and the remaining dead spots are called *Pharisees*. (The concept of neighbor is quite subtle—in Fig. 9 we show the two different ways in which two dead spots can be neighbors of a live one.)

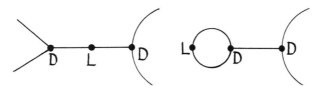

Figure 9. Two Live Spots (L) and their Dead Neighbors (D).

Now no dead spot can be a neighbor of two different live spots, for otherwise we could join these two spots and continue the game. So the number ϕ of Pharisees is given by the equation

$$\phi = (n+m) - (l+2l) = (n+m) - 3(3n-m) = 4m-8n$$

and we have the *Moribundity Equation*:

$$m = 2n + \tfrac{1}{4}\phi.$$

From this equation we can deduce several things:

(i) The number of moves is at least $2n$.
(ii) The number of Pharisees is a multiple of 4.
(iii) If at any time in the game we can ensure that the final position has at least P Pharisees, then the game will last at least $2n+\tfrac{1}{4}P$ moves.

There is a corresponding result to (iii) in the opposite direction:

(iv) If at any time in the game we can ensure that the final position has at least l live spots, then the game will last at most $3n-l$ moves.

So, according to our previous ideas, one player will try to lengthen the game by producing Pharisees, while his opponent tries to shorten it by producing spots which must remain alive.

There is a useful way to estimate the number of live spots there will be at the end of the game. *If any region defined by curves of the game has a live spot strictly inside, then there will be a live spot inside that region at all later times.* So in Fig. 10 we can regard, if we like, the plane as divided

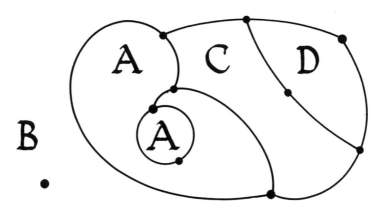

Figure 10. A Sprouts Position with One Pharisee.

into four regions A, B, C, D, and the regions A and B each have live spots strictly inside. Any move made in either of these regions creates a new live spot, and so each of A and B will contain a live spot at the end of the game. We cannot say the same of C and D, whose only live spots lie on their borders, but if we regard C and D together as forming a single region, then this new region has just one spot strictly inside. So we can see that the game will have at least 3 live spots in its final position. It also has presently one Pharisee P, and so (since it developed from an initial position with $n = 4$ spots) we can see that it will last *at most* $3n - 3 = 9$ moves, and *at least* $2n + \frac{1}{4} = 8\frac{1}{4}$ moves. Since it is difficult to see how the game could last for *exactly* $8\frac{1}{4}$ moves, we conclude that the total length of the game will be 9 moves, however it is played from now on! (Actually, 6 moves have already been made, so just 3 more moves are to follow.) Accordingly, this is either a normal play game about to be won by the first player, or a misère play one being won by the second player.

Using these ideas, it is fairly easy to give analyses of games with small numbers of spots. We give the results we have obtained in Table 10, which shows the number of moves that the winner can arrange for the game to last.

no. of spots:	0	1	2	3	4	5	6
normal play:	0P	2P	4P	7N	9N	11N	14P
misère play:	0N	2N	5P	7P	9P		

Table 10. Outcomes of the Smallest Sprouts Games.

The fact that 6-spot normal Sprouts is a $\mathscr{P}$-position was first proved (to win a bet) by Denis Mollison, whose analysis of the game ran to 47 pages! Using the ideas above, we can shorten this considerably, but we have not yet been able to analyze 5-spot Sprouts with misère play.

BRUSSELS SPROUTS

Here is another game, which should be more interesting than Sprouts. We start with a number of crosses, instead of spots. The move is to continue one arm of a cross by some curve which ends at another arm of the same or a different cross, and then to add a new cross-bar at some point along this curve. A 2-cross game of Brussels Sprouts is shown as Fig. 11. After playing a few games of Brussels Sprouts, the skilful reader will be able to suggest a good starting strategy.

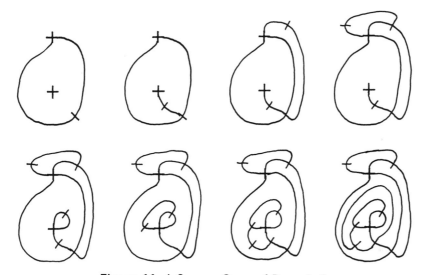

Figure 11. A 2-cross Game of Brussels Sprouts.

STARS-AND-STRIPES

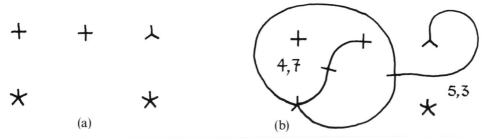

Figure 12. A Game of Stars-and-Stripes.

Suppose we make addition of the cross-bar optional in Brussels Sprouts. It is natural at the same time to allow "stars" with any number of arms instead of just crosses with exactly 4 arms, and to call the cross-bar a *stripe*. An initial position (5, 5, 4, 4, 3) is shown in Fig. 12(a), along with a position 3 moves later (Fig. 12(b)). In the analysis, the game becomes a disjunctive sum of regions, and we can pretend that each region contains only stars. In general, a connected portion of the picture which has just n arms sticking into the region concerned counts as an n-arm star inside the region. (Even the boundary of the region counts as a star.) In Fig. 12(b) we have therefore labelled each region with numbers showing the sizes of the stars in that region.

The one-star game is isomorphic to the octal game **4·07**, since a move with cross-bar essentially splits an n-arm star into two stars of sizes a and b, with $a+b = n$, $a, b \neq 0$, and the move without crossbar splits it into stars of sizes a and b with $a+b = n-2$. The nim-values for this game (Chapter 4, Tables 7(a), 6(b)) are $0.\dot{0}12\dot{3}$ and the genus appears in Table 11.

n	0	1	2	3	4	5	6	7	8	9	10	11
genus of n	0	0	1	2	3	0	1_a^{431}	2	3_b^{31}	$0_{a_1}^{520}$	1_c^{431}	2_d^{0420}

$$a = 2_2 320 \qquad b = a_1 a 2_2 20 \qquad c = b_1 b a_3 a_1 2_2 20 \qquad d = c b_2 b a_2 a_1 a 3_2 3$$

Table 11. The Genus of Stars-and-Stripes Positions.

BUSHENHACK

is another pencil and paper game. It's played with a number of rooted trees, but now when you chop an edge, all edges connecting it to the ground disappear, leaving a number of floating bits of tree to be rerooted as in Fig. 13. Its theory involves yet another property of Nim.

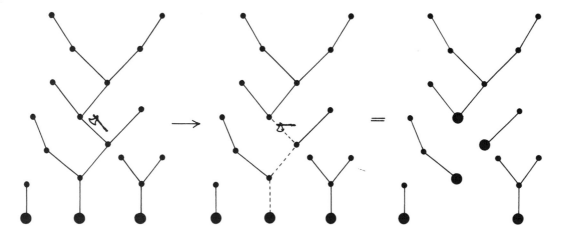

Figure 13. A Bushenhack Move.

GENETIC CODES FOR NIM

If you tell me that you're in a Nim-position of some nim-value (e.g. 9) and can move to positions having exactly so many (e.g. 13) other nim-values, I can tell you exactly what (in this case 0, 1, 2, 3, 4, 5, 6, 7, 8, 12, 13, 14, 15) those values are!

To see why, we enlarge upon a notation from the Extras to Chapter 7, in which the single Nim-heaps are

$$0_{\{\ \}},\ 1_{\{1\}},\ 2_{\{2,3\}},\ 3_{\{1,2,3\}},\ 4_{\{4,5,6,7\}},\ 5_{\{1,4,5,6,7\}},\ \cdots,$$

and in general $n_{[n]}$, where $[n]$, the *variation set*, is the set of changes in nim-value that are possible in one move. The variation set $[n]$ for an arbitrary Nim-heap consists of all numbers whose leftmost binary digit 1 is present in the binary expansion of n, and so it can be found as the union of the appropriate selection of

$$[1] = \{1\}, \quad [2] = \{2,3\}, \quad [4] = \{4,5,6,7\}, \quad [8] = \{8,9,\ldots,15\}, \quad \ldots$$

E.g., since $13 = 1+4+8$, $[13] = \{1,4,5,6,7,8,9,\ldots,15\}$.

We'll say that a position has **genetic code** A if it has the same variation set as the Nim-heap of size A. Arbitrary Nim-positions have genetic codes, because when you *add* positions you *unite* their variation sets; e.g., $5+12$ has genetic code 13, because

$$5 + 12 = 5_{\{1,4,5,6,7\}} + 12_{\{4,5,6,7,8,9,\ldots,15\}} = 9_{\{1,4,5,6,7,8,9,\ldots,15\}} = 9_{[13]},$$

and the options of $9_{[13]}$ can be found by nim-adding 9 to the members of the variation set $[13]$.

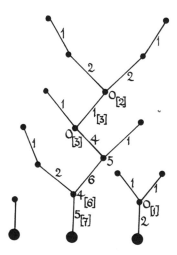

Figure 14. What's the Winning Move? (see the Extras).

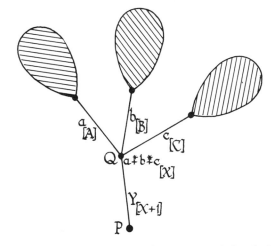

Figure 15. Calculating the Value and the Code.

BUSHENHACK POSITIONS HAVE GENETIC CODES!

In Fig. 14 the symbol $a_{[A]}$ against any edge gives the value and genetic code for the subtree whose trunk is that edge, while at every node where there are several branches we've given this information for the sum of the corresponding subtrees. (An isolated digit a means $a_{[a]}$.) The numbers are calculated as in Fig. 15 where X is the number whose binary expansion has a 1 wherever there is a 1 in *any* of A, B, C, so that

$$[X] = [A] \cup [B] \cup [C]$$

and Y is the smallest number greater than $a \overset{*}{+} b \overset{*}{+} c$ that is divisible by exactly that power of 2 which divides $X + 1$.

Suppose that X has binary expansion

$$\ldots \; ? \; ? \; ? \; 0 \; 1 \; 1 \; 1 \; \ldots \; 1 \quad \text{(ending in } k \text{ 1's)}.$$

Then that of $a \overset{*}{+} b \overset{*}{+} c$ will have the form

$$\ldots \; p \; q \; r \; 0 \; t \; u \; v \; \ldots \; z$$

We already know why these numbers are the code and value for the sum of the three subtrees above Q in Fig. 15. So we need only show that

$$X + 1 = \ldots \; ? \; ? \; ? \; 1 \; 0 \; 0 \; 0 \; \ldots \; 0$$

and

$$Y = \ldots \; p \; q \; r \; 1 \; 0 \; 0 \; 0 \; \ldots \; 0$$

are the code and value for the subtree with trunk PQ. The options for this tree have nim-values

$$a \overset{*}{+} b \overset{*}{+} c \quad \text{(chop } PQ) \quad \text{and} \quad a \overset{*}{+} b \overset{*}{+} c \overset{*}{+} \Delta$$

for any number Δ whose first digit 1 is present in X. In particular, we can move to all nim-values that are $\leqslant a \overset{*}{+} b \overset{*}{+} c$ or differ from it only in the last k places. So we can move to all numbers smaller than Y, which differs from $a \overset{*}{+} b \overset{*}{+} c$ in the $(k+1)$st place from the right, corresponding to the rightmost zero in X. The nim-values of the options are exactly those binary numbers whose leftmost difference from Y corresponds to a digit 1 in $X + 1$, which is therefore the genetic code.

VON NEUMANN HACKENBUSH

when played on trees, is an exactly equivalent game in which the move is to delete a *node* together with all nodes on the path connecting it to the ground and all edges meeting these. To convert to Bushenhack, just add a new trunk to every tree. Von Neumann proved, by a strategy-stealing argument, that a single tree was always an $\mathcal{N}$-position, and Úlehla gave an explicit strategy for trees, which prompted our own discussion.

Bushenhack is really just the theory of $A + B$ and $A:*$, whereas ordinary Hackenbush is concerned with $A + B$ and $*:B$. The most general version of von Neumann Hackenbush is played on any directed graph (remove a node and all nodes it points to). Its analysis involves the properties of $A + B$ and $A:B$ for arbitrary variation sets (Extras to Chapter 7).

EXTRAS

THE JOKE IN JOCASTA

is that the n-spot game always last for n moves, because each spot has two lives and each move uses two. The game is therefore just another form of She-Loves-Me, She-Loves-Me-Not.

THE WORM IN BRUSSELS SPROUTS

is similar but more subtle. The n-cross game always lasts for just $5n-2$ moves, but Brussels Sprouts is definitely more interesting on surfaces of higher genus, e.g. the torus.

BUSHENHACK

The winning move in Fig. 14 is that shown in Fig. 13.

REFERENCES AND FURTHER READING

Piers Anthony, "Macroscope", Avon, 1972.

Hugo D'Alarcao and Thomas E. Moore, Euler's formula and a game of Conway, J. Recreational Math. **9** (1977) 249–251; Zbl. 355.05021.

Martin Gardner, Mathematical Games: Of sprouts and Brussels sprouts; games with a topological flavor, Sci. Amer. **217** #1 (July 1967) 112–115.

Martin Gardner, "Mathematical Carnival", Alfred A. Knopf, New York 1975, Chapter 1.

Emmanuel Lasker, Brettspiele der Völker,

E. Lucas, "Récréations Mathématiques", Gauthiers-Villars, 1882–94; Blanchard, Paris, 1960.

Gordon Pritchett, The game of Sprouts, Two-Year Coll. Math. J. **7** #4 (Dec. 1976) 21–25.

J.M.S. Simões-Pereira and Isabel Maria S.N. Zuzarte, Some remarks on a game with graphs, J. Recreational Math. **6** (1973) 54–60; Zbl. 339.05129.

J. Úlehla, A complete analysis of von Neumann's Hackendot, Internat. J. Game Theory, **9** (1980) 107–115.

Chapter 18

The Emperor and His Money

For good ye are and bad, and like to coins,
Some true, some light, but every one of you
Stamp'd with the image of the King.
   Alfred, Lord Tennyson, *The Idylls of the King, The Holy Grail,* l.25.

Figure 1. The Emperor's Declaration.

"...Emperor Nu took power by overthrowing the divisive My-Nus dynasty. The Nu régime introduced many positive reforms, and in particular abolished the old (An-Tsient) irrational currency, which had his predecessor's head on it, and introduced the Nu system. The masters of the Imperial Mint, Hi and Lo, were alternately to decide the value of each new denomination, and after each decision, sufficiently many coins of this value were to be struck. All went well until Hi ordered the striking of a coin of value one, so throwing the Workers of the Mint into unemployment. They rose in a body, and threw the unfortunate Hi from the tower at the quiet end of the capital, which has been known as the Hi Tower ever since."

My-Nus—Some Divisive Times.

575

SYLVER COINAGE

Had Hi and Lo read this book, they would have realized they were only playing a game, the game of **Sylver Coinage**. In this the players alternately name different numbers, but are not allowed to name *any* number that is a sum of previously named ones. So, if 3 and 5 have been named, for example, neither of the players is allowed to play any of the numbers

$$3, \quad 5, \quad 6 = 3+3, \quad 8 = 3+5, \quad 9 = 3+3+3, \quad 10 = 5+5, \quad 11 = 3+3+5, \quad \ldots$$

When will this game end? If neither player has played 1, 1 will still be playable. But, of course, as soon as 1 has been played, every number

$$1, \quad 2 = 1+1, \quad 3 = 1+1+1, \quad 4 = 1+1+1+1, \quad 5 = 1+1+1+1+1, \quad \ldots$$

is illegal, and so the game ends. Because the player who names 1 is declared the *loser*, Sylver Coinage is a *misère* game. (Skilful players won't spend much time on the normal play version!).

We had better point out that because the old currency had been rather irrational (with coins of value $\sqrt{2}$, e and π) the Emperor declared that there was to be a new monetary unit, the **You-Nit**, and the value of each coin was to be an integral number of You-Nits. (You can see the Emperor making this declaration in Fig. 1!).

And recalling how people were nonplussed by the great financial scandal of the My-Nus dynasty when they had to take away Teh Kah-Weh for issuing currency of negative value, Emperor Nu decided that each coin's value must be a *positive* number of You-Nits.

HOW LONG WILL IT LAST?

It might take quite a long time. To see that it can last for a thousand moves, we need only consider the game

$$1000, 999, 998, \ldots, 4, 3, 2, 1.$$

And of course a thousand can be replaced by any other number, so that the game is **unbounded**. Many other games have this property, for example Green Hackenbush (Chapter 2) played with an infinite snake, but are *boundedly* unbounded because after some fixed number of moves the end will be in sight. Thus after the first move in the Hackenbush game only a finite amount of snake is left.

But Sylver Coinage is not like that! No matter what number you choose, Hi and Lo can find a way to play that number of moves so that what's left of the game will still be unbounded. Their first thousand moves might be

$$2^{1000}, 2^{999}, 2^{998}, \ldots, 2^4, 2^3, 2^2, 2^1$$

and the rest of the game can still last as long as you like:

$$1000001, 999999, 999997, \ldots, 7, 5, 3, 1.$$

In other words Sylver Coinage is *unboundedly unbounded*. And this isn't all. It's *unboundedly unboundedly unbounded* and unboundedly like that, and so (unboundedly) on!

Nevertheless, it can't go on for ever; in the language of Chapter 11 it's an *ender*. It is because the little theorem which proves this is due to the famous mathematician J.J. Sylvester that we have called the game *Sylver* Coinage.

For, at any time after the first move, let g be the greatest common divisor (g.c.d.) of the moves made. Then it's not hard to see that only finitely many multiples of g are *not* expressible as sums of numbers already played. So after at most this known number of moves the g.c.d. must be reduced. Eventually we must arrive at a position with $g = 1$ and can bound the number of moves yet to be made. So although we may not be able to bound the game after any given number of moves, we *can* bound the number of moves it will take to reduce the g.c.d.

SOME OPENINGS ARE BAD

The proof we gave in the Extras to Chapter 2 shows that from any position in Sylver Coinage there *is* a winning strategy for one of the two players *but* because of the infinite nature of the game we cannot work through all positions and guarantee to find winning strategies when they exist. In fact we do not know of (and there may not exist) any way of working out in a finite time who wins from an arbitrarily given position. But we do know the answers for some easy positions.

If at any time you name 1, you lose by definition.

If you name 2, my reply will be 3 if it's still available, and then all larger numbers

$$4 = 2+2, \quad 5 = 2+3, \quad 6 = 2+2+2, \quad 7 = 2+2+3, \quad 8 = 2+2+2+2, \quad \ldots$$

are excluded and you will be forced to name 1.

If you name 3, then for the same reason, 2 is a good reply.

So whoever first names any of 1, 2 and 3 will lose. In particular the first three numbers are bad opening moves. What will you reply if I open with 4? Maybe 5? If so the g.c.d. becomes 1 and there will be only finitely many numbers left. We can find out which by arranging the numbers as in Fig. 2. The circled numbers are excluded because they're multiples of 5 and these exclude the lower numbers by adding 4's. So only 1, 2, 3, 6, 7, 11 remain.

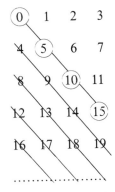

Figure 2. What's Left After {4, 5}.

I won't take 1, 2 or 3. If *I* say 6 or 7, you'll say the other, since these dismiss 11 and leave only 1, 2, 3 for me. So I'll say 11 and make *you* say 6 or 7 instead.

{4,5,11} is a $\mathscr{P}$-position.

Here's what happens after 4 and 6.

```
  ⓪   1   2   3

  4̸   5   ⑥   7

  8̸   9   1̸0̸  11

  1̸2̸  13  1̸4̸  15

  1̸6̸  17  1̸8̸  19
```

....

Since 5 and 7 exclude all large numbers, they kill each other. Similarly for 9 and 11, and for 13 and 15, and so on.

> After $\{4,6\}$ the pairs
> $(2,3), (5,7), (9,11), \ldots, (4k+1, 4k+3)$,
> for $k \geqslant 1$, are mates.

So if you open with 4, I shall respond with 6; if you open with 6, I shall respond with 4. A few similar strategies are known.

> After $\{8,12\}$ the pairs
> $(2,3), (5,7), (9,11), \ldots, (4k+1, 4k+3)$
> and
> $(4,6), (10,14), (18,22), \ldots, (8k+2, 8k+6)$,
> for $k \geqslant 1$, are mates.

There is a slightly more complicated strategy showing that another good reply to 6 is 9.

> After $\{6,9\}$ mate the pairs
> $(4,11), (5,8), (7,10)$ and $(3k+1, 3k+2)$ *for* $k \geqslant 4$,
> but *then*
> after 4,11 mate 5 with 7
> after 5,8 mate 4 with 7
> after 7,10 mate 4 with 5. 8 with 11.

We have proved that

> $\{2,3\}$ $\{4,6\}$ $\{6,9\}$ $\{8,12\}$
> are all $\mathscr{P}$-positions,

and so

> $\{1\}$ $\{2\}$ $\{3\}$ $\{4\}$ $\{6\}$ $\{8\}$ $\{9\}$ $\{12\}$
> are all $\mathscr{N}$-positions.

The numbers 1,2,3,4,6,8,9 and 12 are the only first moves for which explicit strategies have been found. You might expect that pairs $(2,3)$, $(4k+1, 4k+3)$, $(4,6)$, $(8k+2, 8k+6)$, $(8,12)$, $(16k+4, 16k+12)$ provide a strategy after $\{16,24\}$ but unfortunately 12 is *not* a legal move from the position $\{16,24,5,7,8\}$. On the other hand, for the strategies given above, both members of a pair are legal whenever one is. In fact 8 is a good reply to $\{16,24,5,7\}$ because it makes 16 and 24 irrelevant and we shall soon see that

> $\{5,7,8\}$ *is a* $\mathscr{P}$-*position*.

We don't know whether 24 is a good reply to 16, nor even whether 16 *has* any good reply.

ARE ALL OPENINGS BAD?

If on observing the fate of 1, 2 and 3 you thought maybe that all openings were bad, then probably our discussions of 4, 6, 8, 9 and 12 have tended to confirm your suspicions. In this section we'll try to analyze 5 and 7. The discussion of possible replies is made a lot easier by the **clique technique**.

You've already seen some cliques: The number 1 forms a rather special clique all by itself; 2 and 3 form another because they exclude all larger numbers. In our discussion of $\{4,5\}$, 6 and 7 formed a clique since they excluded 11. Cliques have the property that any reply to a clique member must also be a clique member and these two numbers must together exclude all numbers outside the clique.

We illustrate the clique technique by discussing $\{6, 7\}$ (Fig. 3).

$$\begin{array}{llllll}
⓪ & \underline{1} & 2 & 3 & 4 & 5 \\
⑦ & 8 & 9 & 10 & 11 \\
⑭ & 15 & 16 & 17 \\
㉑ & 22 & 23 \\
㉘ & 29 \\
㉟
\end{array}$$

$$\begin{array}{l}
(1) \\
(2,3) \\
(4,5) \\
(8,10)\ (9,11) \\
(15,23)\ (17,22)\ 16! \\
29?
\end{array}$$

Figure 3. The Cliques after (6, 7).

As usual, we can disregard 1, 2 and 3 which form the innermost cliques in *every* position. Now 4 and 5 *together* exclude all larger numbers and so form a third clique. *No matter what larger numbers have been named*, 4 will answer 5 and 5 will answer 4. We can therefore afford to neglect them in discussing larger numbers.

Now we assert that 8, 9, 10 and 11 form the next clique, because 8 and 10 together exclude all but 9 and 11, and these together exclude all but 8 and 10. Even when some larger numbers have already been named, 8 will answer 10, 9 will answer 11, and vice versa, and we can dismiss all four from the subsequent discussion.

We now know that any good reply to any of the remaining numbers

$$15 \quad 16 \quad 17$$

$$22 \quad 23$$

$$29$$

must be another of these. We see that 15 answers 23 and vice versa since these leave only 16 and 17. Similarly 17 and 22 are mates. But since 16 excludes *both* 22 and 23, leaving only 15 and 17, it's a good move by itself. These five numbers form a clique, since 29 is always excluded.

> 16 is the unique
> good reply to {6,7}.

Table 6 in the Extras exhibits complete strategies in a similar way for all the positions

$$\{4,5\}, \quad \{4,7\}, \quad \{4,9\},$$
$$\{5,6\}, \quad \{5,7\}, \quad \{5,8\}, \quad \{5,9\},$$
$$\{6,7\}, \quad \{7,8\}, \quad \{7,9\}.$$

In particular it shows that

> $\{4,5,11\}, \quad \{4,7,13\}, \quad \{4,9,19\},$
> $\{5,6,19\}, \quad \{5,7,8\}, \quad \{5,9,31\},$
> $\{6,7,16\}, \quad \{7,9,19\}, \quad \{7,9,24\},$
> are $\mathscr{P}$-positions.

We deduce that any good reply to 5 or 7 must be at least a two-digit number. The smallest two-digit number, 10, isn't a legal answer to 5; is it a good answer to 7? No!

> $\{7,10,12\}$ is a $\mathscr{P}$-position.

This is proved by Fig. 4. Since the clique technique isn't as helpful as it might have been, we've added extra notes for three of the pairs.

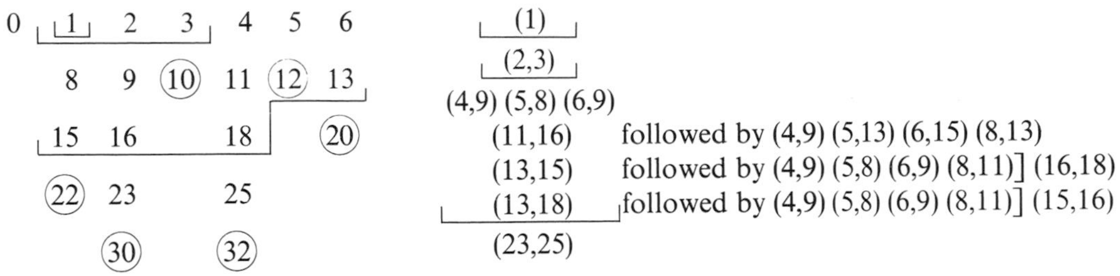

```
0   1   2   3   4   5   6              (1)
    8   9  (10) 11 (12) 13             (2,3)
                                (4,9) (5,8) (6,9)
   15  16      18      (20)          (11,16)    followed by (4,9) (5,13) (6,15) (8,13)
                                     (13,15)    followed by (4,9) (5,8) (6,9) (8,11)] (16,18)
  (22) 23      25                    (13,18)   followed by (4,9) (5,8) (6,9) (8,11)] (15,16)
      (30)    (32)                   (23,25)
```

Figure 4. The Position $\{7, 10, 12\}$.

NOT ALL OPENINGS ARE BAD

R.L. Hutchings has proved that there can't be any good replies to 5 or 7! His main theorem is

> If a and b are coprime ($g = 1$)
> and $\{a,b\} \neq \{2,3\}$, then $\{a,b\}$
> is an $\mathcal{N}$-position.

From this he deduces his **p-theorem**:

> If $p \geqslant 5$ is a prime number,
> $\{p\}$ is a $\mathscr{P}$-position,

p-positions are $\mathscr{P}$-positions.

(For any legal reply produces a position with a g.c.d. of 1.) And from the p-theorem he deduces in turn his **n-theorem**:

> If n is a composite number
> not of the form $2^a 3^b$, then
> $\{n\}$ is an $\mathcal{N}$-position,

n-positions are $\mathcal{N}$-positions.

(Since n has a prime divisor $p \geqslant 5$, which is a good reply.) Together these account for the first few missing numbers:

> $\{5\}, \{7\}, \{11\}, \{13\}, \{17\}, \ldots$ are $\mathscr{P}$-positions.
> $\{10\}, \{14\}, \{15\}, \{20\}, \{21\}, \ldots$ are $\mathcal{N}$-positions.

Our explicit strategies accounted for the eight smallest numbers $2^a 3^b$:

> $\{1\}, \{2\}, \{3\}, \{4\}, \{6\}, \{8\}, \{9\}, \{12\}$
> are $\mathcal{N}$-positions.

But

> Nobody knows about
> $\{16\}, \{18\}, \{24\}, \{27\}, \{32\}, \{36\}, \ldots!$

(We'd be glad to be proved wrong.)

STRATEGY STEALING

Hutchings proves his main theorem by a fine piece of strategy stealing. He considers the topmost number, t, that is not excluded by $\{a,b\}$ and proves that if t is *not* a good reply, then some other number *is*!

We shall call $\{a,b\}$ an **end-position** because, as we'll see in a moment, the topmost number is excluded by every other legal move.

Now let's ask:

Is t a good reply to $\{a,b\}$?

If the answer is "yes", then $\{a,b\}$ is an $\mathcal{N}$-position.

If the answer is "no", then either the game is over or there is a good reply s to $\{a, b, t\}$. But since a, b and s exclude t, s is itself a good reply to $\{a,b\}$. We can say that the player to move from $\{a,b\}$ finds his strategy by stealing the second player's strategy, if he has one, for $\{a,b,t\}$.

In some cases, e.g. $\{5,9\}$, t (here 31) is a good reply. But in others, e.g. $\{5,7\}$ (where $t = 23$) it *isn't*. The strategy stealing argument only tells us that good moves exist, not what they are. Theft is no substitute for honest toil!

In general,

> An end position with $t > 1$
> is an $\mathcal{N}$-position,

end-positions are $\mathcal{N}$-positions.

But the end-position $\{2,3\}$ is *not* an $\mathcal{N}$-position. This is because $t = 1$ and the only legal move ends the whole game.

Why is $\{a,b\}$ an end-position if its g.c.d. is 1? In Fig. 5 we illustrate with $\{9,11\}$ for which the authors know no good reply.

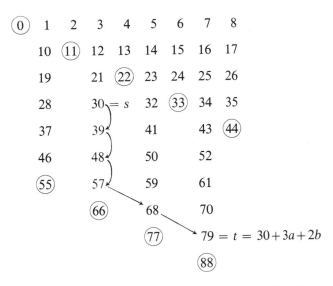

Figure 5. Hutchings's Theorem for $a = 9$, $b = 11$.

Writing the numbers in a columns, as is our wont, we see that in each column the *first excluded* (circled) number is a multiple of b, so the *last included* numbers must differ by multiples of b. Now from any legal move s we can get to the last legal number in its column by adding a's and from this we can get to t by adding b's showing that s excludes t (e.g. $s = 30$ in Fig. 5). The argument also provides a proof of Sylvester's well-known formula.

$$t = (a-1)b - a = ab - (a+b).$$

QUIET ENDS

Suppose Hi and Lo have named two coprime numbers a and b and Hi is considering making the move s. Then we know that the topmost number t will be obtainable using sufficiently many coins of values s, a and b. But our argument proved that only *one* copy of the new coin will be needed:

$$t = s + ma + nb.$$

More generally from a position $\{a,b,c,...\}$ we shall say that s **quietly** excludes t if t can be made up using any numbers of $a,b,c,...$ together with *just one* copy of s:

$$t = ma + nb + ... + s.$$

A **quiet end-position** is one in which the topmost legal move is *quietly* excluded by every number not already excluded.

> If a is coprime with each of
> b and b_1, then
> $$S = \{a, bc, bd, be, \ldots\}$$
> is a quiet end-position if
> and only if
> $$S_1 = \{a, b_1c, b_1d, b_1e, \ldots\}$$
> is.

THE QUIET END THEOREM

Thus

$$\{7, 1 \times 3, 1 \times 4\},$$

which is really the same position as $\{3,4\}$, is a quiet end-position, so that

$$\{7,9,12\} = \{7, 3 \times 3, 3 \times 4\}$$

and

$$\{7,15,20\} = \{7, 5 \times 3, 5 \times 4\}$$

are. In particular, these are end-positions and so are $\mathcal{N}$-positions by the strategy stealing argument. As usual we aren't told what the good replies are.

   We shall use $\{7,9,12\}$ and $\{7,15,20\}$ to illustrate our proof of the quiet end theorem. Once again we write out the numbers in a (here 7) columns and circle the first excluded number in every column (Fig. 6). We assert that these numbers for the positions S and S_1 are in the proportion $b:b_1$ (3 :5 in the example; see Fig. 7).

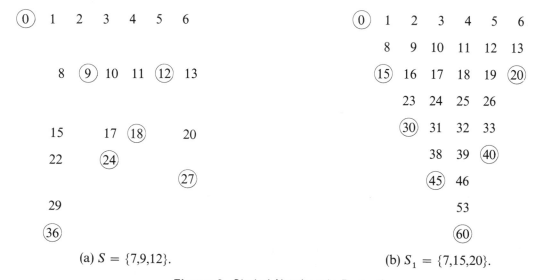

Figure 6. Circled Numbers in Proportion.

$$29 \quad 2 \quad 17 \quad 11 \quad 5 \quad 20 \qquad \text{in the proportion}$$

$$S: \quad ⓪ \ (36) \ (9) \ (24) \ (18) \ (12) \ (27) \qquad 3$$

to

$$53 \quad 8 \quad 33 \quad 23 \quad 13 \quad 38$$

$$S_1: \quad ⓪ \ (60) \ (15) \ (40) \ (30) \ (20) \ (45) \qquad 5$$

Figure 7. The Circled Numbers Sorted.

We first see that the circled numbers for S really are multiples of b. Recall that we **circle** n for S if n is excluded by S, but $n-a$ is not. Since n is excluded, it has the form

$$n = ak + bm$$

where m would be excluded by $\{c,d,e,\ldots\}$. But if k were positive,

$$n - a = a(k - 1) + bm$$

would also be excluded by S, so $k=0$ and we have simply

$$n = bm.$$

Now our assertion is that bm is circled for S only if $b_1 m$ is circled for S_1. Now $b_1 m$ is certainly *excluded* by S_1 and so is circled unless

$$b_1 m - a$$

is also excluded. But then we must have

$$b_1 m - a = ak + b_1 m'$$

for some m' excluded by $\{c,d,e,\ldots\}$, and

$$b_1 m = a(k + 1) + b_1 m',$$

showing that b_1 divides $k+1$ since it is coprime with a. We can now divide by b_1 and multiply by b to obtain

$$bm = ak' + bm'$$

for some positive number k', showing that

$$bm - a = a(k' - 1) + bm'$$

was excluded, and bm was *not* circled for S.

In its modest way, the quiet end theorem is quite powerful. It often gives the quietus to infinitely many replies with a single blow.

> No odd number is a good reply to $\{16,24\}$.

For 1 clearly isn't and if a is any other odd number then $\{a,2,3\}$ is really the same as the quiet end position $\{2,3\}$. By the quiet end theorem $\{a,16,24\}$ is a quiet end-position and so an $\mathscr{N}$-position.

In a similar way it proves that $\{4,6\}$ and $\{6,9\}$ are $\mathscr{P}$-positions without bothering to provide a detailed strategy. Let's use it to discuss the position $\{8,10\}$. After $\{4,5\}$ we found that the only remaining moves were

$$1, \quad 2, \quad 3, \quad 6, \quad 7, \quad 11,$$

so after $\{8,10\}$ the only remaining even numbers will be twice these,

$$2, \quad 4, \quad 6, \quad 12, \quad 14, \quad 22.$$

The quiet end theorem enables us to say that any good reply to $\{8,10\}$ must be in one of these two sets, for otherwise it is an odd number a excluded by $\{4,5\}$ so $\{a,4,5\}$ and therefore $\{a,8,10\}$ will be quiet end-positions. Now,

1	loses instantly,
(2,3)	are mated as usual,
(4,6)	eliminate 8,10 and will mate, as will
(7,11)	(see $\{6,7\}$ in Table 6 in the Extras) and
(12,14)	by our strategy for $\{8,12\}$.

So 22 is the only hope for a good reply to $\{8,10\}$. We shall see later that

> $\{8,10,22\}$ is a $\mathscr{P}$-position.

DOUBLING AND TRIPLING?

Note that the $\mathscr{P}$-position $\{8,10,22\}$ is the *double* of $\{4,5,11\}$. Our $\{8,12\}$ strategy shows that all $\mathscr{P}$-positions arising in the $\{4,6\}$ strategy have doubles that are also $\mathscr{P}$-positions. Maybe every $\mathscr{P}$-position doubles to another? No! For $\{5,6,19\}$ is $\mathscr{P}$, but $\{10,12,38\}$ is answered by 7 since $\{10,12,38,7\}$ is really the same as $\{7,10,12\}$.

Maybe the *triple* of every $\mathscr{P}$-position is another? No! This time $\{4,5,11\}$ is $\mathscr{P}$, but $\{12,15,33\}$ is answered by 5 since $\{5,12,33\}$ is a $\mathscr{P}$-position, as we'll soon see.

HALVING AND THIRDING?

Nevertheless there are many $\mathscr{P}$-positions whose doubles and triples are still $\mathscr{P}$. We conjecture:

¿If $\{2a,2b,2c,...\}$ is $\mathscr{P}$ so is $\{a,b,c,...\}$?	and	¿If $\{3a,3b,3c,...\}$ is $\mathscr{P}$ so is $\{a,b,c,...\}$?

FINDING THE RIGHT COMBINATIONS

How should you start a game of Sylver Coinage? Now that you know so much you will perhaps name 5 for your first move. You now have a strategy for every move I might make and probably feel a little safe. But those stolen strategies are firmly locked inside that little safe you're feeling and more than sensitive fingers are needed to find the right combinations.

You know the first few: 1 needs no reply and you should make the pairs (2,3), (4,11), (6,19), (7,8) and (9,31). Is there any general rule? In trying to answer this question for you we went to a lot of trouble and eventually found a fairly efficient way of breaking open the safe. But the winning combinations it reveals (Fig. 8) suggest that there is no simple answer.

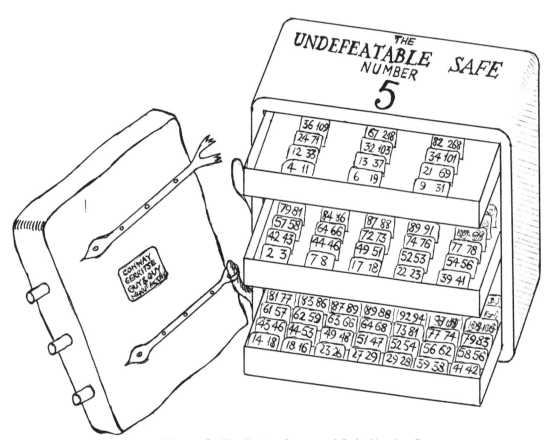

Figure 8. The Stolen Secrets of Safe Number 5.

Let's take a closer look at a position in which 5 and some other numbers have been named. If we were to write the numbers in five columns as usual we would circle 0 and just four other numbers a,b,c,d in the 1-,2-,3-,4-columns respectively, as in Fig. 9. We now make a three-dimensional table of $\mathscr{P}$-positions using just three of these numbers as headings and the fourth as an entry.

Table 1(a) shows the case in which a is the entry and b,c,d the row, column and layer headings. Tables 1(b,c,d) have b,c,d as entries.

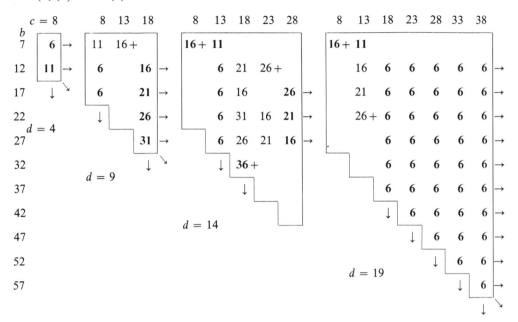

Table 1(a) Entries a for $\mathscr{P}$-positions $\{5,a,b,c,d\}$.

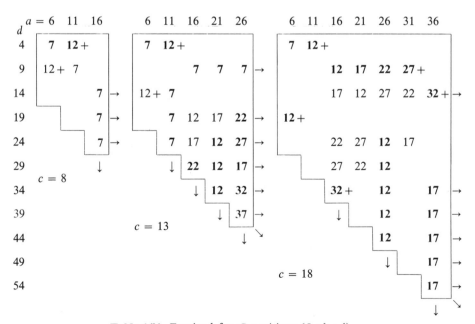

Table 1(b). Entries b for $\mathscr{P}$-positions $\{5,a,b,c,d\}$.

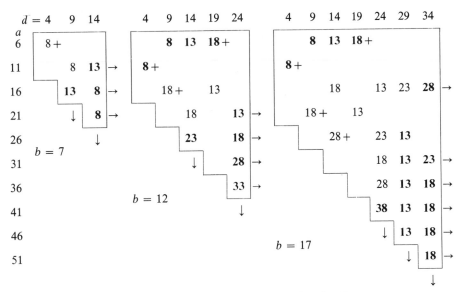

Table 1(c). Entries c for $\mathscr{P}$-positions $\{5,a,b,c,d\}$

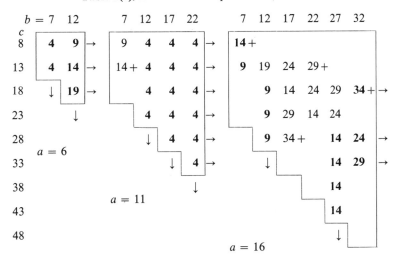

Table 1(d). Entries d for $\mathscr{P}$-positions $\{5,a,b,c,d\}$.

Some positions will appear repeatedly because a heading is redundant. These are indicated by bold figures. For example

$$\{5,6,12,13,14\}, \quad \{5,6,17,13,14\}, \quad \{5,6,22,13,14\}, \quad \dots$$

are really the same position because $12 = 6+6$ is redundant and so we have a column of **6**'s in layer 14 of Table 1(a). In $\{5,6,12,18,19\}$ both 12 and 18 are redundant, so the 19 layer of that table is almost entirely made up of **6**'s.

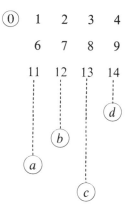

Figure 9. The General Position $\{5,x,y,\ldots\}$.

In $\{5,16,7,13,9\}$ it is the *entry* $16 = 7+9$ that is redundant, so 16 can be replaced by any of

$$21, 26, 31, 36, 41, \ldots$$

and we have written $16+$ to indicate this. Really an entry $n+$ is short for infinitely many entries

$$n, n+5, n+10, n+15, n+20, \ldots .$$

The entries in Table 1(a) were computed in lexicographic order, by making due allowance for these repetitions and otherwise entering the least number $5k+1$ not appearing earlier in the same row, column or file.

You'll probably find the method easier to follow in Table 2 which deals with positions $\{4,a,b,c\}$ in a similar way. This time each entry is the smallest number $b = 4k+2$ which has not appeared earlier in its row or column and an entry $b+$, shorthand for

$$b, b+4, b+8, b+12, b+16, \ldots$$

is made when $b=2a$ or $2c$. It can be deduced from the quiet end theorem that other kinds of repetition will not appear.

Table 3 gives pairs $x<y$ for which $\{4,x,y\}$ is already a $\mathscr{P}$-position, extracted from an extended version of Table 2, kindly calculated for us by Richard Gerritse. It seems that the ratio y/x approaches $2{\cdot}56\ldots$.

As soon as 4 or 5 arises in your game you should refer to the appropriate one of these tables. If 6 turns up first, see the corresponding Table 7 in the Extras.

a \ $c=$	7	11	15	19	23	27	31	35	39	43	47	51	55	59	63	67	71	75	79	83	87	91
5	6	10+																				
9	10	6	14	18+																		
13	14+		6	10																		
17			10	6	14	18	22	26	30	34+												
21			18	14	6	10	26	22	34	30	38	42+										
25				22	10	6	14	18	26		30	34	38	42	46	50+						
29				26	18	14	6	10	22		34	30	42	38	50	46	54	58+				
33				30+	22	26	10	6	14	18												
37					26	22	18	14	6	10	42	38	30	34	54		46	50	58	62	66	70
41					30	34	38	42	10	6	14	18	22	26	58		50	46	54	66	62	74
45					34	30	42	38	18	14	6	10	26	22	62		58	54	46	50	70	66
49					38	42	30	34	46	22	10	6	14	18	26		62		50	54	58	78
53					42	38	34	30	50	26	18	14	6	10	22		66		62	46	54	58
57			46+						38		22	26	10	6	14	18	30	34	42			
61				46	50	54	42				26	22	18	14	6	10	34	30	38	58	74	62
65				50	46	58	54				62		34	30	10	6	14	18	22	26	38	42
69				54+			46				50				18	14	6	10	26	22	30	34
73					54	50	58		46				62	66	30	22	10	6	14	18	26	38
77					58	62	66		54				46	50	34	26	18	14	6	10	22	30
81					62+				58				50	46	38	30	22	26	10	6	14	18
85						66	62		70				54	58	42	34	26	22	18	14	6	10
89						70+			66				58	54		38	42		30	34	10	6
93							70		74				66	62	78	42	38		34	30	18	14
97							74		78				70	82	66		86	38	90	42	34	22
101							78+						74	70				42	66	38	46	26
105								82				78	74	70			90		86	94	42	46
109								86				82	78	74			70		94	90	50	54
113								90				86	94	82			74		70	78	98	50
117								94+				90	86				78			74	70	82

Table 2. Values of b for which $\{4,a,b,c\}$ is a $\mathscr{P}$-position.

x	y	x	y	x	y	x	y	x	y	x	y	x	y
5	11	107	269	205	531	303	777	405	1043	501	1291	603	1549
7	13	109	279	207	529	305	783	407	1045	503	1289	605	1555
9	19	111	277	211	541	311	797	409	1051	505	1299	607	1557
15	33	113	287	213	547	313	807	411	1053	511	1309	609	1567
17	43	119	301	219	557	315	805	413	1063	513	1319	615	1577
21	51	121	307	221	567	317	819	415	1065	519	1329	617	1583
23	57	123	309	223	569	321	823	419	1077	521	1339	621	1595
25	67	125	319	227	585	323	829	421	1079	523	1341	623	1593
27	69	129	331	229	583	325	839	425	1095	525	1347	625	1603
29	75	131	333	231	593	327	841	427	1097	527	1349	627	1609
31	81	133	343	233	595	329	851	429	1103	533	1371	633	1627
35	89	135	345	237	611	335	857	431	1105	535	1373	635	1625
37	95	141	363	239	613	337	871	433	1115	537	1379	637	1635
39	101	143	365	241	619	339	869	439	1125	539	1381	639	1637
41	103	147	373	245	631	341	879	441	1135	543	1393	643	1649
45	115	149	379	247	629	347	885	447	1145	545	1395	645	1655
47	117	151	385	251	641	349	899	449	1151	549	1411	651	1665
49	127	153	391	253	647	351	901	451	1157	551	1413	653	1679
53	139	155	397	255	649	353	911	455	1165	553	1423	655	1681
55	137	157	399	257	659	355	909	457	1171	555	1425	657	1687
59	145	163	417	259	665	357	919	459	1177	559	1433	661	1699
61	159	165	423	261	671	359	917	461	1183	561	1443	663	1697
63	161	169	435	265	683	361	927	463	1189	563	1445	667	1709
65	167	171	437	267	685	367	941	465	1195	565	1451	669	1719
71	177	173	443	271	697	369	951	469	1207	571	1465	673	1731
73	183	175	445	273	699	371	953	471	1209	573	1471	675	1729
77	195	179	453	275	705	375	961	473	1215	575	1477	677	1739
79	193	181	467	281	723	377	971	479	1225	577	1483	679	1741
83	209	185	475	283	725	381	983	481	1235	579	1485	681	1751
85	215	187	477	285	731	383	981	485	1247	581	1495	687	1757
87	217	189	483	289	743	387	993	487	1245	587	1505	689	1771
91	225	191	489	291	745	389	1003	491	1257	589	1511	691	1769
93	235	197	507	293	755	393	1011	493	1267	591	1517	693	1783
97	243	199	509	295	757	395	1013	495	1269	597	1531	695	1781
99	249	201	515	297	767	401	1031	497	1279	599	1537	701	1803
105	263	203	517	299	765	403	1029	499	1277	601	1543	703	1801
												707	1813

Table 3. Pairs x,y for which $\{4,x,y\}$ is a $\mathscr{P}$-position.

WHAT SHALL I DO WHEN g IS TWO?

Example: $\{8,10,22\}$

Apparently we have to examine infinitely many possible replies. Fortunately there is a way of doing this in a finite time. A similar method will work for *any* position with $g = 2$.

Let's see how the position will look after some play from $\{8,10,22\}$. If 1, 2 or 3 has been played, we know what to do. Otherwise the only even numbers that can have been played are

$$4, 6, 12, 14$$

and the even part of the position must look like one of

$$\{4,6\} \ \{4,10\} \ \{6,8,10\}$$
$$\{8,10,12,14\} \ \{8,10,12\} \ \{8,10,14\} \ \{8,10,22\}$$

What odd numbers have been played? If the least of them is n, then since $\{8,10,22\}$ excludes all of

$$16, 18, 20, 22, 24, \ldots$$

we can suppose that the only relevant odd numbers are among

$$n, n+2, n+4, n+6, n+12, n+14.$$

And if any even moves have been made they will restrict the possibilities still further. For instance if 6 has been played we can suppose that the odd numbers are one of the sets

$$n, n+2, n+4 \qquad n, n+2 \qquad n, n+4 \qquad n$$

Table 4 shows the status of the positions classified in this way. Since the last four columns repeat indefinitely, this finite table contains the information for every odd n. How was it computed and why is it periodic?

Let's take a typical entry:

$$\{8,10,14,n,n+6,n+12\}.$$

From this position there are three kinds of option:

(a) the *even* numbers 4, 6 or 12,
(b) the *small odd* numbers $m \leqslant n-14$,
(c) the *large odd* numbers $n-12, n-10, n-8, n-6, n-4, n-2, n+2, n+4$.

Case (a) leads to a position (in an earlier segment of the table) with even part

$$\{4,10\}, \{6,8,10\} \text{ or } \{8,10,12,14\}$$

and we can suppose that these have already been analyzed and found to be ultimately periodic in n.

A case (b) move leads to

$$\{8,10,14,m\}$$

since m excludes n and all larger odd numbers. If there is any odd m for which this is a $\mathscr{P}$-position, then $\{8, 10, 14, n, n+6, n+12\}$ will be an $\mathscr{N}$-position for all $n \geqslant m+14$. If not, we can reject moves in case (b).

Finally, case (c) moves either leave n unchanged or decrease it by at most 12. We conclude that the outcome of every position in the table is computed in a fixed way from

ultimately periodic information (case (a)),
ultimately constant information (case (b)), and
information in the last few columns (case (c));

it must therefore be ultimately periodic in n.

Position		5	7	9	11	13	15	17	19	21	23	25	27	29	31	33	35	37	39	41	43	45	47	49	51
{4,6} (P)	$n, n+2$	P	–	P	–	P	–	P	–	P	–	P	–	P	–	P	–	P	–	P	–	P	–	P	–
	n	–	–	–	–	–	–	–	–	–	–	–	–	–	–	–	–	–	–	–	–	–	–	–	–
{4,10} (N)	$n, n+2$	–	P	–	–	–	P	–	–	–	P	–	–	–	P	–	–	–	P	–	–	–	P	–	–
	$n, n+6$	P	–	–	–	P	–	–	–	P	–	–	–	P	–	–	–	P	–	–	–	P	–	–	–
	n	–	–	–	–	–	–	–	–	–	–	–	–	–	–	–	–	–	–	–	–	–	–	–	–
{6,8,10} (N)	$n, n+2, n+4$	–	P	–	P	–	–	–	–	–	–	–	–	–	–	–	–	–	–	–	–	–	–	–	–
	$n, n+2$	–	–	–	–	–	–	–	–	–	–	–	–	–	–	–	–	–	–	–	–	–	–	–	–
	$n, n+4$	P	–	–	–	–	–	–	–	–	–	–	–	–	–	–	–	–	–	–	–	–	–	–	–
	n	–	P	–	P	–	–	–	–	–	–	–	–	–	–	–	–	–	–	–	–	–	–	–	–
{8,10,12,14} (P)	$n, n+2, n+4, n+6$	P	–	P	–	P	–	P	–	P	–	P	–	P	–	P	–	P	–	P	–	P	–	P	–
	$n, n+2, n+4$	–	–	–	–	–	–	–	–	–	–	–	–	–	–	–	–	–	–	–	–	–	–	–	–
	$n, n+2, n+6$	–	–	–	–	–	–	P	–	–	–	–	P	–	–	–	P	–	–	–	P	–	–	–	P
	$n, n+2$	P	–	P	–	P	–	P	–	P	–	P	–	P	–	P	–	P	–	P	–	P	–	P	–
	$n, n+4, n+6$	–	P	–	P	–	–	–	P	–	–	–	P	–	–	–	P	–	–	–	P	–	–	–	P
	$n, n+4$	–	–	P	–	–	–	–	P	–	–	–	P	–	–	–	P	–	–	–	P	–	–	–	P
	$n, n+6$	–	–	P	–	–	–	–	P	–	–	–	P	–	–	–	P	–	–	–	P	–	–	P	–
	n	–	–	–	–	–	–	–	–	–	–	–	–	–	–	–	–	–	–	–	–	–	–	–	–
{8,10,12} (N)	$n, n+2, n+4, n+6$	P	–	–	–	–	–	–	–	–	–	–	–	–	–	–	–	P	–	–	–	P	–	–	P
	$n, n+2, n+4$	–	–	P	–	–	–	P	–	–	–	–	–	–	–	–	–	–	–	–	–	–	–	–	–
	$n, n+2, n+6$	–	–	P	–	–	–	–	–	–	–	–	–	–	–	–	–	–	P	–	–	–	P	–	–
	$n, n+2$	P	–	–	–	–	–	–	–	–	–	–	–	–	–	–	–	P	–	–	–	P	–	–	P
	$n, n+4, n+6$	–	P	P	–	–	P	–	–	–	–	–	–	–	–	–	–	–	–	–	–	–	–	–	–
	$n, n+4$	–	–	–	–	P	–	–	–	P	–	–	P	–	–	–	P	P	–	–	P	P	–	–	P
	$n, n+6$	–	–	–	–	–	–	P	–	–	–	–	P	–	–	–	P	–	–	–	P	–	–	–	P
	$n, n+14$	–	–	P	–	–	P	–	–	–	–	–	–	–	–	–	–	–	–	–	–	–	–	–	–
	n	–	–	–	–	–	–	–	–	–	–	–	–	–	–	–	–	–	–	–	–	–	–	–	–
{8,10,14} (N)	$n, n+2, n+4, n+6$	P	–	–	–	–	–	–	–	–	–	–	–	–	–	–	–	P	–	–	–	–	–	–	–
	$n, n+2, n+4$	–	–	P	–	–	–	–	–	–	–	–	–	P	–	P	–	–	–	–	–	–	–	–	–
	$n, n+2, n+6$	–	–	P	–	–	–	–	–	–	–	–	–	P	–	P	–	–	–	–	–	–	–	–	–
	$n, n+2$	–	–	–	–	–	–	–	–	–	–	–	–	–	–	–	–	–	–	–	–	–	–	–	–
	$n, n+4, n+6$	–	–	P	–	–	P	–	–	–	–	–	–	P	–	–	–	–	P	–	–	–	–	–	–
	$n, n+4$	–	P	–	–	–	–	–	P	–	–	–	–	–	–	–	–	–	–	–	–	P	–	–	–
	$n, n+6, n+12$	–	–	–	–	–	–	–	P	–	–	–	–	–	P	–	P	–	–	–	–	–	–	–	–
	$n, n+6$	–	–	–	–	–	–	–	–	–	–	–	–	–	–	–	–	–	–	–	–	–	–	–	–
	$n, n+12$	P	–	P	–	P	P	–	–	–	–	–	–	–	P	–	P	–	P	–	–	–	–	–	–
	n	–	–	–	–	–	–	–	–	–	–	–	–	–	P	–	P	–	–	–	–	–	–	–	–
{8,10,22} (P)	$n, n+2, n+4, n+6$	P	–	P	–	P	–	P	–	P	–	P	–	P	–	P	–	P	–	P	–	P	–	P	–
	$n, n+2, n+4$	–	–	–	–	–	–	–	–	–	–	–	–	–	–	–	–	–	–	–	–	–	–	–	–
	$n, n+2, n+6$	–	–	–	P	–	–	–	–	–	–	–	P	–	–	–	P	–	–	–	P	–	–	–	P
	$n, n+2, n+14$	–	–	P	–	P	–	P	–	P	–	P	–	P	–	P	–	P	–	P	–	P	–	P	–
	$n, n+2$	P	–	–	–	–	–	–	–	–	–	–	–	–	–	–	–	–	–	–	–	–	–	–	–
	$n, n+4, n+6$	–	–	–	–	–	–	–	–	–	–	–	–	–	–	–	–	–	–	–	–	–	–	–	–
	$n, n+4$	–	P	P	–	–	P	P	–	–	P	P	–	–	P	P	–	–	P	P	–	–	P	P	–
	$n, n+6, n+12$	–	–	P	–	–	–	P	–	–	–	P	–	–	–	P	–	–	–	P	–	–	–	P	–
	$n, n+6$	–	–	–	–	–	–	–	–	–	–	–	–	–	–	–	–	–	–	–	–	–	–	–	–
	$n, n+12, n+14$	–	–	–	–	–	–	–	–	–	–	–	–	–	–	–	–	–	–	–	–	–	–	–	–
	$n, n+12$	–	–	–	–	–	–	–	–	–	–	–	–	–	–	–	–	–	–	–	–	–	–	–	–
	$n, n+14$	P	–	–	–	–	–	–	–	–	–	–	–	–	–	–	–	–	–	–	–	–	–	–	–
	n	–	–	–	–	–	–	–	–	–	–	–	–	–	–	–	–	–	–	–	–	–	–	–	–

Table 4. The Position {8,10,22}.

Every position with $g = 2$ can be handled in this way. When we have computed enough to verify the period, we can decide in particular whether there is any good reply. For {8,10,22} there isn't one, so it is a $\mathscr{P}$-position.

THE GREAT UNKNOWN

We can best describe our knowledge in terms of the number g. When

$$\boxed{g = 1}$$

the position is bounded so you can find what to do by working through all positions. Of course this might take a long time even if one of our theorems already tells you the outcome. We know that there must a be good reply to {31,37} but don't know any method which guarantees to find one in the next millenium. When

$$\boxed{g = 2}$$

the method we have just described will compute the outcome in a finite but probably even longer time. If

$$\boxed{g \text{ is divisible by a prime } p \geqslant 5}$$

then p is a good reply when it hasn't already been named, when of course there isn't any.

The authors have only been able to examine a few particular positions with other values of g. Table 8 in the Extras contains a complete discussion of {6,9}. Although this is a two-dimensional table, a periodicity develops which enables us to analyze the position to infinity. Maybe a similar thing happens for some other positions with $g = 3$. We computed a much larger three-dimensional table for {8, 12} ($g = 4$), but could detect no structure outside the range covered by our explicit strategy.

16 is the first opening move whose status is in doubt. We don't know whether {16} has a good reply nor even any way of finding out in any finite time. You might consider working upwards testing each possible reply in turn and hoping to detect some structure, but even this is impossible. We don't know any way to test the reply 24, say, in any finite time. We don't even know how to test 100, say, as a possible reply to {16,24}!

The quiet end theorem often eliminates infinitely many replies, for example all odd replies to {16} or to {16,24}, but it never eliminates any reply that would be infinitely hard to analyze.

	{7,9,11}	{7,9}	{7,11}	{7}	{9,11}	{9}	{11}	{}
{6,8,10}	[]	[11]	[11]	[]	[4,5,7]	[5]	[]	[4,7,11]
{6,8}	[10]	[]	[]	[9,10,11]	[4,5]	[5,7]	[7,10]	[4]
{6,10}	[8]	[]	[15]	[8,9]	[4]	[7]	[8,13]	[4]
{6}	[]	[8,10,11]	[8,9]	[16]	[4,7]	[]	[26]	[4,9]
{8,10,12}	[4,5,6]	[4]	[13]	[5,6]	[13,14,15]	[23]	[6]	[14]
{8,12}	[5]	[6]	[6]	[5]	[]	[11,15]	[9,13]	[]
{10,12}	[4]	[4,6]	[16]	[]	[]	[11,13,14]	[9	[7
{12}	[6]	[15]	[27]	[10	[8,10]	[6]	[	[8
{8,10}	[4,5,6]	[4]	[]	[5,6,11]	[23]	[13,15]	[6,7]	[22]
{8}	[5]	[6]	[6,10]	[5]	[12]	[21	[	[12
{10}	[4]	[4,6]	[8]	[12]	[12]	[	[	[5
{}	[6]	[19,24]	[24,34]	[]	[	[6]	[]	[5,7,11,13,...]

Table 5. Status of Subsets of {6,7,8,9,10,11,12} and Known Good Replies.

Even members of set at Left; Odd members at head. Bracket is closed when *all* good replies are known, so that [] indicates a $\mathscr{P}$-position, but [always indicates an $\mathscr{N}$-position for which no good reply is known. The last entry contains all primes greater than 3; and *may* contain some entries $2^a 3^b$.

Table 5 tells you the outcome and all the good replies we know to every position made from the numbers

$$6, 7, 8, 9, 10, 11, 12$$

(if 4 or 5 is involved, Tables 2, 3, 1 and Fig. 8 go much further). If you can add any more to this table or decide whether any number $2^a 3^b$ is a good opening move we would like to hear from you.

ARE OUTCOMES COMPUTABLE?

We can prove that there *must be* a way of programming a computer to find the outcome of $\{n\}$ even though we don't know what that way *is*! The reason is:

> There can only be finitely
> many good opening moves
> $2^a 3^b$.

For no one of these can divide any other, so that no two can have the same value of a or the same value of b. So if $2^{a_0} 3^{b_0}$ is such a number with a_0 as small as possible, and $2^a 3^b$ is any other, then we must have $b < b_0$ and so there are at most $b_0 + 1$ such numbers, say $n_1, n_2, ..., n_k$. We suspect there are none!

If you only knew what these numbers were, then you could program your machine with PORN (Fig. 10) and work out the outcome of any $\{n\}$. This argument shows that in the purely technical sense this is a computable function of n, even though we don't know what function it is.

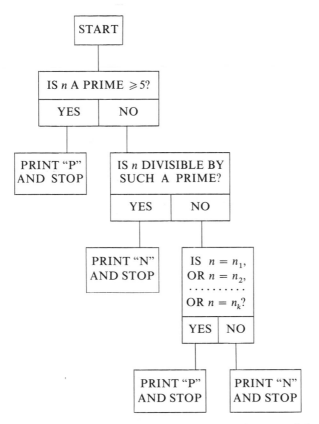

Figure 10. PORN, A Program Which Decides if $\{n\}$ is $\mathscr{P}$ or $\mathscr{N}$.

THE ETIQUETTE OF SYLVER COINAGE

Few Western readers can understand the subtleties of etiquette in the oriental country from which our game comes. But at least we can save you from the more obvious gaffes by pointing out that in Sylver Coinage it is customary for a player who knows he is winning to resign by naming 1, 2 or 3. This quaint custom is said to originate in the tradition that Hi, who could see much further than Lo, nobly took upon himself the fate that was about to befall his beloved brother.

When it's plain to all the world that you have a win, any move but 1 will insult your opponent, but in other cases we advise you to name 3 (2 is possible, but may be misunderstood). If your opponent concurs in your analysis, he will respond with 2, but you have allowed him to express another opinion by naming 1. (Replies to 3 other than 1 or 2 may also be available but their nuances are harder to interpret.)

Of course, one of the greatest insults you can offer is to name 1, 2 or 3 at the very start of the game, for this is the philosopher Hu Tchings' prerogative, at least until someone finds a new way to win.

EXTRAS

CHOMP

Here is a game with similar rules to Sylver Coinage. For some fixed number N, the players alternately name divisors of N which may not be multiples of previously named numbers. Whoever names 1 loses. If $N = 432 = 2^4 3^3$, for example, a move is essentially to eat a square (e.g. 36) from the chocolate bar in Fig. 11, together with all squares below and/or to the right of it. Square number 1 is poisoned!

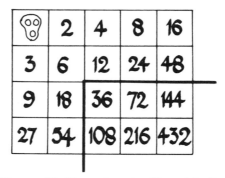

Figure 11. Chomping at a Chocolate Bar.

The first few $\mathscr{P}$-positions are shown in Fig. 12. Strategy stealing shows that rectangles larger than 1×1 are $\mathscr{N}$-positions; the replies are unique if either side is at most 3, but Ken Thompson found that 4×5 and 5×2 bites both answer 8×10.

The arithmetic form of the game is due to Fred. Schuh, the geometric one to David Gale.

ZIG-ZAG

Two players alternately name distinct numbers (which are allowed to be fractional or negative) and the game ends as soon as the resulting sequence contains either an increasing subsequence (**zig**) of length a or a decreasing one (**zag**) of length b. The normal play $a+1$, $b+1$ game is really the same as the misère a, b game, and so we consider only the latter.

Zig-Zag, which was suggested to us by S. Fajtlowicz, sounds difficult to analyze, but fortunately there is a rather clever transformation into a geometrical game like Chomp. We regard square (r, s) in Fig. 13 as eaten if the number sequence so far contains a rising zig of length r and a sagging zag of length s that end with the same number. Then the moves are as in Chomp except that the first move may eat square $(1,1)$ only, and the innermost square eaten on any subsequent move must be adjacent to a previously eaten square. The squares $(a,1)$ and $(1,b)$ are poisoned, so play really goes on inside the outlined $a-1$ by $b-1$ **chocolate bar** of Fig. 13.

598

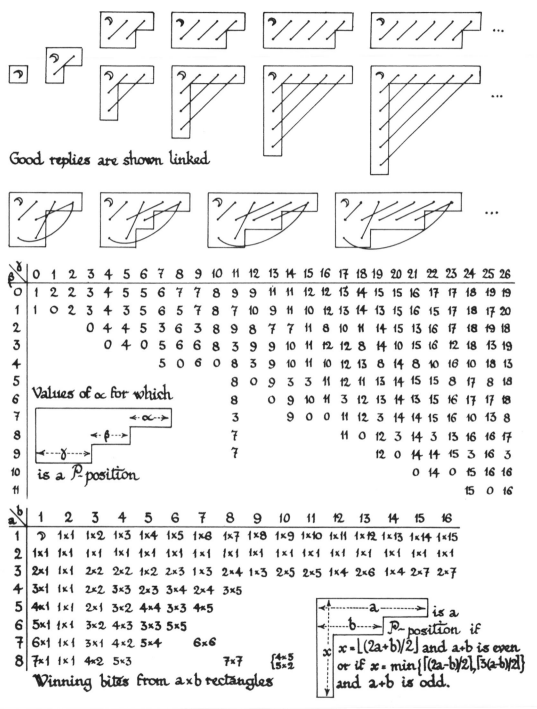

Good replies are shown linked

Values of α for which [staircase diagram with labels α, β, γ] is a $\mathcal{P}$-position

Winning bites from $a \times b$ rectangles

[diagram] is a $\mathcal{P}$-position if $x = \lfloor (2a+b)/2 \rfloor$ and $a+b$ is even or if $x = \min\{\lceil (2a-b)/2 \rceil, \lceil 3(a-b)/2 \rceil\}$ and $a+b$ is odd.

Figure 12. $\mathcal{P}$-positions in Chomp.

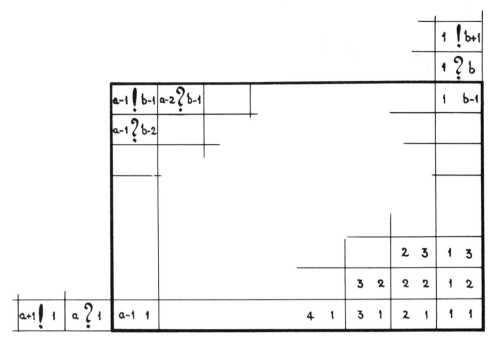

Figure 13. The Chocolate Bar Form of Zig-Zag.

If $a \geqslant 3$, $b \geqslant 3$ and $a+b \leqslant 17$, the first player wins the misère a-Zig, b-Zag game, because David Seal's calculations show that the corresponding $a-1$ by $b-1$ chocolate bars are $\mathcal{N}$-positions.

By assigning Heads to Horizontal edges and Tails to verTical ones we get an equivalent game with coin sequences, involving moves of a head rightwards over tails or a tail leftwards over heads, and Seal used this idea to compute Fig. 14 showing all $\mathcal{P}$- positions for which the uneaten part of the chocolate bar fits inside a 5×5 square.

To find $\mathcal{P}$-positions in both Chomp and Zig-Zag, we used the tabular technique of Chapter 15, and the Clique Technique of this one.

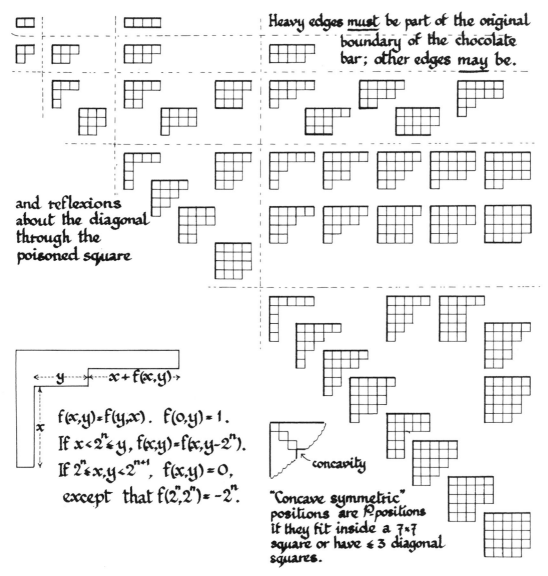

Heavy edges <u>must</u> be part of the original boundary of the chocolate bar; other edges may be.

and reflexions about the diagonal through the poisoned square

$$f(x,y) = f(y,x). \quad f(0,y) = 1.$$
$$\text{If } x < 2^n \leqslant y, \; f(x,y) = f(x, y-2^n).$$
$$\text{If } 2^n \leqslant x, y < 2^{n+1}, \; f(x,y) = 0,$$
$$\text{except that } f(2^n, 2^n) = -2^n.$$

concavity

"Concave symmetric" positions are $\mathscr{P}$-positions if they fit inside a 7×7 square or have ≤ 3 diagonal squares.

Figure 14. $\mathscr{P}$-positions for Zig-Zag.

MORE CLIQUES FOR SYLVER COINAGE

To follow the cliques in Table 6, we advise you to set out the remaining numbers as we did in Figs. 2, 3, 4 for the cases {4,5}, {6,7} and {7,10,12}. Numbers not mentioned are excluded by a good reply.

position	replies	strategy, with cliques indicated by]
{4,5}	11!	1?](2,3)](6,7)]11!
{4,7}	13!	1?](2,3)](5,6)](9,10)]13!
{4,9}	19!	1?](2,3)](5,11)(6,11)(7,10)](14,15)]19!
{5,6}	19!	1?](2,3)](4,7)](8,9)](13,14)]19!
{5,7}	8!	1?](2,3)](4,6)(9,13)(11,13)8!
{5,8}	7!	1?](2,3)](4,11)(6,9)7!
{5,9}	31!	1?](2,3)](4,11)(6,8)(7,13)](12,16)](17,21)](22,26)]31!
{6,7}	16!	1?](2,3)](4,5)](8,9)(8,10)(8,11)(9,10)(9,11)](15,23)(17,22)16!
{7,8}	5!	1?](2,3)](4,13)(6,9)(6,10)(6,11)5!
{7,9}	19!24!	1?](2,3)](4,10)(5,13)(6,8)(6,10)(6,11)](12,15)(17,20)(22,26)(29,33)19!24!

after {7,9,22,26} (12,17)(19,24)(15,20)
      {7,9,29,33} (12,15)(17,20)(19,31)(22,26)(24,26) ...
      {7,9,19}   (12,15)(15,17)(15,20)](22,24)(29,31)
      {7,9,24}   (12,15)(17,20)(19,22)](26,29)

Table 6. Some Complete Strategies for Sylver Coinage.

5-PAIRS

The safe combinations {5,x,y} are of three types. In the top drawer in Fig. 8 are those with y so much larger than x that the coordinates {a,b,c,d} are {x,2x,3x,y}. For these it seems that y/x tends to 3. But are there infinitely many numbers in the top drawer?

The middle drawer contains the remaining ones for which x+y is a multiple of 5. It seems that for these, x and y always differ by 1 or 2.

In the bottom drawer we have arranged the pairs with coordinates {x, y, x+y, 2y} where x and y are in the order given. It seems that here, as in the second drawer, y/x tends to 1.

POSITIONS CONTAINING 6

As in our other analyses, we write the numbers in six columns and circle 0 and five other numbers a,b,c,d,e, one in each of the 1-, 2-, 3-, 4- and 5-columns respectively. We tabulate $\mathscr{P}$-positions by entries c in a 4-dimensional table (Table 7) whose coordinates, a,b,d,e are congruent to 1,2,4,5, modulo 6.

Entries outside the areas enclosed by full lines are found by repeating entries according to the arrows, where appropriate. The tables for $b=8$, $d=4$ and $b=8$, $d=16$ can be extended indefinitely by repeating the portions between the pecked lines and increasing all entries by 12 or 60 respectively. The two tables with $d=10$, $b=8$ or 14 contain no further entries. All further entries in that for $b=14$, $d=16$ are **15**.

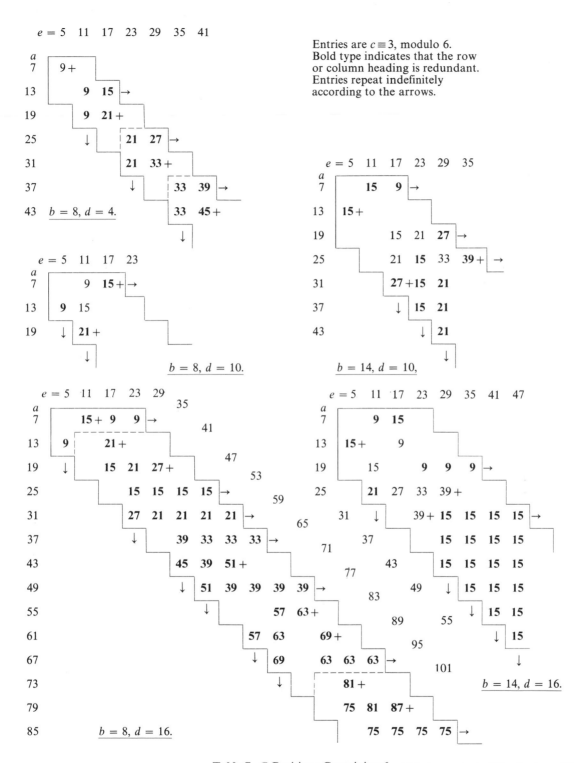

Entries are $c \equiv 3$, modulo 6.
Bold type indicates that the row
or column heading is redundant.
Entries repeat indefinitely
according to the arrows.

Table 7. $\mathscr{P}$-Positions Containing 6,

	5,8 5	8,11 8	11,4 11	14,17 14	17,20 17	20,23 20	23,26 23	26,29 26	29,32 29	32,35 32	35,38 35	38,41 38	41,44 41	44,47 44	47,50 47	50,53 50	53,56 53	56,59 56	59,62 59	62,65 62	65,68 65	68,71 68	71,74 71
4,7	+ +	− −	− −	− −	− −	− −	− −	− −	− −	− −	− −	− −	− −	− −	− −	− −	− −	− −	− −	− −	− −	− −	− −
4	− −	+ −	+ +	− −	− −	− −	− −	− −	− −	− −	− −	− −	− −	− −	− −	− −	− −	− −	− −	− −	− −	− −	− −
7,10	− −	+ −	− −	+ +	+ +	+ +	+ +	+ +	+ +	+ +	+ +	+ +	+ +	+ +	+ +	+ +	+ +	+ +	+ +	+ +	+ +	+ +	+ +
7	− −	− +	+ +	− −	− −	− −	− −	− −	− −	− −	− −	− −	− −	− −	− −	− −	− −	− −	− −	− −	− −	− −	− −
10,13	+ −	− −	− −	− −	− −	− −	− −	− −	− −	− −	− −	− −	− −	− −	− −	− −	− −	− −	− −	− −	− −	− −	− −
10	+ −	− −	− −	− −	− −	− −	− −	− −	− −	− −	− −	− −	− −	− −	− −	− −	− −	− −	− −	− −	− −	− −	− −
13,16	+ −	− −	− −	+ −	− −	+ −	− −	+ +	+ +	+ +	+ +	+ +	+ +	+ +	+ +	+ +	+ +	+ +	+ +	+ +	+ +	+ +	+ +
13	+ −	− −	− −	− +	+ −	− −	− −	− −	− −	− −	− −	− −	− −	− −	− −	− −	− −	− −	− −	− −	− −	− −	− −
16,19	+ −	− −	− −	− +	+ −	− −	− −	− −	− −	− −	− −	− −	− −	− −	− −	− −	− −	− −	− −	− −	− −	− −	− −
16	+ −	− −	− −	− −	− +	− +	− −	− −	− −	− −	− −	− −	− −	− −	− −	− −	− −	− −	− −	− −	− −	− −	− −
19,22	+ −	− −	− −	+ −	− −	+ −	− −	+ −	− −	+ −	− −	+ +	+ +	+ +	+ +	+ +	+ +	+ +	+ +	+ +	+ +	+ +	+ +
19	+ −	− −	− −	− −	− +	− +	− −	− −	− −	− −	− −	− −	− −	− −	− −	− −	− −	− −	− −	− −	− −	− −	− −
22,25	+ −	− −	− −	− −	− −	− −	+ −	− −	+ −	− −	+ −	− −	= −	− −	− −	− −	− −	− −	− −	− −	− −	− −	− −
22	+ −	− −	− −	− −	− −	− −	− +	− +	− −	− −	− −	− −	− −	− −	− −	− −	− −	− −	− −	− −	− −	− −	− −
25,28	+ −	− −	− −	+ −	− −	+ −	− −	+ −	− −	+ −	− −	+ −	− −	+ −	− −	+ +	+ +	+ +	+ +	+ +	+ +	+ +	+ +
25	+ −	− −	− −	+ −	− −	− −	− +	− +	− −	− −	− −	− −	− −	− −	− −	− −	− −	− −	− −	− −	− −	− −	− +
28,31	+ −	− −	− −	− −	− −	− −	+ −	− −	+ −	− −	+ −	− −	+ −	− −	+ −	− −	= −	− −	− −	− −	− −	− −	− −
28	+ −	− −	− −	− −	− −	− −	− −	− −	− +	− +	− −	− −	− −	− −	− −	− −	− −	− −	− −	− −	− −	− −	− −
31,34	+ −	− −	− −	− −	− −	+ −	− −	+ −	− −	+ −	− −	+ −	− −	+ −	− −	+ −	− −	+ −	− −	+ +	+ +	+ +	+ +
31	+ −	− −	− −	− −	− −	− −	− −	− −	− +	− +	− −	− −	− −	− −	− −	− −	− −	− −	− −	− −	− −	− −	− −

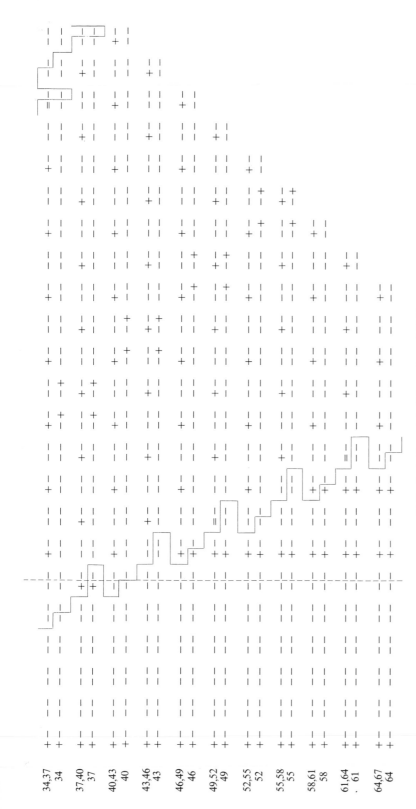

Table 8. A Complete Discussion of $\{6,9\}$.

The table represents a complete discussion of positions containing $\{6,9\}$. Reduced positions contain one, or possibly two neighboring, numbers of form $3k+1$, and of form $3k+2$; pairs of rows and columns refer to the latter and former possibilities. Positions represented by cells outside the crenellated line are not reduced. The pattern within the rectangular quadrant continues indefinitely. The minus signs denote $\mathcal{N}$-positions, the plus signs $\mathcal{P}$-positions and the "$=$" signs $\mathcal{N}$-positions which, at a casual glance at the pattern, might be mistaken for $\mathcal{P}$-positions.

SYLVER COINAGE HAS INFINITE NIM-VALUES

If we make naming 1 an *illegal* rather than a *stupid* move, Sylver Coinage becomes a normal play rather than a *misère* play game and we could consider adding it to other games using the Sprague–Grundy theory. However since some positions have infinitely many options, we can expect infinite nim-values and indeed they happen!

For example, $\mathcal{G}(2,2n+3)=n$ $(n\geqslant 0)$, so $\mathcal{G}(2)=\omega$. On the other hand, $\mathcal{G}(3,3n+1,3n+2)=1$ $(n\geqslant 1)$, so $\mathcal{G}(3)=1$. Here are some other nim-values:

k	= 4 5 6 7 8 9 10 11 13 14 15 16 17 19 20 22 23 25 26 28 29 31 32
$\mathcal{G}(3,k)$	= 2 3 1 4 6 1 7 8 9 11 1 12 14 15 15 17 19 20 21 23 24 26 27
$\mathcal{G}(4,k)$	= ? 3 0 5 ? 8 1 9 14 4 15 ? 16 19 ?

$$\mathcal{G}(4,6,4n-1,4n+1)=1 \qquad \mathcal{G}(4,6,4n+1,4n+3)=0 \qquad (n\geqslant 1)$$

$$\mathcal{G}(5,6)=7, \ \mathcal{G}(5,7)=8, \ \mathcal{G}(5,8)=10, \qquad \mathcal{G}(6,7)=9, \qquad \mathcal{G}(3,3n-1,3n+1)=5 \ (n\geqslant 6),$$

$$\mathcal{G}(3,9n-8,9n-4)=\mathcal{G}(3,9n+2,9n+7)=\mathcal{G}(3,9n+8,9n+13)=10 \qquad (n\geqslant 3).$$

A FEW FINAL QUESTIONS

Is there any effective technique for computing the outcome and all good replies for the *general position*?

If the game is played "between intelligent players", is the first person to make the game bounded the loser?

Is there a winning strategy of bounded length?

Is there an $\mathcal{N}$-position with $g>1$ for which *all* good replies lead to positions with $g=1$?

Is $\mathcal{G}(4)=\omega+1$? or is $\mathcal{G}(4)=6$, say?

REFERENCES AND FURTHER READING

Morton Davis, Infinite games of perfect information, Ann. of Math. Studies, Princeton, **52** (1963) 85–101.

David Gale and F.M. Stewart, Infinite games with perfect information, Ann. of Math. Studies, Princeton, **28** (1953) 245–266.

Martin Gardner, Mathematical Games, Sci. Amer. **228** 1, 2, 5 (Jan, Feb, May 1973)

Richard K. Guy, Twenty questions concerning Conway's Sylver Coinage, Amer. Math. Monthly, **83** (1976) 634–637.

Michael O. Rabin, Effective computability of winning strategies, Ann. of Math. Studies, Princeton, **39** (1957) 147–157: M.R. 20 #263.

Fred. Schuh, The game of divisions, Nieuw Tijdschrift voor Wiskunde, **39** (1952) 299–304.

J.J. Sylvester, Math. Quest. Educ. Times, **41** (1884) 21.

Chapter 19

The King and the Consumer

For fools rush in where angels fear to tread.
Alexander Pope, *Essay on Criticism.*

... because your adversary the devil, as a roaring lion,
walketh about, seeking whom he may devour.
1 Peter 5:8

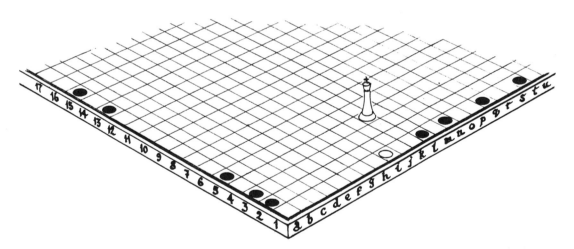

Figure 1. Chas. Plays Geo.

CHESSGO, KINGGO AND DUKEGO

These games are played on some *i* by *j* board. One player, Chas., plays Chess with a lone chess piece which might be a King, or a Knight, or a Duke, or a Ferz, whose moves are shown in Fig. 2. The variants of Chessgo are named for various real and Fairy Chess pieces, Kinggo for a King, etc. Only Kinggo and Dukego will be considered in any detail here.

607

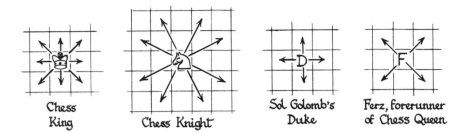

Figure 2. Various Chesspersons.

Chas.'s opponent, Geo., has a number of black (blocking) Go stones and a number of white (wandering) ones. The game starts with the chess piece on a specified square of the otherwise empty board. At each turn the chess piece moves to any legitimate empty square and Geo. then does one of the following:

(a) puts a new Go stone (of either color) on any empty square,
(b) moves a wandering (white) stone already on the board to any other empty square,
(c) passes.

If the chess piece reaches any square on the edge of the board, Chas. wins. If Geo. succeeds in surrounding the chess piece so that it has no legal moves, he wins. A game that continues for ever is declared a draw.

QUADRAPHAGE

This is the special case, invented by R. Epstein, where there are no wandering stones and enough blocking ones to cover the whole board. The title of this chapter refers to the case of Quadraphage in which the chessperson is the King. In Epstein's language, Geo. is a square-eater (graeco-latin *tesseravore*, latino-greek *quadraphage*). Because Geo. eats a square at every turn, this game ends after at most $ij - 1$ turns on an i by j board. The starting position for the chessperson is conventionally the middle of the board, or as near as possible if i or j is even.

Since having the first move is never a disadvantage, a strategy-copying argument shows that there are only three possible outcomes for a well-played Quadraphage game from a given starting position on a finite board. Either Geo. wins (even if Chas. moves first) or Chas. wins (even if Geo. moves first) or the first player to move wins. A **fair position** is one in which the first player to move can win.

We'll show that the fair starting positions for the Duke on a quarter-infinite board are all of the squares on the third rank or file, *except* those that are also on the first or second file or rank. We'll also show that the fair starting positions for the King on this board are all of the squares on the ninth rank or file, except those which are also on a lower file or rank. Finally we'll show that the square board which is fair (from the conventional starting position) for a Duke is the ordinary 8 by 8 chessboard, and we assert that the only fair and square boards for a King are 33 by 33 and 34 by 34. On boards smaller than these, Chas. should win even if Geo. starts first and the reverse should happen on larger boards.

THE ANGEL AND THE SQUARE-EATER

The game of Chessgo is not well understood and it's very difficult to exhibit explicit winning strategies for Chas. even on modest sized boards. For example it seems very likely indeed that the Knight can draw on an infinite board although this seems extremely difficult to prove.

Indeed it's never been shown that there is *any* generalized chess piece that can draw on the infinite board. This suggests the following problem. An **angel** (of power 1000) is a chessperson who can fly in one move to any empty square which could be reached by a thousand King moves. Angels, of course, have wings, so it won't matter if some of the intervening squares have been eaten.

Figure 3. The Angel and the Square-Eater.

We'll say the angel wins by continuing forever (i.e. drawing the game of Quadraphage) against a square-eating **devil** (who can devour *any* square of the board, no matter how far away it is from his previous moves). The devil, of course, wins if he can surround the angel with a sulphurous moat, a thousand squares wide, of eaten squares. Can you give an explicit strategy that's *guaranteed* to win for the angel?

If the devil adopts certain cunning tactics worked out for him by Andreas Blass and John Conway, then infinitely often the angel will find itself decreasing its distance from the centre by arbitrarily large amounts. Although the angel never seems to be in any real danger, its path must also contain arbitrarily convoluted spirals.

STRATEGY AND TACTICS

In both Dukego and Kinggo it's possible to distinguish between strategic moves and tactical ones. In either game Geo. wins, on large enough boards, by first playing a few *strategic* stones on squares far away from the chess piece. When the chess piece gets closer to the edge of the board, Geo. switches to *tactical* moves fairly close to him. Whenever the chess piece is driven away from the edge towards the centre of the board, Geo. reverts to strategic moves.

DUKEGO

Dukego is much simpler than Kinggo and so we consider it first. You might like to try playing it yourself before reading this section. The optimal strategies we present here were first discovered by Solomon Golomb. We consider various infinite boards first.

On an infinite half-plane the Duke can win only if he can get to the edge at his first move. In any other situation Geo. can draw by playing directly between the Duke and the edge. In fact Geo. needs only one white (wandering) stone.

On an infinite strip of width i with $i \leqslant 4$ the Duke, moving first, can win immediately. If $i \geqslant 4$ and Geo. moves first he can draw by playing between the Duke and the nearest edge and again needs only one stone, if it's a wandering one.

On an infinite quarter-plane the Duke, moving first, can win if he starts within a three squares wide border. His initial move attacks the edge and Geo. has no choice but to move directly between Duke and edge. The Duke then charges towards the corner. At each move Geo. is forced to play between the Duke and the edge and eventually the Duke wins by reaching one of the two squares next to the corner.

If Geo. moves first against the Duke on the third rank or file of an infinite quarter plane, he can draw using just one blocking stone and one wandering one. He first puts his blocking stone at the strategic position diagonally next to the corner (Fig. 4). This blocks the only square from which the Duke might attack two boundary squares at once. Whenever the Duke moves onto a lower case letter, Geo. puts his wandering stone on the corresponding capital letter.

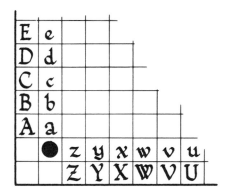

Figure 4. Geo. Beats the Duke on a Quarter-Infinite Board.

On an 8 by j board for any value of *j*, the Duke can win if he moves first no matter how many stones Geo. has. The Duke first advances towards the nearest edge, getting onto the third rank or file. If Geo. blocks his advance, the Duke charges along the edge to win in one of the corners. If Geo. does not immediately block his advance, the Duke's second move places him next to an edge square and Geo. puts a second stone on the board. One of Geo.'s stones must be on the edge square next to the Duke; if the other is to the left of this, the Duke charges to the right, and if to the right, he charges leftward. In either case the Duke eventually wins in the other corner.

On a 7 by j board the Duke can win even if Geo. starts, by attacking whichever half of the board does not contain Geo.'s opening stone.

		E	F	G	H		
	A	abe	abf	abg	abh	B	
T	adt	abd	ab	ab	abc	bci	I
S	ads	ad	a	b	bc	bcj	J
R	adr	ad	d	c	bc	bck	K
Q	adg	acd	cd	cd	bcd	bcl	L
	D	cdp	cdo	cdn	cdm	C	
		P	O	N	M		

Figure 5. Geo. Beats the Duke on an Ordinary Chessboard.

On the 8 by 8 board Geo. can draw using only three wandering stones (Fig. 5). He always arranges to have his stones on the capital letters corresponding to the small letters covered by the Duke. Since the combinations of small letters on any two contiguous squares never differ by more than one letter, this is always possible. Geo. can draw with just two wandering stones and two blocking ones, by placing the blocking stones on A and C. This works because every square with three letters includes just one of a and c. He can also draw with just one wandering stone and four blocking ones placed at A, B, C, D. It's much harder to find how many blocking stones Geo. needs when he has no wandering ones. Table 1 summarizes the fair starting positions in Dukego.

Size of Board	Starting Position	Least Number of Stones Giving Geo. at least a Draw, Moving First
$4 \times \infty$	centre.	1 wandering.
quarter-infinite.	3rd rank or file, excluding 1st or 2nd file or rank.	1 wandering, 1 blocking.
$8 \times j, j \geqslant 8$	centre.	3 wandering, *or* 2 wandering, 2 blocking, *or* 1 wandering, 4 blocking, *or* ? blocking.

Table 1. Fair Boards for Dukego.

THE GAME OF KINGGO

The remaining sections of this chapter are devoted to Kinggo.

THE EDGE ATTACK

Figure 6 shows how the King can force his way to a nearby edge of the board if this is in-adequately defended. The solid line indicates the edge of the board and the dot shows the present

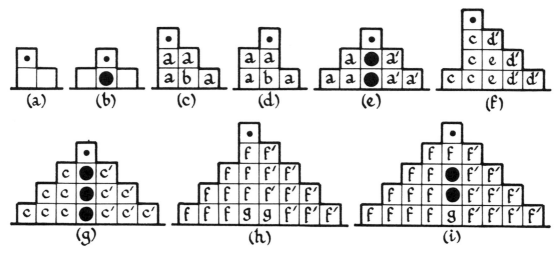

Figure 6. How the King Gets to the Edge.

position of the King. We suppose that the lettered squares are empty; Go stones may occupy any or all of the other squares. In each case Geo. is to move.

If Geo. moves outside the region shown, the King simply advances towards the edge, while if Geo. moves on to a letter x or x' ($x = a, b, \ldots, g$) the King makes a move which results in a case of Fig. 6(x) or its reflexion. If, for example, Geo. puts a stone in the lower right corner (labelled d') of Fig. 6(f), the King moves downwards and achieves a reflexion of Fig. 6(d),

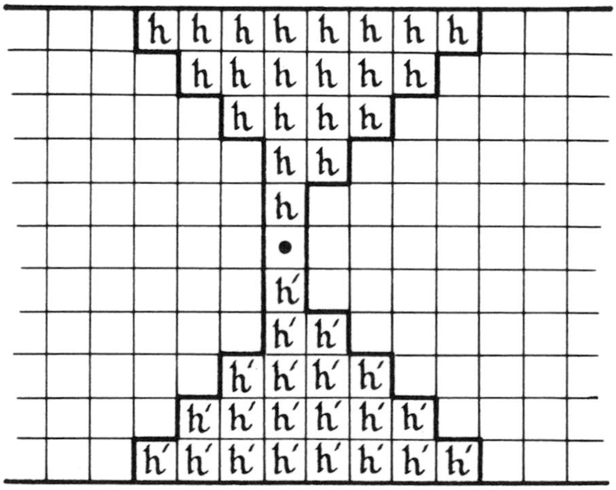

Figure 7. How the King Wins on an Infinite Strip of Width Eleven.

Now a glance at Fig. 7 and Fig. 6(h) shows that:

> the King can win
> on an infinite strip
> of width at most 11,
> even if Geo. goes first.

THE EDGE DEFENCE

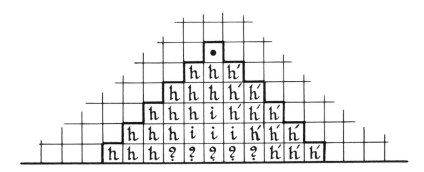

Figure 8. How Geo. Guards the Edge Against the King.

Figure 8, which again refers back to Fig. 6, shows that there are only five possible moves (?, ?, ?, ?, ?) which give Geo. any chance of stopping the King approaching from the sixth rank of an empty board. Figure 9(k) shows how Geo. can successfully defend the edge with any of these five moves. The King may move from any of the shaded squares. If he remains on such a square Geo. passes. When the King moves on to a letter x or x' $(x=j, k, l, ..., q)$ Geo. can move into a case of Fig. 9(x) or its reflexion (as he did in Fig. 6). Note that the proof of each of Figs. 9(j) to 9(q) depends on the others, because the King can nip from one of these positions to another in ingenious ways.

Since none of these positions has more than three stones, Geo. can defend the edge with only three wandering stones.

A MEMORYLESS EDGE DEFENCE

Figure 10, which uses the same conventions as Fig. 5, shows another way that Geo. can stop the King approaching from the sixth rank of an empty board using just three wandering stones. Unlike Fig. 9, this is memoryless in the sense that the positions of these stones depend only on the position of the King and not on how he got there.

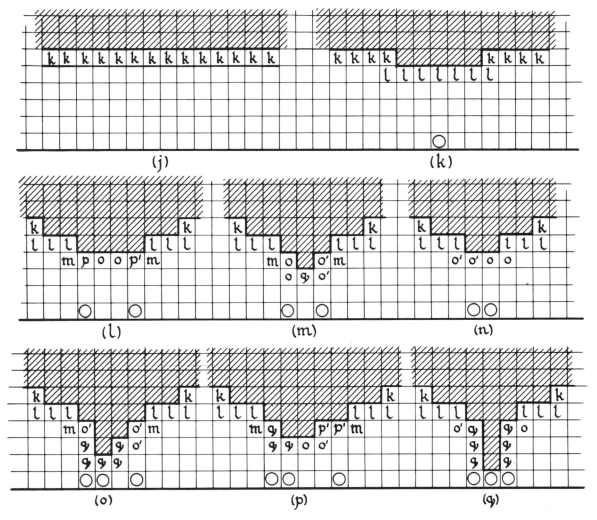

Figure 9. Three Wandering Stones Ward Off the King.

Figure 10. A Memoryless Kinggo Edge Defence.

In later sections of this chapter Geo. will want to patch together several copies of this defence (Figs. 11 and 12). Figure 11 shows how it may be joined to its left-right mirror image, and Fig. 12 shows how to change its phase by one square. Many other memoryless edge defences can be obtained by joining various combinations of Figs. 10, 11, 12 and their translates and reflexions.

		e	g	g	i	i	k	k	k'	k'	i'	i'	g'	g'	e'		
•··	eg	eg	gi	gi	ik	ik	kk	kk	i'k'	i'k'	i'g'	i'g'	g'e'	g'e'		•··
•··	ceg	egi	egi	gik	gik	ikk	ikk	kki	kki	kig	kig	ig'e	ig'e	g'e'c		•··
•··	efg	egh	ghi	gij	ijk	ikl	kkl	k'lk'	l'k'i'	k'j'i	j'i'g'	i'h'g'	h'g'e'	g'f'e'		•··
•··	efg	fgh	ghi	hij	ijk	jkl	kll'	l'l'k'	l'k'j'	k'j'i'	j'i'h'	i'h'g'	h'g'f'	g'f'e'		•··
·•·	E	F	G	H	I	J	K	L	L'	K'	J'	I'	H'	G'	F'	E'	·•·

Figure 11. Wedding Figure 10 With Its Reflexion.

		e	e	g	g	i	i	k	k	k	m	m	o	o	q	q		
•··	ce	eg	eg	gi	gi	ik	ik	ik	km	km	mo	mo	oq	oq	qs		•··
•··	ceg	ceg	egi	egi	gik	gik	ijk	ikm	kmn	kmo	kmo	moq	moq	oqs	oqs		•··
•··	cde	deg	efg	fgi	ghi	hik	ijk	jkm	klm	kmn	mno	mop	opq	oqr	qrs		•··
·•·	bcd	cde	def	efg	fgh	ghi	hij	ijk	jkl	klm	lmn	mno	nop	opq	pqr	qrs	rst	•··
·•·		C	D	E	F	G	H	I	J	K	L	M	N	O	P	Q	R	S	·•·

Figure 12. Getting Figure 10 One Square Out of Step with Itself.

Some results for infinite strips follow immediately from Figs. 9, 10, 11, 12:

> On an infinite strip
> of width at least 12,
> Geo., moving first, can draw
> with just 3 wandering stones.
>
> ———
>
> On an infinite strip
> of width at least 13,
> he can draw even if
> the King moves first.

If the King advances towards the edge he will be stopped at Fig. 9(q) and if the King refuses to attack the edge, Geo. can still obtain 3 consecutive stones as in that figure.

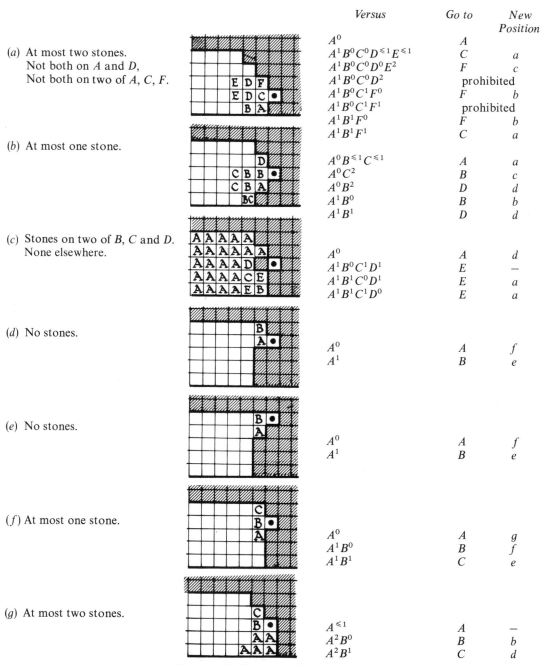

	Versus	Go to	New Position
(a) At most two stones. Not both on A and D, Not both on two of A, C, F.	A^0	A	
	$A^1B^0C^0D^{\leqslant 1}E^{\leqslant 1}$	C	a
	$A^1B^0C^0D^0E^2$	F	c
	$A^1B^0C^0D^2$	prohibited	
	$A^1B^0C^1F^0$	F	b
	$A^1B^0C^1F^1$	prohibited	
	$A^1B^1F^0$	F	b
	$A^1B^1F^1$	C	a
(b) At most one stone.			
	$A^0B^{\leqslant 1}C^{\leqslant 1}$	A	a
	A^0C^2	B	c
	A^0B^2	D	d
	A^1B^0	B	b
	A^1B^1	D	d
(c) Stones on two of B, C and D. None elsewhere.			
	A^0	A	d
	$A^1B^0C^1D^1$	E	—
	$A^1B^1C^0D^1$	E	a
	$A^1B^1C^1D^0$	E	a
(d) No stones.			
	A^0	A	f
	A^1	B	e
(e) No stones.			
	A^0	A	f
	A^1	B	e
(f) At most one stone.			
	A^0	A	g
	A^1B^0	B	f
	A^1B^1	C	e
(g) At most two stones.			
	$A^{\leqslant 1}$	A	—
	A^2B^0	B	b
	A^2B^1	C	d

Figure 13. The Edge-Corner Attack.

THE EDGE-CORNER ATTACK

On an infinite strip of width 13, the King can't *win*, but *can* force his way to the second rank, as in Fig. 9(q). He may then charge along this rank in either direction, forcing Geo. to accompany him. Even if Geo. has a large supply of stones he can do no more than build up a solid wall along the first rank and on a finite board the edge-charging King will eventually reach a corner.

We now claim that for an adequate defence, Geo. must have at least three strategic stones stationed somewhere between the edge-charging King and the corner. All of these three stones must be positioned somewhere in the first five ranks. The proof of this follows from Fig. 13, which lists the appropriate moves for the King against all positions not satisfying these conditions. There are squares with one of the first seven capital letters and infinitely many squares with no letters at all. At Geo.'s move he has at most 3 stones in the figure. The line

$$\text{``Versus } A^0, \text{ go to } A, \text{ position } -\text{''}$$

means that if none (superscript 0) of the 3 stones are on A, then the King moves to A and wins at once. The line

$$\text{``Versus } A^1 B^0 C^0 D^{\leqslant 1} E^{\leqslant 1}, \text{ go to } C, \text{ position } a\text{''}$$

means that if Geo. has one stone on A, none on B or C, and at most one (superscript $\leqslant 1$) on each of D and E, the King should move to C and obtain a translate of the position shown in Fig. 13(a).

Since in every case the King counters Geo.'s moves to any of Figs. 13(a) to 13(g) by a move resulting in another of these figures, Geo. can never force the King above the fifth rank or prevent him from continuing the edge-corner attack, although he *can* keep him moving to and fro among these seven figures.

On the other hand, almost all combinations of three strategic stones along the first rank of the board *will* suffice for Geo. to stop the edge-corner attack. Figure 14 shows the only exceptions.

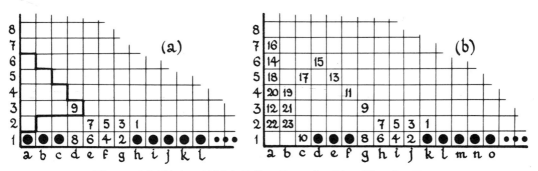

Figure 14. Triplets Which Fail to Stop the Edge-Charging King.

In Fig. 14(a) Geo. has three strategic stones at a1, b1, c1, as well as his tactical stones, h1, i1, ..., defending the edge near the King. The King moves to 1; Geo. is forced to put a stone at 2; the King moves to 3; and so on. The King's move to 9 guarantees him a win by Fig. 6(f) (reflected).

Figure 14(b) uses a similar notation to show how the King wins if Geo.'s strategic stones are at d1, e1, f1.

STRATEGIC AND TACTICAL STONES

Since Geo. can stop an edge corner attack with just three extra stones, and most combinations of three stones suffice, it's convenient to call his three most distant stones in the first five ranks along any edge of the board **strategic** stones; his other stones are **tactical** ones. The tactical stones try to stop the King winning along the side and the strategic ones then prevent him from winning the ensuing edge-corner attack.

Let's consider for instance the game on an infinite strip of width 23 (Figure 15). The King starts at 1; Geo. puts a stone at 2; the King moves to 3; Geo. puts a stone at 4; and so on. The crucial position arises when Geo. puts a stone at 16. Where should the King move now? Although various moves look plausible, only one succeeds!

You must distinguish between strategy and tactics if you're to find the right move. The stones 4, 6 and 8 defend the right flank, so 10, 12 and 16 are needed to defend the left one. Since the stone at 16 is required for *strategic* purposes it is *tactically* worthless.

So the King pretends that 16 is empty and moves to 17, which would give him a tactical victory via Fig. 6(g)! Any other King move would lose to a defence at α or β.

Of course, since 16 *isn't* empty, the game *won't* end on the lower edge, for Geo. can stop the edge attack, but only by using the stone at 16. Eventually the King would have an opportunity to move to 16 if it were vacant. Instead of doing this he embarks on an unstoppable edge-corner attack, running along the second rank towards the left. Geo. can eventually use his stones 10 and 12 to divert the King into various positions of Fig. 13 but can't halt the edge-corner assault.

This sort of argument shows that:

> if Geo. is required to place
> his first 10 stones on the
> top and bottom ranks, the
> King can draw on an
> infinite strip of width 23,
> even when Geo. moves first

We believe that this remains true when we remove the constraints on Geo.'s initial moves, since it seems very unlikely that he gains any advantage by putting his stones nearer to the middle. Although such moves seem futile, we haven't managed to exhibit a precise strategy by which the King can refute them.

CORNER TACTICS

Figure 16 shows how Geo. defends the corner against an attack from either edge using three consecutive blocking stones and three wandering ones. The edges can be continued using Fig. 10 to give a strategy for Geo. on a quarter-infinite board.

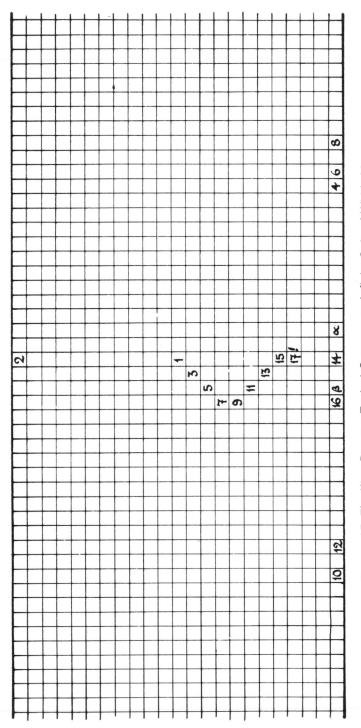

Figure 15. The King Draws a Typical Game on an Infinite Strip of Width 23.

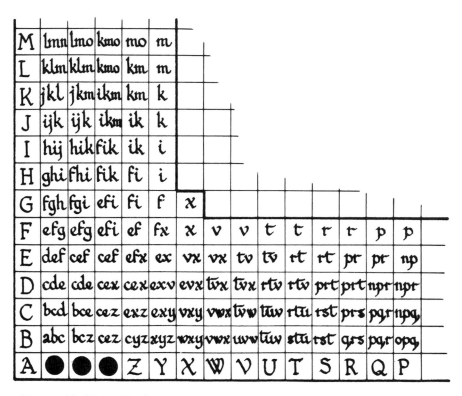

Figure 16. Three Blocking and Three Wandering Stones Defend the Corner.

Although it defends the corner from attack along either edge, it provides only a weak defence against a direct attack towards the corner along the diagonal. It defends against a King on the tenth rank and tenth file of an empty board *only* when Geo. moves first. Since Geo. must first enter his three strategic stones, if the King moves first he will arrive at the sixth rank and file before Geo. has put any wandering stone on the board, and Fig. 16 now requires Geo. to put wandering stones on both F and X. In fact Fig. 17 (which should be used in conjunction with Fig. 6) shows that the King can now win against *any* strategy for Geo., even if there are stones on all the indicated squares of Fig. 17(a). This figure depends on Figs. 17(b) to 17(e) whose proofs are left to the reader.

Figure 17 shows that Geo.'s only hope of defending the corner against a diagonally attacking King, starting from the tenth rank and file, requires that his first three stones be placed elsewhere. One promising possibility uses squares a2, a3, a5 along one edge, when Geo.'s major problem is to find an appropriate continuation when the King arrives on the sixth rank and file. Figure 18(a) shows that there is only one possibility (indicated by ?). The proof of Fig. 18 depends on Fig. 17 and Fig. 6, but we again leave some of these proofs to the reader.

So there's only one move with which Geo. can successfully defend Fig. 18(a)! His complete strategy appears in Fig. 19 with the edges extended by Fig. 10. With the three blocking stones positioned as shown, he defends the corner against attacks along edges or diagonal.

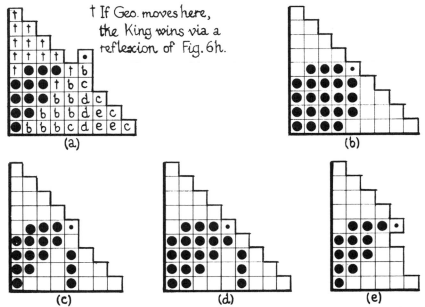

Figure 17. Three Consecutive Blocking Stones Won't Defend the Corner Against the King on the Sixth Rank and File.

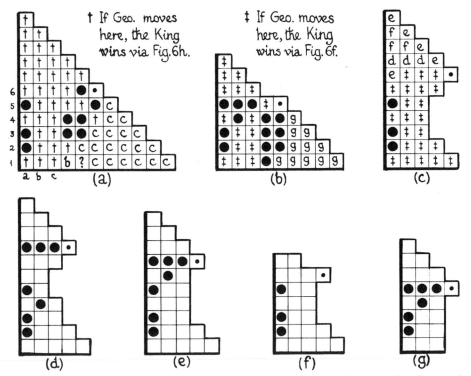

Figure 18. With Three Well Placed Stones and the Initial Move, Geo. Defends the Corner Against the Diagonal Attack.

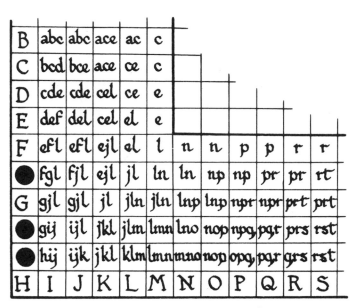

Figure 19. Memoryless Corner Defence.

Combining Figs 13 and 19 we have:

> the fair starting positions
> on the quarter-infinite board
> are those on the ninth rank or file,
> excluding lesser files or ranks.

Geo., moving first, can defend any such position with just three blocking stones and three wandering ones according to Fig. 19. But if the King moves first, he attacks the nearest edge, ignoring the three further stones between him and the corner as in the sample game of Fig. 15. Since Fig. 13 shows that Geo. needs three strategic stones to defend the corner, the King can *either* win on the edge *or* divert to a winning edge-corner assault as in Fig. 13.

DEFENCE ON LARGE SQUARE BOARDS

We've seen that Geo. can defend a corner with three blocking stones and three wandering ones, so he can defend a large enough square board with twelve blocking stones (three in each corner) and three wandering ones. He first puts the twelve blocking stones in their permanent places. If the board is 35 × 35 or bigger, the King begins at least 18 squares from any edge, so he's still at least 6 squares away from the edge after Geo. has placed his 12-strategic stones. So,

> Geo., moving first,
> can win on a square board
> of size 35 × 35 or larger.

THE 33 × 33 BOARD

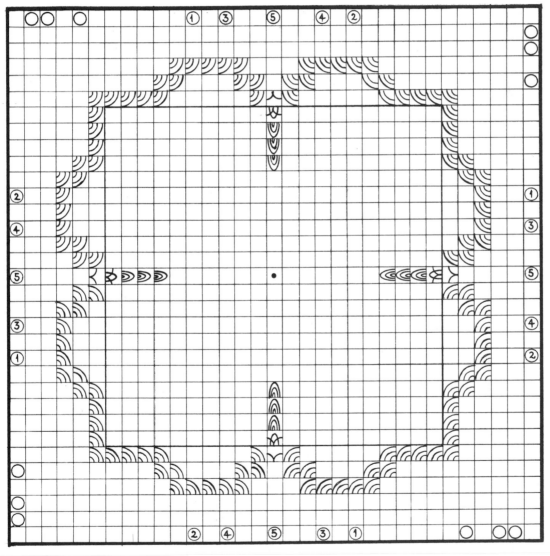

Figure 20. The Centred King on a 33×33 Board.

We'll now show you a more intricate defence which allows Geo., moving first, to survive on a 33×33 board with just 12 (wandering) stones. The details are in Figs. 20 to 26.

THE CENTRED KING

So long as the King stays in the central region of Fig. 20, Geo. puts stones on certain strategic squares, marked with circles on the perimeter of the board. There are 32 of these, 3 near each corner and 5 on each edge. Geo. puts the first four stones one on each edge, and the distribution of his stones after the King has made four or more moves is shown in Fig. 21, a close-up of part of Fig. 20 (the four quarters of the board are congruent). Most of the squares in the central region are divided into nine subsquares, the central one of which is always empty. The other eight subsquares tell Geo. how many stones he should have in each corresponding area. For example, if the King moves to a square marked

3		
1	4	

then Geo. moves so that he has three stones on the left edge, one near the bottom left corner and four on the bottom edge. The order in which Geo. puts his stones in the three squares near the corner doesn't matter, but of the five strategic squares on each edge, it's the middle one that must be occupied last. A reasonable order is indicated by the numbers 1,2,3,4,5 in the circles in Figs. 20 and 21.

A few squares on the main diagonals of Fig. 21 contain arrows:

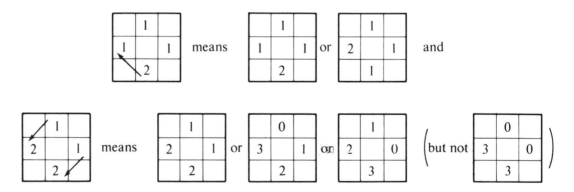

Geo. can use any of these alternatives as a satisfactory defence.

LEAVING THE CENTRAL REGION

If the King leaves the central region of Fig. 20 via a square marked as in Fig. 22(a), we'll say that he's **cornered** in the lower left of the board, and then Geo. will keep him inside the region

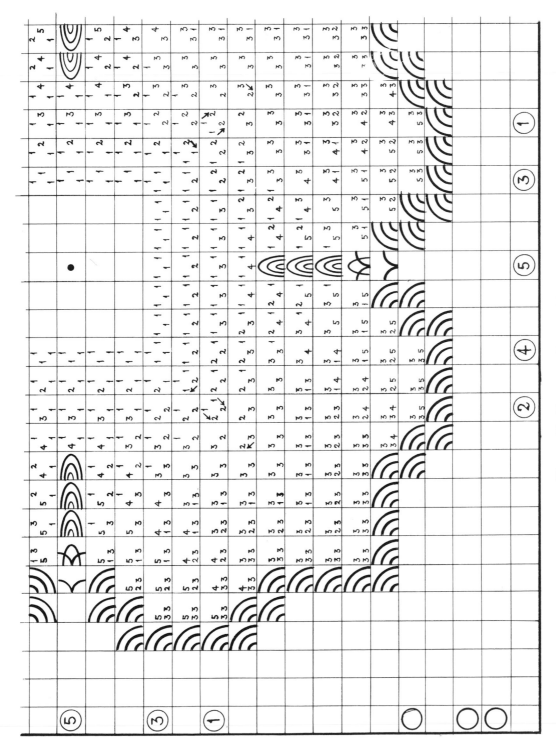

Figure 21. Close-up of Figure 20.

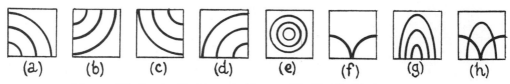

Figure 22. Key to Markings in Figures 20, 21, 23, 24, 25 (see text).

shown in Fig. 23 by making tactical moves which prevent the King from reaching a shaded square, so that he can only "re-centre" himself by moving to a square marked as in Fig. 22(e).

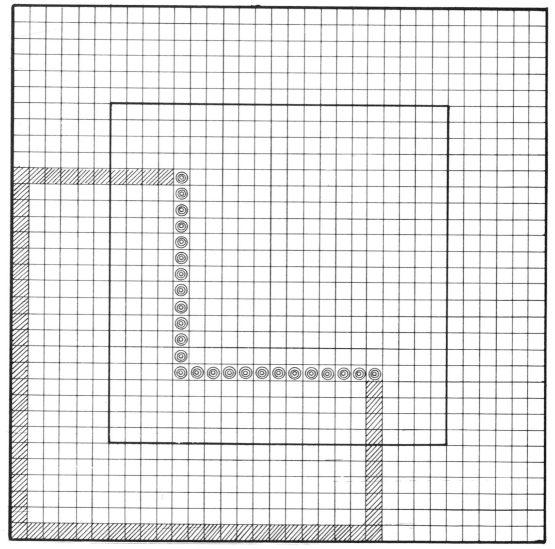

Figure 23. The Cornered King.

If the King moves to squares marked as in Fig. 22(b), (c) or (d) he is correspondingly cornered in the upper left, upper right or lower right of the board. If the King moves to a square labelled as in Fig. 22(f) he is cornered in the lower left or lower right of the board, depending on the direction he came from. If he moves to a label like Fig. 22(g) he is **sidelined** (see later) and when he moves to one like Fig. 22(h) he is either sidelined or cornered, again depending on which way he came; if diagonally, he's sidelined; if horizontally then he'll be pushed back to the corner whence he came.

THE CORNERED KING

Figure 24, a close-up of Fig. 23, reveals the tactical details that Geo. uses to keep the King cornered with just three wandering stones and nine **static** ones (semi-stationary, both strategic and tactical). Of course, when the King first becomes cornered by moving to a square marked as in Fig. 22(a), Geo. may not have his nine static stones in the exact places shown in Fig. 24, but he will have three stones between the King and the lower left corner, and three on the bottom edge and three on the left edge. Geo. uses the stones already on the boundary as substitutes for any stones missing from Fig. 24. When the tactics call for placing a stone on a square already occupied, Geo. places a stone on an unoccupied circle in Fig. 24.

Suppose, for example, that the King leaves the central area of Fig. 20 by moving to square $k4$ (see Fig. 1). He must have come from $l5$, marked

so there are already three stones on the left-edge, three as indicated near the lower left corner and five in the squares 2, 4, 5 and those next to Z and A and between them ("3" and "1"). The King is now on a square labelled "$s24$" so Geo. puts his last stone (the white one in Fig. 1) on S and continues to follow Fig. 24 with the stone on "5" substituting for the missing one between Z and A.

The right arrow in certain squares near the top right of Fig. 24 means that the third genuinely wandering (non-static) stone belongs on a strategic square on the right edge.

THE SIDELINED KING

If the King leaves the central area of Fig. 20 by moving onto a square marked as in Fig. 22(g) he is sidelined as in Fig. 25. Geo. tactically keeps the King off the shaded squares and the King can only re-centre himself by moving onto a square marked as in Fig. 22(e).

The notation in Fig. 26 (a close-up of Fig. 25) is as in Figs. 21 and 24, but we now have some squares

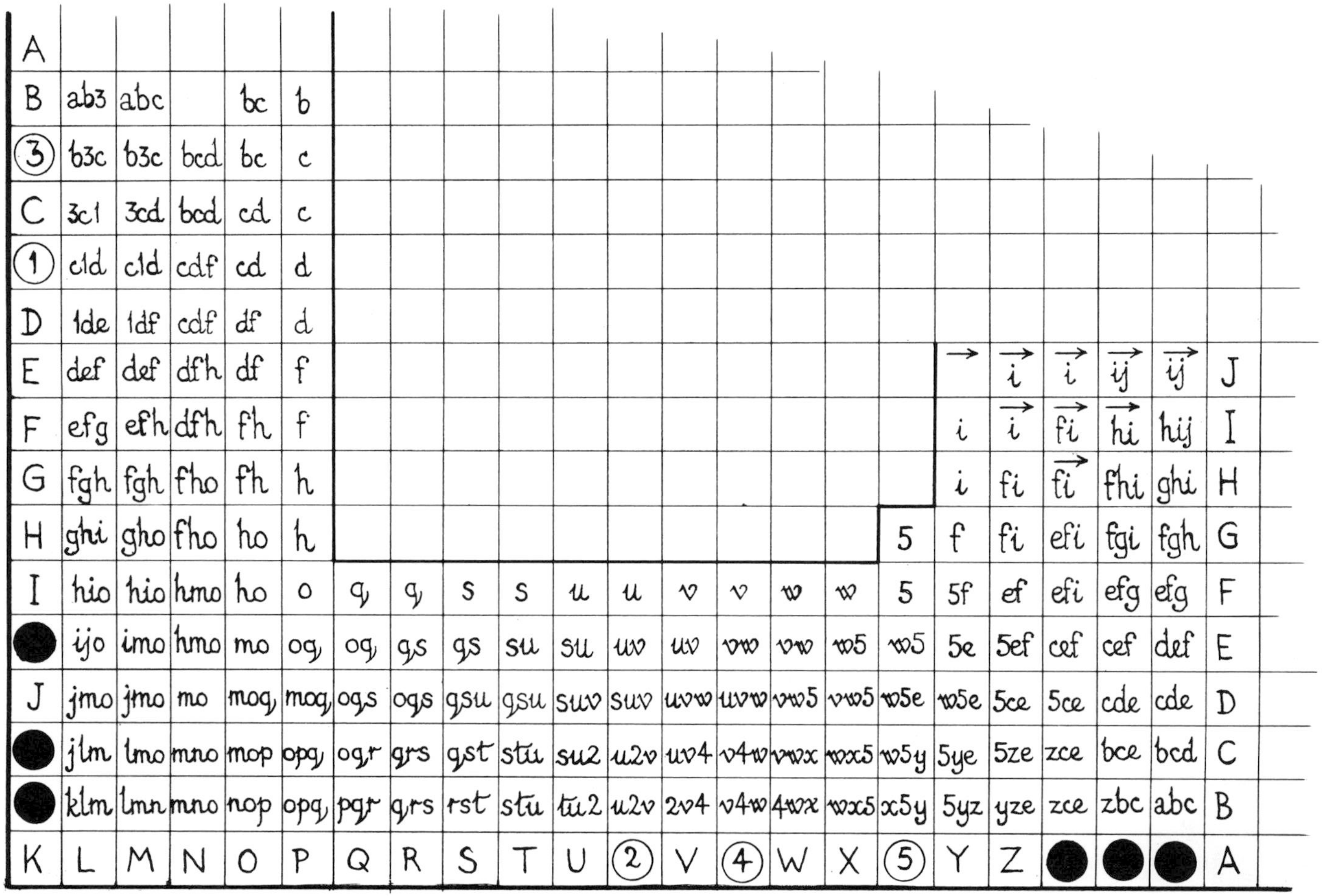

Figure 24. Close-up of Figure 23.

These advise Geo. to have one stone on each of the left and right edges (shown in Fig. 25 in their lowest and highest positions) and *six* on the bottom edge, not only the usual five but one on J or Q as well. [Assume in Fig. 26 that Geo. has 6 static stones on 1, 2, 3, 4, J, Q, and that one of the last two is substituting for 5.]

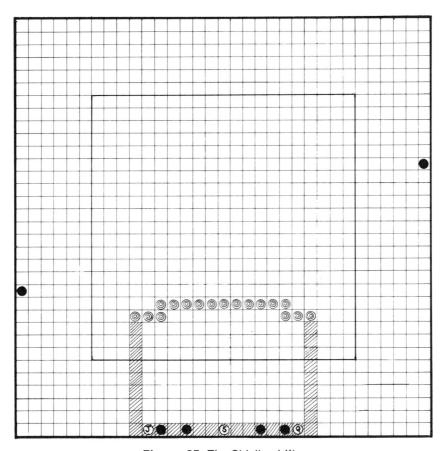

Figure 25. The Sidelined King.

HOW CHAS. CAN WIN ON A 34 × 34 BOARD

Geo., going first, can survive in Kinggo with 12 wandering stones on a 33 × 33 board, so he can certainly survive on a 35 × 35 or larger board, even if the King goes first.

However it seems that the King can win on a 34 × 34 board if he moves first. Here's how he does it. His first three moves diagonally attack the nearest corner. He then turns left or right and attacks the adjacent corner in the half of the board where Geo. has at most one stone. After 9 more moves he is at *l6*, say, and Geo. has been unable to get 9 useful stones on the board. If the corner is adequately defended (with 3 stones), then one flank or the other is weak and a carefully executed edge-corner attack eventually leads to victory.

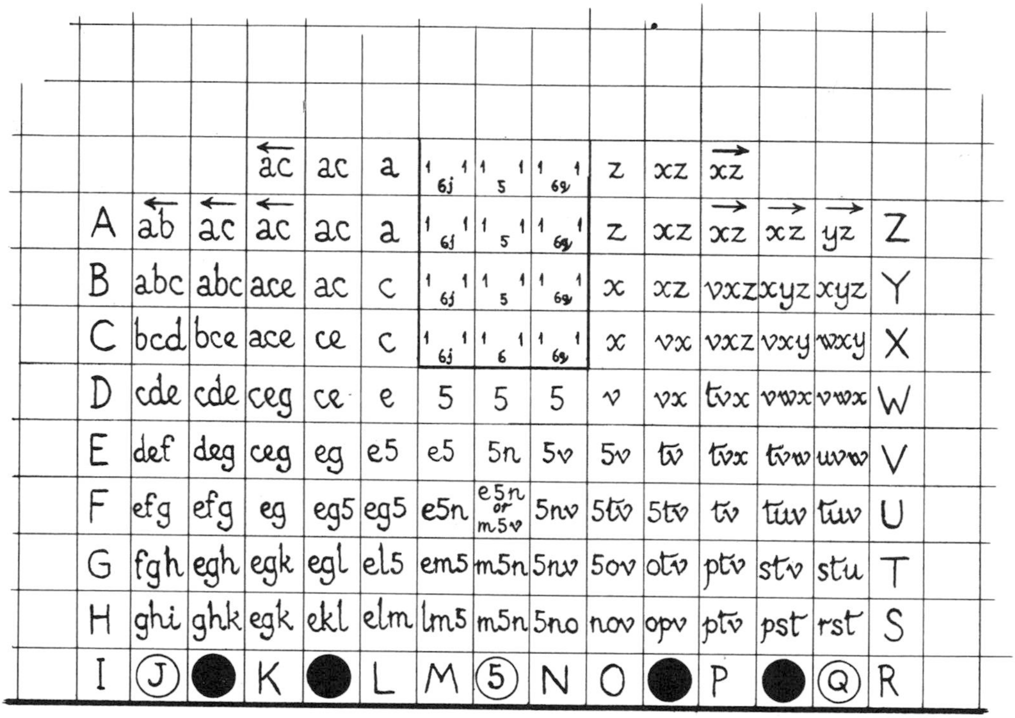

		$\overleftarrow{ac}$	ac	a	$\frac{1}{6j}$ 1	1 5 1	1 $\frac{1}{6y}$	z	xz	$\overrightarrow{xz}$				
A	$\overleftarrow{ab}$	$\overleftarrow{ac}$	$\overleftarrow{ac}$	ac	a	$\frac{1}{6j}$ 1	1 5 1	1 $\frac{1}{6y}$	z	xz	$\overrightarrow{xz}$	$\overrightarrow{xz}$	yz	Z
B	abc	abc	ace	ac	c	$\frac{1}{6j}$ 1	1 5 1	1 $\frac{1}{6y}$	x	xz	vxz	xyz	xyz	Y
C	bcd	bce	ace	ce	c	$\frac{1}{6j}$ 1	1 6 1	1 $\frac{1}{6y}$	x	vx	vxz	vxy	wxy	X
D	cde	cde	ceg	ce	e	5	5	5	v	vx	tvx	vwx	vwx	W
E	def	deg	ceg	eg	e5	e5	5n	5v	5v	tv	tvx	tvw	uvw	V
F	efg	efg	eg	eg5	eg5	e5n	e5n or m5v	5nv	5tv	5tv	tv	tuv	tuv	U
G	fgh	egh	egk	egl	el5	em5	m5n	5nv	5ov	otv	ptv	stv	stu	T
H	ghi	ghk	egk	ekl	elm	lm5	m5n	5no	nov	opv	ptv	pst	rst	S
I	Ⓙ	●	K	●	L	M	⑤	N	O	●	P	●	Ⓠ	R

Figure 26. Close-up of Figure 25.

Unfortunately we haven't been able to formalize these remarks into a strategy for Chas. that's even as explicit as Geo.'s 33×33 one.

RECTANGULAR BOARDS

Geo. can't beat the King on the infinite strip of width 23, even if he moves first and has an unlimited supply of stones. However, if he moves first on a 24 by n board, he can win for sufficiently large n. The minimum value of n seems to be about 63. The King is immediately sidelined along whichever long edge he's nearest to. The King can circumvent the pseudocorners (I and R in Fig. 26) of Geo.'s sideline defence, but only by moving back to squares about midway between the two long edges. Geo. can then defend a second pseudocorner between the real corner and the first one. By the time the King reaches the corner, Geo. has prepared defences of both corners along a short edge of the board and a pair of opposite pesudocorners somewhere between the King and the unattacked short edge.

For each value of i, $24 \leqslant i \leqslant 37$, there appears to be a range of values of j for which the i by j board is a fair battleground for a Quadraphage game against the Chess King. We believe that the 32×33 board is fair and that Geo., moving first, wins with a strategy similar to that we gave for the 33×33 board. We leave the problem of determining the dimensions of all fair Quadraphage boards as a challenge for Omar.

EXTRAS

MANY-DIMENSIONAL ANGELS

can escape from the corresponding hypercube-eaters. This has been proved by Tom Körner who thinks that his proof could conceivably be adapted to the two-dimensional game. Don't write to us with *your* solution to the Angel problem unless you've taken account of the remarks on p. 609!

GAMES OF ENCIRCLEMENT

The games of this Chapter, and of the next two, are ones of *encirclement* or *escape*. There are many games, going a long way back in history, in which this idea is combined with varying kinds of *capture*. Here are a few examples.

WOLVES-AND-SHEEP

There are several games played on Solitaire-like boards (Chapter 23). In **Wolves-and-Sheep** (Fig. 27(a)) the shepherd has 20 sheep, which have first move. They move one place forward or sideways only, onto unoccupied places. The two wolves can move similarly but on any of the indicated lines and can capture in these directions by jumping as in checkers (draughts), including multiple captures. A wolf failing to make a possible capture may be removed by the shepherd, so the sheep may be used as decoys. The shepherd wins if he gets nine sheep into the *fold* (top 9 positions of board).

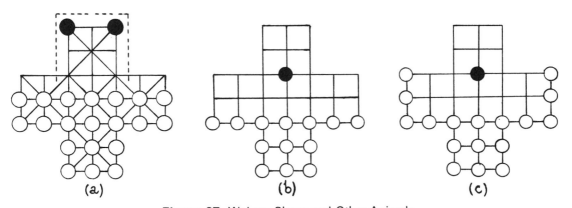

Figure 27. Wolves, Sheep and Other Animals.

The games shown in Figs. 27(b) and (c) are called Fox and Geese, although we use this name for a different game in the next chapter. They are similar to Wolves-and-Sheep, but there are no diagonal moves. The fox starts in any unoccupied position, and the geese try to crowd the fox into a corner. In Fig. 27(b) the 13 geese can move in any of the four orthogonal directions, but the 17 geese of Fig. 27(c) can't move backwards; they move like the sheep in Wolves and Sheep.

Hala-tafl (the Fox Game), and **Freystafl** are mentioned in the later Icelandic sagas. As in the Chapter 20 version of Fox and Geese, the more numerous animals win with correct play, but it's very easy to make mistakes!

TABLUT

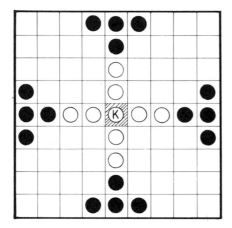

Figure 28. The Start of a Game of Tablut.

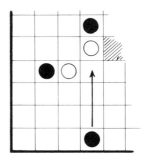

Figure 29. A Muscovite Captures Two Swedes.

Linnaeus, on his 1732 visit to Lapland, recorded a game played on a 9 × 9 board (Fig. 28) whose centre square, the **Konakis** or throne, may only be occupied by the Swedish King. He is protected by 8 blond Swedes and confronted by the 16 swarthy Muscovites. All the pieces move like the rook in Chess, any distance orthogonally. Capture of the King is by surrounding him, N, S, E and W by four Muscovites or by three Muscovites with the Konakis as the fourth square. Any other piece is removed by **custodian** capture, i.e. by placing two opposing pieces to the immediate N and S, or E and W of it. Figure 29 shows a Muscovite capturing two Swedes. A piece may move "into custody" without being captured. The aim of the Swedes is to get their King to the edge of the board.

SAXON HNEFATAFL

Only a fragment of a board has been found; it is probable that the game was played using the 19 × 19 positions of a modern Go board. See R.C. Bell's excellent little book for a possible reconstruction from a tenth century English manuscript. The game was evidently like Tablut apart from the size of the board and the number and position of the pieces.

We finish this chapter with two Chess problems which also involve escape or encirclement.

KING AND ROOK VERSUS KING

Most beginning Chess players soon learn how to win this ending, so it's a surprise to find a couple of non-trivial problems which use just this material, albeit on a quarter-infinite board.

In Fig. 30, can White win? If so, in how few moves? Simon Norton says it's better to ask, "what is the smallest board (if any) that White can win on if Black is given a win if he walks off the North or East edges of the board?" Can Omar prove that it's 9×11?

Figure 31 shows Leo Moser's problem: can White win if he's allowed to make *only one move with the Rook*? If you find yourself frustrated by this, partition the squares in the first three columns into the four sets

a1,a3,a5,...,c2,c4,c6,...
b1,b3,b5,...
a2,a4,a6,...,c1,c3,c5,...
b2,b4,b6,....

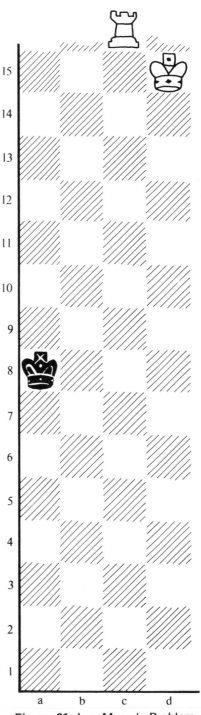

Figure 30. Simon Norton's Problem.

Figure 31. Leo Moser's Problem.

REFERENCES AND FURTHER READING

Robert Charles Bell, "Board and Table Games from Many Civilizations", Oxford University Press, London, 1969.

Richard A. Epstein, "Theory of Gambling and Statistical Logic", Academic Press, New York and London, 1967, p. 406.

Martin Gardner, Mathematical games: Cram, crosscram, and quadraphage: new games having elusive winning strategies, Sci. Amer. **230** #2 (Feb. 1974) 106–108.

C. Linnaeus, "Lachesis Lapponica", London, 1811, ii, 55.

H.J.R. Murray, "A History of Board Games other than Chess", Clarendon Press, Oxford, 1952.

David L. Silverman, "Your Move", McGraw–Hill, 1971, p. 186.

Chapter 20

Fox and Geese

While the one eludes, must the other pursue.
Robert Browning, *Life in a Love*.

The twelve good rules, the royal game of goose.
Oliver Goldsmith, *The Deserted Village*, l.232.

Figure 1. Playing a Game of Fox and Geese.

635

The game of Fox and Geese is played on an ordinary checkerboard between the *Fox*, who has just one black or red piece, and the *Geese*, who have four white ones. The players use squares of only one color (as in Checkers), and the Geese are initially placed in the squares marked **O** in Fig. 2. The Fox is usually placed at **X** in Fig. 2, but since the Geese seem to have the better chances, it is perhaps wiser to allow the Fox to choose his own starting square (provided this has the correct color), and then let the Geese have first move.

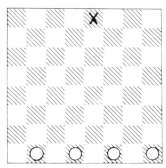

Figure 2. The Usual Starting Position.

The Geese move diagonally one place forward—like ordinary checkers they may not retreat. The Fox also moves diagonally one place, but like a King in Checkers, he may move in any one of the four diagonal directions. There is no taking or jumping. The Geese aim to trap the Fox so that he has no legal move, while conversely the Fox tries to break through the barrier of Geese so that he can stay alive indefinitely. We can therefore say simply that the first player unable to move is the loser, the usual normal play convention.

It is the general opinion that between expert players the Geese should win, but even against most moderately competent players a wily Fox can usually win a game every now and then, and if we let him choose his starting position, he should be able to defeat most novices for quite a long time. Perhaps those of our readers who have not met the game should take some time off to play a few games before reading further.

The question we shall ask and answer in this chapter is just how much of an advantage do the Geese have in this game? Perhaps we should first of all prove that the Geese really do have a winning strategy, even when the Fox is allowed the extra dispensation we suggest. In Fig. 3 we show the five types of position that our own favorite strategy relies on. The O's indicate the positions of the Geese, and the **X**'s indicate particularly critical positions for the Fox. When the Fox is in one of these places, we shall say that the Geese are *in danger*.

If the Geese follow our advice, they will play the game as follows. Most of the time they should play with their eyes closed, so that they will not be alarmed unnecessarily by the Fox's manoeuvres. We can offer them a guarantee that whenever they open their eyes the position will be like one of *A,B,C,D,E*, possibly left-right reflected, and that all they need do before closing their eyes again is see whether or not they are in danger. If not, they should make the moves indicated by the digits before the solidus (/) in Fig. 3, and if in danger, those indicated by the digits after the solidus. We also show by letters before and after the solidus which type *A,B,C,D,E* of position will be seen next. The indicated moves can be made with eyes closed, since we can also guarantee that the Fox will never be in the way, and so the Geese need only open eyes again when the sequence has been completed and the position is once again one of *A,B,C,D,E*.

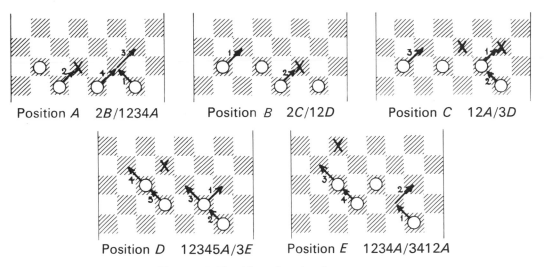

Figure 3. The Most Concise Strategy.

It is very easy to prove that the strategy works, when once the Geese have got into position *A*. As an example, we consider the position *D*. If the Geese have been behaving as we suggest, they can only have arrived at a position *D* from a position *B* or *C* in which they were in danger, and so the Fox can only be in one of a limited number of places. In fact he will be in one of **X,Y,Z,T** of Fig. 4_0.

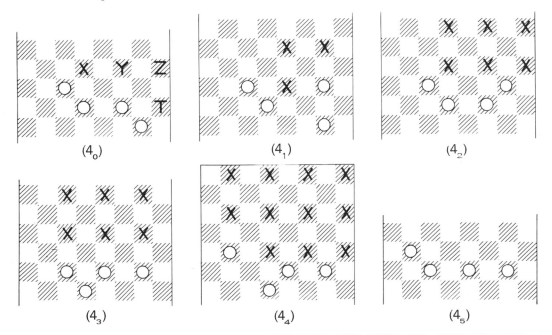

Figure 4. Analysis of Position *D*.

Now if the Geese are in danger (i.e., the Fox is at **X**), they make a single move and arrive immediately at position E. So we can suppose that the Fox is at **Y**, **Z**, or **T**, and the Geese are told to make moves 1,2,3,4,5. Figures 4_1, 4_2, 4_3, 4_4, 4_5 show the position after each of these, and show why the next move in the sequence is legal, for in Figs 4_1 to 4_4 we have marked **X** in every possible place the Fox can be in just before the next move takes place. Since the position shown in Fig. 4_5 is of type A, this verifies that the strategy works from positions of shape D. Note that if the Fox were at **T** in Fig. 4_0 then he lost instantly after move 1, being trapped at the edge of the board.

We leave to the reader the corresponding discussion for positions of shapes A,B,C,E, noting merely that since E can be reached only from a position D with the Geese in danger, we need consider just two places for the Fox in position E, namely that marked **X** in Fig. 3, and the place two squares to the right of it. But for positions A,B,C the Fox may be on any square of the right color that is above the line of Geese.

How do the Geese start the strategy? The answer is that they can move into a position A on their first move, unless the Fox chooses the starting position F of Fig. 5. In this case, we advise them to make moves 1,2,3 and then open their eyes again to behold another anomalous position, G, from which we can put them back on track by giving them another sequence of three moves to be performed with eyes closed.

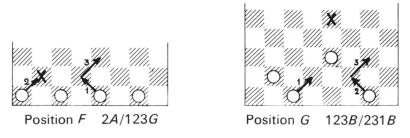

Position F $2A/123G$ Position G $123B/231B$

Figure 5. The Anomalous Starting Position.

SOME PROPERTIES OF OUR STRATEGY

From the standard starting position, and indeed from any position except the anomalous position F of Fig. 5, our strategy leads only to positions in which the Geese never occupy places in either the leftmost or the rightmost column. This is interesting because most reasonably competent players like to move the Geese so that they straddle a horizontal row whenever possible. But if the Geese do this, a cunning Fox can force them into a wider variety of positions than occurs in our strategy, so that the Geese then need to know a lot more about the game to be certain of winning. In fact a competent Fox can force the Geese into positions of all the types A,B,C,D,E, no matter what winning strategy they adopt. However, only if they adopt our strategy is he unable to force them into any other position in which they need open their eyes because their action cannot be automatic. Since our strategy is the only one with as few as five positions in which the Geese need to take a decision, it is the unique *minimal* winning strategy.

Many people who think they know winning strategies can be caught out every now and then by a clever Fox who seduces them into an unfamiliar part of the game. In fact it takes considerable skill to play the Fox against ordinary players so as to exploit to the full any deficiencies in their knowledge. We can give few hints here beyond remarking that the Fox should stay near to the Geese and try to bring them into the middle of the board around him before stepping sideways to slip through any gap they may leave at either side. The best starting position is from the square near to the Geese and directly below the **X** of Fig. 2 (and so two squares right of **X** in position *F*), but position *F* itself is also useful.

THE SIZE OF THE GEESE'S ADVANTAGE

Since the loser in Fox and Geese is the first player unable to move, we should be able to apply the general theory of the rest of the book and evaluate the size of the advantage for the Geese, at least approximately. Is it perhaps $\frac{1}{2}$ of a move? Or maybe ↑? More probably it is some very complicated value about which we can say little of any use.

The answer is something of a surprise, in that we can evaluate the advantage very precisely indeed, and it turns out to have a rather unusual nature. Let us show first that the advantage is strictly greater than 1 move. To see this, of course, we play the game

Fox and Geese − 1

(with the Geese being Left), and show that the Geese can still win. The new game is just Fox and Geese in which the Fox is allowed to pass just once in the game (i.e., when he moves in the component −1). In fact it seems that this allowance is not of very much use to the Fox, and in almost all positions it will only help the Geese if the Fox passes.

However, the analysis illustrated in Fig. 4 shows that our minimal strategy no longer works, because it often makes heavy use of parity to keep the Fox out of the way. In Fig. 4_1, for instance, the Fox might be in the position nearest the Geese and then stay there in Fig. 4_2, making the move to Fig. 4_3 illegal. But such antics are not of much use, and in every case the Geese can survive, although they need to know about a larger number of positions. It even appears that the Geese can allow the Fox to pass arbitrarily many times, provided that he does not pass on two successive moves. In any case, these remarks are enough to show that

Fox and Geese > 1.

We now argue that on the other hand we have

Fox and Geese < 2.

The idea is that the Fox waits until the Geese are very near the top of the board, and then passes twice in succession. The Geese are then forced to advance past him, and the Fox can slip between them and wait until they lose by being jammed at the top of the board. It would be very difficult to give a formal proof of this, because of the very great number of possible moves for the Geese. However, if the Fox hugs the barrier formed by the Geese and seizes any opportunity to get past, all but a few moves of the Geese from any given position are plainly disastrous, and the Geese will necessarily advance in a fairly straight formation. It seems that the Fox can then arrange to move into an advantageous position, perhaps *H* or *I* of Fig. 6. In position *H* he should pass twice, as soon as the Geese have moved, and when they have moved from position *I*, the

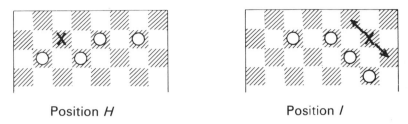

Position *H*   Position *I*

Figure 6. When Should the Fox Pass?

Fox makes one of the indicated moves and then passes twice. Of course this does not amount to a formal proof, but the interested reader should play a few games for himself to see how very easy it is to force such a position, if the Geese haven't in fact lost much earlier. A complete proof should not be difficult, but would certainly be very long, since there are many tedious cases to consider. We prefer to suppose that the above argument will convince the reader.

Obviously, the next value to examine is $1\frac{1}{2}$. The tree for $-1\frac{1}{2}$ appears as Fig. 7, and shows that the game

$$\text{Fox and Geese } - 1\tfrac{1}{2}$$

is Fox and Geese in which the Fox (Right) is allowed to pass twice, and the Geese may also pass, but only once, and only provided that the Fox has not yet passed.

Figure 7. Minus One and a Half.

We need not examine this any further. The Geese obviously can't afford to waste time by passing just when they need all the moves they can get to stop the Fox slipping through, so they will not be amused at our suggestion that they might like to do so. It might have been some use to allow them to pass *after* the Fox's first pass, because then their problem is that they are forced to move past him, but of course this is exactly what we don't intend to permit. So $1\frac{1}{2}$ is too big.

Exactly the same argument shows that $1\frac{1}{4}$, $1\frac{1}{8}$, etc., are also too big. The Geese will only be insulted by the suggestion that they be allowed to pass up to three times (say) provided they do so before the first of the Fox's allowance of two passes. But Fig. 8 shows that this is equivalent to subtracting $1\frac{1}{8}$ from the game. It is plain that we can now assert that

$$1 < \text{Fox and Geese} < 1 + \frac{1}{2^{n}}$$

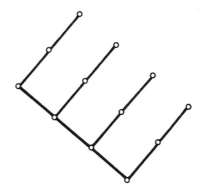

Figure 8. Minus One and One Eighth.

for all $n = 0,1,2,3,\ldots$. In other words, Fox and Geese is only greater than 1 by an infinitesimal amount.

It's amusing that we can say such a thing about a real-life children's game, but of course we need not stop with this assertion. We know many games that are positive but smaller than every positive number, the game ↑ being the most notorious. How does Fox and Geese compare with $1 + {\uparrow}$?

The difference

$$\text{Fox and Geese} - (1 + {\uparrow})$$

is best thought of as the game

$$\text{Fox and Geese} + {\downarrow}$$

with an additional allowance of one pass for the Fox. What should the Geese do? They plainly want to eliminate the component ↓, for we already know that a single pass for the Fox will not prevent the Geese from winning.

So before they make any move in the game of Fox and Geese proper, the Geese should move in ↓, leaving ∗, and then if the Fox doesn't do so, at the next move the Geese should replace ∗ by 0. If the Fox moves in ↓ or ∗, so much the better. So in fact

$$\text{Fox and Geese} > 1 + {\uparrow},$$

and an exactly similar argument shows that we have

$$\text{Fox and Geese} > 1 + n.{\uparrow}$$

for $n = 1,2,3,\ldots$. The point is that $n.{\uparrow}$ is an all small game, since whenever there is still a legal move for one player, so is there for the other. The Geese can therefore gobble up all the all small component before starting the game proper, and it doesn't really matter what the Fox does meanwhile—he can either idle away this time on the checkerboard or chew up some of the all small game himself, since it would be rather foolish of him to waste his free pass—but whatever he does, his retribution will come when the real game starts.

THE PARADOX

At this point, we seem to have found a contradiction. No matter who starts, a game of Fox and Geese can last at most 57 moves, since each of the four Goose pieces can advance at most seven places, and alternating with these 28 moves of the Geese there can be at most 29 moves for the Fox. But one of our theorems asserts that every finite game that is less than every positive number is necessarily less than some finite multiple of ↑, and we seem to have shown that

$$n.\uparrow < \text{Fox and Geese} - 1 < \frac{1}{2^n}$$

for all n. What is the explanation?

Perhaps the trouble lies with the admittedly rather fluid argument which purported to make it plain that the Fox could win with two passes? Or maybe he can win with two, but the extension suggesting that $1 + \frac{1}{2^n}$ was still enough is not quite so insultingly trivial after all? The arguments about 1, and $1+n.\uparrow$, seems pretty safe, but maybe we overlooked something even there?

It's easy for you to make such suggestions, but rather harder to substantiate them. I'm absolutely certain you can't beat me if I play the Geese in

$$\text{Fox and Geese} - (1 + n.\uparrow),$$

and would be prepared to bet quite a large sum that on the other hand I can win playing the Fox in

$$\text{Fox and Geese} - \left(1 + \frac{1}{2^n}\right),$$

no matter what number n you choose.

Oh, of course! I see it now! Fox and Geese isn't really a finite game at all! It's true that it can last at most 57 moves if played by itself, but we are no longer playing a single game but a sum, and when we do that the Fox may make several consecutive moves in the Fox and Geese game while the Geese are moving elsewhere. So Fox and Geese is really an infinite game, and we know from Chapter 11 that there are infinite games (even some numbers) greater than all multiples of ↑, yet still less than $\frac{1}{2^n}$ for every finite number n, for example

$$\frac{1}{\omega} = \{0|1,\tfrac{1}{2},\tfrac{1}{4},...\}.$$

We've just got to examine Fox and Geese a little more closely, that's all. Let's start by comparing it with $1 + \frac{1}{\omega}$. What does that amount to? We allow the Fox to pass just twice, as before, but this time the Geese can pass any finite number of times provided they do so before the Fox's first pass, and provided they announce when making their first pass just how many passes they intend to allow themselves. In other words, at their first pass they can choose what allowance to give the Fox from then on from the numbers $-2, -1\tfrac{1}{2}, -1\tfrac{1}{4}$, etc., in conformity with the equation

$$-1 - \frac{1}{\omega} = \{-2, -1\tfrac{1}{2}, -1\tfrac{1}{4}, \ldots \mid -1\}.$$

Just how offensive can you get? The Geese weren't amused when we offered them one or two passes under these insulting restrictions, and to offer them an unbounded number only adds injury to insult. Obviously

$$\text{Fox and Geese} < 1 + \frac{1}{\omega}.$$

Let's *see* just how offensive we *can* get, if we really try. The equation

$$-1 - \frac{1}{2\omega} = \left\{-1 - \frac{1}{\omega} \,\middle|\, -1\right\}$$

gives us a hint. For every ordinal number β, we have the equation

$$-1 - \frac{1}{2^{\beta+1}} = \left\{-1 - \frac{1}{2^\beta} \,\middle|\, -1\right\},$$

and more generally

$$-1 - \frac{1}{2^\alpha} = \left\{-1 - \frac{1}{2^\beta} \text{ (for all } \beta < \alpha) \,\middle|\, -1\right\}$$

for every ordinal number α, with β ranging over all smaller ones. We can make the following superb offer to the Geese. They can choose any ordinal number α they like, no matter how large say $\omega, \omega^2, \omega^\omega, \omega^{\omega^\omega}, \ldots$. Then whenever they pass they must replace the number by a strictly smaller one, and at their next pass by a smaller one again, and so on. There's just one small restriction which we hope they won't mind, after all this generosity. The Fox will be allowed to pass just twice, even though the Geese may have passed a million times, but would the Geese kindly not pass *after* the Fox has done so even once. The Geese's probable reaction suggests very strongly that

$$\text{Fox and Geese} < 1 + \frac{1}{2^\alpha}$$

for every ordinal number α, no matter how infinite it may be.

On the other hand, we can compare Fox and Geese with 1 plus infinite multiples of ↑. Such games exist, but even the infinite multiples of ↑ are all small games, and the argument we gave for the finite multiples of ↑ still applies. The only difference is that we can no longer give a bound for the length of time it will take the Geese to gobble up the ups. So we can strengthen our previous result to

$$1 + any \text{ multiple of } ↑ < \text{Fox and Geese} < 1 + any \text{ positive number.}$$

Even for infinite ending games such a thing can't happen. However in Fox and Geese the Fox can move infinitely many times even if the Geese don't. So Fox and Geese *isn't* an ender, even though it *is* a stopper (see Chapter 11).

PUNCHING THE CLOCK

We can make Fox and Geese into a genuine ending game by giving the Fox a kind of time clock, as in Fig. 1. At any time, the Fox's side of the clock bears a number, and whenever he moves, he must *punch the clock*—that is, replace this number by a smaller one. We could, say, restrict him to at most 100 moves by starting the clock with 100 showing. After our recent discussion, this seems much too restrictive, however, and we should allow him to choose any ordinal number, even an infinite one, to start with. Of course the Geese's clock need never show any number larger than 28, and could even be dispensed with, because a clock for the Geese is built in to the very nature of the game.

Let's call the modified game, with the Fox's clock started at α, (Fox and Geese)$_\alpha$. We've made things worse for the Fox, and so should expect

$$\text{(Fox and Geese)}_\alpha > \text{Fox and Geese.}$$

In fact we can show that

$$\text{(Fox and Geese)}_{\alpha+30} < 1 + \frac{1}{2^\alpha} < \text{(Fox and Geese)}_\alpha.$$

For, the Geese can win

$$\text{(Fox and Geese)}_\alpha - 1 - \frac{1}{2^\alpha}$$

by making use of those extremely insulting passes we offered them. Whenever the Fox punches the clock, replacing β by γ, say, the Geese make use of their pass move which replaces $-1 - \frac{1}{2^\beta}$ by $-1 - \frac{1}{2^\gamma}$. The Geese make no move in the Fox and Geese game proper, for the Fox will lose on time before they need to!

On the other hand, the Fox can win

$$\text{(Fox and Geese)}_{\alpha+30} - 1 - \frac{1}{2^\alpha}$$

in a similarly underhand way. He can keep his clock showing at least 30 more moves than the number of passes left to the Geese, and when the Geese have run out of pass moves, can win the game making use of his own two passes. This takes at most 30 moves.

So how big *is* Fox and Geese? It seems natural to regard Fox and Geese as the limit of the truncated version (Fox and Geese)$_\alpha$ as α increases indefinitely through the Class **on** of all ordinal numbers. Or in symbols

$$\text{Fox and Geese} = \text{(Fox and Geese)}_{\mathbf{on}},$$

since the name **on** is also used for the limit of all the proper ordinal numbers. The concept **on** is not really an ordinal number itself (just as ∞ is not really an integer, but the limit of the integers) but it does no harm to think of **on** as if it were the largest ordinal number (which doesn't really exist but can be thought of as the absolutely largest infinite number).

Since $\alpha + 30$ tends to **on** as α does, this makes it sensible to write

$$\text{Fox and Geese} = 1 + \frac{1}{\textbf{on}}$$

in which the left-hand side isn't a genuine game, and the right-hand side isn't a genuine number! Although our argument doesn't amount to a formal proof, it seems very likely that this equation holds exactly in the loopy game sense of Chapter 11.

There is a famous mathematical argument called the Burali–Forti paradox, according to which there should really be a largest ordinal number. We can say that the amount by which Fox and Geese fails to be a genuine game is exactly the same as the extent to which the Burali–Forti argument is genuinely paradoxical!

EXTRAS

MAHARAJAH AND SEPOYS

As we said in the Extras to Chapter 19, there are very many games involving encirclement, often mixed with various forms of capture. The name Fox and Geese, for example, has also been used for various games played on the English Solitaire board (Chapter 23) a couple of which are described in the Extras to Chapter 19. Most of these games are typified by a considerable numerical imbalance between the opposing forces. This is compensated by much greater mobility of the numerically inferior pieces. An extreme example is Maharajah and Sepoys which is played like ordinary Chess. White has a standard set of 16 pieces, starting from their usual positions, while Black has a single piece, the Maharajah, who starts on any unoccupied square and can move like a Chess Queen *or* a Chess Knight. The object of both sides is checkmate, of either the White King or the Maharajah. As in most of these games the Lord is on the side of the big battalions, and White wins with correct play.

Other games, where the forces are more equal in number and character are mentioned in Chapter 22.

REFERENCES AND FURTHER READING

Robert Charles Bell, Board and Table Games from Many Civilizations'', Oxford University Press, London, 1969.

Maurice Kraitchik, "Mathematical Recreations", George Allen and Unwin, London, 1943.

Fred. Schuh, "The Master Book of Mathematical Recreations", transl. F. Göbel, ed. T. H. O'Beirne, Dover, N.Y., 1968. Chapter X: Some Games of Encirclement, pp. 214–244.

Chapter 21

Hare and Hounds

I like the hunting of the hare
Better than that of the fox.
                    Wilfred Scawen Blunt, *The Old Squire*.

THE FRENCH MILITARY HUNT

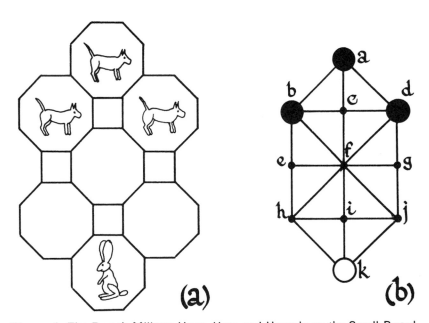

Figure 1. The French Military Hunt. Hare and Hounds on the Small Board.

This little game is very like Fox and Geese. It features a hunter whose three hounds (dogs) try to trap a hare (rabbit) on the board shown in Fig. 1(a). If you can't persuade enough animals to make the right manoeuvres, you can play with four coins on the nodes of the equivalent board shown in Fig. 1(b). It becomes more interesting on the larger board of Fig. 2. At each

647

turn the hunter moves any one hound to a neighboring empty place, and the hare makes a similar move. However the hounds, starting from the top, may not retreat, although a hound may go back and forth horizontally as between *e* and *f* in Fig. 1(b). The hare is completely free to advance or retreat or move horizontally. The hounds win by trapping the hare so that he cannot move at his turn. If the hounds fail to advance in ten consecutive moves, the game is usually declared a win for the hare.

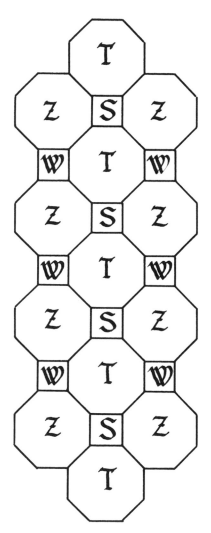

Figure 2. The Larger Board, With Four Types of Place.

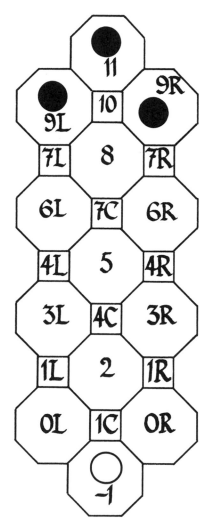

Figure 3. The Larger Board, Numbered for the Trace.

TWO TRIAL GAMES

If you want to see how the game goes, first set up the board and watch an expert hunter against a novice hare:

hounds: *abd cbd fbd fed fhd fhg fhj ihj* (wins)
hare: *k   i   j   g   j   i   k*

First game.

The chase looks so easy that the novice decides to direct the hounds in pursuit of an expert hare:

hounds: *abd cbd fbd fed feg fhg fig eig fig fij*
hare: *k   j   i   h   k   j   k   j   k   h*

Second game.

and now the hare will escape by *e* or *f*.

If expert hounds chase an expert hare on Fig. 1, who wins? And what if the hare makes the first move? Or starts from a different place? (See the Extras.) And (when you've become more expert) what about Fig. 3?

HISTORY

According to Lucas the game (on Fig. 1) was popular among French military officers in the nineteenth century. Some say it was invented by Louis Dyen; others attribute it to Constant Roy. It was solved by Lucas (1893) and Schuh (1943) and popularized (again) by Martin Gardner (1963). Schuh's analysis was based on a list of 18 classes of winning positions for the hounds (reproduced in the Extras) and he recognized that "the opposition" plays a key role, but he had no exact definition for it. In a later section we'll give a definition which simplifies the game on Fig. 1 and also allows us to solve that on Fig. 3.

THE DIFFERENT KINDS OF PLACE

Let's look at the board more closely. There are really two types of octagon: central ones (T in Fig. 2) and side ones (Z). There are also two types of square: central squares (S) and side squares (W). Except near the very top or bottom of the figure, each T or Z is next to at least one place of every other type, but each W or S is only next to octagons, T and Z. Since W and S are never adjacent, it's sometimes convenient to lump them together into a single class, N. Of the three types T, Z and N, every place, even the ones at the top and bottom, is next to at least one place of each other type, but to none of its own type. The letters correspond to remainders after division by 3 of the numbers from Fig. 3:

| Remainder Zero : Z |
| Remainder oNe : N = Weak or Strong |
| Remainder Two : T |

In Fig. 3 the difference of two numbers in adjacent places is always 1 or 2.

The sum of the numbers occupied by the four animals is an important property of the position; we call it the **trace**. Every move changes the trace by 1 or 2. If the hounds succeed in trapping the hare at the bottom of the board, then the hounds are at 0, 1, 0 against the trapped hare at −1 and the trace is 0. If instead the hounds trap the hare on the side of the board, say at 1L, then the hounds end on 3, 2, 0 against the hare on 1, and the trace is 6. It can easily be checked that

> No matter where
> You trap the hare,
> The trace you'll see
> Divides by *three*

TRIALITY TRAPS!

THE OPPOSITION

The best way for the hounds to make their trap is to move so that they leave the trace a multiple of 3 at every turn. We call this "keeping the opposition". If they do this, the hare's move must be to a non-multiple of 3, because it changes the trace by 1 or 2. But whenever the trace is not divisible by 3 the hunter usually has a choice of several hound moves which restore it to a multiple of 3, and among these he should find one which restores a winning position.

> Threefold traces
> Win most chases.

KEEPING THE OPPOSITION

If you check the traces for our first game, with the board numbered as in Fig. 4, you'll see that the hounds always kept the opposition:

hare:	*k*	*i*	*j*	*g*	*j*	*i*	*k*
hounds:	*cbd*	*fbd*	*fed*	*fhd*	*fhg*	*fhj*	*ihj*
trace:	9	9	6	6	3	3	0

Since the hare doesn't want to be trapped, he doesn't want the hunter to move to positions whose trace is divisible by 3. The best way to prevent this is for the hare to grab the opposition by moving to such a position himself. Then any hound move will change the trace to a non-multiple of 3 and the hare is likely to be able to regrab the opposition. This is the way the hare won our second game. The hounds blundered on their second move by playing from 4 to 2, giving a trace of 8, and from then on the hare managed to retain the opposition at every turn:

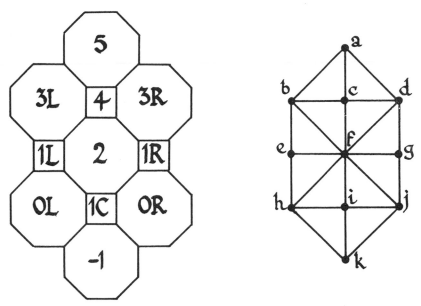

Figure 4. The Board Numbered for Determining the Opposition.

hounds:	*abd*	*cbd*	*fbd?*	*fed*	*feg*	*fhg*	*fig*	*eig*	*fig*	*fij*
hare:	*k*	*j*	*i!*	*h*	*k*	*j*	*k*	*j*	*k*	*h*
trace:	10	10	**9**	6	3	3	3	3	3	3

So whoever can move to a position whose trace divides by 3 is said to have the opposition. The opposition is certainly a valuable commodity which both players desire. But it's not all there is to the game, because sometimes the *hounds* may have the opposition but be unable to keep it without letting the hare escape behind them. In other cases the *hare* may have the opposition for several moves, but then lose it because the hounds block his only moves to places which would restore it. However, such positions are rather rare, and the average player who combines the principle with a little commonsense will usually trap a novice hare on the small board. An annotated example appears on p. 652.

WHEN HAS THE HARE ESCAPED?

He has **escaped** if he has passed or is passing two hounds, unless he is on a *square* place (W or S) and the hounds can immediately occupy the neighboring octagons (Z or T) aside or ahead of him.

Although he may have not escaped, the hare is **free** in some other positions in which the hounds can never force him to retreat. This certainly happens if he's strictly passed a hound and is not on a Weak (W) square, or, if he's on a central octagon (T) and is past or passing at least one hound.

Third Game

Hounds	Hare	Trace	Comments
3L, 5, 3R	−1	10	
3L, 4, 3R		9	Taking the opposition
	0R	10	
2, 4, 3R		9	⎰A novice hunter might have moved 4 to 2, giving a "solid" ⎱ position, but losing the opposition.
	1C	10	
2, 3L, 3R		9	⎧The other "reasonable" move, 3R to 1R, changes the trace by ⎨the wrong amount. Since the move from 2 to 1 would allow ⎩the hare to escape, there's really only one choice.
	−1	7	
1C, 3L, 3R(!)		6	⎧Because the hounds can't retreat, they can never increase the ⎪trace by 2, so to gain the opposition they must decrease 7 to 6 ⎨by moving a hound from 2 to 1. A move to 1R or 1L won't lose, ⎪but wastes time, since the hare can force the hounds back to ⎩the present position position by going to 1C.
	0R	7	
1C, 2, 3R		6	⎰The other two moves (3R to 2, 1C to 0L) that restore the trace ⎱to 6 would let the hare escape.
	−1	5	
1C, 2, 4(!)		6	⎧Once again, the other moves (3 to 1, 2 to 0) keeping the opposi- ⎨tion would let the hare escape, leaving only this unlikely ⎩looking move.
	0R	7	
0L, 2, 4(!)		6	⎰4 to 3R repeats; 2 to 1 allows escape; only 1C to 0L makes ⎱progress
	1R	7	
0L, 2, 3R		6 ⎱	
	0R	5 ⎬	Obvious
0L, 2, 1R		3 ⎰	
	−1	2	Hare's last gasp.
0L, 0R, 1R		0	The novice hunter might now lose by playing from 1R to 0R.
	1C	2	
0L, 0R, 2		3	⎰The only time the hounds reach a trace larger than their ⎱previous one.
	−1	1	
0L. 0R. 1C		0	Wins.

LOSING THE OPPOSITION

To analyze the exceptional positions, when someone wins in spite of not having the opposition, it's best to consider the types of place the animals occupy. For example, all the positions where the hounds have just won are of type Z^2NT, meaning that 2 animals are on Z places, 1 on N and 1 on T.

Some of the exceptional cases arise from the difference between the Strong and the Weak types of N places. Each Strong (central) N square is next to *four* other places, while each Weak (side) square is next to only three. Other things being equal, an animal should prefer a Strong place to a Weak one, since both make the same contribution to the opposition; but the Strong place is likely to offer him more choices later. For example, one exceptional case arises when the hounds move to Fig. 5. Despite the fact that the hounds have the opposition (trace 3), the

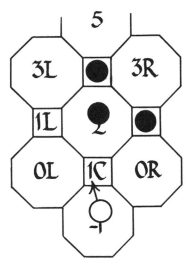

Figure 5. An Exceptional Hare and Hounds Position.

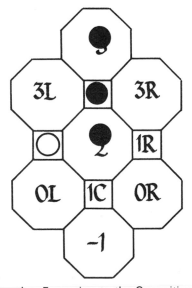

Figure 6. Another Exception to the Opposition Principle.

hare wins by playing to 1C, because now the only hound moves which keep the opposition let the hare escape. In some sense this N^2T^2 position loses because the hound at 1R is on a Weak square. On the other hand, we saw in our third game that a hare on -1 has no defence against hounds on 4C, 2, 1C (another N^2T^2 position). Unless the hare has passed one or more hounds, S^2T^2 wins for the hounds, but SWT^2 often loses.

As another example, suppose the *hare* has just moved to the position of Fig. 6. He has the opposition, but after the hound on 4C moves to 3L, the hare must retreat to 0L, losing the opposition and the game. But a hare in place 1C against these hounds would have both the opposition and a winning position. Once again, the difference between a Strong and a Weak square means the difference between winning and losing, this time for the hare.

A STRATEGY FOR THE HARE

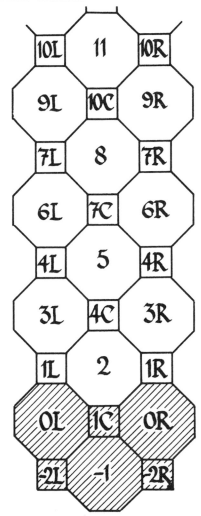

Figure 7. Keeping the Opposition on a Semi-infinite Board.

We'll show that an expert hare that has the opposition on the semi-infinite board of Fig. 7 can either keep it indefinitely or escape, unless he has to start from the **Scare'm Hare'm** position (Fig. 8). In fact the hare will always stay on the six shaded places numbered 1C, 0L, 0R, -1, -2L and -2R, unless the hounds let him out. His basic strategy is to keep the opposition.

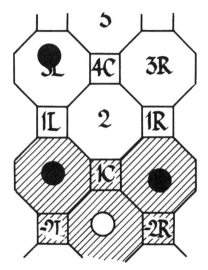

Figure 8. The Scare'm Hare'm Position.

If possible, escape or gain your freedom!
Otherwise, keep on the six shaded places, and if you can keep the opposition by a move to a non-Weak place, do so.
If a move to S(1C) is blocked, then
(A) against hounds on T^2S, move to W(-2L or -2R),
(B) against hounds on ZN^2, advance to Z (losing the opposition) on the other side of the board from the hound-occupied Z.
If a move to Z (0) is blocked,
(C) go to T (-1) (losing the opposition).

THE HARE'S STRATEGY

If these rules allow two or more moves, choose any one. If they allow none, resign (or hope for a mistake)!

First we show that if the hounds reach Fig. 8, a recent hare's move must have been of type (A), (B) or (C). For if the hounds came from a position in which they *had* the opposition, then the hare, after his last move, *didn't*, and the present position must have been reached by (B) or (C). Otherwise the hounds have come from a position whose trace was congruent to 1, mod 3, and hence from Z^2N, since they are on Z^3 in the figure. At the hare's last move 2 was vacant and either 0L or 0R was occupied by a hound. But if the hare came from 0L, 1C or 0R he could have escaped by moving to 2 and so he must have come from the Weak square -2, which he can only have reached by a move of type (A).

Suppose you've just made a move of this strategy which was not of type (A), (B) *or* (C). *Then you* have *the opposition and you're* not *on a Weak square and the table below shows that the Hare's Strategy always gives you another move, unless you're faced with the Scare'm Hare'm Position.*

To From	Z	S	T
Z	—	(A) or gain freedom by advance to T.	already free
S	escape by advance to T.	—	already free.
T	escape, since *not* Fig. 8.	(A) or (B)	—

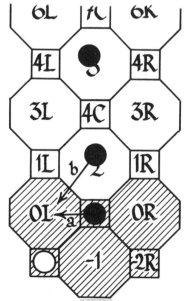

Figure 9. Position After a Move of Type (A).

Next suppose you've just made a move of type (A). Then in the next few moves you can either escape or regain the opposition by a move *not* of type (A), (B) or (C), and from which the hounds can't immediately move to Fig. 8. This is because when (A) is applied, the Strong square 1C must be occupied and also two central octagons (not including − 1 because the hare has not escaped); see Fig. 9. Now the only way the Hare's Strategy can lose the opposition from an N square is by a move of type (C) after a hound moves to 0L. But after move (a) in Fig. 9 the hare regains the opposition, while after move (b) he soon escapes. The hounds can't reach the Scare'm Hare'm Position in time.

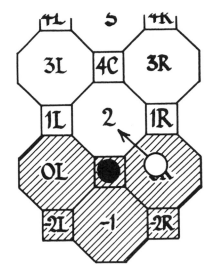

Figure 10. Position After a Move of Type (B).

Now suppose you've just made a move of type (B) (Fig. 10). Then you threaten to escape by moving to the empty T place ahead of you. If the hounds fill this from N, you escape by advancing to W, and if a hound from Z fills it you can reacquire the opposition by retreating to T. The hounds can't straight away reach the Scare'm Hare'm Position.

Finally, *if you've just made a move of type* (C), and were on a Strong square, *both* adjacent Z's must be occupied and you could have escaped. So you were on a Weak square and we have already discussed the situation following your previous move, which must have been of type (A).

ON THE SMALL BOARD

The Hare's Strategy shows that if they don't have the opposition the hounds can only win on the small board by keeping a hound on 5 until they can grab the opposition by moving him to 4 or 3. If they move first from 3L, 5, 3R the hounds can beat a hare starting anywhere except 4. Here is a sample game.

Hounds	Hare	Remarks
3L, 5, 3R	1C	(Or the hare could start on 1L or 1R.)
3L, 5, 2		
	−1	If instead to 0, the hounds take the opposition by moving from 5 to 4.
1L, 5, 2		
	1C	If instead to 0, the hounds take the opposition by moving from 5 to 3.
0L, 5, 2		
	−1	If instead to 0, the hounds take the opposition by moving from 5 to 4.
1C, 5, 2		
		Now, since there is no place −3 on this board, the hare is forced to give the hounds the opposition and the game.

ON THE MEDIUM AND LARGER BOARDS

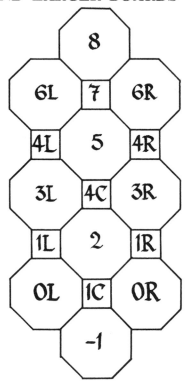

Figure 11. The Medium Board

By a slight extension of this argument, the hounds, moving from 6L, 8, 6R on the Medium Board (Fig. 11) can trap a hare starting on −1, 0, 2, 3 or 5. Since they have the opposition they can certainly win on the Small Board got by dropping numbers −1, 0 and 1 (Fig. 1). The hare on 2 may reach one of the positions of Fig. 12, forcing the hounds to give him the opposition in return for his retreat, but it is too late, since the hounds can play to 3L, 5, 3R, which wins for them, even without the opposition, because places numbered −2 are not on the board. What if the hare now goes to 0L? See the Extras.

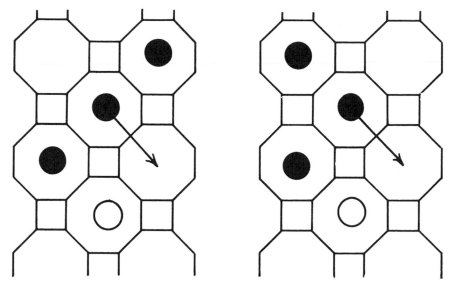

Figure 12. A Sound Bound for a Hound?

It is interesting that the hounds win if the configuration of Fig. 12(a) occurs at 3L, 5, 6R against 2, but not if it is higher (on the Larger Board of Fig. 3) at 6L, 8, 9R against 5. After the hound moves from 8 to 6, the Hare snatches the opposition by retreating to 3 and then follows his Strategy, but using the next set of six squares (4C, 3L, 3R, 2, 1L and 1R) up the board.

It should now be clear that the Hare's Strategy can be improved. If the Hare doesn't have the opposition, he should try to reach a position like 5 against hounds on 6L, 8, 9R (all such positions have trace 28). The way to force the hounds to move into such a position is to move to one whose trace is larger than the desired one by a small multiple of 3. In fact we can prove that

---

on the Larger Board (Fig. 3) the
hounds can win from a position
of trace 31 only if the Hare is on a
Weak square or the position is
6, 10, 11 *versus* 4C (Fig. 13).

THE THIRTY-ONE THEOREM

The proof is sketched in the Extras.

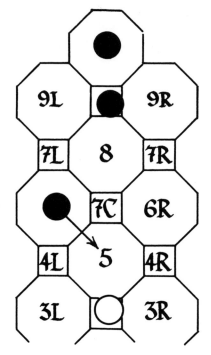

Figure 13. The Hound-Dog Position.

EXTRAS

ANSWERS TO QUESTIONS

Against the hounds placed as in Fig. 1, the hare can win only if he starts at *c* and requires the hounds to start first.

With the hounds on 9L, 11, 9R in Fig. 3 the hare can win from any position provided he has first move. The hardest case is when he starts on 1C, so that the hounds have the opposition. He wins by playing to 2 and using the Thirty-one Theorem. Of course if he *starts* on 2 he plays to the Strong square 4C *and* gains the opposition.

If the hounds move first they can win *only* if the hare starts on -1. They must play with great care, not only maintaining the opposition but also preventing the hare from escaping or achieving the trace 31. Surprisingly, even though it gains the opposition, the opening move from 11 to 10 loses! The difficulty is that if the hare advances via 0, 1 and 3 to 5, the hounds must then be able to reach 6L, 10, 6R. The defence 6L, 7, 6R is unattainable against a hare who is determined to keep the trace at least as high as 27. The defence 6L, 7R, 9R fails when the hare moves from 5 to 7C, forcing the 7R hound to occupy 8, and then retreats to 5 again and wins as in Fig. 12. If the hounds try to prevent the hare from reaching 5 by occupying 5, 9, 10, say, when the hare is on 3, then he escapes via a weak 4. But how can the hounds reach 6L, 10, 6R if the hare plays via 0, 1 and 3 to 5? They must have come from 6, 8, 10 if they had the opposition with the hare on 3; but where were they before that with the hare on 1? There is no position leading to 6, 8, 10 in which they had the opposition!

A SOUND BOUND FOR A HOUND?

If the hare is 0L and the hounds are on 3L, 5, 3R, how do they win? Answer 3R to 2. If hare takes the opposition by going to -1 then 2 to 0R, and if hare to 1C, then 3L to 2. If hare to -1 again, 0R to 1C wins; the trick is to hold back the hound on 5 until they're ready for the kill.

ALL IS FOUND FOR THE SMALL BOARD HOUND

In this chapter we've normally taken the point of view of the hare. To redress the balance, Figs. 14 and 15, which are adapted from Figs. 92 and 93 on pp. 241, 243 of Fred. Schuh's Master Book of Mathematical Recreations, show all the winning positions for the hounds on the Small Board. Figure 14 is a minimal set of 24 $\mathscr{P}$-positions (hounds win if hare has to move) which will ensure victory in all the positions the hounds deserve to win. Figure 15 shows 13 other $\mathscr{P}$-positions for the hounds which they can use for variety in seeking to hide their strategy from inquisitive hares. In each of the 37 positions the hare's place is indicated by a number, the remoteness function for the position.

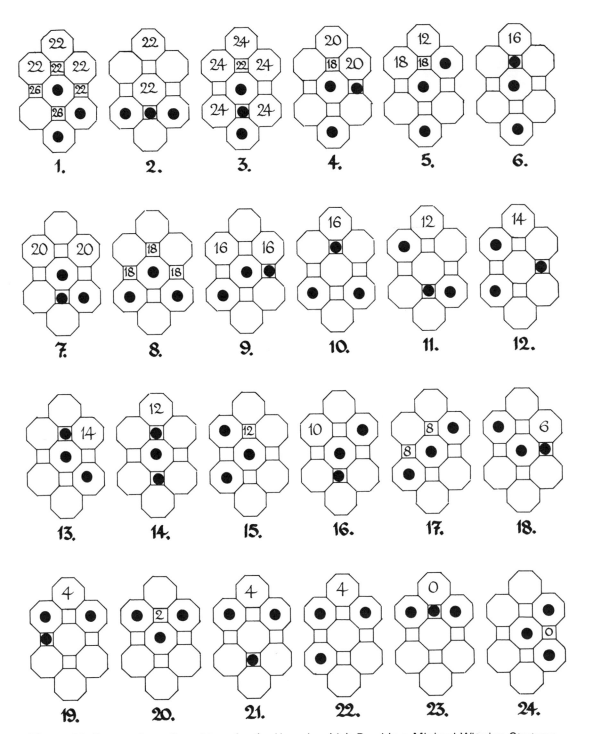

Figure 14. Twenty-four $\mathscr{P}$-positions for the Hounds which Provide a Minimal Winning Strategy.

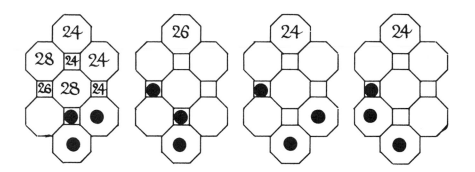

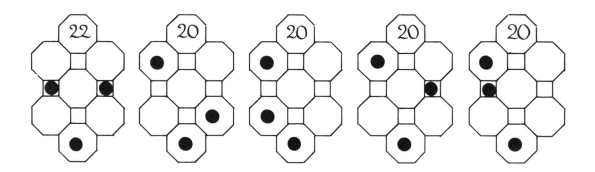

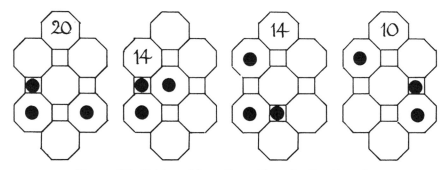

Figure 15. Thirteen More 𝒫-positions for the Hounds.

Table 1 gives a winning strategy for the hounds, based on the 20 $\mathscr{P}$-positions of Fig. 14. The remarks are listed here (L and R are *hare's*; in Figs. 14, 15 left and right are the *hounds'*):

(a) the hounds do not have the opposition, but the hare is now forced to 1R, whereupon the hounds go to 3R, 5, 2 (position 1, reflected), still without the opposition, but the hare is forced again. After he goes to 0R, the hounds to go 3R, 4, 2 (position 7, reflected).

(b) also without the opposition, but see position 4.

(c) still without the opposition, but see position 5.

(d) even now the hounds don't have the opposition, but (position 6) the hare is forced to a zero place and the hounds go to position 13 or its reflexion.

(e) if now or later the hare goes to −1, play as from position 18: the hound on 2 goes to 0, (position 21 or 22), and then the rear hound comes to 2 (position 20).

From:	if hare plays on:	hounds reply by moving to:			arriving at:	with remoteness:	and trace:	Remarks
initial	4,1R,1C,0,−1	3L	5	2	1.	26,26,22,22,22	14,11,11,10,9	
position	2	3	4	3	2.	22	12	
1.	3R	4	5	2	3.	24	14	(a)
	−1	1L	5	2	4.	20	7	(b)
1. or 2.	0	3L	4	2	7.	20	9	
	1	3	2	3	8.	18	9	
4.	1C!	0L	5	2	5.	18	8	(c)
	0	1L	3R	2	9.	16	6	
5.	−1!	1C	5	2	6.	16	7	(d)
	0R	0	4	2	16.	10	6	
6.	0L	1C	3L	2	13.	14	6	
7.	1!	3	3	2	8.	18	9	
	−1	3L	4	0R	11.	12	6	
8.	0	1L	2	3R	9.	16	6	
	−1	3	1C	3	10.	16	6	
9.	−1!	1L	3R	0R!	12.	14	3	
	1	0L	2	3R	17.	8	6	
10.	0L	3L	1C	2	13.	14	6	
11.	0L	2	4	0R	16. refl.	10	6	
	1C	3L	2	0R	17. refl.	8	6	
12.	1C	2	3R	0R	15.	12	6	
	0L	1L	2	0R	18.	6	3	
13.	−1	4	1C	2	14.	12	6	
	1L?	3L	0L	2	trapped!	0	6	
14. or 15.	0L	4	0R	2	16. refl.	10	6	(e)
16.	1	3R	0L	2	17.	8	6	(e)
17.	0R	1R	0L	2	18. refl.	6	3	(e)
18.	−1	1L	0	0	19.	4	0	
	1C	0	0	2	20.	2	3	
19.	1C	2	0	0	20.	2	3	
20.	−1	1C	0	0	trapped!	0	0	

Table 1. A Winning Strategy for the Hounds Using Just the Positions of Figure 14.

PROOF OF THE THIRTY-ONE THEOREM

The hounds can only keep the opposition from a position of trace 31 by moving to 30 (a move to 33 would involve an illegal retreat). If they go to 30, the hare will move to 31 if he can; the hounds will move back to 30 and the hare will win by repetition. The hounds can only win by getting the hare on to a Weak square, or by preventing him from moving to 31. How might they do that? If the hare is on r, the hounds must be blocking any strong neighboring place $r+1$. Suppose the other hounds are on x and y where $x+y \leqslant 11+10$.

$$r + (r + 1) + x + y = 30,$$

$2r+1 \geqslant 9$, $r \geqslant 4$. If $r \geqslant 8$, $x+y \leqslant 13$ and the hare has escaped.

If $r=7$, a hound must be blocking 8, $x+y=15$, and, unless the hare has escaped, $x=6$, $y=9$. The hare moves to 5 and reaches Fig. 12.

If $r=6$, a Z place, the hounds must be blocking 7C and also $x=8$, to prevent escape, so $y=9$. The hare plays to 5. If the hounds restore the trace to 30 the hare returns to 6 and wins by repetition.

If $r=5$, a T place, the hounds must be blocking 6L, 6R and $y=13$, off the board.

If $r=4$ and not a Weak square, the hare is on 4C. A hound must be blocking 5, so $x+y=21$, $x=10$, $y=11$. This is the exceptional Hound-Dog Position (Fig. 13) which the hare can't win. If he goes to 3, the hound on 10 moves to 8. If the hare then moves to 4R, a hound moves from 8 to 6R forcing hare to retreat to 3R, after which the hound moves from 11 to 10C and regains control.

REFERENCES AND FURTHER READING

Martin Gardner, Mathematical Games: About two new and two old mathematical board games, Sci. Amer. **209** #4 (Oct. 1963) 124–130.

Martin Gardner, "Sixth Book of Mathematical Games from Scientific American", W.H. Freeman, San Francisco, 1971, Ch. 5.

Édouard Lucas, Récréations Mathématiques, Blanchard, Paris, Vol. III, 1882, 1960, 105–116.

Sydney Sackson, "A Gamut of Games", Random House, 1969.

Frederick Schuh, Wonderlijke Problemen; Leerzam Tijdverdrijf Door Puzzle en Spel, W.J. Thieme & Cie, Zutphen, 1943, 189–192.

Frederick Schuh, "The Master Book of Mathematical Recreations" (transl. F. Göbel, ed. T.H. O'Beirne) Dover Publications, New York, 1968, 239–244.

Chapter 22

Lines and Squares

And I say to them, "Bears,
Just look how I'm walking in all of the squares!"
And the little bears growl to each other, "He's mine,
As soon as he's silly and steps on a line."
A.A. Milne, *When We Were Very Young.*

On the square, to the left, was elegantly engraved in capital
letters this sentence: ALL THINGS MOVE TO THEIR END.
François Rabelais, *Pantagruel,* V, 37.

If you find you're bored to pieces with our other games, you should find your board and pieces to play these ones. The chapter contains several old friends and some new ones, but we'll avoid the really grown-up games like Chess and Go.

TIT-TAT-TOE, MY FIRST GO,
THREE JOLLY BUTCHER BOYS ALL IN A ROW

Oxford Book of Mother Goose Rhymes, 1951, p. 406.

The game is more usually known as Tic-Tac-Toe, or Noughts-and-Crosses, depending on which side of the Atlantic you are. Whoever moves first puts a cross (**X**) in one of the nine spaces in the board of Fig. 1. His opponent then puts a nought (**O**) into any other space and then they alternate **X**'s and **O**'s in the remaining empty spaces until one player wins by getting three of his own kind on one of the eight lines of Fig. 2. If teacher isn't listening he then shouts a suitably

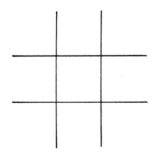

Figure 1. Tic-Tac-Toe Board.

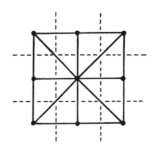

Figure 2. Its Eight Lines.

667

triumphant phrase, which in some parts of America is

"Tic-Tac-Toe, three in a row",

and, in Holland, according to Fred. Schuh, is

"Boter, melk en kaas, ik ben de baas".

When neither player is able to make a line we have a tied game. We have no doubt that most of our readers were bright enough as children to discover that this always happens when the game is properly played, and only the authors of books like *Winning Ways* retain sufficient interest to study the game in any detail.

But have you ever tried a complete analysis? If so, you've probably found that it took more space than you first thought it should. Later on we'll give a more concise analysis than most, though we admit that our rough work took more than one sheet of paper. But first let's look at three non-board games.

MAGIC FIFTEEN

In this game the players alternately select numbers from 1 to 9 and no digit may be used twice. You win by getting three numbers whose sum is 15. This game was suggested by E. Pericoloso Sporgersi.

SPIT NOT SO, FAT FOP, AS IF IN PAN!

                                                is a sentence for which we are indebted to Anne Duncan. It suggests the following game. Write the nine words on nine separate cards and have the two players alternately select cards, a player winning if he can collect all the cards which contain a given letter. This game was suggested by Leo Moser's game of **Hot** in which the nine words were HOT, FORM, WOES, TANK, HEAR, WASP, TIED, BRIM, SHIP, and the winner must collect *three* words with a common letter.

JAM

John A. Michon's game of **Jam** is played on Fig. 3. The players alternately select roads (straight lines) and whoever manages to take all the roads through a town wins.

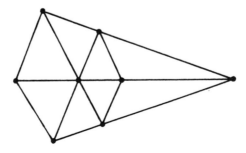

Figure 3. A Jam Board.

HOW LONG CAN YOU FOOL YOUR FRIENDS?

We'll bet you can fool most of them for quite a long time, playing any one of the above games. But they're all Tic-Tac-Toe in disguise, so you should be able to make the right moves while they are floundering! You can see why these games are all the same by arranging the numbers for Magic Fifteen as a magic square (Fig. 4(a)); the words for Spit, Etc. as in Fig. 4(b); and naming the towns or numbering the roads for Jam as in Fig. 4(c). For Hot you can prove the same thing by writing the words on Fig. 1 in the order we gave them. Can you find a better sentence than Anne's, possibly using redundant letters as in Hot? It would be nice if the words of your sentence could be written across the board in order!

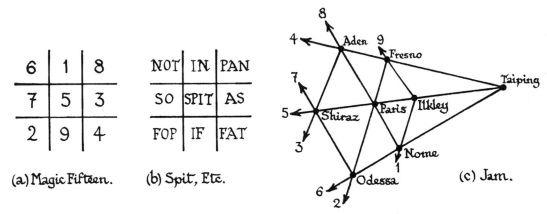

Figure 4. The Game's the Same By Any Name.

ANALYSIS OF TIC-TAC-TOE

For convenience we number the board as in Magic Fifteen and suppose by symmetry that the first move (**X**) is in 5 (Fig. 5), 6 (Fig. 6) or 7 (Fig. 7). We'll also suppose that each player is sensible enough to

(a) complete a line of his kind if he can, and
(b) prevent his opponent from doing so on his next move.

In the analysis,

bold numbers represent such **forced** moves,
! denotes a move that's better than some others,
? denotes a move that's worse than some others,
X denotes a win for Cross,
O denotes a win for Nought,
⊗ denotes a tied game,
~ denotes an arbitrary move, and
v. is a cross-reference to another column in the analysis.

The plays are given in numerical order, apart from the convention about the initial digit.

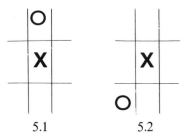

Figure 5. Starting in the Centre.

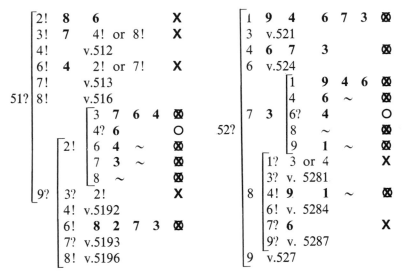

```
      ⌈2!  8    6                 X
      │3!  7    4! or 8!          X
      │4!       v.512
      │6!  4    2! or 7!          X
      │7!       v.513
  51? │8!       v.516
      │                   ⌈3  7  6  4  ⊗
      │                   │4? 6        O
      │             ⌈2!   │6  4  ~     ⊗
      │             │     │7  3  ~     ⊗
      │             │     ⌊8     ~     ⊗
      │         9?  │3?   2!              X
      │             │4!   v.5192
      │             │6!   8  2  7  3  ⊗
      │             │7?   v.5193
      ⌊             ⌊8!   v.5196
```

```
      ⌈1  9  4      6  7  3  ⊗
      │3  v.521
      │4  6  7      3        ⊗
      │6  v.524
      │                   ⌈1     9  4  6  ⊗
      │                   │4     6  ~     ⊗
  52? │7  3         6?    │8        ~     ⊗ ... 
      │                   │        4        O
      │                   ⌊9     1  ~     ⊗
      │             ⌈1?   3 or 4            X
      │             │3?   v. 5281
      │         8   │4!   9     1  ~     ⊗
      │             │6!   v. 5284
      │             │7?   6              X
      │             ⌊9?   v. 5287
      ⌊9  v.527
```

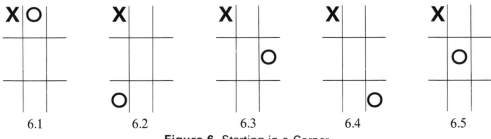

Figure 6. Starting in a Corner.

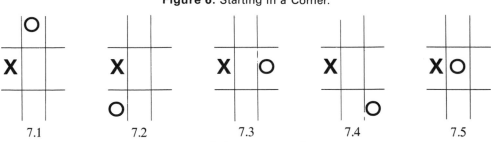

Figure 7. Starting on a Side.

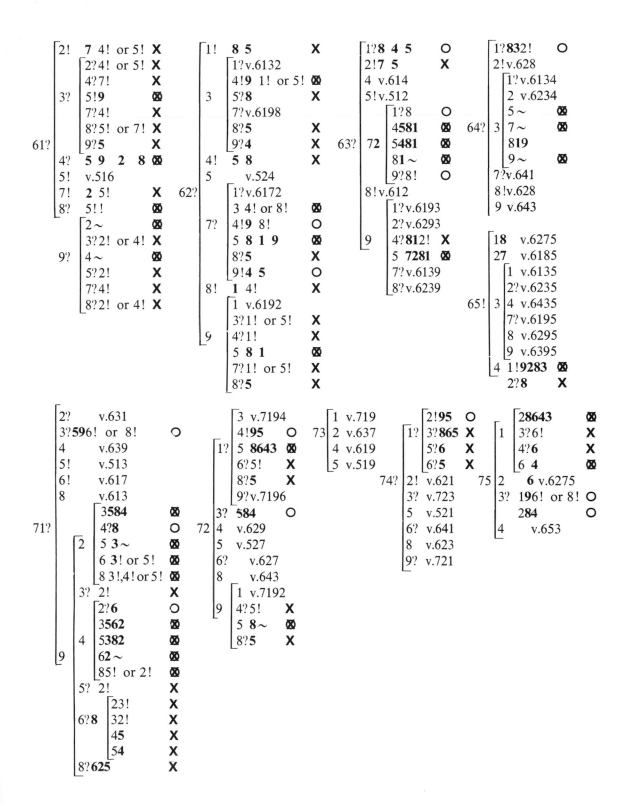

```
61?  2!  [ 7  4! or 5!      X
          2?4! or 5!        X
          4?7!              X
     3?  [ 5!9              ⊠
           7?4!             X
           8?5! or 7!       X
           9?5              X
     4?   5 9  2  8         ⊠
     5!   v.516
     7!   2 5!              X
     8?   5!!               ⊠
     9?  [ 2~               ⊠
           3?2! or 4!       X
           4~               ⊠
           5?2!             X
           7?4!             X
           8?2! or 4!       X


     1!   8 5               X
     3   [ 1?v.6132
           4!9 1! or 5!     ⊠
           5?8              X
           7?v.6198
           8?5              X
           9?4              X
     4!   5 8               X
     5       v.524
62?  7?  [ 1?v.6172
           3 4! or 8!       ⊠
           4!9 8!           O
           5 8 1 9          ⊠
           8?5              X
           9!4 5            O
     8!   1 4!              X
     9   [ 1 v.6192
           3?1! or 5!       X
           4?1!             X
           5 8 1            ⊠
           7?1! or 5!       X
           8?5              X


          1?8 4 5           O
          2!7 5             X
          4 v.614
          5!v.512
63?  72 [ 1?8               O
          4581              ⊠
          5481              ⊠
          81~               ⊠
          9?8!              O
          8!v.612
     9  [ 1?v.6193
          2?v.6293
          4?812!   X
          5 7281   ⊠
          7?v.6139
          8?v.6239


          1?832!            O
          2!v.628
     3  [ 1?v.6134
          2 v.6234
          5~                ⊠
     64?  7~                ⊠
          819
          9~                ⊠
          7?v.641
          8!v.628
          9 v.643

          18   v.6275
          27   v.6185
        [ 1 v.6135
          2?v.6235
     65! 3 4 v.6435
          7?v.6195
          8 v.6295
          9 v.6395
        4 1!9283            ⊠
          2?8               X


          2?      v.631
          3?596! or 8!      O
          4       v.639
          5!      v.513
          6!      v.617
          8       v.613
        [ 2 [ 3584          ⊠
              4?8           O
              5 3~          ⊠
              6 3! or 5!    ⊠
              8 3!,4!or 5!  ⊠
          3?  2!            X
          4 [ 2?6           O
              3562          ⊠
71?     9     5382          ⊠
              62~           ⊠
              85! or 2!     ⊠
          5?  2!            X
          6?8 [ 23!         X
                32!         X
                45          X
                54          X
          8?625             X


          3 v.7194
          4!95              O
     1? [ 5 8643            ⊠
          6?5!              X
          8?5               X
          9?v.7196
     3?   584               O
72   4    v.629
     5    v.527
     6?    v.627
     8     v.643
     9  [ 1 v.7192
          4?5!             X
          5 8~             ⊠
          8?5              X


        1 v.719
73    2 v.637
        4 v.619
        5 v.519


        1? [ 2!95           O
             3?865          X
             5?6            X
             6?5            X
74?     2!  v.621
        3?  v.723
        5   v.521
        6?  v.641
        8   v.623
        9?  v.721


        1 [ 28643           ⊠
            3?6!            X
            4?6             X
            6 4             ⊠
75    2     6 v.6275
        3?  196! or 8!      O
            284             O
        4      v.653
```

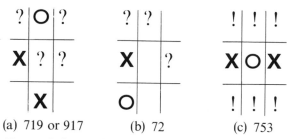

(a) 719 or 917   (b) 72   (c) 753

Figure 8. Lesser Known Byways of Tic-Tac-Toe.

In "The Scientific American Book of Mathematical Puzzles and Diversions" Martin Gardner remarks (and we agree) that many players have the mistaken impression that because they are unbeatable they have nothing more to learn. He gives three examples (Fig. 8) showing how a master player can take the best possible advantage of a bad play. In Fig. 8(a) **X**'s last move was chosen so as to give **O** four losing chances out of six (the Enough Rope Principle). Against **X**'s opening of 7, Gardner recommends **O** to reply with 2 since this offers **X** three losing chances (Fig. 8(b)). In Fig. 8(c) **O** can let **X** choose his move for him, since it is impossible for **O** to play without setting a winning trap!

OVID'S GAME, HOPSCOTCH, LES PENDUS

In his *Ars Amatoris*, Ovid advises young women to learn certain games to amuse their lovers. He mentions in particular a certain *ludus terni lapilli* played on a *tabella* which is conjectured to be a moving form of tic-tac-toe, played with 3 black pebbles and 3 white ones. Several such games are known to have been popular in ancient China, Greece and Rome and in medieval England and France.

In the version nowadays known as **Ovid's Game**, the players take turns placing their pebbles on the board until all 6 are down. If neither player has won by getting the 3 of his kind in a row they continue playing by moving on each turn a single one of their pebbles to any orthogonally adjacent square. The first player has a sure win by playing in the centre:

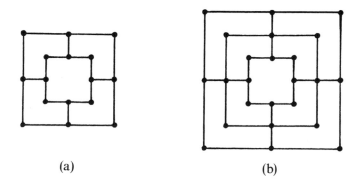

(a)   (b)

Figure 9. Six and Nine Men's Morris Boards.

$$5! \begin{bmatrix} 1 \ 4 \ 6 \ 8 \ 3, \ 4 \ \text{to} \ 9, \ \text{any}, \ 9 \ \text{to} \ 2, \ \text{or} \\ 2 \ 1 \ 9 \ 4 \ 6, \ 1 \ \text{to} \ 8, \ \text{any}, \ 5 \ \text{to} \ 3, \end{bmatrix}$$

so the central opening is usually forbidden, making the game a draw. However, the loopiness of the game allows many variations to occur in a single play and the game teems with traps.

We will use the name **Three Men's Morris** for the version in which, in the moving part of the game, the players are allowed any chess king move along the 8 lines of Fig. 2. An American Indian version, which has been called **Hopscotch**, allows any king move, whether on the 8 lines or not. It is a draw, even when the central opening move is allowed, as is the French version, **Les Pendus**, in which a pebble can be moved to *any* empty space.

SIX MEN'S MORRIS

is played on the board of Fig. 9(a). Each player has 6 counters and the game has two phases as in Ovid's Game. First the counters are placed alternately by the two players. Then the counters are moved from one of the 16 nodes to an adjacent one along a line of the board. If a player gets three in a row he removes an opposing counter. A player wins when he reduces the opposing force to two counters.

NINE MEN'S MORRIS

is played similarly with 9 counters for each player on a square or rectangular board designed as in Fig. 9(b). When a player forms a **mill** (gets three in a row) he again removes an opposing counter, but is not allowed to take one from an opposing mill. There are a number of variations and many names (Merrilees, Morelles, Mill, Mühle); see the books of R.C. Bell or H.J.R. Murray for details.

THREE UP

This is a vertical three-in-a-row game. Each player starts with six checkers of his own color. They play alternately by putting a checker onto the table or onto a previous stack, and each tries to complete a stack three high of his own color. When all the checkers are placed, the players continue by alternately transferring single checkers of their own color from the top of one stack to the top of another, or possibly onto the table. At no time may any stack be more than three high.

It's very easy for a skilled player to beat a novice at this game, which has many cunning features. But Vasek Chvátal has shown that if you never try to win (by putting two of your pieces in a stack) then you can't lose! For if your opponent has set up t ($\geqslant 1$) threats (stacks beginning with two of his pieces) then he can cover at most $6 - 2t$ of your checkers, so you have at least $2t$ uncovered ones—more than enough to deal with his threats.

FOUR-IN-A-ROW

It's clear that the first player can get 1-in-a-row on a 1×1 board, and 2-in-a-row on a 2×2 board, and we have seen that he can't get 3-in-a-row on a 3×3 board, but it's not hard to show

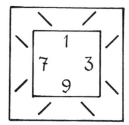

Figure 10. Four-in-a-Row is a Second Player Tie on a 5×5 Board.

that he can get 3-in-a-row on any bigger board, even with just one extra square. How big a board is needed to get 4-in-a-row? C.Y. Lee observes that the second player can tie on a 5 × 5 board. His strategy is to play as in Tic-Tac-Toe whenever the first player plays in the central 3 × 3 square. You won't have too much difficulty if you remember this and note that when you play in the squares marked with a diagonal line in Fig. 10 you sabotage your opponent's chance of getting 4-in-a-row on the border, and also on a diagonal involving two of the squares 1, 3, 9 and 7.

Lustenberger has used a computer to show that 4-in-a-row is a win for the first player on a 4 × 30 board.

By far the most interesting and popular version is the 3-dimensional one, played on a 4 × 4 × 4 cube. Oren Patashnik has shown that the first player can always win at 4 × 4 × 4 **tic-toc-tac-toe**. Patashnik's solution now includes a computerized dictionary of several thousand openings. This dictionary was obtained by patient and skilful interaction between Patashnik and a computer over a period of many months. It is too large to be accessible other than by computer. Several skeptical computer scientists have recently examined Patashnik's dictionary and it is now accepted as complete and correct.

FIVE-IN-A-ROW

It's quite a good game just to try to get 5 in a row orthogonally or diagonally on any reasonably large board. Mathematicians will prefer to play **Five-in-a-Row** on an infinite board.

In this kind of game there are several well defined degrees of threat and when playing with children and good friends it's nice to announce these by suitable cries. We recommend

SHOT! for a threat to win next move, e.g.

SHOTS! for two or more SHOTs at once, e.g.

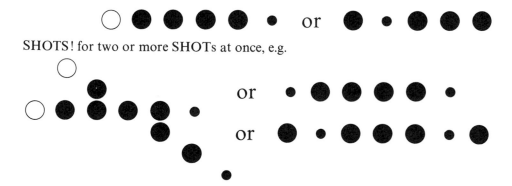

POT! if you can guarantee a SHOT next move, e.g.

● ● ⬤ ⬤ ⬤ ● ●   or   ● ⬤ ● ⬤ ⬤ ● ⬤ ●

POTSHOT! for a POT and a SHOT at the same time, e.g.

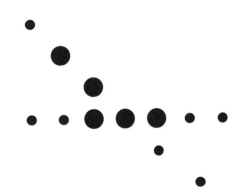

  and

POTS! for two or more POTs at once, e.g.

These can be of great help in understanding the effects of forced moves, for example:

A SHOT, typically a line of 4 open at one end, must be blocked instantly. So a pair of SHOTS wins next move.

A POT, typically a line of 3 open at both ends, must either be blocked immediately or staved off with a SHOT. So a POTSHOT wins unless possibly the move that blocks the SHOT is a countering SHOT. Against a pair of POTS you can only hope to defend by making a sequence of SHOTS until one of them happens to block one of the POTS.

These terms can be applied to many games of this type, for instance in 4-in-a-row,

○ ⬤ ⬤ ⬤ ●

is a SHOT and

● ● ⬤ ⬤ ● ●

is a POT. Similar cries are used in Phutball (see later in this chapter); there are obvious connexions with the notion of *remoteness* in Chapter 9.

Five-in-a-row has been called Go-Bang in England for at least a hundred years and has more recently been called Pegotty or Pegity (Parker Bros., U.S.A.).

GO-MOKU

In Japan there are several perfect players who can always claim their win in their version, **Go-Moku**, of 5-in-a-row on a Go board, size 19×19, even though the first player is handicapped by not being allowed to make the **fork threat** of a pair of open lines of 3 (we'd cry POTS! for this) and *six* in a row is *not* counted as a win.

SIX, SEVEN, EIGHT, NINE, ..., IN A ROW

A.W. Hales and R.I. Jewett have produced an ingenious pairing strategy which shows that many games of this type are tied or drawn. For instance here is a quick proof that 5-in-a-row is tied on a 5×5 board. All you have to do is to make sure that for every move of your opponent in a marked square in Fig. 11 you take the similarly marked square in the direction indicated by the mark. So you could give her the centre square *and* let her make the first move as well. If the position you're presented with already satisfies the condition, make a random move. At the end of the game there will be at least one of your counters in every conceivable winning line.

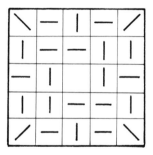

Figure 11. A Hales-Jewett Pairing.

You can see that 9-in-a-row is a draw on an infinite board with the Hales–Jewett pairing of Fig. 12. When your opponent takes the cell at one end of a line in the figure, you take the one at the other. The result was first proved in 1954 by Henry Oliver Pollak and Claude Elwood Shannon, using the following strategy. Tile the board with H-shaped heptominoes: the second player plays ordinary tic-tac-toe in each of these regions, concentrating on preventing a line of 3 in either a diagonal, or the horizontal, or the right vertical. John Lewis Selfridge also gave a Hales–Jewett pairing on an 8×8 board, which could be used to tile an infinite one and give the same result.

T.G.L. Zetters (nom de guerre of some Amsterdam combinatorists) recently showed that the second player can even draw 8-in-a-row. Their proof uses a parallelogram-shaped tile of 12 cells, and goes some way towards showing that 7-in-a-row is also a draw.

Figure 12. Nine-in-a-Row is a Draw on an Infinite Board.

S.W. Golomb has found a Hales–Jewett pairing for 8-in-a-row on an $8 \times 8 \times 8$ cube. It will be easier to explain if we first describe the analogous two-dimensional solution for 6-in-a-row on a 6×6 square. Figure 13(a) is like Fig. 11 except that you may reply to a move on a diagonal with *any* other move on the same diagonal. Note that the figure has the mirror symmetries indicated by the two thick lines, so it would suffice to indicate only one quadrant as in Fig. 13(b).

Figure 14 indicates one octant of Golomb's $8 \times 8 \times 8$ pairing in a similar way. The symbols —, | and \ are in the horizontal layer shown, while ● is all you can see of a vertical line. The arrows pierce the layers and represent lines of obvious directions in various diagonal planes. The three mid-planes of the $8 \times 8 \times 8$ cube (represented by the thick lines in Fig. 14) are reflecting planes and, as in the 6×6 pairing of Fig. 13, you may respond to *any* move on a body diagonal with another on the same diagonal. In fact Golomb can give you *any* six cells on *each* of the four body diagonals *and* allow you to have first move and still tie the game.

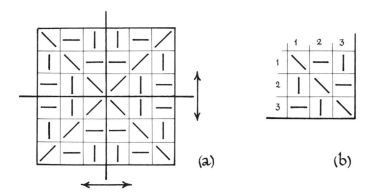

Figure 13. A Pairing for Six-in-a-Row on a 6×6 Board.

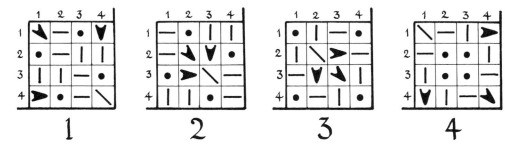

Figure 14. Golomb's Pairing for Eight-in-a-Row on an 8×8×8 Cube.

n-DIMENSIONAL k-IN-A-ROW

Hales and Jewett consider the game of k-in-a-row on the n-dimensional

$$k \times k \times k \times \ldots \times k$$

board. They prove that if k is sufficiently large, namely

$$k \geqslant 3^n - 1 \qquad (k \text{ odd}) \text{ or}$$
$$k \geqslant 2^{n+1} - 2 \quad (k \text{ even})$$

the game is tied by a suitable pairing strategy, and on the other hand that if n is sufficiently large compared to k, it is a first player win by the strategy stealing argument described below. They conjecture that the game is tied if there are at least twice as many cells as lines.

How many lines are there? Leo Moser has remarked that each line is determined by either one of the two cells which extend it into the surrounding

$$(k+2) \times (k+2) \times (k+2) \times \ldots \times (k+2)$$

cube, so that the total number of lines is exactly

$$\tfrac{1}{2}\{(k+2)^n - k^n\}.$$

The Hales–Jewett conjecture is therefore that the game is tied whenever

$$k^n \geqslant (k+2)^n - k^n,$$

i.e.

$$2k^n \geqslant (k+2)^n.$$

So it should be true if $k \geqslant 3n$, for example; Leo Moser has proved that it's true if $k > cn \log n$ for some constant c.

STRATEGY STEALING IN TIC-TAC-TOE GAMES

For almost all forms of tic-tac-toe game there is a strategy stealing argument which shows that the second player cannot have a winning strategy. Though earlier authors probably knew it, this was formally proved by Hales and Jewett. We suppose that each player has an indefinite supply of his own kind of piece, that the pieces don't move after they're once put down, and that each player's aim is to produce a winning configuration with some of his pieces.

The assertion is that all such games in which the winning configurations for the two players are similar, are either wins for the first player or are tied under best play. For if the second player had a winning strategy, then the first player could steal it as follows. After a random first move he could pretend to *be* the second player, ignoring his opening move and making a random move whenever the stolen strategy would otherwise repeat a move already made. We conclude that if the second player had a winning strategy, so would the first, since an additional piece on the board can never harm him! Obviously *both* players can't win at once, so the supposed winning strategy for the second player cannot exist.

The argument applies to n-in-a-row on any shape of board, provided no special restrictions, like those of Go-Moku, are added. In this case the winning configurations are just the appropriate lines of n, and are exactly the same for each player.

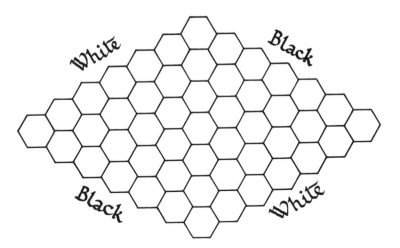

Figure 15. A 7×7 Hex Board.

However, in the most notorious cases of strategy theft the winning configurations are not identical but related by a symmetry of the board (and so are still *similar*). These are, in chronological order,

HEX,

played on a rhombus of hexagons like that of Fig. 15. Black wins if his pieces connect one pair of opposite sides of the board and White if his connect the other pair.

Hex was invented by Piet Hein and the strategy stealing argument found by Nash.

BRIDGIT

(or Gale) is played on two interlaced n by $n+1$ lattices. Left joins two adjacent (horizontal or vertical) spots of the black lattice and Right makes similar moves in the white one. No two moves may cross. In Fig. 16 Left has just won since he has formed a chain connecting a topmost spot to a bottommost one. Bridgit was invented by David Gale and its strategy stealing argument by Tarjan.

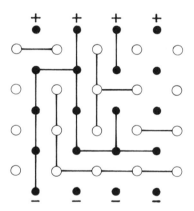

Figure 16. Left Forms a Black Chain in Bridgit.

HOW DOES THE FIRST PLAYER WIN?

In these cases, as in the examples considered by Hales and Jewett, it is impossible for a completed game to be tied, so that the argument actually proves that the first player can win, but does not give much help in finding an explicit winning strategy for him. No explicit strategy for Hex is known, and Tarjan and Even have shown that, in the technical sense, generalized Hex is hard. But for Bridgit an explicit pairing strategy was found by Oliver Gross, and many other strategies can be deduced from Alfred Lehman's subsequent theory of

THE SHANNON SWITCHING GAME

which generalizes Bridgit. It is played on a graph representing an electrical network in which certain nodes are labelled + and some others are labelled −. Each edge (begin the game with them drawn in *pencil*) represents a permissible connexion between the nodes at its ends. *Mr. Shortt*, at his move may *establish* one of these connexions permanently (*ink over* a pencilled edge) and attempts to form a chain between some + node and a − one. His opponent, *Mr. Cutt* may permanently *prevent* a possible connexion (*erase* a pencilled edge) and tries to separate + from − forever. Figure 17(a) shows a Shannon game equivalent to our Bridgit one. You can always suppose that there's only one positive node and one negative one by making identifications as in Fig. 17(b).

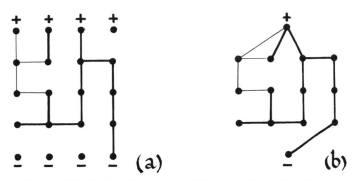

Figure 17. Bridgit Played as a Shannon Switching Game.

Supposing this, Lehman has proved that Mr. Shortt can win as second player if and only if he can find two edge-disjoint trees which each contain all the nodes of some subgraph containing + and − . The "only if" part is hard, but there's an easy strategy which proves "if": whenever Mr. Cutt's move separates one of the trees into two parts, *A* and *B*, Mr. Shortt makes a move on the other tree joining a vertex of *A* to one of *B*.

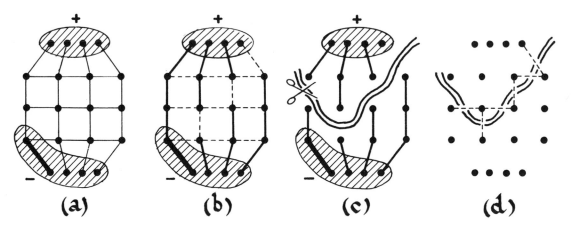

Figure 18. How Mr. Shortt Wins a Game of Bridgit.

Let's use Lehman's theory to show how the first player, who should regard himself as Mr. Shortt, can win in Bridgit. After his first move (Fig. 18(a)) Mr. Shortt (who's now *second* in line to move) can see the two edge-disjoint trees indicated by the thick and pecked lines of Fig. 18(b) (remember to regard each of the + and − sets as connected, including the node that has been Shortted to −). If now Mr. Cutt disconnects one of the trees, for example by erasing the scissored edge in Fig. 18(c), then Mr. Shortt should secure one of the six bridges (Fig. 18(d)) across the imaginary river which now separates the two parts of the tree severed by Mr. Cutt.

The game can be generalized to make the winning configurations for Mr. Shortt just those which contain a specified family P of sets of edges. (In the original game P was the family of paths from + to −.) Lehman proves the "only if" part of his theorem by taking P to be the family of all trees containing every vertex (spanning trees).

If Mr. Shortt, as second player, has a win in the modified game, it's *very* easy to see that there must be two edge-disjoint spanning trees. For since an extra move is no disadvantage, both players can play Mr. Shortt's strategy! If they do this, *two* spanning trees will be established, using disjoint sets of edges. Conversely, if two such trees exist, our previous strategy for Mr. Shortt actually wins for him as second player, even in the modified game.

The more detailed part of Lehman's argument establishes that, in a suitable sense, the modified game reduces to the original one.

THE BLACK PATH GAME

This elegant little game was invented by Larry Black in 1960. You can play it on a rectangular piece of paper ruled into squares as in Fig. 19. At any time the squares that have been used will each contain one of the three patterns shown in Fig. 19(b) and will include a path like the black path in Fig. 19(a) which begins at the starting arrow. The player to move must continue the black path by drawing one of the permissible patterns in the next square. You lose if your move makes the black path run into the edge of the board. The numbers 1 to 8 show the order of the first eight moves in our sample game, and the next player must now move in the square marked 9. You'll see that pattern 1. loses instantly, 2. wins quickly and 3. loses slowly.

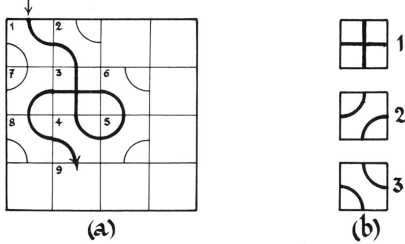

Figure 19. Forming a Black Path.

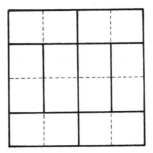

Figure 20. Black Path Game Board Divided into Dominoes.

We have a pairing strategy by which the first player can win on any rectangular board with an even number of squares. He imagines the board divided into 2×1 dominoes in any way he likes, for instance Fig. 20, and then plays so as to leave the end of the path in the middle of a domino (which can never be the edge of the board!). On an odd by odd board it is the second player who can win, by dividing all of the board except the opening square into dominoes.

LEWTHWAITE'S GAME

Domino pairing (e.g. Fig. 21(b)) also enables the second player to win a game invented by G.W. Lewthwaite in which 12 white and 12 black squares are slid alternately in a 5×5 box from the starting position of Fig. 21(a), and a player who, at his turn, cannot move any piece of his color, loses. What happens if a player is also allowed to slide a row or column of 2, 3 or 4 squares, provided both end squares are of his color?

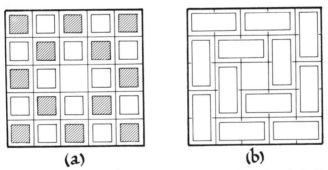

(a)　　　　　**(b)**

Figure 21. Pairing Gives a Second Player Win in Lewthwaite's Game.

MEANDER

was also invented by Lewthwaite and is also played with 24 tiles in a 5×5 box, but the tiles are now patterned as in Fig. 22(a), and are slid by either player. Figure 22(b) shows the starting position. The winner is the first player to produce a continuous curve connecting the boundary to itself and involving at least three tiles, as in Fig. 22(c). There are two versions of the game. In the first, players alternately slide just one tile; in the other, a row or column of 1, 2, 3 or 4 tiles may be slid as a single move.

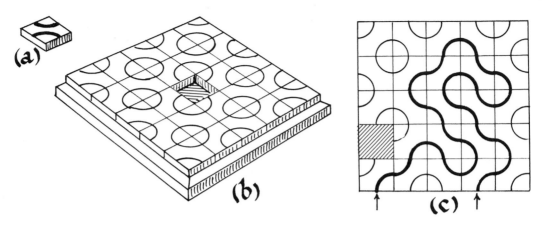

Figure 22. Meander.

WINNERS AND LOSERS

Frank Harary has proposed a family of games, one for each polyomino, P, all played on an infinite board. On alternate turns, Left makes a square black, and Right makes one white, and Left's aim is to produce a black copy of P, while Right tries to foil him. Harary calls P a **winner** if Left has a winning strategy—otherwise a **loser**.

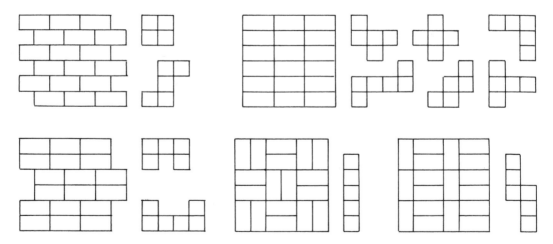

Figure 23. Hales–Jewett Pairings Make Twelve Polyomino Losers.

The twelve polyominoes of Fig. 23 can be proved to be losers using the indicated Hales–Jewett pairings, mostly found by Andreas Blass. If P contains one of these it is therefore a loser. The only polyominoes *not* containing one of these twelve are the twelve shown in Fig. 24. Eleven of these are known to be winners, with known strategies which win in m moves on a $b \times b$ board (see the figure). The last, called "snaky" by Harary, is also conjectured to be a winner.

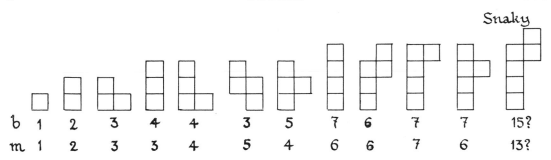

Figure 24. Twelve Polyomino Winners with Board Sizes and Numbers of Moves
(but Snaky's is a bit shaky).

DODGEM

Colin Vout invented this excellent little game played with two black cars and two white ones on a 3 × 3 board, starting as in Fig. 25(a). The players alternately move one of their cars one square in one of the three permitted directions (E, N or S for Black; N, E or W for White) and the first player to get *both* of his cars off the board wins. Black's cars may only leave the board across its right-hand edge and White's cars only leave across the top edge. Only one car is permitted on a square, and you lose if you prevent your opponent from moving.

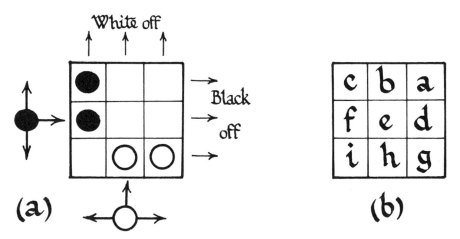

Figure 25. Colin Vout's Game of Dodgem.

Although the board is the same size as that for Tic-Tac-Toe, this game is much more interesting to play. Table 1 contains the outcome of every position; the column gives the positions of the black cars, the row those of the white, labelled by pairs of letters from Fig. 25(b). A blank entry represents an illegal position, since only one car is allowed on each square.

+ is a win for Black (Left),
− is a win for Right (White),
○ is a win for the second player,
∗ is a win for the first player.

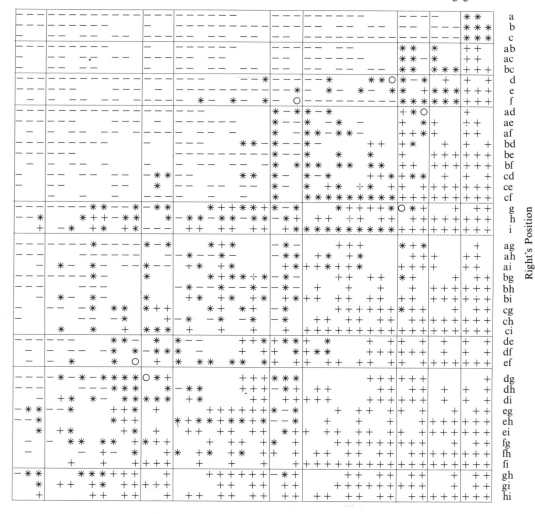

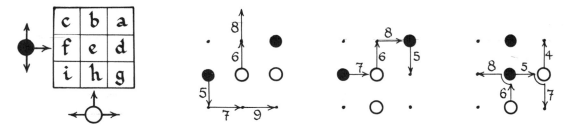

Table 1. Outcomes of Positions in Dodgem and Some Good Moves.

If you haven't got our table drawn on the back of your hand, you'll find this little game hard to play against an expert, who'll spring all sorts of little traps for you. It's often *not* a good idea to push your car off as soon as you can since it may be more useful blocking your opponent. In many situations it's a good idea to aim for the top right hand corner.

When you are expert, you can try playing Dodgem with $n-1$ cars of each color, on an $n \times n$ board, starting in the first column and row, with the SW corner empty.

DODGERYDOO

This game is played with two Dodgem cars on a quarter-infinite board. Now either player may move either car any distance North or West in a single move, provided it does not jump on to or over the other car. If you can't move you lose.

It's not hard to see that

> any position in which
> the two cars are
> on neighboring squares
> is a $\mathcal{P}$-position,

because whatever the next player does you can continue to shadow him. As a consequence,

> any other position with
> the cars in the
> same row or column,
> or in adjacent ones,
> is an $\mathcal{N}$-position,

because the next player can immediately creep one car up to the other. So in analyzing later positions we might as well make it illegal to have both cars in the same row or column, or in adjacent ones.

Let (x_1, y_1) and (x_2, y_2) be the positions of the two cars in this restricted game. Then on these numbers we are playing a nim-like game with four heaps in which we can reduce any one of the four numbers x_1, x_2, y_1, y_2 provided we ensure that neither $x_1 - x_2$ nor $y_1 - y_2$ is 0 or ± 1. Since the x's and the y's don't interact, we can regard this as the sum of two games, one played on the x's, the other on the y's. Table 2 gives the nim-values for either of these games—apart from the positions described in the boxes above. An X denotes an illegal position in the restricted game.

> The position (x_1, y_1), (x_2, y_2)
> is a Dodgerydoo $\mathcal{P}$-position
> just if $f(x_1, x_2) = f(y_1, y_2)$,

(since their nim-sum is then 0), where $f(x_1, x_2)$ is the function given in Table 2.

x_1 \ x_2	0	1	2	3	4	5	6	7	8	9	10	11	12	13	14	15	16
0	X	X	0	1	2	3	4	5	6	7	8	9	10	11	12	13	14
1	X	X	X	0	1	2	3	4	5	6	7	8	9	10	11	12	13
2	0	X	X	X	3	1	2	6	4	5	9	7	8	12	10	11	15
3	1	0	X	X	X	4	5	2	3	8	6	10	7	9	13	14	11
4	2	1	3	X	X	X	0	7	8	4	5	6	11	13	9	10	12
5	3	2	1	4	X	X	X	0	7	9	10	5	6	8	14	15	16
6	4	3	2	5	0	X	X	X	1	10	11	12	13	6	7	8	9
7	5	4	6	2	7	0	X	X	X	1	3	11	12	14	8	9	10
8	6	5	4	3	8	7	1	X	X	X	0	2	14	15	16	17	18
9	7	6	5	8	4	9	10	1	X	X	X	0	2	3	15	16	17
10	8	7	9	6	5	10	11	3	0	X	X	X	1	2	4	18	19
11	9	8	7	10	6	5	12	11	2	0	X	X	X	1	3	4	20
12	10	9	8	7	11	6	13	12	14	2	1	X	X	X	0	3	4
13	11	10	12	9	13	8	6	14	15	3	2	1	X	X	X	0	5

Table 2. Dodgerydoo Values, $f(x_1, x_2)$.

There doesn't seem to be much pattern in the table, once we get away from the edge, but at least the first few rows (and columns) are arithmetico-periodic. The (ultimate) periods and salt-uses in the first five rows are 1, 1, 3, 9, 36, and are valid outside the heavy line. The same table solves two-car Dodgerydoo in three dimensions, for which the $\mathscr{P}$-position condition becomes

$$f(x_1,x_2) \stackrel{*}{+} f(y_1,y_2) \stackrel{*}{+} f(z_1,z_2) = 0.$$

PHILOSOPHER'S FOOTBALL

or PHUTBALL (registered J.H. Conway) for short, is a very playable game that you can read about for the first time in this book. It is usually played on the 15×19 intersections of the board shown in Fig. 26, or on a 19×19 Go board, using one black stone (the **ball**) and a large supply of white ones (**men**). All pieces are common to both players and indeed both players have the same legal moves although their aims are different.

Start with the pitch empty except for the ball which starts at the central spot. Then each player, when he moves, must

> either place a new man at any unoccupied intersection
> *or*   **jump** the ball, removing the men jumped over.

(He may not do both.)

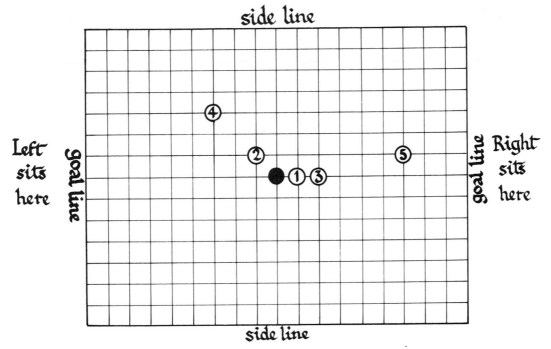

Figure 26. The Phutball Pitch and the First Five Moves of a Game.

A single jump of the ball may be in any of the eight standard compass directions, N, NE, E, SE, S, SW, W, NW on to the first empty point in that direction provided at least one man is jumped over. All the men jumped over are removed instantly. A player may take several consecutive such jumps in various of the eight directions as a single move. But because the men are removed instantly, the same man cannot be jumped over more than once in a move, and no man can be placed on the board in a jumping move.

It is legal for the ball to land on any of the goal lines or side lines. It is also legal for the ball to leave the board, but only by jumping over a man on the goal line, and only as the last move of the game. In fact Left's aim is to arrange that at the *end* of a move the ball is either *on or over* Right's goal line, while Right's is to get it on or over Left's. However a defender can sometimes successfully use his own goal line by jumping the ball onto and off it during a single move.

In the standard opening,

Left, Right, Left, Right, Left,

will place the stones

1, 2, 3, 4, 5,

of Fig. 26, building chains towards their opponents' goals. Right is now frightened by Left's threat to make a long jump over 1 and 3 and later establish a chain through 5. He therefore makes two short jumps himself over 2 and 4.

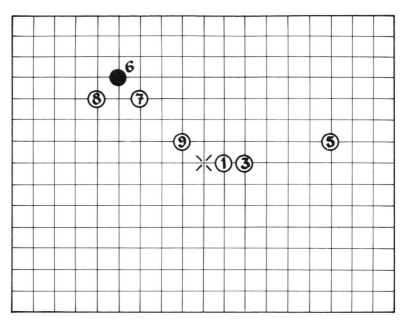

Figure 27. The Next Four Moves.

In the subsequent moves

7, 8, 9,

of

Left, Right, Left,

Left tries to reëstablish his chain while Right prepares the way for a sideways jump to defend against this. If it were Left's turn to move in Fig. 27 he could in one move make two jumps over 7 and 9 and a longer jump over 1 and 3 (it would probably be better for him not to make this last jump; as in Chess, a threat is often more powerful than its execution). However, it's Right's turn so he jumps over 8, and the next few moves are shown in Fig. 28.

These are all rather subtle. Left's move 11 is much better than reïnstating 8, which Right could too easily **tackle** by placing a man where the ball was in Fig. 27 (after a jump of these two stones, Left would find it very difficult to reëstablish a useful connexion with the rest of his chain). Right's move 12 is even more subtle! A direct threat to win at this point would make Left jump over 11 and 7, and arrive at a commanding position. Move 12 provides a way back after this jump and also prepares the way for a move at 14, followed by a roundabout triple jump over 11, 12 and 14, which both gets Right near to the Left goal line and removes some pieces useful to his opponent. The move 12 has even more hidden secrets: if Left places 13, *Right* can make the jump over 11 and 7, and then any Left threat to connect with his old chain equally helps Right to connect with 13 and 12.

Almost all these moves have become standard, but from now on experts differ. The game has many subtle tactics (tackling, poisoning one's opponent's threats, devastating U-turns, ...), and we'll only offer a few hints.

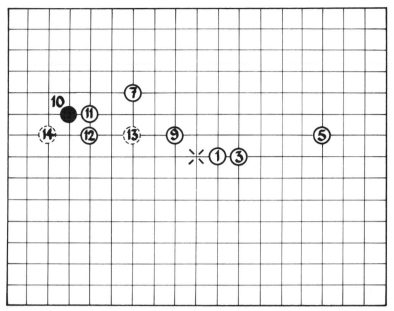

Figure 28. The Game Continues.

Try not to jump until you really have to, and then only as far as you really must. If you will have a stone within three of the place your opponent will jump to, but *not* a knight's move away, you can probably use it to get back and needn't be too frightened by his jump (which he probably shouldn't be making!). Remember that a stone a knight's move away from the ball is almost always useless. Such stones are called **poultry** (a corruption of paltry and parity). A threatened chain becomes much more useful if it can be jumped along in several different ways. Don't forget that the stone you place may be useful to your opponent—possibly in a devastating U-turn.

A pleasing feature of the game is that an expert can still enjoy a game against a novice provided they start with the ball much nearer the expert's goal-line.

Like Chess and Go, and unlike most of the games in this book, Phutball is *not* the kind of game for which one can expect a complete analysis.

EXTRAS

REFERENCES AND FURTHER READING

William N. Anderson, Maximum matching and the game of Slither, J. Combinatorial Theory Ser. B, **17** (1974) 234–239.

Charles Babbage, Passages from the Life of a Philosopher, Longman, Green, Longman, Roberts and Green, London, 1864; reprinted Augustus M. Kelley, New York, 1969, pp. 467–471.

J.P.V.D. Balsdon, Life and Leisure in Ancient Rome, McGraw–Hill, New York. 1969, pp. 156 ff.

A.G. Bell, Kalah on Atlas, in D. Michie (ed.) "Machine Intelligence, 3", Oliver & Boyd, London, 1968, 181–193.

A.G. Bell, "Games Playing with Computers", George Allen & Unwin. London, 1972, pp. 27–33.

Robert Charles Bell, "Board and Table Games from Many Civilizations", Oxford University Press, London, 1960, 1969.

Richard A. Brualdi, Networks and the Shannon Switching Game, Delta, **4** (1974) 1–23.

Gottfried Bruckner, Verallgemeinerung eines Satzes über arithmetische Progressionen, Math. Nachr. **56** (1973) 179–188; M.R. **49** #10562.

L. Csmiraz, On a combinatorial game with an application to Go-Moku, Discrete Math. **29** (1980) 19–23.

D.W. Davies, A theory of Chess and Noughts and Crosses. Sci. News, **16** (1950) 40–64.

H.E. Dudeney, "The Canterbury Puzzles and other Curious Problems", Thomas Nelson and Sons, London, 1907; Dover, New York, 1958.

H.E. Dudeney, "536 Puzzles and Curious Problems", ed. Martin Gardner, Chas. Scribner's Sons, New York, 1967.

J. Edmonds, Lehman's Switching Game and a theorem of Tutte and Nash-Williams, J. Res. Nat. Bur. Standards, **69B** (1965) 73–77.

P. Erdös and J.L. Selfridge, On a combinatorial game, J. Combinatorial Theory Ser. B, **14** (1973) 298–301.

Ronald J. Evans, A winning opening in Reverse Hex, J. Recreational Math. **7** (1974) 189–192.

Ronald J. Evans, Some variants of Hex, J. Recreational Math. **8** (1975–76) 120–122.

Edward Falkener, "Games Ancient and Oriental and How to Play Them", Longmans Green, London, 1892; Dover, New York, 1961.

G.E. Felton and R.H. Macmillan, Noughts and Crosses, Eureka. **11** (1949) 5–9.

William Funkenbusch and Edwin Eagle, Hyperspacial Tit-Tat-Toe or Tit-Tat-Toe in four dimensions, Nat. Math. Mag. **19** #3 (Dec. 1944) 119–122.

David Gale, The game of Hex and the Brouwer fixed-point theorem, Amer. Math. Monthly, **86** (1979) 818–827.

Martin Gardner, "The Scientific American Book of Mathematical Puzzles and Diversions", Simon & Schuster, New York, 1959.

Martin Gardner, Mathematical Games, Scientific Amer., each issue, but especially **196** #3 (Mar. 1957) 160–166; **209** #4 (Oct. 1963) 124–130; **209** #5 (Nov. 1967) 144–154; **216** #2 (Feb. 1967) 116–120; **225** #2 (Aug. 1971) 102–105; **232** #6 (June 1975) 106–111; **233** #6 (Dec. 1975) 116–119; **240** #4 (Apr. 1979) 18–28.

Martin Gardner, "Sixth Book of Mathematical Games from Scientific American", W.H. Freeman, San Francisco, 1971; 39–47.

Martin Gardner, Mathematical Carnival, W.H. Freeman, San Francisco 1975, chap. 16.

Richard K. Guy and J.L. Selfridge, Problem S. 10, Amer. Math. Monthly, **86** (1979) 306; solution T.G.L. Zetters **87** (1980) 575–576.

A.W. Hales and R. I. Jewett, Regularity and positional games, Trans. Amer. Math. Soc. **106** (1963) 222–229; M.R. **26** #1265.

Professor Hoffman (Angelo Lewis), "The Book of Table Games", Geo. Routledge & Sons, London, 1894, pp. 599–603.

Isidor, Bishop of Saville, "Origines", Book 18, Chap. 64.

Edward Lasker, "Go and Go-Moku", Alfred A. Knopf, New York, 1934; 2nd revised edition, Dover, New York, 1960.

Alfred Lehman, A solution of the Shannon switching game, SIAM J. **12** (1964) 687–725.

E. Lucas, "Récréations Mathématiques", Gauthier-Villars, 1882–1894, Blanchard, Paris, 1960.

Carlyle Lustenberger, M.S. thesis, Pennsylvania State University, 1967.

Leo Moser, Solution to problem E773 [1947,281], Amer. Math. Monthly. **55** (1948) 99.

Geoffrey Mott-Smith, "Mathematical Puzzles", Dover. New York, 1954; ch. 13 Board Games.

H.J.R. Murray, "A History of Board Games other than Chess", Oxford University Press, 1952; Hacker Art Books, New York, 1978; chap. 3, Games of alignment and configuration.

T.H. O'Beirne, New boards for old games, New Scientist, **269** (62:01:11).

T.H. O'Beirne, "Puzzles and Paradoxes", Oxford University Press, 1965.

Ovid, "Ars Amatoria", ii, 208, iii, 358.

Jerome L. Paul, The q-regularity of lattice point paths in R^n, Bull. Amer. Math. Soc. **81** (1975) 492; Addendum, ibid. 1136.

Jerome L. Paul, Tic-Tac-Toe in n dimensions, Math. Mag. **51** (1978) 45–49.

Jerome L. Paul, Partitioning the lattice points in R^n, J. Combin. Theory Ser. A, **26** (1979) 238–248.

Harry D. Ruderman, The games of Tick-Tack-Toe, Math. Teacher, **44** (1951) 344–346.

Sidney Sackson, "A Gamut of Games", Random House, New York, 1969.

John Scarne, Scarne's Encyclopedia of Games. Harper and Row, New York, 1973.

Fred. Schuh, "The Master Book of Mathematical Recreations", trans. F. Göbel, ed. T.H. O'Beirne, Dover, New York, 1968; ch. 3, The game of Noughts and Crosses.

SOLITAIRE DIAMONDS!

Twinkle, twinkle, little star,
How I wonder what you are!
Up above the world so high,
Like a diamond in the sky!
         Jane Taylor, *The Star*.

We are all in the dumps, For diamonds are trumps;
The kittens are gone to St. Paul's.
The babies are bit, The Moon's in a fit,
And the houses are built without walls.
       Nursery Rhyme.

If you've followed everything in *Winning Ways* so far, you're probably finding it hard to get people to play with you, so will need something to do on your own. Here are our favorite solitaire diamonds:

The classical games of Peg Solitaire, treated by old and new methods in Chapter 23.

A host of puzzles, pastimes and other party tricks in Chapter 24.

And finally, every automaton will enjoy playing the notorious game of Life (Chapter 25).

Chapter 23

Purging Pegs Properly

We can merely mention bean-bags, peg-boards, size and form boards,
as some of the apparatus found useful for the purpose of amusing
and instructing the weak-minded.
Allbutt's Systematic Medicine, 1899, VIII, 246.

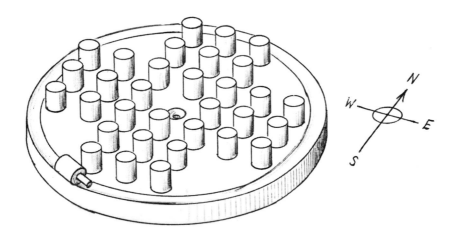

Figure 1. The English Solitaire Board.

Figure 1 shows the English Board on which the game of Peg Solitaire is usually played. It's easier to refill the board if you use marbles, but pegs are steadier when it comes to analysis.

The game is played (by one person of course) as shown in Fig. 2. If in some row or column two adjacent pegs are next to an empty space as in Fig. 2(a), then we may jump the peg *p* over *r* into the space *s* (Fig. 2(b)). The peg *r* that has been jumped over is then removed (Fig. 2(c)). Jumps are like captures in Draughts or Checkers, but they *never* take place diagonally, but only in the East, South, West or North directions.

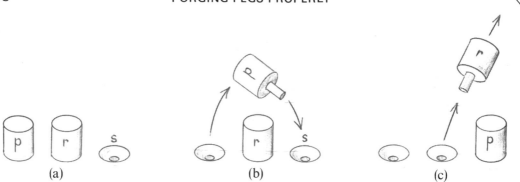

Figure 2. Making a Solitaire Jump.

CENTRAL SOLITAIRE

The standard problem is to start as in Fig. 1, with a peg in every hole except the centre, and then aim, by making a series of these jumping moves, to reduce the situation to a single peg in the central hole (Fig. 3).

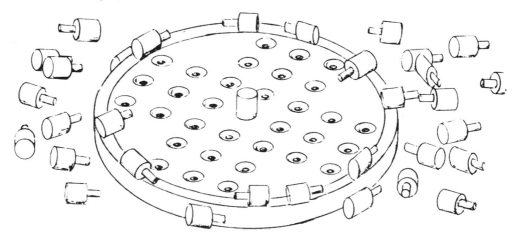

Figure 3. Success!

Like many card solitaire ("Patience") games, Solitaire is probably called a *game* rather than a puzzle because one often feels one is playing against an invisible opponent. Many people not normally interested in puzzles will recall some period of their lives when they have struggled with this opponent for days at a time; yet it seems that most of those who can readily solve simple Solitaire problems have been taught the trick by someone else as a child. It is rare indeed to find someone who has acquired the knack single-handed, and surely Peg Solitaire (nowadays selling in many parts of the world under the trade name of Hi-Q) must be the hardest game of its kind to have gained substantial popularity. It is an ideal game to while away hours of enforced idleness during illness or long journeys, and perhaps we should believe those old books which tell us that the game was invented by a French nobleman who first played it on the stone tiles of his prison cell.

If you haven't played this game before, put down this book, go out right now, buy a board, and try to solve the Central Solitaire Game. Those of you who are left will have plenty of time to read the chapter before the novices come back in a week or so—why not learn a particularly elegant solution to impress them all?

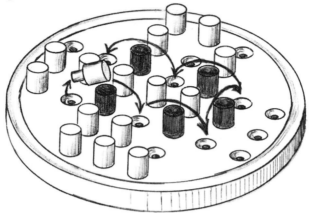

Figure 4. A Move of Five Jumps.

DUDENEY, BERGHOLT AND BEASLEY

Since you must already know how to solve the problem, you'll want to do it quickly, so let's agree to count any number of consecutive jumps made with a single peg as just one **move**. Figure 4 shows such a move—the five shaded jumped-over pegs are to be taken off as part of the move.

		a	b	c		
	y	d	e	f	z	
g	h	i	j	k	l	m
n	o	p	x	P	O	N
M	L	K	J	I	H	G
	Z	F	E	D	Y	
		C	B	A		

Figure 5. Labelling the Places.

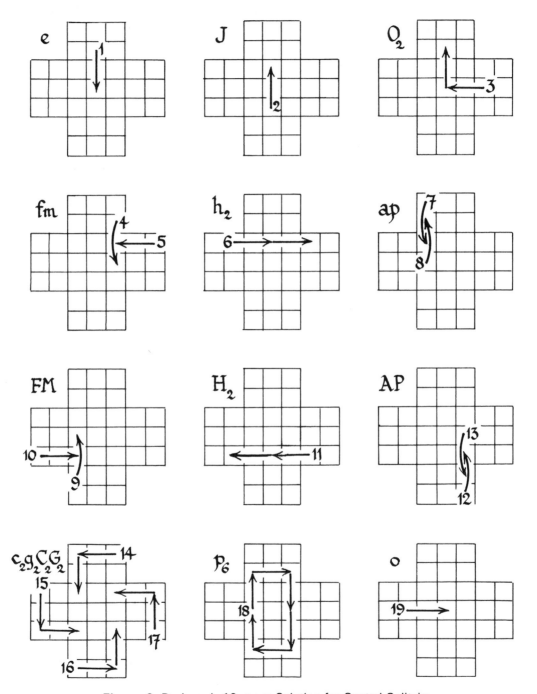

Figure 6. Dudeney's 19-move Solution for Central Solitaire.

In order to describe a solution concisely, we label the places as in Fig. 5, and write S_t for a jump from S to t and shorten this to S when we don't need to indicate the direction. The 5-jump move of Fig. 4 is L_{JHljh} which we will abbreviate to L_5 when it is unambiguous (we can't do that here since L_5 could also mean L_{hjJHl} and various other things). In this notation, Dudeney's elegant 19-move solution of his Central Solitaire problem is

$$eJO_2 \; fmh_2ap \; FMH_2AP \; c_2g_2C_2G_2 \; p_6o,$$

and this is set out in Fig. 6.

Dudeney thought that the number 19 could not be improved, but, in *The Queen* four years later, Ernest Bergholt gave an 18-move solution, unfortunately not quite as symmetrical as Dudeney's:

$$elcPDGJm_2igL_5CpA_2M_2a_3d_5o.$$

Here the notation L_5 is ambiguous, but the intended 5-jump move is the one depicted in Fig. 4. The move d_5 is also ambiguous, but either interpretation leads to the same result.

The whole truth emerged only 52 years later, in 1964, when John Beasley used the methods described in this chapter to prove that a solution in fewer than 18 moves is impossible. With Beasley's kind permission we publish his proof for the first time in the Extras to this chapter. It is very condensed, so the reader who wishes to follow it should first study the chapter diligently!

PACKAGES AND PURGES

It's nice to be able to know the effect of a whole collection of moves before you make them, so let us sell you some of our instant **packages**. When a package is used to clear all the pegs from a region, we call it a **purge**.

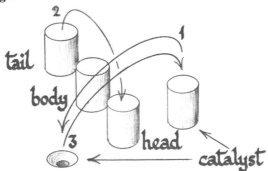

Figure 7. Purging Three Pegs.

Figure 7 shows the handy little **3-purge**, our most popular package. When three pegs—the *tail*, the *body* and the *head*—are adjacent in line, this will remove them all, provided the head has an additional peg on one side of it, and an empty space on the other, as in the figure. Move 1 of the package jumps the additional peg *over* the head; move 2 jumps tail over body *into* head; and move 3 jumps *over* the head, back to its original position. Since the peg and the space on either side of the head are essential to the package, but are restored to their original state, we call them the **catalyst**.

In Figs. 8(a) to 8(h), ● indicates a peg to be purged, ○ a space to be filled, and **XX** indicate catalyst places of which one must be full and the other empty. In most of the purges there are two catalyst moves in opposite directions over the same position (which may be a peg or an empty space) and the remaining moves form one or two packages which deliver pegs to that place. For the 3-purge (8(a)), one peg was already in place and the second is delivered by a single jump which we might call the "2-package" (8(b)). The 6-purge is usually accomplished (8(c)) using a 2-package to deliver the first peg and a 4-package (8(d)) for the second.

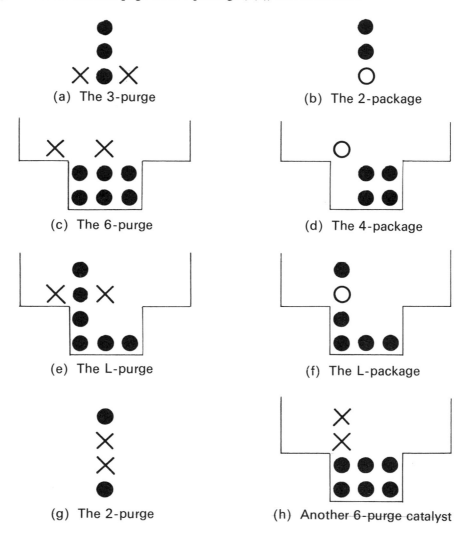

Figure 8. A Parcel of Packages.

The L-purge (8(e)) and L-package (8(f)) are very useful indeed. The first peg for the L-purge is already in place and an L-package supplies the second. The first two moves of the L-package form a 2-purge (8(g)) which can also be used in other situations. The catalyst for the 2-purge is restored in a rather unorthodox way, as is the alternative catalyst for the 6-purge shown in Fig. 8(h).

PACKAGES PROVIDE PERFECT PANACEA

Plenty of problems are performed with panache by people who purchase our packages.

In Fig. 9 we can see at a glance a solution for Central Solitaire, consisting of two 3-purges (1 and 2) followed by three 6-purges (3, 4 and 5) and an L-purge, leaving only the final jump to be made. You should check that every purge has the catalyst it needs.

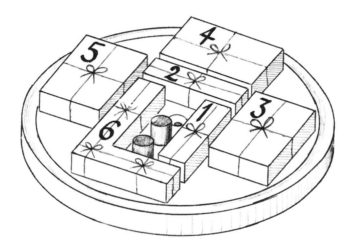

Figure 9. Central Solitaire Painlessly Packaged.

Instead of Central Solitaire we can consider other one-peg reversal problems: start with only one empty space and finish with only one peg in the same place. Figures 9 and 10 show that most such problems can be solved by purely purgatory methods, but in Fig. 10(e) we start with a 4-package indicated by the arrow (1), and the notorious problem (b) needs more complicated methods.

To clarify our notation we explain our solution for (b) in detail. For the first jump we have no choice but to jump from the place marked 1 in the figure. Our second jump, from the place marked 2, clears a space which enables us to make the L-*package*, indicated by the bent arrow (3). We now have a catalyst for the L-purge (4) which is followed by a single jump from the place marked 5. We are now on the home run with purges 6, 7 and 8 followed by a single jump from place 9. If the reader plays this through she will find that we have set up a spectacular 5-jump move from the place marked 10_5.

The reader might like to try her hand at some *two*-peg reversal problems—start with just two spaces on the board and end with just two pegs in those places.

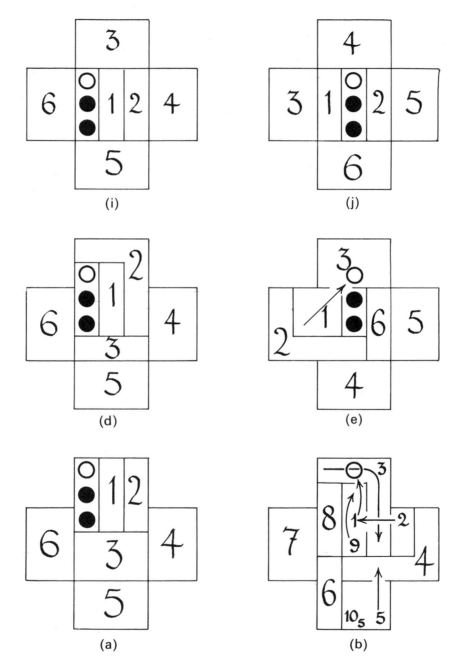

Figure 10. The Other Six One-Peg Reversals.

THE RULE OF TWO AND THE RULE OF THREE

Here is another type of problem (Fig. 11). We start with just one empty space and declare that some particular peg is to be the **finalist** (last on the board). In the example the initial hole is at position *d* and we want the finalist to be the peg that starts at *b*. Where must it end?

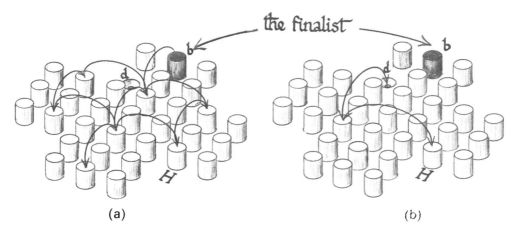

Figure 11. Find Where the Finalist Finishes!

There is an obvious **Rule of Two**—the peg can only jump an even number of places in either direction, as indicated by the arrows in Fig. 11(a). But there is a much more interesting **Rule of Three**. One of the consequences of this is that if we start with a single space on the English board and end with a single peg, then we can move in steps of three from the initial space to that of the finalist, as in Fig. 11(b).

The Rule of Two and the Rule of Three, taken together, can lead to surprises. See how they point to the unique finishing place *H* in Fig. 11(a) and (b). Now that we know that *H* is the only place permitted by both the Rule of Two and the Rule of Three, the problem is a lot easier than it might have been. Figure 12 shows a neatly packaged solution; how did we find it?

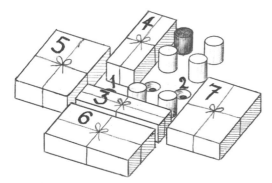

Figure 12(a). The Position After the First Two Moves.

Figure 12(b). The Position Before the Last Two Moves.

What we did was plan the 3-jump move 9_3 which puts the finalist in his place, and our second jump was to clear a space for this. But after we made this second jump most of the pegs parcelled themselves up naturally. The one apparent exception was the peg starting just right of the finalist, and the best way of clearing this seemed to be to use it as in move 8_2 to provide the final jump.

For other problems, gentle reader, we recommend a similar procedure. Plan the last few moves of your solution and let the first few be used to smooth the way for these and leave the remaining pegs in tidy packages. Remember that the catalyst for the very last purge must be among the pegs in your planned finale.

Here's a nice finalist problem for you. Let the initial hole be in position B and the finalist be the peg which starts at J. Can you end with only this peg?

SOME PEGS ARE MORE EQUAL THAN OTHERS

How do we explain the Rule of Three? The best way is to introduce "multiplication" for Solitaire positions. In Fig. 13(a) the two adjacent pegs s and t can obviously be replaced by a single peg at r, so we write

$$st = r,$$

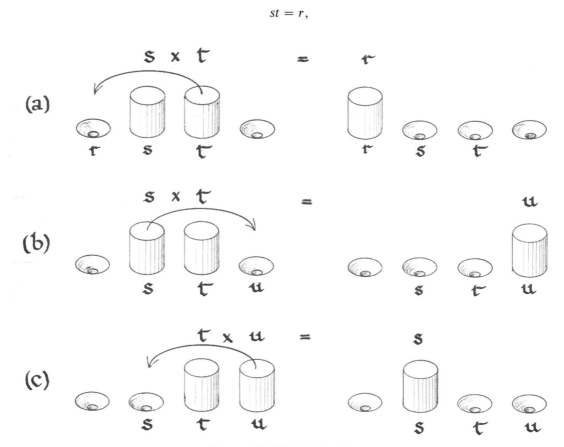

Figure 13. Multiplying Pegs.

but Fig. 13(b) shows that we can also write

$$st = u.$$

Now Euclid tells us that things that are equal to the same thing are equal, so we must agree that $r = u$.

> Places three apart
> in any line are
> considered equal.

Let's see what other rules of algebra tell us. Combining Figs. 13(b) and 13(c), we have

$$st = u, \qquad tu = s,$$

$$st^2u = us,$$

or, cancelling,

$$t^2 = 1,$$

which seems to tell us that

> two pegs in the
> same place cancel.

Remember how catalysts do precisely this—they remove two pegs which are delivered to the same place by the other moves of a purge. In fact it follows from our algebra that

> any set of pegs
> that can be
> purged cancel.

For example, in Fig. 13(c), $tu = s$, so

$$stu = ss = 1.$$

> Three adjacent pegs   (3-purge)
> in line cancel,

and since $r=u$,

$$ru = uu = 1.$$

Two pegs at
distance three cancel.   (2-purge)

r But in the algebra there are less obvious equalities: for since $s^2 = 1 = rst$, we find

$$s = rt.$$

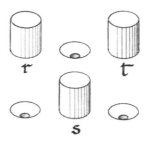

Figure 14. $s = rt$.

REISS'S 16 SOLITAIRE POSITION CLASSES

We've now said enough to see how our algebra cuts the Solitaire board down to size, for since places three apart are algebraically equal, every place is equal to one of the nine in the middle of the board (Fig. 15); for example $a = p$. Now we can use our most recent rule to express each of these nine in terms of the four corner ones, i, k, I, K:

$$
\begin{array}{ll}
j = ik & P = Ik \\
p = iK & J = IK \\
x = jJ = ikIK.
\end{array}
$$

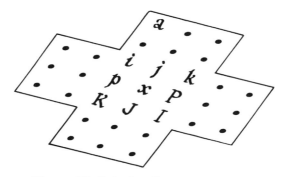

Figure 15. Stripping Down to Essentials.

Since equal pegs cancel,

> every Solitaire position
> is algebraically equal to
> one of the 16 combinations
> of the places i, k, I, K.

THE SIXTEEN REISS CLASSES

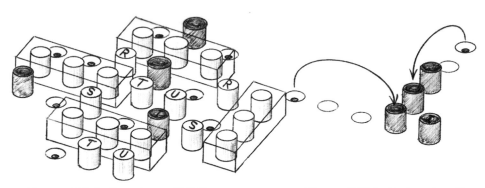

Figure 16(a). Found near Split?   **Figure 16(b).** Reduced to Size.

The position of Fig. 16(a) was found unattended in a Jugoslav railway train. Those filmy packages and letters weren't there—but just came into our mind's eye when we pondered the possibility of reducing the position to a single peg. Where must this single peg be?

Our rules allow us to cancel those four packages of three and then the four pairs RR, SS, TT, UU, so that the position is algebraically equal to the four shaded pegs. We then can move two of these three spaces and cancel another 3-package as in Fig. 16(b) to see that the position equals a single peg at I. So the Rule of Three says that the finalist must be at I, L or f. For which of these places can you find solutions?

How do we know that Reiss's sixteen classes are really different? Might not our algebraic rules imply perhaps that $i = kK$? No! For consider the numbers ± 1 shown in the places of Fig. 17(i). Whenever three of these numbers

$$r, s, t$$

are adjacent in line, we really do have

$$rs = t,$$

and from this we can see that all our algebraic rules hold for these numbers. But in this system we have

$$i = -1, \qquad k = K = +1,$$

so we can't prove $i = kK$! In fact Figs. 17(i, k, I, K) show that all 16 combinations of the pegs i, k, I, K are algebraically distinct: for example the value on Fig. 17(i) is -1 just if i is involved in the combination. Making a Solitaire move or applying any of our algebraic rules will never change the value in any of the four Figures.

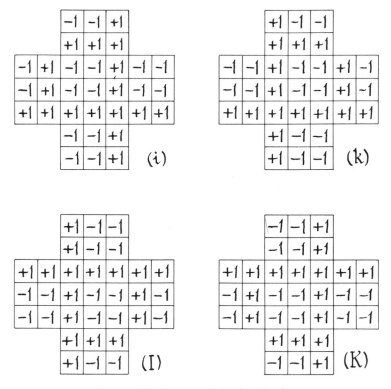

Figure 17. "Answers" to the Algebra.

In algebraic language, the first thing we told you about the Rule of Three may be restated—a position with just one empty space is algebraically equal to the **complementary** position in which *only* that place is full. More generally,

> any position on the English board
> is algebraically equal to the
> complementary position which has
> empty spaces replacing pegs
> and pegs replacing empty spaces.

For our rules allow us to complement any line of three adjacent places and the whole board can be parcelled into such threes.

This property fails for

THE CONTINENTAL BOARD

which has the four extra holes at y, z, Y, Z in Fig. 5. So no reversal problems are possible on this board. Which of the problems which start with a single hole and end with a single peg are solvable on this board? See the Extras.

PLAYING BACKWARDS AND FORWARDS

"The game called Solitaire pleases me much. I take it in reverse order. That is to say that instead of making a configuration according to the rules of the game, which is to jump to an empty place and remove the piece over which one has jumped, I thought it was better to reconstruct what had been demolished, by filling an empty hole over which one has leaped."

Leibniz.

The famous philosopher plainly thought that playing Solitaire backwards was different from playing it forwards, but really it's exactly the same game! For let's see what happens when he makes one of his backward moves from Figs. 18(a) to 18(c). Leibniz regards this as jumping *piece t* into *hole r* and *filling* the empty *hole s* over which he has leaped, but Fig. 18(b) shows that we can regard him as jumping the *hole* at r over the *hole* at s into the *piece* at t and removing the *hole* over which he has jumped. (Of course to *remove* a hole he *inserts* a piece!)

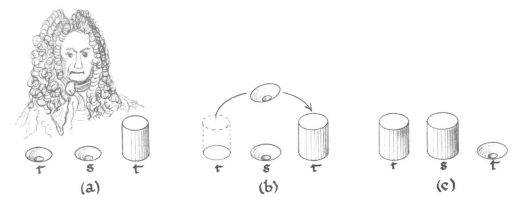

Figure 18. The Philosophy of Leibniz.

> Backwards Solitaire is just forwards Solitaire with the notions "empty" and "full" interchanged.

TIME-REVERSAL = ANTI-MATTER?

This can be useful as well as interesting. A quite spectacular Solitaire finale happens in Beasley's remarkable 16-move solution of the *i*-reversal problem:

$$apc_2F_2gdM_2IAP_\downarrow f_\downarrow C_3Gm....$$

After 14 of the 16 moves the board still seems quite full (Fig. 19(a)) but can be cleared to a single peg in just 2 moves. (Can you find them?)

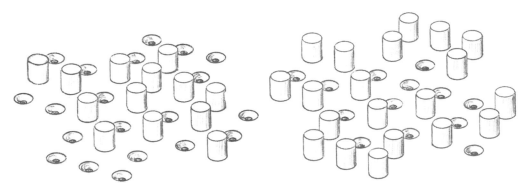

Figure 19. Two moves to Go!   . . .   And How to Get Back?

How would *you* find the moves leading up to this position? The time-reversal trick should make it easy. Instead of reducing a position with only one space, at *i*, to Fig. 19(a), try to reduce the complementary position (Fig. 19(b)) to just one peg at *i*. If you've been doing your homework and practising diligently, you won't find this too hard. You too can astonish your friends with grand finales to other Solitaire problems set up by the time-reversal trick.

PAGODA FUNCTIONS

Reiss's algebraic theory (known to many!) applies even when we allow you to make moves backward in time (like Leibniz) as well as the ordinary forward ones. Of course this lets you take back any of your bad moves, but you may also "undo" moves you haven't even made! If two positions are in different Reiss classes, then we can never get from one to the other by normal moves, by Leibniz's backward moves nor by any mixture of the two.

Unfortunately this means, of course, that the Reiss theory can never tell you when you've made a bad move, because the Reiss class never changes. You need something like the **Pagoda Functions** (known to few!) we are about to show you, that can *change* when you make a move, albeit in a restricted way. Mike Boardman was one of those who helped us to develop these.

Those friends of yours should now be back from the store with their Solitaire boards, so why not present them with a couple of innocent-looking problems? Since these are *reversal* problems, your friends won't be able to prove them impossible even if they've got as far as the last section.

The two problems are shown in Figs. 21(a) and (b) where circles show the only places which are initially empty and which must also be the only places which are finally full. Figures 21(c) and (d) show two pagoda functions which prove the problems impossible. In general, if pag is any such function and *X* any Solitaire position, we shall write

$$\text{pag } X$$

for the *sum* of the numbers that pag assigns to the pegs which are present in X. If X is partitioned into smaller positions Y and Z, then, in our algebraic notation we have

$$X = YZ,$$

and

$$\text{pag } X = \text{pag } Y + \text{pag } Z.$$

so that pagoda functions behave like logarithms.

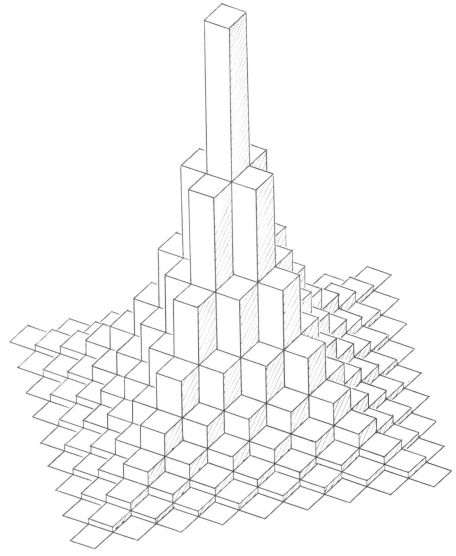

Figure 20. The Golden Pagoda.

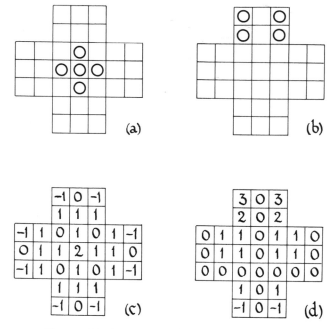

Figure 21. Two Impossible Reversal Problems.

The essential property which defines pagoda functions is that *no move may increase the value.* To check this condition you must make sure that

THE PAGODA FUNCTION CONDITION

$$\text{pag } r + \text{pag } s \geqslant \text{pag } t$$

holds for every conceivable Solitaire jump *r* over *s* into *t*.

CHECK THIS CONDITION NOW IN FIGURES 21(c) AND (d)!

When you've done that you will see the impossibility of our two problems, since the pag (Fig. 21(c)) of the initial position in 21(a), namely 4, can't be increased to 6, the pag of the final position; nor can 8 be increased to 10 (Figs. 21(b) and (c)).

In Fig. 22 we show the pagoda functions you're most likely to find useful; so you'd better check the Pagoda Function Condition for each of them! The values in the blank spaces are zero and you can make any of the indicated swaps. Figures 22(c, d, h, and v) are obvious pagoda functions since they just indicate all the places that a given peg can go to. The 12 places in 22(c) are called **corners** and the 5 in 22(d) are the **dodos**, because one of the easiest mistakes you can make is to let your dodos become extinct when you need one in your final position. Those extra minus ones often make 22(a) and (b) more useful than (h) and (v).

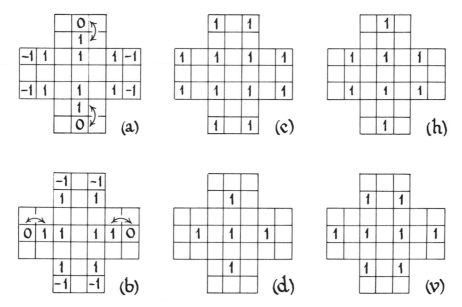

Figure 22. Some Useful Pagoda Functions.

THE SOLITAIRE ARMY

A number of Solitaire men stand initially on one side of a straight line beyond which is an infinite empty desert (Fig. 23). How many men do we need to send a scout just 0, 1, 2, 3, 4, or 5 paces out into the desert?

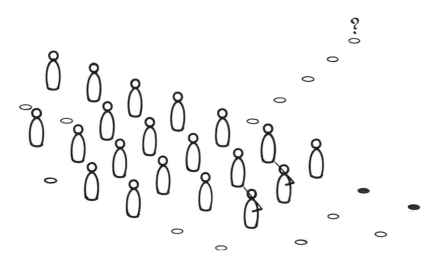

Figure 23. How About Sending a Scout Out?

It's not hard to see that the answers for 0, 1, 2 and 3 paces are 1, 2, 4 and 8 men, so you might guess that the next two answers are 16 and 32. But in fact no less than 20 men are needed to get 4 paces out. Can you find the two possible configurations of 20 men? (See the Extras.)

For 5 paces the answer is even more surprising—it is *impossible* to send a scout five paces into the desert, no matter how large an army we hire! The pagoda function which proves this is shown in Fig. 24. It was the shape of the graph of this function (Fig. 20) which first suggested the name "pagoda". The number σ is determined by the golden ratio:

$$\sigma = \tfrac{1}{2}(\sqrt{5} - 1) = 0\cdot 618\ldots,$$

$$\sigma^2 + \sigma = 1.$$

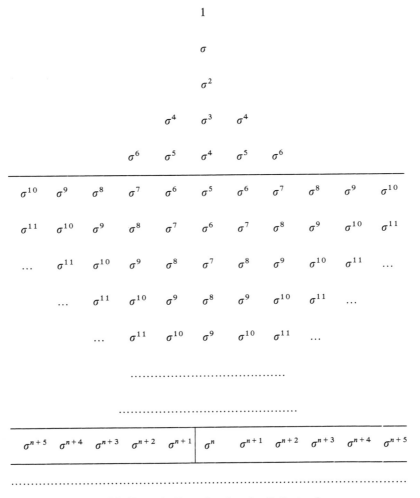

Figure 24. Pagoda Function for the Solitaire Army.

By some easy mathematics we have

$$\sigma^n + \sigma^{n+1} + \sigma^{n+2} + \ldots = \frac{\sigma^n}{1-\sigma} = \sigma^{n-2},$$

so that the total score of the line whose middle element is σ^n is

$$\sigma^{n-2} + \sigma^{(n+1)-2} = \sigma^{n-3},$$

and the total score of this line and all lower lines is

$$\frac{\sigma^{n-3}}{1-\sigma} = \sigma^{n-5}.$$

In particular, the sum of *all* the men on or below the σ^5 line is *exactly* 1, so no finite number of these men will suffice to send a scout to the place whose score is 1. But infinitely many men are *almost* enough, because we once showed that if any man of our army is allowed to carry a comrade on his shoulders at the start, then no matter how far away the extra man is, the problem can now be solved.

MANAGING YOUR RESOURCES

Your score on a pagoda function is in some sense a measure of your resources, which you should not consume too rapidly. But mere worldly goods are not enough: they must be capably managed to preserve a balance between your commitments in various directions.

The **Balance Sheet** of Fig. 25 has been cunningly devised to do just this. The subtlety of the English board is that you are often forced to consume assets in order to maintain the **balance**,

		b^{-1}	β	$b^{-1}\beta$		
		b	$\alpha\beta$	$b\beta$		
a^{-1}	a	1	a	1	a	a^{-1}
α	$b\alpha$	b	$c\alpha\beta$	$b\beta$	$b\alpha\beta$	α
$a^{-1}\alpha$	$a\alpha$	1	$a\alpha$	1	$a\alpha$	$a^{-1}\alpha$
		b	$a\alpha\beta$	$b\beta$		
		b^{-1}	β	$b^{-1}\beta$		

$\beta^2 = 1$

$\alpha^2 = 1$

Figure 25. The Balance Sheet.

as measured by the greek letters α and β, of your position in the North-South and East-West directions. The latin letters *a, b* and *c* measure the **assets** on a number of pagoda functions simultaneously (*a* and *b* for Figs. 22(a) and 22(b) and abc^2 for Fig. 21(c)).

To estimate the overall capacity of a position, find the product of the resources of all its pegs in Fig. 25, using the relations

$$\alpha^2 = \beta^2 = 1.$$

A problem has two such products, the **raw product** (for its initial position), which must be taken to the **finished product** (for the final position) while consuming the **available resources**:

$$\frac{\text{raw product}}{\text{finished product}} = \text{available resources}.$$

In Fig. 26, all the jumps that change the product are shown to do so in **units** of sizes

$$
\begin{array}{ccccc}
a & a\alpha & c\alpha & a^2 c^{-1}\alpha = A & a^2 \\
b & b\beta & c\beta & b^2 c^{-1}\beta = B & b^2
\end{array}
$$

so your available resources will only be **productive** if they can be made up of such units.

Central Solitaire, for example, has raw product $a^4 b^4$ and finished product $c\alpha\beta$ so that its available resources are

$$\frac{a^4 b^4}{c\alpha\beta} = a^4 b^4 c^{-1}\alpha\beta.$$

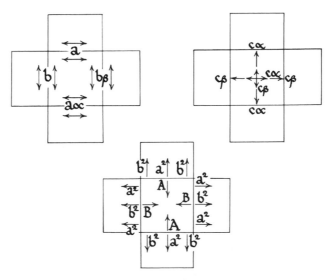

Figure 26. Using Resources in Various Units.

In Dudeney's solution only the opening and closing few moves actually use any of these:

move	e	J	O_2	$fmh_2apFMH_2APc_2g_2C_2G_2$	P_6	o
resources	A	$c\beta$	$B.c\alpha$	⟵ —— free moves —— ⟶	$1.a.1.1.a\alpha.1$	B

UNPRODUCTIVITY AND THE PRODIGAL SON

Many problems are impossible for the simple reason that

$$b^2\alpha \text{ and } a^2\beta$$
$$\text{are unproductive!}$$

Why is this? In the case $b^2\alpha$, for example, we are hamstrung for lack of a's, so the α forces us to make a jump $c\alpha$, leaving only b^2c^{-1} for the remaining moves, in which c^{-1} demands a move $b^2c^{-1}\beta = B$, and we then have no assets with which to adjust the remaining β.

THE PRODIGAL SON'S OPENING

Jump into centre; jump over centre;
jump into centre; jump back over centre;

is the only way Central Solitaire can go wrong in as few as four moves. What's so bad about these moves? The prodigality lies in the second and fourth moves which both use $c\alpha$ or both use $c\beta$ and therefore leave only

$$a^4b^4c^{-1}\alpha\beta/c^2 = a^4b^4c^{-3}\alpha\beta$$

for the remaining moves. But

$$a^4b^4c^{-3}\alpha\beta$$
$$\text{is unproductive!}$$

For the only way to cope with c^{-3} without overspending either a or b is to use the units

$$A,A,B \text{ or } A,B,B$$

which leave only the unproductive products

$$b^2\alpha \text{ or } a^2\beta.$$

Of course the same argument shows that *no* two moves in *any* solution of Central Solitaire can have product c^2.

Can you find the only way (**Fool's Solitaire**) of getting absolutely pegbound (unable to move) in six jumps? And can you **Succour the Sucker** by solving the position reached after five of these moves? And can you flag yourself down to *another* pegbound position in as few as ten jumps from the start?

DEFICIT ACCOUNTING AND THE G.N.P.

The **deficit** of a problem is the amount by which its initial position lacks the resources of the entire board, combined with the total resources of the final position and the costs of any moves you intend to make. Since the resources of the entire board are

$$a^4 b^4 c \alpha \beta \text{ (the (English) Gross National Product)}$$

we have

$$\text{remaining resources} = \frac{a^4 b^4 c \alpha \beta}{\text{deficit}}.$$

The deficit is found very easily by multiplying the initial hole values by the final peg values. For Central Solitaire, the basic deficit is

$$c \alpha \beta . c \alpha \beta = c^2,$$

which the Prodigal Son's bad moves extravagantly enlarged to c^4. He clearly didn't know the **Deficit Rule**:

> If deficit$/c^4$ *IS* productive,
> your remaining resources *AREN'T*!

This is because (G.N.P.)$/c^4$ is our unproductive product $\alpha^4 \beta^4 c^{-3} \alpha \beta$.

ACCOUNTING FOR TWO-PEG REVERSAL PROBLEMS

We know that all the one-peg reversal problems are possible, but there are just four different impossible two-peg reversal problems. The first of these is **Hamlet's Memorable Problem** (to be or not to be):

Get to only b, e present   (to be)
from only b, e absent   (not be).

Deficit account for Hamlet's Problem

To:

Initial holes @ b & e :	$\beta . a\beta = a$
Final pegs @ b & e :	$\beta . a\beta = a$
First & last jumps into e :	$c\alpha . c\alpha = c^2$
Jump into b :	a^2
Deficit :	$a^4 c^2$

Since

$$\frac{a^4c^2}{c^4} = a^4c^{-2} = A^2 \ldots$$

is productive, Hamlet's Problem succumbs to the Deficit Rule. The other three impossible two-peg reversals are the **Dodo Problems**, for which the two places are two of the five dodo pegs (Fig. 22(d)). Deficit accounts for the typical problems *eo, ex* and *eE* are:

Dodo Problem	*eo*	*ex*	*eE*
Initial holes and final pegs	$(a\beta.bd)^2$	$(a\beta.c\alpha\beta)^2$	$(a\beta.a\alpha\beta)^2$
Required moves	$c\alpha.c\beta$	$c\alpha$	$c\alpha.c\alpha$
Deficit	$a^2b^2c^2\alpha\beta$	$a^2c^3\alpha$	a^4c^2
Deficit/c^4	$A.B$	A	$A.A$

The reader who has been paying attention will have no difficulty in finding solutions to any other two-peg reversal problem.

John Conway, Mike Guy and Bob Hutchings have shown that the only impossible *three*-peg reversals are typified by

(1) The **Bumble-bee Problems** (*b,e* and any third place other than *g,m,M,G*),
(2) The **Deader Dodo Problems** (two dodos and any third place other than an outside corner *acgmMGCA*),
(3) The **Three B'ars Problems** (any three of the unlucky 13 places in the three rows *def, nopxPON, FED*).

These can be shown to be impossible by deficit accounting. In fact in any reversal problem, an additional peg other than an outside corner merely aggravates the deficit.

FORGETTING THE ORDER CAN BE USEFUL

If you allow yourself to have 2 or more, or −1 or less, pegs in a hole, you can make your moves in any order! It's a good idea to alter a hard problem in this way, and when you've solved the altered problem, go back and find a sensible order for the original one.

We'll do out loud for you the tricky 3-peg reversal:

start with 0 pegs in *b, N, n*;   1 peg everywhere else;
end   with 1 peg in *b, N, n*;   0 pegs anywhere else.

In the altered problem it's easier to

start with −1 peg in *b, N, n*;   1 peg everywhere else;
end   with 0 pegs anywhere.

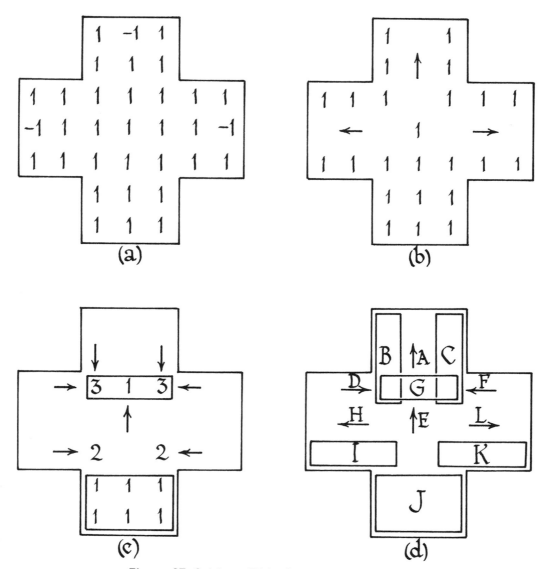

Figure 27. Solving a Tricky 3-peg Reversal Problem.

From the starting position, Fig. 27(a), we'll need, at some time, to make three jumps to fill those −1's, so we make these three jumps *now*, reaching Fig. 27(b). The only plausible way to deal with the six isolated corner pegs in this is to jump them inwards, and after the indicated upward jump over the centre we reach Fig. 27(c). The remaining pegs in this can be cleared by a 3-purge, a 6-purge and four double jumps over the inner corners.

If you follow Fig. 27(d) in the order A to L you'll find yourself making all the above moves in a legal way. The double jumps have been incorporated into the 3-purges B, C, I and K.

BEASLEY'S EXIT THEOREMS

Sometimes you can work out exactly what moves to make in a problem, but find it hard to get them into the right order. The following remarks can help you get your moves in order, or prove that it can't be done.

> A region of at least three squares that starts full *or* ends empty needs at least one *exit move*.
> A region of at least three squares that starts full *and* ends empty needs at least two exit moves.

BEASLEY'S FIRST AND SECOND EXIT THEOREMS

An **exit move** for a region is a jump that empties some square in the region and fills some square outside the region. To justify Beasley's Second Exit Theorem, note that the first and last moves affecting a region must both be exits. We'll illustrate with

A STOLID SURVIVOR PROBLEM

Suppose we want to do an *a*-reversal, with the added condition that peg K is the **stolid survivor**, i.e. that the first move of K is also the final move from K to a. Can the grand finale be a 6-chain?

The ideas of the first part of our discussion are often useful in long chain problems. Then we'll try to put the moves we've found into order, using Beasley's Exit Theorems.

How do we use the 16 side pegs $h^8 v^8$ of Figs. 22(h) and (v)? Each of the outer corner pegs must at some time be jumped into the central 3×3 square, and those at C and M must sidestep first to avoid the stolid survivor at K. So the jumps mentioned use up side pegs as follows:

$$
\begin{array}{ccccccc}
c & m & G & A & C & M & g \\
v & h & h & v & hv & vh & h
\end{array}
$$

leaving $h^3 v^4$ for the remaining jumps. Since the first move uses one side peg and the final chain six, we have accounted for all the side pegs and no *other* move can destroy one.

This forces us to make the first move c_a, since the alternative, i_a, would move an inside corner peg to the outside and make us use another side peg to bring it back later. Next k_c would use another side peg, so the second move is j_b and this peg must stay at b until the grand finale because a move refilling e would use yet another side peg. We now know that the final 6-chain uses $h^2 v^4$ and involves a horizontal jump over b, so it must be as in Fig. 28(a).

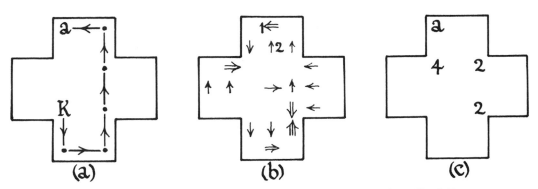

Figure 28. Can the Stolid Survivor Make a Grand 6-chain Finale?

Since K doesn't move till the end, L can't be jumped over and can only be cleared by the upward jump L_h. We need to make two jumps over B, once to get corner peg C out, and once in the finale, so we must deliver an extra peg there by a downward jump J_B. For similar reasons *two* extra pegs are needed at D, so we must make two downward jumps P_D. For the second of these, and for the finale, we need two more pegs delivered at P; these must come from N and p. We've now found 23 (Fig. 28(b)) of the 31 jumps. If we make these we arrive at Fig. 28(c). The two pegs on each of I and k must be cleared by pairs of vertical or horizontal to and fro jumps, and the four on i by two such pairs.

To find the right order in which to make these moves we use Beasley's Second Exit Theorem. Consider the region of Fig. 29(a). The moves we've copied from Fig. 28(b) incorporate just one exit from the region; the vertical jump across P. To make sure there's another we must remove the two pegs on k by a *vertical* pair of to and fro jumps as in Fig. 29(b). But the region of *that* figure can now have only one exit, the vertical jump across f. So our problem's impossible!

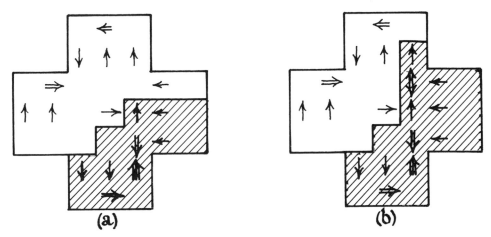

Figure 29. Using Beasley's Second Exit Theorem.

ANOTHER HARD PROBLEM

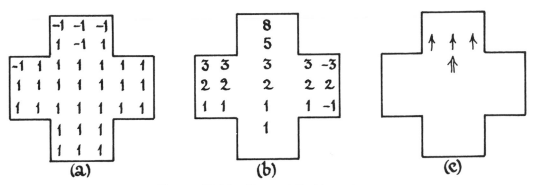

Figure 30. The Reversal Problem *abceg*.

We'll try the 5-peg reversal problem *abceg*, i.e. start with the board full except for spaces at *a, b, c, e, g*, and finish with pegs in just those places. An equivalent problem is to clear the board of Fig. 30(a), which has negpegs (or **negs**) in each of the places *a, b, c, e, g* and pegs in the other 28 places.

For the original problem the pagoda function of Fig. 30(b) changes from 20 to 16, or, in the form of Fig. 30(a), from 4 to 0. This pag kills any possible move across *b*, which would lose 8, so the jumps i_a, k_c shown in Fig. 30(c) are forced, as is the jump j_b to fill *b*. In order to make this last jump a peg must be delivered to *e*, and *e* must also be full by the end, so two jumps x_e are also needed. If we make these five jumps, using negs where needed, we arrive at Fig. 31(a), whose

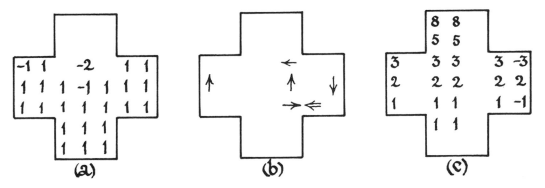

Figure 31. We Make Some Progress.

resources are $a^2 b^4 c^{-1} \alpha \beta$, showing a deficit of $a^2 c^2$. The Deficit Rule tells us we can't make another move of value a^2, since $a^4 c^2 / c^4 = A^2$, so the jump M_g (Fig. 31(b)) is forced. Now use the pagoda function of Fig. 31(c). Its value for Fig. 31(a) is 2, so the peg at *N* can't jump inwards, nor can we jump over it upwards, since these moves lose 4 on this pag. So the jump m_G (Fig. 31(b)) is forced. The two pegs at *G* must now both jump to *I*, and a peg must be delivered to *H* for the second of these. This can't come from l, as this loses 4 on the 1st pag, so the jump J_H is also forced. Moreover, as l can't jump downwards, and can't be jumped over (this would lose a^2) it must make the jump l_j over k. This needs delivery of a peg at k, which can't come from i (loses 6 on the last pag) so the jump I_k is forced. If we make all these moves, which have been collected in Fig. 31(b), we arrive at Fig. 32(a), for which the resources are now

$$a^2 b^3 c^{-1}\alpha = Ab^3 \quad \text{or} \quad A.B.b.c\beta \quad \text{or} \quad B.a.a\alpha.b\beta.$$

so there is no jump $c\alpha$.

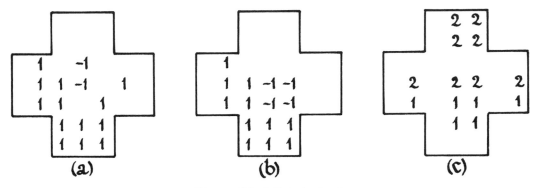

Figure 32. A Cul-de-Sac!

There are two ways in which we might remove the peg at O: by j_{IHJ} or by O_x. The former (after the necessary delivery I_k) leads to Fig. 32(b) which is impossible to clear, as the pag of Fig. 32(c) shows. So O_x is forced (Fig. 33(a)) and this requires the delivery D_P (horizontal delivery is prohibited by the pag of Fig. 31(c)). These two jumps lead to a position whose resources $a^2\alpha\beta$ are uniquely productive: $(a^2 c^{-1}\alpha)(c\beta)$ and the jump E_x is forced. The L-package of Fig. 33(a) will deliver a second peg to K and the board is cleared by L_J and h_{LJj}.

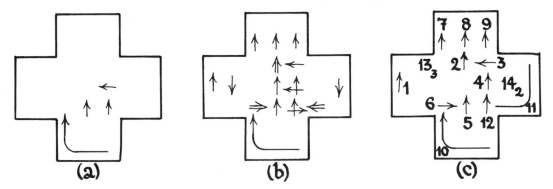

Figure 33. The Problem Solved.

The 23 jumps are shown in Fig. 33(b). How do we do them in practice? In what order? The answer isn't unique, but one possibility is given in Fig. 33(c). It involves two L-packages, 10 and 11, and two chain moves, 13_3 and 14_2.

THE SPINNER

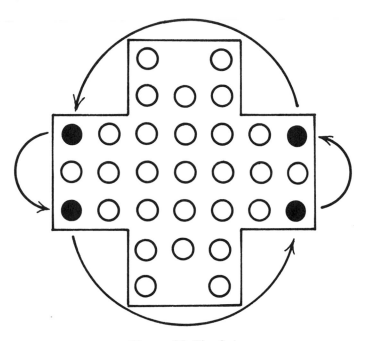

Figure 34. The Spinner.

If you start with empty spaces at *b*, *B* and marked pegs at *g*, *M*, *G*, *m*, can you finish with just the four marked pegs on the board in the respective positions *M*, *G*, *m*, *g*?

OUR FINE FINALIST

The Rule of Two and the Rule of Three together tells us that if the initial hole is at B, then a finalist that starts at J must end in either B or b. Here's a solution for b:

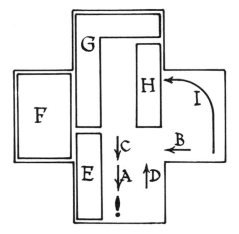

The letters indicate the order of the successive moves, except for the finalizing flourish. The bent arrow we've used for move I is our notation for an L-*package*, as distinct from an L-*purge*.

However, it's impossible for the finalist to finish at B. This is because there are forced moves

$$J_B \qquad x_E \qquad x_E \qquad J_B$$

which consume

$$a^2 \qquad c\alpha \qquad c\alpha \qquad a^2$$

on the Balance Sheet, giving a deficit of $a^4 c^2$. Since

$$\text{deficit}/c^4 = a^4 c^{-2}$$

is productive, your remaining resources *aren't*.

DOING THE SPLITS

If you start from Fig. 16(a) and make the moves A to I indicated in Fig. 35, where the pairs of circles C, F, G indicate 2-purges, you'll reach a 5-peg configuration which can easily be reduced to I, L or f. (We found this solution by the ordering process after subtracting this 5-peg configuration from the starting position.)

728

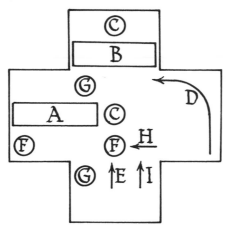

Figure 35. The Train was going to *l*vanicGrad, *L*jubljana or *f*oća.

ALL SOLUBLE ONE-PEG PROBLEMS ON THE CONTINENTAL BOARD

were found by Reiss using his theory. In our language, the Continental board is algebraically equal to its centre, and so for a one-peg problem to be soluble we must have

(initial hole) × (final peg) = centre,

in our algebraic sense. You can easily check that the initial hole and final peg are at opposite ends of an arrow in

$$(a\,p\,C\,O) \leftrightarrow (A\,P\,c\,o) \qquad (e\,G\,J\,M) \leftrightarrow (E\,g\,j\,m).$$

There is a 41-hole board for which Lucas gives all the soluble problems; but see the appendix to his *second* edition, because he first conjectured that most of the problems were insoluble!

THE LAST TWO MOVES

in Fig. 19(a) are $n_9 G_3$.

A 20-MAN SOLITAIRE ARMY

can get a scout 4 places out by arranging itself as shown in Fig. 23. The two men with guns can be moved to the shaded places so as to obtain the only other arrangement.

FOOL'S SOLITAIRE, ETC.

If each of your moves is confined to the middle row or column you'll reach a position like Fig. 36(a) after six jumps. The next pegbound position is the Hammer and Sickle position of Fig. 36(b), reached after ten jumps.

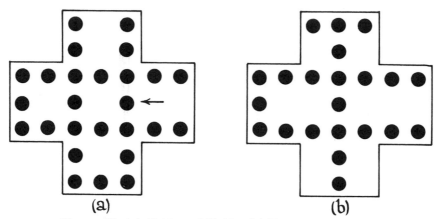

Figure 36. (a) Sickle and Sickle. (b) Hammer and Sickle.

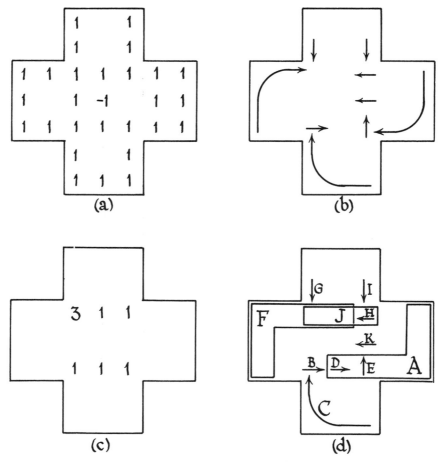

Figure 37. Succouring the Sucker.

To succour the sucker who's made five of the six moves leading to Fig. 36(a) it's best to try to clear Fig. 37(a) to zero. If you set this up on the board (use an upside down peg for the -1!) you should see how the moves of Fig. 37(b) suggest themselves in order, leading to the easily cleared position, Fig. 37(c). The L-moves in Fig. 37(b) are L-*packages*, not L-purges. You then have the tricky little problem of arranging the moves in order, one solution of which is given in Fig. 37(d), in which A and F are L-*purges*, but C is an L-*package*.

BEASLEY PROVES BERGHOLT IS BEST

Suppose there were a 17-move solution to Central Solitaire. Then Beasley first uses the scoring function of Fig. 38(a) ("score" refers to this function—which is *not* a pagoda function—throughout the proof) and his First Exit Theorem, to show that no move begins or ends on b, n, B or N. The initial and final scores are 20 and 0. Moves which begin or end on b, n, B or N *increase* the score by at least 1. Others decrease it by at most 2 (the careful reader will make a table of score changes for each type of move).

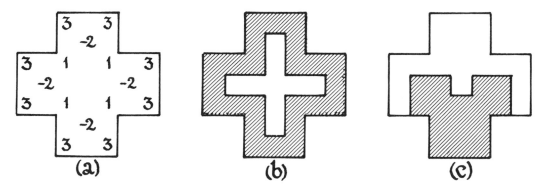

Figure 38. Scoring Function and Regions Used in Beasley's Proof.

Any solution to Central Solitaire contains 11 **reserved** moves:
the first, which we'll take to be e_x,
the last, a single jump into the centre,
the penultimate one, taking a peg to j, p, J or P, and
eight moves bringing the outside corner pegs to inside corner
squares so they may be captured.

The first and last moves each increase the score by 2, the penultimate one decreases it by at most 1 and each of the other eight decreases it by at most 2. So the other six (**loose**) moves must decrease the score by at least 7.

The second move is a loose move, either J_j or h_j, say. The move J_j doesn't change the score and it leaves the region of Fig. 38(b) full. The first exit from this region is a loose move, either of type b_j or of type (ending with) h_j. The former increases the score by 2 and the other four loose moves would have to decrease it by at least 9, which is impossible. The latter decreases the score by 1, and our four loose moves have to reduce it further by at least 6. If any of these increased the score, the others could not then reduce it to zero, so moves starting or ending on b, n, B or N

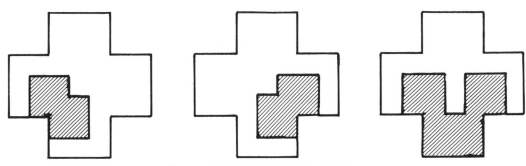

Figure 39. What is the First Exit?

are again impossible. Such a move *might* occur as the penultimate one, but the six loose moves would then have to reduce the score by 10, and the same argument shows this is impossible.

The second move h_j reduces the score by 1 *and* is a first exit from the region of Fig. 38(b). The other five loose moves must reduce the score by at least 6. What is the first exit from the region of Fig. 38(c)? There are several possibilities, all of them loose moves, which we'll leave the reader to pursue. In some cases he'll want to ask a further question about one of the regions of Fig. 39, whichever is still full. From now on we'll assume that no move begins or ends on b, n, B or N.

How do we clear a, b and c? We've proved that b can't jump out, so there must be a jump over it, say c_a. The two pegs at a now force two jumps a_i and a jump into d, which we shall call a **side delivery**. The four jumps

$$c_a \quad a_i \quad a_i \quad ?_d$$

are parts of at least three moves

$$a_i\ldots \quad ?_{\ldots d} \quad c_{ai}\ldots \quad \text{(the normal case), or}$$

$$a_i\ldots \quad ?_{\ldots d} \quad ?_{\ldots kcai} \quad \text{(a U-turn).}$$

However a U-turn demands a previous clearance of c and an extra side delivery to f.

Since the same argument applies at n, B and N, we shall need at least four side deliveries, none of which can be among our 11 reserved moves, and none of which can be the first exit from Fig. 38(b). This accounts for 16 moves; call the other the **spare**. Moreover, if a U-turn is involved we have a further side delivery, and so no spare. Note that after eha, p is a side delivery, but j doesn't count as one while g is still occupied, because we'll still need one to clear gnM.

The final stage of Beasley's proof just enumerates all the variations. In the list below the spare move is in **bold**. In the first two variations the first exit from Fig. 38(b) is L, and in all the others it's h. Each variation ends with ‡, § or a colon and a number.

    ‡   means that the next move can't be a corner move
        or a side delivery and the spare has already been used,
    §   means that there aren't enough moves left to reduce
        the score to zero, and
    :9 refers to variation number 9, for example.

This list of variations covers the cases where no U-turns are used. If there is a U-turn there is *no* spare move so we have only the variation $ehapc_2$‡ (cf. 56).

1 $eJLCpA_2\ddagger$	17 $ehKMJg_2\ddagger$	33 $ehajgpL\S$	48 $ehapFc_3\ddagger$
2 $D\S$	18 $CD\S$	34 $c_2L\S$	49 $M_2\ddagger$
	19 $P_2g_2\ddagger$	35 $J_2M_2\ddagger$	50 $c_2MJg_2\ddagger$
3 $ehxaf\ddagger$	20 $A_2\ddagger$	36 $l_2M_2\ddagger$	51 $Mc_2{:}50$
4 $pc_2\ddagger$	21 $d_2g_2\ddagger$	37 $L\S$	52 $Jc_3\ddagger$
5 $Lap\S$	22 A_2	38 $J_2M_2p_dc_2\ddagger$	53 $g_3\ddagger$
6 $gj\S$	23 $j_2\S$	39 $l_2M_2p_dc_2\ddagger$	54 $c_2{:}50$
7 $kcPa_2\ddagger$	24 $CD\S$		55 $g_2c_2\ddagger$
8 $mH\S$	25 $P_2A_2\ddagger$	40 $ehapc{:}30$	56 $c_2P_2\ddagger$
9 $J_2a_2\ddagger$	26 $MJ{:}19$	41 $k_2\S$	57 $F_2MJg_2\ddagger$
10 $G_2\ddagger$	27 $j_2\S$	42 $x{:}4$	58 $x{:}4$
11 $L_3\S$	28 $d_2A_2\ddagger$	43 $L{:}5$	59 $L\S$
12 $mH\S$	29 $MJ{:}21$	44 $kmH\S$	60 $jgL\S$
13 $J_lG_2\ddagger$		45 $J_lG_2\ddagger$	61 $J_2M_2\ddagger$
14 $cP{:}9$	30 $ehacpa\ddagger$	46 $L_3\S$	62 $l_2M_2\ddagger$
15 $L_3G_2ap\S$	31 $x{:}3$	47 $Pc_2\ddagger$	63 $P\ddagger$
16 $c_2\S$	32 $L{:}5$		64 $FMj_2\S$
			65 $Jg_2\ddagger$

THE CLASSICAL PROBLEMS

These are: start with one empty space, finish with a single peg. They include the reversals, for which Bergholt's results were:

	a-	b-	d-	e-	i-	j-	x-	reversal
in	16	18	16	19	16	16	18	moves.

We've just seen that his x-reversal is best possible, but Harry O. Davis has given a 15-move solution of the i-reversal:

$$kmh_2cPKCD_{PF}A_3MG_2H_4a_2d_5g_3.$$

And here are his solutions, which equal Bergholt's, for the b- and j-reversals:

$$jhapc_2xl_hIf_PA_2GJm_2gL_{Hh}M_2CB_5,$$

$$hKCd_2MJkmH_{Jl}G_3cA_2D_{Fd}g_2ab_7.$$

Hermary identified the 21 distinct problems, one place empty to one place full (see Lucas) and Davis has made a table of best known solutions (see Martin Gardner, "The Unexpected Hanging and Other Mathematical Diversions"). The numbers of moves are:

aa	ap	aO	aC	bb	bn	bx	bB	dd	dK	dH	ee	eM	eJ	ii	il	jj	jg	jE	xx	xb
16	16	17	16	18	17	18	18	16	15	16	19	17	17	15	16	16	16	17	18	17

For this information we thank Wade E. Philpott, who has copies of the solutions. Omar will want to find better ones, or prove them best possible.

REFERENCES AND FURTHER READING

J.D. Beasley, Some notes on Solitaire, Eureka, **25** (1962) 13–18.

E. Bergholt, The Queen, May 11, 1912; and "The Game of Solitaire", Routledge, London, 1920.

N.G. de Bruijn, A Solitaire game and its relation to a finite field, J. Recreational Math. **5** (1972) 133–137.

Busschop, "Recherches sur le jeu de Solitaire" Bruges, 1879.

M. Charosh, The Math. Student J., U.S.A, March 1961.

Donald C. Cross, Square Solitaire and variations, J. Recreational Math. **1** (1968) 121–123.

Harry O. Davis, 33-solitaire, new limits, small and large, Math. Gaz. **51** (1967) 91–100.

H.E. Dudeney, The Strand Magazine, April, 1908; and see "Amusements in Mathematics", problems 227, 359, 360, Nelson, London 1917, pp. 63–64, 107–108, 195, 234.

M. Gardner, Sci. Amer. **206** #6 (June 1962) 156–166; **214** #2 (Feb. 1966) 112–113; **214** #5 (May 1966) 127.

M. Gardner, "The Unexpected Hanging and other Mathematical Diversions", Simon and Schuster, 1969, p. 126.

Heinz Haber, Das Solitaire-Spiel, in "Das Mathematische Kabinett", Vol. 2, Bild der Wissenschaft, D.V-A., Stuttgart 1970, pp. 53–57.

Irvin Roy Hentzel, Triangular puzzle peg, J. Recreational Math. **6** (1973) 280–283.

Hermary, Sur le jeu du Solitaire, Assoc. franc. pour l'avancement des sci., Congrès de Montpellier, 1879.

Ross Honsberger, "Mathematical Gems II", Mathematical Association America, 1976, chap. 3, 23–28.

M. Kraitchik, "Mathematical Recreations", George Allen & Unwin, London, 1943, pp. 297–298 quotes letter 1716:1:17 Leibniz to Monmort.

E. Lucas, "Récréations Mathématiques", Blanchard, Paris 1882, Vol. 1, part 5, 89–141 is mainly concerned with the continental board (37 places) but pp. 132–138 refer to the English board and much of the whole is applicable. He attributes (pp. 114–115) the 3-*purge* to Hermary.

M. Reiss, Beitrage zur Theorie der Solitär-Spiels, Crelle's J., **54** (1857) 344–379.

Ruchonet, Théorie du solitaire, par feu le docteur Reiss, librement traduit de l'allemand, Nouv. Corr. math., t. III p. 231, Bruxelles 1877.

B.M. Stewart, "Theory of Numbers," Macmillan, New York, 1952, 1964, pp. 20–26. Analyzes Solitaire on a 7×5 rectangular board. He colors the diagonals with 3 colors in either direction and obtains the Rule of Three as an example of congruences (mod 3). Exercise 4.5 on p. 24, due to F. Gozreh, asks you to start from an even length row of pegs with the second peg missing and finish with just the second peg from the other end. A pattern of 2-purges does the trick. If you start with the fifth peg missing, then a 2-purge and a double jump by the 1st peg reduces the problem to the earlier one. Can you clear the row with other pegs missing? Which missing pegs enable you to clear an *odd* length row?

Chapter 24

Pursuing Puzzles Purposefully

The chapter of accidents is the longest chapter in the book.
John Wilkes

I shall proceed to such Recreations as adorn the Mind; of
which those of the Mathematicks are inferior to none.
William Leybourne; *Pleasure with Profit.*

We know you want to use your winning ways mostly when playing with other people, but there are quite a lot of puzzles that are so interesting that you really feel you're playing a game against some invisible opponent—perhaps the puzzle's designer—maybe a malevolent deity. In this chapter we'll discuss a few cases where some kind of strategic thinking simplifies the problem. But because we don't want to spoil your fun we'll try to arrange not always to give the *whole* game away.

SOMA

This elegant little puzzle was devised by Piet Hein. Figure 1 shows the seven non-convex shapes that can be made by sticking 4 or fewer $1 \times 1 \times 1$ cubes together. Piet Hein's puzzle is to assemble these as a $3 \times 3 \times 3$ cube.

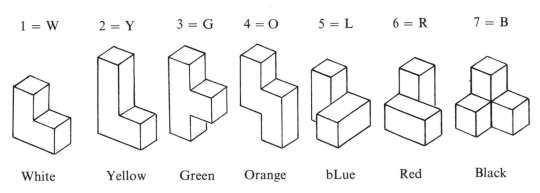

1 = W	2 = Y	3 = G	4 = O	5 = L	6 = R	7 = B
White	Yellow	Green	Orange	bLue	Red	Black

Figure 1. The Seven Pieces of Soma.

735

We advise you to use seven different colors for your pieces as in the figure. Many people solve this puzzle in under ten minutes, so it can't be terribly hard. But we've got a distinct feeling that it's much harder than it ought to be. Is this just because the pieces have such awkwardly wriggly shapes?

BLOCKS-IN-A-BOX

Here is another puzzle invented by one of us some years ago, in which all the pieces are rectangular cuboids but it still seems undeservedly hard to fit them together. We are asked to pack one $2 \times 2 \times 2$ *cube*, one $2 \times 2 \times 1$ *square*, three $3 \times 1 \times 1$ *rods* and thirteen $4 \times 2 \times 1$ *planks* into a $5 \times 5 \times 5$ box (Fig. 2). It's quite easy to get all but one of the blocks into the box, but somehow one piece always seems to stick out somewhere. A friend of ours once spent many evenings without ever finding a solution. Why is it so much harder than it seems to be?

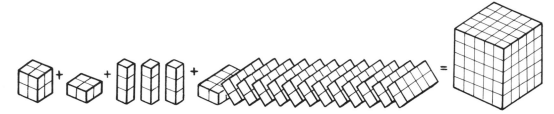

Figure 2. The Eighteen Pieces for Blocks-in-a-Box.

HIDDEN SECRETS

In our view the good puzzles are those with simple pieces but difficult solutions. Anyone can make a hard puzzle with lots of complicated pieces but how can you possibly make a hard puzzle out of a few easy pieces?

When a seemingly simple puzzle is unexpectedly difficult, it's usually because, as well as the obvious problem, there are some hidden ones to be attended to. Both Soma and Blocks-in-a-Box have such hidden secrets, but let's look at a much simpler puzzle, to fit six $2 \times 2 \times 1$ squares into a $3 \times 3 \times 3$ box, leaving three of the $1 \times 1 \times 1$ cells empty—the *holes* (Fig. 3). This now seems fairly trivial, but even so there's a hidden secret which sometimes makes people take more than 5 minutes over it. This hidden problem comes from the fact that the square pieces can only occupy

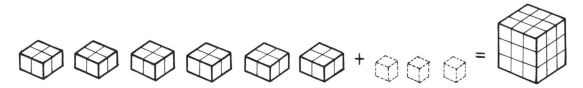

Figure 3. A Much Simpler Puzzle.

an even number of the cells in each horizontal layer. So since 9 is odd each horizontal layer must have a hole and there are only just enough holes to go round. Of course these holes must also manage to meet each of the three layers in each of two vertical directions—you can't afford to have two holes in any layer, because some other layers would have to go without.

The problem wasn't really to fit the *pieces* in but rather the *holes*. Only when you've realized this do you see why the unique solution (Fig. 4) has to be so awkward looking, with the holes strung out in a line between opposite corners rather than neatly arranged at the top of the box.

Perhaps you'd like to try the big Blocks-in-a-Box problem now, before looking at the extra hints in the Extras.

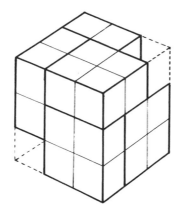

Figure 4. Six Squares in a 3×3×3 Box.

THE HIDDEN SECRETS OF SOMA

It's because the Soma puzzle pieces have to satisfy some hidden constraints as well as the obvious ones, that it causes most people more trouble than it should. Let's see why.

The $3 \times 3 \times 3$ cube has 8 *vertex* cells, 12 *edge* cells, 6 *face* cells and 1 *central* cell as in Fig. 5.

Figure 5. The Vertex, Edge, Face and Central (invisible) Cells.

Now the respective pieces can occupy at most

$$\begin{array}{ccccccc} W & Y & G & O & L & R & B \\ 1, & 2, & 2, & 1, & 1, & 1, & 1 \end{array}$$

of the vertex cells, so just one piece, the **deficient** one, must occupy just one less vertex-cell than it might. The green piece can't be deficient without being doubly so, and therefore:

> the Green piece has
> its spine along an
> edge of the cube.

Now let's color the 27 cells of the cube in two alternating colors,

> Flame for the 14 FaVored cells, F and V,
> Emerald for the 13 ExCeeded ones, E and C.

Then in *one* solution that we know, the respective pieces occupy

$$\begin{array}{ccccccc} W & Y & G & O & L & R & B \\ \end{array}$$
$$2+2+3+2+2+2+1 = 14 \text{ F, V cells.}$$
$$1+2+1+2+2+2+3 = 13 \text{ E, C cells,}$$

but the Yellow, Orange, bLue and Red pieces, and we now know also the Green piece, *must* occupy these numbers in *every* solution, and therefore so must the White and the Black, since an interchange of colors in either or both of these would alter the totals.

> The White piece occupies
> 2 FV cells, 1 EC cell.

> The Black piece occupies
> 1 FV cell and 3 EC ones.

For the placing of a single piece within the box, these considerations leave only the positions of Fig. 6 (which all arise). You'll see that up to rotations of the cube, the placement of any single piece is determined by whether or not it is deficient and whether or not it occupies the central cell.

The hidden secrets of Soma make it quite likely that one of the first few pieces you put in may already be wrong, when of course you'll spend a lot of time assembling more pieces before such a mistake shows its effect. This would happen for instance if you started by putting the corner of

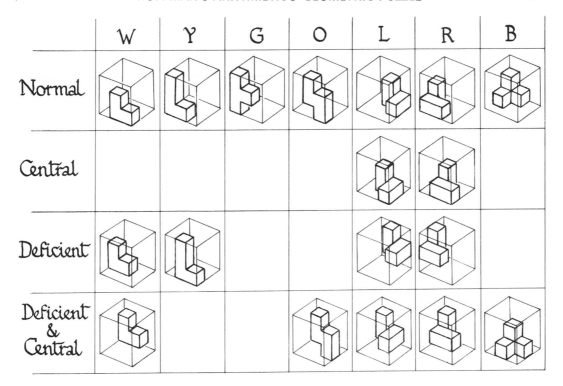

Figure 6. All Possible Positions for the Seven Soma Pieces.

the White piece into a corner of the cube. But if you only put the pieces into the allowed positions, you'll find a solution almost as soon as you start. The complete list of 240 Soma solutions was made by hand by J.H. Conway and M.J.T. Guy one particularly rainy afternoon in 1961. The SOMAP in the Extras enables you to get to 239 of them, when you've found one—*and* located it on the map!

HOFFMAN'S ARITHMETICO-GEOMETRIC PUZZLE

A well-known mathematical theorem is the inequality between the arithmetic and geometric means:

$$\sqrt{ab} \leqslant \frac{a+b}{2}.$$

Figure 7 provides a neat proof of this in the form

$$4ab \leqslant (a+b)^2$$

and the three variable version

$$27abc \leqslant (a+b+c)^3$$

has prompted Dean Hoffman to enquire whether 27 $a \times b \times c$ blocks can always be fitted into a cube of side $a+b+c$. This turns out to be quite a hard puzzle if a, b, c are fairly close together

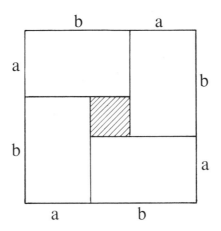

Figure 7. Proof of the Arithmetico-Geometric Inequality.

but not equal. A good practical problem is to fit

$$27 \qquad 4 \times 5 \times 6 \text{ blocks into a } 15 \times 15 \times 15 \text{ box.}$$

With these choices, as for any others with

$$\tfrac{1}{4}(a + b + c) < a < b < c,$$

it can be shown that each vertical stack of three blocks must contain just one of each height a,b,c, while there must be just three of each height in each horizontal layer. There must be the same unused area on each face (just 3 square units in the $4 \times 5 \times 6$ case).

It's almost impossible to solve the puzzle if you don't keep these hidden secrets constantly in mind because you'll make irretrievable mistakes like making a stack of three height 5 blocks, or leaving a 2×2 empty hole on some face. When you *do* keep them in mind, the puzzle becomes much easier, being only extremely difficult! You'll find some information about solutions to Hoffman's puzzle in the Extras.

COLORING THREE-BY-THREE-BY-THREE BY THREE, BAR THREE

In Hoffman's $3 \times 3 \times 3$ puzzle, the three lengths along any line of three had to be different. Can you color the cells of a $3 \times 3 \times 3$ tic-tac-toe board with

> three different colors,

using all

> three colors the same

number (9) of times, in such a way that *none* of the $\tfrac{1}{2}(5^3 - 3^3) = 49$ tic-tac-toe lines uses

> three different colors,

nor has all its

> three colors the same?

WIRE AND STRING PUZZLES

Figure 8 shows a number of topological puzzles which can be made with wire and string. It's a pity that manufacturers don't seem to know about all of these.

You wouldn't expect to be able to say much about such varied looking objects, but in fact there's a quite general principle which helps you to solve a lot of them.

THE MAGIC MIRROR METHOD

We'll just take the one-knot version of the puzzle shown in Fig. 8(c) which has been commercially sold as The Loony Loop (Trolbourne Ltd., London). You're to take the string off the rigid wire frame in Fig. 9(a).

If only that rigid wire were a bit stretchable, the puzzle would be quite easy. After squashing the string up (Fig. 9(b)) so as not to get in the way, we could stretch the loops over the ends (Fig. 9(c)) and shrink them again (Fig. 9(d)). After this we can take the string right off (Fig. 9(e)) and then put the loops back as they were (Fig. 9(f)) so as not to upset the owner.

Now the change from Fig. 9(b) to Fig. 9(d) could be accomplished by continuously distorting space. Think of embedding the puzzle in a flexible jelly, if Mother has one made up. Now old-fashioned fairgrounds had special mirrors which seemed to distort space in very funny ways. Now let's imagine a magic mirror with the wonderful property that the distortion is just what's required to make Fig. 9(b) look like Fig. 9(d). Hold the wire frame absolutely still before the magic mirror (Fig. 10(a)) and bunch the string up until it's almost a single point on the axis. Because the space distortion was continuous, its image will also be almost a single point on the image axis.

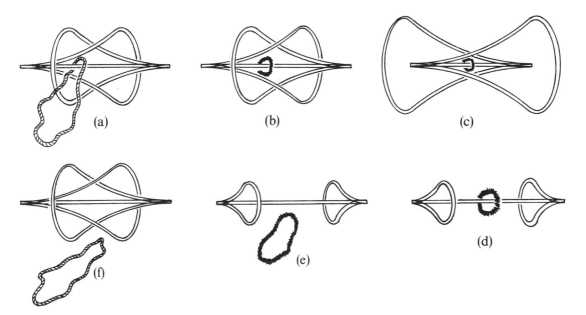

Figure 9. Solving The Loony Loop.

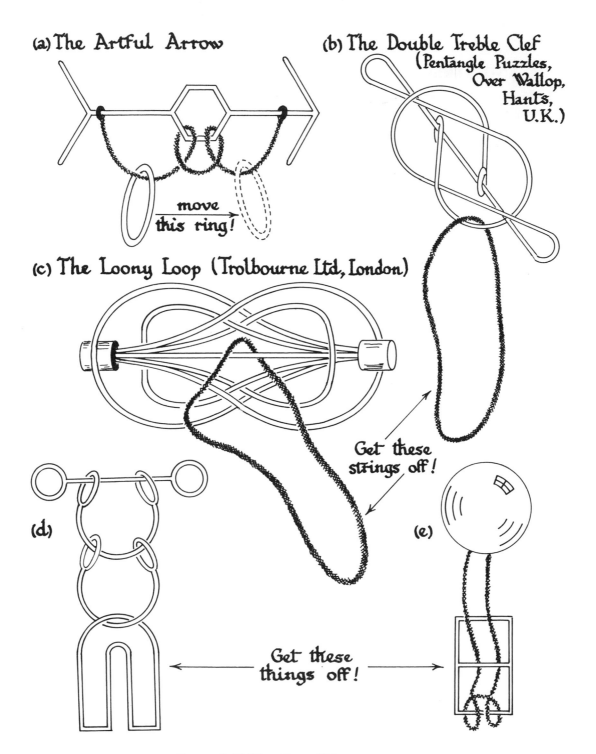

(a) The Artful Arrow

move
this ring!

(b) The Double Treble Clef
(Pentangle Puzzles,
Over Wallop,
Hants,
U.K.)

(c) The Loony Loop (Trolbourne Ltd, London)

Get these
strings off!

(d)

(e)

Get these
things off!

Figure 8. Shifting Rings, Strings . . . . . .

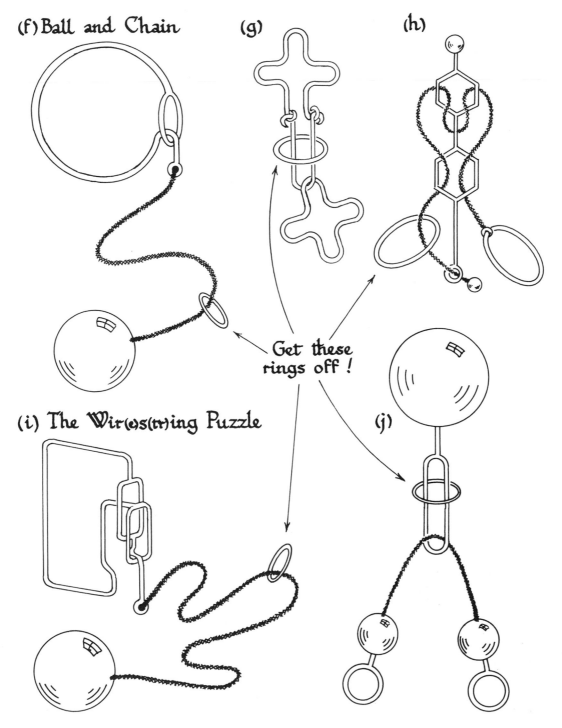

(f) Ball and Chain

(g)

(h)

Get these rings off!

(i) The Wir(e)s(tr)ing Puzzle

(j)

. . . . . . and Other Things.

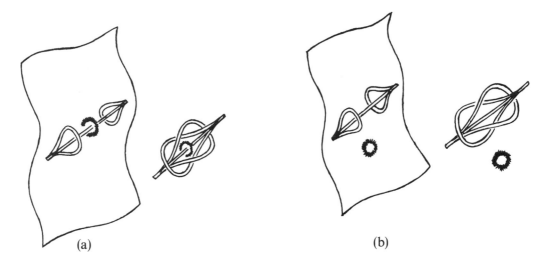

Figure 10. The Magic Mirror.

Now, very carefully, move the string in just such a way that its *image* in the magic mirror moves completely away from the wire and shrinks to a small point at some little distance from it. Once again, because the distortion was continuous, the real string must now be almost a point, some distance from the wire, and you've solved the puzzle. Easy, wasn't it?

In such cases it often helps to imagine an intermediate distortion. In Fig. 11 we show two stages in an intermediately distorted one-knot Loony Loop. Perhaps you're ready for the two knot version (Fig. 8(c))? Or the Double Treble Clef (Fig. 8(b)) (Pentangle Puzzles, Over Wallop, Hants, U.K.)?

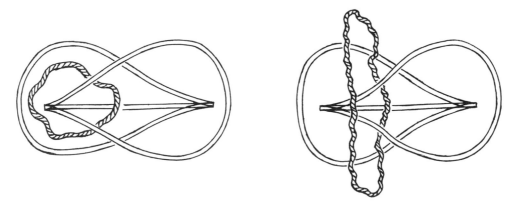

Figure 11. A Less Distorting Mirror.

If a puzzle has got just one completely rigid piece and a number of completely flexible pieces then you can often use the magic mirror method to pretend that the rigid piece is also flexible. For instance, although it may seem impossible to make the braided piece of paper in Fig. 12

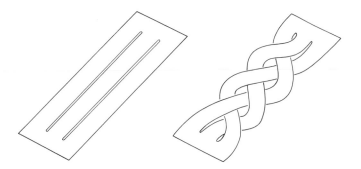

Figure 12. Can You Braid this Strip of Paper?

without glue, it can be undone quite easily. This principle is quite familiar to craftsmen in leather. (To make it you should start braiding at one end and undo the tangle which forms at the other.) The

BARMY BRAID

problem appears for the first time in this book. It's to take the string off the rigid wire frame in Fig. 13(a). You know you can do it, because in a suitable magic mirror it looks like Fig. 13(b).

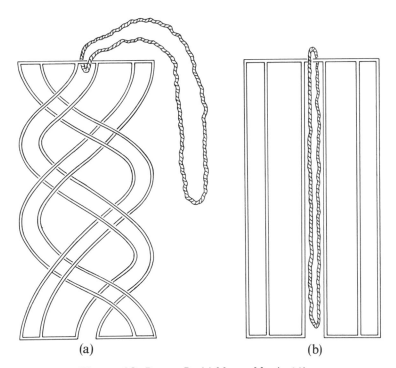

(a)   (b)

Figure 13. Barmy Braid Meets Magic Mirror.

THE ARTFUL ARROW

Figure 8(a) is our version of a puzzle that appears in many different forms. The basic framework is often a bar of wood with a drill hole in place of our hexagon. We have even seen a version in which the ends of our arrow are a giant's arms and the central hole his nostrils, but the solution is always the same! You can solve this puzzle, and some similar ones, by a modification of the Magic Mirror Method which we call

THE MAGIC MOVIE METHOD

If the Artful Arrow had a much smaller ring, there'd be no difficulty about solving it; we'd just slide the ring along the string from the tail of the arrow to its head. Let's suppose we have a kinematic friend who takes a movie of this, but that through some accident with his filters, the string doesn't show up too well, so that what the movie shows is the rigid arrow framework and a little ring that wanders about in space. In fact the ring moves downward through the hexagon (1 to 2 to 3 in Fig. 14(a)), sweeps around (3 to 4 to 5) and then comes safely back up again (5 to 6 to 7).

What we want to do is to watch this movie in a sort of hyperspace magic mirror which

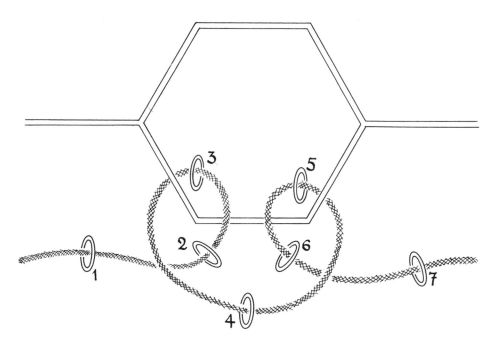

Figure 14(a). The Magic Movie M_o.

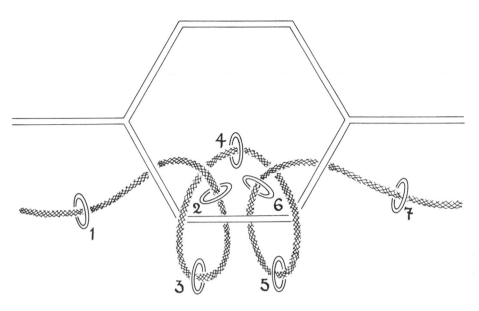

Figure 14(b). An Intermediate Half-Magic Movie.

distorts both space and time. Our friend can arrange this for us by taking the movie M_0 to the animation department where they can change the whole movie bit by bit, first to M_1, in which the ring goes down through the hexagon and wanders about a bit less before it comes back up again, then to M_2, in which it wanders hardly at all before coming up, then to M_3 in which it only takes a timid dip through the hexagon, then in M_4 not at all, while in M_5, M_6, ... the size of the ring gradually increases until it is too big to go through the hexagon.

The trouble with all these movies is that we can't see the string! But since we intend the sequence of movies to realize a continuous distortion of space-time, we can ask the animation department to work overtime and fill in the position of the string as well. The final movie, M_{10} say, should satisfy the producer as representing a solution to the puzzle.

As usual, it helps if the whole process is only half-magic. What must actually happen in this sequence of movies is that the excursion of the ring through the hexagon is gradually replaced by a pulling up of the central loop of string (Mahomet coming to the mountain). In Fig. 14(b) we show an intermediate movie in which you can hardly tell whether this loop, as it passes through the ring in position 4, is above or below the hexagon. You can therefore solve this puzzle by passing the ring from 1 to 2 to 3 while the loop is *below* the hexagon, then lifting the loop a bit while you slide the ring from 3 to 4 to 5 and drop it again so that you can go from 5 to 6 to 7. Since all these movies can be made with a full-sized ring, this will solve the puzzle.

This argument allows us to extend the idea we noted when introducing the Barmy Braid. Suppose that a puzzle has *any number* of rigid pieces (like our arrow and ring) and some arbitrarily flexible ones (e.g., our string) and you could find a solution if the rigid pieces were made flexible. Then, if the motion of the rigid pieces in your solution can be continuously distorted into a rigidly permissible motion, you can use the Magic Movie Method to solve the original puzzle. In topologists' technical language we are using the *Isotopy Extension Principle*.

PARTY TRICKS AND CHINESE RINGS

Figure 15. Girl Meets Boy.

You must have met the party trick where the boy and the girl have to separate themselves without untying the knots in the string. Usually they have lots of fun stepping through one another's arms without effect before they find the real answer.

Let's look at one of those fists more closely (Fig. 16(a)). With a really magic mirror this looks like (Fig. 16(b)) and the solution is obvious, but as usual it's slightly easier to see what to do if your mirror is only half magic (Fig. 16(c)).

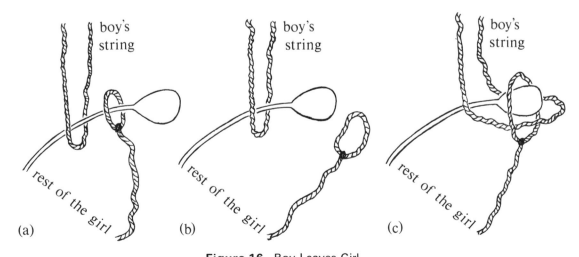

Figure 16. Boy Leaves Girl.

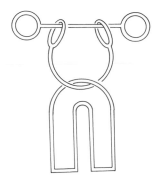

Figure 17(a). Pajamas on Hanger.

One of our wire and string puzzles is very like this. The pajama-shaped frame at the bottom of Fig. 17(a) is made of wire rather than string, but it happens to be just about the shape that a piece of string would need to get to while being taken off. In Fig. 8(d) you'll see there's a similar puzzle, but with an extra piece.

The magic mirror in Fig. 17(b) shows that this puzzle can certainly be solved if the wire pajama shape is replaced by a completely flexible string—once again this funny shape is sufficient to overcome its lack of flexibility.

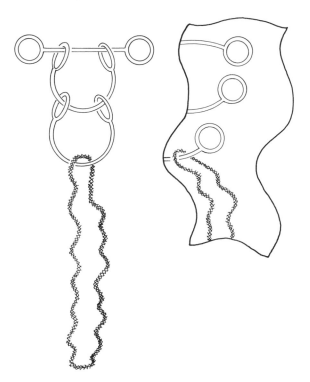

Figure 17(b). Another Look in the Magic Mirror.

The Chinese rings are an indefinite extension of this principle. The magic mirror method shows that the string in Fig. 18(a) can be taken right off. In the course of doing so it reaches a position like that of the wire loop in Fig. 18(b), and removal of this is the usual Chinese Rings puzzle.

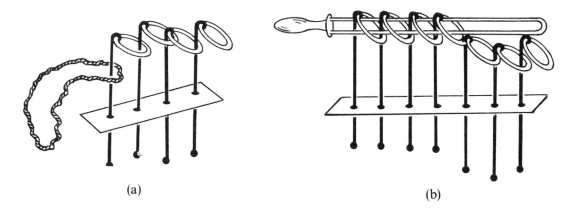

(a)   (b)

Figure 18. The Chinese (st)ring Puzzle.

CHINESE RINGS AND THE GRAY CODE

Figure 19(a) shows a certain position of a 7-ring Chinese Rings puzzle. We call this position

1   0   1   1   1   0   0

because the rings we've numbered

64   32   16   8   4   2   1

are respectively

on off on on on off off

the loop. ("On" means that the ring's retaining wire passes through the loop.) Which positions neighbor this?

You hardly need a magic mirror to see how the state of the rightmost ring, number 1, can always be changed (Fig. 19(b)), showing that our position neighbors

1   0   1   1   1   0   1.

But it also neighbors

1   0   1   0   1   0   0

as well!

To see this, slip ring number 8 up over the end of the loop as suggested by the dotted arrow in Fig. 19(a) and then drop it down through the loop as hinted in Fig. 19(c).

In general the rightmost ring, number 1, can always be slipped on or off the loop, so that

… ? ? ? 0 neighbors … ? ? ? 1.

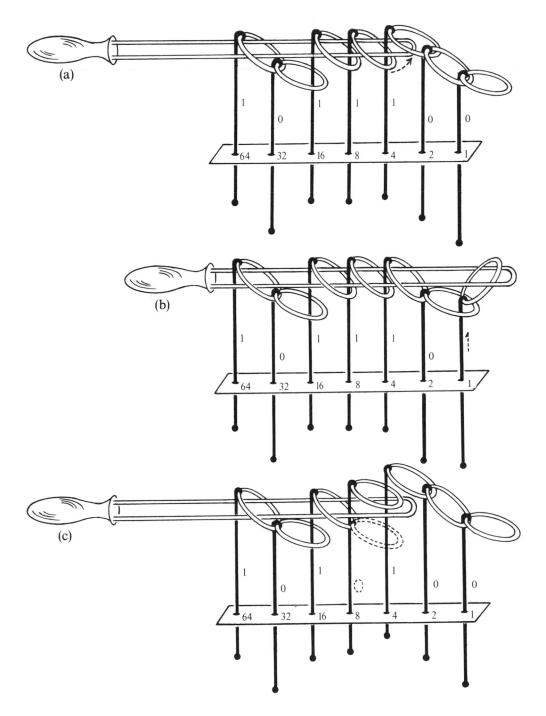

Figure 19. Gray Code and Chinese Rings.

But also a ring can be slipped on or off provided that the ring just right of it is *on* and all rings right of *that* are *off*, so that

$$... \ ? \ 1 \ 1 \ 0 \ 0 \ \text{neighbors} \ ... \ ? \ 0 \ 1 \ 0 \ 0 \ 0.$$

With these neighboring rules the entire set of 2^n positions in the *n*-ring puzzle form one continuous sequence, which for $n = 4$ is:

ring #	8	4	2	1	
state # 8, i.e.	1	0	0	0	is 15 moves from being off,
state # 9, i.e.	1	0	0	1	is 14 moves from being off,
state # 11, i.e.	1	0	1	1	is 13 moves from being off,
state # 10, i.e.	1	0	1	0	is 12 moves from being off,
state # 14, i.e.	1	1	1	0	is 11 moves from being off,
state # 15, i.e.	1	1	1	1	is 10 moves from being off,
state # 13, i.e.	1	1	0	1	is 9 moves from being off,
state # 12, i.e.	1	1	0	0	is 8 moves from being off,
state # 4, i.e.	0	1	0	0	is 7 moves from being off,
state # 5, i.e.	0	1	0	1	is 6 moves from being off,
state # 7, i.e.	0	1	1	1	is 5 moves from being off,
state # 6, i.e.	0	1	1	0	is 4 moves from being kff,
state # 2, i.e.	0	0	1	0	is 3 moves from being off,
state # 3, i.e.	0	0	1	1	is 2 moves from being off,
state # 1, i.e.	0	0	0	1	is 1 moves from being off,
and state # 0, i.e.	0	0	0	0	is OFF!

How do we tell how many moves it takes to get all the rings off if we're given only the state number, i.e. the sum of the numbers of the rings that are on? The answer displays a remarkable connexion with nim-addition! When you're in state number n, it will take you exactly

$$n \overset{*}{+} \lfloor n/2 \rfloor \overset{*}{+} \lfloor n/4 \rfloor \overset{*}{+} \lfloor n/8 \rfloor \overset{*}{+} \ ... = m$$

moves to get off. For example in state 13 you're just

$$13 \overset{*}{+} 6 \overset{*}{+} 3 \overset{*}{+} 1 = 9$$

moves away. And if you're given a number m, then state number

$$m \overset{*}{+} \lfloor m/2 \rfloor = n$$

is the one that's just m moves from off. For example

$$9 \overset{*}{+} 4 = 13.$$

Let's find the position that's 99 moves from off in the 7-ring puzzle. Because the binary expansions of 99 and $\lfloor 99/2 \rfloor$ are

$$
\begin{array}{ccccccc}
1 & 1 & 0 & 0 & 0 & 1 & 1 \\
  & 1 & 1 & 0 & 0 & 0 & 1 \\
\end{array}
$$

and

the answer is   1 0 1 0 0 1 0.

How many moves is state

$$1 \quad 1 \quad 0 \quad 1 \quad 1 \quad 1 \quad 1$$

from off? The answer is found by the 7-term nim-sum

$$
\begin{array}{ccccccc}
1 & 1 & 0 & 1 & 1 & 1 & 1 \\
  & 1 & 1 & 0 & 1 & 1 & 1 \\
  &   & 1 & 1 & 0 & 1 & 1 \\
  &   &   & 1 & 1 & 0 & 1 \\
  &   &   &   & 1 & 1 & 0 \\
  &   &   &   &   & 1 & 1 \\
  &   &   &   &   &   & 1 \\
\end{array}
$$

$$= 1 \quad 0 \quad 0 \quad 1 \quad 0 \quad 1 \quad 0,$$

which is the binary expansion of 74.

In various kinds of control device it's important to code numbers in such a way that the codes from adjacent numbers differ in only one place and the code that appears above, known to engineers as the Gray code, has this useful property. It has also been used in transmitting television signals. However, its connexion with the Chinese Rings puzzle was known to Monsieur L. Gros, more than a century ago. Incidentally, the multiknot Loony Loop is connected with a ternary version of the Gray code.

The Chinese Rings, despite their name, appear to be a medieval Scandinavian discovery, having originally been used as a sort of combination lock. In recent years several mechanical and electronic puzzles, completely different in appearance, but employing the same mathematical structure, have appeared on the market.

THE TOWER OF HANOÏ

In happier times, Hanoï was mainly known to puzzlers as the fabled site of that temple where monks were ceaselessly engaged in transferring 64 gold discs from the first to the last of three pegs according to the conditions that

only one disc may be moved at a time, and
no disc may be placed above a smaller one.

Figure 20(a) shows the initial position in a smaller version of the puzzle and Fig. 20(b) shows the position 13 moves later.

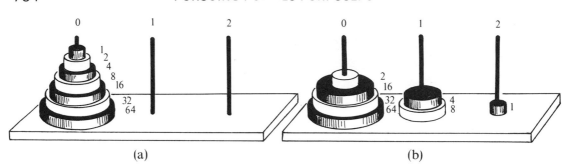

Figure 20. The Tower of Hanoï.

In this puzzle it's possible to make mistakes, unlike in the Chinese Rings where the only mistake you can make is to start travelling in the wrong direction. However, you won't make too many mistakes if you use discs that are alternately gold and silver and

> never place a disc immediately above another of the same metal.

To find out where you should be after m moves, expand m in binary, and then, according as the total number of discs is

	even	or	odd,
replace a 1 digit by the ternary number	1	or	2,
replace a 2 digit by the ternary number	21	or	12,
replace a 4 digit by the ternary number	122	or	211,
replace an 8 digit by the ternary number	2111	or	1222,
replace a 16 digit by the ternary number	12222	or	21111,
replace a 32 digit by the ternary number	211111	or	122222,
replace a 64 digit by the ternary number	1222222	or	2111111,

... ...

These ternary numbers, when added mod 3 without carrying, show you what peg each disc should be on. For 13 moves and a 7-disc tower, since 7 is odd and

$$\left.\begin{array}{r} 1 \\ +4 \\ +8 \end{array}\right\} \qquad \text{we find the ternary numbers} \qquad \left\{\begin{array}{l} 2 \\ 211 \\ 1222 \end{array}\right.$$

$$= 13. \qquad\qquad\qquad\qquad\qquad\qquad 0001102,$$

showing that disc 1 should be on peg 2, discs 4 and 8 on peg 1, and the rest on peg 0 as in Fig. 20(b).

The Tower of Hanoï puzzle and the fable which usually accompanies it were invented by Monsieurs Claus (Édouard Lucas) and De Parville in 1883 and 1884.

A SOLITAIRE-LIKE PUZZLE AND SOME COIN-SLIDING PROBLEMS

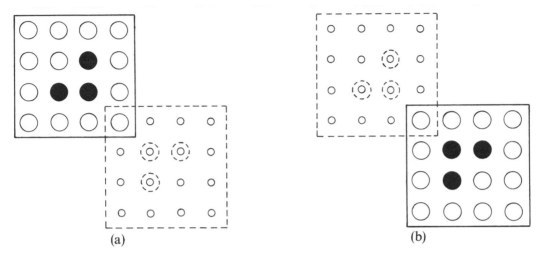

Figure 21. A Solitaire-Like Puzzle.

A little puzzle we came across recently is played in a way very similar to the game of Peg Solitaire, except that the pegs are not removed after jumping. Starting from the position of Fig. 21(a), go to the "opposite" position of Fig. 21(b) jumping only in the N–S and W–E directions. The three special pegs are to move to the three special places.

H	H	H		T	T	T

Figure 22. Swap the Hares and Tortoises.

This is rather like various two-dimensional forms of the familiar Hares and Tortoises (or sheep and goats) puzzle (Fig. 22) in which the animals (you can use coins) have to change places and the permitted moves are as in the game of Toads and Frogs in Chapter 1. Other problems with the same coins are:

(i)   get from Fig. 23(a) to Fig. 23(b) with just 3 moves of 2 contiguous coins (the coins to be slid on the table, remaining in the same orientation and touching throughout);
(ii) the same, but reversing the orientation of each pair of coins as it is moved;
(iii) similar problems, but with more coins;
(iv) form the six coins of Fig. 24(a) into a ring (Fig. 24(b)) with just three moves. At each move one coin must be slid on the table, without disturbing any of the others, and positioned by touching it against just two coins. For example, you might try Fig. 24(c) for your first move, but then you wouldn't be able to slide the middle one out.

Figure 23. Make Three Moves of Two Contiguous Coins.

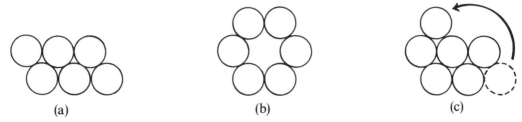

Figure 24. Ringing the Changes.

THE FIFTEEN PUZZLE AND THE LUCKY SEVEN PUZZLE

Figure 25. Sam Loyd's Fifteen Puzzle.

The most famous sliding puzzle is Sam Loyd's *Fifteen Puzzle* in which the home position is Fig. 25 and the move is to slide one square at a time into the empty space. You are required to get home from the random position you usually find the puzzle in. Nowadays the puzzle is usually sold with pieces so designed that it is impossible to remove them from the base.

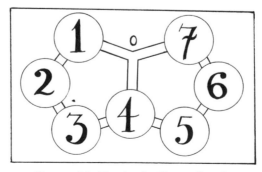

Figure 26. The Lucky Seven Puzzle.

A more interesting puzzle is the **Lucky Seven Puzzle** for which the home state is displayed in Fig. 26 and similar rules apply.

In such puzzles there are certain basic permutations of the pieces that bring the empty space back to its standard position. For the Seven Puzzle you can either move the four discs in the left pentagon in the order 1, 2, 3, 4, 1, leading to the position of Fig. 27(a) or treat the right pentagon similarly, moving 7, 6, 5, 4, 7, leading to the position of Fig. 27(b).

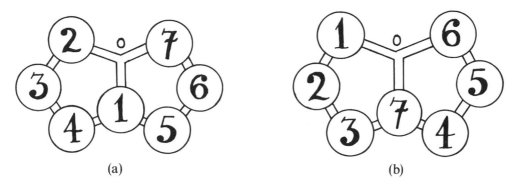

(a)   (b)

Figure 27. After a Few Moves.

In the first case we have effected the permutation α in which

$$\left.\begin{array}{llllllll} \text{disc} & 1 & 2 & 3 & 4 & 5 & 6 & 7 \\ \text{goes to place} & 4 & 1 & 2 & 3 & 5 & 6 & 7 \end{array}\right\} \text{or, for short,} \quad (1432)\,(5)\,(6)\,(7),$$

and in the second case the permutation β in which

$$\left.\begin{array}{llllllll} \text{disc} & 1 & 2 & 3 & 4 & 5 & 6 & 7 \\ \text{goes to place} & 1 & 2 & 3 & 5 & 6 & 7 & 4 \end{array}\right\} \text{or } (1)\,(2)\,(3)\,(4567).$$

We can obviously combine these basic permutations to any extent. For instance, by performing the sequence

$$1 \xrightarrow{\alpha} 4 \xrightarrow{\beta} 5 \xrightarrow{\alpha} 5 \xrightarrow{\alpha} 5 \xrightarrow{\beta} 6$$
$$2 \rightarrow 1 \rightarrow 1 \rightarrow 4 \rightarrow 3 \rightarrow 3$$
$$3 \rightarrow 2 \rightarrow 2 \rightarrow 1 \rightarrow 4 \rightarrow 5$$
$$4 \rightarrow 3 \rightarrow 3 \rightarrow 2 \rightarrow 1 \rightarrow 1$$
$$5 \rightarrow 5 \rightarrow 6 \rightarrow 6 \rightarrow 6 \rightarrow 7$$
$$6 \rightarrow 6 \rightarrow 7 \rightarrow 7 \rightarrow 7 \rightarrow 4$$
$$7 \rightarrow 7 \rightarrow 4 \rightarrow 3 \rightarrow 2 \rightarrow 2$$

$$\left.\begin{array}{llllllll} \text{disc} & 1 & 2 & 3 & 4 & 5 & 6 & 7 \\ \text{gets to place} & 6 & 3 & 5 & 1 & 7 & 4 & 2 \end{array}\right\} \text{or } (164)\,(2357).$$

By combining any given permutations in all possible ways we get what mathematicians call a **group** of permutations. Is there an easy way to see which permutations belong to the group of the Lucky Seven Puzzle? Yes! The trick, as always in such cases, is to find some permutations which keep most of the objects fixed. In the case of the Seven Puzzle it seems best to regard the outer edges as forming a complete circle across which there is a single bridge between places 0 and 4 (Fig. 28). In this form the seven discs can be freely cycled round the outer circle (which

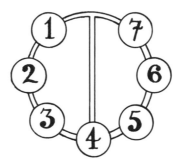

Figure 28. Crossing Bridges.

we hardly count as a move) or else a single disc may be slid across the bridge (remember that in the actual form of the puzzle the bridge is too short for several discs to traverse it at once). It doesn't really matter whether the disc we slide across the bridge goes upwards or downwards, since this has the same effect on the cyclic order, so we'll always slide our discs *downward*.

If we think of the puzzle in this way and, starting from the home position, slide discs 2, 4, 2, 4, 2 down the bridge, we reach the position of Fig. 29 in which discs 2 and 4 have been interchanged

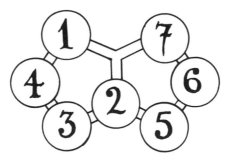

Figure 29. Swapping Two and Four.

and all the others are in their original places. Obviously we can interchange any pair of discs which are two places apart round the circle in this way. It's not hard to see how *any* desired re-arrangement can be reached by a succession of such interchanges. For instance if we wanted to get

$$\text{discs } 1 \; 2 \; 3 \; 4 \; 5 \; 6 \; 7$$
$$\text{to places } 7 \; 6 \; 5 \; 4 \; 3 \; 2 \; 1$$

we might perform the interchanges of the following scheme

$$
\begin{array}{ccccccc}
1 & 2 & 3 & 4 & 5 & 6 & 7 \\
3 & 2 & 1 & 4 & 5 & 6 & 7 \\
3 & 2 & 5 & 4 & 1 & 6 & 7 \\
3 & 2 & 5 & 4 & 7 & 6 & 1 \\
3 & 4 & 5 & 2 & 7 & 6 & 1 \\
3 & 4 & 5 & 6 & 7 & 2 & 1 \\
5 & 4 & 3 & 6 & 7 & 2 & 1 \\
5 & 4 & 7 & 6 & 3 & 2 & 1 \\
5 & 6 & 7 & 4 & 3 & 2 & 1 \\
7 & 6 & 5 & 4 & 3 & 2 & 1
\end{array}
$$

Get 1 in position first,
then 2,
then 3,
then 4,
then 5 (6 and 7).

leading to a solution in which 45 discs have crossed the bridge. This method is not very efficient but it has the great advantage of providing an almost mechanical technique by which you can obtain any position. Can you find a shorter solution to the above problem?

ALL OTHER COURSES FOR POINT-TO-POINT

The history of the Fifteen Puzzle has been given too many times to bear further repetition here. Exactly half of the

$$15! = 1 \times 2 \times 3 \times \ldots \times 15 = 1\,307\,674\,368\,000$$

permutations (the so called *even* permutations) can be obtained. In technical language, the available permutations form the **alternating group**, A_{15}, whereas for the Lucky Seven Puzzle we have the full **symmetric group**, S_7, of $7! = 7 \times 6 \times 5 \times 4 \times 3 \times 2 \times 1 = 5040$ permutations.

You can make a puzzle of this type by putting counters on all but one of the nodes of any connected graph and then sliding them, point to point, always along an edge into the currently empty node. We can afford to ignore the *degenerate* cases, when your graph is a cycle, or is made by putting two smaller graphs together at a single node, because then the puzzle is trivial, or degenerates into the two smaller puzzles corresponding to the two smaller graphs.

Rick Wilson has proved the remarkable theorem that for every non-degenerate case but one we get either the full symmetric group (if some circuit is odd) or the alternating group (otherwise). The single exception is the graph of the **Tricky Six Puzzle** (Fig. 30) for which the group consists of all possible Möbius transformations

$$x \to \frac{ax + b}{cx + d} \ (\text{mod } 5)$$

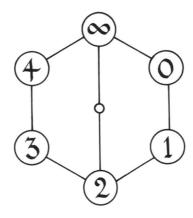

Figure 30. Rick's Tricky Six Puzzle.

THE HUNGARIAN CUBE—BÜVÖS KOCKA

The Hungarian words actually mean "magic cube". If you're crazy enough to get one of these you'll see that when it comes to you from the manufacturer it has just one color on each face (Fig. 31(a)) but your Hungarian cube is unlikely to stay in this beautiful state because you can rotate the nine little **cubelets** that make up any face (Fig. 31(b)) and so disturb the color scheme. For example, if you complete the turn started in Fig. 31(b), and then turn the top face clockwise you'll arrive at Fig. 31(c). After three more turns the colors are all over the place (Fig. 31(d)) and you'll find it very hard to recover the original arrangement; in other words to get each of the cubelets back into its own **cubicle**, *and* the right way round.

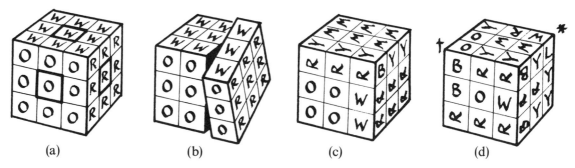

| (a) | (b) | (c) | (d) |

Figure 31. The Hungarian Magic Cube.

There are really two problems about this elegant little puzzle. The first is how its brilliant designer, Ernö Rubik, can possibly have managed to make all those motions feasible without all the cubelets falling apart. We'll leave that one to you! The other is, of course, to provide a method by which we can guarantee to get home from any position our friends have muddled the cube into.

JUST HOW CHAOTIC CAN THE CUBE GET?

At least there are six permanent landmarks: the cubelets at the centres of the faces always stay in their own cubicles although they may be rotated. We call these the **face cubelets** and have framed them in Fig. 31(a). No matter how confused your cube looks, you can tell what the final color of each face should be, just by looking at the face cubelet at its centre. So, for instance, in Fig. 31(d) we call the top face **white** even though only one third of it really is.

So you can work out the home cubicle for any cubelet by just looking at its colors and thinking which faces these belong to. For instance the LWO cubelet ∗ in Fig. 31(d) should end up at † (in our cube the colors opposite R, W, O are L, B, Y). We recommend the nervous novice always to hold the cube with its white face uppermost and then to take a careful note of the color of the bottom face, which we call the **ground** color.

Since the other 20 visible cubes are of two types,

       8 **corner cubes**, which have 3 possible orientations in their cubicles,

and 12 **edge cubes**, which have 2,

there are at most

$$3^8 \times 2^{12} \times 8! \times 12! = 519\,024\,039\,293\,878\,272\,000$$

conceivable arrangements. However, Anne Scott proved that only one-twelfth of this number, namely

$$43\,252\,003\,274\,489\,856\,000$$

are attainable.

CHIEF COLORS AND CHIEF FACES

These notions help us keep track of the orientations of cubelets, even when they're not in their home cubicles. We'll call the **chief face** of a *cubicle* the one in the top or bottom surface of the cube, if there is one, and otherwise the one in the right or left wall. The **chief color** of a *cubelet* is the color that should be in the chief place when the cubelet gets home. In other words White or the Ground color if possible, and otherwise the color that should end up in the left or right wall of the cube.

If a cubelet, no matter where it is, has its chief color in the chief face of its current cubicle we'll call it **sane** and otherwise **flipped** (if it's an edge cubelet) or **twisted** (if it's a corner one). There's only one way to make an edge-flip (e), but a corner may be twisted anticlockwise (a) or clockwise (c).

Now, as shown in Fig. 32, turning the top (or bottom) preserves the chiefness of every cubelet. Turning the front (or back) changes the chiefness at four corners and turning the left (or right) changes it at four corners and four edges. Since each turn flips an even number of edges, you can see that for attainable positions

> the total number of edge-flips
> will always be even.

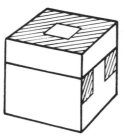 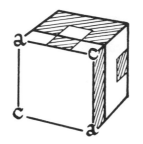 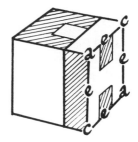

Figure 32. Changes in Chiefness.

And since each turn produces equal numbers of clockwise and anticlockwise twists

> the total corner twisting
> will always be zero, mod 3.

In computing corner twists we count $+1$ for clockwise and -1 for anticlockwise — of course three clockwise twists of a cubelet produce no effect. Finally, for reasons as in the Fifteen Puzzle

> the total permutation of all the
> 20 movable cubelets must be *even*.

An **even permutation** is one we might imagine making by an even number of interchanges.

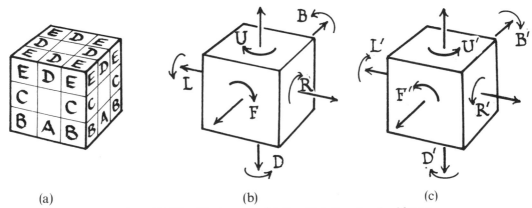

(a)   (b)   (c)

Figure 33. The Six Stages and Our Notation for the Moves.

CURING THE CUBE

Benson, Conway and Seal have simplified Anne Scott's proof that you really can get home from any position for which

(i) the total edge flipping is zero, mod 2,

(ii) the total corner twisting is zero, mod 3, and

(iii) the total permutation of all 20 movable cubes is even.

We have adapted our names for the moves (Fig. 33) so as to agree with David Singmaster's in the hope that a single notation will rapidly become universal. Note that the unprimed letters L,R,F,B,U,D, refer to *clockwise* turns, and the primed letters L′,R′,F′,B′,U′,D′ to *anticlockwise* ones. Our notation for the **slice moves** is illustrated in Fig. 34. Note that in these moves only the *middle* layer of the cube is turned. We shall also use the common notation in which, for example, X^2 means "do X twice" and X^{-1} means "undo X".

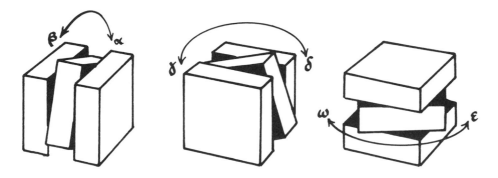

Figure 34. Slice Moves.

Our method has six stages which correspond roughly to the letters in Fig. 33(a).

A: Aloft, Around (Adjust) and About.

B: Bottom Layer Corner Cubelets.

C: Central Layer Edge Cubelets.

D: Domiciling the Top Edge Cubelets.

E: Exchanging Pairs of Top Corners.

F: Finishing Flips and Fiddles.

We've collected the figures for these stages in Fig. 35 for easy reference, so keep a finger on page 765.

Warning: Be very careful when applying this algorithm. Think of "tightening" or "loosening" a screw-cap, so that you never mistake a clockwise turn for an anticlockwise one, even from behind. Be aware at all times which way up you are holding the cube, and don't stop to think in the middle of a sequence of moves. Remember that if you make a tiny mistake you'll probably have to go all the way back to Stage A.

> THE CUBE SELDOM FORGIVES!

A: ALOFT, AROUND (ADJUST) AND ABOUT

Our first stage (Fig. 35A) gets the bottom edge cubelets (A in Fig. 33(a)) into their correct cubicles, the right way round. You bring the ground (=chief) color of such a cubelet into the topmost surface (Aloft) then turn the top layer Around to put this cubelet into the correct side wall which can be turned About to home the cubelet. Sometimes this disturbs a bottom edge cubelet that's already home, but this can be Adjusted by turning the appropriate side wall just before the About step.

B: BOTTOM LAYER CORNER CUBELETS

Now, without disturbing the bottom layer edge cubelets, you must get the bottom layer corner cubelets home.

If the cubelet that's to stand on the shaded square of Fig. 35B is in the top layer, turn the top layer until this cubelet's ground color is in one of the three numbered positions. Then do the appropriate one of

$$\text{B1: } F'U'F \qquad \text{B2: } RUR' \qquad \text{B3: } F'UF.RU^2R'$$

If the cubelet is already *in* the bottom layer, but wrongly placed, use one of these to put any corner cubelet from the top layer into its current position, thereby evicting it into the top layer. Then work as above to put it into the proper place. Repeat this procedure for the other three bottom layer corner cubelets.

C: CENTRAL LAYER EDGE CUBELETS

This stage corrects the central layer edge cubelets without affecting the bottom layer.

If the cubelet destined for the shaded cubicle of Fig. 35C is in the top layer, turn the top layer until you want to move this cubelet in one of the two ways of Fig. 35C (its side face will then be just above the face cubelet of the same color). Then do the appropriate one of

$$\text{C1: } URU'R'.U'F'UF \qquad \text{C2: } U'F'UF.URU'R'$$

If the cubelet is already *in* the central layer, but wrongly placed, use one of these to evict it into the top layer. Then work as above. Repeat the procedure for the other three central layer edge cubelets.

D: DOMICILING THE TOP EDGE CUBELETS

i.e. putting the top layer edge cubelets into their own home cubicles without as yet worrying about their orientations.

You can do this by a sequence of swaps of adjacent edge cubelets as in Fig. 35D for which the moves are

$$UF.RUR'U'.F'$$

Of course you can first turn the top layer to reduce the number of swaps needed.

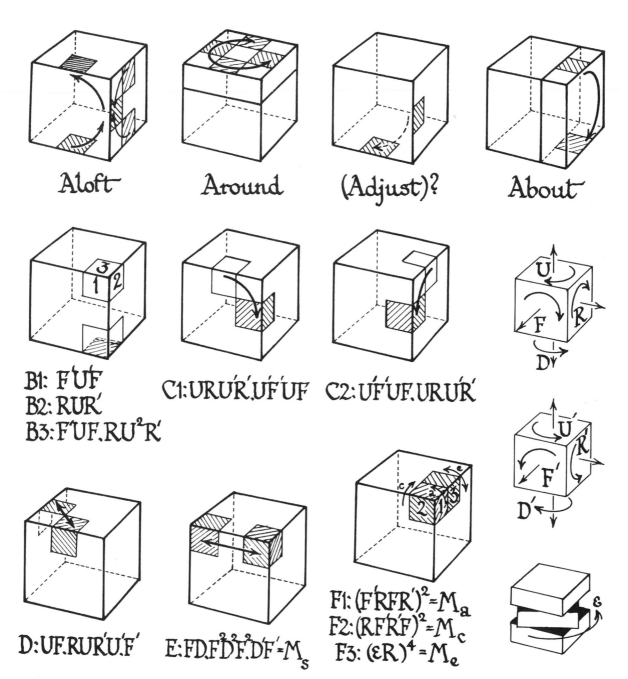

Aloft Around (Adjust)? About

B1: F'UF
B2: RUR'
B3: F'UF.RU²R'

C1: URUR'.UF'UF C2: UF'UF.URUR'

D: UF.RURU'.F' E: FD.FD²F.DF'=M$_s$

F1: (F'RFR')²=M$_a$
F2: (RF'R'F)²=M$_c$
F3: (ER)⁴=M$_e$

Figure 35. Six Simple Stages Cure Chaotic Cubes.

E: EXCHANGING PAIRS OF TOP CORNERS

Now you must get the top layer corner cubelets into their own cubicles by moves that, when they are finally completed, won't have affected the bottom two layers or moved the top layer edge cubelets. Usually you can do this in just two swaps of adjacent corners, but sometimes four will be needed.

Correct performance requires some care. Work out a pair of successive swaps of adjacent corner cubelets that will improve things. Then turn the cube until the first required swap is as in Fig. 35E and do our

$$\text{monoswap, } M_S = FD \cdot F^2 D^2 F^2 \cdot D'F'$$

Then turn THE TOP LAYER *ONLY* to bring the second desired swap into the position of Fig. 35E, do another monoswap, and then return the top layer to its original position.

Since the bottom two layers are disordered by a single monoswap, but restored by a second one, it's important not to move these layers (by turning the cube, say) between the two mono-swaps of each pair.

F: FINISHING FLIPS AND FIDDLES

Since every cubelet should now be in its own cubicle, the only remaining problems can be solved by edge-flips and corner twists in the top layer. To tackle any particular top layer cubelet, turn THE TOP LAYER *ONLY* to bring that cubelet into one of the two shaded cubicles of Fig. 35F and then, according as its white face is in position

| 1, | 2 | or | 3 |

do our

| **anticlockwise monotwist,** | **clockwise monotwist** | or | **edge monoflip** |
| $M_a = (F'RFR')^2$ | $M_c = (RF'R'F)^2$ | | $M_e = (\varepsilon R)^4$ |

where ε is a slice move (Fig. 34).

Once again it's important not to move the bottom two layers by turning the cube between operations, since individual monotwists and monoflips affect these layers. However, the entire set of operations needed to correct the top layer will automatically correct the bottom two layers as well.

EXPLANATIONS

Stage E works because our monoswap operation M_S leaves the top layer unchanged except for the desired swap of the two near corner cubelets, while two copies of the monoswap cancel ($M_S^2 = 1$).

So a sequence such as

monoswap, turn top clockwise, monoswap, turn top back

doesn't really disturb the bottom two layers, which "feel" only the two cancelling monoswaps. The top layer, however, effectively undergoes a swap of the two near corners followed by a swap of two right corners, which are brought into position by the first top turn and returned by the second.

Stage F works similarly because M_a, M_c and M_c have exactly the desired effects on the top layer, and enjoy the properties

$$M_e^2 = M_c^3 = 1, \qquad M_c M_e = M_e M_c, \qquad M_a = M_c^{-1}.$$

So Anne Scott's laws ensure that the bottom two layers feel a cancelling combination of operations, while the top layer undergoes the desired flips and twists.

IMPROVEMENTS

Our method is easy to explain, perform and remember, but usually takes more moves than an expert would. If you're prepared to take more trouble and have a rather larger memory, you can often shorten it considerably. For instance, the original monoflips and monotwists (due to David Seal and David Goto) are shorter:

$$m_e = R\varepsilon R^2 \varepsilon^2 R \qquad m_e^{-1} = R'\omega^2 R^2 \omega R' \qquad m_c = R'DRFDF' \qquad m_a = m_c^{-1} = FD'F'R'D'R$$

but with these you must always be careful to follow a mono-operation by the corresponding inverse one.

Explore the effects of the following moves, which many people have found useful. The first few only affect the top layer. Here and elsewhere we've credited moves to those who first told them to us. We expect that many facts about the cube were found by clever Hungarians long before we learnt of them. For the Greek letter slice moves, see Fig. 33.

David Benson's "special" $RUR^2.FRF^2.UFU^2$
David Singmaster's "Sigma" $FURU'R'F'$
Margaret Bumby's top edge-tricycle $\beta U^{\pm 1}\alpha . U^2 . \beta U^{\pm 1}\alpha$
Two more top edge-tricycles $U^2F.\alpha U\beta . U^2.\alpha U\beta .FU^2$; $FUF'UFU^2F'U^2$
Top corner tricycle $RU'L'UR'U'LU$
Clive Bach's cross-swap $(\alpha^2 U^2 \alpha^2 U)^2$
Kati Fried's edge-tricycle $\beta F^2 \alpha F^2$
Tamas Varga's corner tricycle $((FR'F'R)^3 U^2)^2$
Two double edge-swaps $(R^2 U^2)^3$; $(\alpha^2 U^2)^2$
Andrew Taylor's Stage C moves $F^2(RF)^2(R'F')^3$; $(FR)^3(F'R')^2F^2$
Other Stage C moves $FUFUF.U'F'U'F'U'$; $R'U'R'U'R'.URURU$

In the Extras you'll find lists of the shortest known words (improvements welcome!) to achieve any rearrangement, or any reorientation of the top layer. These are quoted from an algorithm due to Benson, Conway and Seal which guarantees to cure the cube in at most 85 moves (a half turn still counts as one move, but a slice counts as two). Morwen Thistlethwaite has recently constructed an impressive algorithm which never takes more than 52 moves.

Because there are 18 choices for the first move, but only 15 (non-cancelling) choices for subsequent ones, the number of positions after 16 moves is at most

$$18 \times 15^{15} = 7\,882\,090\,026\,855\,468\,750 < 43\,252\,003\,274\,489\,856\,000$$

proving that there are many positions that need 17 or more moves to cure. We can improve this to 18 moves by using the estimates $u_1 = 18, u_2 = 27 + 12u_1 = 243, u_{n+2} \leqslant 18u_n + 12u_{n+1}$, which take into account relations like $LR = RL$.

ELENA'S ELEMENTS

Elena Conway likes making her cube into pretty patterns. Here are some ways to do this, most of which she discovered herself.

"4 Windows"	"6 Windows"	"Chequers"	"Harlequin"
$\alpha\gamma^2\beta\delta^2$	$\alpha\gamma\beta\delta$	$\alpha^2\gamma^2\varepsilon^2$	$\alpha\gamma\beta\delta\alpha^2\gamma^2\varepsilon^2$

"Stripey"	"Zigzag"	"4 Crosses"	"6 Crosses"
$(L^2F^2R^2)^2 . LR'$	$(LRFB)^3$	$(LRFB)^3(FBLR)^3$ or $(\gamma^2L'\gamma^2R)^3$	$(\gamma^2L'\gamma^2R)^3(\alpha^2B'\alpha^2F)^3$

And try following "6 Crosses" with any of the earlier ones.

ARE YOU PARTIAL TO PARTIAL PUZZLES?

It's interesting to see what you can do using only *some* of the available moves. You might restrict yourself to just a specified selection of faces, to half-turns, to slice moves, or to the **helislice moves** like LR. Mathematically these correspond to subgroups we call the 2-, 3-, 4- and 5-**face groups**, the **square group**, the **slice group** and the **helislice group**.

Beginners are recommended to stay in the slice group because they cannot get lost. From any position you can cure the edge-cubes in 3 slices, getting to "4 Windows" or "6 Windows" and so home in 4 more slices. Frank O'Hara has shown that in fact at most 5 slices are needed in all. The slice group has order $4^3.4!/2 = 768$ and the helislice group has order $2^{11}.3 = 6144$.

The 2-face group has been intensively studied by Morwen Thistlethwaite. It's interesting to notice that it involves both the lucky Seven Puzzle (on the edge cubelets that move) and Rick Wilson's Tricky Six Puzzle (on the corners).

Roger Penrose first proved that everything can be done using just 5 faces. David Benson has a simple proof:

$$RL'F^2B^2RL'.U.RL'F^2B^2RL' = D.$$

OTHER "HUNGARIAN" OBJECTS

A $2\times2\times2$ cube and $2\times3\times3$ "domino" have also been manufactured. Their design seems even more mysterious, although as puzzles they're much easier. One can *imagine* Hungarian tetrahedra, octahedra, dodecahedra, icosahedra, etc. Although, as far as we know, these have neither been manufactured nor completely solved, Andrew Taylor has found a neat proof that (for any choice of chief faces and colors)

the total permutation on edges and corners is even,
the number of edge-flips is even, and
the total corner twisting is zero, modulo the corner valence.

Despondent Domino dabblers should need but three little words (with effects):

X = EhEhEh	Y = EcEhNcE	Z = cYcYc
(28)	(13)(26)(1'3')(2'6')	(13)(26)

(c is a clockwise $\frac{1}{4}$-turn of the top; h,E,N $\frac{1}{2}$-turns of top, East, North).

A TRIO OF SLIDING BLOCK PUZZLES

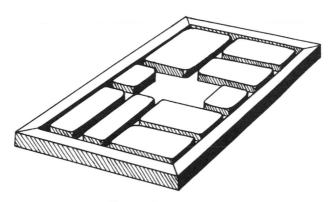

Figure 36. Dad's Puzzler.

Dad's Puzzler (Fig. 36) is unfortunately almost the only sliding block puzzle that's generally available from toy stores. although it goes under many different names. The problem is to slide the pieces without lifting any out of the tray, until the 2×2 square arrives in the lower left hand corner. Fifty years ago the puzzle represented Dad's furniture-removing difficulties, and the 2×2 block was the piano; at other times it has been depicted as a pennant, a car, a mountain, or space capsule but the puzzle has remained unchanged, probably for a hundred years. Some more enterprising manufacturer should sell a set containing one 2×2, four 1×1 and six 2×1 pieces which can be used either for Dad's Puzzler or for the following more interesting puzzles.

In the **Donkey** puzzle the initial arrangement is as in Fig. 37(a) and the problem is to move the 2×2 square to the middle of the bottom row. The name arises from the picture of a red donkey which adorned the 2×2 square in the original French version (L'Âne Rouge, which probably goes back to the last century) but we think that our choice of starting position already looks quite like a donkey's face.

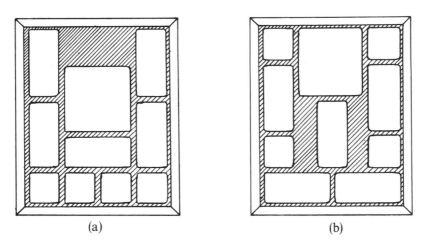

(a)   (b)

Figure 37. The Donkey and The Century (and a Half).

The **Century Puzzle**, published for the first time in *Winning Ways*, was discovered by one of us several years ago as a result of a systematic search for the hardest puzzle of this size. Start from Fig. 37(b) and, as in the Donkey, end with the 2×2 block in the middle of the bottom row. Or, if you're a real expert, you might try the **Century-and-a-Half Puzzle** in which you're to end in the position got by turning Fig. 37(b) upside-down.

TACTICS FOR SOLVING SUCH PUZZLES

As in our previous sliding puzzles the basic idea is to see what can be done while quite a lot of the pieces are kept fixed. In all three of these examples one occasionally sees one of the configurations of Fig. 38 somewhere, and any of these can be exchanged for any other, moving only the

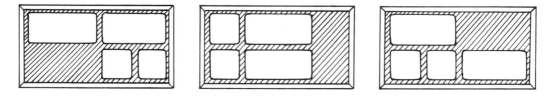

Figure 38. A Micropuzzle.

pieces in the area shown. They form a kind of micro-puzzle within the larger one. Figure 39 is a complete "map" of Dad's Puzzler showing how it consists of a dozen of these micro-puzzles joined by various paths of moves that are more or less forced. Using this map, you'll find it easy to get from anywhere to anywhere else.

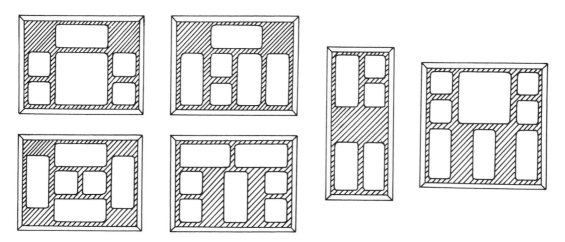

Figure 40. Micro- and Mini-puzzles Found in Donkey and Century.

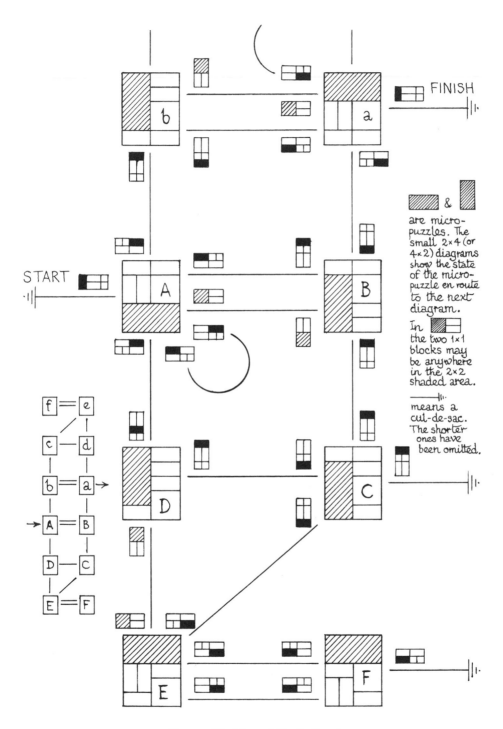

Figure 39. Map of Dad's Puzzler.

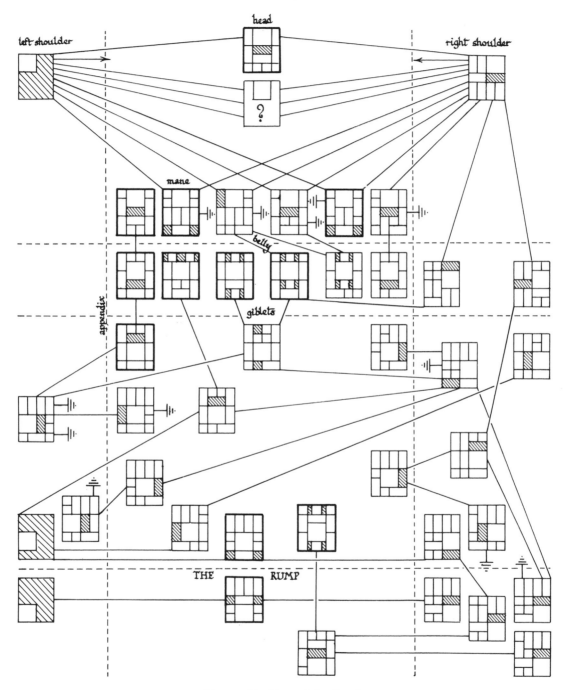

Figure 41. Map of the Donkey.

In the Donkey and Century puzzles there are several micro- and mini-puzzles: see what moves you can make inside the regions shown in Fig. 40. The Century and Donkey puzzles will never become easy but it will help if you become an adept at these minipuzzles. Figure 41 is our map of the Donkey. The positions are classified according to the location of the 2×2 square and in most cases we have only drawn one of a left-right mirror-image pair. Some unimportant culs-de-sac will be found in the directions indicated by the signs ⊣||ıı and the rectangle containing (?) represents many positions connected to the left and right shoulders. The arrows indicate other connexions to the shoulders. Left-right symmetric positions are boldly bordered.

The Century puzzle is very much larger, and we need more abbreviations to draw its map within a reasonable compass. The positions are best classified by the position of the large square together with information about which of the two horizontal pieces should be counted as "above" or "below" the square. We remark that in Fig. 42 both horizontal pieces should be counted as *below* the square despite their appearance, because the only way to move these pieces takes the horizontals *down* and the square *up*.

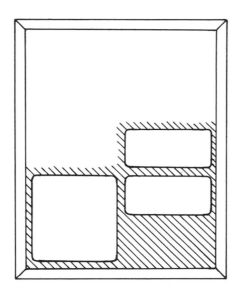

Figure 42. The Two Horizontal Pieces are Below the Square!

The key to the puzzle is to find one of the two possible **narrow bridges** in the map at which the first horizontal piece changes from *below* the square to *above* it. In fact it's best to think out the possible configurations in which this can happen and then work the puzzle backwards and forwards from one of these. Very few people have ever solved the puzzle by starting at the initial configuration and moving steadily towards its end. A much abbreviated map appears as Fig. 43.

Our maps were prepared with much help from some computer calculations made by David Fremlin at the University of Essex, who found incidentally that the Donkey pieces may be placed in the tray in 65880 positions and the Century pieces in 109260 ways. Although the Century puzzle can be inverted (this is our Century-and-a-Half problem) Fremlin's computer found that the Donkey cannot. It would be nice to have a more perspicuous proof of this.

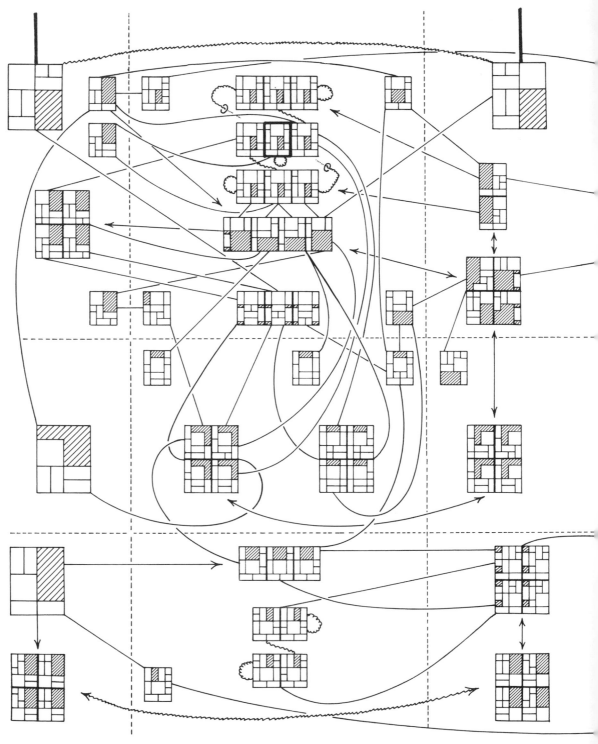

Figure 43. Map . . . .

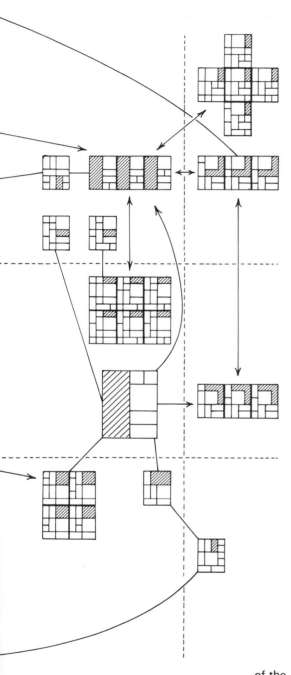

The starting position is heavily outlined; see centre column of opposite page, near top

Positions are classified thus:

   overleaf: Square "between" horizontals.
   opposite: Two verticals left, one right.
   this page: Three verticals left.

They are further classified according to the location of the square:

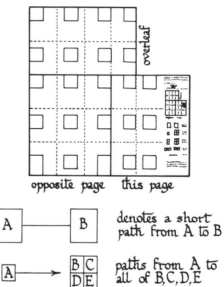

opposite page   this page

| A | — | B | denotes a short path from A to B |

A ⟶ B C / D E   paths from A to all of B,C,D,E

A / B   C D / E F   from A to D, B to C and E only

A B C   D E F   from A,B,C to D,E, F, perhaps respectively

〜〜〜〜   Reflecting connexions

The "narrow bridges" are the two thick connexions between the top of the opposite page and the left of overleaf.

. . .   .   of the   . .   . .

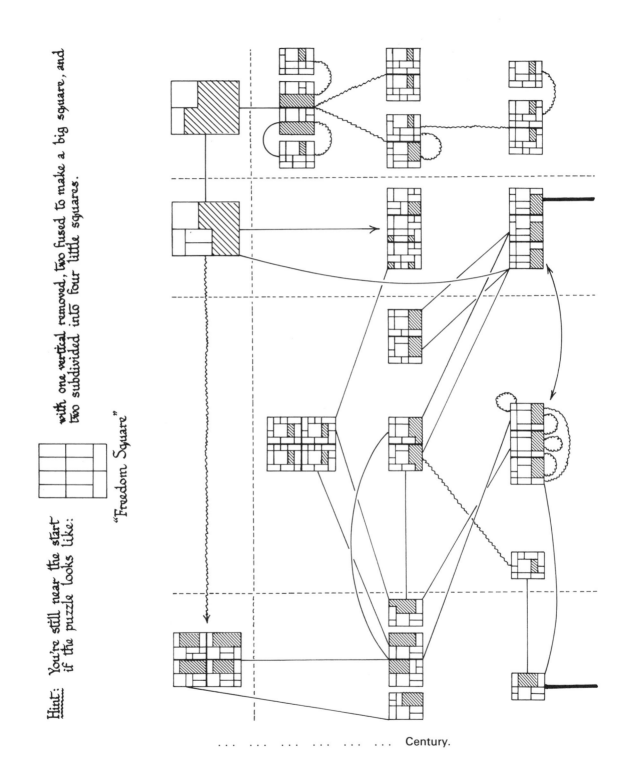

Hint: You're still near the start
if the puzzle looks like:

with one vertical removed, two fused to make a big square, and
two subdivided into four little squares.

"Freedom Square"

. . . . Century.

COUNTING YOUR MOVES

It's customary to follow Martin Gardner and declare that any kind of motion involving just one piece counts as a single move. It takes 58 moves to solve Dad's Puzzler and 83 to solve the Donkey. How many do you need to solve the Century puzzle? And how many for the Century-and-a-Half?

PARADOXICAL PENNIES

You tell me your favorite sequence of three Heads or Tails and then I'll tell you mine. We then spin a penny until the first time either of our sequences appears as the result of three consecutive throws. I bet you 2 to 1 it's mine!

The graph

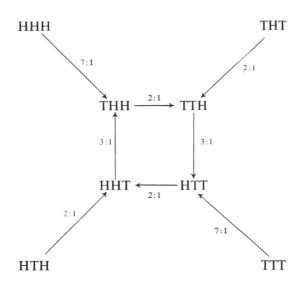

shows the sequence I'll choose for each possible sequence of yours, together with the odds that I win. You'll see that it's always at least 2 to 1 in my favor.

Here's a rule for computing the odds. Given two Head-Tail sequences a and b of the same length, n, we compute the **leading number**, aLb, by scoring 2^{k-1} for every positive k for which the last k letters of a coincide with the first k of b. Then we can show that the odds, that b beats a in Paradoxical Pennies, are exactly

$$aLa - aLb \quad \text{to} \quad bLb - bLa.$$

Leo Guibas and Andy Odlyzko have proved that, given a, the best choice for b is one of the two sequences obtained by dropping the last digit of a and prefixing a new first digit. Notice the paradoxical fact that in the length 3 game:

THH beats HHT beats HTT beats TTH beats THH.

PARADOXICAL DICE

You can make three dice, A, B, C, with a similar paradoxical property, using the magic square:

	D	E	F
A	6	1	8
B	7	5	3
C	2	9	4

Each die has the numbers of one row of the square on its faces (opposite faces bearing the same number). For these dice

$$A \text{ beats } B \text{ beats } C \text{ beats } A,$$

all by 5 to 4 odds! Similarly for the three dice, D, E, F, obtained from the columns. The only other paradoxical triples of dice using the same numbers are those obtained from A, B, C by interchanging 3 with 4 and/or 6 with 7. These interchanges improve the odds.

It's possible to put positive integers on the faces of two dice in a unique non-standard way that gives the same probability for each total as the standard one. Algebraically, the problem reduces to factorizing

$$x^2 + 2x^3 + 3x^4 + 4x^5 + 5x^6 + 6x^7 + 5x^8 + 4x^9 + 3x^{10} + 2x^{11} + x^{12}$$

into the form $f(x)g(x)$ with $f(0)=g(0)=0$ and $f(1)=g(1)=6$. The two factorizations are

$$(x + x^2 + x^3 + x^4 + x^5 + x^6)^2 \qquad \text{and}$$

$$(x + 2x^2 + 2x^3 + x^4)(x + x^3 + x^4 + x^5 + x^6 + x^8),$$

so the new pair of dice have the numbers

$$1, 2, 2, 3, 3, 4 \qquad \text{and} \qquad 1, 3, 4, 5, 6, 8.$$

MORE ON MAGIC SQUARES

It's an old puzzle to arrange the numbers from 1 to n^2 in an array so that all the rows and columns and both the diagonals have the same sum, which turns out to be $\frac{1}{2}n(n^2+1)$. The only 3×3 magic square (see the last section), often called the Lo-Shu, was discovered several dynasties ago by the Chinese. We also used it in Chapter 22. In 1693 Frenicle de Bessy had worked out the 880 magic squares of order 4. In this section we'll show you how to find all these.

It's handy to subtract 1 from all the numbers, because the numbers 0 to 15 are closed under nim-addition. With this convention the magic sum is 30. We shall call a square **perfect** if we can nim-add *any* number from 0 to 15 to its entries and still obtain a magic square; if only $\frac{1}{2}$ of these additions are possible we'll call it $\frac{1}{2}$-**perfect**, and so on. Since nim-adding 15 is the same as complementing in 15, it always preserves the magic property, showing that *every* square is at least $\frac{1}{8}$-perfect. We shall also classify the squares by the disposition of complementary pairs as in Fig. 44.

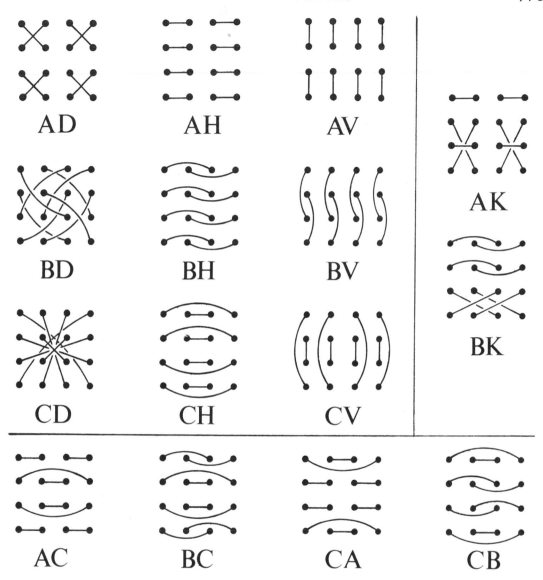

Figure 44. Classifying Squares by Complementing Pairs.

There are essentially just three ways to write the numbers from 0 to 15 as an addition table:

0	1	2	3
4	5	6	7
8	9	10	11
12	13	14	15

0	1	4	5
2	3	6	7
8	9	12	13
10	11	14	15

0	2	4	6
1	3	5	7
8	10	12	14
9	11	13	15

but you can then freely permute the rows and columns in any of these. Take any table obtained in this way, say

$$
\begin{array}{cccc}
15 & 11 & 14 & 10 \\
13 & 9 & 12 & 8 \\
7 & 3 & 6 & 2 \\
5 & 1 & 4 & 0
\end{array}
$$

Apply the interchanges indicated by our **Quaquaversal Quadrimagifier**

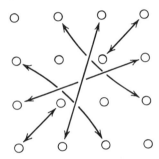

and you get a magic square:

$$
\begin{array}{cccc}
15 & 2 & 1 & 12 \\
4 & 9 & 10 & 7 \\
8 & 5 & 6 & 11 \\
3 & 14 & 13 & 0
\end{array}
\qquad
\begin{array}{cccc}
16 & 3 & 2 & 13 \\
5 & 10 & 11 & 8 \\
9 & 6 & 7 & 12 \\
4 & \boxed{15 \quad 14} & & 1
\end{array}
$$

Adding 1 to this particular example we obtain the right hand square which features in Albrecht Dürer's famous self-portrait, *Melencolia I*, in which the boxed figures indicate the date of the work. In this case complementary numbers appear according to the scheme called *central* in Fig. 44, and so this square is called central.

By applying the Quaquaversal Quadrimagifier to the other forms of addition table we can get 432 essentially different perfect magic squares. The complementary pairs enable us to classify these as:

    48 Adjacent Diagonal (AD),
    48 Broken Diagonal (BD),
    48 Central Diagonal (CD),
    96 Adjacent Horizontal (AH) or Adjacent Vertical (AV),
    96 Broken Horizontal (BH) or Broken Vertical (BV), and
    96 Central Horizontal (CH) or Central Vertical (CV).

Because we don't count squares different when they are related merely by a reflexion or a rotation of the diagram, we must regard adjacent-horizontal and adjacent-vertical squares as the same type. You can find out what type your square will be by looking at the position occupied by the complement of the addition table's leading entry before Quadrimagification:

$$\ast \quad \circ \quad \circ \quad \circ$$
$$\circ \quad AD \quad CH \quad BV$$
$$\circ \quad CV \quad BD \quad AH$$
$$\circ \quad BH \quad AV \quad CD$$

Now take the above 96 central-horizontal squares and apply the flip operation

$$\circ \quad \circ \quad \circ \quad \circ$$
$$\circ \quad \circ \quad \circ \quad \circ$$
$$\updownarrow \qquad\qquad\qquad \updownarrow$$
$$\circ \quad \circ \quad \circ \quad \circ$$
$$\circ \quad \circ \quad \circ \quad \circ$$

and you'll get 96 more central-horizontal squares. All squares so far found are perfect.

There are 112 more central-horizontal squares that are only $\frac{1}{4}$- or $\frac{1}{8}$-perfect. They can be found by taking any of the seven squares:

6	10	5	9		14	2	13	1						10	1	14	5
13	12	3	2	a_8	5	4	11	10					c	13	8	7	2
0	7	8	15	↔	8	15	0	7		0	13	2	15	4	15	0	11
11	1	14	4		3	9	6	12		11	8	7	4	3	6	9	12
	↓d				↓d				14	3	12	1			↓c		
12	5	10	3		13	4	11	2		5	6	9	10	12	11	4	3
11	9	6	4	a_1	10	8	7	5					c	1	8	7	14
0	14	1	15	↔	1	15	0	14					2	5	10	13
7	2	13	8		6	3	12	9					15	6	9	0

$$\underbrace{\hspace{7cm}}_{\frac{1}{4}\text{-perfect}} \qquad \underbrace{\hspace{5cm}}_{\frac{1}{8}\text{-perfect}}$$

and applying any combination of the four operations:

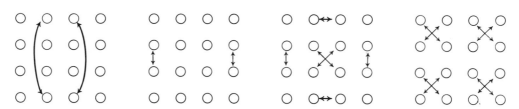

Now take the 14 squares of Fig. 45 and apply any combination of complementation and the last three of our operations and you'll get a total of 224 squares, 56 of each of the types

Adjacent Central (AC),
Broken Central (BC),
Central Adjacent (CA), and
Central Broken (CB).

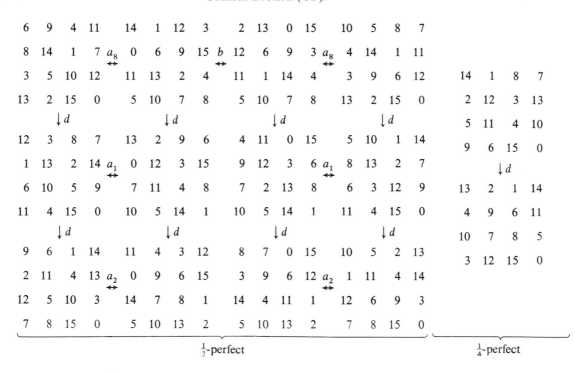

Figure 45. Adjacent and Broken Central and Central Adjacent and Broken Squares.

There remain only 16, rather irregular, squares to be found. You can get them by applying any combination of complementation and the last *two* of our operations to the two $\frac{1}{2}$-perfect squares

$$
\begin{array}{cccc}
1 & 14 & 9 & 6 \\
10 & 3 & 4 & 13 \\
7 & 8 & 15 & 0 \\
12 & 5 & 2 & 11
\end{array}
\qquad \xrightarrow{\;d\;} \qquad
\begin{array}{cccc}
2 & 13 & 3 & 12 \\
5 & 6 & 8 & 11 \\
14 & 1 & 15 & 0 \\
9 & 10 & 4 & 7
\end{array}
$$

and they're 8 each of the types

Adjacent Knighted (AK),
Broken Knighted (BK).

There are various permutations of the 16 numbers that occasionally lead from one magic square to another, namely

a_n: nim-*add n*, for example $a_6 = (0\ 6)(1\ 7)(2\ 4)(3\ 5)(8\ 14)(9\ 15)(10\ 12)(11\ 13)$
b: the *big* swap $(0\ 12)(1\ 13)(14\ 2)(15\ 3)$
c: *circle* $(0\ 10\ 12)(1\ 11\ 13)(14\ 4\ 2)(15\ 5\ 3)$
d: *double*, mod 15 $(1\ 2\ 4\ 8)(3\ 6\ 12\ 9)(5\ 10)(7\ 14\ 13\ 11)$

and we've indicated some of these in the figures.

THE MAGIC TESSERACT

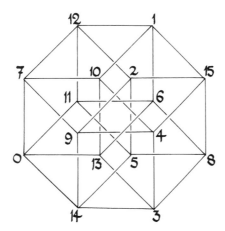

We'll leave it to you to rediscover the many remarkable relations between the 48 BD squares, sometimes called **pandiagonal** or **Nasik** squares, and our **Magic Tesseract** in which the vertices of every square add to 30. By projecting this along three different directions, you can find three magic cubes in which each face adds to 14. These are the duals of the three octahedral dice found by Andreas and Coxeter. Alternate vertices in the magic tesseract are the odious and evil numbers, and if you replace each odious number by its opposite (nim-sum with 15) you'll see how the tesseract was made.

ADAMS'S AMAZING MAGIC HEXAGON

Starting from the pattern

$$
\begin{array}{ccccc}
 & & 1 & & \\
 & 2 & & 3 & \\
4 & & 5 & & 6 \\
 & 7 & & 8 & \\
9 & & 10 & & 11 \\
 & 12 & & 13 & \\
14 & & 15 & & 16 \\
 & 17 & & 18 & \\
 & & 19 & &
\end{array}
$$

can you reorder the numbers from 1 to 19, taking less than 47 years, so that all five rows in each of the three directions have the same sum?

THE GREAT TANTALIZER

This is a tantalizing puzzle which surfaces every now and then with a new alias. We've chosen one of the older names. An early American version was the Katzenjammer puzzle, but most recently it has emerged under yet another name, Instant Insanity. The manufacturers seem to be very good at selecting new names, but they never change the underlying puzzle. The problem

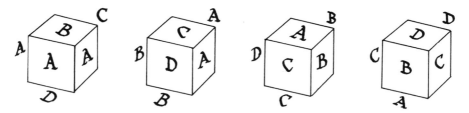

Figure 46. Pieces for The Great Tantalizer.

is to assemble the four cubes of Fig. 46 (in which the outer letters refer to the hidden faces) into a vertical $1 \times 1 \times 4$ tower in which each wall displays all four "colors", A, B, C, D. If you don't go instantly insane on playing with the cubes, you'll probably be greatly tantalized by them.

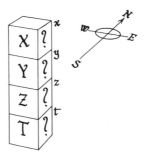

Figure 47. The Tantalizer Solved?

T.H. O'Beirne seems to have been the first to publish a general way of solving such problems and we think his solution is still the best. Let's imagine the problem solved and concentrate on the North and South walls of the tower (Fig. 47). Then X, Y, Z, T will be A, B, C, D in some order, as will x, y, z, t. Write the four letters A, B, C, D on a piece of paper and join

$$\text{X to x,} \quad \text{Y to y,} \quad \text{Z to z} \quad \text{and} \quad \text{T to t.}$$

What you'll get will probably be a way of joining ABCD into a circuit, but it might perhaps be several circuits which together include each letter just once. For example if

$$\text{X Y Z T x y z t}$$

are

$$\text{A B C D D C A B}$$

we get the single circuit

while if they were

$$\text{A B C D D A C B}$$

you'd get two circuits of different lengths

There will be a similar circuit, or system of circuits, for the East–West walls. Each of the two systems will contain every vertex just once and have one edge for each cube.

It's now easy to solve the puzzle by drawing the following graph (Fig. 48). The vertices of the graph are the colors A, B, C, D and the *i*th cube yields three edges labelled *i* joining pairs of vertices corresponding to its pairs of opposite faces. All you have to do is to select from this graph the two separate systems of circuits which each use all four numbers and all four vertices just once.

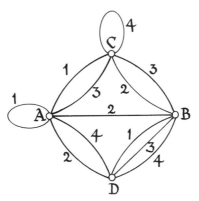

Figure 48. Solving the Tantalizer.

What are the possibilities for such circuit systems in the example? By considering each possibility

$$1\ 1\ 1\ 1,\qquad 2\ 1\ 1,\qquad 2\ 2,\qquad 3\ 1,\qquad 4$$

for the circuit lengths, you'll rapidly conclude that both systems must consist of a single 4-circuit which can only use the letters in the cyclic order ACBD. There is only one way of selecting two such systems without using any edge twice:

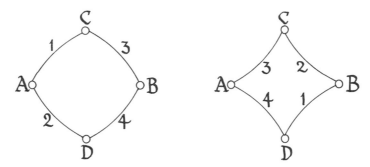

So the Great Tantalizer has a unique solution (up to reordering the cubes and rotating or inverting the whole tower). You can get it by pushing the cubes of Fig. 46 together left to right and tipping the result on end.

O'Beirne takes as his basic example a five cube puzzle of this type which dates from the first World War (Fig. 49) and uses the flags of the allies Belgium, France, Japan, Russia and the United Kingdom. You might like to check his assertion that this has just two essentially different solutions.

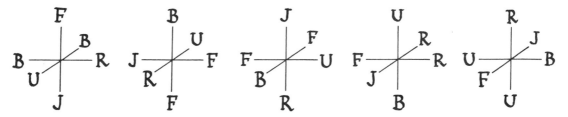

Figure 49. The "Flags of the Allies" Puzzle.

POLYOMINOES, POLYIAMONDS AND SEARCHING POLICY

A domino is made of two squares stuck together, so S.W. Golomb has suggested the words tromino, tetromino, etc. for the figures that can be made by sticking 3, 4, or more equal squares together. He has registered the particular names pentomino (5 squares) and polyomino (*n* squares) as trade-marks. Unfortunately few of the puzzles that have been proposed have hidden secrets, so they yield to nothing better than trial and error (or systematic search). As Rouse Ball says about Tangrams in early editions of *Mathematical Recreations and Essays*, "the recreation is not mathematical and I reluctantly content myself with a bare mention of it".

Here is the type of puzzle that arises. Up to rotations and reflexions there are just 12 pentominoes, for which you'll find our naming system in Chapter 25, with a total area of 60 square units. Which of the candidate rectangles

$$3 \times 20 \quad 4 \times 15 \quad 5 \times 12 \quad 6 \times 10$$

can be packed with them? Figure 50 shows a way of solving two of these problems at once, and also, if the pieces are regarded as made of five cubes each, of packing the $2 \times 5 \times 6$ box (they will also pack a $3 \times 4 \times 5$ box). Such problems are peculiarly susceptible to idle computers and the 6×10 pentomino rectangle was one of the first to be tackled in this way when C.B. Haselgrove found its 2339 solutions in 1960.

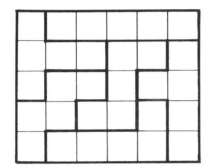 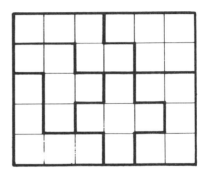

Figure 50. Packing Pentominoes.

Noting that two equilateral triangles can form a diamond, T.H. O'Beirne has proposed the terms triamond, etc., for figures made from three of more. Counting reflexions as distinct this time we find there are 19 hexiamonds, named in Fig. 51, which will pack into the shape of Fig. 52 in many thousands of different ways. The packing shown in the figure is probably the most symmetric about the North-South line. We'd like to see a similarly symmetric one for the East–West line.

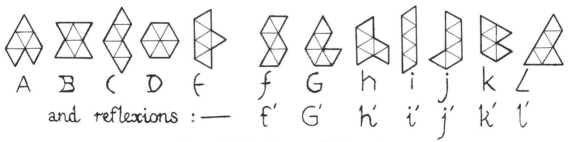

Figure 51. The Nineteen Hexiamonds.

This prompts a few remarks about sensible search procedures when solving puzzles or finding strategies for games that may be too large for complete discussion. Even when you have a large computer it's wise to have some idea where to look. Symmetry is usually a valuable consideration. For instance the (nearly) left-right symmetric solutions of the hexiamond puzzle admittedly form

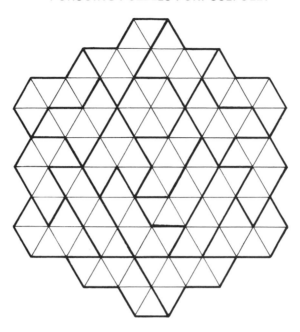

Figure 52. The Most Symmetric Hexiamond Solution?

only a small corner of the space to be searched, but this one is likely to be a profitable one because the constraints on opposite sides of the board are satisfied simultaneously. However, symmetry is not the only consideration. In analyzing a game it's wise to try to find out what the players are really fighting for (the game's hidden secrets). For example the French Military Hunt game on the Small Board is small enough that you can give an exhaustive analysis without needing to understand what's really going on. But when you've discovered that the players are really just fighting over the opposition you can extend the analysis to much larger boards for which a complete analysis would be prohibitive, even by computer.

Many of the analyses in *Winning Ways* were found in this way. Only when we realized that Dots and Boxes was really more concerned with parity than with box counting were we able to make any headway. And it's impossibly complicated to evaluate a reasonably sized position in Hackenbush Hotchpotch exactly, but we got a head start when we realized that often the atomic weight was the only thing that really mattered. In Peg Solitaire the hidden secret turned out to be the notion of balance represented by α and β in Chapter 23.

Even though polyomino type problems may have no hidden secrets, some people are much better at them than others because they subconsciously search in more likely places. Experienced polyominists don't undo their good work by repeatedly starting from scratch but keep most of the puzzle in place while fiddling with just a few pieces at any time. When they've found one solution, they can usually transform it into others by similar manipulation. For example, from Fig. 50 you can obtain another solution by repacking pentominoes R and S, and in Fig. 52 we can interchange the two (f, h) pairs or rotate the central (A,D,E, j, j') hexagon.

Exercise for Experts: For what values of n can you pack n^2 copies of hexiamond A into a replica of A on n times the scale?

ALAN SCHOEN'S CYCLOTOME

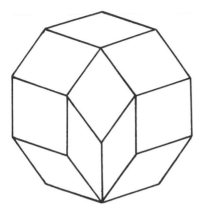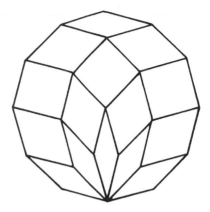

Figure 53. Dissections of $2n$-gons into Rhombs, n = 5 and 6.

Alan Schoen is patenting the interesting sequence of puzzles he derived from the well-known dissections of $2n$-gons into $\binom{n}{2}$ rhombs of angles $\pi k/n$, $1 \leqslant k \leqslant n-1$ (Fig. 53). He takes one of each of the $\lfloor n/2 \rfloor$ shapes of rhomb and one of each of the shapes you can make by joining two rhombs in every possible way to form a hexagon. The hexagon must not contain a straight angle, since he observes that no packing of rhombs in the $2n$-gon contains a pair of parallel edges, except those which form the rungs of the "ladders" which run between each pair of opposite sides in every packing. This non-convexity condition is similar to that imposed by Piet Hein in designing the Soma pieces, but here it arises naturally. Reflexions are not counted as different. This set of rhombs and hexagons (cyclotominoes?) will pack into the original $2n$-gon. In fact for

$$n = 2 \quad 3 \quad 4 \quad 5 \quad \text{and} \qquad 6$$
$$\text{there are } 1 \quad 1 \quad 3 \quad 14 \quad \text{and} \quad \text{more than } 150$$

essentially different packings. Schoen gave one of us a set of pieces for $n = 8$ and we were able to assemble them as in Fig. 54. We've numbered the pieces with the values of k, where $\pi k/n$ is the smaller angle of the rhomb. Where two shapes of piece are made from the same pair of rhombs, the one with the straighter reflex angle has its digits in natural order.

Solutions can be obtained from one another much as in O'Beirne's Hexiamond, or as on our Somap. In Fig. 54 the pieces 4 and 22 may be rotated or exchanged with 2 and 24, which in turn can be rotated or reflected. After this exchange, with 2 touching 11 and 34, we have a rotatable decagon, 1,2,34,11,32,3 & 4 of which the last four pieces form a rotatable octagon. As 3 & 4 are contiguous, they will exchange with 34, after which 4 & 1 and 2 & 3 are contiguous, and will swap with 14 and 23. After the original exchange, 2 may instead have two sides in common with 13 and these two will rotate, after which 21 and 12 may be interchanged if 1 & 2 are moved as well. Or again, 2 may touch 23 & 24, so that after the 34 exchange, 2 & 3 will swap with 32, and then 2 & 11 form a symmetric hexagon. And so on and on, yielding well over a hundred solutions.

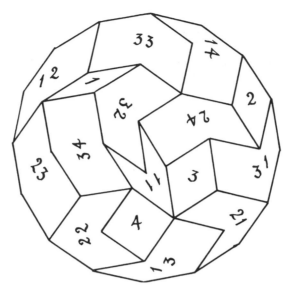

Figure 54. Schoen's 16-piece 16-gon. A Century or So of Solutions.

How many pieces are there in a set of cyclotominoes? According as $n = 2m$ or $2m + 1$, there are $m^2 - m$ or m^2 hexagons, and m rhombs in either case, so there are m^2 or $m^2 + m$ altogether. You can use sets for a variety of games and puzzles, ranging from Tangram-like pictures (Fig. 55) to quite sophisticated packing problems. It's early to say if these last contain any hidden secrets (though Alan Schoen has noted the one about parallel edges); there's perhaps a better chance since there is more structure in the shapes than there was in polyominoes and polyiamonds.

Many pleasing patterns can be produced: for example, take r^2 sets of pieces and pack them in nesting $2n$-gons of side lengths $1, 2, \dots, r$.

The exponential difficulty of this sequence of puzzles prompts us to add another remark about searching. A typical combinatorial puzzle or search of "size" n takes something like $n!$ trials to complete, and this is much more like n^n than c^n, no matter how big you take c. On the other hand the number of solutions may only be c^n, and while this goes up fast, your chance of finding one of them is only $(c/n)^n$ and this gets very small very fast as soon as n is bigger than c.

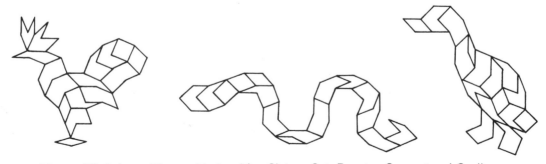

Figure 55. Schoen-Shapes Made with a Sixteen Set: Rooster, Serpent and Gosling.

MACMAHON'S SUPERDOMINOES

In his *New Mathematical Pastimes*, MacMahon proposed a different kind of generalized domino, got by dividing a regular polygon into colored triangles. We'll discuss just two examples. If we use just four colors, there are exactly 24 ways of coloring a triangular superdomino, and the standard problem is to pack these into a regular hexagon with an all black perimeter and adjacent colors alike, as in Fig. 56.

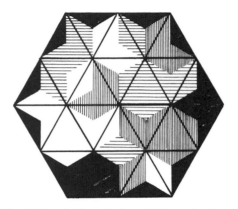

Figure 56. MacMahon's Four-Colored Triangular Superdominoes.

In this case it's hard to keep the secret hidden for very long. There are barely enough black edges to go round, and once you've found a suitable arrangement for them the rest is fairly easy.

When we consider the 24 three-colored square superdominoes, with which the usual problem is to make a 4×6 rectangle under similar conditions, the black edge problem is much more subtle. It can be shown that every solution to this problem has a column of four squares in which every horizontal edge is black (the **ladder**). In Fig. 57(a) the ladder occupies the second column and in Fig. 57(b) it occupies the third. In the Extras you'll find every possible configuration for the black edges.

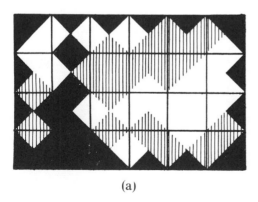 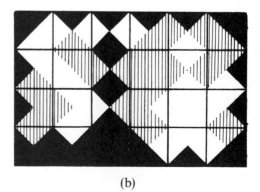

(a)   (b)

Figure 57. Three-Colored Square Superdomino Solutions Showing the Ladder.

MacMahon's superdomino problems can be made into jigsaw puzzles by using differently shaped edges in place of colors. Thus for the three colors in MacMahon's square problem one can use either the three edge shapes of Fig. 58(a) or those of Fig. 58(b) (which alter the matching condition).

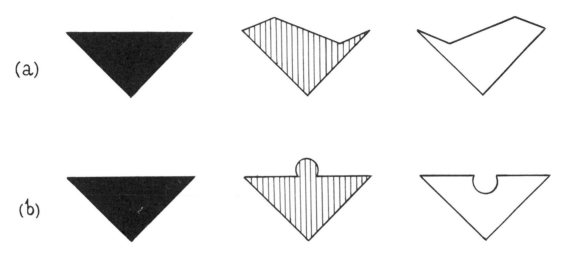

Figure 58. Two Ways of Making a MacMahon Jigsaw Puzzle.

Some years ago one of us sent out a Christmas card (Fig. 59) in the form of a jigsaw puzzle based on Fig. 58(b). The assembly in Fig. 59 is *not* a solution because it contains heads connected directly to hands and necks connected directly to arms. Can you turn it into an anatomically correct solution? Figure 60 is M.S. Paterson's modification of this idea, using another shape system. You must rearrange the pieces so that each wrestler has a properly connected body consisting of one head, one torso, one pair of shorts, two arms and two legs!

QUINTOMINAL DODECAHEDRA

The MacMahon superdominoes with five or more sides have not received much attention, but here's a nice little problem. There are 12 different **quintominoes** if we use five different colors once each and allow turning over. Can you fit them, colors matching, onto the 12 faces of a regular dodecahedron?

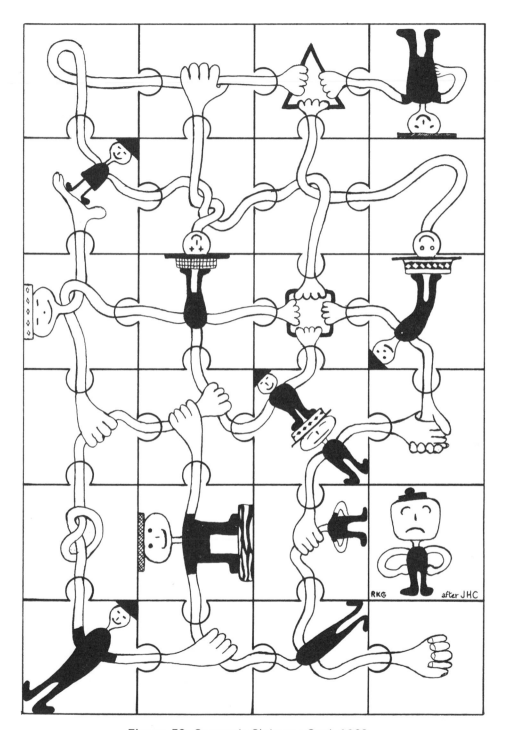

Figure 59. Conway's Christmas Card, 1968.

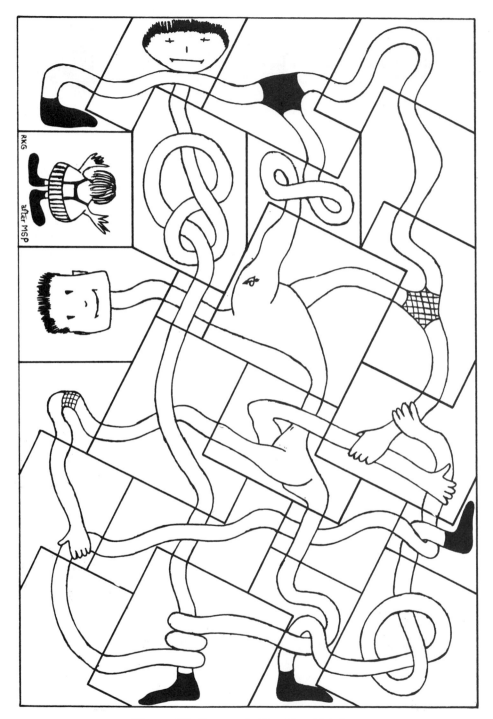

Figure 60. Paterson's Wrestling Match.

THE DOOMSDAY RULE

Here's an easy way to find the day of the week for an arbitrary date in an arbitrary year. The day of the week on which the last day of February falls in any given year will be called the **doomsday** for that year. For instance, in year 1000, doomsday (Feb. 29) was a Thursday (THOUSday). Then the following dates in *any* year are all doomsdays:

$$\text{Feb } 28/29 \qquad \text{Jan } 31/32$$

(the second alternative in leap years), otherwise for even months,

$$\text{Apr } 4 \qquad \text{Jun } 6 \qquad \text{Aug } 8 \qquad \text{Oct } 10 \qquad \text{Dec } 12$$

(the number of the month in the year), and for odd ones,

$$\text{Mar } 3+4 \qquad \text{May } 5+4 \qquad \text{Jul } 7+4 \qquad \text{Sep } 9-4 \qquad \text{Nov } 11-4$$

(add 4 for the 31-day, **long**, months; subtract 4 for 30-day, **short**, ones). Here's a summary with memos.

Jan	Feb	Mar	Apr	May	Jun	Jul	Aug	Sep	Oct	Nov	Dec
31/32	28/29	7	4	9	6	11	8	5	10	7	12
"last"	last	long 3	even 4	long 5	even 6	long 7	even 8	short 9	even 10	short 11	even 12

You should get used to finding other doomsdays in each month by changing the given one by weeks or fortnights; for example, since

Jul 11 is a doomsday, so is Jul 4 (Independence Day),

and since

Dec 12 is a doomsday, so is Dec 26 (Boxing Day).

On what day of the week was May-Day in the year 1000? May 9, and so May 2, were doomsdays (Thursdays in year 1000), so May 1 was a Wednesday.

It's easy to go wrong when adding numbers to days, so we suggest you use our mnemonics

NUN-day	ONE-day	TWOS-day	TREBLES-day	FOURS-day	FIVE-day	SIXER-day	SE'EN-day
Sunday	Monday	Tuesday	Wednesday	Thursday	Friday	Saturday	Sunday

Let's suppose we want Michaelmas Day (Sep 29) in the year 1000: we say

Sep 5 (short 9) and so Sep 26 are doomsdays (Thursdays—FOURS-days) so
Sep 29 is 3 on FOURS-day = SE'EN-day (Sunday).

To find doomsday for any year in a given century, you should add to the doomsday for the century year,

the number of *dozens* after that year,
the *remainder* after this, and
the number of *fours* in the remainder.

For example, for the year 1066 we say

$$\left.\begin{array}{l}\text{THOUS}\\\text{Thurs}\\\text{FOURS}\end{array}\right\}\text{day,}$$

$$
\begin{array}{ccccc}
 & 5\ \text{dozen,} & 6 & \text{and} & 1, & \text{and since}\\
 & (60) & (\text{remainder}) & & (4\text{'s in }6) & \\
4 & +5 & +6 & + & 1 & \equiv 2,\ \text{mod }7,
\end{array}
$$

doomsday in 1066 was a TWOS-day, and so the Battle of Hastings (Oct 14) was fought on a

4 on TWOS-day = SIXER-day (Saturday).

Let's do some years in our own century, given that 1900 = Wednesday = TREBLES-day.

Aug 4,   19————————14
4 off   TREBLES-day, 1 dozen, 2 (and 0) = TWOS-day (Tuesday),

Nov 11,   19————————18
4 on   TREBLES-day, 1 dozen, 6 and 1 = 15-day = ONE-day (Monday).

Of course, whole weeks can be cancelled, so the parentheses in

(4 on TREBLES)   1,   (6 and 1)

can be forgotten, making the answer immediate.

In the Julian calendar (as instituted by Julius Caesar) each century was one day earlier than the last, and so

0	100	200	300	400	500	600
700	800	900	1000	1100	1200	1300
1400	1500	1600	1700	…		

were

Sunday Saturday Friday Thursday Wednesday Tuesday Monday.

But in the modern, Gregorian, calendar (as reformed by Pope Gregory XIII)

		…	1500
1600	1700	1800	1900
2000	2100	2200	…

are

Tuesday Sunday Friday Wednesday

because each century year that is *not* a multiple of 400 drops its leap day, and so is *two* days earlier than the previous one. In practice, remember that 1900 was a Wednesday, and that each step *backwards* to 1800, 1700, 1600 *adds* two days.

Thus, since Jul 4 is a doomsday,

Jul 4,   17————————76

was

exactly   Sunday, 6 dozen, 4 and 1 = Thursday.

Various countries adopted the Gregorian reform by omitting various days; for example,
in Italy, France and Spain,   Oct 5–14, 1582.
in Britain and the American colonies,   Sep 3–13, 1752,
in Sweden,   leap days, 1700–1740,
elsewhere, various dates between 1583 (Poland) and 1923 (Greece).

You should also remember that the start of the year has not always been Jan 1. For some time before 1066 it was Christmas Day of the previous year, and for several centuries it was Mar 25 (so called Old Style dating, which was abolished in 1752). Such things are ignored in the Doomsday Rule, but, along with varying national conventions, must be accounted for in subtle examples:

Apr 23, 1616 (England) = 2 off Friday, 1 dozen, 4 and 1 = Tuesday (Shakespeare's deathday),
Apr 23, 1616 (Spain) = 2 off Tuesday, 1 dozen, 4 and 1 = Saturday (Cervantes' deathday),
Feb 29, 1603 (England) = exactly Friday, 0 dozen, 4 and 1 = Wednesday (Whitgift's deathday).

This "1603" must obviously be 1604 (New Style). Archbishop Whitgift was Queen Elizabeth's "worthy prelate" and first chairman of the commission which eventually produced the Authorized Version of the Bible.

The ambiguous days from Jan 1 through Mar 24 in years between about 1300 and 1752 were usually written in the "double dating" convention; e.g. Queen Elizabeth's deathday was Mar. 24, 1602/3 for which we find "3 on Fri + 3" = Thursday.

When calculating a B.C. date, it's best to add a big enough multiple of 28 (or 700) years to make it into an A.D. one, remembering that there was no year 0 (1 B.C. was immediately followed by 1 A.D.). Thus, in the Julian system we add 4200 to

$$\text{Oct 23, 4004 B.C.,} \quad \text{getting} \quad \text{Oct 23, 197 A.D. (}not\text{ 196),}$$

and giving

$$\text{1 off SIXER-day, 8 dozen, 1 (and 0)} = \text{SE'EN-day} = \text{Sunday}$$

for the day of Creation, according to Archbishop Ussher.

Problems   1. A man was nearly 48 years old on celebrating his first birthday. Where, when and what day of the week was it?
2. On what weekday is the 13th of the month most likely to fall in the Gregorian calendar?

... AND EASTER EASILY

A number of sources give more or less complicated rules for determining Easter. These usually apply only over limited ranges and are sometimes incorrect, even in reputable works, because they neglect the exceptions in the simple rule below.

Easter Day is defined to be the first Sunday strictly later than the **Paschal full moon**, which is a kind of arithmetical approximation to the astronomical one. The Paschal full moon is given by the formula

$$(\text{Apr 19} = \text{Mar 50}) - (11G + C)_{\text{mod } 30}$$

except that when the formula gives

Apr 19   you should take   Apr 18

and when it gives

Apr 18 *and* $G \geqslant 12$,   you should take   Apr 17.

In the formula,

$$G(\text{the } \mathbf{Golden\ number}) = \text{Year}_{\text{mod }19} + 1 \ (\text{never forget to add the 1!})$$

$$C(\text{the Century term}) = +3 \text{ for all Julian years}$$

$$\left.\begin{array}{l} -4 \text{ for 15xx, 16xx} \\ -5 \text{ for 17xx, 18xx} \\ \mathbf{-6} \text{ for } \mathbf{19xx}, \text{20xx, 21xx} \end{array}\right\} \text{Gregorian}$$

The general formula for C in a Gregorian year Hxx is

$$-H + \lfloor H/4 \rfloor + \lfloor 8(H+11)/25 \rfloor.$$

The next Sunday is then easily found by the Doomsday rule. Example

$$1945 \equiv 7, \text{ mod } 19 \text{ so } G = 8 \text{ and we find for the Paschal full moon:}$$

$$\text{Mar } 50 - (88-6)_{\text{mod }30} = \text{Mar } 50 - 22 = \text{Mar } 28.$$

Because this is a Doomsday, it's very easy to work out that it is

$$\text{"exactly Wed } (+3+9+2)\text{"}.$$

Easter Day, 1945, was therefore Mar 32, April Fool's Day.

For 1981 ($\equiv 5$, mod 19) the formula gives

$$\text{Apr } 19 - (66-6)_{\text{mod }30} = \text{Apr } 19,$$

so the Paschal full moon is

$$\text{Apr } 18 = \text{Doomsday, } 1981 = \text{Saturday,}$$

so Easter Sunday, in 1981, is Apr 19.

Here is an example in the Julian system:

$$1573: \text{P.F.M.} = \text{Mar } 50 - (176+3)_{\text{mod }30} = \text{Mar } 50 - 29 = \text{Mar } 21 = \text{Saturday,}$$

so Easter Day, 1573 was Mar 22. Since this date is still in the Old Style 1572, we can say that that year contained two Easters!

You should use the Julian system even today if you want to know when the Orthodox churches celebrate Easter. Example:

$$\text{Julian P.F.M. } 1984 = \text{Apr } 19 - (99+3)_{\text{mod }30} = \text{Apr } 7.$$

The next Doomsday is Apr 11, which is, still in the Julian system,

$$\text{Tuesday,} \qquad 7 \text{ dozen} = \text{Tuesday,}$$
$$(\text{Julian } 1900)$$

so that Orthodox Easter Day, 1984 is the Julian date, Apr 9. Since the Julian calendar is now 13 days out of date, this is Apr 22 in the Gregorian system.

Differences between Julian and Gregorian dates:

15xx,	16xx,	17xx,	18xx,	19xx,	20xx,	21xx,	...
10 days,	10 days,	11 days,	12 days,	13 days,	13 days,	14 days,	....

HOW OLD IS THE MOON?

If you stand on the earth and watch the sun and moon going round you, you'll see that they take about $365\frac{1}{4}$ [365·242199] and 30 [29·530588 or $29\frac{5}{9}$] days to do so, on average [brackets like these contain better approximations to various numbers].

From these facts you can deduce that the number of days that have passed since the last new moon is approximately:

$$(\text{day number}) + (\text{month number}) + (\text{year number}) + (\text{century number}),$$

all reduced mod 30 [$29\frac{5}{9}$].

The **day number** is the number of the day in the month.

The **month number**

for	Jan	Feb	Mar	Apr	May	Jun	Jul	Aug	Sep	Oct	Nov	Dec
is	3	4	3	4	5	6	7	8	9	10	11	12
	[$2\frac{2}{3}$	4	$2\frac{1}{3}$	$3\frac{8}{9}$	$4\frac{4}{9}$	6	$6\frac{5}{9}$	8	$9\frac{5}{9}$	$10\frac{1}{9}$	$11\frac{5}{9}$	$11\frac{8}{9}$]

(or just remember that the rule is about $\frac{1}{2}$ a day late/early in the long/short odd months).

The **year number** for a year whose last two digits are congruent, modulo 19,

to 0	± 1	± 2	± 3	± 4	± 5	± 6	± 7	± 8	± 9
is 0	± 11	± 22	± 03	± 14	± 25	± 06	± 17	± 28	± 09
[0	$\pm 10\frac{8}{9}$	$\pm 21\frac{7}{9}$	$\pm 3\frac{1}{9}$	± 14	$\pm 24\frac{8}{9}$	$\pm 6\frac{2}{9}$	$\pm 17\frac{1}{9}$	± 28	$\pm 9\frac{1}{3}$]

[with an additional

	$\frac{1}{2}$		$\frac{1}{4}$	0	$-\frac{1}{4}$	$-\frac{1}{2}$
in years	$4n$ (after leap day)		$4n+1$	$4n+2$	$4n+3$	$4n+4$ (before leap day)].

The **century number** for the Gregorian centuries

	15xx	16xx	17xx	18xx	19xx	20xx	21xx	22xx	23xx	24xx
is	$16\frac{1}{3}$	12	$6\frac{2}{3}$	$1\frac{1}{3}$	-4	$-8\frac{1}{3}$	$-13\frac{2}{3}$	-19	$-24\frac{1}{3}$	$-28\frac{2}{3}$

and, for the Julian centuries

	8xx	9xx	10xx	11xx	12xx	13xx	14xx	15xx	16xx	17xx
	27	$22\frac{2}{3}$	$18\frac{2}{3}$	14	$9\frac{2}{3}$	$5\frac{1}{3}$	$+1$	$-3\frac{1}{3}$	$-7\frac{2}{3}$	-12

To remember these,

the day number is easy,
the month number also, except for Jan = 3, Feb = 4.
the year number's tens digit is its units digit reduced, modulo 3,
the centuries 14xx and 19xx are $+1$ and -4; and a short century (36524 days)
    drops back $5\frac{1}{3}$ days, while a long century (36525 days) drops back $4\frac{1}{3}$ days
    (because 1273 lunations take $36529\frac{1}{3}$ [36529·337] days).

Thus (using only the rough numbers) on Christmas Day, 1984, the moon will be

$$25 + 12 + (+28) - 4 \ (\text{mod } 30) = 1 \text{ day old,}$$

since $84 \equiv +8$, mod 19 and $8 \equiv 2$, mod 3. But, applying the formula to New Year's Day 1985 we find

$$1 + 3(!) + (+09) - 4 = 9 \text{ days old}$$

despite the interval of exactly 7 days. The true motion of the moon is very complicated, and such a simple rule can only hope to give answers to within a day or so. If you're watching the moon late at night, for instance, remember that 11:00 p.m. is nearer tomorrow than today because the rule is attuned to the start of the day.

Of course a moon's age of about

$$0, \qquad\qquad 7\tfrac{1}{2}, \qquad\qquad 15, \qquad\qquad 22\tfrac{1}{2},$$

days corresponds to

New Moon,   First Quarter,   Full Moon,   Last Quarter.

Those who like to keep mental track of the moon throughout a year should remember the total number for that year, e.g.

in 1982, day number + month number +2,
in 1983, day number + month number +13 etc.

1984,	1985,	1986,	1987,	1988,	1989,	1990,	1991,	1992,	1993,	1994
−6,	+5,	−13,	−2,	+9,	−10,	+1,	+12,	−7,	+4,	−15

JEWISH NEW YEAR (ROSH HASHANA)

The Jewish New Year's Day in a Gregorian year Y A.D. (i.e. the first day of the Jewish year Y + 3761) happens on September N, where

$$\{\lfloor Y/100 \rfloor - \lfloor Y/400 \rfloor - 2\} + \frac{765433}{492480}(12G)_{\text{mod }19} + \tfrac{1}{4}(Y)_{\text{mod }4} - \frac{313Y + 89091}{98496} = N + \text{fraction}$$

and G is the Golden number, except that it must be postponed from any

			TUE	MON
SUN	WED	FRI	if fraction $\geqslant \dfrac{1367}{2160}$	if fraction $\geqslant \dfrac{23269}{25920}$
			and if $(12G)_{\text{mod }19} > 6$	and if $(12G)_{\text{mod }19} > 11$

to the following

| MON | THU | SAT | THU (*not* WED) | TUE |

(omit the terms { } for Julian years).

EXTRAS

BLOCKS-IN-A-BOX

The key to this puzzle is that every piece except the three $3 \times 1 \times 1$ rods occupies as many "black" cells as "white" in every layer. The rods must therefore be arranged so as to correct the color compositions in all fifteen layers simultaneously. It turns out that there is a unique arrangement which does this. Figure 61 also shows the only three dispositions for the $2 \times 2 \times 2$ cube and $2 \times 2 \times 1$ square. With these five pieces in place, the puzzle becomes easy.

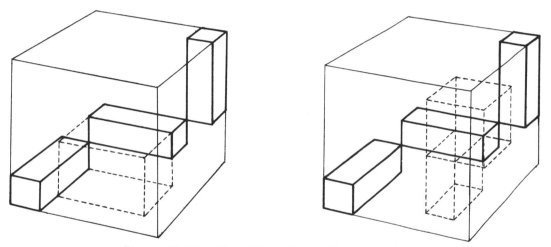

Figure 61. Were You Able to Fit the Blocks-in-a-Box?

A much harder puzzle is to pack 41 $1 \times 2 \times 4$ planks (together with 15 $1 \times 1 \times 1$ holes) into a $7 \times 7 \times 7$ box (see reference to Foregger, and to Mather, who proves that 42 planks can't be packed.)

THE SOMAP

The Soma pieces $1 = W$, $2 = Y$ and $4 = O$, while themselves symmetrical, may appear on the surface of the cube in either the *dexter* fashion

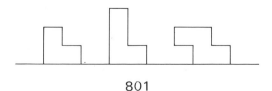

801

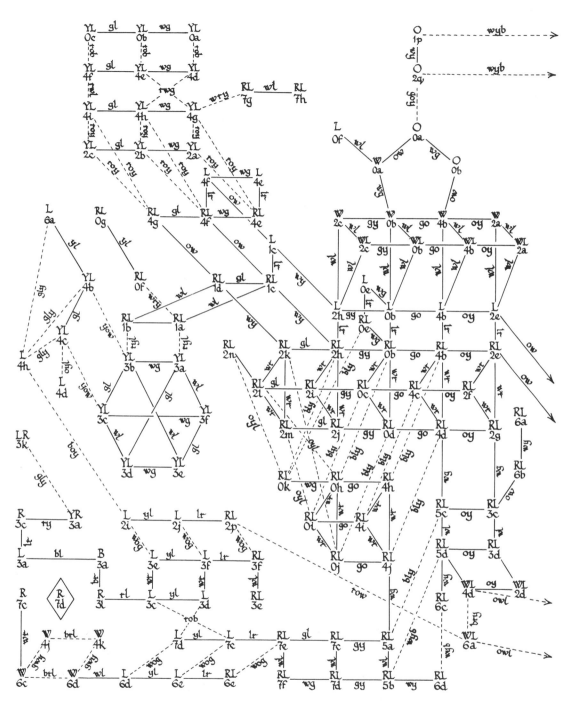

The diamond's gory secrets are seven seas away!

Figure 62. The   . . .   .

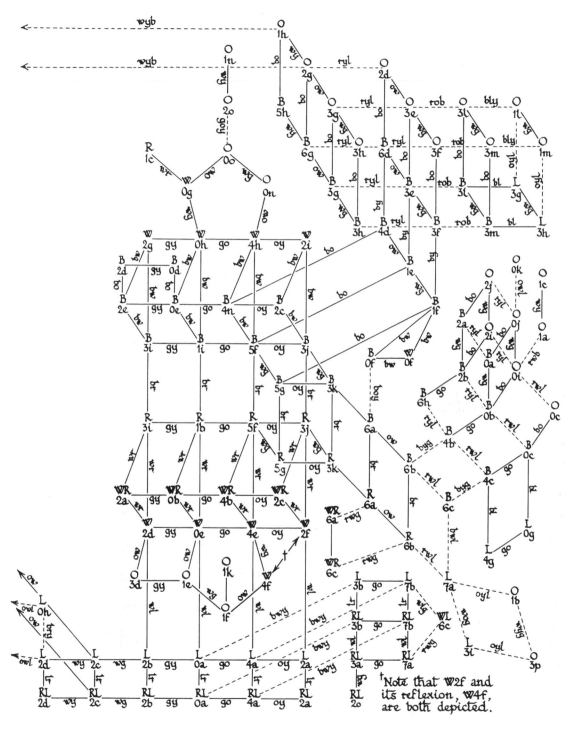

†Note that W2f and
its reflexion, W4f,
are both depicted.

. . . . Somap.

or the *sinister* one

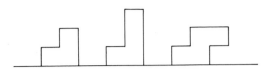

so you can tell which of these pieces are dexter by giving the sum of their numbers, which we call the **dexterity** of the solution. The symbols

DC   DC   DC
na   *nb*   *nc*

refer to different solutions having deficient piece D, central piece C and dexterity *n*, a single capital letter indicating that the same piece is both deficient and central. Thus

RL   RL   RL   RL
5a   5b   5c   5d

are four solutions in which Red is deficient, bLue is central and pieces 1 and 4 are dexter ($1+4=5$), while

B   B   B
6a   6b   6c ···

are solutions in which Black is deficient *and* central while 2 and 4 are dexter.

Along with the solutions in Fig. 62, there are their reflexions whose names are found by interchanging R and L and replacing *n* by

$3-n$, $6-n$, $7-n$,

in the cases

O central,   W central,   otherwise.

When two solutions are related by changing just two pieces, P and Q, this is indicated by a solid line PQ. Some three-piece changes are indicated by dashed lines in a similar way. So all that's left for you to do is to find a suitable solution which you can locate on the Somap which will then lead you to all the others except R7d.

SOLUTIONS TO THE ARITHMETICO-GEOMETRIC PUZZLE

Figure 63 shows how we indicate layers in this puzzle by using *a* or *α*, according to orientation, for an *a*-high block, etc. The 21 solutions to Hoffman's puzzle are exhibited in Table 1 in this notation. When, as usual, only the middle layer is shown, another layer is separated from it by a letter S, and the remaining one is the special layer of Fig. 63. The meanings of the other letters in Table 1 are:

    R: reflect the special layer across the dotted diagonal,
    S: swap the two non-special layers,
    S′: swap two adjacent layers in a different direction,
    T: tamper with a $2 \times 2 \times 2$ corner, not involving the special layer,
    T′: tamper with a $2 \times 2 \times 2$ corner, which does involve the special layer.

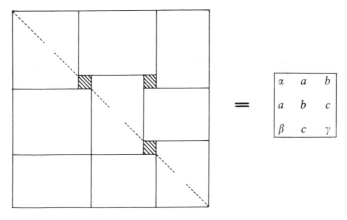

Figure 63. The Special Layer.

We'll leave it to you to work out why this gives just 21 solutions, and to verify that of these, exactly 17 have **duals**, obtained by replacing the dimensions a, b, c by c, b, a. Just one of the solutions (which?) is self-dual. This solution has the remarkable property that it can be repeatedly transformed (into rotations of itself!) by transporting either of two special faces to the opposite side.

Raphael Robinson and David Seal have found ways of combining solutions to the Arithmetico-Geometric puzzle in various dimensions to produce higher-dimensional ones. For example, if

$$a = a_1 + a_2 + a_3 \quad \text{and} \quad b = b_1 + b_2 + b_3$$

we know how to pack 27

$$a_1 \times a_2 \times a_3 \quad \text{or} \quad b_1 \times b_2 \times b_3$$

blocks into an

$$a \times a \times a \quad \text{or} \quad b \times b \times b$$

cube. The Cartesian product of these gives us a way of packing $27^2 = 729$

$$a_1 \times a_2 \times a_3 \times b_1 \times b_2 \times b_3$$

6-dimensional hyperblocks into a single

$$a \times a \times a \times b \times b \times b$$

hyperblock. But now the Cartesian product of three copies of Fig. 7 gives us a way to pack $4^3 = 64$ of these

$$a \quad \times \quad b \quad \times \quad a \quad \times \quad b \quad \times \quad a \quad \times \quad b$$

hyperblocks into an

$$(a+b) \times (a+b) \times (a+b) \times (a+b) \times (a+b) \times (a+b)$$

hypercube.

In general the method combines m-dimensional and n-dimensional solutions to give an mn-dimensional one. We hope Omar will tell us how to deal with dimensions 5, 7, 11 and so on.

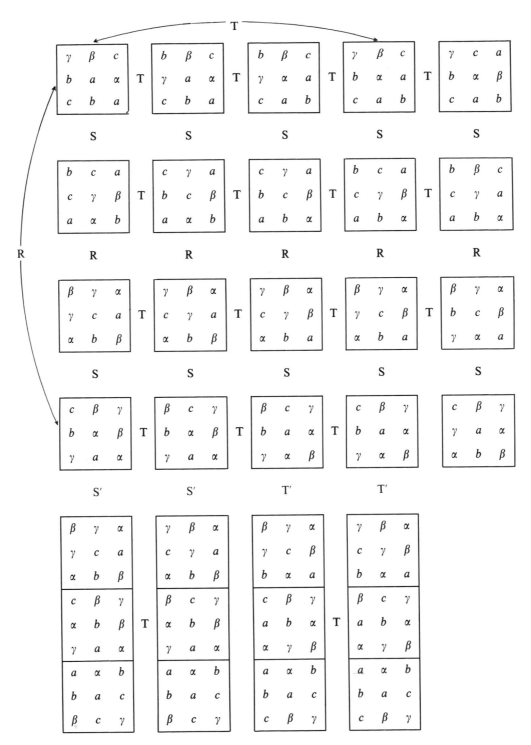

Table 1. The 21 Solutions to Hoffman's Puzzle.

... AND ONE FOR "THREE" TOO!

$$0 \quad 0 \quad 2 \qquad 1 \quad 1 \quad 0 \qquad 1 \quad 0 \quad 0$$

$$0 \quad 0 \quad 2 \qquad 1 \quad 2 \quad 1 \qquad 1 \quad 2 \quad 2$$

$$2 \quad 2 \quad 1 \qquad 0 \quad 1 \quad 1 \qquad 0 \quad 2 \quad 2$$

There's only one other solution. Hint: add $x + y + z$.

HARES AND TORTOISES

Make the moves in this order (jumps are bold):

H, T, T, H, H, H, T, T, T, H, H, H, T, T, H.

If you move only one kind of animal for as long as you can before moving the other kind, you'll soon see how to swap 57 Hares with 57 Tortoises.

Solutions to the other coin problems (heads are **bold**) are:

Start from 012**345**; move   01 to 67, **56** to **89** and 23 to **56**;

or   01 to 76, 23 to **98** and **56** to **65**.

Start from 0123**4567**; move 12 to 89, **45** to **12**, 78 to 45 and 01 to 78;

or   **67** to **98**, 01 to 76, 34 to 43 and 78 to 87.

M. Delannoy has shown that the first problem with n pairs of coins can always be solved in just n moves. However the second problem, due to Tait, requires $n + 1$ moves if $n > 4$. For some reason which we don't understand, we have always found these little problems confusing and can never remember their solutions!

The last little coin puzzle is one of the simplest examples we know of a psychological block. You notice that four coins are already in position (Fig. 64(a)), so you're reluctant either to move one of them (Fig. 64(b)) or to waste time by replacing it (Fig. 64(c)), but that's the only way to get to Fig. 64(d) in three moves. There's a four-move version in which you start with a triangle.

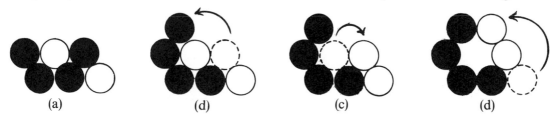

    (a)   (d)   (c)   (d)

Figure 64. How to Infuriate Your Friends.

THE LUCKY SEVEN PUZZLE

has a solution in which just seven discs are slid down the bridge, alternately from the left and right sides:

1, 7, 2, 6, 3, 5, 4.

TOP FACE ALTERATIONS FOR THE HUNGARIAN CUBE

We give the shortest known sequences for all permutations (Table 2) and for all combinations of flips and twists (Table 3) in the top layer. The numbers are the numbers of moves, but not counting any final top turns (U^k) which can all be saved to the end. David Seal has proved that most of these are best possible.

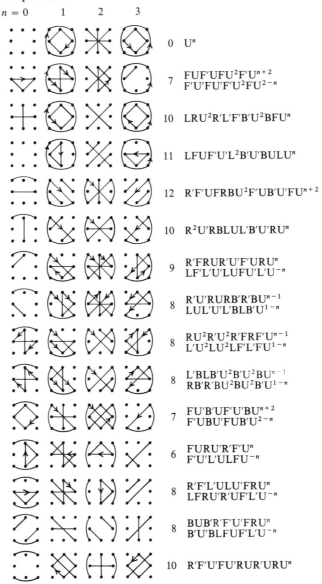

$n = 0 \quad 1 \quad 2 \quad 3$

0 U^n

7 $FUF'UFU^2F'U^{n+2}$
$F'U'FU'F'U^2FU^{2-n}$

10 $LRU^2R'L'F'B'U^2BFU^n$

11 $LFUF'U'L^2B'U'BULU^n$

12 $R'F'UFRBU^2F'UB'U'FU^{n+2}$

10 $R^2U'RBLUL'B'U'RU^n$

9 $R'FRUR'U'F'URU^n$
$LF'L'U'LUFU'L'U^{-n}$

8 $R'U'RURB'R'BU^{n-1}$
$LUL'U'L'BLB'U^{1-n}$

8 $RU^2R'U^2R'FRF'U^{n-1}$
$L'U^2LU^2LF'L'FU^{1-n}$

8 $L'BLB'U^2B'U^2BU^{n-1}$
$RB'R'BU^2BU^2B'U^{1-n}$

7 $FU'B'UF'U'BU^{n+2}$
$F'UBU'FUB'U^{2-n}$

6 $FURU'R'F'U^n$
$F'U'L'ULFU^{-n}$

8 $R'F'L'ULU'FRU^n$
$LFRU'R'U'F'L'U^{-n}$

8 $BUB'R'F'U'FRU^n$
$B'U'BLFUF'L'U^{-n}$

10 $R'F'U'FU'RUR'URU^n$

Table 2. Top Layer Permutation Sequences.
(the lower sequence of a pair refers to the left-right reflected picture)

Pattern	n	Sequence
`• • •` / `• • •` / `• • •`	0	no moves required
`• • •` / `• • e` / `• e •`	12	F'U'F²DRUR'D'U'F²U²FU'
`• e •` / `• • •` / `• e •`	13	LF'UL'FB'UR'FU'RF'BU'
`• e •` / `e • e` / `• e •`	13	L²F²L²U²R'LFL'RU²L²F²L²U
`• • a` / `• • •` / `• • c`	12	R'U'LU²R'F²RF²U'RU²L'U² RU²L'UB²L'B²LU²R'ULU²
`• • a` / `• e •` / `• e c`	13	RU'LU²R²F'U'FUR²U²R'L'U BFU²F²U'L'ULF²U²B'UF'U'
`• e a` / `• e •` / `• e c`	13	R'UL'U²R²BUB'U'R²U²RLU' F'B'U²B²ULU'L'B²U²FU'BU
`e • a` / ` ` / `• e c`	14	F²DF'UFD'FL'U'LUF²U²F'U LU²L²U'B'UBL'DL'U'LD'L²U'
`• e a` / `e • •` / `• • c`	14	B²D'BU'B'DB'LUL'U'B²U²BU' L'U²L²UFU'F'LD'LUL'DL²U
`• e a` / `• • •` / `• c c`	14	RUR²F²D'R²BL'B'R²DF'RF'U² BLBD'L²FRF²L²DB²L²U'L'U²
`• • a` / `e • •` / `• • c`	14	LF'D'L'BL'B²U²L'BDF'L²F²U² B²R²BD'F'RU²F²RF'RDBR'U²
`• e a` / `e • e` / `• e c`	15	BU²BR²FD²FLFL²F²D²F'R²B²U R²F²LD'L²B²L'B'L'D²L'F²R'U²R'U'
`a • •` / `• • •` / `• • •`	11	R'BD²B'RU²R'BD²B'RU²
`a • •` / `• • •` / `• e c`	14	B'UFU'BU²F²L'U'LUF²U²F' LU'R'UL'U²R²BUB'U'R²U²R
`a • •` / `e • •` / `• e c`	13	L'UBL'D'BD²R²D'B²L²UF²U² B²U'R²F²DL²D²F'DRFU'RU²
`a e •` / `• • •` / `• • •`	13	R'B²F'L'DF'L²FD'LFB²RU²
`a • •` / `e • e` / `• • c`	13	BR²LFD'LF²L'DF'L'R²B'U²
`a e •` / `e • e` / `• e c`	16	BUB²RBR²URL'U'L²F'L'F²U'F'
`c • c` / `• • •` / `• • c`	12	RU'L'UDB²D'R²U²LU'RU' B'UF'U²B²DL²U'D'FUB'U
`c • c` / `• e •` / `• e c`	11	LR'U'R²B'R'B²U'B'U²L' LU²BUB²RBR²URL'
`c e c` / `e • •` / `• • c`	11	F'U²R'U'R²B'R'B²U'B'F F'BUB²RBR²URU²F
`c • c` / `e • •` / `• e c`	14	F²R²FU'F²R'F'R²U'R'U²F²R²F² F²R²F²U²RUR²FRF²UF'R²F²
`c e c` / `• e •` / `• • c`	8	B'U'B²L'BL²U'L'U² RUR²FRF²UFU²
`c e c` / `• • •` / `• e c`	12	BLU²B'U'B²L'BL²U'L²B' BL²UL²BLB²UBU²L'B'
`c • c` / `e • e` / `• • c`	12	R'F²U'F²R'F'R²U'R'U²FR R'F'U²RUR²FRF²UF²R
`c e c` / `• • •` / `• e c`	12	L'U'B²UBLBLUL'U'B'U² FURU'R'F'R'F'U'FURU²
`a • c` / `• • •` / `a • c`	14	R²B²R²U'RL'DL²U²LD'L²U²R'U
`a • c` / `• e •` / `a e c`	12	LUFU'F'L'R'U'F'UFR R'F'U'FURLFUF'U'L'
`a e c` / `• • •` / `a • c`	12	RBUB'U'R'L'B'U'BUL L'U'B'UBLRUBU'B'R'
`a e c` / `• • •` / `a e c`	14	F'U'F²UL'U'RLU'R'UF²U'F'U²
`a • c` / `e • e` / `a • c`	14	R'U'F'L'R'U'F'UFRLUFR
`a e c` / `e • •` / `a e c`	13	LU²F'U'F²LF²L'F²UFU²L'U'
`c • a` / `• • •` / `a • c`	15	R'U²RU²R²B'D'R'FR²F'DBU'R'U'
`c • a` / `• e •` / `a e c`	15	R'F²U'D'L'F'LFDULFL'FR R'F'LF'L'U'D'F'L'FLDUF²R
`c e a` / `• • •` / `a e c`	14	R'UB'R²U'RUR²BU²R²B'R'BU² F'LFL²U²F'L²U'L'UL²FU'LU²
`c e a` / `e • e` / `a e c`	14	B'D²FU²RF'D²BLU²FU²F'LU

Table 3. Top Layer Flip and Twist Sequences.
(the lower sequence of a pair refers to the picture with a and c swapped)

THE CENTURY PUZZLE

is so called because it takes exactly 100 moves, and the Century-and-a-Half takes 151 according to the official rules, but since the first and last are only half-moves, we can obviously count it as 150 whole moves. You can see solutions to both puzzles in Fig. 65, and by turning the book upside-down you'll see the only other 100-move solution to the Century.

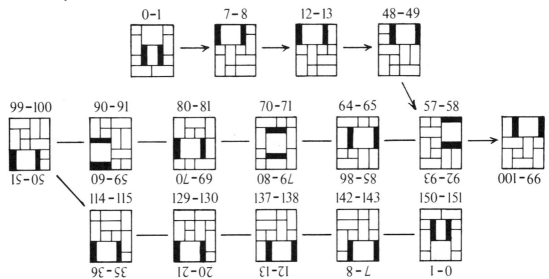

Figure 65. Solutions to the Century and Century-and-a-Half Puzzles.

ADAMS'S AMAZING MAGIC HEXAGON

```
              15
          14      13
       9      8      10
          6      4
      11      5      12
          1      2
     18      7      16
         17      19
              3
```

In Martin Gardner's *Sixth Book of Mathematical Games* you can read the remarkable history of Clifford W. Adams's discovery and of Charles W. Trigg's uniqueness proof. It's easy to see that a diameter d magic hexagon uses the numbers from 1 to $(3d^2 + 1)/4$, which add to

$$\frac{1}{2}\left(\frac{3d^2 + 1}{4}\right)\left(\frac{3d^2 + 5}{4}\right) = \frac{1}{32}(9d^4 + 18d^2 + 5),$$

so that each of its d columns must add to

$$\frac{1}{32}\left(9d^3 + 18d + \frac{5}{d}\right)$$

which can only be an integer if d divides 5.

FLAGS OF THE ALLIES SOLUTION

If you use the O'Beirne method you will find the two pairs of 5-circuits

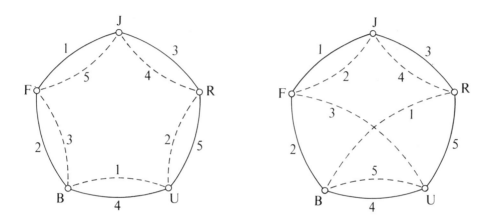

which lead to the solutions shown in Fig. 49 and Fig. 66.

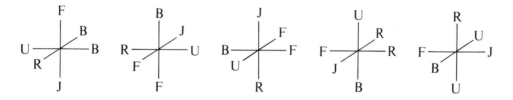

Figure 66. The Other Solution to the Flags of the Allies Problems.

ANSWER TO EXERCISE FOR EXPERTS

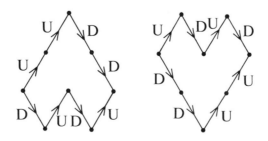

We have a rather complicated proof that n^2 copies of hexiamond A can be used to replicate A on a larger scale only if $n \equiv 0$ or ± 1 mod 6. Our proof establishes that these are the only values of n for which the relations (look at the foot of the previous page)

$$U^2D^2 = DUDU \quad \text{and} \quad D^2U^2 = UDUD$$

imply

$$U^{2n}D^{2n} = D^nU^nD^nU^n.$$

We've also shown that none of the usual kinds of coloring argument excludes other values of n.

WHERE DO THE BLACK EDGES OF MACMAHON SQUARES GO?

Round the outside, of course, but there are six more inside. These can be arranged in 20 different ways. In the first two the ladder is in the *third* column, otherwise it's in the second. The last row of Fig. 67 contains $6 + 6 + 2$ arrangements: the dotted lines are alternative positions for the sixth black edge.

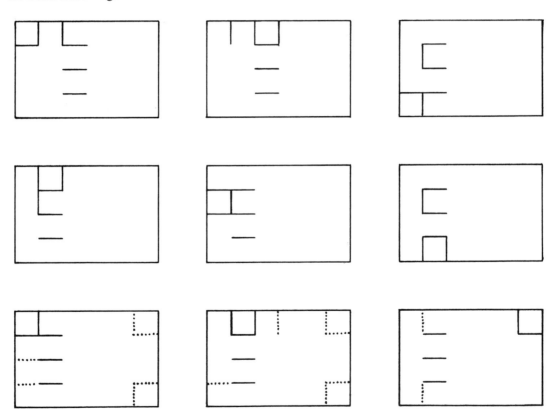

Figure 67. The Twenty Black Edge Arrangements for MacMahon Squares.

THE THREE QUINTOMINAL DODECAHEDRA

should be recoverable from

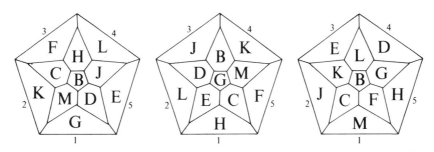

$$12345 = A \quad 12354 = B \quad 12435 = C \quad 12453 = D \quad 12534 = E \quad 12543 = F$$
$$13245 = G \quad 13254 = H \quad 13425 = J \quad 13524 = K \quad 14235 = L \quad 14325 = M.$$

DOOMSDAY ANSWERS

1. In Sweden there were no leap-days between Saturday 29 Feb 1696 and Saturday 29 Feb 1744, so the answer is Sweden, 29 Feb 1744, Saturday. At the time he was 11 days short of being 48 years old. This riot-avoiding scheme for losing the controversial 11 days was mooted in 1645 by John Greaves, an Oxford professor of astronomy.

2. A tedious enumeration shows that in the 400 years of the Gregorian cycle Doomsday is

	Sun	Mon	Tue	Wed	Thu	Fri	Sat	
for	43	43	43	43	44	43	44	ordinary years
and	13	15	13	15	13	14	14	leap years

From this you can work out that the 13th day falls on

	Sun	Mon	Tue	Wed	Thu	Fri	Sat	
in	687	685	685	687	684	688	684	months,

verifying B.H. Brown's assertion that the 13th of a month is just a little bit more likely to be a Friday than any other day of the week!

REFERENCES AND FURTHER READING

W.S. Andrews, "Magic Squares and Cubes", Open Court, 1917, reprinted Dover, 1960.

A.K. Austin, The 14–15 puzzle, Note 63.5, Math. Gaz. **63** (1979) 45–46.

W.W. Rouse Ball and H.S.M. Coxeter, "Mathematical Recreations and Essays", 12th edn. University of Toronto Press, 1974, pp. 26–27 (calendar problems), pp. 116–118 (shunting problems), p. 121 (sliding coins), pp. 193–221 (magic squares), pp. 312–322 (Fifteen Puzzle, Tower of Hanoï, Chinese rings). See early editions for Tangrams. Pages 141–144 on equilateral zonohedra and the references there, are related to Schoen's Cyclotome puzzles.

C.J. Bouwkamp, Catalogue of solutions of the rectangular $2 \times 5 \times 6$ solid pentomino problem, Nederl. Akad. Wet. Proc. Ser. A, **81** (1978) 177–186; Zbl. 384.42011.

Bro. Alfred Brousseau, Tower of Hanoï with more pegs, J. Recreational Math., **8** (1975–76) 169–176.

B.H. Brown, Problem E36, Amer. Math. Monthly, **40** (1933) 295 (calendar).

T.A. Brown, A note on "Instant Insanity", Math. Mag. **41** (1968) 68.

Cardan, "De Subtilitate", book xv, para 2; ed. Sponius vol. III, p. 587 (Chinese rings).

F. de Carteblanche, The coloured cubes problem, Eureka, **9** (1947) 9–11 (Tantalizer).

T.R. Dawson and W.E. Lester, A notation for dissection problems, Fairy Chess Review, **3** (Apr 1937) 5, 46–47 (polyominoes).

M. Delannoy, La Nature, June 1887, p. 10 (sliding coins).

A.P. Domoryad, "Mathematical Games and Pastimes", Pergamon, 1963, pp. 71–74 (Chinese rings); pp. 75–76 (Tower of Hanoï); pp. 79–85 (Fifteen puzzle); pp. 97–104 (magic squares); pp. 127–128 (sliding coins); pp. 142–144 (cf. Schoen's puzzle).

Henry Ernest Dudeney, "The Canterbury Puzzles", Nelson, London, 1907, 1919 reprinted Dover, 1958, No. 74 The Broken Chessboard, pp. 119–121, 220–221 (pentominoes).

Henry Ernest Dudeney, "536 Puzzles and Curious Problems", ed. Martin Gardner, Chas. Scribner's Sons, New York 1967, No. 383 The six pennies, pp. 138, 343; No. 377 Black and white, pp. 135, 340; No. 516 A calendar puzzle, pp. 212, 409–410; No. 528 A leap year puzzle, pp. 217, 413.

T.H. Foregger, Problem E2524, Amer Math. Monthly, **82** (1975) 300; solution Michael Mather, **83** (1976) 741–742.

Martin Gardner, Mathematical Games, Sci. Amer., **196** #5 (May 1957) (Tower of Hanoï); **197** #6 (Dec. 1957) **203** #5 (Nov 1960) 186–194, **207** #5 (Nov 1962) 151–159 (Polyominoes); **199** #3 (Sept 1958) 182–188 (Soma); **210** #2 (Feb 1964) 122–126, **222** #2 (Feb 1970) (Fifteen puzzle. Sliding block puzzles); **210** #3 (Mar 1964) 126–127 (Magic squares); **219** #4 (Oct 1968) 120–125 (MacMahon triangles; Conway's "three" puzzle); **223** #6 (Dec 1970) 110–114 (non-transitive dice; quintominal dodecahedra).

Martin Gardner, "The Scientific American Book of Mathematical Puzzles and Diversions", Simon and Schuster, New York 1959, pp. 15–22 (magic squares); pp. 55–62 (Tower of Hanoï); pp. 88 (Fifteen puzzle); pp. 124–140 (polyominoes).

Martin Gardner, "The 2nd Scientific American Book of Mathematical Puzzles and Diversions", Simon and Schuster, New York, 1961, pp. 55–56, 59 (sliding pennies); pp. 65–77 (Soma); pp. 130–140 (Magic squares); pp. 214–215, 218–219 (another Solitaire-like puzzle).

Martin Gardner, "Sixth Book of Mathematical Games from Scientific American", Chas. Scribner's Sons, New York, 1971, pp. 23–24 (magic hexagon); pp. 64–70 (sliding block puzzles); pp. 173–182 (polyiamonds).

Martin Gardner, "Mathematical Puzzles of Sam Loyd", Dover, New York 1959, No. 73 pp. 70, 146–147.

S.W. Golomb, Checkerboards and polyominoes, Amer. Math. Monthly, **61** (1954) 675–682.

S.W. Golomb, The general theory of polyominoes, Recreational Math. Mag. **4** (Aug 1961) 3–12; **5** (Oct 1961) 3–12; **6** (Dec 1961) 3–20; **8** (Apr 1962) 7–16.

S.W. Golomb, "Polyominoes", Chas. Scribner's Sons, New York, 1965.

A.P. Grecos and R.W. Gibberd, A diagrammatic solution to "Instant Insanity" problem, Math. Mag. **44** (1971) 71.

L. Gros, "Théorie du Baguenodier", Lyons, 1872 (Chinese rings).

L.J. Guibas and A.M. Odlyzko, Periods in strings, J. Combin. Theory Ser. A **30** (1981) 19–42.

L.J. Guibas and A.M. Odlyzko, String overlaps, pattern matching and non-transitive games, J. Combin. Theory Ser. A **30** (1981) 183–208.

Béla Hajtman, On coverings of generalized checkerboards, I, Magyar Tud. Akad. Math. Kutato Int. Köz, **7** (1962) 53–71.

Sir Paul Harvey, "The Oxford Companion to English Literature", 4th ed., Oxford, 1967, Appendix III, The Calendar.

C.B. and Jenifer Haselgrove, A computer program for pentominoes, Eureka, **23** (1960) 16–18.

Kersten Meier, Restoring the Rubik's Cube. A manual for beginners, an improved translation of "Puzzlespass mit dem Rubik's Cube" 4c Hulme, Escondido Village, Stanford CA 94305 USA or Henning-Storm-Str. 5, 221 Itzehoe, W. Germany, 1981:01:20.

J.A. Hunter and Joseph S. Madachy, "Mathematical Diversions", Van Nostrand, New York, 1963, Chapter 8, Fun with Shapes, pp. 77–89.

Maurice Kraitchik, "Mathematical Recreations", George Allen and Unwin, 1943, pp. 89–93 (Chinese rings, Tower of Hanoï); pp. 109–116 (calendar); pp. 142–192 (magic squares); pp. 222–226 (shunting puzzles); pp. 302–308 (Fifteen puzzle).

Kay P. Litchfield, A 2 × 2 × 1 solution to "Instant Insanity", Pi Mu Epsilon J. **5** (1972) 334–337.

E. Lucas, "Récréations Mathematiques", Gauthier-Villars 1882–94; Blanchard Paris, 1960.

Major P.A. MacMahon, "New Mathematical Pastimes", Cambridge University Press, 1921.

Douglas R. Hofstadter, Metamagical Themas: The Magic Cube's cubies are twiddled by cubists and solved by cubemeisters, Sci. Amer. **244** #3 (Mar. 1981) 20–39.

J.C.P. Miller, Pentominoes, Eureka, **23** (1960) 13–16.

T.H. O'Beirne, "Puzzles and Paradoxes", Oxford University Press, London, 1965, pp. 112–129 (Tantalizer); pp. 168–184 (Easter).

T.H. O'Beirne, Puzzles and Paradoxes, in *New Scientist*, **258** (61:10:26) 260–261; **259** (61:11:02) 316–317; **260** (61:11:9) 379–380; **266** (61:12:21) 751–752; **270** (62:01:18) 158–159.

Ozanam, "Recreations", 1723, vol. IV 439, (Chinese rings).

De Parville, La Nature, Paris, 1884, part i, 285–286 (Tower of Hanoï).

B.D. Price, Pyramid Patience, Eureka, **8** (1944) 5–7.

R.C. Read, Contributions to the cell growth problem, Canad. J. Math. **14** (1962) 1–20 (polyominoes).

J.E. Reeve and J.A. Tyrrell, Maestro puzzles, Math. Gaz. **45** (1961) 97–99 (polyominoes).

Raphael Robinson, Solution to problem E36, Amer. Math. Monthly, **40** (1933) 607.

Barkley Rosser and R.J. Walker, On the transformation group for diabolic magic squares of order four, Bull. Amer. Math. Soc. **44** (1938) 416–420.

Barkley Rosser and R.J. Walker, The algebraic theory of diabolic magic squares, Duke Math. J. **5** (1939) 705–728.

T. Roth, The Tower of Bramah revisited, J. Recreational Math. **7** (1974) 116–119.

Wolfgang Alexander Schocken, "The Calculated Confusion of Calendars", Vantage Press, New York, 1976.

Leslie E. Shader, Cleopatra's pyramid. Math. Mag. **51** (1978) 57–60 (Tantalizer variant).

David Singmaster, Notes on the 'magic cube', Dept. Math. Sci. & Comput. Polytech. of S. Bank, London SE AA, England, 1979, 5th edition, 1980, £2·00 or $5·00.

W. Stead, Dissection, Fairy Chess Review, **9** (Dec 1954) 2–4 (polyominoes).

James Ussher, "Annales Veteris Testamenti", Vol. 8, Dublin ed. 1864, p. 13 ("beginning of night leading into Oct. 23").

Joan Vandeventer, Instant Insanity, in "The Many Facets of Graph Theory", Springer Lecture Notes **110** (1969) 283–286.

Wallis, "Algebra", latin edition 1693. Opera, Vol. II, Chap. cxi, pp. 472–478 (Chinese rings).

Harold Watkins, "Time counts; the story of the calendar", Neville Spearman, London, 1954.

Richard M. Wilson, Graph puzzles, homotopy and the alternating group, J. Combin. Theory Ser. B **16** (1974) 86–96.

Chapter 25

What is Life?

Life's not always as simple as mathematics, Abraham!
    Mrs. Abraham Fraenkel.

Life's too important a matter to be taken seriously.
    Oscar Wilde.

... in real life mistakes are likely to be irrevocable.
Computer simulation, however, makes it economically practical
to make mistakes on purpose. If you are astute, therefore,
you can learn much more than they cost. Furthermore, if you
are at all discreet, no one but you need ever know you made
a mistake.
    John McLeod and John Osborn, *Natural Automata*
    and *Useful Simulations*, Macmillan, 1966.

Most of this book has been about two-player games, and our last two chapters were about one player games. Now we're going to talk about a no-player game, the **Game of Life**! Our younger readers won't have learned much about Life, so we'd better tell you some of the facts.

Life is a "game" played on an infinite squared board. At any time some of the cells will be **live** and others **dead**. Which cells are live at time 0 is up to you! But then you've nothing else to do, because the state at any later time follows inexorably from the previous one by the rules of the game:

BIRTH. A cell that's *dead* at time t becomes *live* at $t+1$ only if *exactly three* of its eight neighbors were live at t.

DEATH by overcrowding. A cell that's live at t and has four or more of its eight neighbors live at t will be dead by time $t+1$.

DEATH by exposure. A live cell that has only one live neighbor, or none at all, at time t, will also be dead at $t+1$.

These are the only causes of death, so we can take a more positive viewpoint and describe instead the rule for

SURVIVAL. A cell that was live at time t will remain live at $t+1$ if and only if it had just 2 or 3 live neighbors at time t.

> Just 3 for BIRTH
> 2 or 3 for SURVIVAL

A fairly typical Life History is shown in Fig. 1. We chose a simple line of five live cells for our generation 0. In the figures a circle denotes a live cell.

Which of these will survive to generation 1? The two end cells have just one neighbor each and so will die of exposure. But the three inner ones have two living neighbors and so will survive. That's why we've filled in those circles.

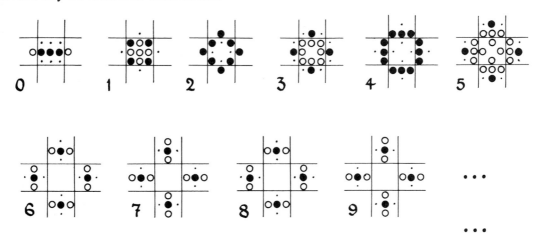

Figure 1. A Line of Five Becomes Traffic Lights.

What about births at time 1? There are three cells on either side of the line that are dead at time 0, but have exactly three live neighbors, so will come to life at time 1. We've shown these prospective births by dots in the figure.

So at time 1 the configuration will be a solid 3 × 3 square. Let's briefly follow its later progress.

Time 1–2: The corners will survive, having 3 neighbors each, but everything else will die of overcrowding. There will be 4 births, one by the middle of each side.

2–3: We see a ring in which each live cell has 2 neighbors so everything survives; there are 4 births inside.

3–4: Massive overcrowding kills off all except the 4 outer cells, but neighbors of these are born to form:

4–5: another survival ring with 8 happy events about to take place.

5–6: More overcrowding again leaves just 4 survivors. This time the neighboring births form:

6–7: four separated lines of 3, called **Blinkers**, which will never interact again.

7–8–9–10–... At each generation the tips of the Blinkers die of exposure but the births on each side reform the line in a perpendicular direction.

The configuration will therefore oscillate with period two forever. The final pair of configurations is sufficiently common to deserve a name. We call them **Traffic Lights**.

Time	0	1	2	3	...	
(a)	o●o	⊙	o●o	⊙	...	A Blinker
(b)					...	A Blanker
(c)					...	A Block

Figure 2. If Three Survive, They'll Make a Blinker or a Block.

The Blinker is also quite common on its own (Fig. 2a). Most other starting configurations of three live cells will blank out completely in two moves (Fig. 2(b)). But if you start with three of the four cells of a 2×2 block, the fourth cell will be born and then the **Block** will be stable (Fig. 2(c)) because each cell is neighbored by the three others.

STILL LIFE

It's easy to find other stable configurations. The commonest such **Still Life** can be seen in Fig. 3 along with their traditional names. The simple cases are usually loops in which each live cell has two or three neighbors according to local curvature, but the exact shape of the loop is important for effective birth control.

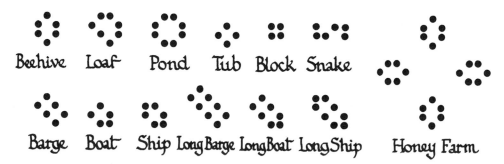

Beehive Loaf Pond Tub Block Snake

Barge Boat Ship Long Barge Long Boat Long Ship Honey Farm

Figure 3. Some of the Commoner Forms of Still Life.

LIFE CYCLES

The blinker is the simplest example of a configuration whose life history repeats itself with period > 1. Lifenthusiasts (a word due to Robert T. Wainwright) have found many other such configurations, a number of which are shown in Figs. 4 to 8.

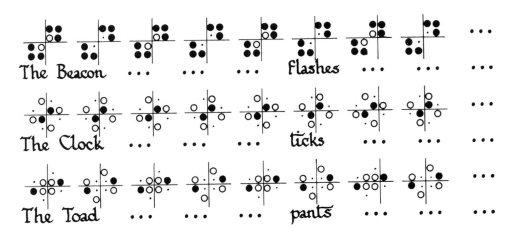

Figure 4. Three Life Cycles with Period Two.

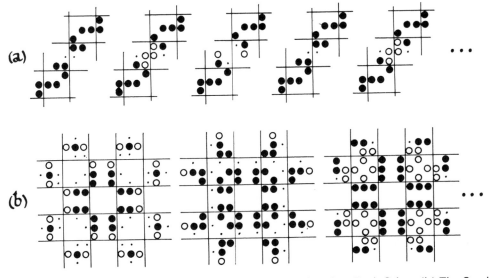

Figure 5. Two Life Cycles with Period Three. (a) Two Eaters Gnash at Each Other. (b) The Cambridge Pulsar CP 48-56-72.

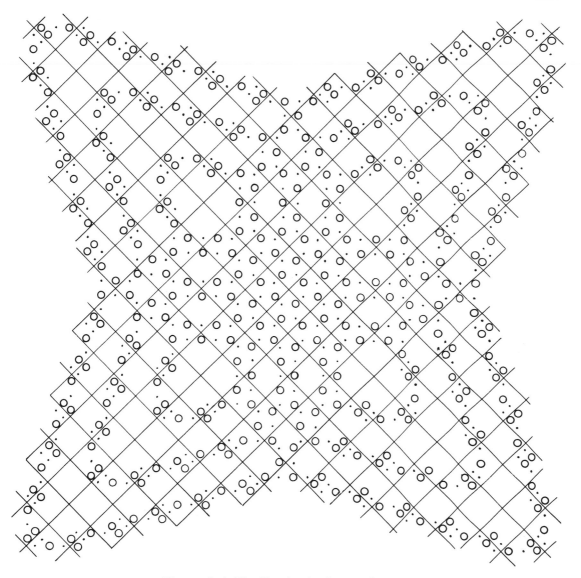

Figure 6. A Flip-Flop by the Gosper Group.

THE GLIDER AND OTHER SPACE SHIPS

When we first tracked the *r*-pentomino (you'll hear about that soon) some guy suddenly said, "Come over here, there's a piece that's walking!" We came over and found Fig. 9.

You'll see that generation 4 is just like generation 0 but moved one diagonal place, so that the configuration will steadily move across the plane. Because the arrangements at times 2, 6, 10, ... are related to those at times 0, 4, 8, 12, ... by the symmetry that geometers call a *glide reflexion*, we call this creature the **glider**. But when you see Life played at the right speed by a computer

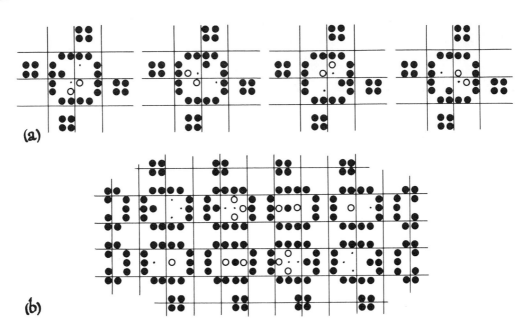

Figure 7. (a) Catherine Wheel. (b) Hertz Oscillator. Still Life Induction Coils Keep Field Stable.

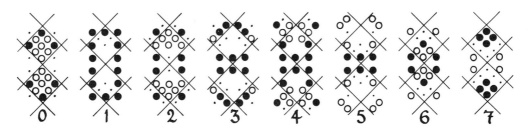

Figure 8. Figure 8.

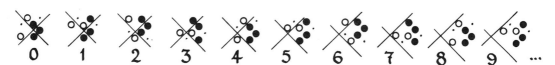

Figure 9. The Glider Moves One Square Diagonally Each Four Generations.

on a visual display, you'll see that the glider walks quite seductively, wagging its tail behind it. We'll see quite a lot of the glider in this chapter.

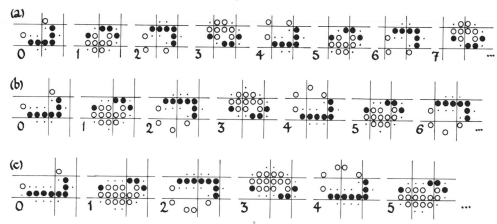

Figure 10. (a) Lightweight, (b) Middleweight, (c) Heavyweight Spaceships.

It was at just such a visual computer display that one of us first noticed the **spaceship** of Fig. 10(a) (and was very lucky to be able to stop the machine just before it would have crashed into another configuration). This **lightweight spaceship** immediately generalizes to the **middleweight** and **heavyweight** ones (Figs. 10(b) and (c)) but longer versions turn out to be unstable. It was later discovered, however, that arbitrarily long spaceships can still travel provided they are suitably escorted by small ones (Fig. 11). All the spaceships, as drawn, move Eastwards.

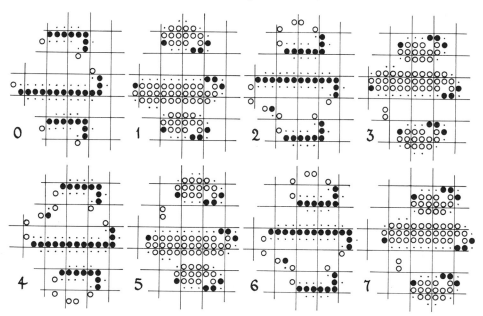

Figure 11. An Overweight Spaceship Escorted by Two Heavyweight Ones.

THE UNPREDICTABILITY OF LIFE

Is there some way to foretell the destiny of a Life pattern? Will it eventually fade away completely? Or become static? Oscillate? Travel across the plane, or maybe expand indefinitely?

Let's look at what *should* be a very simple starting configuration—a straight line of n live cells.

$n = 1$ or 2 fades immediately,

$n = 3$ is the Blinker;

$n = 4$ becomes a Beehive at time 2,

$n = 5$ gave Traffic Lights (Fig. 1) at time 6,

$n = 6$ fades at $t = 12$,

$n = 7$ makes a beautifully symmetric display before terminating in
               the **Honey Farm** (Fig. 3) at $t = 14$;

$n = 8$ gives 4 blocks and 4 beehives,

$n = 9$ makes two sets of Traffic Lights,

$n = 10$ turns into the **pentadecathlon**, with a life cycle of 15,

$n = 11$ becomes two blinkers,

$n = 12$ makes two beehives,

$n = 13$ turns into two blinkers,

$n = 14$
and   ⎫ vanish completely,
$n = 15$ ⎭

$n = 16$ makes a big set of Traffic Lights with 8 blinkers,

$n = 17$ becomes 4 blocks

$n = 18$
and   ⎫ fade away entirely,
$n = 19$ ⎭

$n = 20$ makes just 2 blocks,

and so on.

What's the general pattern? Even when we follow the configurations which start with a very small number of cells, it's not easy to see what goes on. There are 12 edge-connected regions with 5 cells (S.W. Golomb calls them pentominoes). Here are their histories:

Figure	Our mnemonic	Destiny

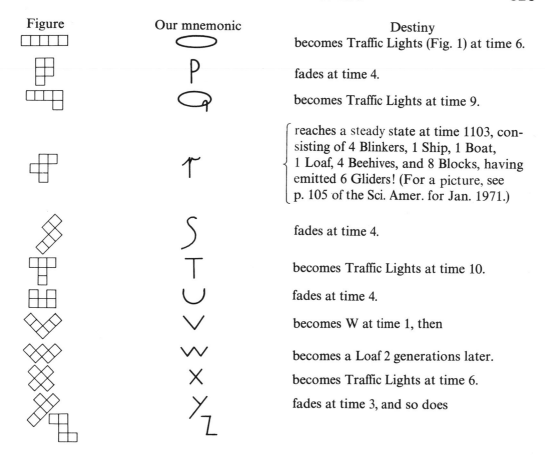

becomes Traffic Lights (Fig. 1) at time 6.

fades at time 4.

becomes Traffic Lights at time 9.

reaches a steady state at time 1103, consisting of 4 Blinkers, 1 Ship, 1 Boat, 1 Loaf, 4 Beehives, and 8 Blocks, having emitted 6 Gliders! (For a picture, see p. 105 of the Sci. Amer. for Jan. 1971.)

fades at time 4.

becomes Traffic Lights at time 10.

fades at time 4.

becomes W at time 1, then

becomes a Loaf 2 generations later.

becomes Traffic Lights at time 6.

fades at time 3, and so does

Once again, it doesn't seem easy to detect any general rule.

Here, in Figs. 12 and 13 are some other configurations with specially interesting Life Histories, for you to try your skill with.

Can the population of a Life configuration grow without limit? Yes! The $50.00 prize that one of us offered for settling this question was won in November 1970 by a group at M.I.T. headed by R.W. Gosper. Gosper's ingenious **glider gun** (Fig. 14) emits a new glider every 30 generations. Fortunately it was just what we wanted to complete our proof that

> Life is really unpredictable!

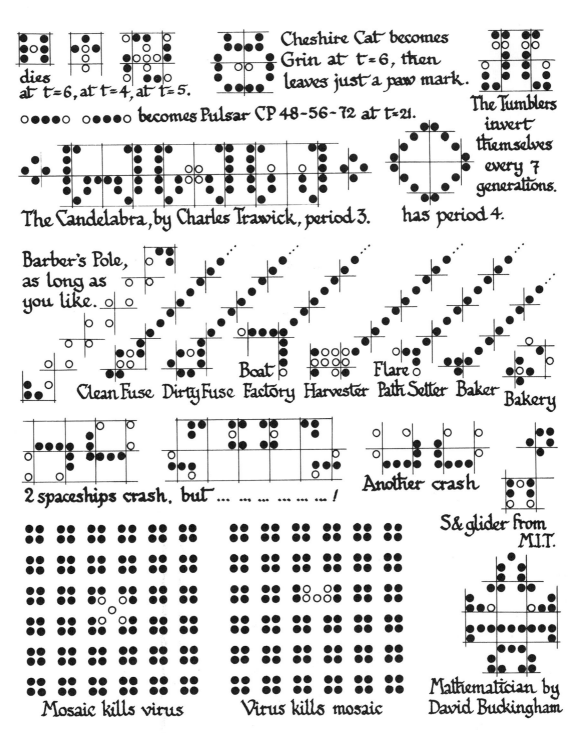

Figure 12. Exercises for the Reader.

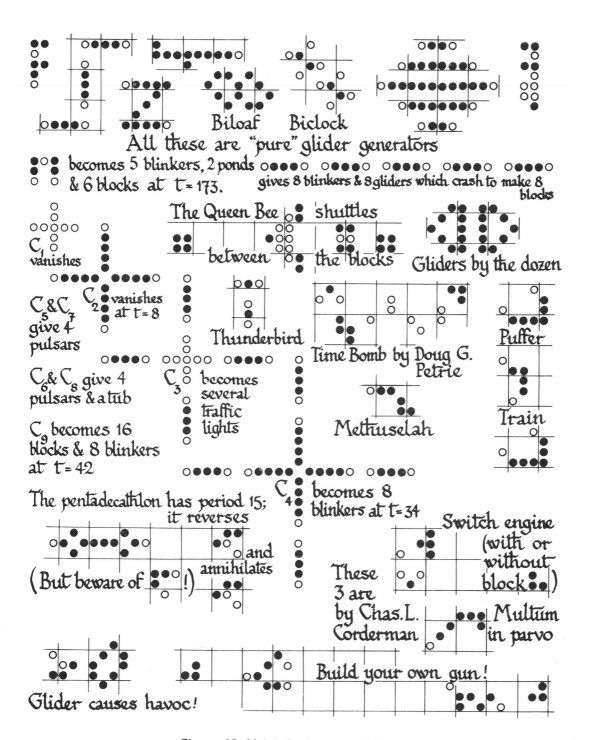

Biloaf   Biclock

All these are "pure" glider generators

becomes 5 blinkers, 2 ponds & 6 blocks at $t = 173$.

gives 8 blinkers & 8 gliders which crash to make 8 blocks

The Queen Bee   shuttles

C_1 vanishes

between   the blocks   Gliders by the dozen

C_5 & C_7 give 4 pulsars

C_2 vanishes at $t = 8$

Thunderbird

Time Bomb by Doug G. Petrie

Puffer

C_6 & C_8 give 4 pulsars & a tub

C_3 becomes several traffic lights

Methuselah

Train

C_9 becomes 16 blocks & 8 blinkers at $t = 42$

C_4 becomes 8 blinkers at $t = 34$

The pentadecathlon has period 15; it reverses

and annihilates

(But beware of   !)

These 3 are by Chas. L. Corderman

Switch engine (with or without block   )

Multum in parvo

Glider causes havoc!

Build your own gun!

Figure 13. Mainly for Computer Buffs.

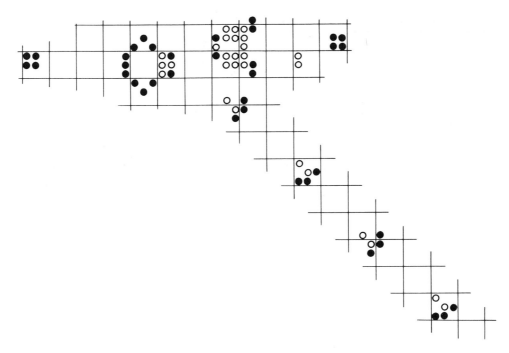

Figure 14. Gosper's Glider Gun.

GARDENS OF EDEN

There are Life configurations that can only arise as the initial state, because they have no ancestors!

We'll prove that if n is sufficiently large, there is some configuration within a $5n-2$ by $5n-2$ square that has no parent. It will suffice to examine that part of a prospective parent that lies in the surrounding $5n \times 5n$ square (Fig. 15). If any one of the component 5×5 squares is empty, it can be replaced as in Fig. 15(b) without affecting subsequent generations. So we need consider only

$$(2^{25} - 1)^{n^2} = 2^{24 \cdot 999999957004337\ldots n^2} \text{ of the } 2^{25n^2}$$

configurations in the $5n$ by $5n$ square. However, there are exactly

$$2^{(5n-2)^2} = 2^{25n^2 - 20n + 4}$$

possible configurations in the $5n-2$ by $5n-2$ square, so that if

$$24 \cdot 999999957004337\ldots n^2 < 25n^2 - 20n + 4,$$

one of these will have no parent! We calculate that this happens for $n = 465163200$, so that there is a Garden of Eden configuration that will fit comfortably inside a

2325816000 by 2325816000 square!

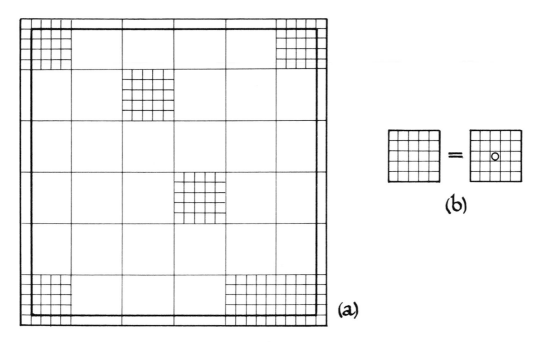

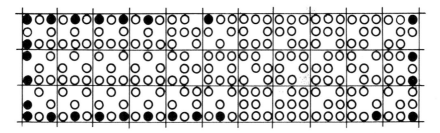

Figure 15. Location of the Garden of Eden.

This type of argument was first used by E.F. Moore in a more general context. More careful counting in the Life case has brought the size down to 1400 by 1400. However, using completely different ideas and many hours of computer time the M.I.T. group managed to produce an explicit example (Fig. 16).

Figure 16. An Orphan Found by Roger Banks, Mike Beeler, Rick Schroeppel, Steve Ward, *et al.*

LIFE'S PROBLEMS ARE HARD!

The questions we posed about the ultimate destiny of Life configurations may not seem very mathematical. After all, Life's but a game! Surely there aren't any difficult mathematical problems there?

Well, yes there are! Indeed we can prove the astonishing fact that *every* sufficiently well-stated mathematical problem can be reduced to a question about Life! Those apparently trivial problems about Life histories can be arbitrarily difficult!

Here, for instance, is a tricky little problem that's kept mathematicians busy ever since Pierre de Fermat proposed it over 300 years ago. Is it possible for a perfect *n*th power to be the sum of two smaller ones for any *n* larger than 2? Despite many learned investigations by many learned mathematicians we still don't know! But if you had an infallible way to foretell the destiny of a given Life configuration, you'd be able to answer this question!

The reason is that we can design for you a finite starting pattern P_0 which will fade away completely if and only if there is a way of breaking an *n*th power into two smaller ones. If you had a mechanical method which would accept as input an arbitrary finite Life pattern *P*, and is guaranteed to respond with

FADE, if the rules of Life will eventually cause *P* to disappear completely, and
STAY, if not,

then you could apply it to P_0 and settle Fermat's question.

Even better, we could design a pattern P_1 which will tell you what those perfect powers are. If

$$a^n + b^n = c^n$$

 is the first solution of Fermat's problem in a certain dictionary order, then eventually P_1 will lead to a configuration in which there are

> *a* gliders, travelling North–West,
> *b* gliders, travelling North–East,
> *c* gliders, travelling South–West,
> *n* gliders, travelling South–East,

and nothing else at all! We can do the same sort of thing for other mathematical problems.

MAKING A LIFE COMPUTER

Many computers have been programmed to play the game of Life. We shall now return the compliment by showing how to define Life patterns that can imitate computers. Many remarkable consequences will follow from this idea.

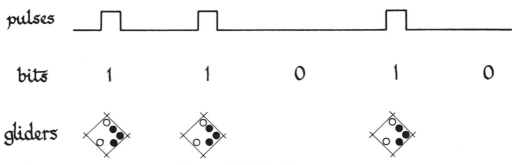

Figure 17. Gliding Pulses.

Good old fashioned computers are made from pieces of wire along which pulses of electricity go. Our basic idea is to mimic these by certain lines in the plane along which gliders travel (Fig. 17). (Because gliders travel diagonally, from now on we'll turn the plane through 45°, so they move across, or up and down, the page.) Somewhere in the machine there is a part called the **clock** which generates pulses at regular intervals and most of the working parts of the machine are made up of logical **gates**, like those drawn in Fig. 18. Obviously we can use Glider Guns as pulse generators. What should we do about the logical gates? Let's study the possible interactions of two gliders which crash at right angles.

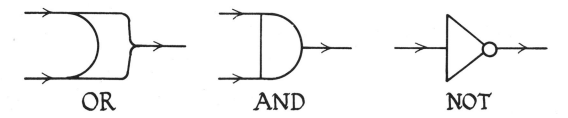

Figure 18. The Three Logical Gates.

WHEN GLIDER MEETS GLIDER

There are lots of different ways in which two gliders can meet, because there are lots of different possibilities for their exact arrangement and timing. Figure 19 shows them crashing (a) to form a blinker, (b) to form a block, (c) to form a pond, or (d) in one of several ways in which they can annihilate themselves completely. This last may seem rather unconstructive, but these **vanishing reactions** turn out to be surprisingly useful!

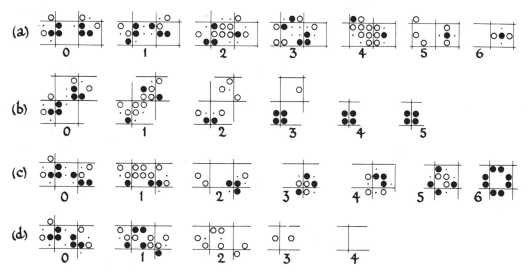

Figure 19. Gliders Crashin' in Diverse Fashion.

HOW TO MAKE A NOT GATE

We can use a vanishing reaction, together with a Glider Gun, to create a NOT gate (Fig. 20). The input stream enters at the left of the figure, and the Glider Gun is positioned and timed so that every space in the input stream allows just one glider to escape from the gun, while a glider in the stream necessarily crashes with one from the gun in a vanishing reaction (indicated by ✳). Figure 20 shows the periodic stream

$$1\ 1\ 0\ 1\ 1\ 0\ 1\ 1\ 0 \ldots$$

being complemented to

$$0\ 0\ 1\ 0\ 0\ 1\ 0\ 0\ 1 \ldots.$$

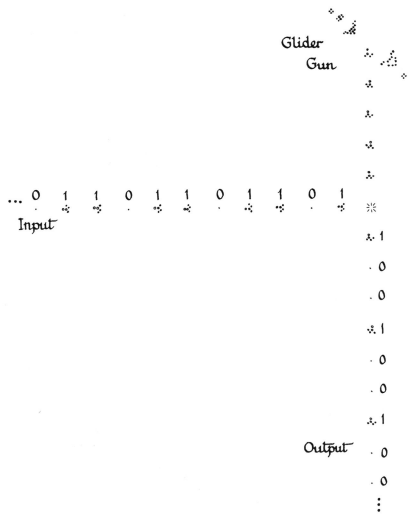

Figure 20. A Glider Gun and a Vanishing Reaction Make a NOT Gate.

Fortunately there are several vanishing reactions with different positions and timings in which the decay is so fast that later gliders from the same gun stream will not be affected (Fig. 21). This means that we can reposition a glider stream arbitrarily by turning it through sufficiently many corners (Fig. 22).

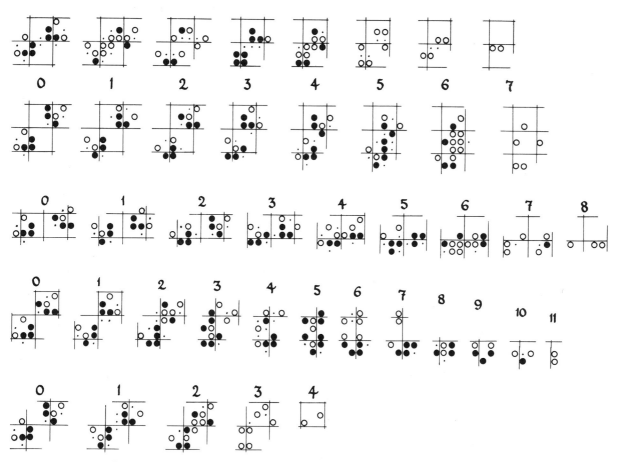

Figure 21. A Variety of Vanishing Reactions Between Crashing Gliders.

THE EATER

What else can happen when glider meets glider? Lots of things! One of them is to make an **eater** (Fig. 23) and an eater can eat lots of things without suffering any indisposition. The eater, which was discovered by Gosper, will be very useful to us; in Fig. 24 you can see it enjoying a varied diet of (a) a blinker, (b) a pre-beehive, (c) a lightweight spaceship, (d) a middleweight spaceship, and (e) a glider. If it attempts a heavyweight spaceship it gets indigestion and leaves a loaf behind; if it tries a blinker in the wrong orientation it leaves a baker's shop!

Sometimes glider streams are embarrassing to have around, so it's especially useful then— it just sits there and eats up the whole stream!

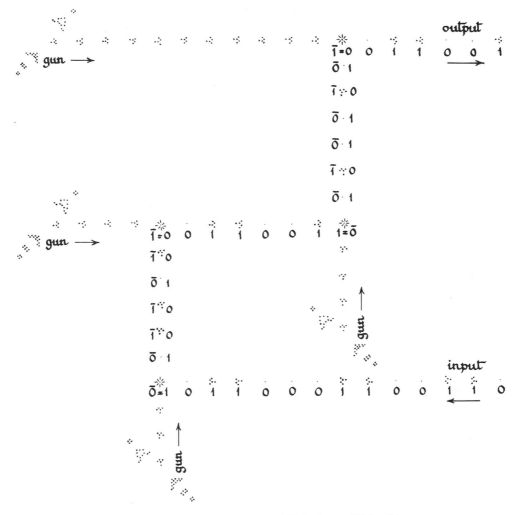

Figure 22. Repositioning and Delaying a Glider Stream.

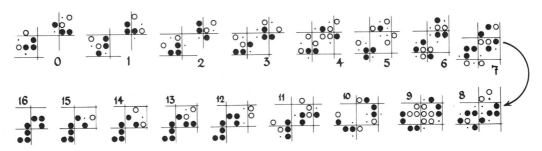

Figure 23. Two Gliders Crash to Form an Eater.

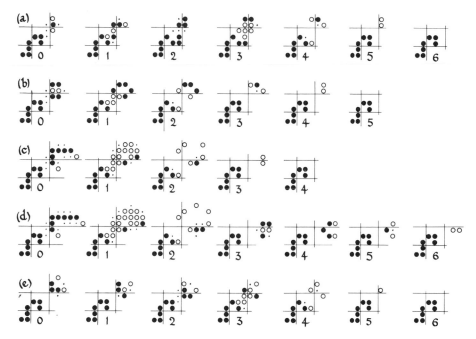

Figure 24. The Voracious Eater Devours a Varied Meal.

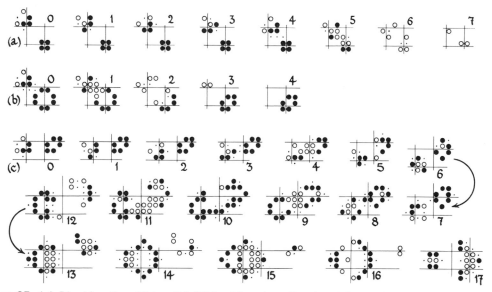

Figure 25. (a) Blockbusting Glider. (b) Glider Dives into Pond and Comes Up With Ship. (c) Glider Crashes into Ship and Makes Part of Glider Gun.

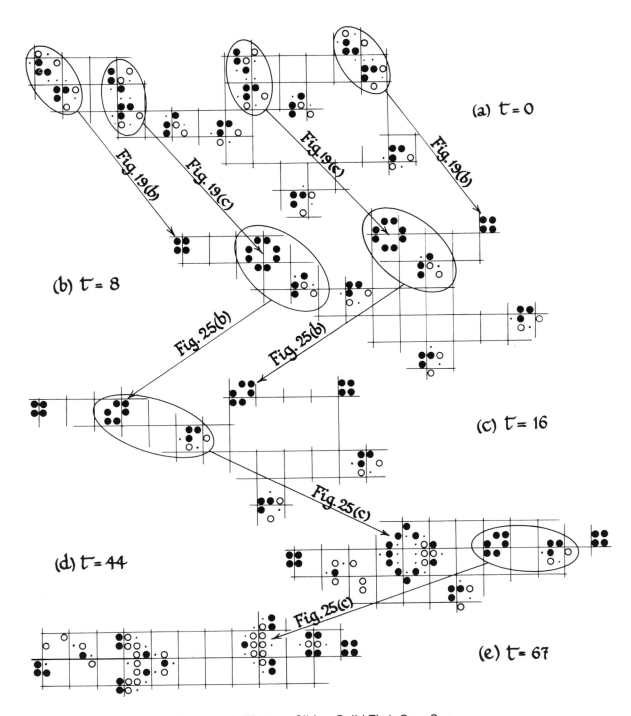

(a) $t = 0$

Fig. 19(b)

Fig. 19(c)

Fig. 19(c)

Fig. 19(b)

(b) $t = 8$

Fig. 25(b)

Fig. 25(b)

(c) $t = 16$

Fig. 25(c)

(d) $t = 44$

Fig. 25(c)

(e) $t = 67$

Figure 26. Thirteen Gliders Build Their Own Gun.

GLIDERS CAN BUILD THEIR OWN GUNS!

What happens when a glider meets other things? We have seen it get eaten by an eater. It can also annihilate a block (and itself! Fig. 25(a)). But more constructively it can turn a pond into a ship (Fig. 25(b)) and a ship into a part of the glider gun (Fig. 25(c)). And since gliders can crash to make blocks (Fig. 19(b)) and ponds (Fig. 19(c)), they can make a whole glider gun! The 13 gliders in Fig. 26(a) do this in 67 generations. Figures 26(b,c,d) show the positions after 8, 16 and 44 generations. The extra glider then slips in to deal with an incipient beehive, and by 67 generations (Fig. 26(e)) the gun is in full working order and launches its first glider 25 generations later.

THE KICKBACK REACTION

Yet another very useful reaction between gliders is the **kickback** (Fig. 27(a)) in which the decay product is a glider travelling along a line closely parallel to one of the original ones, but in the opposite direction. We think of this glider as having been *kicked back* by the other one. Figure 27(b) shows our notation for the kickback.

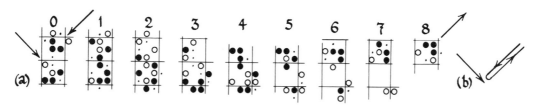

Figure 27. The Kickback.

All the working parts of our computer will be moving glider streams, meeting in vanishing and kickback reactions. The only static parts will be glider guns and eaters (indicated by G and E in the figures).

THINNING A GLIDER STREAM

The glider streams that emerge from normal guns are so dense that they cannot interpenetrate without interfering. If we try to build a computer using streams of this density we couldn't allow any two wires of this kind to cross each other, so we'd better find some way to reduce the pulse rate.

In Fig. 28 the guns G_1 and G_2 produce normal glider streams in parallel but opposite directions. But there is a glider g which will travel West until at A it is kicked East by a glider from the G_1 stream. The timing and phasing are such that at B it will be kicked back towards A again, so that it repeatedly "loops the loop", removing one glider from each of the two streams per cycle. After this every Nth glider is missing from each of these streams. We don't want the G_1 stream, so we feed it into an eater, but we feed the G_2 stream into a vanishing reaction with a stream from a third gun G_3. Every glider from G_2 now dies, but every Nth one from G_3 escapes through a hole in the G_2 stream! So the whole pattern acts as a **thin gun**, producing just one Nth as many gliders as the normal gun. To get the phasing right, N must be divisible by 4, but it can be arbitrarily

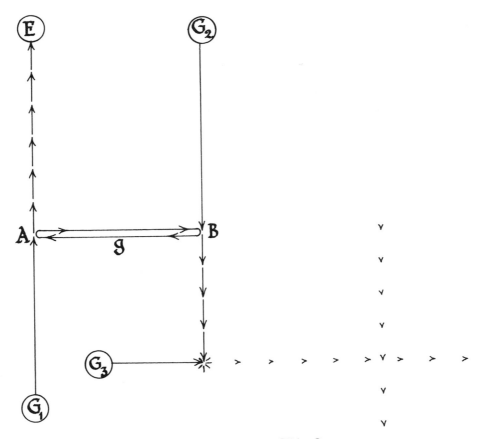

Figure 28. Thinning a Glider Stream.

large and so we can make an arbitrarily thin stream. Now two such streams can cross without interacting as in the right hand part of Fig. 28, provided things are properly timed. So from now on we can use the word **gun** to mean an arbitrarily thin gun. Perhaps a thinning factor of 1000 will make all our constructions work.

BUILDING BLOCKS FOR OUR COMPUTER

In Fig. 29 we see how to build logical gates using only vanishing reactions (we've already seen the NOT gate in more detail in Fig. 20). But there's a problem! The output streams from the AND and OR gates are *parallel* to the input, but the output stream from the NOT gate is at *right angles* to the input. We need a way to turn streams round corners without complementing them, or of complementing them without turning them round corners. Fortunately the solution to our *next* problem automatically solves *this* one.

The new problem is to provide several copies of the information from a given glider stream, and we found it a hard problem to solve. To get some clues, let's see what happens when we use one glider to kick back a glider from a gun stream.

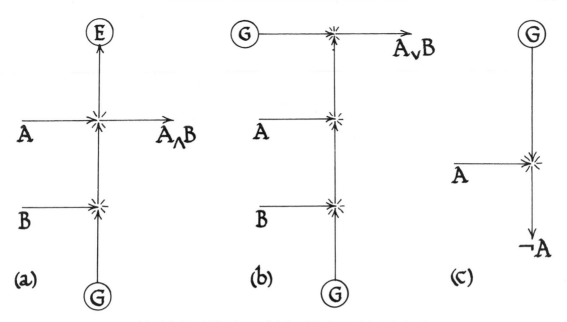

Figure 29. (a) An AND Gate. (b) An OR Gate. (c) A NOT Gate.

We suppose that the gun stream, the **full stream**, produces a glider every 120 generations (a quarter of the original gun density; $N = 4$ in the previous section). Then it turns out that when we kick back the first glider, the effect is to remove just three gliders from the stream! This happens as follows:

(i) The first glider is kicked back (Fig. 27) along the full stream.
(ii) The second glider crashes into the first, forming a block (somewhat as in Fig. 19(b)).
(iii) The third glider annihilates the block (Fig. 25(a)).
(iv) All subsequent gliders from the full stream escape unharmed.

We can use this curious behavior as follows. Suppose that our information-carrying stream operates at one tenth, say, of the density of the full stream, so that the last 9 of every 10 places on it will be empty, while the first place might or might not be full. If we use 0 for a hole and block the places in tens, our stream looks like

$$\ldots \; 000000000D \; 000000000C \; 000000000B \; 000000000A \to$$

We first feed it into an OR gate with a stream of type

$$\ldots \; 00000000g0 \; 00000000g0 \; 00000000g0 \; 00000000g0 \to$$

the g's denoting gliders that are definitely present. The result is a stream

$$\ldots \; 00000000gD \; 00000000gC \; 00000000gB \; 00000000gA \to$$

in which every information-carrying place is definitely followed by a glider g. This stream is used to kick back a full stream whose gliders are numbered:

$$\ldots \; \ldots\ldots\ldots\ldots \; \ldots\ldots\ldots\ldots \; X987654321 \; X987654321 \to$$

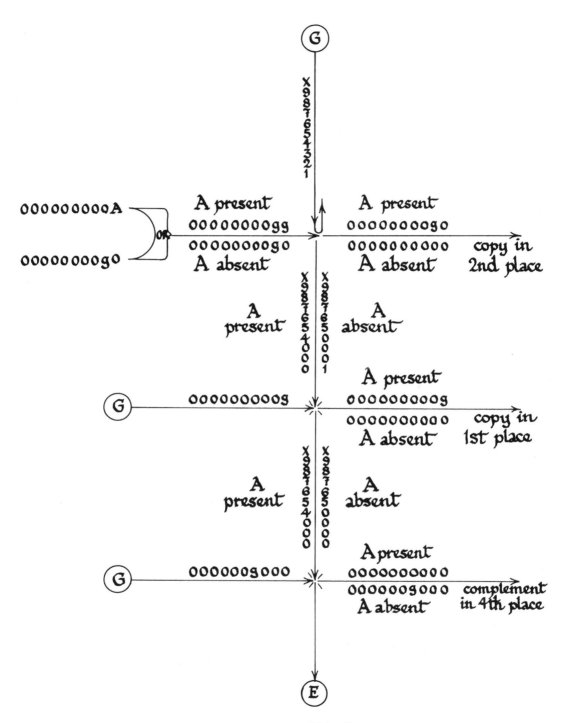

Figure 30. Copying a Glider Stream.

If glider A is *present*, it will obliterate gliders 1, 2 and 3 of the full stream and the following glider g can escape in the confusion. But if A is *absent*, then full stream glider 1 escapes and gliders 2, 3, 4 are removed instead by the following glider g. So the stream which emerges is definitely empty except for the second of every ten places and these places carry a copy of the input stream. The original full stream now manages to carry the information *twice*, in the first and fourth digits of each block, the first digit carrying the *complemented* version (which has *not* been turned through a right angle). By feeding this stream into vanishing reactions with suitably thin streams we can recover the original stream either complemented or not, and freed from undesirable accompanying gliders! Figure 30 shows these techniques in action.

From here on it's just an engineering problem to construct an arbitrarily large finite (and very slow!) computer. Our engineer has been given the tools—let him finish the job! We know that such computers can be programmed to do many things. The most important ones that we will want it to do involve emitting sequences of gliders at precisely controlled positions and times.

AUXILIARY STORAGE

Of course the engineer will probably have designed an internal memory for our computer using circulating delay lines of glider streams. Unfortunately this won't be enough for the kind of problem we have in mind, and we'll have to find some way of adjoining an *external* memory, capable of holding arbitrarily large numbers. To build this memory, we'll need an additional static piece (the block).

For instance we might ask the computer to compute

$$a^n + b^n \text{ and } c^n$$

for *all* quadruples (a,b,c,n) in turn and stop when it finds a quadruple for which

$$a^n + b^n = c^n.$$

We don't know how big a, b, c and n might get, and they'll almost certainly get too large even to be written in the internal memory.

So we're going to adjoin some auxiliary storage registers, each of which will store an arbitrarily large number. Figure 31 shows the general plan. Each register contains a block, whose distance from the computer (on a certain scale) indicates the number it contains. In the figure, register A contains 3, B contains 7, C contains 0 and D contains 2. When the contents of a register is 0, the block is just inside the computer. All we have to do is to provide a way for the computer to

> *increase* the contents of a register by 1,
> *decrease* the contents of a register by 1, and
> *test*   whether the contents are 0.

Fortunately each of these can be accomplished by a suitable fleet of gliders. One such fleet is off to increase register B by one! And another glider is about to discover that register C contains 0.

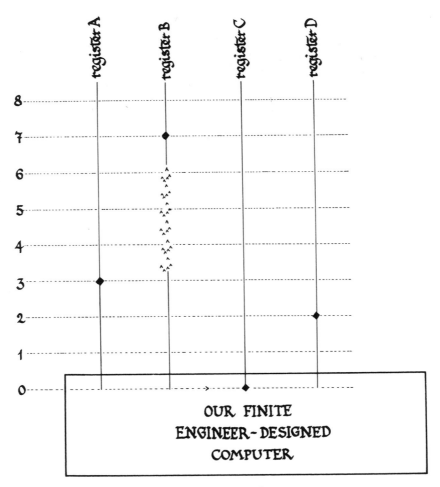

Figure 31. Auxiliary Storage.

HOW WE MOVE BLOCKS

To find these fleets we studied the six possible glider–block crashes. One of them does indeed bring the block in a bit, but unfortunately by a knight's move. However the block can be brought back onto the proper diagonal by repeating the process with a reflected glider on a parallel course. The combined effect of this pair of gliders is to pull the block back three diagonal places (Fig. 32).

Unfortunately there is no single glider-block crash which moves the block further away, but there is a crash which produces the arrangement of 4 beehives we call a honey farm, and two of these four are slightly further away, and so we can send in second, third and fourth gliders to annihilate three of the beehives, and then a fifth glider which converts the remaining beehive back into a block. The total effect again pushes the block off the proper diagonal, but a second team of five gliders will restore this, resulting in a block just one diagonal place further out! (Fig. 33).

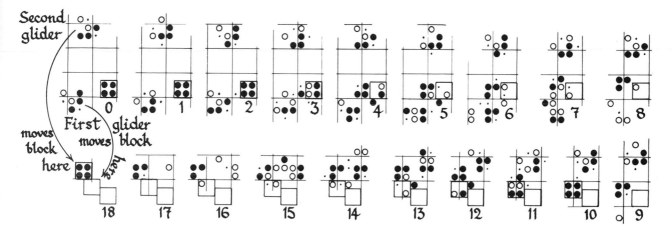

Figure 32. Two Gliders Pull a Block Back Three Diagonal Places.

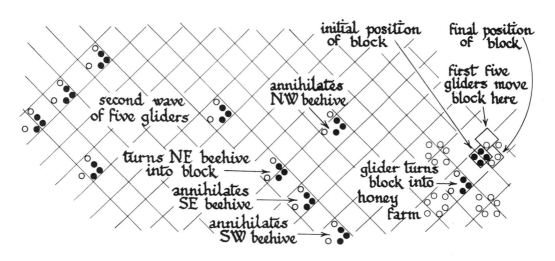

Figure 33. Ten Gliders Move a Block Just One Diagonal Place.

We therefore choose a diagonal distance of 3 to represent a change of 1 in a register and can decrease the contents of a register using a pair of gliders, or increase it using 3 flotillas of 10.

Apart from the difficulty discussed in the next section we have now finished the work, for Minsky has shown that a finite computer, equipped with memory registers like the ones in Fig. 30, can be programmed to attack arbitrarily complicated mathematical problems.

A LITTLE DIFFICULTY

But now comes the problem. Every glider in our finite computer has at some time been produced by a glider gun, so how could we arrange to send those gliders along closely parallel, but distinct paths? Surely one gun would have to fire right through another (Fig. 34)? Our technique of **side-tracking** uses three computer controlled guns G_1, G_2, G_3 as in Fig. 35. These are programmed to emit gliders exactly when we want them to.

Figure 34. How Can One Gun Fire Through Another?

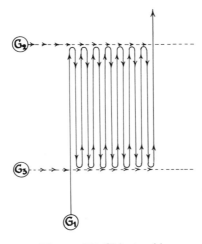

Figure 35. Side-tracking.

Firstly, G_1 emits a glider g travelling upwards,

Secondly, G_2 emits a glider at just the right time to kick g back downwards,

Thirdly, G_3 kicks g back up again,

and so on, alternately, until at a suitable time G_2 fails to fire and g is released. By controlling the number of times G_2 and G_3 fire, the *same* guns can be used to send a succession of gliders along distinct parallel paths.

MISSION COMPLETED—WILL SELF-DESTRUCT

Side-tracking can be used for a much more spectacular juggling act! We can actually program our computer to throw a glider into the air *and* bring it back down again. In Fig. 36, G_1, G_2, G_3 behave as before and can be programmed to arrange that a glider g ends up travelling Eastwards arbitrarily far above the ground. But G_4 has been arranged to emit a glider which will be kicked back down by g. We could even arrange to kick it back up again, then down again, then up again,… as suggested by the dotted lines in Fig. 36.

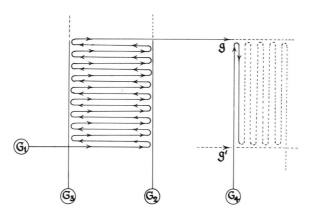

Figure 36. Double Side-tracking.

Using such techniques we can design a program for our computer which will send large numbers of gliders far out into space and then turn them round so that they head back towards the computer along precisely defined tracks (Fig. 37).

Now comes the clever part. Figures 38(a), 38(b) and 25(a) show that the eaters, the guns' moving parts, and blocks, can all be destroyed by aiming suitably positioned gliders from behind their backs. If the computer is cleverly designed we can even destroy it completely by an appropriate configuration of gliders!

Here's the idea. We design the computer so that every glider emitted by a gun or circulating in a loop would, if not deflected by meeting other gliders, be eventually consumed by an appropriately placed eater. Then we design our attacking force of gliders to shoot the computer down, guns first. After each gun is destroyed we wait until any gliders it has already emitted have percolated through the system and either been destroyed by other gliders, or swallowed by eaters, before attacking the next gun. When all the guns are destroyed we shoot down the eaters and blocks.

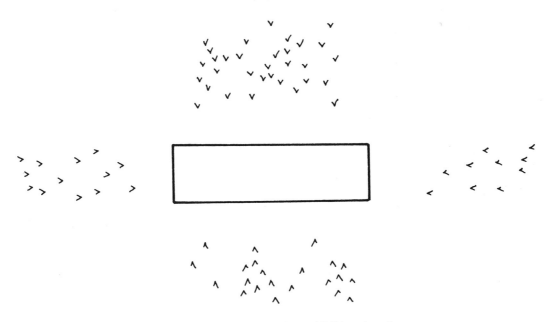

Figure 37. Self-attack from All Directions!

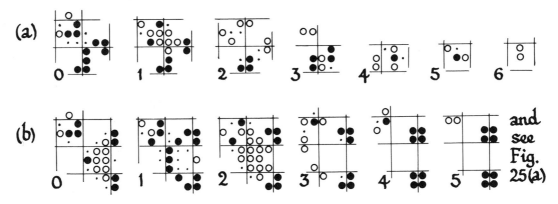

Figure 38. (a) The Eater Eaten! (b) The Gun Gunned Down!

The whole process requires some care. Each gun G_i must have a matching eater E_i, and G_i and E_i lie in a strip of the plane which contains no other static parts of the computer (Fig. 39). The gliders $g_1, g_2, g_3,\ldots$ with which we shoot down a given gun can be arbitrarily widely spaced in time provided they come in along the right tracks. Moreover we can arrange to shoot down the successive guns, eaters and blocks after increasingly long intervals of time.

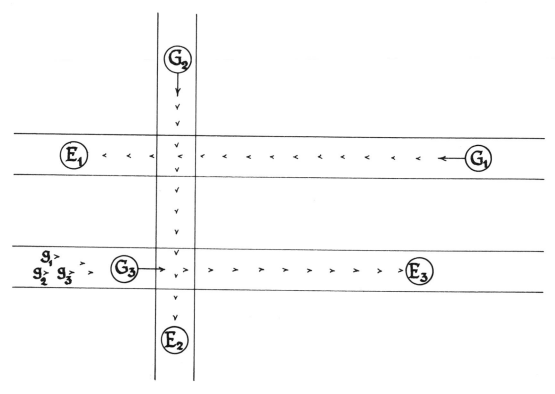

Figure 39. Arranging Destroyable Guns.

However, it *can* be done! We intend to use it like this. Program the computer to look for a solution of an arbitrarily hard problem, such as Fermat's. If it never finds a solution it will just go on forever. However, if it *does* find a solution we instruct it to throw into the air a precisely arranged army of gliders, then reduce all its storage numbers to zero (this brings all the blocks inside the computer), switch off, and await its fate. The attacking glider army, of course, is exactly what's needed to obliterate the computer, leaving no trace. It's important to realize that a *fixed* computer can be programmed to produce many different patterns of gliders and in particular the one required to kill itself. The information about this glider pattern can be held by the numbers in the memory of the computer and not in the computer's design.

Since mathematical logicians have proved that there's no technique which guarantees to tell when arbitrary arithmetical problems have solutions, there's no technique that's guaranteed to tell even when a Life configuration will fade away completely. The kind of computer we have simulated is technically known as a *universal machine* because it can be programmed to perform any desired calculation. We can summarize our result in this answer to our chapter heading:

> LIFE IS UNIVERSAL!

EXTRAS

LIFE COMPUTERS CAN REPRODUCE!

Eaters and guns can be made by crashing suitable fleets of gliders, so it's possible to build a computer simply by crashing some enormously large initial pattern of gliders. Moreover, we can design a computer whose sole aim in Life is to throw just such a pattern of gliders into the air. In this way one computer can give birth to another, which can, if we like, be an exact copy of the first. Alternatively, we could arrange that the first computer eliminates itself after giving birth; then we would regard the second as a reincarnation of the first.

> There are Life patterns which behave like self-replicating animals.

> There are Life patterns which move steadily in any desired rational direction, recovering their initial form exactly after some fixed number of generations.

GENETIC ENGINEERING

We've now shown that among finite Life patterns there is a very small proportion behaving like self-replicating animals. Moreover, it is presumably possible to design such patterns which will survive inside the typical Life environment (a sort of primordial broth made of blocks, blinkers, gliders, ...). It might for instance do this by shooting out masses of gliders to detect nearby objects and then take appropriate action to eliminate them. So one of these "animals" could be more or less adjusted to its environment than another. If both were self-replicating and shared a common territory, presumably more copies of the better adapted one would survive and replicate.

WHITHER LIFE?

From here on is a familiar story. Inside any sufficiently large random broth, we expect, *just by chance*, that there will be some of these self-replicating creatures! Any particularly well adapted ones will gradually come to populate their territory. Sometimes one of the creatures will be accidentally modified by some unusual object which it was not programmed to avoid. Most of these modifications, or **mutations**, are likely to be harmful and will adversely affect the animal's chances of survival, but very occasionally, there will be some *beneficial* mutations. In these cases the modified animals will slowly come to predominate in their territory, and so on. There seems to be no limit to this process of evolution.

> It's probable, given a large enough
> Life space, initially in a random state,
> that after a long time, intelligent
> self-reproducing animals will emerge and
> populate some parts of the space.

This is more than mere speculation, since the earlier parts are based on precisely proved theorems. Of course, "sufficiently large" means very large indeed, and we can't prove that "living" animals of any kind are likely to emerge in any Life space we can construct in practice.

It's remarkable how such a simple system of genetic rules can lead to such far-reaching results. It may be argued that the small configurations so far looked at correspond roughly to the molecular level in the real world. If a two-state cellular automaton can produce such varied and esoteric phenomena from these simple laws, how much more so in our own universe?

Analogies with real life processes are impossible to resist. If a primordial broth of amino-acids is large enough, and there is sufficient time, self-replicating moving automata may result from transition rules built into the structure of matter and the laws of nature. There is even the possibility that space-time itself is granular, composed of discrete units, and that the universe, as Edward Fredkin of M.I.T. and others have suggested, is a cellular automaton run by an enormous computer. If so, what we call motion may be only simulated motion. A moving particle in the ultimate microlevel may be essentially the same as one of our gliders, appearing to move on the macrolevel, whereas actually there is only an alteration of states of basic space-time cells in obedience to transition rules that have yet to be discovered.

REFERENCES AND FURTHER READING

Clark C. Abt, "Serious Games: The Art and Science of Games that Simulate Life", The Viking Press, 1970.

Michael A. Arbib, Simple self-reproducing universal automata, Information and Control, 9 (1966) 177–189.

E.R. Banks, Information Processing and Transmission in Cellular Automata, Ph.D. thesis, M.I.T., 71:01:15.

E.F. Codd, "Cellular Automata", Academic Press, New York and London, 1968.

Martin Gardner, Mathematical Games, Sci. Amer. **223** #4 (Oct. 1970) 120–123; **223** #5 (Nov. 1970) 118; **223** #6 (Dec. 1970) 114; **224** #1 (Jan. 1971) 108; **224** #2 (Feb. 1971) 112–117; **224** #3 (Mar. 1971) 108–109; **224** #4 (Apr. 1971) 116–117; **225** #5 (Nov. 1971) 120–121; **226** #1 (Jan. 1972) 107; **233** #6 (Dec. 1975).

M.J.E. Golay, Hexagonal parallel pattern transformations, IEEE Trans. Computers **C18** (1969) 733–740.

Chester Lee, Synthesis of a cellular universal machine using the 29-state model of von Neumann, Automata Theory Notes, Univ. of Michigan Engg. Summer Conf., 1964.

Marvin L. Minsky, "Computation: Finite and Infinite Machines", Prentice-Hall, Englewood Cliffs, N.J., 1967.

Edward F. Moore, Mathematics in the biological sciences, Sci. Amer. **211** #3 (Sep. 1964) 148–164.

Edward F. Moore, Machine models of self-reproduction, Proc. Symp. Appl. Math. **14**, Amer. Math. Soc. 1962, 17–34.

Edward F. Moore, John Myhill, in Arthur W. Burks (ed.) "Essays in Cellular Automata", University of Illinois Press, 1970.

C.E. Shannon, A universal Turing machine with two internal states, in C.E. Shannon and J. McCarthy (eds.) "Automata Studies", Princeton University Press, 1956.

Alvy Ray Smith, Cellular automata theory, Tech. Report No. 2, Digital Systems Lab., Stanford Electronics Labs., Stanford Univ., 1969.

J.W. Thatcher, Universality in the von Neumann cellular model, Tech. Report 03105-30-T, ORA, Univ. of Michigan, 1964.

A.M. Turing, Computing machinery and intelligence, Mind, **59** (1950) 433–460.

Robert T. Wainwright (editor) Lifeline; a quarterly newsletter for enthusiasts of John Conway's game of Life, **1–11**, Mar., Jun., Sep., Dec. 1971, Sep., Oct., Nov., Dec. 1972, Mar., Jun., Sep. 1973.

Index

GLOSSARY OF SYMBOLS

See also the Appendix (pp. 225–228) to ONAG (reference on p. 24).

$\mathbf{A} = \mathbf{ace} = \{0 \mid \mathbf{tiny}\}$, 337

$\overline{\mathbf{A}} = -\mathbf{ace} = \{\mathbf{miny} \mid 0\}$, 339

$\mathbf{A}- = \{\mathbf{on} \mid \mathbf{A} \parallel 0\}$, 339

$\overline{\mathbf{A}}+ = \{0 \parallel \overline{\mathbf{A}} \mid \mathbf{off}\}$, 339

$\aleph_0$, aleph-zero, 309

$\lceil\ \rceil$, "ceiling", least integer not less than, 453

$(x)_n, \{x \mid -y\}_n$, Childish Hackenbush values, 230

$\overline{1}\clubsuit = \{\clubsuit \mid 0\}$
$\clubsuit = 0\ \clubsuit = \{1\clubsuit \mid 0\}$, clubs, 339
$1\clubsuit = \{\mathbf{deuce} \mid 0\}$

$a\langle b\rangle$, class a and variety b, 343

● ❶ ○ ⓧ, Col and Snort positions, 49, 142

$\gamma°$, degree of loopiness, 341

$2\clubsuit = \{0 \mid \mathbf{ace}\} = \mathbf{ace} + \mathbf{ace} = \mathbf{deuce}$, 337

$\overline{1}\diamondsuit = \{\overline{\mathbf{J}} \mid 0\}$
$\diamondsuit = 0\ \diamondsuit = \{\mathbf{ace} \mid \overline{1}\diamondsuit\}$, diamonds, 339
$1\diamondsuit = \{0 \mid \diamondsuit\}$

$\Downarrow = \{\downarrow* \mid 0\} = \downarrow + \downarrow$, double-down, 70, 71, 73

$\Uparrow = \{0 \mid \uparrow*\} = \uparrow + \uparrow$, double-up, 70, 71, 73

$\Uparrow* = \{0 \mid \uparrow\} = \uparrow + \uparrow + *$, double-up-star, 73

$\downarrow = \{* \mid 0\}$, down, 66

$\downarrow_2 = \{\uparrow* \mid 0\}$, down-second, 227, 228

$\downarrow_3 = \{\uparrow + \uparrow^2 + * \mid 0\}$, down-third, 227, 228

$\downarrow_{abc...}, \downarrow_{\overline{abc}...}$, 252

$\curlyvee$, downsum, 316, 337

$\mathbf{dud} = \{\mathbf{dud} \mid \mathbf{dud}\}$, **deathless universal draw**, 317

ε, epsilon, small positive number, 308

$\doteqdot$, equally uppity, 233, 238, 240

$\lfloor\ \rfloor$, "floor", greatest integer not greater than, 53

$\parallel 0$, fuzzy, 31, 34, 35

G, general game, 30–33

$G \parallel 0$, G fuzzy, 2nd player wins
$G < 0$, G negative, R wins
$G > 0$, G positive, L wins , 31
$G = 0$, G zero, 1st player wins

$G + H$, sum of games
G^L, (set of) L option(s) , 33
G^R, (set of) R option(s)

$\mathscr{G}(n)$, nim-value, 82

$G.\uparrow = \{G^L.\uparrow + \Uparrow* \mid G^R.\uparrow + \Downarrow*\}$, 238, 246, 249

$>$, greater than, 34

$\geqslant$, greater than or equal, 34

$|\triangleright$, greater than or incomparable, 34, 37

$\gtrdot$, at least as uppity, 233, 238

$\frac{1}{2} = \{0 \mid 1\}$, half, 9, 22

$\overline{1}\heartsuit = \{\heartsuit \mid 0\}$
$\heartsuit = 0\heartsuit = \{1\heartsuit \mid \overline{\mathbf{A}}\}$, hearts, 339
$1\heartsuit = \{0 \mid \mathbf{joker}\}$

$\mathbf{hi} = \{\mathbf{on} \parallel 0 \mid \mathbf{off}\}$, 335

$\mathbf{hot} = \{\mathbf{on} \mid \mathbf{off}\}$, 335

$\parallel$, incomparable, 37

$\infty = \mathbb{Z} \parallel \mathbb{Z} \mid \mathbb{Z}$, infinity, 309, 314, 371

$\pm\infty = \infty \mid -\infty = \mathbb{Z} \mid \mathbb{Z} = \int^{\mathbb{Z}} *$, 314

$\infty \pm \infty = \infty \mid 0 = \mathbb{Z} \mid 0$, 314

$\infty + \infty = 2.\infty = \mathbb{Z} \parallel \mathbb{Z} \mid 0$, double infinity, 314

$\infty_{abc...}$, 367–375

$\infty_{\beta\gamma\delta...}$, 313

$\int$, integral, 163–176, 314, 346, 347

$\mathbf{J} = \{0 \mid \overline{\mathbf{A}}+\} = \mathbf{ace} \curlywedge (-\mathbf{ace}) = \mathbf{joker}$, 338

$\overline{\mathbf{J}} = \{\mathbf{A}- \mid 0\} = \mathbf{ace} \curlyvee (-\mathbf{ace}) = -\mathbf{joker}$, 339

L, Left, 4

LnL, LnR, RnR, positions in Seating games, 46, 130, 251

$<$, less than, 34

$\leqslant$, less than or equal, 34

$\triangleleft|$, less than or incomparable, 34, 37

$\mathbf{lo} = \{\mathbf{on} \mid 0 \parallel \mathbf{off}\}$, 335

$\mathfrak{D}$, loony, 377–387

$\gamma, \gamma\dot{}, \gamma^+, \gamma^-$, loopy games, 315

$s\&t$ loopy game, 316

$-1 = \{\ \mid 0\}$, minus one, 21

$-\mathbf{on} = \{\mathbf{on} \mid 0 \parallel 0\}$, **miny**, 333

$-\frac{1}{4} = \{\frac{1}{4} \mid 0 \parallel 0\}$, miny-a-quarter, 133

$-_x = \{x \mid 0 \parallel 0\}$, miny-$x$, 124

$\stackrel{*}{\times}$, nim-product, 443

$\stackrel{*}{+}$, nim-sum, 60, 75, 82, 108

$\mathbf{off} = \{\ \mid \mathbf{off}\}$, 316–320, 337

$\omega = \{0, 1, 2, ... \mid\ \}$, omega
$\omega + 1 = \{\omega \mid\ \}$, omega plus one
$\omega \times 2 = \{\omega, \omega+1, \omega+2, ... \mid\ \} = \omega + \omega$, 309–313
$\omega^2 = \{\omega, \omega \times 2, \omega \times 3, ... \mid\ \} = \omega \times \omega$

$\mathbf{on} = \{\mathbf{on} \mid\ \}$, 316–321

I

$1 = \{0 \mid \ \}$, one, 9, 21

ono $= \{\mathbf{on} \mid 0\}$, 335–336

oof $= \{0 \mid \mathbf{off}\}$, 335–337

over $= \{0 \mid \mathbf{over}\} = \dfrac{1}{\mathbf{on}}$, 321

$\pi = 3\cdot141592653\ldots$, pi, 308–309

$\pm 1 = \{1 \mid -1\}$, plus-or-minus one, 118–120

$(\pm 1).\!\uparrow = \{\Uparrow* \mid \Downarrow\downarrow\}$, 239

$\Downarrow = \{\Downarrow* \mid 0\} = 4.\!\downarrow$, quadruple-down, 327

$\Uparrow = \{0 \mid \Uparrow*\} = 4.\!\uparrow$, quadruple-up, 73, 327

$\tfrac{1}{4} = \{0 \mid \tfrac{1}{2}\}$, quarter, 8, 22

$\tfrac{1}{4} = \tfrac{1}{4}.\!\uparrow = \{\Uparrow* \mid 1\tfrac{1}{2}.\!\downarrow+*\}$, quarter-up, 228

$\tfrac{1}{4}* = \tfrac{1}{4}.\!\uparrow+* = \{\Uparrow \mid 1\tfrac{1}{2}.\!\downarrow\}$, quarter-up-star, 228

R, Right, 4

$\tfrac{*}{2} = \{*,\uparrow \mid \downarrow*,0\}$, semi-star, 350

$\tfrac{1}{2} = \tfrac{1}{2}.\!\uparrow = \{\Uparrow* \mid \downarrow*\}$, semi-up, 228, 239

$\tfrac{1}{2}* = \tfrac{1}{2}.\!\uparrow+* = \{\Uparrow \mid \downarrow\}$, semi-up-star, 228

$\tfrac{3}{2} = 1\tfrac{1}{2}.\!\uparrow = \{\Uparrow* \mid *\}$, sesqui-up, 228

sign( ), 328–330

$|,\|,\|\|,\ldots$, slash, slashes, … separate L and R options, 8, 127, 346

$\overline{2}\spadesuit = \{\overline{A} \mid 0\}$

$\overline{1}\spadesuit = \{0 \mid \overline{2}\spadesuit\}$

$\spadesuit = 0\spadesuit = \{0 \mid \overline{1}\spadesuit\}$ $\Big\}$, spades, 339

$1\spadesuit = 0 \mid \spadesuit$

$\star$, far star, remote star, 222–224, 236–243

$* = \{0 \mid 0\}$, star, 40

$*2 = \{0,* \mid 0,*\}$, star-two, 43

$*n = \{0,*,\ldots,*(n-1) \mid 0,*,\ldots,*(n-1)\}$, star-$n$, 43

$*\alpha$, star-alpha, 313

$\hat{*} = *.\!\uparrow = \{\Uparrow* \mid \downarrow*\}$, starfold-up, 228, 239

$*\bar{n}$, all nimbers except $*n$, 377

$*n\!\rightarrow$, all nimbers from $*n$ onwards, 377

$\odot = 0*\!\rightarrow$, sunny, 377–381, 384

$\uparrow_{abc\ldots} = -\downarrow^{abc\ldots}$, superstars, 252

$\tfrac{3}{4} = \{\tfrac{1}{2} \mid 1\}$, three-quarters, 18

$+_{\mathbf{on}} = \{0 \mid \mathbf{oof}\} = \{0 \| 0 \mid \mathbf{off}\} = $ **tiny**, 333, 337

$+_{\tfrac{1}{4}} = \{0 \| 0 \mid -\tfrac{1}{4}\}$, tiny-a-quarter, 124

$+_2 = \{0 \| 0 \mid -2\}$, tiny-two, 124

$+_x = \{0 \| 0 \mid -x\}$, tiny-x, 124

tis $= \{\mathbf{tisn} \mid \ \} = 1\&0$, 322, 354

tisn $= \{\ \mid \mathbf{tis}\} = 0\&-1$, 322, 354

$(l,r),(l,r)_c$, Toads-and-Frogs positions, 125, 135, 348, 355, 356

$\Downarrow = \{\Downarrow* \mid 0\} = 3.\!\downarrow$, treble-down, 73, 327

$\Uparrow = \{0 \mid \Uparrow*\} = 3.\!\uparrow$, treble-up, 73, 327

$3\spadesuit = \{0 \mid \mathbf{deuce}\} = $ **trey** $= $ **ace** $+$ **deuce**, 337

$\triangle$, triangular number, 244

$2 = \{1 \mid \ \}$, two, 9, 21

under $= \{\mathbf{under} \mid 0\} = -$ **over**, 321

$\uparrow = \{0 \mid *\}$, up, 66, 73, 252

$\uparrow^{\alpha}$, up-alpha, 321

$\uparrow^2 = \{0 \mid \downarrow*\}$, up-second, 227, 228, 321

$\uparrow* = \{0,* \mid 0\}$, up-star, 67, 221

$\uparrow^3 = \{0 \mid \downarrow+\downarrow_2+*\}$, up-third, 227, 321

$\uparrow_{abc\ldots}$, 252

upon $= \{\mathbf{upon} \mid *\}$, 321, 355

upon$* = \{0, \mathbf{upon}* \mid 0\}$, 321

$\curlywedge$, upsum, 316, 337

$0 = \{\ \mid \ \} = 0* = 0.\!\uparrow$, zero, 9, 43

---

abacus positions, 478–481
Abacus Strategy, 479–480
abnormal move, 305
absorbancy, downsum, 340
Abt, Clark C., 849
accounts-payable, 125, 720–721
ace, 337
acrostic
  games, 450–455
  Mock Turtle Fives, 455
  product, 450–451, 454
  Turnips, 451
  Twins, 441–442, 451
action, in hottest game, 163
active position, 146
acute triangle, 245
Adams's magic hexagon, 784, 810
Adams, Clifford W., 784, 810
Adams, E.W., 116
Adders $= \cdot73$, 409, 424
Adders-and-Ladders, 366

addition
  of games, 32–34
  of loony games, 379
  of loopy games, 370
  misère, 399
  nim-, 60–61, 75–76, 89, 101, 108–109, 115, 185, 190, 370, 398, 431, 441, 443–444, 463–464, 472–474, 476, 522, 524, 571–572, 688
  ordinal, 214
  of switches, 120
Additional Subtraction Games, 375
additives of no atomic weight, 220
adjacency matrix, 216
age, moon's, 799
Air on a $\mathscr{G}$-string, 96
ajar, 388–390
Algorithm
  Secondoff, 501, 503
  Zeckendorf, 501
Alice in Wonderland, 3, 5, 59, 221, 429–430

all small games, 221
All Square, 385
All the King's Horses, 257–263, 266–269, 272–273
almonds, 359, 373
also-ran, 266
alternating group, 759
alternating moves, 48–49
amazing jungle, 203, 216–217
ambient temperature, 161
ambitious distraction, 451
ambivalent Nim-heaps, 406
American colonies, 796
anatomy of Toads-and-Frogs, 65
AND gate, 831, 838–839
Anderson, William N., 692
Andersson, Göran, 117
Andreas, J.M., 783
Andrews, W.S., 813
angel, 609, 631
anger, fit of, 297
Animal Farm, 142, 706

Animals
    dead, 133
    Grundy's wild, 411
    tame, 405–410
    tracking, 200
annihilation games, 218
Anthony, Piers, 573
Antipathetic Nim, 459–462
Antonim, 459–462
Arbit, Michael A., 849
Archangel, 9, 30, 1916
Argument, Tweedledum and Tweedle-dee, 5, 37, 329–330
arithmetic periodicity, 99, 112–116, 140, 688
Arithmetico-Geometric Puzzle, 739–740, 804–806
army, 94, 715–717, 729
arrays, Nimstring, 548
arrow, 517, 677, 729, 742, 746
Ars Amatoria, 672, 693
Artful Arrow, 742, 746
Arthur, 507–509, 511, 517
assets, 718–719
asymmetrical heating, 169
atomic weight = uppitiness, 195–196, 220, 222–234, 236–243, 246, 249
    calculus, 223, 240, 250
    of lollipops, 230
    of nimbers, of up, 224
    rules, 233
atomic weight
    eccentric, 223–224, 231, 242–243
    fractional, 226–227
    properties of, 228
atoms
    Lucasta, 554–556
    superheavy, 313
Austin, A.K., 813
Austin, Richard Bruce, 54, 95, 101, 116, 505
average versus value, 12
averages, playing the, 163, 169

Babbage, Charles, 692
baby-sitting, 393
Bach, Clive, 349
back-handed compliment, 385
Backgammon, 16
Backsliding Toads-and-Frogs, 347, 355–356
backwards
    playing, 711
    thinking, 364
bad child, 410
bad move, 513, 712
Baked Alaska, 301–303
baker, bakery, 826

balance, 361, 717, 788
    sheet, 717
ball, 95, 688
Ball and Chain, 743
Ball, W.W. Rouse, 116, 505, 786, 813
Balsdon, J.P.V.D., 692
Banks, E. Roger, 829, 849
bargain, 156
barge, 819
Barmy Braid, 745
Baseball, Basketball, 17
Battle, 255
battle, 5
    hot, 141, 279–288, 303
Battleships, 16
beacon, 820
bead = bivalent node, 528
Beasley's Exit Theorems, 723–724, 731–732
Beasley, John D., 699, 701, 712, 731–734
bed, redwood, 206, 210–212, 216
bee, queen, 827
beehive, 819, 824–825, 833, 843
Beeler, Michael, 829
beetle, 566
behavior for Princes, 503
Belgium, 786
Bell, A.G., 692
Bell, Robert Charles, 632, 634, 673, 692
Belladonna, 494
Benson, D.C., 116
Benson, David J., 763, 767, 768
Berge, Claude, 80
Bergholt, Ernest, 699, 701, 731, 733–734
Berlekamp, Elwyn Ralph, 79–80, 121, 182, 298, 505, 550
Berlekamp's Rule, 79–80
Bertha, 507–513, 517, 520–521
Bessy, Frenicle de, 778
Bicknell-Johnson, Marjorie, 80
biclock, 827
big firms, 403
big game, 67, 200, 204, 216, 397
biloaf, 827
binary (base 2), 98, 449, 830
    tree, 25
bipartite graph, 212, 219, 549
birth, 817
    control, 819
birthday, 298, 397, 795
bit = binary digit, 98, 830
Black Path Game, 682–683
black stone, *see also* blocking, 608, etc.
Black, Farmer, 141
Black, Larry, 682
blanker, 819
Blass, Andreas, 609, 684

blatantly loopy, 371
blatantly winning ways, 390
blinker, 818–819, 825, 827, 833
block, 819, 824–825, 827, 831, 837–838, 841–843, 845–847
    puzzles, 735–740, 756, 769–777, 784–792, 801–807, 810–812
blocking stones, 608, 610–611, 618, 620, 622
Blocks-in-a-Box, 736, 801
blossom, 191, 193, 232
bLue edge, 4, 191 =
Blue Flower Ploy, 193, 232
Blue Jungle Ploy, 196
blue tinted nodes, 199
Blue-Red Hackenbush, 3–8, 22, 31, 33, 38, 44, 191, 206–212, 220
Blue-Red-Green Hackenbush, *see also* Hackenbush Hotchpotch, 31, etc.
board
    Continental, 711, 729
    English, 697
    games, 427, 607–734
    sizes, 608, 611, 613, 615, 618, 622–623, 629–630
Boardman, Mike, 712
boat, 819, 825–826
body, 468, 701
bogus Nim-heap, 57–58
bomb, time, 827
Bond, James, = ·007, 94
Bono, Edward de, 364, 388, 392
bonus move, 385
booby prize, 499
Borosh, I., 80
bottle, 213, 220
boundary
    left, 150
    right, 150, 160
Bounded Nim, 483–484
Bouton, Charles L., 44, 54, 80, 426
Bouwkamp, C.J., 814
box, 456, 507–550, 558–559
Boxing, 456
Boxing Day, 795
boy leaves girl, 748
boys by billions, 513
braiding paper, 745
branch, 24, 36, 185, 554–563, 572
brazils, 373
Bridge, 17
bridge, 183, 188–190, 758, 807
Bridgit, 680–682
Britain, 796
Brousseau, Bro. Alfred, 814
Brouwer, Andreas E., 676
Brown, B.H., 813–814
Brown, T.A., 814
Brualdi, Richard A., 692
Bruckner, Gottfried, 692

Bruijn, N.G. de., 458, 734
Brussels Sprouts, 569, 573
Buckingham, David, 826
bugs, 563
bulls, 141
Bumble-Bee Problems, 721
Bumby, Margaret, 767
Burali-Forti paradox, 645
Bushenhack, 570–572
Busschop, 734
Büvös Kocka, 760–768, 808–809
Bynum's Game = Eatcake, 134, 225, 269
Bynum, James, 134, 225, 269
bypassing reversible options, 62–66, 72–73, 78

cabbages, 563
CABS, 368–373
cabs, 344–346
Caesar, Julius, 551, 796
cake, 28, 53, 190, 215, 264–266, 269–272, 275–277, 279–284, 288–290, 301–303
Calculus, Atomic Weight, 2, 3, 240, 250
calendar
    Gregorian, 796–800
    Julian, 796–800

candelabra, 826
canonical form for numbers, 24
capturable coin, 521–522
capture, 631, 646
capture, custodian, 632
Cardan, 814
Cards, House of, 337
carousal, 360
carousel, 349, 360, 362
Carpenter, 429–430
carpet, greatly-valued, 448
Carpets, 446–448
Carpets, Fitted, 447
Carteblanche, Filet de, 491, 505, 814
cash flow, 124
cashews, 373
Cashing Cheques, 120–122, 141, 155, 231
Cat, Cheshire, 826
catalyst, 701–703, 706–707
caterpillar, 468, 563
Catherine Wheel, 822
ceiling, 453
Celoni, James R., 220
central Solitaire, 698–701, 703
central Soma piece, 739
centralizing switches, 121
centred king, 623–625

Century Puzzle, 769–770, 773–777, 810
Century-and-a-Half, 769–770, 773, 777, 810
Cervantes' deathday, 797
chain of boxes, 508–516, 518–520
Chain,
    Ball and, 743
    green, 42
    long, 512–513, 515, 518–522, 527, 529–531, 540–541, 543–546
    Lucasta, 554–556, 558, 563
    short, 513, 520, 540
    snapping, 530–531, 533
    Snort, 174–179
chair,
    redwood, 206
    swivel, 329
chalk-and-blackboard game, 3
chance moves, 16
Chandra, Ashok K., 218, 220
change of heart, 255
change, phase, 164–165
charge, electric, 243–245
Charming Antipodean Beauty Spot, 371
Charming Charles, 491
Charosh, M., 734
Chas., 607–609, 629–630
Checkers = Draughts, 218, 220, 697
cheque-market exchange, 155
Cheshire Cat, 826
Chess, 116, 219, 607, 632–633, 646
Chess,
    complete analysis, 16, 691
    Dawson's, 88–91, 100–101
    problems, 623
Chessgo, 607, 609
chesspersons, 88, 607–609, 632–633
child,
    bad, 410
    good, 407
Childish Hackenbush, 45, 54, 153, 229–232
childish lollipops, 229–232
childish picture, 45
children's party, 130, 174
Chinese Nim = Wythoff's Game, 407
Chinese Rings, 748–753
chocolate bar, 598, 600
Chomp, 598–600
chopping, 530, 570
Christmas, 793, 799
Cuvatal, Vasek, 673
class and variety, 342–343
class, outcome, 30, 83
classes, Reiss's Solitaire, 708
Claus = Lucas, 754
clean and dirty, 826
Clef, Double Treble, 744
climbing bars, 206

Clique Technique. 579, 581
cliques, 579–581, 602
clock, 635, 644, 820
closed, 388–390
cloud, 32, 38, 119, 146
clubs, 339, 427
coalitions, 17, 499
cockroach, 566
Cocoons, 563
Codd, E.F., 849
code digits, 91–92, 98–100, 102–107, 112
code,
    of behaviour, 503
    genetic, 571–572
    Gray, 750–753
coin sequence game, 600
Coinage, Sylver, 17, 576–598, 602–606
coins, 121–122, 427, 432–438, 440–451, 454–456, 516–524, 575, 755–756, 777, 807
Col, 39–41, 49–53, 69–70, 77, 141, 218, 468
cold game, 279–280, 287
cold position, 285–286, 302
cold war, 280–282, 284, 286
cold work, 296
Coldcakes, 280
Colon Principle, 184–185, 214, 335
coloring, 39, 141
Commandment,
    lukewarmth, 286, 290
    markworthy, 297
common cosets, 109
comparing games, 37, 328
compendium, 101, 367
complementary position, 710
complementing effect, 385
complete graph, 549
complete in Pspace, 218
complete information, 16
completing a box = complimenting move, 507
complimenting move, 359, 385–387, 507, 518
component, 32–34, 37, 255, 258, 261, 266, 268–269, 279–282, 287, 292, 305–306, 376–378, 395
component,
    cold, 279
    hot, 279–280
    loopy, 390
    tepid, 306
compound,
    conjunctive, 258, 266
    continued conjunctive, 266
    disjunctive, 258
    impartial, 376
    selective, 279
    severed selective, 292

shortened selective, 292
subselective, 376, 499
compound game, 32, 255
compound thermograph, 160
computable function, 596–597
computers, reproducible, 848
computing power, 159
confused, 32, 71
confusion interval, 119, 146, 154, 159
congruence modulo 16
conjecture, 111, 503, 586
conjunctive compound, 258, 266
Connell, Ian G., 80
Continental board, 711, 729
continued conjunctive compound, 266
Contours, 553–554
contract, 124
control, 510–511, 540, 567
convention, normal play, 16
Conway, Elena, 768
Conway, John Horton, 19, 24, 54, 80, 116, 121, 140, 182, 220, 253, 278, 357, 426, 456, 468, 505, 564, 587, 606, 609, 688, 721, 739, 793, 813
Cook, Stephen A., 219–220
Coolcakes, 288–289
cooling, 147–148, 174–175
formula, 147
coprine, 384
Corderman, Charles L., 827
Corinthians I, 13, 12, 71
corkscrew, left-handed, 359
Corner, 441–443, 446, 627, 714–715, 721–722
defence, 618, 620–622
tactics, 618–620, 627
cornered king, 624, 626–628
cosets, common, 109
cost, 157
counters, heaps of, 43
Couples, Seating, 46–47, 94
cousin, 101–106, 113, 115, 420
coverlet, 216
cows, 141
Coxeter, Harold Scott Macdonald, 80, 116, 505, 783, 813
Cram = Impartial Domineering, 139, 468–472
Cricket, 17
criminal, minimal, 188, 209
critical temperature, 163–167
Cross, Donald C., 734
Crosscram = Domineering, 117
crosses, tendrilled, 547
crowd, three or more's a, 527
Csirmaz, Lásźlo, 692
Csmiraz, *Discrete Math.* misprint for Csirmaz, 692
cube
Hungarian, 760–768, 808–809

magic, 760–768, 808–809
Rubik, 760–768, 808–809
cul-de-sac, 726
Curtis, Robert Turner, 436–437
custodian capture, 632
Cutcake, 26–27
Hickerson's, 53
Cutcakes, 264–265, 272–274, 280
cutting, 264, 272
cycles, 186–188, 209, 296, 517, 544, 820–822
Cyclotome, Alan Schoen's, 789–790

D.A.R., 340
D.U.D.E.N.E.Y., 487–489
Dad's Puzzler, 769
D'Alarcao, Hugo, 573
Damß, J.E., 220
date, 374, 390
Davies, D.W., 692
Davis, Harry O., 733–734
Davis, Morton, 606
Dawson's Chess = ·137, 88–91, 100–101
Dawson's Kayles = ·07, 17, 92, 94, 100–101, 251, 418, 424, 466, 470, 532
Dawson's-vine, 532, 535
Dawson, Thomas Rayner, 88, 116, 814
dead animal, 133
dead cell, 817
Deader Dodo Problems, 721
deadly dodge, 514
death, 817
Death Leap Principle, 125–127, 133
deathday, 797
deceptive defence, 514
decomposing, 466, 532–535
deficient Soma piece, 739
deficit, 720
accounting, 720–721
Rule, 720, 725
degree of loopiness, 340
degree of **upon**, 355
degree, cooling by one, 175
Delannoy, 807, 814
deleting dominated options, 64, 78
delphinium, 49, 193, 234, 324
Denim, 500
deriders of zero, 451
Descartes, Blanche, 96, 116
desert, 715
deuce, 337
devastating U-turns, 690
devil's label, 189
devil, square-eating, 609
dexterity, 801, 804
diamonds, 339
dice, paradoxical, 778

dictionary
Col, 49–53
Cram, 468–472
Domineering, 118, 137–140,
Nimstring, 525–526, 531, 547–549
Snort, 143, 173, 175–179
Difference Rule, 76, 384
digit
binary, 98, 830
code, 91–92, 98–100, 102–107, 112
Dim, 97, 422
with Tails, 384
disarray, 94
discount, 157
disguise, 94, 430, 552, 669
disincentive, 144
dissection, 126, 132
dissociation, thermal, 164
distributive law, 443, 451
Dividing Rulers, 416–417, 438
do or die donation, 514
dodecahedra, quintominal, 813
Dodgem, 685
Dodgerydoo, 687
Dodie Parr: odd parity, 511–516, 535–536, 538, 541, 544–546
Dodo Problems, 721
dodos, 714
dog with leftward leanings, 6
dogs, 647
Dollar Game, Silver, 457, 501
dominated option, 64, 78
Domineering = Crosscram, 117–120, 137–140, 149, 173–174, 346, 468
Domineering, Impartial = Cram, 139–140, 278
Dominoes, 117
Domoryad, A.P., 814
Don't-Break-It-Up Theorem, 208–209, 211
Donkey Puzzle, 769–770, 772–773, 777
Doomsday Rule, 795–797, 813
Doors, 446–450, 456
dots + doublecrosses = turns, 537
Dots-and-Boxes, 17, 219, 507–550, 788
Dots-and-Pairs = Cram, 139
Double Duplicate Nim, 113
Double Hackenbush, 323
Double infinity, 314
Double Kayles, 98
Double Treble Clef, 742, 744
double-crossed, 507, 509
double-dealing, 508–509
double-down, $\Downarrow$, 70–71, 73
double-six, 385
double-up, $\Uparrow$, 70–71, 73, 222
doubling, 93, 586
down, $\downarrow$, 65–66
down-second, 227–228
downsum, 316, 335, 337, 340

Draughts = Checkers, 697
drawn ≠ tied, 16, 315
dual, 517
dud = deathless universal draw, 317–318, 333
Dudeney, Henry Ernest, 82, 116, 487, 505, 692, 699, 701, 719, 734, 814
Duffus, Dwight, 292
duke, 607
Dukego, 607–611
Duncan, Anne, 668
Duplicate Kayles, 98, 424
Duplicate Nim, 113, 115
duplication of nim-values, 93, 97, 113, 115, 424–425
Durer, Albrecht, 780
Dyen, Louis, 649

Eagle, Edwin, 692
earwig, 566
Easter, 797
Eatcake = Bynum's Game, 134, 225, 269
Eatcakes, 266, 269–272, 275–277
Eater, 820, 833–835
eating, 270–271, 833, 835
eccentric cases of atomic weights, 223–224, 231, 242–243
economy, underlying, 147
Eden, Garden of, 828
edge, 42, 45, 325
    attack, 611–613
    defence, 613–616
edge-corner attack, 617–618
edges
    bLue and Red, 4–8, 31, 79, 191, 229, 242, 309, 323
    grEen, 31, 42, 184–191, 229, 242, 310
    pale and pink, 323–324
Edmonds, Jack, 692
effective computability, 606
Eggleton, Roger Benjamin, 488
electric charge, 243
Eliot, Thomas Stearns, 429, 499–500
Elizabeth, Queen, 797
Emperor Nu, 575
empty numbers, 439
empty set, 82, 379
encirclement, games of, 607–665
end, 528
end, quiet, 583
end-position, 582
ender, 309–310, 576
Endgame, 396
endgames, loony, 543
ending condition, 16, 48–49, 309
England, 497, 797
English board, 697
enlarged flow, 201

Enough Rope Principle, 17, 513, 672
entailing, 359, 376–385
Epp, Robert J., 505
Epstein's Game, 484–486, 501–502
Epstein, Richard A., 608, 634
equally favorable, 37
equally uppity, 233, 238, 240
equitable, 153, 155–157, 166
equivalences
    Nimstring, 531
    Twopins, 466
Erdös, Paĺ, 692
escaped hare, 651–652
essential echo, 514
eternal games, 48, 359
etiquette, 597
Euler's Theorem, 537, 550
Eureka, 96, 116, 244
Evans, Ronald J., 692
even, 259, 261
Even Alteration Theorem, 477
even evicts! 286
even timers, 285
Even, Shimon, 218, 220
evil = even, 267, 287
evil numbers, 109, 431, 453, 783
Ex-Officers Game = ·06, 102, 425, 470
exactly periodic, 85
exceptional values, 89–91, 100, 107
excitable, 153, 155–157, 166–168
excluded tolls, 285
excluded values, 110
exemptions, tax, 147
exit move, 723–724, 732
Exit Theorems, Beasley's, 723–724, 731–732
explosive nodes, 51
exponential-time algorithms, 218–219
exposure, death by, 817
extended thermograph, 157–159
Extras, 16, 48, 75, 100, 132, 176, 214, 246, 272, 304, 349, 388, 422, 456, 501, 537, 571, 598, 631, 646, 661, 692, 728, 801, 848

fair board, 611, 630
fair position, 608, 611
Fair Shares and Unequal Partners, 360, 374
Fair Shares and Varied Pairs, 359, 390
fairy chess, 116, 607
fairy tale, 292
Fajtlowicz, S., 598
Falada, 292–294, 299–301, 304–305
Falkener, Edward, 692
Fano's fancy Antonim finder, 461
far star = remote star, 222
farm, 142, 706, 824, 843

faux pas, 640
favorite, 253, 258, 262
Felton, G.E., 692
fence, 456
Fencing, 456
Ferguson, Thomas S., 86, 116, 410, 422, 426, 496–497, 505
Fermat powers of two, 444
Fermat problem, solution of, *see* margin of page, 830
Fermat, Pierre de, 444, 830
ferz = fers, 607–608
Fibonacci, Leonardo Pisano, 483–484, 486, 501
Fibonacci Nim, 483
Fibonacci numbers, 483–484, 486, 501, 503
Fibulations, 486, 501
fickle, 393, 403–405, 409, 412, 414, 480, 499
field, 292–293, 304, 450
Fifteen Puzzle, Sam Loyd's, 756, 759
fifth column, 391
figure eight, 822
finalist, 705, 728
fine print, 124
finicky figures, 303
finished product, 718
finishing line, 387
firm 393, 403–405, 409, 412, 480
first
    bite, 302–303
    cousin, 101–102, 104–106, 113, 115
    eaten strip, 275
    home, 260, 300–301
    horse stuck, 260
    off, 292
    one-by-one cake, 265
    player wins, 30
    strip, 275
fit, 24, 243
Fitted Carpets, 447
Five-in-a-Row, 674
Fives
    Acrostic Mock Turtle, 455
    Ruler, 438
    Staircase, 465
    Triplet, 438
fixed, 315
Flags of the Allies Puzzle, 786, 811
Flanigan, James Alan, 357, 425, 470, 505
Flanigan's Game = ·34, 470
flare path setter, 826
flat, 410
flip-flop, 821
floor, 53, 453
flow, 197–205, 220
flow, cash, 124
Flow Rule, 197, 199, 205

flower, 31, 38, 49, 68–69, 183, 189, 192–195, 205, 222, 232–234, 236–238, 324
flower garden, 183, 192, 221–222, 232
flowerbed, 233–234, 236, 238
    should be posy, 35
flowerstalk = stem, 38
Fool's Solitaire, 720, 729
foot, 206
Football, Philosopher's, 688–691
Ford, Lester R., 200, 220
Foregger, T.H., 801, 814
forging, 369
fork, 312
    threat, 676
form
    canonical, 24
    simplest, 24
    standard, 100–106
Formula, Cooling, 147
foundations for thermographs, 151
Four-in-a-Row, 673
Fox Game = Hala-Tafl, 632
Fox-and-Geese, 17, 632, 635–645, 647
fractional atomic weights, 226
fractional multiples, 246
Fraenkel, Aviezri S., 80, 218, 220, 392
Fraenkel, Abraham, 817
France, 786, 796
free, 315, 651
freezing point, 150, 166
Fremlin, David, 773
French Military Hunt, 17, 647–658, 788
Freystafl, 632
Fried, Kati, 767
frieze patterns, 475–478, 501
Frogs, see Toads, 14, etc.
FTOZOM, 564
Fulkerson, Delbert Ray, 200, 220
Full Moon, Paschal, 797–798
function
    computable, 596–597
    pagoda, 712–717, 725
    remoteness, 259, 661–664
    ruler, 97, 438, 487
    score ≠ pagoda, 731–732
    Steinhaus, 259
    Welter, 472–474, 476–481
fundamental insects, 566
Fundamental Theorem of Zeroth Order Moribundity, 564
Funkenbusch, William, 692
furniture, redwood, 206–212, 216
fuse, 186, 826
Fusion Principle, 186–188
fuzzy flowers, 31
fuzzy games, 32
fuzzy positions, 30, 34–35

𝒢-ness, 402
G-raph, 200, 202
𝒢-sequence = nim-sequence, 82, etc.
𝒢-string, Air on a, 96
g-string, 489–490
𝒢-value = nim-value, 82, etc.
Gale, David, 598, 606, 680, 692
gallimaufry, 69–70, 77
Galvin, Fred, 244
galvinized games, 243–245
game
    birthdays, 397
    identification, 67
    in the jungle, 204
    locator, 101, 103, 424
    of encirclement, 607–665
    of Life, 817
    of pursuit, 17, 607–665
    reserves, 394
    tracking, 67, 216–217
    trees, 42
    with cycles, 356
Game
    Acrostic, 450–455
    Additional Subtraction, 375
    annihilation, 218
    big, 67, 200, 204, 216
    Black Path, 682–683
    Bynum's = Eatcake, 134, 225, 269
    cheap, 367
    coin sequence, 600
    cold, 141, 280
    comparisons of, 37
    compendium, 101, 367
    compound, 32
    coolest, 169
    eating, 134, 225, 266, 269–272, 275–277
    entailed, 359, 376–385
    Epstein's, 484–486, 501–502
    equitable, 153, 155–157, 166
    eternal, 48, 359
    Ex-Officers = ·06, 102, 425, 470
    excitable, 153, 155–157, 166–168
    Falada, 300–301
    finite, 48, 114
    Flanigan's = ·34, 470
    Fox = Hala-tafl, 632
    fuzzy, 32
    galvinized, 243–245
    Grundy's 17, 96, 111, 414, 419–420, 424, 441, 456
    half-tame, 403, 415–417, 424–425
    hard, 206, 212, 218–219
    hexadecimal, 115–116
    hot, 123, 131, 141–182, 219, 279–288, 296, 303
    impartial, 17, 42, 82, 190, 214, 271, 310, 359, 376
    impartial loopy, 255, 359–392

impartial misère, 255, 393–426
    Kenyon's = ·3f, 115
    L-, 364–366, 388–389
    Lewthwaite's, 683
    loopy, 255, 307, 314–357, 376
    many-dimensional, 215, 456, 678–679
    map-coloring, 39, 141
    misère Grundy's, 396–400
    misère octal, 423–425
    misère Welter's, 480–481
    negative of, 35–37
    no-player, 817
    Northcott's, 56
    NP-hard, 219
    octal, 101–115, 423–425
    one-horse, 258
    ordinal sum, 𝒢:ℋ, 214
    Ovid's, 672
    partizan, 17, 67, 255, 275, 292, 356, 359
    Put-or-Take-a-Square, 484–486, 501–502
    reduced, 426
    restive, 405–406, 412–418
    restless, 412–415, 423
    Ruler, 437–438, 446, 451, 487
    Sato's Maya = Welter's, 407
    Shannon switching, 680–681
    short hot, 219
    silver dollar, 457–458, 501
    simplifying, 62–65, 78–79
    subtraction, 83–86, 97, 375, 410, 422, 483, 487–500
    switch, 119–123, 153
    take-and-break, 82, 91–92, 95, 109
    take-away, 82, 87, 100, 487–500
    tame, 397, 402–418, 423–426, 480
    tameable, 405, 426
    tartan, 445–446
    tepid, 286, 288, 296, 306
    The 37 Puzzle, 487
    tiniest, 123–124
    two-dimensional, 312–313, 441–455
    Welter's, 407, 472–474, 476–481
    wild, 410
    Wythoff's, 17, 62, 76, 407
    zero, 4, 9, 43
gaming tables, 458
garden, 35, 192, 221, 232, 492
Gardner, Martin, 19, 54, 140, 278, 468, 505, 573, 606, 634, 649, 665, 672, 692–693, 733–734, 777, 810, 814, 849
Garey, Michael R., 212, 218–220
gates, logical, 831–832, 839
gathering fruit, 334
Gauss, Karl Friedrich, 244
gee-up, 238
Geese, see Fox, 17, 632, 635–645, 647

Generalized Geography, 218
Generalized Hex, 218
Generalized Kayles, 218
genetic codes for Nim, 571
genetic engineering, 848
genus, 402–426, 467, 470–472, 553–554, 562–563, 570, 573
Geo., 607–613, 615–624, 627, 629–630
geranium, 49, 193, 234
Gerritse, Richard, 587, 590
Gibberd, R.W., 814
gift horses, 74, 79
Gift Horse Principle, 74, 79
Gijlswijk, V.W., 364, 392
Ginny, 367–371
giraffe, 200–202
girl meets boy, 748
glass of wine, 359–360
glass, magnifying, 71, 147
glider, 821–822, 826–827, 830, 834, 843
    gun, 825, 827, 832, 834
    stream, 837–839
Go, 17, 157, 219, 607
    complete analysis, 691
    My First, 667
    stones, 608, 612
Go-Bang, 676
Go-Moku, 16, 676, 679
Goats, see Sheep, 754
Göbel, Fritz, 116, 505, 665, 693
godd, 189, 220
Golay, M.J.E., 849
Gold Moidores, 432
Goldbach, Christian, 381
Goldbach position, 362
Goldbach's Nim, 381
Golden number, 798
golden number (ratio), 77, 114, 501, 716–717
Golden Pagoda, 713
Goller, Nicholas E., 366, 388
good = odd, 267, 287
good child, 407
good move, 17, 377
Good, Irving John, 220
Goose Girl, 292
gosling, 790
Gosper, R.W., 821, 825, 828
Goto, David, 767
Gozreh, F., 734
grafting plumtrees, 334
graph, 142–143, 521–525, 528
    bipartite, 212, 219, 549
    complete, 549
    spanning tree of, 212, 219
    Nimstring, 518–535, 543–544
    non-planar, 517
graphic picture of farm life, 142
grass, 42
Gray Code, 750–753

Great Hall, 352
Great Tantalizer, The, 784
Great-Aunt Maude, 367
greatly-valued carpet, 448
Greaves, John, 813
Grecos, A.P., 814
Greek gift, 74, 513
Greek letters, loopy, 315
green
    chain, 42
    edges, 31, 42, 184–191, 229, 242, 310
    girl, 186
    Hackenbush, 40, 42, 44, 183–190, 220
    jungle, 191–192, 195–196
    snake, 42
    tinted nodes, 199
    tracks = paths, 197
    trees, 184–187
greenwood tree, 36
Gregorian caldendar, 796
grin, 826
Gros, Monsieur L., 753, 814
Gross, Oliver, 680
ground (=earth), 187, 516
group
    alternating, 759
    symmetric, 759
grown-up picture, 45
Grundy, Mrs., 290
Grundy, Patrick Michael, 44, 54, 58, 80, 116, 215, 313, 397, 424, 426
Grundy scale, 87, 89, 93, 96, 100, 378–379, 386
Grundy Skayles, 90
Grundy's Game, 17, 96, 111, 414, 419–420, 424, 441, 456
    misère, 396–400
    wild animals, 411
Grunt, 440–441, 449, 456
Guibas, Leo J., 777, 814
Guiles = ·15, 93, 102, 416, 424
gun
    glider, 825, 827, 832, 834
    thin, 837
Guy, Michael John Thirian, 432, 486, 501, 587, 721, 739
Guy, Peter Richard Thirian, 735
Guy, Richard Kenneth, 88, 101, 116, 121, 366, 456, 505, 587, 606, 693, 821

Haber, Heinz, 734
Hackenbush, 3–8, 21–22, 29, 44–45, 77, 183–220
    Hotchpotch, 31, 39, 49, 68–70, 191–206, 220, 222, 229, 242, 788
    is hard!, 206, 212
    number system, 80

picture, 3–4
string, 25, 79, 309
Hackenbush, Blue-Red, 3–8, 22, 31, 33, 38, 44, 191, 206–212, 220
    Childish, 45, 54, 153, 229
    Double, 323
    Green, 40, 42, 44, 183–190, 220
    infinite, 307, 312, 324
    loopy, 323–324
    von Neumann, 572
Hajtman, Béla, 814
Hala-tafl, 632
Hales, A.W., 676–680, 684, 693
half move, 6, 9, 22
half-hearted handout, 513
half-off, 336
half-on, 336
half-perfect square, 778, 782
half-tame, 394, 403, 415, 424
halving, 189, 586
Hamlet's Memorable Problem, 720
hammer and sickle, 729–730
handouts, 513
Handsome Hans, 491
Hanner, Olof, 182
Hanoï, Tower of, 753
Harary, Frank, 684
hard problems, 218–220
hard redwood bed, 212, 216.
hard-headed, 167
hard-hearted, 513
hardness, 206, 212, 218–220
Hare and Hounds, 647–665
Hares and Tortoises, 754, 807
harmless mutation, 528
Harry Kearey, 298
harvester, 826
Harvey, Sir Paul, 814
Haselgrove, C.B., 787, 815
Haselgrove, Jenifer, 815
havoc, 827
head, 701
    losing your, 216
    severed, 292
heap, quiddity, 500
heaps, see Nim-heaps, 43, etc.
heart, change of, 255
hearts, 339
heat, 123, 130, 141, 160, 279
heating, 163, 169
Hein, Piet, 680, 735, 789
Hentzel, Irvin Roy, 734
hereditarily tame, 405
Hermary, 734
Hertz oscillator, 822
Hex, 218, 679, 680, 692
hexadecagon, 790
hexadecimal games, 115–116
hexagon, 680, 784, 810
Hexiamond, O'Beirne's, 787–789

Hi, 575
hi, 335–336
Hi-Q, 698
Hickerson, Dean, 53, 487
Hickory, Dickory, Dock, 487
hidden secrets, 736–738, 740, 786, 788, 790–791
hierarchy, 95
highway, 344, 371
hilarity, 360
Hilbert Nim, 313
Hillman, A.P., 80
Hnefatafl, Saxon, 632
Hockey, 17
Hoffman, Dean, 739, 804
Hoffman, Professor = Lewis Angelo, 693
Hoffman's Puzzle, 739–740, 804–806
Hofstadter, Douglas R., 815
Holladay, John C., 507, 550
hollyhocks, 38
home, 257, 260, 263, 266, 268, 299–301, 366–367
Honest Joe, 155
horse, 29, 74, 257–258, 260–264, 266, 272–273, 192, 299–301, 386–387
    also-ran, 266
    favorite, 258, 261
    gift, 74, 79
    outsider, 266
    slow, 266, 268
    working out a, 30
Horsefly, 375, 391
hot, 335–336
hot, 123, 131, 141, 145, 147, 167, 169, 219, 280, 284, 287, 296
    battle, 141, 279–288, 303
    component, 279–280
    game, 169, 219, 287
    position, 145, 284
    work, 296
Hotcakes, 279–284
Hotchpotch, Hackenbush, 31, 39, 49, 68–70, 191–206, 220, 222, 229, 242, 788
Houng-Dog Position, 660
Hounds, *see*
house and garden, 35
House of Cards, 337–341
Howells, D.F., 505
Hudson, Paul D.C., 499, 505
Hungarian Cube, 760–768, 808–809
Hunter, J.A.H. "Fun with Figures", 815
Hutchings, Robert L., 576, 721

Icelandic sagas, 632
illegal, 300, 302, 384
imminent jump, 11

impartial, 17, 42, 82, 190, 214, 271, 310, 359, 376
    Cutcakes, 273
    Domineering = Cram, 139
    horse-moving, 263
    loopy games, 255
    remoteness, 276
incentive, 144, 246, 249
incomparable, 37
Independence Day = Doomsday, 795
induction, 114
inequalities for stoppers, 331
Inequality Rule, 328–329
infected should be infested, 566
infinite
    delphinium, 49
    ender, 309
    frieze pattern, 478
    geranium, 48
    Hackenbush, 307, 312, 324
    Nim, 310
    nim-values, 606
    ordinal numbers, 309
    remoteness, 362
    repetition, 16, 364
    Smith theory, 313
    tolls, 295–300, 305–306
infinitesimal, 38, 164–169
infinitesimally close, 147
infinitesimally shifted, 173–175, 191
infinity, 309, 314, 371, 435, 490, 644
ink, waste of, 362
input, 832, 834
Instant Insanity, 784
integral, 163–176, 314, 346–347
Intermediate Value Theorem, 406, 418
interval, confusion, 119, 146, 154, 159
intriguing women, 490
inverting Welter's function, 477
invoices and cheques, 124
irrational, 576
irregular values, 89–91, 100, 107
ish = Infinitesimally SHifted, 173
Isidor, Bishop of Seville, 693
isomorphism, 552, 570, 600, 668–669
Isotopy Extension Principle, 747
Italy, 796

Jam, 668
Japan, 786
Jelly Beans = ·**52**, 408, 424
Jenkyns, Thomas A., 499, 505
Jewitt, R.I., 676–680, 684, 693
Jewish New Year, 800
jig-saw puzzles, 787, 792–794
Jimmy, 367–371, 393
Jocasta, 564, 573
Johnson, David S., 212, 218–220

join, 257–278, 280
joints, 528, 535
joker, 338
jump, 9–15, 65–66, 77–78, 125–130, 132–136, 697–706, 711, 714, 719–720, 722–726, 729, 731–732
jumpee, 13
jumper, 10
jungle
    clearing, 216–217
    green, 191, 195
    parted, 196
    sliding, 192
    smart game in, 204
    tracking, 199
    unparted, 205
jungle warfare tactics, 205

Karp, Richard M., 212, 219
Katzenjammer Puzzle, 784
Kayles = ·**77**, 81–82, 88, 90, 92, 94, 109–111, 218, 397, 424, 466, 470, 532, 552
Kayles, Dawson's = ·**07**, 17, 92, 94, 251, 418, 424, 466, 470, 532
    Double, 98
    Misère, 411–412
    Quadruple, 98
    Triplicate Dawson's, 251
Kayles-vine, 533–534
Kenyon, John Charles, 101, 114, 116
Kenyon's Game = ·**3f**, 115
kickback reaction, 837
killing mutation, 528
Kindervater, G.A.P., 364, 392
king, 607–608
    centred, 623–625
    cornered, 624, 626–628
    edge-charging, 617
King
    Kimberley, 216
    sidelined, 627, 629–630
Kinggo, 607, 609, 611–630
King's Horses
    All the, 257–263, 266–269, 272–273
    Some of the = Falada, 292
kite-strategy, 234, 238
Klarner, David A., 505
knight, 258, 607
Knight, White, 58–61, 258
Knuth, Donald, 19, 53
Konakis, 632
Körner, Thomas W., 631
Kotzig's Nim, 481
Kraitchik, Maurice, 734, 815
Kriegspiel, 16

L-game, 364–366, 388–389
L-package, 702–703, 726, 728, 731
L-purge, 702–703, 728, 731
Lacrosse, 17
ladder, 367, 472, 791
L'Âne Rouge, 769
Lasker, Emmanuel, 573
Lasker, Edward, 99, 116, 693
Lasker's Nim, 99, 112–113
last cut, 274
last home, 268
last horse, 266
last move, 167
last player losing, 255, 426
last player winning, 4, 10, 14, 16, 255
latent heat, 130, 287
latent loopiness, 355, 371
latent phase change, 164
lateral thinking, 364, 392
latin squares, 463
Lee, Chester Y., 674, 850
Left, 4
    boundary, 150
    excitable, 155
    remoteness, 259, 261
    stop, 145–146
    tally, 281
Lefty, 26, 264, 279
leg, 206
Lehman, Alfred, 680–682, 692–693
Leibniz, Gottfried Wilhelm von, 711–712, 734
Lemma
    Norton's, 214, 235, 334
    Snort, 176
Lemon Drops = ·56, 408, 424
Lenstra, Hendrik Willem, 429, 456
Les Pendus, 672–673
Lester, W.E., 814
Let them eat cake!, 269
Lewis, Angelo, 693
Lewthwaite, G.W., 683
Lewthwaite's Game, 683
Li Shuo-Yen, Robert, 323, 353, 357, 499, 505
lice, infestation with, 566
Lichtenstein, David, 220
Life, 17, 55, 817, 850
    computer, 830, 848
    configuration, 825, 830, 847
    cycle, 820–822
    environment, 848
    history, 818, 825–827, 830
    is universal!, 847
    pattern, 824, 830, 848
    sole aim in, 848
    space, 849
    still, 819, 822
Life's but a game!, 829
Life's problems are hard!, 829

Life's impredictability, 824–825
Lifeline, 850
Lifenthusiasts, 820
lightning bolts, 52
limbs, stretching, 531
line
    real number, 25
    wiggly, 526, 546–547
Linnaeus, Carolus, 632, 634
Litchfield, Kay P., 815
little safe, 587
live cell, 817–819
live spots, 564, 567, 573
Lo, 575
lo, 335–336
Lo-Shu, 778
loaf, 819, 825
logical gates, 831–832, 838–839
lollipops, 229–230
long, 512
    barge, boat, 819
    chain, 509–513, 515–516, 518–522, 527, 529–531, 540–541, 543–546
Long Chain Rule, 512, 515
    cycle = loop, 519–520, 531
    path, 528–533
    period, 108
    ship, 819
loony, 302, 377–387, 523–525, 527, 529, 542, 545–546
loony endgames, 543
Loony Loop, 741–742, 753
loop, 819
    long, 520
    looping the, 837
    short, 520
loopiness, 341–343
    blatant, 371
    degree of, 340
    latent, 355, 371
    patent, 356, 371
Loops-and-Branches = ·**73**, 552
loopy component, 370, 390
loopy game, 255, 307, 314–357, 359, 376
loopy Hackenbush, 323–325
loopy option, 390
loopy position, 369, 388
loopy value, 367, 369–371
lose control, 540
lose slowly!, 258
lose your shackles!, 531
losing, last player, 255, 393–426
Lost World, 393–394
louse, 566
Loyd, Sam, 82, 116, 756
Lucas, Edouard, 554, 573, 649, 665, 693, 733–734, 754, 815
Lucasta, 554–563
Lucky Seven Puzzle, 756–759, 768, 807

lucky star, 237
Ludo, 16
Lukewarmth Commandment, 286, 290
Lustenberger, Carlyle, 674, 693

m-plicate, 97
MacMahon jig-saws, 792–794
MacMahon, Major Percy A., 815
MacMahon squares, 791–794, 812
MacMahon superdominoes, 791–794
MacMahon triangles, 791
Macmillan, R.H., 692
Madachy, Joseph S., 815
Magic
    Cube, 760–768, 808–809
    Fifteen, 668
    hexagon, 784, 810
    Mirror, 741, 744–746, 748–750
    Movie, 746–747
    square, 669, 778–783
    tesseract, 783
Mahomet, 746
making tracks, 199
management of cash flow, 124
Many-way Maundy Cake, 215
map, 39, 141, 394, 771–776, 801–804
Mark, 4, 25; Matthew 13, 12, 385
markup, 157
Markworthy Commandment, 297
mast, 148
mast value = mean value, 162
mate, 472–473
mathematician, 826
Mather, Michael, 801, 814
Mating Method, 472–473
mattress, 210
Mauhin, Patrick, 29
Maundy Cake, 28–29, 53, 190, 215
max, 268
maxim, 259, 267
maximal flow, 197
May-Day, 795
Maya Game Sato's, 407
Mayberry, John P., 499, 505
mean value, 145, 147–150, 162
Meander, 683
Meier, Kersten, 815
Melencolia I, 780
men = Phutball players, 688
Merrilees, 673
Method
    Magic Mirror, 741–746
    Magic Movie, 746–747
    Mating, 472–473
Methuselah, 827
mex = Minimal EXcluded, 57, 82, 398, 522, 524
Mill, 673

Miller, J.C.P., 815
Milnor, John, 182
minimal criminal, 188, 209
minimal spanning tree, 212, 219
Minsky, Marvin L., 844, 850
miny, 124, 126, 133
miny, 333
Miracle Octad Generator, 436–437
Mirror, Magic, 741, 744–746, 748–750
misère
    birthdays, 397
    Contours, 553–554
    Cram, 468–472
    Cutcakes, 273
    Grundy's Game, 396–400
    Kayles, 411–412
    Loops-and-Branches, 552
    Lucasta, 556–563
    Mex Rule, 398
    Nim, 393
    octal games, 423–425
    play, 17, 258, 261, 393, 576, 606
    remoteness, 261
    Rims, 552
    Sprouts, 567–568
    Stars-and-Stripes, 570
    theory, 395–399
    Twopins, 467
    unions, 292
    Welter's Game, 480–481
    Wyt Queens, 407
mistake, inevitable, 362
mixed, 315
Möbius, August Ferdinand, 435
Möbius transformation, 435, 759
Mock Turtle, 429–435, 437
    Fives, 438
    Theorem, 434
Mock Turtles, 431–433
Moebius, 432–435
    Nineteens, 438
MOG = Miracle Octad Generator,
    436–437
Mogul, 432–435
Moidores, 432–433
Mollison, Denis, 564, 568
money, 167, 575
moneybag, 457–458
Monopoly, 17
moon, 359, 797–800
moon
    age of, 799
    new, 800
    Paschall Full, 797–798
Moore, Edward F., 829, 850
Moore, Eliakim Hastings, 498, 505
Moore, Thomas E., 573
Moore and More, 499
Moore's Nim_k, 407, 498–499
Morelles, 673

Morgenstern, Oskar, 505
moribundity, 564, 567
    Equation, 567
Morra, Three-Finger, 16
Morris, Lockwood, 219
mosaic, 826
Moser, Leo, 633, 668, 678–679, 693
Motley, 437, 445, 451
Mott-Smith, Geoffrey, 468, 693
mountain, 9, 746
mountain, purple, 191–192
move set, 481–483
moves, 16, 42
    abnormal, 305
    alternating, 48
    bad, 17, 513, 712
    bonus, 385
    chance, 16
    complimenting, 359, 385–387, 507,
        518
    consecutive, 255, 385
    entailing, 359, 376–385
    equitable and excitable, 157
    exit, 723–724, 732
    five-eighths, 22
    futile, 618
    good, 17, 377
    half, 6
    horse. 386
    hotter, 169
    illegal, 300–302, 384
    legal, 384
    loony, 377–387, 391, 527, 529, 542,
        545–546
    non-entailing, 377–378, 380
    non-suicidal, 302, 528
    normal, 395
    overriding, 292, 294, 297, 299, 300,
        306
    pass, 263, 266, 318, 332, 335
    plausible, 618
    predeciding, 292, 300
    quarter, 8
    repainting, 323
    reversible, 56, 62, 72, 78, 208, 395
    reversible misère, 395
    reverting, 405
    strategic, 609
    suiciding, 292, 300, 524
    sunny, 377–381, 384, 387, 391
    tactical, 609
    temperature-selected, 129
    three-quarter, 17
    trailing, 382
    worthwhile, 208–211
Movie, Magic, 746–747
Mr. Cutt and Mr. Shortt, 681–682
Mrs. Grundy, 290
Mühle, 673
multiples of up, 73, 238, 249

multiples, fractional and non-integral,
    246
multiplying pegs, 706–710
multum in parvo, 827
Munro, Ian, 220
Murray, H.J.R., 634, 673, 693
Muscovites, 632
musical series, 116
mutation, 528–529, 849
Myhill, John, 850

$\mathcal{N}$-positions, 83, 259, 361–364, 388,
    390, 419, 482–483, 485–486, 501,
    503, 539, 555, 558, 560–561, 568,
    579, 581–582, 597–598, 600, 604–
    606, 687
n-dimensional k-in-a-row, 678
n-theorem, 581
Nash, John F., 680
Nasik squares, 783
negative
    charge, 243
    numbers, 21, 310
    of a game, 35–37
    positions, 30–31, 70
negs = negpegs, 725
neighbor, 567
von Neumann Hackenbush, 572
von Neumann, John, 505, 850
Nim, 17, 42–43, 55–56, 113, 169, 367,
    426, 430, 432, 457, 459, 463, 473–
    474, 486, 498–500, 552, 687
    Antipathetic, 459
    Bounded, 483
    Chinese = Wythoff's Game, 407
    Double Duplicate, 113
    Duplicate, 113, 115
    Entailing, 380
    Fibonacci, 483
    genetic codes for, 571–572
    Goldbach's, 381
    Hilbert, 313
    infinite, 310, 606
    Kotzig's, 481–483
    Lasker's, 99, 112–113
    misère, 393, 398, 486
    Moore's, 407, 498–499
    Poker, 55
    Similar Move, 462
    Sympathetic, 460
    Triplicate, 113, 115
    two-dimensional, 312–313
    Welter's, 407
nim-addition, 60–61, 75–76, 89, 101,
    108–109, 115, 185, 190, 370, 398,
    431, 441, 443–444, 463–464,,472–
    474, 476, 524, 571–572, 688
Nim Additional Rule, 75, 522
    in hot games, 169

nim-heaps, 43–44, 57–61, 82, 369, 373, 393, 398–404, 406, 410, 414, 416, 422, 430, 480, 571
  ambivalent, 406
  bogus, 57–58
nim-multiplication, 443–445
Nim-position, 43, 368, 393, 405–406, 426, 457, 571
nim-product, 443–446, 449
nim-sequence, 82–87, 93, 97–100, 102, 104–108, 112–113, 115, 495–496, 553
nim-sum, 61, 75–76, 82, 89–90, 108–111, 430, 432, 439, 443, 449, 474, 552, 687
nim-values, 82–87, 89–98, 109–116, 185–190, 367–388, 390–391, 405–406, 422, 431–434, 437–441, 443, 446, 448–452, 454–456, 472–473, 479–480, 487, 499, 503, 524, 532–535, 545–549, 552–556, 563, 570–572, 606, 687
  doubling, 93
  duplication, 93, 97, 113, 115, 424–425
  halving, 189
  periodic, 83–85, 90–91, 93, 97, 99–108, 111–116
  reflected, 108
  relevant, 376
  replication, 97
nimbers, 42–43, 58, 76, 117, 193–194, 253, 377–381, 385–386, 398, 522, 524
  adding, 44, 60
  infinite, 310
Nim_k, Moore's, 407, 498–499
Nimstring, 516, 518–535, 541–549
Nine Men's Morris, 672–673
No Highway, 344–347
no-player game, 817
Noah's Ark Theorem, 403, 412–415, 423
node-disjoint cycles, 544
nodes
  Col, 49–53
  explosive, 51–52
  game position, 42, 321–323, 334–338, 349–350
  Hackenbush, 185–188, 196–199, 216–218
  Nimstring, 517, 526–528, 530, 542–546
  Snort, 142–143, 176–179
  tinted, 199, 202–205, 217
  untinted, 199, 204
non-abacus positions, 480
non-arithmetic-periodicity, 114
non-number, 144, 156
normal move, 305

normal play, 14, 16, 258
normal Soma piece, 739
Northcott's Game, 56
Norton, Simon J., 141, 164, 182, 214, 235, 238, 246, 334, 462, 486, 501, 633
NOT gate, 831, 832, 838–839
Noughts-and-Crosses = Tic-Tac-Toe, 16, 667–672, 674, 678–679, 685
novice, 362
NP-complete, 212, 218–220
NP-hard, 218–219, 543–544
Nu, 344, 575
Number Avoidance Theorem, 144, 179
number system
  Hackenbush, 80
  tree and line, 25
numbers, 24, 117, 280
  canonical form, 24
  empty, 439
  evil, 109, 431, 453, 783
  Fibonacci, 483–484, 486, 501, 503
  i-, j-, k-, 439–440
  infinite ordinal, 309, 644
  odious, 109, 431, 439–440, 453, 783
  overheated, 170–172, 346
  simplest, 21, 24, 285, 288
  Surreal, 19
  suspense, 266, 273
  thermographic thicket of, 172
  triangular, 244, 486
  whole, 21
nut-crackers, impossible, 359

$\mathcal{O}$-positions, 362, 364, 370–371, 388, 390
O'Beirne, Thomas H., 116, 481, 505, 665, 693, 785–789, 811, 815
obtuse triangle, 245
octad, 435–437
octal games, 101–115, 423–425
octal notation, 101, 432–433
odd, 259, 261, 267, 285–287, 511
odious numbers, 109, 431, 439–440, 453, 783
Odlyzko, Andrew M., 777, 814
off, 316–320, 333, 335–338
Off-Wyth-Its-Tail!, 382
Officers = ·6, 94, 419–420, 424
offside, 316–317, 320, 324–325, 328, 334–335, 349–350
O'Hara, Frank, 768
Omar, 44, 74, 108, 136, 253, 483–484, 495, 503, 624, 630, 633, 733, 805
on, 316–318, 333, 644
On-the-Rails, 386–387
ONAG = On Numbers and Games, 19, 24, 116, 137, 140, 182, 253, 278,

356, 397, 411, 426, 443, 446, 456, 472, 476, 505
oNe = Weak or Strong place, 649
One-for-you, Two-for-me, . . ., 299
one-horse game, 258
One-Star = 4·07, 570
One-step, Two-step, 495
One-upmanship Rule, 232
ono, 335–337
onside, 316–317, 320, 324–327, 334–335, 349–350
oof, 335–338
open, 362, 364, 370–371, 388, 390
option, 16, 151
  best, 283
  dominated, 64, 78
  Left, 33
  loony, 524
  loopy, 388
  non-loopy, 369
  questionable, 367
  reversible, 56, 62–66, 72–73, 78, 208, 367
  Right, 33
  suicidal, 297, 524
  worthwhile, 208–211
optional extras, 84
OR gate, 831, 838–839
ordinal numbers, 309, 644
ordinal sum, 214
outcome, 30
  classes, 30, 83
  of sum, 33–34
output, 832, 834
outsider, 266
over, 321, 333
overcrowding, 817
overheating, 170–172, 346
overriding, 292, 294–297, 306
Ovid, 672, 693
Ozanam, 815

-positions, 83, 259, 361–365, 388, 390–391, 396–397, 399–404, 406, 411–412, 423, 430, 432, 434–435, 437, 459–465, 482–488, 492–495, 501, 503, 514, 538–539, 553, 555, 558, 560–561, 563, 568, 577, 579–581, 586, 588–601, 603–605, 661–664, 687–688
p-theorem, 581
packages, 701–706, 709, 728, 730–731
pagoda functions, 712–717, 725
Pairing Property, Ferguson's, 86, 422, 496–497
pairs, restive and tame, 405
pale twig, 324
panacea, panache, 703

pandiagonal squares, 783
Pandora, 326, 514
paradox, 499, 505, 645
paradoxical dice, 778
paradoxical pennies, 777
parity, 492, 511, 788
Parity Principle, 185
Parker, Richard, 501
parody, 266
Parrotty girls, 511
parted jungle, 196
particles, 163, 166
partizan, 17, 67, 255, 275, 292, 339, 356
party tricks, 748
Parville de ¿ = Lucas?, 754
Paschal Full Moon, 797–798
Patashnik, Oren, 674
patently cold and hot, 287
patently loopy, 356, 371
Paterson, Michael Stewart, 564, 792, 794
path, 197, 528–529, 682–683
Path of Righteousness, 513–514
paths = tracks, 197, 199, 216–217
Patience = Solitaire, 17, 698
Paul, Jerome L., 693
Paul, Wolfgang J., 220
paw mark = block, 826
pearls, 488–489
Peek, 218
Peg Solitaire, 17, 695–734, 788
Pegity, Pegotty, 676
pegs, 697–734, 753–754
pencil-and-paper game, 3
Penfield, Wilder, 394
Penrose, Roger, 768
pentadecathlon, 824, 827
pentominoes, 786–787, 825
perfect square, 778
periodicity, 89–93, 99–101, 108, 112–114, 116, 826
    arithmetic, 99, 112–116, 140
    Dawson's Chess, 89–90
    Domineering, 140
    Eatcakes, 269, 271
    exact, 85
    Guiles, 93
    Kayles, 90–91
    octal games, 102–108, 112–114
    subtraction games, 83–85, 495–498
    ultimate, 111, 269, 488–489, 495, 688
petal, 49, 68–69, 193, 232, 324
Petrie, Douglas G., 827
pharisees, 567
phase change, 163–165
Philosopher's Football = Phutball, 676, 688–691
Philpott, Wade E., 733
Phutball, 676, 688–691

picture, 3, 45, 186, 435–437
    of farm life, 142
piebald spot, 142
pink twig, 324
place (Zero, oNe, Two), 648–657, 661, 664
placing plumtrees, 334
play
    misère, 17, 258, 261, 393, 576, 606
    normal, 14, 16, 258
player, symmetrical, 513
playing backwards, 711
playing the averages, 163
Ploy
    Blue Flower, 193, 232
    Blue Jungle, 196
Plugg = Cram, 139, etc.
plumtrees, 332, 334, 337
poisoning, 690
Poker, 17
Poker-Nim, 55, 457
pole, barber's, 826
Policy
    Searching, 786–787, 790
    Temperature, 122–123, 128–130
Pollak, Henry Oliver, 676
polyiamonds, 786
polyominoes, 137–138, 684, 786
pond, 819, 827
Pond, I.C., 505
PORN, 596–597
position
    abacus, 478–481
    active, 146
    ajar, 388–390
    closed, 388–390
    cold, 285–286, 302
    complementary, 710
    Domineering, 118, 137–140, 149, 173–174
    exceptional, 653
    fickle, 393, 403–405, 409, 412, 414, 480
    firm, 393, 403–405, 409, 412, 480
    fuzzy, 30, 34–35
    Goldbach, 362
    hot, 145, 284
    Houng-Dog, 660
    loony, 302, 377–387, 523–524
    loopy, 369, 388
    $\mathcal{N}$-, 83, etc.
    negative, 30–31, 70
    non-abacus, 480
    $\mathcal{O}$-, 362, etc.
    $\mathcal{P}$-, 83, etc.
    positive, 30, 70
    Scare'm Hare'm, 655
    starting, 16
    sunny, 377–378, 381, 384
    tepid, 286

terminal, 4, 9, 30, 43
positive
    charge, 243
    house, 39
    house and garden, 35
    positions, 30, 70
    posy, 31 (35)
POT(S), POTSHOP, 675
poultry, 691
predecider, 292
pretending, 401, 419, 425
Price, B.D., 815
Prim, 97, 384, 422
Prince Charles, 491–492
Princes' code of behavior, 503–504
Princess and the Roses, 490–494, 503–504
Principle
    Bogus Nim-heap, 58
    Colon, 184–185, 214, 335
    Complimenting Move, 385
    Death Leap, 125–127, 133
    Enough Rope, 17, 513, 672
    Fusion, 186–188
    Gift Horse, 74, 79
    Isotopy Extension, 747
    Parity, 185
    Star-Shifting, 241, 249
    Translation, 145, 149, 154
    Uppitiness Exchange, 238
Pritchett, Gordon, 573
Problem
    Bumble-Bee, 721
    Deader Dodo, 721
    Dots-and-Boxes, 536, 544–546
    Hamlet's Memorable, 720
    hard, 218–220, 725
    Three B'ars, 721
Prodigal Son, 719–720
product
    acrostic, 450
    finished, 718
    Gross National, 720
    nim-, 443–446, 449
    raw, 718
    ugly, 451
productive, 718
professional boxer, 514
profit, 157, 458
profit-consciousness, 167
program cycle, 296
projective, 410
proof, 114, 144, 179, 196, 207–209, 211–212, 239–242, 246–250, 320, 328–330, 350–353, 388, 415, 422–423
Proviso, Endgame, 396–397
pruning plumtrees, 334
pseudocorner, 630
PSPACE-complete, 218–220

PSPACE-hard, 218–220
puffer train, 827
pulsar CP 48-56-72, 820, 826–827
pulses, 830
punching the clock, 644
purchasing contract, 125
purges, 701–703, 722, 728, 731
purple mountain, 191–192
pursuit, 17, 607–665
Put-or-Take-a-Square = Epstein's
    Game, 484–486, 501–502
putative nim-value, 439
Puzzle
    Century, 769–770, 773–777, 810
    Donkey, 769–770, 772–773, 777
    Fifteen, 756, 759
    Flags of the Allies, 786, 811
    Hoffman's, 739–740, 804–806
    jigsaw, 787, 792–794
    Lucky Seven, 756–759, 768, 807
    Solitaire-like, 754
    The 37, 487
    Tricky Six, 759–760

Quadraphage, 140, 278, 608–609
Quadruple Kayles, 98
quality of quaternity, 494
Quam, 500
quantity beats quality!, 195
Quaquaversal Quadrimagifier, 780–
    781
quarter-infinite board, 264, 272, 292,
    313, 687
quarter-move, 8, 22
quarter-perfect square, 781–782
queen bee, 827
Queen Elizabeth, 797
quiddity heap, 500
quiet end, 583
    position, 583–584, 586
    theorem, 584–586, 590, 595
quietly excludes, 583
quietus, 585
quintessential quinticity, 494
quintominal dodecahedra, 813
quintominoes, 792
quotation marks: eccentric cases, 223–
    224, 231, 242–243

rabbit, 647
Rabin, Michael O., 606
Rademacher, Hans, 537, 550
rademacher, rado, radon, 351
Rails, 552
randomness reigns, 494
range, 463
rapid join, 266
rare values, 109–111

raw product, 718
reaction
    kickback, 837, 839, 844–845
    vanishing, 831–833, 837–838, 841
Read, Ronald C., 815
reader
    assiduous, 44
    gentle, 706
    more mathematical, 342
    persevering, 89
    skeptical, 127
real number line, 25
rectangles, 26–29, 139, 225, 630
Red
    edges, 4, 191
    tinted nodes, 199
    twig, 208
Red-Blue Hackenbush, see Blue-Red
    Hackenbush
reduced game, 426
redwood
    bed, 206, 210–212, 216
    furniture, 206–210
    tree, 209–210
    twig, 208, 211
Reeve, J.E., 815
References, 54, 80, 116, 140, 182, 220,
    253, 278, 356, 392, 426, 456, 505,
    550, 573, 606, 634, 646, 665, 692,
    734, 813, 849
reflexion of nim-values, 108
register, storage, 842
Reisch, Stefan, 220
Reiss, M., 708–709, 712, 734
remote horse, 258
remote star, 222–224, 229–232, 235–
    243, 249–250
Remote Star Test, 237–238, 240
remoteness, 169, 258–266, 269, 272–
    273, 275–277, 295, 297, 361–366,
    501–503, 661–664, 676
    even, 259, 261, 361
    horse's, 260–264, 272–273
    infinite, 361–362
    Left, 259, 261
    misère, 261–265, 272–273, 275
    normal, 259
    odd, 259, 261, 361
    Right, 259, 261
    rules, 259, 261
repainting moves, 323
replication of nim-values, 97, 495
reproduction of computers, 848
resetting the thermostat, 181
resources, available, 718, 720
restive, 394, 405–406, 412–418, 563
restless, 394, 412–415, 423
Restricted Translation Rule, 252
reversal problem, 703–704, 714, 720–
    721, 725–726, 733

reversible moves, 56, 62, 72, 78, 208,
    395
reverting moves, 405
rhombs, 789–790
Right, 4
    boundary, 150
    excitable, 155
    remoteness, 259, 261
    slant, 159
    stop, 145–146
    tally, 281
Rims, 551–552
ring, 818
rings and strings, 742–743
rings, Chinese ¿ Scandinavian?, 748–
    753
Rip Van Winkle's Game = Kayles, 82
ripening plums, 334
Rita, 26, 264, 279
Robertson, Edward, 220
Robinson, Raphael M., 805, 815
Rolling Stones, 326
Romantica, 491, 494
rook, 633
rooster, 790
rooted trees, 570
rose-garden, 491, 503–504
Rosh Hashana, 800
Rosser Barkley, 815
Roth, T., 815
round the world, 361
roundabout, 307, 349, 360
Roy, Constant, 649
Rubik's Cube, 760–768, 808–809
Rubik, Ernö, 760
Ruchonet, 734
Ruderman, Harry D., 693
Rugs, 446
Rule of Three, 705–706, 709–710
Rule of Two, 705
Rule
    Atomic Weight, 233
    Berlekamp's, 79–80
    C.A.B.S., 368–373
    Deficit, 720, 725
    Difference, 76, 384
    Downsum Absorbancy, 340
    Doomsday, 795–798
    Flow, 197, 199, 205
    Inequality, 328–329
    Long Chain, 512, 515–516, 535
    Loony addition, 379
    Mex, 57, 398, 522, 524
    Misère Mex, 398
    Misère Nim, 398
    Misère Play, 17, 258, 261, 383
    misère remoteness, 261
    Nim-Addition, 61, 75–76, 370, 398,
        522
    Normal Play, 14, 16, 258

One-upmanship, 232
remoteness, 259, 261
Restricted Translation, 252
Simplicity, 23–27, 29, 40, 47, 50, 285, 287, 296–297
Smith's, 368–369, 372–373
suspense, 267, 283
Tally, 284–285, 288, 305–306
Two-Ahead, 194, 232
With, 247
Without, 247
Wythoff's Difference, 76, 384
Ruler
  Eights, 438
  Fifteens, 438
  Fives, 438
  Fours, 438
  function, 97, 417, 438
  Game, 437–438, 446, 451, 487
  Sevens, 438
  Sixes, 438
rules, 16
rules, Li's Loopy Hackenbush, 324
Russia, 786

Sackson, Sidney, 665, 693
saltus, 99, 113, 116, 140, 688
Sarsfield, Richard, 80
Saskatchewan landscape, 153
Sato's Maya Game = Welter's Game, 407
Saville, misprint for Seville, 693
scale, Grundy, 87, 89, 93, 96, 100, 378–379, 386
Scare'm Hare'm Position, 655
Scarne, John, 693
Schaefer, Thomas J., 108, 116, 218
Schaer, Jonathan, 45
Schocken, Wolfgang Alexander, 815
Schoen, Alan, 789–790, 813
Schroeppel, Rick, 829
Schuh, Prof. Frederick, 116, 489–491, 495, 503, 505, 598, 606, 649, 661, 665, 668, 693
Schuhstrings, 489–490
Schwenk, Allen J., 505
Scissors-Paper-Stone, 16
score function, 731–732
scorpion, posing as insect, 566
Scott, Elizabeth Anne, 761, 763, 767
scout, 715–717, 729
scrap-heap, 371–372
Seal, David J., 600, 763, 767, 805
seasoned campaigner, 160
Seating Boys and Girls, 130–131, 174–175, 253, 346
Seating Couples, 46–47, 130–131, 253
Seating Families, 94, 251–253
Secondoff Algorithm, 501, 503

secrets, hidden, 736–738, 740, 786, 788, 790–791
Select Boys and Girls, 290
selective compound, 279–280, 292, 376
selective compound, shortened = severed, 292
Selfridge, John Lewis, 488, 676, 692–693
sente, 157
serpent, 790
set
  empty, 82, 379
  move, 482
  subtraction, 84–86, 422
  variation, 215, 571
Seven-up, 213, 220
severed head, 200, 292
severed selective compound, 292
sex
  opposite, 130
  significance, 494
shackles, 531
Shader, Leslie E., 815
Shakespeare, William, 797
Shaki, Ahiezer S., 357
Shannon, Claude Elwood, 676, 680, 692, 850
shatter, 360
She-Loves-Me, She-Loves-Me-Not, e.g. ·05, 101, 113, 115, 253, 456, 495, 573
She-Loves-Me-Constantly, e.g. ·51, 102, 484
Sheep and Goats, 754
Shepherd, Geoffrey C., 475, 505
shifting by stars, 241, 249
  infinitesimally, 173, 191
ships, 819, 821, 823
short
  chains, 513, 520, 540
  hot games, 219
  loops, 520
  paths, 528
shortened selective = severed, 292
short-sighted view, 156
shortlist, 283–284
Shortt, Mr., 681–682
SHOT(S), 674
sickle and sickle, 730
side, 316–317, 320–321, 324–328, 330, 334–336, 349
sidelined king, 624
sidling, 318–322, 326, 330, 345, 351–355
Sidling Theorem, 320, 351–353
sign, 328–331, 353
Silber, Robert, 80
Silver Dollar Game, 457, 501
Silverman, David L., 634
Simoẽs-Pereira, J.M.S., 573

Simonim = SImilar MOve NIM, 462–464
simplest form, 21, 24, 73, 350
simplest number, 21, 24, 285, 288
Simplicity Rule, 23–27, 29, 40, 47, 50, 285, 287, 296–297
simplifying games, 62–65, 78–79
singleton, 393
Singmaster, David, 763, 767, 815
sinister, 804
Sipser, Michael, 219–220
Sisyphus, 326–328
Six Men's Morris, 672–673
Ski-Jumps, 9–13
skittles, 81
slant, right = correct, 159
slash, |, 8, 159, 346
slashes, ||, 127, 346
sliding block puzzles, 769–777, 810
sliding jungles, 192
slipper, 10
Slither, 692
slow horses, 266, 268
slow join, 266–271, 280
slower join, 263
small, 38, 221–253
Smith Theory, 313, 375
Smith's Rule, 368–369, 372–373
Smith, Alvy Ray, 850
Smith, Cedric Austen Bardell, 88, 96, 98, 101, 116, 258, 278, 292, 368–369, 371–373, 397, 426, 491, 494, 499
snakes, 42–44, 232, 819
Snakes-and-Ladders, 16, 366
Snaky, 684
Snort, 49, 141–143, 145–154, 157, 163–166, 173–179, 218, 468
  dictionary, 176–179
  lemmas, 176
Solitaire, 17, 695–734, 788
  army, 715–716, 729
  central, 698–701, 703, 731–733
  English, 697
  Fool's, 720, 729
Soma, 735–739, 789, 801–804
Somap, 789, 801–804
sophistication levels, 535
sound bound for a hound, 661
spaceships, 821, 823, 826
spades, 1, 339
Spain, 796–797
span-length, 188
spanning tree of graph, 212, 219,

spar, 456
spare move, 732
Sparring, 456
sparse space, 109–112
species, 415

Spinner, The, 727
spinster, 472–473
splitting the atom, 226–227
spoiler, 157
spokes, 515
spot, 142, 371
Spots and Sprouts, 94, 551, 564
Sprague, Roland Percival, 44, 58, 80, 116, 215, 313, 472, 505
Sprague–Grundy theory, 58, 215, 313, 522–535
Sprouts, 564–568
Squandering Squares, 245
square
  half-perfect, 778, 782
  magic, 669, 778–783
  Nasik, 783
  pandiagonal, 783
  perfect, 778
  quarter-perfect, 781–782
square-eater, 609
Squares Off, 299
Squares, MacMahon, 791–794, 812
Stability Condition, 343
stage, 372–375
Staircase Fives, 465
stalemate = tie, 16
stalk = stem, 69
Stalking = ·31, 409, 424
standard form, 100, 102, 104–107, 113
star, 36, 40, 118, 123, 183, 359, 695
  far, 222
  lucky, 237
  remote, 222–224, 229–232, 235–243, 249–250
  thermograph of, 152
Star-Incentive Theorem, 250
Star-Shifting Principle, 241, 249
Stars- and-Stripes, 569–570
starting position, 16
startling value, 40
Stead, W., 815
Steinhaus function = remoteness, 259
Steinhaus, Hugo, 278, 373
stem, 38, 49, 69, 193, 205, 232, 530
step, 495
Stewart, B.M., 734
Stewart, F.M., 606
still life, 819
Stockmeyer, Larry, 218
stolid survivor, 723
stones, black = blocking, 608, etc.
  blocking, 608, 610–611, 618, 620, 622
  Go, 608, 612
  lifting, 326
  non-static, 627
  rolling, 326
  static, 627
  strategic, 609–610, 617–618, 620–627
  tactical, 618

unlimited supply, 630
useful, 629
wandering, 608, 610–611, 613–615, 618, 622, 624, 627, 629
well-placed, 621
white = wandering, 608, etc.
stop, 526
stop, Left and Right, 145–146
stopper, 317, 320–321, 331–332, 334, 336–337, 342, 349–350
stopping position, 145–162
stopping value, 145, 149, 169
Storer, James, 219
strategic stones, 609–610, 617–618, 620–627
strategy, 169, 609
  Abacus, 479
  copying, 608
  Goller's, 388
  Hare's, 654
  kite, 234
  misère Lucasta, 559
  stealing, 386, 522–523, 572, 582, 584, 598, 678–679
  survival, 351–353
  Swivel Chair, 329
  symmetry, 5, 513–516
  Thermostatic, 154, 159–163, 179–181, 219
  Tweedledum and Tweedledee, 5, 37, 329–330
  winning, 48
streak, 455
stream
  full, 839
  glider, 837
  thin, 838
  thinning, 837
string, 489–490, 516–528, 741–750
  air on a $\mathcal{G}$-, 96
  g-, 489–490
  Hackenbush, 25, 79–80, 309
  of pearls, 488–489
Strings-and-Coins, 516–518
Strip and Streak, 455
Stripping, 451–452
strong squares, 649
structure of periods, 101, 108
subperiods of nim-values, 108
subselective compounds, 376, 499
subtraction games, 83–86, 97, 375, 410, 422, 483, 487–500
  set, 84–86, 422
succour the sucker, 720, 730–731
suicider, 292, 297, 524
sums
  eternal, 48
  galvinized, 243
  of games, 32, 118, 214, 257

of nimbers, 44
NP-hard, 219
ordinal, 214
sunny positions, 377–381, 384
superdominoes, MacMahon's, 791
superheavy atoms, 313
superstars, 252
surprise exam, 499
Surreal Numbers, 19
survival, 328, 351–353, 393, 817
survivor, stolid, 723
suspense, 169, 268
  numbers, 266–272, 274, 295, 297, 501–503
  rule, 267, 283
swanpan, 479
Sweden, 796, 813
Swedes, 632
Swedish King, 632
Swedish nobleman, 797, 813
Sweets and Nuts, 373–374, 390
Swirling Tartans, 444–445
switch, 119–123, 153
  engine, 827
Switching Game, Shannon, 680–681, 692–693
Swivel Chair Strategy, 329
Sylver Coinage, 17, 576–598, 602–606
Sylvester, James Joseph, 576, 606
Sym, 441, 446
symmetric group, 759
symmetrical player, 513
symmetry, 5, 513–516
symmetry rule's O.K., 514
symmetry strategy, 5, 513–516
Sympathetic Nim, 460
Sympler, 441, 447
Synonim, 460, 462

T-move, 161
Tabella, 672
Tablut, 632
tackle, Phutball, 690
tactical move, 609
tactical stone, 617–618
tactically worthless, 618
tactics, 205, 609, 627
  corner, 618, 620–622, 626–628
tail, 701
tails, 376, 382, 384
Tait, Hilary, 290
Tait, Peter Guthrie, 807
take-and-break games, 81–116
take-away games, 82–87, 97, 100, 375, 410, 422, 483–484, 487–500, 505
Taking Squares, 409
tally, 280–306
  machine, 288, 298
  rules, 284–285, 288, 305–306
tame, 397, 402–418, 423–426

tameable, 405, 426
Tangrams, 786
Tantalizer, The Great, 784–786
tardy union, 292
Tarjan, Robert Endre, 218
tartan, 444–445
Tartan Theorem, 445–446
Tartans, Swirling, 444–445
tax exemption, 147, 149–152
Taylor, Andrew, 767–768
temperature, 122–123, 148–151, 160–169, 180
  ambient, 160–161
  critical, 163–167
  policy, 122–123, 128–130
tendril, 530
tendrilled crosses, 547
Tennis, 17
tentative tally, 286
tepid component, 306
tepid game, 288
tepid position, 286
tepid work, 296
terminal position, 4, 362, 396
ternary = base 3, 439–440
ternary Gray Code, 753
Ternups, 438
tesseract, magic, 783
tesseravore, 608
Test
  Remote Star, 237
  Uppitiness, 236
tetromino, 786
Thatcher, J.W., 850
The More the Merrier, 499
Theorem
  At-least-one, 249
  Beasley's Exit, 723–724, 731–732
  Don't-Break-It-Up, 208–209, 211
  Euler's, 537, 550
  Even Alteration, 477
  Exit, 723–724, 731–732
  Fundamental, of Zeroth Order Moribundity, 564
  Half-Tame, 415
  Harmless Mutation, 528
  Intermediate Value, 406, 418
  Max-flow, Min-cut, 196, 200
  Mock Turtle, 432, 434
  n-, 581
  Noah's Ark, 403, 412–415, 423
  non-arithmetic periodicity, 114
  Number Avoidance, 144, 179
  on simplifying games, 78–79
  p-, 581
  Quiet End, 584–586, 590, 595
  Redwood Furniture, 207–209
  Sidling, 320, 351–353
  Simplest Form, 350
  Star-Incentive, 250

Tartan, 445–446
Thirty-One, 659, 661, 665
Twopins Decomposition, 466, 533
Uglification, 454
Zeckendorf's, 483
theory, Green Hackenbush, 183–190, 196
Theory, Smith, 313, 375
thermal dissociation, 164
thermograph, 147–155, 157–162, 164–168, 170–172, 180–181, 338
  compound, 160
  extended, 157–158
  four-stop, 154–155
  of **oof**, 338
thermographic thicket, 172
thermographs of star and up, 152
thermography, 17, 147–175, 219
thermostat, 160, 181
THERMOSTRAT = Thermostatic Strategy, 154, 159–163, 179–181, 219
thinking
  backwards, 364
  forwards, 364
  laterally, 364, 392
thinning a glider stream, 837
third cousin, 113
Third One Lucky, 486–487
thirding, 581
thirteen's unlucky!, 400
Thirty-One Theorem, 659, 661, 665
Thistlethwaite, Morwen, 767–768
Thompson, Ken, 597
Three B'ars Problems, 721
Three Men's Morris, 673
Three Up, 673
Three-Color Hackenbush, see also Hackenbush Hotchpotch, 31, etc.
Three-Finger Morra, 16
three-quarters, 17–18
thumb-twiddling, 385
thunderbird, 827
Thursday, Maundy, 28
Tic-Tac-Toe = Noughts-and-Crosses, 16, 93, 667–672, 674, 678–679, 685
Tic-Toc-Tac-Toe, 674
tie $\neq$ draw, 16
time bomb, 827
time, complete in exponential, 218–219
timer, 280–283, 285, 287–288, 290, 295–298, 305–306
tims, 443
tinted, 39–40, 49–51, 53, 199, 201–202, 204–205
tiny, 333, 337
tiny, 124, 166
tiny-a-quarter, 129
  -two, 124, 166
  -x, 124

tis, tisn, 322, 324, 354
Tit-Tat-Toe = Tic-Tac-Toe, 16, etc.
toad, 820
Toads-and-Frogs, 14–15, 65–66, 70, 72, 77, 125–129, 132–136, 347–348, 355–356, 755
toenail, 154
Toeplitz, Otto, 537, 550
toil, honest, 582
toll, 280–283, 285–286, 288, 292, 295–299, 305
toll, infinite, 292–300, 305–306
Top Entails, 376
Tortoises, see Hares, 754, 807
Tower of Hanoï, 753
trace, 648
tracking, 67, 200, 216
track = path, 197, 199, 216–217
Trading Triangles, 244–245
traffic lights, 818–819, 824–825, 827
trailing, 382–383
train, 382, 827
transition, phase, 165
translation
  by nimbers, 249, 252
  by numbers, 145, 149, 154
  of four-stop games, 154–155
  of switches, 121
travesty, 266
Trawick, Charles, 826
Treblecross, 93–94
tree
  Australian, 25, 210
  binary, 25
  game, 42, 397
  green, 184–187
  greenwood, 36
  infinite, 312
  redwood, 209–211
  spanning, 212, 219, 682
  with extra twig, 211
trey, 337
triality traps, 650
triality triumphs, 492
triamond, 787
triangular numbers, 244, 486
Tribulations, 486, 501–502
Tricky Six Puzzle, 759–760, 768
Trigg, Charles W., 810
Trim, 500
Triplet Fives, 438
Triplets, 437
Triplicate Dawson's Kayles, 251
Triplicate Nim, 113, 115
tripling, 581
tromino, 786
truth, awful, 396
Tschantz, Steve, 54
Tsyan-Shizi = Wythoff's Game, 407
tub, 819, 827

Tubergen, G.J. van, 364, 392
tuft, 469
tumblers, 826
Turing, Alan M., 850
Turn-and-Eatcake, 227
Turning Corners, 441–442, 446
Turning Turtles, 429
Turnips, 438–439, 449–451, 456, 487
Turnips, Acrostic, 451
turns = dots + doublecrosses, 537
Tweedledum and Tweedledee, 4, 5, 37
    Argument, 5, 37, 329–330
twig, 186–187, 190
twigs
    pale and pink, 324
    redwood, 208, 211
Twins, 5, 437, 446
Twins, Acrostic, 441–442, 451
Twisted Bynum, 227
two and two, 399
Two place, 649
Two-Ahead Rule, 194, 232
Two-Dimensional Nim, 312–313
two-dimensional games, 441–456
Twopins, 466–467, 530, 532
    Decomposition Theorem, 466, 533
    equivalences, 466
Twopins-vine, 530, 532–534
Tyrrell, J.A., 815

U-turns. 690, 732
uggles, 451
uglification, 451–454
    table, 453
    Theorem, 454
ugly product, 451
Uléhla, J., 572–573
ultimately periodic, 111, 269, 488–489,
    495, 688
unboundedly unbounded, 576
uncertainty, 222
under, 321, 333
underlying economy, 147
union, 279–306
    misère partizan, 292
    tardy, 292
    urgent, 292, 296
    of variation sets, 571
United Kingdom, 786
units, 403, 718
universal machine, 847
unparted jungles, 205
unpredictability, 824
unproductivity, 719
unrestricted tallies, 294–298
unruly, 115
unsnappable vine, 533
untinted nodes, 199, 204

up, ↑, 65–74, 121, 152, 222, 224, 238,
    249, 641–643
up-second, 227–228, 321
up-onth, 355
upon, 321, 333, 355
upon∗ = delphinium, 321, 324, 333
uppitiness = atomic weight, 222, 233,
    236–238, 240–242
uppity, equally, 233
upset board, 297
upstart equality, 73
upsum, 316, 335, 337
urgent unions, 292, 296
Ussher, Archbishop James, 797, 815

value, 6–15, 18, 21–30, 38–41, 45–47
    mast = mean, 145, 147–150, 162
    startling, 40
    ¨versus average, 12, 145
values
    Childish Hackenbush, 45, 54
    Col, 39–41, 52
    Cram, 472
    Cutcake, 27
    Domineering, 118, 137–140
    entailed, 377–384
    exceptional, 89–91, 100, 107
    Hackenbush, 6–8, 21–22, 29–30
    irregular, 89–91, 100, 107
    loony, 524–525
    loopy, 367, 369–371
    Maundy Cake, 28
    nim-, 82–87, 89–98, 109–116, 185–
        190, 367–388, 390–391, 405–406,
        422, 431–434, 437–441, 443, 446,
        448–452, 454–456, 472–473,
        479–480, 487, 499, 503, 524,
        532–535, 545–549, 552–556, 563,
        570–572, 606, 687
    Nimstring, 525–526, 531, 547–549
    non-loopy, 369
    putative, 439
    rare, 109–111
    redwood bed, 211
    regular, 89–90
    Seating Boys-and-Girls, 131
    Seating Couples, 47
    Ski-Jumpers, 10–13
    small, 38, 167, 221–253
    Snort, 143, 175–179
    Streaking, 452
    Stripping, 452
    switch, 119–123
    Toads-and-Frogs, 14–15, 128, 132–
        136
    ¨vine, 541–543
Vandeventer, Joan, 815
vanishing reactions, 831–833, 837–
    838, 841

Varga, Tamas, 767
variation set, 215, 571
variations, 93
varieties, 342
victory, 159
vines, 530, 532–534, 541–543, 547
virus, 826
voracity, 835
Vout, Colin, 39

Wainwright, Robert T., 820, 850
Walker, R.J., 815
Wallis, John, 815
Walrus, 429–430
waltz, ·6, 95–96
wandering stones, 608, 610–611, 613–
    615, 618, 620, 622, 624, 627, 629
war, cold, 279–280
Ward, Steve, 829
warfare, jungle, 205
Watkins, Harold, 815
weak squares, 649
weight, see also atomic weight, 195, etc.
welt, 472
Welter function, 472–474, 476–481
Welter's Game, 407, 472–474, 476–481,
    505
Welter, C.P., 472, 505
Whim, 500
Whinihan, Michael J., 505
Whist, 255
White Knight, 58–61, 258
white stones, see wandering stones
White, Farmer, 141
Whitgift, Archbishop, 797
whole numbers, 21
wholeness of Hackenbush Hotchpotch,
    242
width, 160, 179–181
wiggly line, 526, 546–547
wild
    animals, 410–411
    games, 410–411, 414–415, 417–418
Wilder, Thornton, 394
Wilson, Neil Y., 116
Wilson, Richard M., 759, 768, 815
win quickly!, 258
Windows, 446–449
winners and losers, 684
winning post, 375, 391
wire and string puzzles, 741–753
Wirestring Puzzle, 743
Wirsing, Edward, 743
Wolves-and-Sheep, 631
women, beautiful and intriguing, 490
    other, 46
wonders, numberless, 117
worthy prelate, 797

working out a horse, 30
world
lost, 393–394
small, 221–253
worthwhile move option, 208–211
wrestling match, Paterson's, 794
Wright House, 352
Wyt Queens, 61, 76, 382, 407–408
Wythoff's Difference Rule, 76, 384

Wythoff's Game, 17, 62, 76, 407
Wythoff, W.A., 80

Yamasaki, Yōhei, 407, 410, 481, 499, 505
Yes!, 55, 111
You-nit, 575–576

Zeckendorf Algorithm, 501
Zeckendorf Theorem, 483
zero, 4, 9, 30, 43, 649
Zero place, 649
zero, deriders of, 451
Zetters, T.G.L., 676, 693
Zig-Zag, 598
zig-zags, Domineering, 173
zoo, Good Child's, 407

Song of Night

Also by Glenville Lovell

Fire in the Canes

Song of Night

Glenville Lovell

For Ianthe and Costella

With special thanks to Bahati for taking time to edit the early draft.
Thanks also to Denise Bukowski for taking up my cause.

Grateful acknowledgement is made to Anthony (The Mighty Gabby)
Carter for permission to reprint a portion of the lyrics of the calypso Jack.

Published by

Soho Press, Inc.
853 Broadway
New York, NY 10003

Library of Congress Cataloging in Publishing Data

Lovell, Glenville,
    Song of night / Glenville Lovell.
        p. cm.
    ISBN 1-56947-122-3 (alk. paper)
    I. Title.
PS3562.08624S66 1998
813'.54--dc21

97-53058
CIP

10 9 8 7 6 5 4 3 2 1

Chapter One

Ah, yes, behold! Like a band of renegade angels thrown down from Heaven they come stealing over the pawpaw trees behind Daisy Padmore's house. The woman in the window has been waiting for them since five-thirty, an hour ago. Her name is Cyan. A tranquil smile envelops her dark face. From her perch on the rotting window sill, she stands to welcome the fireflies.

The streetlamp at the top of the gap flickers when the fireflies appear as if some electronic mind were trying to welcome them, emitting a sound like pebbles shaken together in a bottle, then—nothing. Weekly, workmen from the Department of Communication and Works come to fix the streetlamp. Six weeks now. Every night the streetlamp flicks, then goes dead. Every night it is left to the fireflies to light the village.

They encircle the gallery and light up her garden. How luminous her yellow roses are in their firelight. Following their flight among the almond tree leaves, Cyan's eyes turn skyward. Once-threatening dark clouds in the east are beginning to fade. The moon will be rising early,

Clutching a bag of conkies tightly to her bosom, her elderly neighbor and godmother, Augusta Baptiste, steps intrepidly into this pool of fire to cross the grassy threshold that separates the two houses. On the edge of Cyan's garden she stops, smiles, and says hello in a quiet eager voice. She too has been waiting. Will this be the right moment?

Cyan's apparent disregard of her friendly greeting doesn't alarm her. They haven't been on speaking terms for a long time, but she hoped their little chat a few days before would've been the start of something new. A fresh beginning. Disappointed that morning, she has come to try again.

Still smiling, she calls Cyan's name louder, loud enough to disturb the fireflies' circular flow. The fireflies scatter. Cyan turns. The blankness of her eyes drowns the old woman's hope. Today will *not* be a good day for rekindling old friendships either. Head down, Augusta marches back to her house.

Cyan never saw the old woman that evening. She saw nothing in fact: not the young boy feeding a mangy dog in the street nor the girl leaning against Daisy Padmore's paling across the way while her boyfriend sat at her feet carelessly caressing her ankles. She saw nothing, that is, save the cloud of iridescent dust circling the gallery. She always saw the fireflies.

"Can you tell me where Cyan Cattlewash lives?"

"You mean that crazy girl who father get hang? She live down the gap by the standpipe, the fifth house down. A brown board and shingle house. It right next to a yellow house with a big soursop tree taller than a telephone pole. But don't pick none o' dem soursops, yuh hear. Them two women don't give 'way nothing. But what you want wid that girl? Wunna go lock she up? Officer. . ."

"Thank you."

. . .

Two recently recaned morris chairs, a mahogany center table, and two ladder-back chairs are all the furniture in the small front-house. A vase of freshly cut yellow roses sits on the center table. The drone of a small fan next to Cyan's foot drowns out banging at the back door. The banging stops and a man comes around to the front, passing on the lee side of the house under the soursop tree whose branches scrape the red galvanized-tin roof.

"You ain't hear me knocking at you back door?"

Cyan looks at the reedy balding man as though he were a stranger.

"Girl, what wrong with you? Is me, Lemuel. You look like you see a duppy!"

"You wanna come in?" Cyan asks in a flat lifeless voice.

"Come in, what! I come to tell you that a whole van-load of police-men out the front road asking if anybody know where you live."

"You sure you don't wanna come in?"

"Girl, you hear what I just tell you? You in some kinda trouble?"

"Trouble?"

"Lord have mercy!"

It is Saturday, three days after she sealed her bargain with the brown-skinned woman from Illinois whom she'd met by chance a few weeks earlier at Accra Beach.

Sitting alone under a clump of casuarina trees, the woman had that cold-clear skin American blacks from the snow-bound regions seemed to have, the kind of complexion Bajans who'd lived a long time in New York or Canada brought back home to show off along with the latest styles. Pale next to Cyan's deep sweat-shined hue. Cyan identified her as a potential customer right away. Resolutely, she settled her heavy clothes-laden suitcase at the woman's feet, noticing the woman's toes looked like they'd spent too much time-scrunched up in shoes a size too small.

The woman lowered her book before Cyan could read its title. Her eyes questioned the intrusion.

Cyan answered with learned brashness, "I have some nice bargains for you today, miss. All my clothes handmade of the best materials. All tie-dye done by local artists. The finest you go get anywhere on the island. I personally guarantee it." For good measure she added a cane-syrup-dipped smile to douse whatever impatience the woman might have left.

"Let's see what you have," invited the woman with a smile of her own not quite as practiced, but genuinely friendly.

With some difficulty Cyan bent down to open the battered suitcase Breeze had given her. The same Breeze who'd made love to her one night and flown to Germany next morning with a fat blonde. He'd never written and so didn't know she was about to drop his child. She wouldn't have told him anyway.

She did wish she'd been up to see him leave, to look at his back one last time, to see if he'd slinked away with his shoulders stooped like a beggar or if he'd left her with his six-foot frame straight up like a man. That night the sweet sweaty lovemaking had tired her out so much she'd fallen asleep right away, head on his smooth chest, too exhausted to feel him sliding from under her in the middle of the night or hear the spurt of his motorbike. Gone from her as silently as he'd come. Next morning she woke up with a head cold and a knot in her stomach she'd been working to untie ever since.

Cyan had sold only two inexpensive wrap skirts of African print that day for a total of fifty dollars. She needed to sell one of the more expensive pieces: the black-and-red tie-dyed dress for $200. . . or the sleeveless, ankle-length African-print dress trimmed with gold for $175. Fifty dollars was not enough for her materials and labor plus five hours of walking, stooping and standing in the sun with a big belly. She was tired. One good sale and she'd be able to go home.

The American eyed Cyan's distended belly and fingered her creations with interest. "They're all quite lovely," the woman said, caressing the tie-dyed dress. "You made them yourself?"

"Every last one. With me own hand."

She was a big woman, the American, about five-seven, with legs shaved to the edge of obsession. Some razor nicks were healing, many were quite fresh.

"You from the States, ain't you?" Cyan asked.

"Is it that easy to tell?"

"I meet a lot of Americans, I can usually tell them now. You enjoying our beautiful weather?"

"Yes, it's very nice."

"How long you here for?"

"I'm not sure yet. I only got here yesterday. Maybe a month or two, maybe longer. I don't really have a timetable. I expect to be here a little while, though."

Cyan stood up to stretch her back. Along with stiffness in her legs, back spasms were the only problem she'd had with the pregnancy. Mostly at night after she'd been stooping and bending all day.

"Are you alright?" the woman asked.

"Yes, I fine. Nothing to worry 'bout."

"You ought to sit down."

"No, it better if I stand up. If I sit down, it go be shite to get me back up."

"Looks like it's almost time. . . the baby."

"Oh! Yes, and I can't wait to drop this child outta me, yuh hear."

"I know what you mean. Some of our bodies just can't take the nine month strain. What's your name?"

"Night."

"Night. That's a strange name. Is that your real name?"

"No, but people start calling me Night from small 'cause I was so dark."

"Oh, one of those names some people find funny?"

"You get used to things like that round here quick, or your life become more of a hell than it gotta be. I used to it now. Actually I prefer it to my real name now. Night suit me. I like the night. Most beautiful part of the day. Nothing like starlight for walking on the beach."

"You mean moonlight."

"No, I mean starlight. Pitch black night 'cepting for the stars. That's the time I like."

Two briefcase-carrying vendors sauntered by and stopped a few feet away to monitor Cyan's progress with the American. Cyan warded them off with an icy stare.

"Look wunna better go 'long 'bout wunna business," she shooed. "This one belongs to me."

The vendors, two stocky men showing off their muscular bodies in swim trunks stuffed tight in the front, stood their ground.

Afraid the men might cause trouble for the pregnant girl, the American said, "I'd like to look at your things some more, but I've been sitting here in the sun for quite some time and I'm beginning to feel a bit uncomfortable. Why don't you come up to where I'm staying tomorrow around five in the evening? There you can show me your wares in a more comfortable environment."

"Where you staying? We could go now," said Cyan, not wanting to lose a potential sale.

"Well, it's some distance from here. I'm staying with a friend at a place called . . . I don't even remember the name. It's near a racetrack. On a tiny little road. Very quiet. I think it's called Dayrells Road."

"Oh, yes, I know down there."

"My friend is American. She lives here, though. She's a photographer and runs an art gallery," she said, rising and dusting sand from her legs.

"Wait a minute. . . You don't mean. . . you don't mean Koko?"

"Yes, I do. Do you know her? Good gracious me! It can't be possible. Are you, by any chance. . ."

"Yes, I's Cyan. You must be Amanda. She say you wasn't coming 'til next week."

"My goodness!" exclaimed Amanda. "This is unbelievable. Simply unbelievable. God is forever working miracles. I was supposed to arrive next week, but I had to take an earlier flight. How wonderful! Well, Cyan, now that we've met, no reason why we can't continue this conversation at the house."

She clasped the sweating girl to her like they were long lost friends.

Chapter Two

"Wunna hear what happen to Night?"

"No, what?"

"The police carry she 'way last night."

"Yuh lie!"

"Deed and faith, soulie gal. I get the word early this morning. And yuh won't guess from who?"

"Who?"

"Lemuel. The only body 'bout here she play she had time for. I always know that girl would come to ruin. As the saying goes, the fruit can't fall too far from the tree."

"What the police carry she 'way for?"

"Who knows. Could be anything with that girl. Could be anything. Maybe she thief something from one o' them tourists she say she do business with. She ain't got a uncle lock up this is years now for stealing?"

The sermon in Grady Lord's shop—which sold groceries, too, but mostly rum—was about to begin. Seven people in all were present—two women and five men. Missing was the preacher, the self-proclaimed spiritual leader of this flock who grazed on white rum, corned beef, and biscuits. Being rum drinkers didn't mean they forgot about giving sustenance to the spirit. The effort to get to church on Sundays was too much for them; still a Sunday didn't pass without them praising God. And lately they didn't begin drinking until Lemuel Armstrong—once a pastor with his own church, now an itinerant preacher—dropped in to the shop to deliver his short sermon. There was nothing like debating the existence of Heaven and Hell over a bottle of Mount Gay.

"A shame what happen to poor Night," one woman said.

"Yeah. Pity. Much people didn't like she, but I for one think she had a right to live she life the way she want. She ain't trouble nobody," the other woman said.

"'Cepting she mother."

"That mother of hers shoulda been shame to call sheself a mother."

"What I really want to know right now, though is what happen to Lemuel. He very late today. You sure the police ain't carry he 'way, too?"

The women were thirsty. Ordinarily a bit of ripe news would be enough to distract them—not today. Their throats were too dry. They hadn't had a drink since yesterday morning. Not even something as juicy as a rare police raid could slake their thirst.

"I hear Lemuel was there when the police come," a stout man said.

"See what I tell yuh. I bet Lemuel get carry 'way, too. Lord have his mercy. What we going do now?" a woman cried.

"He won't hear keep from up under that girl. That girl turn he dotish as a ram-sheep," said a tall man. "If he don't show he rass in here in half hour we go begin without he."

The women turned sharply to stare at the man.

"Now you know we don't begin a Sunday without Lemuel. What Lem-Lem do you, though? You like you jealous. He got a right to be dotish behind a woman if he want. Wunna men is all the same any-way. If you wasn't drunk all the time you would be dotish behind somebody right now, I would bet you that," one woman challenged.

"You making blasted sport. Me? No woman can't turn me so. After what that girl do to he, he still up under she like he's she underwear. That is why I stick to rum. Rum can't break yuh heart. I rather rum turn me foolish than be dotish behind a woman."

The door opened. They turned, but it was a little boy who'd come to buy flour. The tall man stroked his mustache and smiled.

The two sisters standing under the awning of the Universal Pentecostal Church of God should've had better things to think about on a Sunday morning with the blue sky perfectly pitched for bright sunshine and soft sea breezes.

Dressed like ibises in similar scarlet floral print, Augusta and Trinidad Baptiste had just listened to their pastor deliver a familiar sermon about the return of Jesus Christ to take his disciples to glory. They fully expected to be among the chosen, but today the sermon had been flat, not quite making it through the clutter of their thoughts. Cyan's arrest crowded out everything else.

Opening their parasols, they left the protection of the church for the short walk across the pasture to their house. The sun rained on them with a gentle yet annoying persistence. The halo it burned around the pair glowed and shimmered, daring the sisters to leave the shade of green parasols. Of fair complexion, these sisters feared the sun; they would close the parasols after stepping through their front door, not before.

Theirs was the sixth house on a dead-end lane—a *gap*—off the main road. Cyan's was fifth. The two houses were close enough for them to hear Cyan's sewing machine on a quiet night. Mango, gooseberry, soursop and golden apple trees bloomed in the backyard of their yellow two-bedroom chattel house. Out front was a tiny garden where they tried unsuccessfully to grow roses to match Cyan's.

Except for a few scattered wall houses, theirs was a typical dwelling in the village of Bottom Rock, a half mile or so from the town of

Oistins and a little more than five miles from Bridgetown, the capital of Barbados.

None of the gaps and tiny streets that crisscrossed the village had any address other than *the gap by the standpipe* and the like, but as in all the tiny villages on an island sold in tourist brochures as the friendliest in the Caribbean, names were unnecessary. Finding where anyone lived was always just a question away.

The gap was barely wide enough for two people to walk side by side; anytime a taxi came to pick the sisters up, which was seldom, the driver would have to park on the main road and blow the horn, hoping they would hear, or walk down the gap to knock on their house, which always annoyed the driver, young or old, but especially the old men in their crumpled caps and white shirts, who would mumble that it was the sisters' job to be waiting on the front road if they knew a car couldn't get to them. With parasols open, the sisters would walk single file behind the driver as if his words had simply bounced off their parasols.

It was a lively green village. Behind every house, fruit trees of some kind bloomed: mango, lime, sugarapple, breadfruit, coconut. In front of every house, flowers: roses, Joseph's coat, tiger lilies, Lady-in-the-Night. In every open space, grass or shrubs or trees offering shade from the scorching sun. Even the open pasture where young boys played cricket was ringed with trees for shade.

The village sprawled away from both sides of Highway 7 to take in several large areas of agricultural land once owned by plantations, since taken over for housing development by the government after the sugar industry died. People from all over were buying small plots to build houses. The small Pentecostal church the sisters attended sat on a hill overlooking the cricket pasture. Most people, however, traveled to the Anglican church in Oistins.

Black and mostly poor, the inhabitants followed many occupations: domestics, schoolteachers, laborers, fishermen, farmers and policemen. Oistins was within walking distance and the fish market, post office, police station, supermarkets, and numerous little shops, made it the center of the village's commercial life. Farmers sold their produce of potatoes, carrots, cucumbers, eddoes—and at Christmas, sorrel—there.

Instead of going inside to have their Sunday dinner of roast pork with peas and rice and diced beets, which Trinidad had prepared before they went to church, the sisters perched on the front step in the shade of the prolific almond tree at the corner of their house, whose wide, high branches kept the sun from turning their home into a cauldron.

The twelve o'clock sun was merciless. It had not rained in weeks. The sisters could smell heat rising from a parched earth. Leaves on the almond tree were wilting. A bare-necked fowl with dingy white feathers, its naked neck raw and red as if it had been fighting, picked away at brown half-baked grass. Otherwise the gap was dead. A greenish haze had settled on the village. The sisters glanced at each other knowingly. Thank God! Rain coming. Experience had taught them that whenever the haze came like this—a grainy green out of nowhere—rain was close.

May was known for its unpredictability in weather and other things too. Strange things always seemed to happen in the village in May.

One May morning six years ago, Poor-Boy Jackson walked through the village telling everybody his wife had given birth to a half-human, half-goat, and anybody willing to pay him five dollars could go see it. It was discovered later that Poor-Boy Jackson wasn't the father at all. His brother was. This caused one of the biggest bassa-bassas the village had seen in years. Every day Poor-Boy and his brother chased each other up and down with cutlasses until Poor-Boy's wife up with the child and took off. On May Day a year later, Suki Padmore, who lived opposite them, came home early from his job in the quarry and burned down his house, seemingly for no good reason. Suki claimed that a spirit had come to him and said his wife was in the house with another man and he was trying to smoke them out. A year later,

Cyan's father killed that young man in the dance hall on a rainy May night. And yesterday, May 9, Cyan had gotten herself arrested. For what?

The sisters knew patience. Someone would bring all the news to their door. Before the day was done they would know everything. They deserved to know. It had nothing to do with being nosy. After all, Cyan was Augusta's goddaughter and their neighbor on top of that. It was their duty to find out what was going on around them. Times were changing fast fast. Ignorance could mean death.

In the old days you could trust anybody, even strangers. But these weren't the old days. The sisters could remember a time when you could leave your door wide open, go to town, and come back to find your house exactly the way you left it. Sleep with a window open nowadays and thieves would steal the bed from under you. They blamed it all on Independence and America. When the country was British, these things didn't go on: stealing, drugs, slackness on the streets. America was the rage, especially with young people and politicians. America this and America that. Everybody wanted to get to America. All the TV shows came from there now, all the clothes, the music, and most of the tourists.

Tourism had replaced sugar at the head of the economy. Cane fields got chopped down for hotels; canecutters who couldn't hack it as waiters became limers. As people bolted for America to make their fortune, their houses were being rented to strangers. Money was becoming the basis of all relationships. Everything was now for sale. No longer could you go next door and borrow a cup of sugar or beg for a breadfruit or a few mangoes. You had to be able to pay. If your neighbor caught you picking her mangoes, it could cause a big kadooment. And the neighbor who just moved in from town might very well be a criminal.

They'd known Cyan all her life. Misguided? Yes. Wild? Absolutely. But a criminal? She was the daughter of a murderer, but that didn't make *her* a criminal. Still, with her bloodline you couldn't be sure.

"But yuh know, she wasn't the same since she father dead," said Augusta.

"Don't go blaming the dead for what happen to that own-way gal," said Trinidad.

"But yuh have to admit."

"Admit what? She father was a nice man 'til he marr'd up with that foreigner woman that come to this country from St. Lucia. If yuh want to blame anybody yuh gotta blame she. She shouldn'ta been allowed in the country in the first place."

"But yuh can't say that, Trin. Foreigners does do a lotta good for the country. Who would cut the canes if not for the foreigners? The men 'bout here want easy job in hotels now. I really think is the way she father dead. . . that had to affect she."

"All the same, Night had a mother, even if she was a foreigner. A mother suppose to guide her children. Look how many men does go 'long and leave them pickney behind 'bout this place. I don't see them doing the things that Night used to do. Yuh gotta blame the mother."

"I feel fuh Night, though, Trin. She used to be such a nice little girl. Remember? Remember when she used to come to our house and we used to take her to church and cook for she and tell she stories? And you teach her how to make her own clothes? Remember?"

At one o'clock Lemuel Armstrong stepped through the red door of Grady Lord's rum shop. Sweaty faces turned to greet him, not a smile among them. These castaways were too thirsty to smile. All they could manage were glazed grins.

Lemuel's peculiar angular walk, his height, his uncompromising stubbled face, his clear pinpoint eyes set in deep sockets like candles in a dry well were even more exaggerated today. His face drooped, and the skin appeared to sag from his jaw and chin. As he shuffled to the bar, his eyes burned with defeat.

A stroke at twenty-five had left his six-foot-four body frail and bent with a walk characterized by a stiff sideways shuffle. His shoulders would never achieve a square position, and when he tried to walk fast, he was crab-like. Still, he was a head taller than most of the men in the rum shop.

Awakened to God after the stroke, he had been a preacher at the Universal Pentecostal Church until just over a year ago when his congregation turned against him. Now he preached on street corners, in rum shops, in the bus stand. Wherever people congregated he took his message.

His friendship with Cyan began a short time after her father died. Today he knew the only message these lost souls were interested in involved the whereabouts of one Cyan Cattlewash. They wouldn't be getting much from him.

All eyes in the rum shop latched on to Lemuel as soon as his feet landed on the sandy floor. He was sucked into the shop by their unassailable hunger to know his secret. What happened to Cyan? What had she done?

"Where you been, man?" all hungry eyes seemed to ask.

But no one spoke. Hearts hardened by the brine of self-pity began to feel the depth of Lemuel's sorrow. They weren't sure if a tale was close to the telling; they could only hope. But every one of them sobered up; every drunk, to the last woman, stood tall—eyes clear, heart open. They were primed and ready. Never had Lemuel had such an eager audience. Not even in his crowning moments as the leader of the Pentecostal church.

If anyone were to tell Cyan's story—and he wasn't sure anyone could—it would begin with her father's death. That, in *his* mind, was where it all started.

But it had begun in fact with Cyan's birth. Or maybe even before.

Chapter Three

Precious Lord, take my hand
Lead me on through this land
I am tired, I am weak, I am sad.
Through the storm, through the night
Lead me on to the Light
Take my hand, Precious Lord
Lead me on.

She didn't cry when she was born. The nurse had slapped her behind five times and, when she didn't cry, had put her down and called her devil-child. For six months she didn't utter a sound. Not a giggle. Not one cry. Hungry, wet, or full-bellied, her demeanor was the same: a look so tranquil, everyone thought she might be retarded. When a squadron of fireflies flew into the house one evening when she was six months old and alighted on her hand, she laughed so loud her parents came running to her side screaming and carrying on like they'd won bingo. Startled, she began to cry. Eighteen years later, Cyan looked at her father's coffin and couldn't find any tears.

She walked out of Christ Church parish graveyard that evening thinking life could not possibly get worse. Never again would she be able to go to the beach with her father to watch him do handstands and push-ups. Their last time together, he'd cried. That sound, the harshness of his sobs, was still starlight-clear in her head. No discreet silent tears these, but a rending of the soul, with snot running from his nose like a child's, as if he were cleansing himself one last time. The next morning at five thirty-five he was hanged.

A fisherman all his life, with his own launch built by his own hands when he was barely twenty, her father was hanged for killing a man who'd flirted with his wife at a dance.

The whole village knew Steel to be a jealous man, with a temper to match the bonny-peppers he ate raw off the tree. He would light up the village on Saturday nights with his swearing if he came home to find his wife gone dancing without him. This made him the butt of jokes throughout the village. "What he so jealous 'bout, though? That poor-ass foreigner woman ain't worth what the dog left back."

Cyan's mother, Obe, tall and gangly, with wide earth-brown eyes and enormous pouting lips, was called a thousand different names behind her back, none of them flattering. *Foreigner, Obeah Woman,* and *Dog-Mouth* were particular favorites in Oistins fish market, where she sold Steel's catch.

The way Cyan looked at it, the man her father killed should've known not to flirt with Obe in front of Steel, especially since all of Oistins had seen them holding hands on the sea rocks behind the District Hospital when Steel was out on his boat. And Obe should've known better than to give the sweet-eye to another man, with Steel a few feet away at the bar. The fight that broke out in the dance that fateful Saturday night left the man, a youngster no more than twenty-five, mortally wounded from Steel's razor-sharp billfish beak, which he brought home still blood-smeared and gave Cyan to hide.

But hiding the weapon didn't help. With no money for a good lawyer, her father couldn't prove that when he left the dance to go home for his weapon, he didn't have murder on his mind. It was his return to the dance with a knife, and the fact that he'd slit the man's throat ear to ear and then stabbed him five times in the chest, that got him a noose instead of life with hard labor.

Cyan knew her father's blood ran hot. Her first taste of his anger came when she was eight. He'd caught her under the house-cellar examining ten-year-old Isaac Small's penis. Enraged, Steel had flogged them both with a heavy leather belt, leaving cuts and bruises all over her back and Isaac's. He then sent the boy to bring his father, Percy, who was so scared of Steel he never came.

But his sense of humor and energetic pursuit of life more than made up for that other side. A stocky, muscular man with a jucking-board for a stomach, his casual, almost condescending manner hid an extraordinarily competitive spirit. Constantly training for the annual road race around the island, he finished third one year, for which he got a silver cup. It excited him so to see his name scrawled on that tiny silver cup. Every year he vowed to claim the winner's gold trophy; when he lost, he'd get drunk and sit on the beach for hours until Cyan would beg him to come home. Then he'd flash two rows of perfect teeth, a smile as dazzling as the green sunlight reflecting off the sea, lift her on his shoulders, and run all the way home.

Cyan got to watch him train near their house on the beach called Miami as the sun turned over its watch. He'd sprint up and down the sand, his muscles gleaming like those of a black racehorse, while she watched from the cover of a casuarina. Sometimes he'd run backward or walk on his hands, knowing this made her laugh and clap. Afterward he'd take her swimming on his back or to PP's shop across from the supermarket in Oistins for ice cream. As he carried her on his neck past men loafing on the library steps, past Oistins Police Station, past rum shops, past fishermen cleaning their nets, the ribbing about his weak race record would come.

"Man, Steel, if you was to run the race wid she on you neck, you'd probably finish the same. Last."

"Steel, boy, you could stop wasting you time say you training. Come and fire one o' these likkers, man."

"Man, Steel, my grandmother with she chigger-foot could run faster than you."

Licking ice cream from her cup, he would promise to make them inscribe her name instead of his on the gold trophy when he won. She believed him, too, though she didn't really care if he won as long as she could continue to watch him train at twilight when the world was perfect.

From the cemetery she walked down Oistins Hill to PP's shop. She ordered an ice-cream cone and left before the misty-eyed owner, who'd hunted crabs in the swamp with her father, could ask about the turnout. What turnout? There was no turnout. Just herself, Celine, her sister; Celine's boyfriend; her mother; her aunt Zuma. . . and a few fishermen. More people had turned out to see her father arrested than buried. No Anglican priest would consent to bury him, though he was baptized in that faith; Lemuel Armstrong, pastor at Universal Pentecostal and a boyhood friend of Steel's came to their rescue.

Deliberately she crossed the street as lilting laughter eased out from the seclusion of a proud-looking evergreen. The culprit was an old woman sitting on a box at the bus stop. Who could she be laughing at?

She turned to drop a nasty word on the woman, noticed that the old lady was deeply engrossed in a letter, and bit her lip. Don't be so damn paranoid, she muttered to herself, stepping off the street and onto the beach.

Though she acted as if she had, she'd never gotten accustomed to the laughter that followed her father's arrest four years earlier—the biggest spectacle the village had yet seen. Bigger than the time the queen passed through the village on her way to Government House, when everyone lined the street waving the Barbados flag; even bigger than the time everybody stood by and watched Daisy Padmore beat her husband for burning down the house. When the police swooped in by the van-loads that Sunday morning to arrest her father, every Manjack and his cousin were on hand.

Taking off her shoes, Cyan immediately felt the day's accumulated heat rising from the dry sand. Spreading out quickly, her toes settled into the warmth, loving the depth of the buried heat that the sand would hoard well into the night, until long after the first lovers had lain in its hearth.

Eyes on the sand, she walked along searching for the footprints her father must've left there in defiance of the sea's power to obliterate anything it touched. His footprints would be right on top of *his* father's, evidence of the years they'd walked this beach and fished together in a boat so tiny it could scarcely hold the catch. Her grandfather, who'd disappeared at sea the year she was born, had had to work as a night-watchman on top of his job as a fisherman to make ends meet.

But she found no footprints to trace. Why hadn't history burned their memory into the sand? Why didn't the sea honor such pain? As unforgiving as ever, the sea licked at her feet, taking everything back, even the drops of ice cream that dripped down her hand onto her dress, then onto the sand.

The black dress her mother had lent her for the funeral hung from her bony frame like rags. Sand flies nipped her ankles; she stamped her feet angrily to dampen their enthusiasm, to no avail. Homing in on the sweet liquid dripping onto her feet, the tiny insects, invisible in the waning light, had already surrounded her.

Ahead of her the sun's molten eye was closing slowly, leaving gold nuggets embedded in the clouds. Gulls in training unfurled and flapped their wings in front of her, making stop-and-go landings on the sand.

The front of the dress was now white-streaked as though some impressionist painter had designed it. Cyan decided there and then she would never wear another black dress as long as she lived.

She dropped the ice cream. Unzipping the dress, she let it crumple to the ground and stepped out of it. Good riddance. To dress and sand flies. The white cotton petticoat she had on, also her mother's, smelled of mothballs. In the front was a tiny hole that looked like it could've been made by a hot teardrop.

She looked at the crumpled dress, wondering what to do with it. Fold it up and take it home or, leave it there to be filled with seawater? Leave it. She walked on as a wave claimed the dress, leaving no memory of it in the sand as it receded from the shore.

There was no one else on the beach. She walked on past the fish market, past boats under repair sprawled in the sand, past the jetty where her father's boat, *Night*—since sold to help pay the one lawyer who would accept what little money they could offer for Steel's defense—used to be moored, past high rocks behind guest houses, and onto a long stretch of beach approaching some hotels. This was where her father would train if Miami was too crowded. She could still see him running effortlessly across the warm sand, black back rippling. As the waves rolled up, he would raise his legs high, skimming the water like a flying fish.

Cyan knew she'd profited from not having a brother to vie for her father's attention. Just one sister. And because Celine's head was always in a book, Cyan got to attend cricket matches alone with her father. By the time she was ten, he'd taught her the names of all the players on the West Indies cricket team and which island they hailed from; she could bowl overhand and underarm, knew the difference between off-spin and leg-spin, understood a hook was more than something to catch fish and was aware that of all the teams they faced, the West Indies enjoyed thrashing England the most.

Something soft and sticky clung to her toes. She looked down. Tar! Tar on her beach? What next? Had he been there, her father would've carried on about pollution destroying the reefs and killing the fish, which made it harder for fishermen to eke out a living. She'd heard this lament from him a million times. It had reached the state of a mantra. He would never have let her leave that ice cream on the beach. Any little thing could start him up: a youth urinating, debris from a picnic. The noxious smell from hotel waste disposed in the sea made him madder than hell. Tourism will eat this country up, he'd say. "Everything in the country depend on the sea living. If the sea dead, Barbados dead. And tourism go kill the sea." And while other fishermen happily sold their catch at better prices to hotels, her father refused. Vilified by them as ignorant and backward, pronounced foolish by his wife, who told him righteousness couldn't put food on their table, he stuck to his guns. No fish he caught ever landed on a hotel plate. Why was her father such an angry man, she often pondered. Was it life? Was it his blood?

And she wondered if he'd prayed or begged God for mercy in his last moments. What went through his mind that split second before his wind stopped? Did he think about her and Celine? She'd been angry at her father since the day he was arrested. More so now. So angry she'd willed herself not to cry for him.

The stretch of beach she was now on was partially hidden from the world by a forest of hotels, casuarinas and sea-almond trees. The sun's weak red rays bounced off broad sea-almond leaves and rode waves out to sea. In this cocoon of dull light, leaves and water, a place where lovers with imagination could run wild, Cyan glimpsed a blur in the distance. She closed slowly on the blur until it became a man.

In three-quarter length khakis, back bared to the sun, the scrawny brown-skinned man almost disappeared into the background. Bobbing and weaving like a hummingbird, he was furiously painting on a large canvas. Every few moments he changed his perspective, looking at the canvas from this angle, then that angle, stooping, squinting, then daubing the brush with paint, making a few lightning stabs at the canvas, then stepping back for another look. She watched, bewildered and fascinated by this strange choreography: stoop, squint, stab, stop. Again. Suddenly he turned, looked in her direction, and, as if he hadn't seen her, bent down to add more paint to his palette.

She inched up. Close enough to make out that he was painting a man standing alone on the stern of a fishing boat. In the picture, huge waves were about to crush the man. Then the painter stopped, hitched up his pants, and turned to reproach her with cold eyes.

"What do you want?" he said.

She wanted to tell him to take his paints, his canvas and his scrawny rass off her beach so she could be alone with her memories. But something about the painting drew her. Smiling, edging still closer, she said nothing.

Downwind the scent of his sweat was high. His tiny shoulders seemed to start at his oversized ears, which flared away from a head of close-cropped reddish hair, like wings. His ribs printed through his skin and his flat-as-a-bake ass offered no assistance to the shorts which hung from his hips much like the black dress had hung from her body. The flared nostrils, large mouth, and black cold-edged eyes behind large horn-rimmed spectacles made him somewhat frightening. Under the easel lay a bunch of recently broken sea-egg shells. Juice oozed from them. He was an ugly thing but had good taste. Sea-eggs were her father's favorite dish.

With a flourish of arms he turned once more to his canvas. She watched as he dabbed green onto the wave, but it was the man on the boat, standing open-faced to the sea, who locked her astonished gaze. It was her father.

She blinked. Her father had been so large in her mind all day it would've been easy enough to superimpose his likeness on a picture, especially since she'd just seen his face in that plain gray coffin her family could barely afford.

• • •

Hard trancelike concentration on the face in the picture—the resemblance to her father as sure as the lazy waves lapping her feet. Everything alive now with dream. The waves dragging her deeper in, nearer the boat. Her smiling father stepping down into the water to lift her onto the deck. Now the boat beginning to move. Where we going? she wanting to ask him. And huge waves crashing on them, washing them, but not moving them. Steady, steady as always, her father steering now, not smiling anymore, but serious as the time he took her out fishing one starlit night. Now the boat passing through diaphanous mist, through white rain, through the maw of a scarlet night lurid with duppies and leviathans. Dauntless into arid light, sailing without wind, without motor. Hearing whispers. Her eyes feeling big and wide, like they'll never close again, like she can see everything. Her head feeling large, infinite, like she knows everything. Excited, turning to say something to her father, the truth of this vision is now revealed. Her father has disappeared. She's alone on the boat.

She's alone in the world.

A burning to learn if this scruffy red man knew her father lifted her out of herself, out of the stupor of her sorrowful dream, and she spoke.

"Who that you painting?" she asked.

The painter kept up his steady bobbing and weaving.

"You hear me? Who that you painting? That look like somebody I know."

He stopped, dropped the brush into a small skillet near the easel, and turned to face her.

The sun's red glare set the man aflame. The noise of a jet ski broke the calm as it raced around the bend where the beach curved away from them, skipping over whitecapped waves. Two more skis followed in quick succession. The noise faded, and the hushed splash of wave-trains methodically coming and leaving reconnected them.

"And who does this painting remind you of, might I ask?" said the painter dryly.

"My father. You knew him?"

"What is his name?"

"Chesterfield. Chesterfield Cattlewash, but everybody call him Steel."

"No, can't say the name rings any bells. I would remember a name like that. Now, if you don't mind, I'm rather busy. I'd prefer that you find someone else to bother."

Cyan was surprised that the stranger's voice did not match his appearance. And then she was glad. He spoke with educated elegance, taking time to measure his words as if he were laying them out on a bed to get dressed in. The only person in her family with any education was Celine. She suspected Celine talked like this when she was in Bridgetown at Queens College High School, but at home she spoke like everyone else, in raw Bajan.

"You sure you ain't know him? How come you painting his picture if you ain't know him?"

The man was squatting now, examining the painting intently. He stood slowly and spat hard in the sand.

He turned to face her, saw the defiance in her eyes, saw that her long neck had stiffened, that her wide sea-cat eyes were watery, and then realized she was half-naked. Nothing on but a petticoat. Seemed too big for her, too. He looked at her lanky body, at her flat nose and pouty black lips, and couldn't hold back a smile. This young girl must have a remarkable sense of herself to walk along the beach in noth-ing but a petticoat, unafraid to challenge a stranger going about his business.

"Look, I don't know your father, never met him, but would certainly like to someday if he's as straightforward as you."

"You can't meet him 'cause he dead."

A low-flying jet spread its silver shadow over them. They both looked up, saw its white underbelly, and watched its noisy disappearance over the trees. In a few minutes it would land and spit out its load of pleasure-seekers from North America or Europe, bringing riches and resentment.

"I wish I could tell you I'd known him." Then his eyes softened, and he set his brush down on a piece of dirty linen on the sand.

"Is that why you look so sad? It happened recently?"

She nodded.

He didn't know her. She didn't know him. What level of communion can strangers reach as to a father's death? He searched for platitudes.

"I'm sorry about your father," he said.

The heavy pause that followed lasted a few minutes. The stranger looked at her with deep penetration as if he were taking a snapshot of her soul. She looked around, suddenly feeling uneasy. Her eyes found the sky. The sun had finally broken the horizon's pane, releasing darkness.

"Look, mistuh, sorry I bother you," Cyan said.

She walked off slowly, unwilling to release him now that she'd gotten his attention. There was something left undone between them. She turned around after she'd taken a few hesitant steps.

"If I was to beg you hard, would you give me that picture?" she said.

"Does it really resemble your father that much?"

"It everything of him. You gotta have meet him somewhere."

"Perhaps. I don't know. I've been working on this for six months. It's almost done. I think it's my best work."

"So you ain't answer my question. You would give it to me?"

"I don't know. It'd be hard to just give it away like that."

"I ain't got no money and I ain't got nothing to give you."

"What's your name?"

"Cyan."

"How old are you?"

"Eighteen."

"Are you in school?"

"I done left school so long I forget what a school look like."

The stranger laughed. He walked to her, his face friendly and open.

"Well, I'll tell you what. I'll give you the painting if you agree to come work for me."

"Work for you doing what, bo?"

"Taking care of my house."

"You mean like a maid?"

"If you want to call it that."

"Look, I ain't nobody maid, you understand that. My father work for heself, my mother work for sheself. And I ain't working for nobody but meself when I ready. Besides, I don't believe you could afford no maid. How you could afford a maid? You's a picture painter. Who does buy them things so you could afford a maid? Bajans don't buy them kinda things so."

The scowl returned to the painter's face. He turned halfway around, then thrust his hands into his pockets and walked back to his canvas.

"I thought you wanted the painting."

"You go give it to me first?"

"You don't trust me."

"Why should I trust you? I ain't know you from Adam."

"That didn't stop you from begging me for the picture."

Out of his back pocket he pulled a thin brown leather wallet, then from it drew a gray card which he handed to her.

"What this for?" she asked.

"My name and address. If you change your mind, let me know."

He returned to his painting with such fervor that she could not help but stand and admire him. Then she read the card:

DR. JONATHAN MAYHEM
WAVERLY AVENUE
BATTS ROCK, ST. MICHAEL.

• • •

The wailing from her mother's room was so loud it frightened away the fireflies that circled briefly around their house and then left. The house smelled of gladiola. She'd cut some to make a wreath, changed her mind, and left them in a jug of water on the shed-roof table. In the bedroom she shared with Celine, wilted rose petals floated about the bed and the floor.

Unable to find her sister anywhere in the house, she paused at the door of her mother's room. Stretched long across the bed like withered sugarcane, her mother was carrying on like there was no tomorrow, something Cyan could not understand. Obe had shown little emotion when Steel was sentenced. Now look at her. Acting like she was facing death herself.

Consoling Obe was Zuma, the only one of her father's sisters who hadn't emigrated to America. None of the others had bothered to come back for the funeral. Cyan saw little of Zuma, a brusque loud woman, because Zuma hated Obe and rarely visited. Anytime those two came within sight of each other, a big cuss-out would start. United by death, just those two enemies, the consoler and the seemingly inconsolable, were in the house.

A family should be like a hand of green bananas. So tight, if you cut one, the blood ran all over the rest. Not her family. Hers was more like different-color fish in the same sea. Couldn't even mourn together. They'd left the cemetery in different directions: Celine with her boyfriend, and Obe . . . Obe left before the coffin was even in the ground good, which Cyan would never forgive her for doing.

But it had not always been so. She remembered those Sunday afternoons when the four of them, forced out of the house by the heat after a big meal of fried fish and rice, used to sit under the wings of the huge akee tree that separated their house from Jewl Bright's to poke fun at people coming home from church. This one's dress too short, that one too fat to wear white, this one's legs too bandy to wear knee-length, that other one looked like a pumpkin in green.

Saturday, the busiest fish-selling day, would catch them in the market feverishly working together to keep the hordes of customers satisfied. After Celine got into Queens College, it became the three of them (Steel said it wouldn't look good for a high school girl to be selling fish in the market). Some Saturdays her father never got the fish to the stall, where she and her mother would be waiting. As people swarmed him, he'd sell the fish right there on the beach at prices far cheaper than the prevailing rate or he'd trust people to pay him later. Her mother would chide him all evening into the night for his lack of business sense, for "giving way the fish to his blasted women," for "not realizing he got three mouths to feed." After the tongue-lashing, her father would disappear, ostensibly to have a drink with friends, and not return until next morning—drunk.

She was about nine the first time she saw her father drunk on a Sunday morning. Her bedroom was in the back part of the two-bedroom gabled house and pointed east. In those days there were no blinds at their bedroom windows. Her sister could sleep through lean morning heat, but almost every day before six-thirty, sunshine would nudge Cyan out of bed.

That morning the sun had been kept at bay by puffy gray clouds that filtered soft light into the room. Unmistakable for its fullness, her father's voice roused her as he passed under her bedroom window on his way to the paling door. He was singing at the top of his lungs.

She opened the window only to see him fall headlong into the gate. To break his fall he grabbed the spinach vine frothing over the fence. Too slight to bear his weight, the vine popped, and he struck his head on the thick limestone block used to keep the gate closed.

He got up cursing. His head was bleeding. He pulled furiously on the door. Latched from the inside, the gate rattled and shook; the whole paling trembled under his assault. The doorpost began to give way as he thundered for someone to open up. Cyan ran to the gate as her mother came out of her room, also cursing. By the time Cyan got to the backyard, her father had ripped the door, post and all, away from the paling. He stumbled into the yard and greeted her with a wide grin, then with a great flourish vomited at her feet. Putrid fumes wafted up from the yellow bile slowly spreading like oil on the gravel.

"What you doing up so early, Night?" her father managed through his drool.

"Is seven o'clock in the morning, Pa."

"Seven o'clock and the sun ain't up yet?" He raised his head to the sky. "God! What happen to you this morning? Where the rass you hiding the sun? Is seven o'clock and you ain't send the sun out yet. Make me get home late. I think is five o'clock and is already seven." And he began to laugh, a wild common-class laugh that filled the yard and set the hens cackling.

"But looka you, though, nuh."

The voice full of contempt came from behind Cyan. It was her mother.

"Look at you, yuh w⁁fless, drunk pig! What the rass yuh had to break off the gate for? It ain't bad enough that yuh come here smelling like yuh fall in somebody toilet. You had to go and destroy the blasted door, too."

"I break off the door? I ain't break off no door, hear? The door was already break off before I touch it."

"Is you have to put it back on, so I don't give a damn. And if you know what good for you, you better go back where you come from and don't come 'bout here to aggravate my soul. If I didn't have these children to think 'bout I would pack my bags and go 'long back where I come from. But you soon know which God you serving. Cyan, come on in here and leave that ungrateful dog out there to lick up his own vomit."

Her mother stood in the kitchen door waiting for Cyan to heed her command, but Cyan was transfixed by the image of her father, weak-kneed, weak-stomached, eyes bulging with a dark vacant look. She'd never seen him like this before. This was unforgivable.

"Cyan, you hear what I tell you?"

"Go 'long when yuh mother call yuh, child," her father mouthed, each word splattered with a thick sour odor. Cyan felt sick; she wanted to cry. This was not her father. Impostor! She wanted to spit on him, kick him out through the gaping space where the door once kept the world out of their yard. She wanted to hug and kiss him, to wash his drooling face, to wipe the blood from his forehead, to straighten his back.

Later, after he'd sleep-sweated the alcohol from his system, he wanted to take her to the beach, but she begged off with a pain in her side. But the real pain was in a place she could not touch, in a place she could not name or even really feel. It was there, haunting, unreachable, and frightening.

But her father, his wits fully about him now, saw through her pretense. She tried to resist his attempt to put her on his lap.

"Girl, you think you too big to sit on me lap?" He laughed.

He became soulful, apologetic. He'd erred in a profound way in his daughter's eyes, and he knew that as young as she was, Cyan could be very unforgiving.

"Daddy wasn't really drunk this morning, you hear," he said. "Is a cold I catch last night that make me throw up."

"A cold make you throw up like that?"

"Daddy feeling a lot better now. Your daddy ain't no drunk, you hear?"

"All right, Pa."

"Don't let nobody ever tell you nothing bad 'bout your daddy, hear?"

"All right, Pa."

"Now you ready to go to the beach?"

"My side hurting me, Pa."

"You side hurting you? Which side? This one?" He tickled her left side. "Or this one?" He tickled her right side.

A tiny giggle slipped out. She tried to grab it back but it exploded. She gave in to the laughter. In seconds she was splayed over his lap laughing wildly. Eager to join the game, Celine fell on top of her, hoping to siphon off a dose of affection. This set off a battle between them for their father's tickles. Two years younger, but stockier and stronger, Celine finally pushed Cyan away only to find that Steel had grown tired of the game.

Chapter Four

"I didn't think you'd come," the painter said.

Cyan heard him but couldn't answer. She was too busy gawking at the fine furniture in the house on Batts Rock, at the size of the living room and at the walls that spoke her name. Splashed on each wall were paintings and photographs of every imaginable scene: young men squatting in a yard nicking dice; old men gazing wistfully at the sea; fishermen, cane-cutters, and hawkers pleading with their eyes. Each scene reminded her of a moment she'd lived. She was thrilled.

"You do all these pictures?" she asked.

"Some of them. Some I bought. The photographs are my wife's. I went back to the beach to look for you, you know. Several times in fact, but I never found you."

Since she'd last seen him, he'd grown a pencil-thin mustache. Face thinner, eyes sharper and clearer, he reminded her of a mongoose.

"You find me easy enough the first time."

"I thought it was the other way around."

She rolled her eyeballs and cast him a doubtful look but said nothing.

He smiled and walked away, muttering to himself, along the tight hallway.

Cyan followed him into the dining room, whose walls were also covered with paintings, past a long shiny mahogany table stained so dark it looked purple, out to a patio overlooking the sea.

A woman with soft-looking honey-colored skin lay prone on a thick blue blanket. Nothing on but a white bikini bottom. No top. A red bandanna corkscrewed around her head.

Jonathan knelt down and shook her firmly. No response. He shook her twice more, which netted the same non-response. He stood up, smiling sheepishly.

"I wanted you to meet my wife, but she's had a little too much to drink," he apologized.

"You mean she drunk?"

"No, she's not drunk. She sleeps very deeply when she drinks."

"Sounds like she drunk to me. She sleeping hard hard like a drunkard. That's the way my father used to sleep when he drunk."

Jonathan took in the obstinate set of Cyan's mouth and saw the futility of arguing with her.

Cyan eyed the smooth-skinned woman again, trying to guess her age. Angular face glossed with sweat, thin lips creased at the edges as though she were smiling, thick but firm legs. Fortyish. Then Cyan noticed that the woman had no eyebrows. How odd? Why would anybody shave their eyebrows?

She turned to Jonathan impatiently. "What 'bout the picture for me, man?"

"Will you be taking the job? I really need somebody. You see how big this place is. We're both very busy."

"Why you ain't say you was a doctor instead of letting me think you was just a picture painter?"

"I *am* just a painter when I'm painting."

"You know what I mean, man. The way you look out there that day, you ain't look like you was nuhbody."

"Does that mean you'll be working for me?"

"Wunna got children?"

He shook his head.

"Wunna shoulda get a smaller place. Why wunna need such a big house for just the two of you?"

"Yes, I suppose you're right, but I like this house. It's big enough that Koko and I don't get in each other's way. And look at that view! I wouldn't give up this view for all the tea in China. I grew up in St. George and always wanted to live by the sea."

"The picture done?"

Jonathan smiled lazily and tilted his head the way a curious animal observes the appearance of an alien in its habitat with a mixture of suspicion and excitement.

Her smile also was one of suspicion and excitement. She liked this big house by the sea, the comeliness of the surroundings: fishing boats angling on shimmering blue-green water, gulls circling in the sky. But she didn't know yet what to make of the expression in his eyes. Three weeks gone now since their chance meeting on the beach. Why hadn't he gotten somebody else to work for him? What was so special about her? Being a doctor, he'd have no problem finding somebody to clean his house. One notice in the paper would draw tons of women from all over the island. But he wanted her enough to have gone looking for her again and again.

The picture, more than the job, had brought her here, though it was time for her to get a job. She'd always thought she'd work alongside her mother and father. With her father gone, her mother had managed to keep working in the fish market scaling and boning fish bound for hotels. But Cyan wasn't sure she wanted to work near fish again.

"Actually the painting isn't quite finished yet," Jonathan said.

"What you mean it ain't finish? Man, you like you making sport. You like you just throwing out bait to see who you could catch."

"No, no, not at all. It's almost done. Wait here. I'll be right back," he said, slipping through the sliding glass doors and into the house.

Voices beneath the patio drew her. Bare-backed little boys were skipping about jagged rocks below. Every thirty seconds the sea hurled itself against the brown-greenish rocks as if attempting to dislodge the boys. Sweat and seawater mixed to form a leathery sheen on their backs, which shone like turtle shells.

At first she couldn't tell what they were doing. Then she saw the little bird—too young to fly or injured—hopping about in their midst. It was rusty green, the color of the rocks, and the boys were exhorting it to fly.

A boat horn blared. Cyan looked up to see a fishing boat and a yacht about to collide on the water. The blue fishing boat tried to swerve. Too late. Its port side smashed against the hull of the yacht, hurling a man who'd been standing on the bow of the yacht headlong into the water. Both boats came to a locked standstill.

A frantic scene now: motorboats and jet skis racing to the spot; an old man in a pirogue paddling wildly to reach the man, who was waving his hands helplessly. They arrived just in time.

The noise of the crash had jarred the woman awake. She sat up and stared at Cyan bewildered. Eyes red and hard.

"Who're you?" she asked. "Was that an explosion I heard, or am I having a bad dream?"

"I ain't know if you having a bad dream or not, but I won't be surprise," Cyan replied.

The woman glowered, not sure whether Cyan's sauciness was malicious or just an example of the peculiar wit of Bajans.

Jonathan's return sliced the taut stares strung between the women. Attention swerved to the large canvas under his arm.

"You're up, dear. Have you met Cyan?"

"I'm not sure I really want to meet her," the woman replied.

"This is the young woman I told you about. The one on the beach."

"She's young enough, but a little on the skinny side, even for you, dear," she said, walking off into the house, leaving Cyan to stare after her mystified.

"What my skinniness do she?" Cyan said.

"Don't mind my wife. She's American. You know how Americans can be. They really don't understand us."

"So how come you went and marr'd one if them don't understand we?"

A fervid cry swelled from the rocks below. Cyan leaned over to look. The boys were huddled tightly together, arms raised, eyes on the mottled sky. Against the background of broken multicolored clouds she could barely make out the little bird struggling to stay aloft. She wanted to let out a cry of her own, then thought better of it.

She stepped off the bus into a downpour. Accompanied by a barking wind intent on blowing the rain up her nostrils, the pebble-sized raindrops struck her such hard blows, they reminded her of Obe's heavy hand.

How could anyone as bony as her mother have hands that heavy and hard? Hands like iron. When Obe hit you, whether a slap across the face or a whack on the back with a belt, the pain stayed with you for days. You'd go to sleep hurting and wake up in deeper agony. Obe's blows penetrated more than skin, they took over the brain, swelled it, rendering you feeble, weepy, and frail. Thank goodness Obe hadn't hit her since she was fourteen. In the years preceding, her mother seemed to get uncommon pleasure from whaling up both her back and Celine's. Belt in hand, her mother would say, "This go hurt me more than it go hurt you." Cyan hated those words. They meant she would be getting twice as many blows as normal.

If her father had been out drinking a Saturday night and didn't come home in time next morning for his scheduled tongue-lashing, the slightest thing she or Celine did could provoke a beating: Forgetting to sweep the house or feed the fowls before setting off for Sunday school or the beach got them called back for some hot blows delivered while the chore was being completed; leaving the back gate open for mongooses to come in and suck the fowl eggs or leaving scales on the fly-ing fish brought a cuff across the head.

Celine often laughed in her mother's face. Cyan took the beatings harder than her sister and would cry herself into uncontrollable fits, with thick snot running down her chin. At this, Obe would fly into a spiteful frenzy, accusing Cyan of faking, of trying to play on her father's feelings. And that meant more blows.

All her father would say when she showed him the welts and bruises was that she must've done something to deserve it.

The three cardinal sins in Obe's house were stealing, lying, and get-ting with child. Violate the first and your fingers would taste fire, the second and your teeth would be knocked down your throat, and the last would result in eviction.

The year Cyan turned fourteen, their neighbor, her own godmother, Augusta Baptiste, had accused her of stealing. The girl denied it, but her mother didn't believe her and decided to make an example of Cyan.

With the accused screaming for her father who wasn't home, and with Celine looking on in horror, Obe dragged her elder daughter to the kerosene stove, where a wild flame was already licking the air. She held the fingers of Cyan's right hand over the fire for what seemed like forever. And then gave her a flogging on top of that.

Running pain kept Cyan awake all night. Rushed to the hospital next morning with a runaway fever and swollen fingers covered with large blisters, she told the doctor she burned herself by accident.

When Steel found out, he got so angry, he couldn't speak. He started to stumble around the house like he was drunk, mumbling and stut-tering until he found his billfish beak, which he held to Obe's throat, threatening to kill her if she ever touched Cyan again. Her mother never had. But Cyan never forgave her mother or Augusta. Every time she looked at the scars on her right hand, she thought of burning down her godmother's house.

• • •

Soaked head to toe, she stepped into the quiet house leaving the rain behind. She stripped and dried off in the bedroom, dropping the wet dress on the floor.

Besides being a fisherman, her father had been a skilled carpenter. Birds in flight were carved into the mahogany headboard he'd made for her bed. Some nights she'd pretend she could hear the birds singing or their wings beating the air, and that sound would put her to sleep. She grabbed her blue home-dress from the headboard, stepped into it, and was about to leave the room when she looked up and saw in one corner a tiny wasp's nest under construction.

The many nails protruding from the ceiling made their house a favorite with pioneering wasps. Taught by her father, she'd become an expert at thwarting their enterprise with smoke for large nests or a long stick for small ones. This one was the long-stick variety. Armed with a broomstick and a paper bag, she dislodged the half-built catacomb. When they were children, she and Celine had saved the nests in boxes until the baby wasps were ready to break out of their individual tombs. And though it was dangerous to let them go free they did anyway. And then they'd laugh at each other as the freed wasps flew around their heads looking to reward them for their kindness.

She disposed of the nest in a pan of kerosene in the kitchen and then made *mauby*. Her parched throat welcomed the sweet bitter taste.

The drone of the rain on the galvanized roof had an insistent beat. She sat down on the bed to listen and fell asleep.

Hunger wakes her around six. She makes a pot of split-pea soup with lots of cabbage. The rain has stopped. A shoal of fireflies drifts past her window. The sisters next door, Trinidad and Augusta, are singing in their rich sopranos. She has almost forgotten what lovely voices they have. But even though their voices evoke goosebumps on her skin, their singing still can't make up for what Augusta has done to her.

She eats in the kitchen door looking out onto the backyard and begins to reflect on the day. In the gloaming the passion fruit and spinach vines creeping over the paling cast fine seinelike shadows on the backyard stones.

She already knows where her first week's pay will go. Forty-five dollars a week isn't much to divide, but she'll have to give her mother something. The rest will be spent on clothes for her and Celine. And then she'll put some money aside to send Celine to evening school.

The doctor's yellow-skinned wife? No problem. Dealing with her mother has prepared her for anybody, even nasty Yankees. The Yankee bitch better get used to seeing her there four days a week. If the doctor doesn't care that hiring her upset his wife, why should she? What reason did the woman have for being so rude this afternoon? Think because she's American, she could treat people like dirt? No nasty Yankee woman was going to come here and treat her so, eyebrows or no eyebrows. She already has a plan to deal with the bitch if she gets on her nerves. A pot of water always on the stove. Just in case.

She and Celine call their mother's room *the hotel* because they are forbidden to enter it when she isn't home. The hotel's bed is big and firm. She can never resist lying in it any chance she gets. Such a great place to daydream.

Midnight brings her mother home with company. Lying in the hotel's bed, Cyan hears the front door open and feels laughter gush in with the subtlety of a hurricane.

Sitting up, she listens to her mother and the man-friend, their reckless laughter.

Her mother totters into the bedroom on loose legs and looks hard at Cyan like something in her eyes is preventing her from seeing well.

"Girl, what the rass you doing in my bed? Ain't I tell you all not to go in my bed? Get up and get out!"

"Who that man out there?" Cyan asks, coolly ignoring her mother's command.

"That ain't none o' you damn business. Get your skinny little tail outta me bed. That sister o' yours in here?"

"No. She at she boyfriend, you know that."

"That boy go soon do for her. And what the rass you was cooking that got the house smell so? You been cooking that cabbage again? Ain't I tell you if you go cook cabbage to make sure you carry out the garbage when you finish? How you expect people to have company with the house smelling like this?"

Any other time an attempt to censure her food choices would start a fight. Not tonight. Not when she has such good news. But first, to get rid of that man. She won't share the news with him.

"Ma," Cyan begins excitedly, "I got something to tell you. Something good. But I ain't telling you 'til you make that man leave."

"Girl, you must be mad to talk to me so fresh. You head can't be on straight. You better understand right now, Cyan. I am the woman in here. I make the rules, not you."

And then Cyan takes in how spicy Obe looks in the yellow pants suit that had come in a box from one of her aunts in America four years ago, the same week her father was arrested. The sparkle in her eyes outshines the bald overhead light. Obe is also wearing more makeup than usual, fake pearls, and enough bangles to start a percussion band. She's never seen Obe look more carefree, more sexy. That thought displeases her and makes her hate the stranger's presence even more.

"I hope you ain't plan to let him sleep here," Cyan says, bristling.

She sees the slap coming but can't get out of the way. Her mother's hand collides with her face in a clang of bangles, the sting vibrating in the taut silence that follows. On that cue the man sticks his head into the room.

"You girls having a good time?" he asks with a smirk.

Eyes clouded with tears, Cyan looks up at the man. The doorway bulges with his massiveness. She wants to scream at him to get out of her father's house, but the slap has welded her lips together.

She rubs her lips as she gets up, trying to wipe away the sting.

"Where you going? I ain't done with you yet," her mother says.

Now standing between her mother and the man, she feels her nose begin to smart at the stench of stale rum.

"What it is you got to tell me?"

"I forget," Cyan answers sullenly.

"Girl, get out me sight before I have to kill you, yuh hear!"

Back in her room she cannot sleep. This is the first time her mother has hit her since the burning. She massages the side of her face with her right hand, the one with the scarred fingers. As if the fire that had withered them had been captured beneath the scorched skin, her fingers kindle her face to life again. She can now taste the salt left on her mouth by her mother's sweaty palm.

Her mother has broken the truce. Bechrist it go be war from now on. I too old for this shite. No more. I ain't taking no more humiliation from she.

She starts to cry, more to drown out the sounds of laughter and pleasure coming from her mother's room than anything else.

Chapter Five

$\mathcal{G}$ray dawn shattered the silent darkness hanging over the village. It surprised Percy Small, creeping out of Trinidad Baptiste's bedroom after leaving his watchman job early. He had to get away before Augusta woke up, and had to get home before his wife went out to water her flowers and to look for him coming from the direction of St. Lawrence. He decided to cut through the banana grove behind Obe's house to minimize the chance of being seen.

With the stealth of a hungry rat, dawn crept into Cyan's room, and she woke up screaming. The nightmare she was having had followed her into the cold light. The man stalking her dreams had just run past her window. Her scream brought her mother's unexpected attention.

"Girl, what you keeping so much noise in the house for?" Obe said.

"Somebody was just looking through the window."

"Somebody like who?"

"I don't know. Look outside."

Obe flung the window open. A light breeze flipped the blinds like a kite's tail.

"You see anybody?" Cyan asked.

"Not a damn soul."

Cyan came to the window. Her eyes scanned the banana patch, then the road.

"That man! Who that going up the road?"

"Who? Porter? You meet him last night."

"I ain't meet nobody last night. What was he doing under my window?"

"Girl, don't talk foolishness. Porter wasn't anywhere near your window."

"I see him with my own two big eyes. He was standing right at the window, Ma."

"Cyan, now you know that ain't no true. Porter just went out through the front door."

"You telling me I lying, Ma? I know what I see."

"I ain't able to fuss with you so early this morning. I too blasted tired. I see yuh sister ain't make it home again last night. She think she's woman in here, eh? It go be me and she in here today. All yuh take advantage of my mourning to do as you please."

"How you could be mourning and bring a man to sleep in here last night?"

"Yesterday was me last day mourning. Things go be different from now on."

"I can't believe you do that."

"Well, believe it, Cyan. I mourn your father long enough. I got a life to live. What you think I been doing while he was in prison these past four long years? Especially since I know he wasn't coming back. You think I been sitting around waiting for him?"

"I know what you was doing, Ma. You don't think I ain't know? You been doing it before he went to prison. The whole village know it. That is why he dead. You's the body kill him."

"Girl, if I was to take you on, I might do something ignorant. But you better watch that mouth of yours, yuh hear me? Your father ain't here to save you no more, yuh know."

"I ain't care what you do to me, Ma. I ain't care. Kill me if you want. I ain't care. You put the noose round his neck and I ain't frighten to say it."

Obe left the room without another word. Cyan felt mighty. A surge of energy, a rushing of blood at her temples made her giddy. She had silenced her mother. How sweet to see Obe scurrying away like a mongoose at the scent of a dog! Her father needed his billfish beak to do it. She'd done it with a few words.

Celine came home that afternoon, her face a mountain of smiles. Her perpetual smile had led old Millicent Davenport—who lived on the main road next to the standpipe, and for whom she did odd jobs like write shopping lists and read the Bible because Millicent's eyes were bad—to remark one day that if she smiled in a canefield, it could start a fire.

There were three fires battling in Celine that afternoon: the desire to get a job so she could save some money and one day finish her O-level studies; the love burning a hole in her chest for her boyfriend, Sylvester; and so much grief over her father that every time she saw the word "hang" she'd start crying. Were it not for Sylvester, she didn't know what would become of her. How could you love somebody as much as she loved Sylvester?

During her father's funeral she'd fainted at the grave, and Sylvester had revived her with smelling salts. After Obe left the grave without her and Cyan, she went with Sylvester to Lodge Road, where he lived with his grandmother and his four sisters. She'd planned to remain a virgin until after her O-levels, to keep her mind focused on education, though she'd been out of school for two years. But that night the pain drilling a hole in her gut drove her to beg Sylvester for sex. He'd refused. You don't really want sex, he'd said, just a shoulder to cry on.

His gallantry was no match for her pain. She stripped naked; he closed his eyes. She threatened to leave; he remained a block of wood.

Only when she threatened to go out and find herself a real man, somebody to give her what she wanted, did he crack in anger.

She fed his fury with her empty longing. As he rammed into her, she cried. Hurt like hell. But nothing like the pain in her heart. She held him tightly through the night feeding him tears, and a piece of her soul. She was afraid to close her eyes. Each time she did, two smiling little girls in frilly white dresses with the most perfect bright teeth came toward her pushing a boxcart made of shiny new pine wood. In it was her father's body crumpled up like old newspaper, half his face eaten away by maggots. Sex kept her awake and away from those demons. Whenever it looked like Sylvester would fall asleep, she'd get him hard and ride him. By morning he was exhausted, she was sore. First thing out of his mouth that morning, even before they'd had a cup of tea, was marrying talk.

She'd dismissed it then as giddy-headedness, intoxication from getting all that sex from her in one night, after he'd been trying with no luck to screw her for months.

Today he'd given her a ring. Not a fancy ring with diamonds or anything. Lord knows Sylvester couldn't afford anything like that, having been laid off from his waiter job at Golden Sands some time back. Just a plain silver ring with an engraved heart. Still, it was the most beautiful ring she'd ever gotten. Well, it was the only ring she'd ever gotten, not counting the ring from the mouth of the Coke bottle Gentel Lord had given her in primary school. What else could she have said but yes?

She'd rushed home to tell the only person she could tell. Cyan. After Cyan, there was no one else. Apart from Millicent, and Sonia Payne, her best friend from primary school who'd just had a baby, nobody else around here talked to her.

But Cyan was nowhere around. She looked up and down the village, going as far as Callenders where, after the dance hall murder, Cyan had hidden their father's billfish beak among the ruins of the old plantation, and where she knew her sister went sometimes to get away from people. But if Cyan was there, the ruins and the casuarinas held her secret.

Dejected, Celine climbed the back steps and sat in the doorway as twilight scaled the tall trees and crept through the banana grove behind the paling, filling it with shadow. Beyond the banana grove the sun had dropped into the woods, setting them on fire.

As the evening darkened, with the separate shadows becoming one solid mass of blackness, and the scent of mayflower and Lady-in-the-Night settled on the breeze, Celine could feel her spirits begin to sink. Up and down her spirits had been going since her father died. Sometimes she thought she was going mad. It was causing her to depend on Sylvester more than she wanted to.

Certain times of the day she'd get a dark longing to see her father. When that happened, it seemed she could not swerve away from the oncoming rush of despair with its waiting demons. She hid from it behind sex with Sylvester. That was why she forced sex on him even during her period.

But she was also afraid that if she didn't get control of herself, he might run away. How could she know if he really loved her or just pitied her unless she conquered the despair on her own?

A closer family would help. She couldn't turn to her mother. Obe was in her own private world. With her father gone, her mother was a prisoner let loose. Obe probably hadn't even noticed that she'd slept at Syl's house every night for the past three weeks.

She wished she was more like Cyan, a loner, frugal with her affection and attention. Her sister didn't let all the talk about their father bother her. And she was sure Cyan didn't need sex to hide from demons; she would stare at them until they fled. Cyan always had things easy, no one minded her lack of interest in reading or school. And who got to go to cricket matches with their father while she was forced to stay home buried in a book? Cyan, of course.

Had she been able to stay in school, she would've been preparing for her O-levels now. She'd also have friends to talk to and something other than Sylvester to keep her mind off her father. But after Steel's arrest, school went to hell. She was kept back two years in 3-A. At the end of the second year, when she failed all her subjects again, the headmistress told her she wouldn't be allowed back. If she was the one everybody said was bright, the one who'd go far in life, how come she couldn't get started on her journey?

Obe came home and found Celine in the back doorway. They looked at each other but nothing was said. Then Obe went outside to fill with water the galvanized tub used for everything—washing, scrubbing, and bathing. She went into the stall to wash the fish smell off her body. Long ago, before things with Steel started going bad, they'd planned to have an indoor bath and toilet. They'd gotten a pipe installed in the backyard, but that was as far as they got. They never saved enough to put a sink in the kitchen or to buy bricks for adding the toilet and bath. When it came to his own family, Steel hadn't been a practical man. Repairs around the house took him months to get to. Before he got into trouble, she'd talked to him about replacing the windows. The wood ants had started to take over the house. Never got done. And he couldn't keep a cent in his pocket. Always giving away his money. If it wasn't women, it was his friends. If somebody needed money for the doctor he'd come to Steel. If the cricket team didn't have enough bats, they asked Steel to help out. If the limers under the plum tree by the standpipe needed money to buy food, Steel was always good for twenty dollars. And where were all these people when he needed money to pay for a lawyer? Couldn't find a one.

But now she'd get her indoor bath and toilet. No more having to pee into a topsie at night. Porter had promised to buy the blocks in the next two months.

Celine was still sitting in the back doorway when Obe returned to the house refreshed. A little coconut oil on her body, especially down there where Porter liked the hair to be silky soft, and she'd be ready when he came over.

Obe came out of the bedroom dressed and prepared to cook. Celine still hadn't moved.

"You go stay in that door all evening?"

"I ain't even think you see me," Celine answered.

"Now what foolishness that you saying?"

"You ain't even say nothing to me when you come in. Like I wasn't even here."

"I see you when you ain't even seeing yuhself, so forget that kinda talk. I don't ever stop seeing you all, yuh hear me? In me sleep I does still be seeing you and yuh sister, as disagreeable as she is. I seeing you getting mix up with that boy in Lodge Road, and I could tell you right now he go get you in trouble."

"What kinda trouble it go get me in, Ma?" Celine challenged.

Obe came and stood over her daughter. She wanted to kneel down to hug her but didn't know how.

"I ain't go stop you from seeing the boy, so don't set yuh face in a rat nest. You's a bright girl, Celine. You got learning. And I know had it not been for what happen to your father, you would be still in high school. You was doing well 'til all this happen, so I know it ain't you fault. We was proud of how you was getting on. I know it go be hard to get over what happen to your father. Yuh can't rush these things. Them does take time. A lotta time. Yuh heart don't heal overnight. When I lost my first baby, my son, in that river, I didn't think I would ever get over it. I leave my family in St. Lucia, got on a boat and come here thinking I could run from the pain. You can't. I ain't really ever get over that boy. His face does still come to me sometimes. And he always vex when he come to me even though he was a happy little boy. I can't forget him, but I learn to get on with life. Be careful. You go be able to get on with your life one day. You still got time. You could still do things with your life. You could still go on and be some-body. I know if I stop you from seeing that boy, you go hide behind my back and do whatever you want to do. And that may be worse. So all I could tell you is be careful. Don't let that boy get you in no trouble. Once you get in trouble, it all over. If I had the money, I woulda sent you to private lessons or private school myself. You still go get you chance in life. Porter is a man with money. He mention that he would like to help you out. So be nice to him when you see him. If we play we cards right, we go get you into private school so you could study for you O-levels one day coming soon."

Chapter Six

$\mathcal{L}$ocated midway between the airport and Bridgetown, Oistins was an odd mix of old and new. Though it reflected a country moving from an agricultural way of life to a service-oriented society—a fact borne out by the appearance of banks and shopping malls across from the fish market, two towering oil storage tanks erected in a former swamp, guest houses, supermarkets, and a modern clinic—it still held on to some of the features of the sleepy fishing village it used to be. Amid all the construction and road-widening to accommodate the increase in traffic, fishermen still built and repaired their boats on the beach, small shopkeepers still gave credit to fishermen who couldn't get the fish to bite, and limers still gathered on the steps of the Oistins public library to watch schoolgirls pass, waiting for a high wind to flip a loose skirt exposing the treasure underneath.

Cyan walked past the Oistins library, past sweaty workmen barbergreening a section of the road, hating the smell of tar, hating their greasy faces wide open to the nothingness offered by the heat.

Yes, block out their wishful stares. Think instead of how good you looked in the new olive green dress made over the weekend. Think of how sweet patchouli smelled on you.

She hoped the patchouli vial at the bottom of the brown patent leather bag borrowed from her mother—though Obe didn't know it yet—which blended so well with her pumps, was screwed tight. If she soiled this bag, she'd have to sleep under the house. This was Obe's favorite bag.

The By-pass bus—so called because it bypassed Bridgetown on its way to Speightstown—went by her, about twenty yards from the stop. She picked up her feet, hoping the bus would be delayed. Luckily it was. By a woman carrying two large crocus bags of yams, one of which had gotten trapped in the doorway.

As Cyan settled into a window seat, the excitement of going to her new job began to build slowly in her body. She felt proud and free. The last time she'd felt such a surge of freedom was the time she went to Bridgetown by herself when she was twelve.

No one knew she'd gone to Bridgetown that day with twenty dollars she'd gotten for staying with her aunt Zuma, who lived alone in St. George, after Zuma had come out of the hospital following a hernia operation. Not even Celine. Feeling big and independent, she'd walked around Bridgetown for four hours, in her mind each step taking her closer to womanhood. The twenty dollars burned a hole in her pocket as she sampled every store.

Hunger had driven her to Patsy's Food Shop and Bar on McGregor Street, a brightly painted run-down place with pillars leaning every which way and as many people holding them up. At the bar, men and women hollered back and forth, steaming up the already-humid room with their alcohol-heated breath. She'd sat in a corner alone and glanced up from her plate of rice and stew only when a man who sounded like her father ordered a shot of white rum. But the man was a skeleton, a shriveled-up old drunk with bloodshot eyes and limp shoulders who, as he threw his head back to let the rum gallop down his throat, leaned so far, he appeared ready to topple.

His flimsy body swayed back and forth like a fig tree in the wind. She had to smile. There was something beautiful and triumphant about his will to defy gravity and the alcohol trying to bully him into submission, something sad and poetic about his motion to and fro like his body was arguing with the space. She remembered thinking at the time how heartbroken she'd be if her father ended up like that.

Now she would've taken that deformed man over what she had of her father.

The bus stopped a few yards from Waverly Avenue. Without returning the driver's knotted smile, she stepped off and walked to the head of the gap where she stood staring down the white gravel road lined with casuarina and coconut trees. On both sides shrubbery and grass grew thick.

A mongoose with two young ones in the middle of the road welcomed her to the neighborhood with a wary stare, head slanted expectantly, testing the air to make sure she wasn't a dog in disguise. Then they sauntered off into the bush. A rustle high in the trees drew her attention to several monkeys springing from branch to branch.

She sniffed her armpits to make sure the dash to the bus hadn't caused her deodorant too much distress. Nothing worse than starting a new job smelling high.

She strutted down the white road. Divots and loose gravel made it difficult to keep her balance, but she felt so boundless in the sun's untarnished brightness bouncing off the road that she made it to the front gate without so much as a stumble.

The doctor's house was one of five on that ridge overlooking the Caribbean Sea. An upstairs house of an uncompromising square design, it was built of old-fashioned limestone, with large columns supporting the overhanging balcony. Ferns and ivy swung from the railings and clung to the columns. The property was fenced in by a ring of coconut trees.

On the lawn stooped Koko, patiently staring at the sun shining through the coconut trees. In her hand, hanging limply at her side, was a large, expensive-looking camera. Sunlight hit the silver of the camera frame and bounced away, shimmering.

Then Koko straightened up and issued instructions to a tall man wearing only shorts and a straw hat. A cutlass gleamed in his hand as he leaned against a tree next to a large bunch of coconuts. Buttered with sweat, his face and muscular chest were glossed black in the sunlight. He started to cut the coconuts off the bunch one by one. Then, holding one close to his chest, he skillfully sliced a drinking hole in the husk. With a grin he upturned the coconut to his mouth and began to drink. All this time Koko had been clicking away with her camera, moving closer, to the side, standing, stooping; it reminded Cyan of the day she met Dr. Mayhem.

Cyan stood, eyes fixed on the man and his virile smile. Suddenly she felt like a little girl again. An unstoppable wave of self-confidence radiated from him. Like an untuned drum her heart pounded against her chest. She didn't like the way he made her feel. Why couldn't she have come at a different time? Like after he'd gone.

Koko swept off her wide-brimmed hat, flashing a bald head. The brazenness of Koko's baldness stunned Cyan. She'd never met a woman so shameless as to shave not only her eyebrows, but all the hair off her head.

As if sensing another presence, Koko turned around.

"So you've finally arrived," she said. Without lingering for a reply, she resumed her work.

"What you mean I finally arrive? Dr. Mayhem tell me to come at ten. It ain't even ten o'clock yet," said Cyan.

"I don't have time to argue with you. The important thing is you're here. I need a pot of coffee right away."

"Coffee? At this time of day? You don't think you'd be better off with some lemonade?"

"If I wanted lemonade, I would've asked for lemonade. Now are you here to work or are you here just to jaw with me?"

"Sorry."

Departing, she heard the young man snickering and wanted to curse him and the woman who gave birth to him.

By the end of the day Cyan had cleaned the house top to bottom: three upstairs bedrooms including the master bedroom, which was bigger than the entire Cattlewash house, a guest room downstairs with no blinds at the window or sheets on the bed, which Koko instructed her to dress in white after pointing her to the linen closet; two upstairs bathrooms and one downstairs, plus a living room and kitchen. She'd swept the sand and leaves off the patio. The work tired her out so much, she dropped asleep on the living room couch afterward.

At six o'clock Koko appeared from her darkroom with the painting. Embarrassed, Cyan jumped up, trying to look like she'd been just reclining and not sleeping. But Koko only smiled and said Jonathan would be late, and that she'd drive her home because the painting was too large to take on the bus.

For a moment Cyan thought of protesting. She did not want to go anywhere with this woman. But she didn't want to wait another day to claim her prize, either.

She best don't say nothing to me 'cause I would 'buse she tonight, Cyan resolved as she got into the car.

With the painting in the backseat they set off into the twilight. As Koko maneuvered the tight turns of the tiny roads with care, Cyan stared out the window, enjoying the rush of the wind, thinking about the young man being photographed.

Round midday he'd come into the house for a glass of lemonade. She thought he'd come to laugh at her some more. But all he did was sit quietly sipping his lemonade. Afterward he took a bracelet of black, red, and green beads from his hand and offered it to her. When she refused it, he laid it on the chair and said, "It yours either way." Then he told her his name was Breeze, and left.

She'd wanted to ask him where he lived, if he had a woman, but the words stuck to her lips, suddenly gone dry. He stayed on her mind all day, a good thing too. Thinking about him made the time fly.

Close up, his smile was even more cocksure. And when he smiled, his weighty brown eyes expanded like the surf, and she had the stupidest desire to strip and play in them. She liked the way his eyes followed her body, too, not seeking to diminish her like other men's did, but intimate and inviting. Her confidence came back. She felt like a woman again. When he sped away on his motorbike, disappointment cleaved the dry corners of her mouth. That was when she picked up the bracelet and slipped it onto her wrist.

"What're you smiling at?"

Koko's voice doused cold water on her cozy memory.

She'd been unaware of herself smiling. Nor had she realized they'd left the confines of the densely housed St. Michael parish and were now bouncing rapidly through the open spaces of Christ Church.

"You probably think I don't like you," Koko said.

For a moment, as she toyed with the bracelet on her wrist, Cyan wasn't sure what to say. The hard edge was gone from Koko's voice. The voice Koko now used was gentle, almost apologetic.

"I would like to know what I do you," Cyan said noncommittally.

"I have nothing against you personally. I just have a great dislike for maids."

"Why? You did ever a maid?"

"I have my reasons."

Silence sat between them again. Cyan toyed with her bracelet, hoping this time the silence would last the rest of the trip. She wanted to return to her daydreaming. Koko nudged silen

"What made you take this job?"

"I need money. I ain't got nobody to support me. And
nobody breaking down me front door to give me a job in a government office."

"Shouldn't you be in school? How old are you, fifteen?"

"Eighteen."

"Eighteen? You seem younger. Is this your first job?"

"Sort of."

"How long do you think you'd be doing this?"

"I dunno."

"A year, two?" Koko persisted.

"Maybe two, I don't know. What's it to you?"

Koko looked at her and smiled.

"If you could do anything with your life right now, what would you
do?" Koko said.

"Live it."

Koko laughed and Cyan relaxed. She wasn't sure where the woman
was going with all these questions, but laughter was always a good
sign.

"If I'd been born here and was your age, I guess I'd say the same
thing. I've been here ten years and the truth is, though I love it here,
I've discovered that living your life in this place is not as simple as it
might first appear to an outsider. When I first came, I saw the trees, the
blue sky, and the sea, and I thought, this is indeed paradise. Why
couldn't I've been born here? Several years ago I was taking pictures
of some women cutting cane near North Point who told me they'd
never been to the Animal Flower Cave. And I thought, how amazing—
within walking distance of them and they'd never gone. And I asked
them why. They said it was a place for tourists. That they didn't feel
right going places that were for tourists. And I didn't understand what
they were telling me until much later. Have you ever gone to the
Animal Flower Cave?"

"No. That too far for me to go."

"It's really not. It wouldn't take more than forty minutes to get there from here."

"For you maybe. You could go anywhere you want. You got a car. No place won't be far for you. You don't know how hard it is to get round this place if you ain't got a car."

"I suppose you're right. But what I'm trying to say is that I've met and talked to a lot of people, photographed them, and what I've realized is that, though most of them don't have to deal with the kind of things black people have to deal with where I come from, like racism—white people that just plain hate you because you're black— they still have a hard time enjoying the beauty around them, they feel that somehow they're not good enough to enjoy the same things white people come here to enjoy. Even if you're surrounded by beauty and tranquility, slavery didn't leave you equipped to deal with your blackness. That for you born in paradise, paradise may not *be* paradise."

"A lot of people leave here and go to America to live. For a lot of them America is paradise."

"Is that what you think? Is that what you want to do?"

"I don't know. Is living with white people that hate you worse than living with black people that hate you? Or it worse than being poor? I would be frighten to leave, though it might be the best thing I could do. I don't blame people who jump at the chance. Life here might be sweet for some people, but other people does got it very hard. I know a woman who went to New Jersey and was working as a maid, and she did making more money than she sister who did working at a bank in town."

"No question you can make money. But how much, and at what price? Is this woman happy working as a maid in New Jersey?"

"I don't know. Her children sure is happy, though. Them does get new clothes and toys every two months or so, and now them building on a wall toilet and bath. You know how long me father did talking 'bout building on a wall toilet and bath. He dead and gone, and it ain't build yet."

"You don't think they'd rather have their mother than new clothes and new toys?"

"Them got a father. Maybe if the mother was here, she'd be so vex 'cause she poor, she would ill-treat them. Them better off not getting ill-treatment."

"You seem like a smart girl. Don't let yourself get stuck in a job like this. Some of the girls my husband has hired started to act as though he'd given them life. As though nothing could be more rewarding than working for a doctor with a big house on the sea. I don't know why, but he likes having a maid. We don't need one, but he always insists on having one. And they never last. They soon begin to think it's their house and act as though I have no right to be there. Then I have to get rid of them. I don't like doing it, but to save my marriage, I have to, if you understand what I mean."

Cyan understood quite well, but kept silent.

"If you're interested in learning a craft or skill I know the woman who runs the adult education program at the YWCA. We're very good friends. I'm sure I can get her to waive the fees for you."

What it matter to her what I do with my life? Cyan wondered as the car pulled up outside her gap. Fetching the painting from the back seat she said thank you and hurried along the gap. Behind her she heard the Triumph drive off.

Rigid back, stone face: that's Porter. That's how he sat at the kitchen table when she walked through the door. Dark brownish sauce from the bowl of coo-coo and red herring he'd just wolfed down dripped from the corners of his mouth along his unshaven chin. Even with his belly full his face was still a stone mask. Like a man without a soul. Rigid back, stone face, greasy mouth: just the kind of man her mother deserved.

Porter left shortly. Said he had to go pick up some rent for land he owned. She didn't mourn his departure. What land could a man like him have to rent? Didn't look like he owned a good pair of shoes, far less land. Bet it's his other woman he's going to see, Cyan wanted to tell Obe.

His departure left mother and daughter alone together.

Obe, who was ironing, had been so engrossed with the way Porter demolished her coo-coo, she'd paid little attention to the large package Cyan brought home. Obe's mind was busy trying to recall the last time she saw a man sit down and eat with such carelessness: juice dripping from his mouth, red herring in his teeth, sauce on the front of his shirt. Not since she was a little girl living on the island of St. Lucia, when she used to sit and watch her father eat. Porter ate like her father, with the abandon of a child, maybe worse. But he ate everything she put on the plate and, more important, came back for seconds. She would try to hold on to this man.

Cyan was about to unwrap the painting in the front-house when her mother spoke from the shed-roof.

"What is that thing you bring in here?"

"I didn't even think you see me come in."

"I see everything, don't forget. What is it?"

"Come and see," Cyan replied, tearing at the newspaper wrapping excitedly. She wanted Obe to like the picture. The only things on the wall of the front-house were a cheap print of *The Last Supper* and a polished mahogany plaque that read: IN GOD WE TRUST. To hang the picture in such company she would need her mother's permission. She turned the picture so Obe could see it from where she stood.

"Look, Ma."

"I can't see it from here. I ain't got on me glasses."

Cyan moved closer, a few feet away from her mother.

"It's a picture, Ma. I want to put it up in the front-house."

"A picture? That's a big able picture. Where you get that big able thing from? That thing nearly as big as the damn house."

"Look at it good. Who it remind you of?"

"Nobody. It look like a man. That's all it look like. It don't look like nobody I know."

"Look good!" Cyan cried. "Look good, good. It don't remind you of Pa?"

Obe's face turned cold. Setting the iron down, she straightened up, drew her shoulders back, and stretched her long neck as if it'd suddenly caught a cramp. She looked at the picture again, not wanting to see Steel's face or any resemblance of the man she'd wanted to love forever. But Steel had cared only about himself and couldn't unhinge jealousy from his hip.

In St. Lucia, Obe had lived with a man whose family owned a lot of land in her village. She'd taken his abuse for three years before leaving. A move precipitated by a tragedy that still pinged in the nadir of her soul. She regretted not leaving Steel long before his jealousy turned their marriage into a farce. Having people stare and point at her in the market was enough to remind her of the mistake she'd made that bright afternoon twenty years before when she saw him at a workbench under a clammy-cherry tree near a yellow house, buried in wood chips and shavings from the boat he was constructing, and stopped to ask him if she could rake up the trash for a few dollars. She'd arrived in Barbados only a few weeks before, had no money and no prospects. He smiled and offered her a drink of mauby from a jug. When she finished raking the trash into a heap, he asked where she was from and if she could cook. And because he was young and knew how to smile, which told her he knew how to enjoy life, she moved in with him that very day.

She looked at the picture and saw what she didn't want to see: the man who'd taught her how to swim, how to slow-dance to Joe Simon and Otis Redding, and how to make coo-coo.

"That don't look a damn thing like you' father."

"I always know you was blind," Cyan joked.

"I wish to God I was blind the day I set eyes on your father under that tree sweating that smile that get me in all this trouble."

"Is just a joke, Ma."

"A joke? I look like I got time to joke?"

"You used to be able to joke. Remember them days when we used to sit down outside on Sunday and—"

"I ain't got time to remember foolishness," Obe interrupted.

"I think it look like Pa, and I go put it up in the front-house," Cyan declared.

"If you want it to look like your father I can't stop you. But you ain't putting that thing in my front-house. Keep it in your bedroom. I don't want to wake up every morning and look at it."

"You must think it look like him. If not, you wouldn't say that."

"I don't care who it look like. Just don't put it in me front-house; otherwise, I go put a match to it."

"You don't ever want to think 'bout him, do yuh. You don't want to keep his memory living. You just wanna forget 'bout him like he was some dog you just happen to throw a bone to. Well, I ain't go let you forget 'bout him just so."

"You worry 'bout his memory. He was your father. You got his blood. When he dead, he cease being anything to me."

"He was your husband."

"And a murderer. Don't forget. He open a man neck like it was a fish belly. Over what? Over nothing."

"Over nothing? That ain't what I hear. I wish he was here to open up Porter greasy face."

Without thinking, Obe swung the hot iron at Cyan's head. But her daughter was ducking and moving away before the iron began to sweep the air. It sailed harmlessly by her.

"Yuh know, sometimes, Cyan, I wish I didn't have you. You is such a disagreeable child."

"Yeah? Well, sometimes I does wish you didn't have me neither," said Cyan as she backed away into her room.

Obe became sick the moment Cyan left. Sick to her stomach at the thought she could've injured her daughter. Again. Even killed her. Was she losing control of her life? She knew she'd lost her elder daughter four years ago. Back then, anger and shame made her act without thinking. What could be worse than having someone accuse your children of stealing? Cyan had had a habit of taking money from her father's pocket. She'd warned Steel about letting her, but as always he laughed and did nothing. It was left up to her to keep the girl straight, from turning into a thief. She never intended to burn Cyan's fingers so badly. She never intended to hold her hand to the fire that long. Just long enough to scare her. But then the flame was there, and she couldn't stop herself, though she heard the girl screaming.

Her actions just now left her trembling and shaking her head. Was she some kind of monster capable of killing her own child? The look in Cyan's eyes as she left the room terrified her. And in that moment, her flat eyes, closed to slits where no light could penetrate, had become claws digging at her mother's heart. A deep emptiness, like her soul had left her body, overcame Obe. Fear that it might not come back dragged her to her knees. Then she felt a sudden feverishness; her soul had returned, consumed by shame. She turned off the iron and left the house in tears.

When she heard her mother leaving, Cyan got the painting and hung it on the wall in her room. Then she waited up, hoping Celine would come home. She was hungry but did not eat. She felt like crying but steeled herself against it. Too old to be crying about such things now. Her mother was capable of anything at anytime. Get used to it.

The swirl of fireflies lighting up the backyard drew her to the window; their fire brightened her spirits. A slight breeze skimmed the fluorescent darkness.

There were no lights on in the house when Celine came home around ten. Cyan listened, smiling to herself as her sister crept through the house. At the bedroom door Celine stood, waiting for her eyes to adjust to the darkness.

"Night, you still up?"

"I still up. I been waiting for you," Cyan answered.

"Something happen?"

"Same shite as always."

"You and Ma get into a bassa-bassa again."

"I don't wanna talk 'bout that. I got something to show you. Turn on the light."

Celine flicked the light switch, shocking the room with light.

"Look," Cyan said, pointing to the painting.

For a moment Celine stood speechless. Then she crept up to the painting like she was afraid it would attack her. She touched it, rubbed her hands all over it, smelled it. She put her head against it as if listening for a heartbeat. And when she thought she heard something, she jumped back.

"Jesus, Cyan. Where you get this from? Who give you this picture of Pa?"

"See, you think so, too! I tell Ma it look like Pa, and she pretend it didn't look like him. Is everything of Pa, ain't it? When I first see it, I couldn't believe it meself."

"God almighty. Yuh know how they say that everybody got a twin? That is Pa twin."

Celine sat on the bed next to her older sister. The two of them stared at the painting until Celine began to cry.

"I wish he could step off the wall now and talk to me!" she cried.

"You gotta stop thinking like that," Cyan said. "It ain't ever go happen. Stop crying and come to bed."

Celine undressed and lay next to her sister, "I got something to tell you." Her face cracked into a smile as she threw her arms around her sister.

Cyan clung to her.

"I did suspect since last week, but I only find out for true-true today," Celine said.

"So tell me then. You got me on pins and needles already."

"I go have a baby. And Sylvester and me want to get married."

Cyan could not believe her ears. This was not her sister talking. This was some other girl, some foolish girl who didn't know any better.

"But I thought you wanted to finish your studying. To get a good job. Ma go have a fit."

"I want to leave this house. I want to get married. I want to get outta this village. That is what I want. I want to be happy, Cyan. Who I fooling? Where I go get the money to go to private lessons? I got a chance to be happy with Silly. Life ain't no good if you ain't happy. And how can I be happy when people looking at you every day like you got shite on your face? And when you pass the rum shop the men holler at you and ask you if is true your father take the hangman's doggie in his boxie before he swing from the gallows. And the women whispering that them shoulda hang the worthless mother too. And them look at you like them would like to hang you too."

"Don't pay them people no mind. I don't pay nobody in this village no mind. I does go 'long like them don't exist. I don't speak to none o' them. I don't care what them say."

"It ain't that easy for me, Night. I ain't like you. I ain't as composed as you. I can't block out things like you."

"You can't let nothing stop you from getting back to your studies, Celine. You gotta get rid of this child before Ma find out."

"No, Night. Sylvester and me want this baby."

"How could you get with child? Bright people don't get with child. Them does get certificates and degrees and get big jobs, and *then* get children. Only ignorant people does get children that them can't afford to feed. You ain't stupid. You bright. I can't believe this happen to you."

"Don't worry 'bout me, Night. I got a man. He want to marry me. We go get we own house. His family got land in St. George. And if you want, you could come and live with we."

"And where this man does work? Answer me that, Celine. You suppose to be smarter than that. You suppose to be smarter than me, and I know yuh don't get a child for a man that don't work. Even I got enough sense not to do that."

"You vex with me, Night? Why you vex with me? I doing what I want to do. I ain't stopping you from doing what you want to do. You vex with me 'cause I got a man and you ain't got none?"

"You idiot! I ain't want no man. What I want a man for?"

"To take your virginity. I bet you's still a virgin."

Cyan forgot her anger and began to giggle.

"You is, ain't you?" Celine asked, adding her own squeaky giggles to her sister's. Soon they were wrapped in each other's arms tittering unstoppably.

"I lost mine long before you," Cyan said.

"You lie!"

"I ain't lie. If I lie I die. I do it once."

"When?"

"When I was fourteen."

"You's such a liar," said Celine, laughing.

"I serious. Remember Banana, the boy from town who used to spend summers and weekends by Sergeant Payne on the main road?"

"Yeah, I remember he. Had a mark that shape like a hand of bananas on his neck. You didn't like he, though. You say he head shape like a pilchard tin."

"And I wish I did never set my eyes on that pilchard tin!"

"I don't believe you, Night."

"All right, then, if you don't believe me. I done."

"Where you do it?"

"Next door. At the witch and them."

"You do it at Augusta and them? Night, you must be crazy."

"It just happen so. It wasn't no plan nothing. One day Trinidad and Augusta went to town and leave me there. Ma had take you shopping to buy cloth to make your uniform. Banana see me through the window and he ask me, who home? And when I say, nobody, he just open the gate and come in. And he say he ain't leaving 'til I kiss him. And then he grabble me up and kiss me. And then he start rubbing me bubbies through me shirt, and it feel so good, girl, Celine, I won't tell a lie. I forget meself. I forget where I was and everything. Everything fly out me head like it did a open cage. The next thing I know, we was on a white sheet on the floor in Augusta's bedroom and he was on top of me. And when we get up, I see these two little spots of blood on the sheet, and I get so frighten, I nearly pee meself. So I juck the sheet in some water with some Clorox hoping to wash it and put it on the line to dry before Augusta and Trinidad come home. But them come home before I could finish washing the sheet. And Augusta ask me why I washing the sheet. I tell her I throw 'way something on it by accident. And she ask me where I get that sheet. And I couldn't remember where I get the sheet from. Then I remember where the sheet come from. Sometimes when I go over there, I used to see her with this fancy-looking white sheet spread out on the bed looking at. It had this fancy gold trim around the edge. And when I come in, she would fold up the sheet and put it in this valise under the bed. This was the same sheet. That day she had the mattress off the springs, and Banana musta seen the sheet in the valise and pull it out. So she slap me 'cross me face and take the sheet from me. I was so surprise, I slap she back and run home crying."

"Wait a minute! That is when she tell Ma that you steal her money?"

"Yes. To this day I ain't know why she tell Ma that lie. She give me that money, as God is me judge. That is why I go hate she to she grave."

"And here I was thinking you did a virgin! Wanna know when I lost mine? The day Pa bury. It was the only thing I could do to make me forget. To make me stop thinking 'bout him. To make me stop thinking my inside was going drop out, thinking we ain't go ever see him again. I know he was in jail and all that and we only used to get to see him once in a while, but at least we coulda seen him if we went to the prison. We can't go to the grave and tell the gravedigger to dig up the coffin so we could look at his face. And even so he can't say nutten. If you can't speak, is the same thing as if you invisible."

Cyan's heart cracked open, and tears began to flow.

Celine put her face to her sister's; their tears mingled. She wrapped Cyan's bird-thin body in her thick arms, and they fell asleep.

Chapter Seven

ℋer mother was a liar.

She lied about Porter not moving in, and she lied about letting Celine stay after she found out about the pregnancy. Oh, what a blasted liar her mother was! If there was a God in Heaven He would punish Obe for those bold-faced lies.

Cyan was ready to fight for her sister. When angry, Obe could be an indomitable presence; her arms grew longer and her eyes pulsated with an unnatural brightness. But Cyan was not afraid.

One morning she cornered her mother setting up jucking-board under the clammy-cherry tree out back to wash Porter's clothes. Celine was at her boyfriend's, where she'd been sent packing. Porter had just pedaled off to see about his boat.

Mother and daughter squared off, hemmed in by their emotions, by their love and at the same time distrust of each other, and by the morning quiet. A few bare-necked hens scratched grass in the yard. Wet air hovered about them; green clouds skimmed close to the ground.

Mother and daughter stood in the yard, enduring the stench of Percy Small's pigs a few houses down. They stood apart, each knowing that the other's heart was pounding expectantly. Obe knew what her daughter wanted and knew she would have to deny it, if for no reason other than she'd already ordered Celine out of the house. She could not appear to be weak. To stand by your convictions, to defend your principles, was the best thing she could teach her children. She knew they didn't believe she had any compassion; when they became women they'd understand. They would look back and thank her for making them strong. No man would ever be able to take advantage of them.

Mother and daughter stood, chests in the air, the blood that bound them together churning like a dark sea, each knowing that the gnawing in her gut, the tightening in her bowels, had a significant history.

"If you don't let Celine come back, then I leaving, too," Cyan bluffed.

"Then you could go 'long. Maybe I would be able to get some peace in this blasted house for a change."

"You can't chase her 'way just so."

"I can't? Tell me why not? This ain't me house?"

"She's your daughter. Your flesh and blood."

"Flesh and blood ain't got nothing to do with nothing. Sometimes yuh gotta harden yuh heart against yuhself if you wanna keep yuh mind. Sixteen years old, and what the rass she got to look forward to? After we spend all this money on books and uniforms and lunch money to send her to school. She get kick outta Queens College, and I forgive her 'cause of the circumstances. But she just gone and end her life. I don't want her in my house. Let that man support her."

"But, Ma, that boy don't work," Cyan pleaded.

"It will teach her a lesson. What is the point of all the hard work and sacrifice me and your father went through? I thought that at least she woulda make something outta her life. God, I remember how proud we was when she pass that exam. I say to Steel, 'At least one o' you all could go on and be somebody.' I do everything. I try not to be too strict, I try to give her some freedom 'cause I figure a girl with her education would know how to take care of herself. She would know what is important. I figure I can't be as strict on her as I is on you. She go need some freedom so she don't feel I keeping her back. But she worse off than somebody with no education."

"Let her come home, Ma. Let her come home. Please. I promise I ain't go ask you for anything ever again. I swear. This one time, Ma, do it for me. I working. I can help out 'til the baby come. Talking to Celine is the only thing I got to look forward to. Nobody in this village don't talk to me. What I go do without Celine? Please, Ma, don't do this to me."

Obe looked at Cyan for a long time, not smiling once, her face drained of emotion. She suddenly felt tired, older than her forty-two years. The world was on her back and she took a deep breath to hold up the load. In the warm morning she felt a coldness come upon her like a nighttime draught. She was a wounded woman. Was defeat around the corner? She still held out hope. Hope for children. Hope for herself and Cyan. Perhaps this was their chance for reversal. But how far would she have to go? Give up Porter too?

"Okay, Cyan. If you wanna work for her and that baby, then you work for them. She's your responsibility now."

Without thinking, Cyan threw her arms around her mother and kissed her. Then feeling the other weight on her mind, she untangled herself and stepped back to look Obe square in the face.

"And what 'bout Porter?" she said.

"What about him?"

"You go let him move in here?"

"Who say anything 'bout Porter moving in here? He got his own house. Porter tell you he moving in here? I don't want no man in this house."

She had wanted to believe in her mother so desperately. Just for once she wanted to be able to go to her mother's room, sit on the bed for some old talk. She wanted nothing more than to sit on the front steps with Obe on dark moonless nights, crickets and whistling frogs singing loud and the smell of almonds and frangipani stirring up magic. And her mother's voice so rich and fluid, drowning out Jewl Bright's baby crying next door with stories about growing up in St. Lucia, where rivers were warm and soundless, mountains tall and green, valleys deep and hungry, where she'd had to flee a man who beat her because their son fell into the river and drowned. But those days were gone. She couldn't talk to Obe anymore. Her mother had changed. Obe had Porter.

He moved in one Saturday morning while Cyan was getting her hair done dreadlock style. She left the hairdresser feeling reckless and confident; a certain mannishness crept into her stride as she passed the young men standing on the steps of Lord's shop sipping rum and arguing. They noticed her new style and frowned.

"Look who play them getting dreads."

"She could really go and eat some food and put some flesh on them bones."

"What, them dreads bigger than she."

She laughed hard to let them know she'd heard and couldn't care less.

Twenty yards from the house she heard his voice. Why did *he* have to laugh so hard? He was laughing at them, that's why. Laughing at her father, who would've sliced open his face like the belly of a flying fish were he still alive.

Porter was drunk. So was Obe. She'd never seen her mother in such a state: dress all awry, without underwear in the middle of the day, showing her sagging breasts, eyes glassy, smelling of rum and stale sweat. Her mother's panties lay on the floor next to a chair that had been broken somehow in the time between Cyan's departure and return. The thought that Obe might've had sex, breaking a chair in the act—right there in the shed-roof in the middle of the day, with people passing by outside—disgusted her. Did her mother have no shame?

On the floor beside the table were two large bags bursting with men's clothes. It was the moment she'd dreaded ever since she laid eyes on Porter. "If you get to know him, you'd like him," Obe had tried to tell her. "He's a hardworking man. Got land. Got his own boat that he rent out." But Cyan didn't want to know anything about the man. Didn't want to get to know him, either. And she had vowed to move out the day he moved in.

But she stayed. She stayed because of Celine. She stayed because the great love of her sister's life, one Sylvester Blanchard, better known as Silly—a name that could not have been better chosen—woke up one day, realized he was going to be a father, and went mad. That was the only explanation Cyan could come up with for his odd behavior. She was sure as the stars he was faking. Everything he did was just an attempt to shed his responsibility: drinking himself to the brink of death one time, walking seven miles barefoot to Hopefield Plantation demanding to see God another time, stepping off the pier because he dreamed he could walk on water. He almost drowned that time, and should've. Would've saved everybody a heap of aggravation. But he was saved by a diver whose hand of freshly mined coral had gotten entangled with Silly's leg as he was sinking. To save his coral, the diver had to save Silly.

Silly's mother tried to have him committed. The doctors who examined him determined there was nothing wrong. The next week his family shipped him off to his father in the States, saying the doctors here didn't know what they were doing.

The whole thing turned Celine inside out. No one could calm her. She ate nothing and threw up slime every day. Cyan became her mother: counseling, cajoling, inspiring, anointing.

Cyan left work on time every day to hurry home to her sister. She liked fussing over Celine. At night they'd watch the fireflies in the backyard, or walk down to the beach to listen to the waves, or sit laughing with the steel-eyed man in the painting. But the way Celine was losing weight instead of gaining worried Cyan.

Her mother was now back to selling fish in the market regularly for the man who rented Porter's boat. And she still boned and cleaned fish for the hotels. Most evenings Cyan would stop for fish—the only thing Celine would let pass her lips and the thing she'd keep down the longest. While she wrapped fish, Obe would ask how Celine was coming along; it was the only time they talked about her pregnancy. Obe and Porter never came home before ten. By then the village would've settled on quiet. Lights would've been doused. Fireflies few. Cyan and Celine long asleep.

She wouldn't say it in public, but Porter seemed to be good for her mother. They seldom quarreled, and Obe seemed more contented. When Cyan visited her mother in the market, Obe seemed genuinely concerned about Celine's physical and mental state. And they even managed a gentle moment every now and then, a reminiscence of the two of them standing side by side slicing fish for impatient customers, when, with the whip and biting candor of a December night's sea wind, her mother would put the buyers in their place with a well-chosen quip: "The fish dead, it ain't go fly away, so if you gotta go take a shit, you can go 'long and come back." It would often bring the intense haggling in the market to a halt for a moment of comic relief.

"Your sister getting any better?" Obe asked one day.

"She ain't throw up yesterday."

"What the doctor say?"

"She won't go."

"What yuh mean she won't go? I thought you tell me you was taking her to the doctor."

"She say she ain't going."

"That girl is such a jackass. When I get home, she and me go have a few words. You too easy on her. I don't know what kinda mother you go make."

"Me? I ain't having no children."

Obe looked at her and laughed. "You plan to like woman then?"

"I ain't liking nobody. Man nor woman."

"It go come, don't worry. And if you take man, you go find yourself where all women does find themself. With a child. And if yuh love the man, it really ain't go be so bad. Yuh go like the feeling. Ain't no feeling in the world like being with child for a man you love that love you back just as much."

"Then why you so hard on Celine? She say she love Sylvester."

"But where this Sylvester is now? Tell me that. I warn her 'bout that boy. It ain't that I ain't expect you all to make mistakes. Is just that some mistakes you just can't recover from. She done gone and get herself in trouble. Ain't nothing nobody could do 'bout that now. The least she could do is take care of herself. She beginning to look like you, and that ain't no good for the baby. When I get home, I go let her know if she don't get her rass to a doctor, she will leave my house."

That evening Cyan flew home on new wings. Celine was asleep and didn't hear her come in. Had she been awake, she wouldn't have heard her sister's footsteps anyhow because Cyan was landing on the soft sand of her mother's promise to take charge of Celine's health. Tough as it was for her to deal with her mother sometimes, Cyan knew that if anyone could get her sister to the doctor it would be Obe.

She whipped up a frothy fish soup for Celine, filled with broad-leaf thyme whose pleasing aroma had the power to erase melancholy. The scent hung from the rafters and protruding nails, thin and persistent like stalactites of memory. It smelled like her mother's fish soup, and she wanted the aroma to last until Obe came home.

Celine woke with a smile when Cyan brought the soup.

"You was dreaming?"

"No. Not really," replied Celine as she boffed the pillow to brace her back.

"Then what you smiling at?"

"I was smelling that fish soup, and it remind me so much of Ma's, I thought she was home."

"I talk to she today."

"So? You does talk to Ma every day."

"No, I really talk to her. She say she go have a word with you when she come home."

Celine lifted her eyes from the thin veil of steam rising from the bowl. The soup tasted good. And she was hungry for the first time in weeks. She hoped Cyan wasn't about to spoil her appetite. Sure she wanted to talk to her mother. But *having a word with* and *talking to* were two different things.

"A word about what?" Celine asked suspiciously. Perhaps whatever *word* her mother had to share wouldn't taste so bad.

"She want you to go to the doctor."

"I don't need to have a word with her about that 'cause I done decide what I go do," Celine said.

"All you gots to decide right now is if you go have this baby healthy or sick," said Cyan.

"I ain't go have this baby sick or healthy. In fact I can tell you right now, I ain't go have this baby at all. I wouldn't have Sylvester's baby if God come and tell me I going to deliver another Jesus."

Cyan looked at her sister in bemusement. She didn't for one minute believe Celine, who still pined for Silly. No way was she going to get rid of that baby, not while she still believed Silly might show up one day, happy to be a father.

Chapter Eight

There was a time when she thought all dead people became blackbirds and that cane flowers were clouds dropped from the sky. She knew better now.

She watched the sun drop like a dead bird from the sky amid a flurry of red clouds. High-school girls going home from netball pulled petticoats between dainty legs the way Mother must've taught them when they were little. Giggling, they brushed past the wind that had just unveiled their cotton panties. Such innocence. Playing hopscotch with Celine and Perlie Blades in the dirt below Perlie's house, listening with her father to cricket on the radio, watching her mother cut up sheep's head to make soup, dueling with her sister for fried sheep's brain, hearing the excitement in Steel's voice as he recounted the time he had a drink with the famous Garfield Sobers, the greatest cricketer in the world. What she would do to return to a world of such innocence.

Cyan was hungry. Sooner or later she'd have to go home. No getting around it. Darkness was poised to swallow her. In the void the hunger would seem even more threatening. Not that she had to go home for food. She had money in her pocket. Were it not for Celine, she probably would run away.

A man crawled out of a nearby shop and braced himself against the kicking wind. Lemuel. In his youth Lemuel had been a strapping cricketer who played for the island, and many said he was good enough to play for the West Indies. Now his body was crooked. Still, there was a residue of virility left to defy Nature.

He was coming toward her. She turned, not knowing whether to flee or stay. She didn't feel like talking.

He stopped in front of her, putting his crookedness under her nose, daring her to ignore him. He was nothing much to look at. Yet something about him seemed to hypnotize her. His eyes were proud and compelling as if they were the only things he had of worth now.

He did not speak. She eyed him in silence.

"What you want?" Her voice as angry as it was puzzled.

"You better watch you'self, girl." His deep voice came out of a cave.

"Who you telling to watch themself?"

"I used to know your father real good. We used to play cricket and nick dice together. I know what people 'bout here think 'bout him. They would like to destroy you for being his daughter. Don't let them."

"Nobody can't do me nothing."

"I used to feel like that, too. I know that feeling good. Young and strong, that's what I was. Indestructible. It don't last forever, yuh hear me. God could take it from you like *that*. Remember that. And watch out for your sister too."

"Why you care what happen to we?"

"Faith ain't measured in nuggets of gold, but in the things you do. You father was the onliest body in this village who truly believe I coulda make the West Indies team. Everybody else try to bring me down, to belittle me. Them cheer for me when I was playing local cricket, but the minute my name get mention for big cricket, the minute I get call to trials, them turn on me, like them couldn't stand to see me get through. Them say I would never be good enough, that I was too worthless. That I drink too much rum, that I had too much women, that I too lazy. Not your father. He believe in me. Used to tell me all the time I was the best fast bowler he ever see. That I was better than Wes Hall. I wasn't very careful with money in those days, and when I didn't have money to get a good pair of shoes for the trials, Steel give me the money. And he come and watch every match I play.

"And when the radio announce that I make the Barbados team and everybody start saying how them know I was gonna make the team, Steel and me, we just stand up and listen to them and laugh.

"I play twelve matches for Barbados, and who knows, if what happen to me didn't happen, I mighta make the West Indies. But I got good memories 'bout cricket days and I would never forget your father. And I promise myself when I hear that he was. . . you know . . . going to be . . .you know, I promise myself I would look out for his children as much as I could."

Then he was gone. Crab-walked across the street so fast, it surprised her. A car zipped past. When she looked again, he had disappeared into the tiny space between two houses.

Cold disappointment crept past her defenses after he'd disappeared. Why would she feel that way about him? A cripple. But after what she'd done today, who was she to pity anybody?

Was it her fault that Obe was such a poor judge of character, such a poor chooser of men, or that Porter turned out to be weak? Was it her fault that her mother had come home and caught him screwing her?

From the time Porter moved in, a day didn't pass when she didn't find him staring at her. She wanted to ask him why he looked at her that way, like he'd paid money for a special close-up view. But she stopped herself, knowing it would lead to a big bassa-bassa.

One morning he addressed her in the yard as she was coming out of the bath nestled in the shade of the lime tree next to the outhouse. She thought he'd long since pedaled off to attend to his boat. With nothing but a towel wrapped around her lanky frame she felt acutely vulnerable.

"You ain't like me, do you?" he said.

She stared at him, so huge and oppressive, so big that he seemed to block out the cold seven o'clock sun.

"Why you ain't like me?" he challenged.

"I ain't got no reason."

"You just don't."

"Yes."

And then she knew why he looked at her that way, why his eyes punctured the silence of her soul and made her fearful. With devilish confidence, showing tobacco-stained teeth, he reached out and touched her bare shoulder. His thick mustache moved with the smile like sea anemone under attack. She stood magnetized by such forwardness. Her mother's man wanted to screw her.

Today when she came home half-day with a headache, the house was empty. The quiet of the house upset her more than the heat. She'd been looking forward to spending the afternoon with Celine, who'd started eating regularly. Where could her sister have gone?

Searching for a breeze, she flung all the windows open. The house remained oppressively hot. Everything was still. Couldn't even smell the roses. Green lizards baked on the window 'til they turned brown. Hazy, languid quiet had settled on the yard.

With a wet towel she wiped sweat from her naked body and stretched across the bed. She'd left the bedroom door unlatched so that if Celine came home while she was asleep, she wouldn't have to get up.

When she woke and saw Porter staring at her nakedness, she was filled with panic, then rage, then nothing. Then exhilaration. She saw the power she had over him. He was big, frightening, weak. Weakness she would later find out all men had for a woman's body. All men could be challenged and conquered by it.

Doing nothing to delay or deny him, she let him come. A sack of potatoes dropped on top of her, crumpling her slender body. As he pumped away, gasping and sputtering like a broken-down engine, she put her hands on his ass and was shocked by his nakedness. She couldn't remember him taking his clothes off. She wanted to laugh. She didn't know what she was doing or why she was doing it. Mother should come through the door and catch her precious man screwing her daughter. That was her only thought.

And then she looked around and wondered if she was dreaming. Serene, almost angel-like, her mother was standing in the doorway as composed as a priest during communion.

For a second their eyes clashed above Porter's pig sounds. Cyan blinked twice. The dark limp shadow in the doorway was coming to life. The eyes began to roll; the mouth was making utterances in loud plangent tones. Then the mass rushed toward them. Porter went flying through the window, and then her body was hers again, light and buoyant.

She lay unmoved, strangely separate from the goings-on outside. Her mother was cursing. And then she looked out the window and saw Porter running naked across the pasture.

Her mother did not speak to her at all for the rest of the day. But there were looks. Wide, insistent stares. Obe's eyes had grown the size of cannon balls, and as black. It was as if her mother were trying to suck her back into her womb through her expanded black eyes.

Cyan stayed in her room. Each time Obe passed, she'd give her elder daughter a look. Cyan latched the door. Her mother broke it down; leaving her unprotected, exposed to that look. She closed her eyes, pretended not to notice Obe when she came to stand in the doorway, but she could feel the eyes boring into her. Soon the blankness of her mother's eyes surrounded her. She felt like she was drowning. She heard Obe crying in the kitchen and tried to swim toward her, to beg forgiveness. But her mother seemed to retreat, recede, as if she were being pulled backward by the undertow of her anger.

When Celine came home, she too was silent. She didn't want to talk and went straight to sleep like she had taken a drug. Silence forced Cyan from the house.

Cyan followed the fireflies home. Celine was still asleep, and her mother had left the house. Relieved, Cyan fell asleep soon after her face touched the pillow.

A burning bladder woke her up round midnight. She heard a voice and stayed still, thinking it was her mother. It was Celine. In front of the painting.

"I ain't go let them get me, Pa. Them got you but I ain't go let them get me," Celine was saying.

"Celine? What you doing, girl?" Cyan whispered loudly.

"Talking to Pa."

"Girl, don't talk craziness. Get back in the bed."

"Why you hide from me that this was Pa here in this picture all along? Why you tell me it ain't Pa? Why you lie to me?"

"Celine, you all right? Come here, let me see if you got a fever."

"I ain't got no fever. This is Pa, Night. He talk to me. I just talk to him."

"Celine, girl, what the shite you talking? You going mad? Get in the bed. You like you stay out in the sun too long today or something."

"Come and see, Night. Come and see. Come and talk to him."

"I don't have to come and see nothing. I's the body bring home that picture, remember. If he was going to talk to somebody he woulda talk to me. Now get your tail in the bed."

"Night, he talk to me. I swear. He wake me up. He say he know I thinking 'bout getting rid of the baby, and he agree with me is the best thing to do. Then I could finish my O-levels and get a good job."

"Celine, get in the bed 'fore I have to call Ma for you. You want Ma to come in here and knock that damn baby outta you for talking foolishness?"

Celine sat on the floor opposite the painting.

"Celine, girl get up!"

"Only if you come and talk to Pa. He say he wanna talk to you, too."

"Get in the bed, Celine. You head going bad. If Ma hear you she go definitely send you down to the Mental," Cyan muttered, as she pulled the topsie from under the bed. "Get in the bed. And if I catch you in front that picture again say you talking to Pa, I go take it down and give it way."

As Cyan hoisted her nightdress to sit on the topsie, she noticed the dark figure standing in the doorway.

"What the rass going on in here, tell me?" Obe fumed. "I shoulda know not to let you put that damn picture in here. It ain't bad enough that she go have a child for a man that gone mad and run away, now she talking to a picture like she going mad, too."

Obe grabbed the painting from the wall. Struggling to wrench the painting from her mother, Cyan knocked over the topsie, spilling stale pee all over the floor. Cyan slipped on the slick floor. Dragging the painting, Obe proceeded to the kitchen, where she grabbed a box of matches before going out the backdoor into the yard.

Cyan jumped up and followed her mother.

"What you go do, Ma? What you go do?" she screamed.

Obe dropped a lit match on the painting. It flared up quickly.

"No, Ma! You can't do that. No!"

"I can do anything I want in this blasted house. After what you do today I don't care nothing 'bout you. You ain't my daughter. You ain't nothing but a slut!"

The oil paint crackled and outlined the darkness with greenish yel low flame. Cyan ran to get water from the pipe, but the painting was already destroyed.

Obe went back inside, leaving her daughter to watch the fine embers and ash

Chapter Nine

Umbrellas moved past her like shapeless memories. Faces hidden underneath black cloth and wire. No one recognized her. She longed to be recognized by somebody. Who was she? Didn't anyone want to know?

Cyan listened to the gusts howling around her, blowing the savage rain against her unprotected face. The umbrellas continued to move swiftly by. Some yielded to the ferocious wind, landing like broken blackbirds with soft splashes in the puddles only to be retrieved by the faces suddenly coming to life with emotion.

"Shite!"

"Fuck!"

"Blasted umbrella gone an' brek!"

She was soaked to the soul. Her shoes, her hair, her clothes, her heart, all waterlogged.

There he was again looking at her. Across the street his body curved against the house like a tree uprooted and flung against a rock.

Now inching toward her in the rain. His eyes looked closed, his legs moving as fast as possible but going nowhere.

"Look like you go need a guardian angel, girl," he said, coming closer.

"I ain't no girl. And I ain't need no guardian angel."

"Yes, you do. And God send me."

"You's a mad man."

"You may be right," he said with a wet smile.

The wind had died down some; rain was still pelting. She looked at him and wondered what was keeping him from falling over.

"God," he said, as if he'd read her mind. "God is what keeping me going. You need God in your life."

"I don't need nutten."

"I know how you feel right now. But God can change all that."

"Can He bring my sister back? Can He bring my father back?"

"Yes. He can do that."

"Then tell Him do it right now."

"Don't expect Him to do it just because you want."

"Then kiss my rass!"

"Come up to the church next Sunday. Let me pray for you."

"People 'bout here pray for me enough. I don't want nobody praying for me. I can pray for meself."

"Don't let your heart dry up from weeping and suffering; let the love of God fill it with sweet joy. God's got a plan for you. He ain't making you suffer for nothing."

And then he was gone.

There was no meaning to life, no meaning to faith, to God. She did not believe in guardian angels. If there was such a thing why were her father and sister gone from her?

Celine died on the second of June 1984, one day after she was taken to the hospital unconscious and hemorrhaging. She had been buried yesterday, the seventh. She died because she was hard-ears if you listened to her mother.

She died because the abortion went bad. An abortion Cyan didn't think she would have. Who did it? Who paid for it? That answer went with Celine to her grave.

Cyan had been wandering the street since the funeral. Last night she slept on the soft turned earth of Celine's grave. Tonight could be anywhere.

She wished she could've saved her sister. And if not Celine, the baby. Something. Anything that said their lives mattered. But her sister had decided that without Silly the baby wasn't worth the trouble. Oh, how Cyan hated men who ran away from responsibility! Was it too much to ask them to treat a woman's love with some respect? To treat you with some dignity after they got what they wanted?

Cyan wore white for Celine. She borrowed money from Koko for the coffin. That was white too. She knew her only sister would've approved.

Nightfall. The rain had stopped. She'd been sitting on the seawall for hours. Surrounded by warm darkness, Cyan wondered if the waves were wailing for her sister. Or if stars that threaded the night like diamonds on a black string would dance to the calypso beat of her sister's heart. If stars were part of Heaven, then they would be dashing about tonight preparing a welcome for their newest angel. She looked up, and Heaven was as still as the flat earth.

Why she didn't jump with fright when the man climbed up on the wall and sat next to her was something she'd never understand. The moment he climbed up, a star darted mockingly across the sky. The irony did not elude her. She'd prayed for dancing stars, but all she got was one stinking star, which skipped weakly before her eyes and died. If she'd blinked, she would've missed it. God was mocking her like he always did, like he mocked Celine.

The man sat to her left. She looked around. It was Breeze. His smile was genuine. That smile had moved her before. She wanted him to stay.

He smelled of beer. Though she'd never had alcohol in her life, she suddenly got the urge to get drunk. In the split second that followed the warm feeling evoked by his smile, she decided what would happen that night. In that heartbeat between the star darting across the face of the moon and waves halting on the bank, waiting for her to drink, she decided to get drunk and to hell with tomorrow.

She awoke next morning in a strange place, numb beyond sleep. It felt like she'd been buried in mud for weeks, causing all her muscles to atrophy.

The house was empty. She was naked. Like the remains of wedding-night frenzy, her white dress dangled from the edge of a chair. Where were her panties? The memory of taking them off was dull: the drunken laughter that accompanied it, loud slurping kisses in the warmest and wettest places. Then the madness of it all came rushing back to her. The frenzy, the wild uncouthness with which he'd taken her. Too rough. But strangely she'd felt no pain.

She slipped the dress over her aching head, not bothering to look for her panties anymore, and went through the door.

The police were waiting with her mother when she got home. Things got ugly fast. So ugly, the police had to restrain her mother and threaten to take her away because they thought she would kill her daughter.

And neighbors came out of their houses to listen while the police waited, hoping the woman would calm down before the rain came. Clouds were getting fatter and fatter, ready to scrape earth; the wind gave off that damp smell of a long hard rain. Goats were scrambling to higher ground. Sparrows were quiet. Not so Obe.

"I swear is an early grave You must have plan for me, Lord. Otherwise You wouldn'ta give me such disagreeable children. But if You think I go beg you to spare me, Yuh wrong. Yuh put me here and I go take whatever You give me. If You testing me, then I go pass this test. Maybe I ain't as strong as I used to be. But I stronger than I look. If You think I go give up, Yuh wrong. I ain't giving up. I ain't giving back this life You give me. If You want it, You go have to come and take it back cause I ain't go let these children kill me. One already gone, and if I have to take this other one so she don't kill me first, then Lord you know I would do it. You give me life and I keeping it. At all costs. So You could stop testing me. Whatever You do to test me, I plan to survive."

After that, weeks went by without a word between them. Cyan left the house to go to work and nowhere else. In the evening she would sit in her room tearing petals off withered roses, or sit in the window to watch fireflies arrive, hoping they would bring a guest, someone whose smile could touch her like their glow. The fireflies always appeared just before six o'clock. Sometimes they came in such large numbers, appearing out of nowhere like fluorescent rain, that Cyan wanted to run and play among them as she used to do.

One week the fireflies did not come. And Cyan cried.

At work she was seeing less of Koko, who was spending more time in her gallery. And if she wasn't in her gallery, she was off taking pictures around the country. The house was lonely when the Mistress wasn't there. She'd gotten used to chatting with Koko in between her chores.

Koko had brought the biggest wreath to Celine's funeral. The following Sunday she had taken Cyan for a drive around the island.

They drove through St. George, past acres of sugarcane and flat open land where sheep and cows grazed. At Welchman Hall Gully they stopped to catch a glimpse of green monkeys, but instead found deeper enjoyment watching a group of tourists prance around the gully's tiny bamboo-bordered tracks behind a family of monkeys. Baby animals clung to the backs of parents and peered wide-eyed at the strangers in their midst while the leader of the lazy-moving pack stroked himself constantly and mugged unabashedly for the cameras. Accompanied by guides using assumed English accents to narrate the historical origins of green monkeys on the island, the tourists marveled at how tame the animals were. One woman pointed out that it was easier to take pictures of the monkeys than of the people. And the animals didn't ask for money.

They left the monkeys and the tourists who seemed to get on so well together to take in the valleys and hills of St. John. They drove past casuarina trees, guinea and khuskhus grass sloping down hillsides; down the East Coast Road, past rows of coconut trees and goats grazing under trees and along hedgerows. They stopped at a small roadside shop in St. Joseph for a lunch of fish cakes and mauby. Before long Koko was up taking pictures of old men playing dominoes and an old woman sitting outside nursing a Ju-C in the hot afternoon. Then they were off again driving along the rough coastline.

They were so close to the sea, Cyan could see water droplets from the sea spray settling on the gleaming backs of fishermen crouched cleaning their nets. A heaving sea smashed against giant green rocks, which rose like monsters from the seabed about fifty yards out. She'd never seen this side of the island before. She asked Koko to stop. They pulled off the road onto the sandy shoulder. Cyan got out and walked across the sand to the edge. For the first time in her life she looked at the sea and felt fear and awe. The water seemed so dark. And the foaming head was heavy and moss-filled. It churned sluggishly around itself, milking its way to the shore as if burdened down with sorrow. She could almost see the rocks trembling when the sea crashed into them. She expected them to split open at any time. How could fisher-men survive these waters? She thought of her father. He would've loved the challenge they presented.

She felt a sweaty arm wrap around her shoulder.

"The Atlantic Ocean is an awesome sight, isn't it?" Koko said.

Cyan didn't reply. She didn't know this was what it was called. It was all just Sea to her. She allowed Koko to draw her closer. It was a com-forting feeling. On one of the huge rocks in the distance she saw her father's face.

"This is where the slave ships landed from Africa," Koko said.

"You mekking sport. Here? On this beach?"

"Not here on this spot, but along this coast. The ships came across the Atlantic. Of all the islands in the Caribbean, Barbados is closest to Africa. A lot of times this was the first stop the slave ships made. Slaves bound for other islands usually saw Barbados first."

"How you know so much 'bout what went on here in them times?"

"I read a lot."

"I does read, too, but I didn't know any of that."

"You know, one of the things that struck me as odd when I first got here was how much the people on this island took things for granted. I thought that since most of the people here were black, black govern-ment and everything, the place would be full of monuments and memorials to slaves and their struggle for freedom. I was surprised that none existed. And then I heard something that seemed like an expla-nation. Someone on television, a politician, I think, was saying that folks here saw their very existence as a living memorial to past struggles. They didn't see the need for monuments, for images, for reminders that they came from slaves. It troubled me, but I decided it must've been my American sensibility. And I was determined to leave my American val-ues locked away. Then one day I was out driving and I saw a group of tourists offering some young white children money so they could take pictures of them in their school uniforms. And after the tourists left I went up to the same group and asked if I could take their picture. They stared at me in bewilderment and shook their heads. When I offered them money, they ran off. The way those children ran from me hurt me. I thought about it for a long time. I started to reflect on everything I felt when I came here. And the absence of monuments and memorials began to trouble me again. Was there some connection between the absence of monuments honoring black heroes and those children running from me? I could no longer escape my background. It sent me searching through the history books, searching the island's literature, searching for the writers on the island. I didn't find much. All the writers lived overseas. All your stories have been forgotten, buried, or lost or there's nobody bold enough to challenge that mind-set of forgetfulness. That's why I decided to open a gallery. I was optimistic that there were people on this island who were uncomfortable enough with their fractured past to create art."

"Maybe the children run because you bald head frighten them," Cyan said.

They looked at each and laughed.

That peculiar weighty smell of fish and seawater so familiar to Cyan followed them as they set off again. The sun was spread out in a blanket of blue above them. A cozy feeling settled in her stomach as they sped along the winding roads. How wonderful it felt sitting next to Koko in the Triumph with the top down, feeling the wind slap her face, breathing the sea, listening to Koko talk about her life in the States.

"You always know you wanted to take pictures of people?" Cyan asked.

"Yes. My mother was a very beautiful woman. The first time I saw a picture of her and realized I could keep it in my room all the time I knew that's what I wanted to do. To take pictures of beautiful people so I could look at them all the time. Unfortunately, a lot of the pictures I had to take weren't beautiful."

"And you' mother ain't try to stop you?"

"My mother didn't care what I did. She was too busy trying to be a star. She was an actress. A great one too. But she hardly worked. She left me with my grandmother while she tried to conquer Hollywood. She got bit parts in a few movies, but nothing substantial."

"That a real place, this Hollywood?"

"Yes, it's real enough for those who believe in it. My mother believed in it. She knew she was forced to live in a box in Hollywood because she was black, but she refused to give up her dream. When she died, she still hadn't given up the dream that she'd get a call to play a great role some day. I left America because I refuse to live my life in a box."

"You don't feel living here is like living in a box? I feel that way sometimes. That I living in a box. And that people throwing stones all the time, trying to smash the box. Actually I does feel that way all the time nowadays. That I ain't never go get out this box. And even if I get out, what's the point? People go still try to put you back in. There got some people, it seem like that is their job. To put you in a box and keep you there. From small, that's the way it was for me. Who ain't call me stupid call me ugly. I don't mind people calling me Night now, but when I did small, I used to cry when people call me so. I used to hate the sun. I used to put a lot of powder on me face, thinking I could hide how dark I was. I wish I did born in America or some place else. I don't understand how you could leave a place like America, where you could be anything, where everything free and you got so much things. I hear everybody got a car and TV in their house. That the hospitals like hotels, and got more doctors than patients. How you could leave that to come and live here?"

"The America you know is Hollywood. That ain't the real America. At least it ain't the America I grew up in. I don't know if I came here because I was in love or because I just wanted to get out of America. I needed a sanctuary. Somewhere along the way I'd given up hope. Looking back on it now, I don't know how I could've done that. Given up hope like that. That was so unlike me. I was used to fighting. I was used to struggle. I grew up in Chicago, a city with a particularly vicious police force. I fought with them. And survived. Was never intimidated. But then I crashed. Lost faith in what I was doing. Plain and simple. I wasn't prepared for the suddenness of it. I went to New York. Then Jonathan came along. Leaving America was an easy decision at the time."

They passed a school with a poster for a drive-in movie pasted on one of the walls.

"You could take me to the drive-in?" Cyan asked timidly. "I never been to the drive-in. They got a picture with Sidney Poiter showing. He look so good. The first time I see him was in a picture call *Warm December*. When he come on the screen, I didn't want to look at nobody else."

"I have a thing for Sidney's smile myself. And those eyes."

"He remind me of Breeze. The way he smile. So confident. Like he know exactly what he go do next, and if you like it or not, he go still do it."

Koko fell silent for a moment.

"Breeze? You've seen Breeze lately?" Koko asked.

"Yes. The day after Celine bury. Can I tell you a secret?" Cyan said.

"Of course, you can."

"I think I love Breeze. Breeze and me, we had sex that night. I think I did drunk, but it did still feel real real sweet."

"How does he feel about you?"

"I don't know. I ain't seen him since. You think I should tell him how I feel when I see him again?"

"I don't know. It might be better to see if he feels the same way."

"How I go know if he feel the same way unless I tell him how I feel?"

"That's a very brave thing to do. Telling a man you love him when you don't know how he feels."

"I don't know 'bout brave. If I don't tell him, he might get away before I get a chance."

They drove through St. Lucy in silence. At Culpepper Bay they got out to stretch their legs. Then they drove on to North Point, where they descended the warm wave-eaten caverns to play among the sea anemone in the Animal Flower Cave. Their colors and the way they cleverly moved away when you tried to touch them reminded Cyan of butterflies. A short distance from them, a thunderous sea carved faces in the rocky coast.

"Do you know who gave your sister the abortion?" Koko said as they left the caverns, slicked with sweat and sea spray.

"Nobody don't know. She ain't tell nobody. And she did unconscious by the time she get to the hospital, and nobody ain't get a chance to talk to she."

"That's a shame."

"I couldn't believe it was Celine when I went to dress her at the funeral home. I wish now I'da let my mother go. But I know if she did gone, she woulda dress Celine in black. And I didn't want that. But that wasn't Celine. She body did so hard, like rockstone. I was putting clothes on rockstone. Not Celine. That is why at the church you ain't see me go near the coffin. I know it did only rockstone inside that box."

Things were not going well with Dr. Mayhem. He seemed nervous all the time, asking questions about Koko that Cyan had no answers for: Who came to see Koko? Who called for her? She had to tell him straight that if he thought his wife was horning him, he should ask her.

He began threatening to fire her. He would give her a list of things to do: what kind of food to cook, which clothes he wanted cleaned or pressed urgently, then he would accuse her of not following his instructions.

Wednesdays he took off; it was like a holy day. Taking a day off in the middle of the week was his way of enforcing his importance on the rest of the world. On that day he did nothing. He would leave the house early in the morning dressed in shorts and sandals, returning just before sundown to eat his favorite meal: saltfish stewed in okra and onions over black-eyed peas and rice.

One Wednesday he instructed Cyan to cook fish and chips. When she pointed out it was Wednesday, his holy day, his saltfish day, he looked at her as if wanting to bite off her head and snapped, "Don't question me, just do as I tell you! I want fish and chips today."

She seasoned and fried flying fish with as much care and attention as if she were cooking for her father. Dr. Mayhem's angry outburst that evening when he sat down to dinner and saw fried fish staring him in the face instead of his okra stew almost made her quit on the spot. Cyan wanted to scream at him the way he screamed at her—Stupid! Incompetent! But she bit her tongue.

Later, as she was changing in a guest room for the trip home, he knocked at the door.

"Cyan?"

She did not answer, fearing he'd come to blame her for something else.

"Cyan? You in there?"

Cold silence lasting about a minute. He spoke again.

"Cyan, I'm sorry. I was wrong. I remember now, I'd told you this morning I wanted fried fish tonight. I wasn't thinking."

She remained silent, hoping he would think she'd gone. Through the stillness she heard him laboring to breathe. Was he all right? The wheezing made her think of blowing soap bubbles in the washtub through a pawpaw reed. Cyan almost laughed out at the sweet memory of dueling with Celine to see who could blow the biggest bubbles. But the sound frightened her. She opened the door, forgetting that she had on only bra and panties.

"You alright, Dr. Mayhem?"

Sweating vigorously, he was leaning against the wall. He looked at her, became unexpectedly aware of an extreme, hard beauty about her, and dropped his eyes. He wasn't even sure he liked her, but Cyan got under his skin. Made him uneasy. Even when she displayed concern, stubbornness showed in her eyes and punctuated her voice. Her big round eyes seemed to take in the whole world but let nothing out. Her face could be so blank. Her defiance was admirable if annoying. And the tight glossy blackness of her skin troubled him, too. He'd never seen anyone in this country bear such blackness so boldly. "Night" did suit her, both her disposition and her complexion. Why couldn't she be like all the others he'd hired? Why wasn't she impressed by the fact that he drank with the chief justice, that he dined at the house of the American ambassador, or that he'd gone to school with the prime minister and most of the members of his cabinet? Why didn't she come to him asking favors, wanting money, giving him the opportunity to charm her?

"It's just an allergy," he said. "I'll be alright."

She turned to go. He wanted her to stay. He wanted to wash his eyes over her sleek black legs, so slender, they could be burnt cane.

His hand fell on the warm flesh of her shoulder as he reached out to stop her from going back into the room.

Cyan recoiled and slapped it away as she turned to face him. Her eyes shot sparks.

"Don't touch me! Don't you ever touch me again, hear!"

"I'm sorry," he said. "Didn't mean nothing. I wanted to tell you something, that's all. Something I'd been hiding from you. Something I should've told you before but didn't know how."

He waited for her to respond. Her wooden stare was eloquent enough.

"That painting I gave you, that *is* your father," he continued. "I met with him in prison a couple of times after he was sentenced. He'd been depressed and acting strange, and they wanted a determination on whether he was suicidal or not. I didn't want to tell you the truth that day we met because I knew he'd been put to death. I could tell you were upset, and I didn't know how you'd react if I'd confirmed it was actually your father who'd inspired the painting. Besides, I just wanted to get it done, get it out of me. He left a big impression on me, as you could tell. All he talked about was the sea. How he wished he'd gone fishing that night. And when he spoke, he stared into my face. Like you're doing now. His eyes never leaving my face. Like he was trying to hypnotize me. . . like he was trying to send me a message. It's hard to explain. Anyway, once I'd lied to you, I didn't know how to tell you the truth later on."

Her silence made him feel ashamed. He couldn't face her eyes, and so didn't see the tears brimming at the corners. With nothing more to say he turned, deflated, and departed.

As she boarded the bus home that night, Cyan knew she would never go back there.

Chapter Ten

$\mathcal{B}$loated dead frogs in his driveway as he set out to work. Two weeks now. That first morning as he backed the car out of the garage onto one of them, the popping sound it made as it exploded frightened him. Stepping out of the Peugeot to check, he glimpsed Koko standing in the doorway, looking as strange and as beautiful as when he'd first met her on the steps of the Metropolitan Museum in New York. There her bald, perfectly round head, dark under the shadowy lights, had brought a taste of licorice rushing to his mouth, and then he was struck with an overwhelming desire to lick her head. So that when she arrived on the island and her hair began to grow back, he was happy she continued to shave it.

Each morning Dr. Mayhem would get out to examine the dead frogs, wondering where they came from, whether they were dying in his driveway or if someone was putting them there, and each morning as he bent down, he would catch Koko watching him from the door, looking strange and beautiful, and he would relive that night in New York, become as excited as the first time he saw her and return to the house filled with the desire to lick her head which always led to lovemaking.

After two weeks he'd had enough of the frogs, though he was tempted not to take action; before their sudden appearance he and Koko hadn't made love in a year.

He called the Health Department to see if there had been other reports of the recurrent dead frogs around the country. The receptionist told him the Chief Health Inspector, an old high school mate, would not be in until twelve o'clock, then before he could hang up, she said, "Mistuh, you sure you wife ain't horning you?"

The woman's question needled him all the way to his office. The suspicion that Koko was having an affair had been riding him for months. There could be no rational connection between the appearance of dead frogs in his driveway and his wife horning him. But it was precisely the irrationality of it that convinced him his suspicions were indeed correct. All he needed was proof.

Following the rational path of science was supposed to remove the hold of superstition left over from his past. But his past was alive with strange and illogical occurrences, where science had no dominion, where rationality was as naked and as helpless as a newborn. A past filled with incredible stories told by Reema, his itinerant grandmother, who traveled the countryside selling potatoes and interpreting dreams, and who promised to look out for him always, even from her grave. And to him Reema's word was still gospel. He believed everything she'd ever told him.

Ever since her death he'd kept up a correspondence with his grandmother: whenever he felt troubled, he'd write her a letter. The act of writing connected them, he'd remember her stories as vividly as if hearing them for the first time and by the end of the session, whatever was troubling him would've melted away. As history sought the storyteller to capture the glory of a culture, he was convinced history had singled him out, an example of logic and faith existing in harmony, and because of this he'd learned to listen even more closely to his patients when they spoke of sightings, or visits from and conversations with deceased loved ones.

His favorite Reema story was about Isaac, her father. Isaac had sworn revenge on a man named Benjamin who'd killed one of his cows after it had strayed onto Benjamin's property and eaten all his young corn. What made Isaac furious was that Benjamin didn't have the decency to eat the meat after he'd slaughtered the cow, but left it for the corbeaus and dogs. He'd vowed to "put two big rocks in Benjamin's chest if it's one minute to Judgment." But Benjamin had died suddenly a few days later leaving Isaac with what seemed like an empty vow. On his deathbed many years afterward, Isaac instructed his family to put two big rocks in his coffin because he expected to butt up on Benjamin somewhere on the Other Side. His outlandish burial instructions were ignored; Isaac was buried with all the ceremony attendant upon a man who'd fathered thirty children from five women, but he went to his grave without his big rocks, under protest from Reema, who'd been overruled by her eldest brother. It did not take long for the mistake to become legend. A week later the family woke up to find little white worms crawling all over the house. The worms were killed and the house sprayed with disinfectant; finally by nightfall, it appeared that all the worms had disappeared. Next morning the worms had returned, this time too many to manage. The Health Department was called, but no one there believed the story. Unable to sleep in the house that night the family huddled together under a makeshift tent outside to decide what to do. Reema convinced them that their father was showing his displeasure at their disobedience. Next night three sons, along with Reema—there to make sure they did it right this time—went to the graveyard to put the big rocks in the coffin. There were no sightings of worms after that.

He arrived at his office on George Street at half past nine. His secretary informed him that his first appointment, a new patient named Augusta Baptiste, had canceled. It didn't surprise him. Most people canceled at least three appointments before coming their first time. She'd probably managed to convince herself at the last minute that she could handle her problems on her own. She'd make it to his office eventually.

His thriving practice floated on the backs of middle class professionals and their distressed teenage children under pressure to excel in school. Most of his time was spent counseling parents, who couldn't understand how their perfectly normal children trained so well in the art of self-control could end up so lost in a society willing to cater to their every whim.

He identified with the parents. Like most of them he'd surmounted poverty with education. Growing up in St. Thomas he'd risen every morning to a cup of scalded cow's milk and two biscuits before setting off to school. He'd recited his times table while his stomach growled with hunger knowing that all he would get for lunch when he ran home would be another cup of scalded cow's milk and two more biscuits. After high school he worked in the civil service for five years before leaving for New York University on half-scholarship.

Armed with a piece of paper testifying to his expertise in psychotherapy, he found himself almost unemployable on his return to the island. His was a country of people with no emotional problems, it seemed. A visit to a psychologist, psychiatrist, or any kind of behavioral specialist was an outright admission of insanity, the greatest infirmity a person could admit to—greater than having cancer or diabetes, or high-blood pressure. To admit to any form of mental dysfunction was equal to or worse than being impotent, each a sign of frail genes, a reason to hang your head in shame.

Reema used to say that only Eke-bekes, her term for white people, went mad. It would not have surprised him if that belief had sprung up among slaves somewhere on a plantation where heat and tropical diseases caused whites to suffer sensory delusions. The reverse was nearer the truth: Slavery must've driven more blacks than whites to madness, he suspected. Still, these descendants of slaves had somehow managed to rise above the inhumanity of that experience. Perhaps only the strongest survived. Were there no weak ones among them? Were there no Barbadians willing to admit to frailties of the mind, to passions they couldn't control?

He knew better. These progeny of slaves used alcohol as therapy, as their chokehold on sanity, and if he kept his shingle up, they'd find him.

After a year of near unemployment spent in the library and the public gallery of the House of Assembly listening to debates, he got his first client, a woman who wanted to commit suicide because her child had failed the eleven-plus exam. Gradually more clients trickled in: men and women chasing the demons of success and having difficulty relating to an unpleasant past, an imperfect present, an uncertain future; men and women trying to come to terms with loss. These were his clients. People who'd left the gossip and superstitions of tiny villages for the wall-and-glass hysteria of the housing development, the Parks. People who didn't want to be reminded that their mothers and grandmothers worked on plantations, who felt assaulted if they heard Bajan dialect, who wished their children weren't so dark, and who couldn't understand why their lives were so empty, though their cupboards were overflowing.

But was his life any better? And what if Koko was having an affair? Hadn't he done the very same thing?

He'd tried to keep his pursuit of young virgins from her eyes, but in an island this small, you couldn't hide a thimble from the blind. Koko had been his first virgin. It was an experience still unparalleled in his mind. He was shocked that someone her age could be a virgin. Still, it unleashed cravings in him he didn't know existed. He found himself fantasizing about it over and over. Wanting to relive it. There was something primal and regenerative about the struggle he had to enter her that first time. And when he finally did, it was with a sense of possession, a sense that what magic lay ahead would be his and his alone, with the power to transform him. He was a pioneer, discovering something new. Columbus discovering the New World.

But what would've transformed him and their marriage most was children. Though he didn't expect to match his grandfather's prodigious harvest of offspring, he'd always fancied the idea of a large family. Had Koko been willing he would've liked four or five children. When she failed to conceive, he was afraid it might've been the feebleness of his seed, until, eight years into marriage, he seduced a young virgin from St. Joseph who'd come to work for them as a maid. She became pregnant and gave birth to a boy who later died of pneumonia. But that buried any doubt about his seed's power. He often wondered what would've happened had the child lived. Would he have left Koko? A childless marriage was not what he'd expected. And he suspected that his wife might've had an abortion at some time during their marriage. But she denied it.

Did it really matter that she was having an affair? Yes. He was a man. And as a man, he had to confront her. But with proof. He didn't want to look stupid.

By Palm Sunday he had the proof he needed. She was dressed for the beach. As she was about to leave he sprung his trap.

"Where're you going?" Jonathan asked.

"Isn't it obvious?" she replied, her dark eyes dimming suspiciously "Why?"

"I thought you might want my company. We haven't been to the beach together in years."

"I'm just going to relax and read a book. I don't really need any company."

"You have a book for that beach bum, Breeze, too, or can't he read?"

Halfway out the door, she stopped.

"What?"

"Don't *what* me! I followed you to that house in Harts Gap, you know. If you were going to horn me, why couldn't you pick somebody with class? Why a beach bum? How is that going to make me look?"

"Sonofabitch!"

"I haven't finished—Koko! Come back here!"

"All of a sudden you're spying on me? What's the matter. No hungry little uneducated whores left for you to impress? Too bad, isn't it?"

"Barren bitch!"

"You've got some nerve. You have the nerve to call *me* barren? You are the emptiest muthafucker to come down the pike."

"Why the hell can't you have any children? Call them what you like, but at least those girls can breed."

"Well, that's about all they seem to do. And with people like you on the island, that's about all they'll ever get to do. I wouldn't be caught dead carrying your child, Jonathan."

"Then why do you stay with me?"

"That's a good question."

"You slut! Come back here or don't come back at all, you hear me!"

She rented a three-bedroom wooden house in Dayrells Road not far from the Garrison Savannah racetrack. It came furnished by its expatriate owners. Yellow chairs and sofa, blue drapes far too heavy for the climate, pink linoleum throughout the house. The furniture, drapes, and linoleum would have to go. And maybe she'd repaint the blue walls white. Once she improved the walls with her own paintings and photographs, the place would take on a more comely look. The garden out front was overrun with ferns gone wild and crotons that had long assumed their colorful foliage gave them rights to the property. Until she came to the island, she'd never had any interest in gardens or gardening, but she'd found their presence around every house on the island pleasing; they seemed to fit well with the tranquillity and submissiveness of the populace. She would hire someone to trim the crotons and restore order to the ferns as well as plant some roses and lilies.

The thought of returning to the States flew away as swiftly as it had hatched. If she had wanted to go back to the States, she would've done so years ago when she found out about the baby Jonathan had fathered. She loved Barbados: its sauna-hot days, its green gentle hills, air rich with the scent of flowers and fruit, and most of all the undulating sea of black people she saw every day going about their business with a complacency that could have bloomed only beyond the reach of racism.

Her bald head had created waves of speculation and fascination in the country's conservative atmosphere and had made her somewhat of a celebrity on the island; her blue Triumph convertible was as recognized in the street as the prime minister's Mercedes. Her frequent appearances on television to talk about exhibitions at her ground-floor gallery in the Hilton Hotel—where she'd sold paintings to Elton John, Mick Jagger and other celebrities—brought the social elite buzzing to her door. Invitations to cocktail parties, luncheons, and dinners piled up on her desk. Men came at her from all angles—doctors, lawyers, businessmen, mostly friends of her husband—and when she told him, he would feign surprise, but beneath it she knew he was proud that his friends coveted his eccentric American wife. However, she preferred the company of the free-spirited beach vendors, fishermen, and artists whom she photographed.

Foreigners had a penchant for romanticizing as exotic an unfamiliar culture, especially one that exhibited so little of the unsettling violence of their own, where the death of a black person caused less concern than the death of a dog. But Koko did not think of herself as a foreigner on the island anymore, though she wondered to herself if that wasn't the ultimate sign of a romantic.

After she'd been in Barbados a number of years, seduced by the lullaby of hushed greenery and violet sunsets that gave way to nights where the moon was so low and big, she felt she could reach up and break off a piece, she wondered how she'd endured the brutality of American life: the noise, the mummified city buildings fixed together row after row like screams in a nightmare, the blizzards, the police always hovering like buzzards, the loneliness. Perhaps she was somewhat romantic about the island, but in her view, there was nothing wrong with that. Life was good to her here.

Cyan came over at ten in the morning to help her get settled in the new house. The music of Ray Charles and the Temptations blared all morning long from the stereo while they unpacked boxes of photographs, clothes, camera equipment, books, and kitchen utensils. From outside came the lively voices of passersby greeting each other, and young boys arguing points in a road tennis game. Across the street, in a little alcove between two houses, men sat on wooden crates dueling at dominoes, while more leaned against an akee tree, awaiting their turn. Bottles of white rum appeared and disappeared with alarming regularity. Nobody got drunk, however.

In between work, Koko and Cyan stopped to sip from a flask of rum punch Koko had made. They hung photographs and paintings, emptied out wardrobes and installed Koko's dresses. They polished the antique brass-handled chests Koko had bought at auction for her finer clothes and underwear, cleaned out cabinets, and stored silver and china. Cyan tried on some of the American's clothes. They sang at the top of their voices and danced over boxes and rubble on the floor. By mid-afternoon they were both tipsy. All but one box had been unpacked. Full-grown sun had brought death to the world outside. The streets were quiet. Tennis players had gone into hiding, chased away by the hot tar road. Domino players had fallen asleep where they sat.

Unpacking the last box, Koko pulled out a photograph in a gold frame, which she put on a gold-adorned kidney-shaped table in her bedroom.

"That picture look like you," Cyan remarked.

"It's my mother. I guess I do look like her."

"She real pretty, for truth. I could see why she wanted to be in pictures. She pretty as a picture. She woulda look good in a movie next to Sidney Poitier."

"Sidney would make anybody look good."

"Even me?" joked Cyan.

"You? Actually, you would make Sidney look good." Koko laughed.

"You really think so?"

"Indeed I do. You're a beautiful girl."

"Sidney, here I come!" Cyan laughed out.

"My mother told me she met Sidney once. At a party. They spoke briefly, and that was it."

"She ever take you to meet anybody famous?"

"Heavens, no. I hardly saw her. She left me with my grandmother when I was seven. Said she would be back for me when she became famous. I wrote her letters all the time asking her when was she coming back. She'd reply saying, soon. She did return. By then she was sick and dying and certainly not famous."

"Your father was in Hollywood too?"

"My father. Ah, he fared a little better than my mother. He didn't have to suffer through a dream unfulfilled. He was shot by a cop at a traffic light. The cop said my father tried to run him over. I was three. I don't remember any of it. What I know is what people told me."

"Girl, you ain't had no luck with you' parents at all."

"No more than you," said Koko with a tight smile.

Cyan laughed. "I suppose you right about that. Ever since I start working for you and Mr. Mayhem I always wondered why wunna ain't had no children."

"I don't know. Fear. I didn't trust myself to take care of another life. I think I would kill myself if I had a child and did something that might cause it to hate me or distrust me."

"I thinking 'bout getting on the pill. You know where I could get that?"

"Of course. I'll take you to my doctor tomorrow if you like."

"You think he could be my doctor?"

"She."

"Oh. You think she could be my doctor?"

"She's one of the best on the island. And expensive. But she's also a very good friend. She buys all her paintings from me, and I always give her a good deal, so I'm sure if I have a talk with her, she would understand that you can't pay her regular fee."

"You would do that for me?"

"Yes, of course. It's nothing, really. It's one of the lovely things about living here. People actually like doing favors for one another."

"That would be nice. I don't know what to say."

"You know what I like about you?" Koko said, looking at Cyan and smiling wickedly. "You've asked me all kinds of questions, but you've never asked me why I shave my head. You're the only person in this country who's never asked me that."

They laughed and Koko went to take a shower.

Chapter Eleven

$\mathcal{S}$he looked out the car's window at the women raking sand free of leaves and debris. The leaves were then piled in a heap for a second group of women to stuff into bags so that a third group of women could carry them on their heads to a truck parked at the side of the road about a hundred yards away. A flirtatious sea breeze tested their patience, stirring up the neat heap of leaves. The workers cursed loudly and threw down their rakes in disgust before the supervisor came over to chide them. Behind them, tourists in dark sunglasses baked in the midday sun.

The car sat in the shade of some casuarinas facing the sea at Accra Beach across from Chefette. It was a gloriously bright day. An orange sun alone in a flat blue sky. The sea still as a pond. The kind of day tourists don't believe exists until they see it.

Cyan had not touched the beef roti Breeze bought her. Only ice was left of the Coke.

"You ain't hungry?"

"Not really," she replied.

"I had a hard time finding where you live, yuh know."

"Everybody know where I live. All you had to do was ask for the girl who father went to the gallows."

"Yes, Koko tell me 'bout that. People never let you forget something like that, eh?"

"I don't care what people say. Talk don't bother me. Is me own mind that don't let me forget. And I don't wanna forget, anyway. He was me father. I ain't shame to admit it. He kill a man. I is to forget him because of that?"

"I woulda move outta that village if it was me."

"I ain't frighten for nuhbody in that village. Ain't no sense in running, anyway. Running ain't go stop me from wishing I could see him, from looking at the sea and seeing his boat bobbing on the water and waiting to see him get off. Where can I run from that? He kill a man. He get hang. Even Anansi can't change that story."

"I suppose you right. Why you didn't stay 'til I get back the other day? When I came back, you was gone."

"I didn't know where I was. I didn't know if it was you' house or somebody else house I was in. I didn't know if you was coming back. Nuhbody wasn't around. I get frighten and went home. I even leave my panties." She laughed.

"Yeah, I find them."

"Where?"

"Under the bed. I wash them and put them in my drawer. I just went to get a sea bath. You didn't think I was coming back?"

"How I suppose to know?" Cyan asked in a soft but agitated voice.

Breeze leaned out the window to greet a passing dreadlocked youth in the company of a blond woman. The youth poked his head into the car and smiled at Cyan. She turned her head away, annoyed that Breeze did not send the dread, whom he called Sailor, on his way. After a brief exchange with Breeze, the interloper left.

She realized she'd already given herself over to the idea of owning this man. She wasn't clear on when it happened. Was it when he entered her that night and she held on to him with a savageness she couldn't take back, or was it this morning, when the rental pulled up outside her house and punctuated the quiet with its piercing horn?

She turned to watch him finish off his Banks beer, remembering that night he found her on the seawall in Oistins and how drunk she got on beer. She didn't regret any of it. The drinking or the sex. Nothing had ever felt that good. She wanted to do it again. But only with Breeze.

"So what we go do after we eat? We going someplace else afterward?" she asked boldly.

He smiled. "Somewhere else like where?"

She liked the way he smiled at her. It was a smile that said "I know what you want," and though it didn't say "I will give it to you," it was still generous. His hairless face was darkly alive, his eyes wide, unsettled, a steady flame. There was a strange remoteness about him that she liked. It left her slightly afraid, exhilarated. This man was going to be hers. He'd have no choice. That she didn't really know him only excited her all the more. She trembled with uncertainty and expectation. Nothing could replace the way her heart skipped when their eyes met.

She'd always thought that the man she fell in love with would be someone she'd known for a long time. Someone who came around every day and followed her like a shadow, bearing sweets and fruits and dreams; someone who'd watch her pass every day on her way to work or the beach, who'd longed to talk, to touch, but was too shy; someone who'd dreamed about her for years without uttering a solitary word.

But it was Breeze who'd found her sitting on that wall thinking all kinds of crazy things. Who knew what would've happened if he hadn't found her! He came and got her when she most needed someone. He would be hers now. This man, looking at her with unsettled eyes like he was weary of the world, would soon be convinced there wasn't another woman in the world like her. She would see to it.

"I ain't never had no boyfriend," she said. "I want you to be my man."

Her honesty and directness surprised him. He was silent for a long time. He'd have to tell this little sparrow she didn't know what she was saying. But something made him squeeze back the words, something in her optimistic smile sent his mind backpedaling. To a time when he was not so full of himself, not so weary of love and its rewards, not so hardened by the vicissitudes of a life lived with the fear of one day waking up unable to stand on his own. Back to a time when his soul was quiet and gentle.

But that was a long time ago. Too long. In this climate of joyless toil he tried to accumulate all the money he could, which left him barely enough time to sleep. Waylaid by dreams of poverty and shame, his sleep was broken by a helter-skelter schedule that saw him moving from South Coast to West Coast around the clock in search of a sale, occasionally pausing to satisfy a touristwoman looking to fulfill a dark fantasy.

He was the king of the beach vendors. He sold more because he worked harder and longer than anyone else. When others got tired of the hot sun and sought refuge under the fat branches of an almond tree, he walked even faster, bartered longer, smiled deeper to get that sale. And he sold anything. From black coral to black-market Guyana gold to herb. Since he was nineteen, he'd been doing this. Now twenty-seven, he wanted to slow down but was afraid.

To some people he knew he'd always be a beach bum. No way anyone could call him a bum, beach or otherwise, to his face. He worked too blasted hard. Making new contacts for gold when the old ones dried up wasn't easy. He paid divers for coral and paid people to clean and polish it. Two youngsters who'd graduated from the best high school on the island with five certificates and couldn't find office work were now on his payroll, selling to tourists on the beach. Up when dawn opened its eye, he didn't go to bed until the last party was over. He worked harder than the prime minister.

But he knew what this name-calling was all about. The high and mighty putting down people who didn't wear a tie, who didn't go to the right school. These same people called the mechanic working on their car a *grease monkey* and the fifty-year-old woman cooking their meals *girl.*

Night wasn't all that good-looking, but her long thin body masked the wonderful energy she possessed. A good thing. Energy and passion far outweighed a pretty face in his mind, and most men, he suspected, would rather have a passionate woman than a pretty wooden doll. Still her youth and inexperience troubled him. Love would be important to a girl like her, and she would never be able to understand his dedication to business.

Even with all this, he found himself thinking about being her man. Life could be so crazy sometimes. His friends would laugh at him. He hadn't been anybody's man since he discovered there were enough white women who came down from the cold for anonymous sex to keep him satisfied.

"Do you know what I do?" he said.

"No, not really. But it don't matter. As long as you ain't kill nobody. My father kill a man and they hang him and I still vex with him for leaving me and my sister. If you's my man, you's my man. Only thing is, you can't leave me. If you leave me, you can't come back. I ain't ever go take back no man that leave me."

He looked at her. Her eyes danced with defiance. If he had any sense, he'd start the car, take her home and never see her again. If he didn't end it now, he'd never be able to forget about her, to leave her alone. But he felt himself breaking, yielding to the desire to feel her wiry body wrap around him. Imprisoning him. And he'd thought he loved his freedom.

He fired the Datsun's engine and said, "Let's go to my house."

She looked at him and said calmly, "That mean you go be my man?"

"Yeah, I go be your man."

• • •

He told her to get on the pill after he came on her belly. She wanted to tell him she already was, but was too happy to speak. Happy feeling the thump of his heart against her breast and the stickiness binding them together. Not far away the sea kept up a steady to and fro, the music of time. She listened, her heart silent and happy.

Dark thoughts about her family fought to subdue her bliss, but she cursed the demons back where they came from. Nothing was going to blunt the sweet feeling of Breeze's come pulling the skin of her belly as it dried, his baby-soft breathing against her neck as he began to fall asleep.

She felt slightly agitated, still in a state of arousal. As soon as he was safely asleep, she knew what she would do. What she always did when she got this aroused. But she wasn't disappointed. She was lying with her man.

The next week she began classes at the YWCA. Dressmaking was an easy choice. She'd learned the basics from Trinidad Baptiste, her neighbor, and made her own clothes sometimes on the sewing machine in her mother's room. She also took jewelry-making. The adult program forced her to study composition and arithmetic, but she fell asleep in those classes.

Breeze offered to pay for the schooling, but she told him Koko had already arranged everything, she didn't have to pay. His eyes opened wide.

"You and she become big friends since that first day, ah?"

"Yeah, man, I like Koko. We get along good now. You know she leave she husband. I like going by her house up there in Dayrells Road. She got so much books up there. She got as much books as the library. I don't think anybody in Barbados does read as much as Koko. She does try to get me to read some of them books, but is too much books for one body to read. You wanna hear a funny story? She lend me a book call *Black Like Me*. Is 'bout a white man who change the color of his skin black so he could see how black people feel living in America. It did a funny story to me at first. 'Cause I didn't really believe it. I never hear 'bout no white person who wanna be black. That would never happen 'bout here. And then Koko tell me it was really a true story."

"I would take that story with a grain of salt, if I was you. America is the land of make believe, you ain't know that? What them make up does be more real than what real. I does deal with a lot of Yankees. Them full of stories."

"I don't believe Koko would tell me a lie."

"You too trusting, you know that?"

"You saying I shouldn't trust you?"

"I ain't saying that at all. All I saying is that you too trusting. Anyway, you ain't tell me why you stop working for that doctor."

"You ain't ever ask me that."

"Well, why you leave?"

"I ain't wanna talk about that."

"That doctor trouble you?"

"I ain't wanna talk 'bout it. You deaf?"

Her dismissiveness left him sulking. He was supposed to pick her up from the YWCA the next day. He did not show.

The next evening she saw him sitting on his bike outside the gate. She took her sweet time coming down the path to the gate and then she walked past him heading down Roebuck Street as if she hadn't seen him.

He caught up with her at the corner of Coleridge Street and told her to get on the bike. Head straight, she kept right on walking.

"How you expect me to be your man, and you wouldn't listen to me?" he hollered at her stiff back.

"You supposed to keep your promise to me. I was looking for you yesterday," she said, turning around.

"I couldn't make it. You know my job. I couldn't get away. Leh we go have something to eat."

"I ain't hungry."

"Girl, you's a hard woman, yuh know."

"You go keep you promises to me from now on?"

"I go keep me promises. Now you go get on the blasted bike?"

She saw his eyes laughing.

"I ain't making no sport, Breeze. I serious. I have to know I can depend on you."

"What you want me to do? Cut out me heart and give it to you so you could believe me?"

"Yes," she smiled as she snuggled in behind him.

She felt the Kawasaki 900 convulse under her as Breeze revved the engine. The noise was deafening. Then they shot off down Coleridge Street with such sudden fury that she was almost dumped on her buttocks in the street.

Chapter Twelve

Dear Pa,

I hope the reaches of this letter fine you in good helth and spirits. I meet a young man the other night. He's very nice. He say he go be my man. He have a motorbike and he live in a nice big house. I think he go treat me good. I don't know what I woulda do that night if he didn't come right at that time. I did thinking bout walking in the sea and just closing my eyes. I did so tired. No I wasn't goin to drown myself or nothing so. You know I wouldn't do that. But I did so tired, Pa. You don't know. I did so tired. That was the night after Celine bury. I didn't want to go home. I didn't want to leave Celine. And I didn't want to have to listen to Ma. I know what she woulda been saying. That Celine shoulda know better. I know all that. What I don't understand is why Ma always hold everything gainst we. From the smallest to the biggest thing. An now that Celine gone is just me. I don't listen to nothin she got to say. It is hard to stay here. She is my mother but she don't understand that I got feelins too. I wish you could come back. That god could give you another chance. But I know that could never happen. But suppose it could? Suppose you could come back. You wouldn't do nothin

like you do before again, would you? You wouldn't kill nobody. I
does dream bout you all the time on the boat. Why you an me cant
go runnin and swimming. I miss you.

  Your lovin daughter
  Cyan

*F*or weeks she's been looking for this letter. She began
writing to him when he went to jail and never stopped, even after his
death. Why this one letter disappeared, she doesn't know. She finds it
in her mother's room. The first wave of anger brings fire to her mind.
To take a match to all her mother's things: her bed, her underwear, her
clothes. Everything. How dare she? This letter was personal. It was her
heart, not for anyone to read. If her father couldn't read it, then nobody
could. How dare her mother read it?

She rips the letters written to her father after his death, all ten of
them, into tiny pieces and scatters them out the window. They float off
among the blooming rosebushes, landing on the fluffy flowers. She
looks out the window and sees the flowers begin to wither.

She has to get away from her mother. If not, she'll do something hor-
rible. The urge to destroy is too powerful, too persuasive. She has to
leave home.

Breeze said no. After a week of hemming and hawing, Breeze told her
she couldn't move in with him. It wouldn't be a good idea right now,
was how he put it. Angered, she left him on the beach in St. James
where they'd been sitting in the lap of a twisted casuarina, teasing fan-
tasies from each other's lips. She went straight to Koko, who didn't
hesitate to say yes.

She planned to announce her decision to leave after her evening sea
bath, a ritual she had given up when her father went to jail. Since his

death she'd reclaimed it. The sea was the only thing in this country her father and people like him could claim as theirs. And soon, with hotels talking of making beaches private, that might be gone, too.

The walk through the village to the beach took her past men and wanna-be men playing dominoes and drinking rum under the hog-plum tree by the standpipe and past women with children waiting for the ice cream van. That walk used to be such fun when her father was alive. Then, everybody spoke to her. Good-natured joshing about her skinny legs. Men asked if her father would be going out the next day. Boys followed her all the way to the beach, hoping she would let them swim with her. Now all she got were hard stares.

At the beach she'd swim for half an hour, then lie and watch the sky change from bone to violet to crimson. After another quick dip, she'd walk home, not bothering to change out of her bathing suit.

Young girls, some younger than herself, would be strolling with babies on their hips. Older women heading home from work with baskets on their heads would pause to rub a little boy's chin or pat a little girl's head before swearing to themselves that young girls shouldn't be getting babies because they didn't know how to take care of them. Water would be dripping from her hair, down her back. Because it used to belong to her mother, her bathing suit would be sagging at the crotch. In the overhanging gloaming she wouldn't bother to hide the fact that she was a full woman now with patches of knotty hair—which Koko had told her to shave, but which she kept as her badge of womanhood—peeking from the edges of her bathing suit.

Walking past these girls with their babies always moved her. At one moment a mother might caress a snotty-nosed child, and at another attack it with a wounded-animal savagery that seemed strangely natural to the mother—one quick hard slap or cuff of the child's head sending it sprawling—but which provided no answer to the child's innocent, questioning stare. *What did I do, Mother, to warrant such pain?* Even at that early age the little one would've already developed the remarkable passiveness that would carry it through the world.

Where did that anger come from? she would wonder as she watched a little child get slapped across her face so hard, she couldn't cry. She took no pleasure from watching. The fascination with these scenes that unfolded like dreams came from their familiarity. She had seen them over and over again. She had experienced them. Still, she didn't understand them. Part of her own childhood was locked away in these dreams, and reliving them sometimes brought her to tears.

Men would stand behind young girls, arms akimbo or hands folded in their pockets, gazing longingly at the tight behinds encased in hip-hugging skirts. On their faces, a look to match the elegiac nature of these languid evenings. The men always looked smug or sad, never happy. What made them smirk with such superiority or cast their eyes down with such forlornness?

But today she was feeling superior to any man, woman or child; today would be the last day they would be seeing her around here.

Chapter Thirteen

$\mathcal{D}$ear Father, I don't often call on You, You know that, so when I come, You know it gots to be something very important. Even when Celine dead I hold up meself on me own without calling on You. Not that I ain't want to, but You know I ain't live the best life I coulda live. And I ain't worship You in the best manner. Maybe is because me mother forced me to go to church so much that when I get on me own I did all the things she tell me I shouldn't do. But I never stop believing in You. I never stop believing that You can bear all our burdens. That is why I come to You today in prayer. That is why I come to the conclusion I reach today to leave Cyan to herself. To put her in Your hands! There come a time when a mother have to let go of her children. Fate force me to let go of Celine and me first boy. And because I see the potential Celine had for doing so much with her life, I feel her loss more than with my first boy. But if Cyan think I going let her plan to leave destroy me, she wrong. My heart breaking to beg her to stay, that is why I had to make the decision I make today. I will not let my heart break anymore. Cyan go have a big surprise waiting for her when she step in here.

Maybe I ain't as good a mother as she would like me to be, but as You is me judge, I doing the best I can. When I was ready to leave my mother house, she was more than happy to kick me out the door. Even though she coulda tell from the long water coming down my cheek-bones that I didn't really want to go. She ain't even fart on me when I stand up in the door wanting her to say to me, "Look, girl, stop this foolishness, put down that bag and come back in here 'fore I knock off your head." I learn my lesson that day: Don't say something your legs can't back up. I went 'long with my heart in me feet that day, but I went 'long and ain't look back. I wasn't even Cyan age yet but I thought I was a woman and I was made to carry a woman's load. My mother had me in church every Sunday. Even if I was sick I had to get up and get to church. And I went long like a dutiful daughter 'til I reach sixteen. But the truth is, Lord, what was outside the church inter-est to me more than what was inside. I wouldn't tell no lie. I wanted to go partying and to moonlight picnics with boys. And my mother would let me do none of that. But I run away from home more to get my mother to notice me than anything else. But she probably knew that. Only life can teach certain lessons and she leave me to learn them on me own 'cause I didn't want to listen to her. And when she start coming round 'cause I take up with an important man in the village, I ain't even remind her how she let me leave. And when my baby die and the man start to beat me, I ain't even tell her nothing. I carry my load like a woman.

I would like to tell Cyan I sorry for putting her hand in the fire. I hurt her more than I expect. But I do it for her own good. You see what kinda family she come from. She already had a uncle lock up for stealing. I do it for her own good.

I don't care how much suffering it bring me, to my grave I will believe I do the right thing. I want her to learn to stand on her own two feet. Don't expect nothing from nobody. Work for everything. That way no man could ever abuse her. I endure it once and wouldn't want any of them to have to go through it. The first day that man in St. Lucia hit me, I shoulda kill him. But I stay. Too long, Lord, too long. I see how me mother stand for it, and I thought I could stand it, too. But I couldn't take it. It wasn't me fault the child drown. The child was fast. I put him to sit down on the grass. I try to keep me eyes on him. It ain't me fault what happen. The father get on like I throw him in the river. Like I just watch him drown. Maybe he would still be alive if I'd left him with his father, but the father claim he was busy. What was I suppose to do? Like I say before, Lord, if You send me Cyan, my own flesh and blood that have no love for me, as punishment for not looking after the boy good enough, then I will take my punishment. I know she hate me. She believe I responsible for her father getting hang. He never hit me, but he was just as bad as that man in St. Lucia. He only abuse me in a different way. His drinking and coming home when he feel like. How he expect me to put up with that? I admit I was trying to get back at him. To hurt him. To make him jealous. That is why I was flirting with the man in the dance. And with all that happen, I ain't sorry. I feel freer than I ever feel. I know she lose her father, but that wasn't my fault. Somebody woulda kill him sooner or later. Or the alcohol. I feel for her, though, cause I know how she worship him. All them letters she write to him though he dead. That is a very strange thing for somebody to do. I just hope she ain't losing her mind. But I understand her doing it. I know she would get vex if she find out I read her letters, but the truth is I ain't sorry 'bout that neither. From reading them letters, I get to understand her much better. Though she make it sound like I's the worst thing. If I had it to do again I woulda just leave Steel. It mighta save Cyan and me. 'Cause I love her. She's the only one left and I hope someday we could find what we had again. When we used to sell fish together, and walk to the beach and swim together. When she used to come outside and watch me bathe and stare at me naked body and laugh when I tell her that one day her body go look just like mine. But you never know what you go have to suffer through once you get out the womb. We have to accept what we get. We don't know how the children we bring in the world go turn out, neither. Man is so small and stupid. We don't know nothing. We look to You for guidance but we don't always know how to interpret the signs. So we always guessing. We guessing and trying to shift with the times and the signs. I did what I had to do. I ain't ashamed of it. And I ain't ashamed of what I about to do now, either. I bring Cyan into this world and I would like her to love me like a daughter should love a mother, like I love my mother. But I can't force her. Maybe she will one day. Maybe deep in her heart she do. Maybe one day she would understand how I feel. That if she ever want me, I go pick up me feet and get to her as fast as I could. But for right now, she on her own. She is her own woman now. She old enough. She taking man now. She could stand on her own feet. I know that. I made sure of that. If I give her nothin, I know I give her that. I go leave her in You hands.

These people 'bout here never did like me. Never did accept me. I ain't do them nutten, but that is how them is, I suppose. Unless you is American or a white tourist, them don't fart on foreigners. I ain't go miss this lot, I tell yuh. Not at all. And to tell the truth, is time I go back to St. Lucia. Is time. I run away from a lot of things there that maybe I shoulda face before I come here. Keep Cyan in Your sight, Lord. Don't let nothing bad happen to her. That is all I come to ask you. Thank you for listening to my prayer.

Thank you, Lord.

Chapter Fourteen

$\mathcal{S}$he plants new flowers as soon as her mother leaves for St. Lucia. Now she has no need to move in with Koko. Everything Obe ever planted in the front garden Cyan disinters from the ground. The roses stay because she had planted them herself.

Next morning she gathers all the flowers together in the front yard. The withered gardenias and lilies look sorrowful. The morning glory is weeping. Ignoring the hint of sweetness from the wilted gladiola, she pours kerosene on the pile and with one match starts a fire and watches the flames leap into the air. The burning flowers belch acrid smoke, billowing out of control like a heart full of hate. The smoke hangs in the almond tree and wafts in the leaves of the soursop tree next door. She feels the lump return to her throat, a lump she felt yesterday as the taxi drove off with her mother and her bandaged suitcases, now emptied of the dreams she'd chosen to abandon.

But there was a dignity in her mother's departure that resonated in the part of her that still loved the woman. There was the way Obe's beige hat, tilted by vanity to one side, remained steady in the heavy wind. As the taxi departed, she'd stood there, eyes wide and frightened, squeezing the blood from her knuckles clenched behind her back. Her mother did not see. Obe's eyes had been filled with tears caught in the tinted net of her dark sunglasses purchased especially for this purpose.

The next day the flower pile still smolders. She leaves it to put itself out.

The evening shadows hug the coastline through the trees, slink through the village, and meet her at the top of the gap. She is ready for Breeze. It's six o'clock. The fireflies are coming. Twilight will have chased the tourists from the beaches, and Breeze will have suspended selling for the time being. Until he hits the clubs. He'll be on his way home now. And if the Crane Hotel has been his last stop, as it almost always is, he'll pass this way after stopping for a beer (he doesn't drink anything stronger). She knows if she stands outside her gap, by six-thirty she'll see him.

She discovered this by chance one evening about a month before her mother left the island. Coming from the beach, she had reached the top of her gap when Breeze's red bike came roaring at her. His peculiar way of sitting straight up on a bike designed for the rider to lean forward gave him away. She waved her hands and screamed his name as he sped by. He pulled up a few yards away next to a rose-bush gone mad in an untidy little garden in front of a yellow house. She ran to him, brushing against the coarse leaves that overhung the street.

"Get on," he said without changing his straight-ahead gaze.

In nothing but a bathing suit she got on. He sped off. Mashing her stomach into the small of his back, she wrapped her arms around his waist. They became one, leaning into narrow spaces between cars and buses, streaking past slow-moving donkey carts, barely noticing the frozen eyes of women and children stationed at bus stops. She sucked at the wind as it pressed into her; chaotic whiffs of burnt cane from lorries and tractors entwined with the sweet nuance of Lady-in-the-Night. The sharp wind set her teeth on edge and lashed at her eyes with such cruelty, they watered. Ever defiant, she laughed in the wind's face, and liking the sound of her own voice in the mouth of the wind, she laughed again and again just to hear her echo.

When they arrived at the house he rented in Harts Gap, she got off and waited while he stored the bike in the yard. She liked when he parked the bike in the backyard and not in front the house; it meant he would not be going out again and she would be spending the night. He did not always let her stay the night. Sometimes after they made love, he took her home. She cursed him when he did that and told him she would never come back, but by the time he dropped her home, she was already missing him.

Emerging from the yard, he stretched for more than a minute in the gloomy light, jogging in place for another five minutes as she watched. Riding made his back stiff. Catlike, he moved with the subtlety of night, everything about him reined in, yet large still. Shadows moved up and down the street, taking no notice of them: her, standing there quiet and watchful; him, dancing and prancing as though preparing for Carnival. Slow-moving cars slid past, carrying packages of families to neat rows of houses on that street, or early-bird lovers looking for a spot on the beach a few yards away.

That day his place was cleaner and neater than she'd ever seen it. She sensed a woman's presence not long gone from the house. It produced an involuntary sucking of her teeth. He looked at her surprised.

"How come it so clean?"

"My sister was here cleaning," he replied. "I paying she to come every Wednesday from today. She suppose to clean and wash and iron my clothes. She ain't got nothing else to do. If she didn't cleaning my house she'd probably be off cleaning somebody else house. This way she get a little money and she don't get ill-treat by none o' these white Bajans or wanna-bes. Them ain't go pay she no more than I does pay she anyway. Probably not as much."

"How come you ain't ask me to do it?"

"No way. I don't want you to be doing that."

"Why not? You does give me money. I don't do nothing for it. It ain't go take nothing offa me to come and clean."

"I don't want you to do that. My sister in she forties. She and she husband just break up. She ain't got no education, ain't nothing else for she to do. I just helping she out. I don't want you thinking that cleaning house is a future. I don't want you getting into that way of thinking. You can do more than that."

"I do it before. Ain't no big deal."

"Stop talking that kinda talk. I ain't want you thinking like that. I ain't want you to ever get the idea into your head to start back cleaning people house again. You in school. Learn something that could carry you through life. You could make clothes good. You got a talent for that. You could support yourself with that. Tourists does come 'bout here with nuff money to spend. You think white people is the only people 'bout here who know how to make money offa tourists? Tourists would spend good money for clothes from local tie-dye cloth and stuff like that. You wanna spend you life cleaning somebody house?"

"But it wouldn't be somebody house. It'd be your house. Our house."

He paused. "I done wid this matter."

"You frighten to death of me moving in wid you, ain't it?"

"As long as I got money in me pocket, I ain't frighten for nothing. As long as I could make a living, I ain't got nothing to worry 'bout."

She knew he made good money. He was always buying her things: shoes, dresses; he'd bought her an electric sewing machine to replace the hand model, and though she never asked him, he gave her a hundred dollars every week. The house he rented was a wall house, and was filled with all the amenities one could think of. The stereo equipment with two huge speakers on the floor and two smaller ones in the roof, the television set, the furniture, everything looked new. There was a washing machine in the garage, a hot-water tank in the bath-room, things that only people who were well-off could afford. Breeze had all the things she saw in Dr. Mayhem's house except the pictures and books.

That night they made love to the distant beat of rocking waves. She held on to him with the same determination as on the bike. She wanted to flow with him as the sand flowed with the sea, to be as vast and as open for his love as the deep of sleep. She wanted this man to be hers and hers alone, but she'd been hearing rumors. She knew how deadly rumors could be, so she tried to ignore them. But they kept after her. What if they were true? What if her man was sleeping with touristwomen? She'd have no choice but to let him go. She didn't want to have to let him go. On this night she would not let go.

Yes, she is ready for Breeze. Yellow rose in her hair. A cool yellow dress reaching just below her knees. Her skin well creamed. Scent of patchouli. She can smell herself. Sweet for days. For him she has a red rose. Earlier she'd aroused her sex rubbing against the petals. Later she'll feed them to him. One by one. Something they started one day after she caught him nibbling rose petals in her bedroom. Skylarking, she'd told him they'd taste better if she rubbed them on her sex. He agreed.

No panties. No bra. He likes that. She likes it because he likes it. As long as he is willing to please her, she will please him. When she gets on the bike, she will press her nipples and her bare sex against his back. It will drive him crazy. He will not be able to wait until they get to the bedroom. He will take her standing in the garage. His kiss will taste bitter of beer. And she will lick his ears and wrap her legs around him. Her spit will clean the sand from his neck. And when they're done, he will carry her to the bedroom with her legs still wrapped around his waist and his cock inside her. He probably tells his friends about it.

He'll be arriving soon. The fireflies are here already. She watches them sail above her head on into the trees and gardens down the gap. Children come out to catch them. She remembers doing the same when she was little. And when she caught one and it set her palms alight, she'd laugh with delight.

She is thinking of catching a firefly when she hears the Kawasaki's boom. It is the sound of a plane taking off. She sees him but doesn't wave. By now he knows she'll be waiting.

The Kawasaki flashes past. She waves her arms wildly. Too late. He's gone.

Anger comes. Fast and demonic. He was not alone, that's why he didn't stop. The woman leaning into him, pressing her nipples into his back, was a touristwoman.

If she had wings, she would chase them and knock them both into a ditch somewhere or under a blasted car. She does not know what to do. She sits on the edge of the road and cries.

Chapter Fifteen

$\mathcal{D}$arkness' pillow snuffed out the day's heat. Night arrived as silently as a stolen kiss. It hugged the tiny houses of Dayrells Road together, making them indistinguishable. In came the Trades off the sea, racing inland across the Garrison Savannah, looking for someone to cool. Koko was waiting on the gallery steps. She liked the nights cool like this.

Saturday night. The hum of buses and cars descended on the neighborhood from the nearby highway. Across the road a streetlamp rained lilac light on young men dueling at the domino table. No job to go to next morning. Sunday worship would be optional, depending on the absence of a hangover. It was time to let loose the demons of the past week, shake off the dry ache of hopelessness, time to smile in somebody's face and feel the electric shock of desire clasp you like a sea-cat, time to abandon the wasted and start something new. Time to go dancing. Calypso, reggae, soul, disco. The neighborhood was already jumping with groups of young men and women parading up and down the avenue modeling the latest fashions from America on their way to a party or club.

Koko put out her cigarette and gazed up at the liquid moon flowing like a dream. The one disappointment about being on her own was not being able to have Breeze. She missed him. Breeze was one lover she hadn't wanted to give up. He commandeered her, possessed her, dominated her in a way she never thought she'd allow any man to do. Not even her husband. And even when she struggled in response, she knew she'd always give in. Still, when she confronted him about Cyan, she was surprised that he admitted being in love with her. Cyan was not the kind of woman she thought Breeze would've fallen in love with. That's why she'd warned Cyan about Breeze's flings with tourist-women. She hadn't wanted to see Cyan hurt. But it'd happened anyway. And for the past three months her friend had been living with the blues. She'd tried mothering, consoling, talking, hugging. She'd taken her to the movies, sailing, even arranged for them to spend a weekend at a friend's beach house on the East Coast. But Breeze had locked his claws around Cyan's heart. Many nights after they'd had dinner together, she'd ask her friend to stay over, but Cyan would insist on going home. Koko knew the reason: She still expected to hear the Kawasaki throttling down her gap. When Cyan confided that Breeze had never taken her dancing, Koko hit on a plan: They'd go out dancing. If calypso music couldn't loosen Breeze's grip on Cyan's heart, nothing could.

A cracked engine block had put her car in the repair shop. The taxi she'd been so patiently awaiting arrived at eleven. She lit another cigarette and got in. The driver told her he didn't allow smoking. She cursed him. He was already half an hour late and should've been glad she was still waiting when he got there. That shut him up.

Her frustration released, Koko relaxed into the clean blue upholstery of the Fairmont to enjoy the ride and her cigarette. She was meeting Cyan at Southern Palms Hotel in St. Lawrence Gap, heart of the tourist district and nightlife on the South Coast. Heavy traffic made the going slow. Cars crept along; people weaved in and out of crowded streets and alleys on their way to the various hotels and clubs on the strip.

Cyan was leaning against a guard wall outside the hotel when the taxi pulled up. Koko paid the fare, got out, and greeted her with a smoky smooch on the cheek.

They walked through the garden surrounding the hotel. Green, yellow, and pink lights planted in the ground bounced off the lilies, orchids and gardenias, sending giant shadows into the electric air.

They entered the hotel's pink lobby. Turning left they walked through an indoor tropical garden, filled with more lilies and orchids, as dramatically lit as the outdoor garden. Beyond was the open-air nightclub in one corner of a wide courtyard featuring palm trees, flowers, and more planted lights.

The tiny space was already packed with tourists and Bajans. Loud calypso music from a band under a thatched-roof kiosk heated up the atmosphere.

There were no empty tables around the crowded circular dance floor; the two women sat at the end of the rectangular bar. From there they could see over the low wall that separated the compound from silent sea. The slate black water moved so quietly as it caught the hotel lights, they could've been watching a wave of fireflies approaching and receding. It was eerie and magical. All around, bamboo tables and caned chairs suggesting a theme of island simplicity. But the muted lights creating shadows, the bartender mixing drinks with an air of grandiosity, the sense of abandon hanging in the air, all were having a mercurial effect. Cyan felt herself smiling; her inhibitions slowly began to crawl away.

Following Koko's example, she ordered rum punch. The pink drinks, with lots of ice and mixers, came in tall glasses adorned with tiny wooden palm trees. Winking at each other as if to say *let's have the time of our lives tonight,* they took their first sips. Bold and long.

They'd been seeing a lot of each other since Cyan's classes began at the YWCA. The first pair of earrings Cyan made, tear drops done in brass, she gave to Koko. Now that she was finished with her studies and competed for business on the beach with other vendors, she would often stop off at Koko's gallery to view the paintings or photographs. Afterward, Koko would drive her home, where they'd sit and chat over boxes of Kentucky Fried Chicken. Koko listened as Cyan loved and hated Breeze out loud. But Cyan didn't cry anymore. She'd cried the night he passed her by and was determined, as bad as it hurt, that she would not cry for Breeze again.

She'd listen raptly as Koko talked about life in America, about marching and demonstrating for freedom for black people, about taking pictures of police beating black people, of getting thrown into jail for trying to take those pictures. None of it made sense to her, and she couldn't understand why Bajans would be so anxious to get to a place like that. She told Koko the real reason the skin on her right hand was so shriveled up, something she'd never told anyone else, not even Breeze. They talked about the books Koko gave her to read; most of which went unopened, but some she read over and over, like the one about the human body with pictures of every organ and muscle. She saw and read about parts of her body she didn't know existed: Fallopian Tubes. Left Ventricle. Right Ventricle. Pituitary Gland. Words she couldn't pronounce that she'd write down and ask Koko. *Oesophagus. Coccyx. Ischium.* The human body fascinated her. How it worked. What kept it all going day after day. Why some people were skinny and some fat; some black, some white, some in between. When she read those books, she wished she'd been smarter in school, like Celine. Wouldn't it have been wonderful if she and her sister could've gone to school together to become doctors? It made her miss Celine all the more.

She wished she could've had with her mother the relationship she had with Koko. To be able to talk about sex, about her father, about anything. Even about Breeze whom she couldn't get out of her mind, though she didn't want him back. In retrospect, she suspected things with Obe might've turned out the same even if her mother hadn't put her fingers in the fire. Obe was just a different kind of person from Koko. Must be the way they were brought up. Maybe reading a lot of books had something to do with it. It wasn't that her mother wasn't as smart as Koko. It was a different kind of smart. Obe defined herself and everybody else in terms of the ability to survive. Koko defined herself by her ability to do things, to influence people, to make her life mean something.

It had taken some persuading by Koko to get Cyan to come here to the hotel. She dealt with tourists on the beach and found them to be friendly enough. But she knew hotel managers frowned on Bajans, unless they were white, coming into hotels. It's as if they believed the tourists left their white enclaves in North America or Europe for a tropical paradise where black people existed only to wait on them. But Koko had been relentless, and finally she'd given in.

After the women had taken only a few sips, a stocky young man came up to them, boldly took Koko's hand, and pulled her onto the dance floor. Koko went along laughing, and Cyan got the impression the man wasn't a stranger to her friend.

Soon a white man sat next to her. He was big, with a friendly sunburnt face that turned crimson when he smiled. He offered to buy her a drink. She said no. He asked her to dance.

"I don't feel to."

"How about later? Should I come back?"

She looked at him and smiled. He had light blue eyes and fair hair that fell in an unruly mop along the side of his face.

"If you want to."

She watched him leave. Why, with so many white women around would this good-looking white man want to dance with her?

The rum punch slammed her brain, and she went reeling toward drunkenness. The lights became brighter, the shadows more murky and inviting. The music insinuated itself deeper into her hips, making her ass wriggle on the chair. She could feel men's eyes, having peeled off her clothes, creeping over her body, and surprisingly she liked it. Ordinarily, she hated when men did that. She finished the drink and ordered another one.

Koko returned, sweating and laughing.

"You ordered another drink for me?" she asked.

"Yours ain't done yet."

"It is now." Koko laughed.

With that, the rest of her drink went down the hatch. Koko ordered another rum punch as the young man who'd dragged her off to the dance floor leaned over and clamped his hand on Cyan's.

"You ain't dancing?"

She pulled her hand back brusquely, which startled him. Then, to indicate she didn't want to hurt his feelings, she got up and walked to the dance floor. She felt him behind her.

They danced for a brief time together: he, trying to bottle her up, she, wanting to dance outside his zone of restriction. Shortly, she abandoned him as a partner, dancing away alone.

When people bounced her she bounced back, giving vent to her pent-up rage. She danced with her soul, with her broken heart, disorderly and unrestrained. She jumped and pranced, she wriggled and corkscrewed her hips. The music and the alcohol drove Breeze from her mind and she laughed at the pleasure of it. Spent and sweating mightily after twenty minutes, she returned to the bar where Koko was sitting with a salty smile.

"I wish you could've seen yourself. You were a wild woman on the floor. Every part of your body was moving. I didn't know you could dance like that."

Cyan beamed. Glistening marbles of sweat fell off her body and rolled away. In the ecstasy of the moment she was a firefly. Her sweating body was aglow. And it seemed that everyone else saw the same thing. Before she could sit down properly, another touristman came to ask her for a dance. She shook him off. Then a burly Bajan. He got the same treatment. Another touristman. And another. It seemed like there was a line of men drawn to her glowing body.

"Everybody wants to dance with you," Koko said.

"I ain't wanna dance with nobody. I wanna dance with you. Why you and me can't dance together?"

Koko looked at her and smiled with glazed, capricious eyes.

"Sounds good to me," she said.

"Lemme catch my breath a minute."

Koko swirled ice with her pinkie. She glanced at Cyan with a question in her eye. Cyan saw it.

"What?"

"Nothing. I was just looking at you, remembering that day we met. I thought for sure you were going to be like all the other girls Jonathan hired. He slept with most of them, you know. Sometimes I wonder if he isn't cursed or something. For a doctor, for a man of reason and logic, his thinking can be so backward. I don't understand it."

"That is why you won't go back?"

"I'd had enough. I stayed too long, to tell the truth. You know what I found in a closet about two years ago. A suitcase full of letters."

"To a next woman?"

"Yes. But not what you'd think. His grandmother Reema, who's been dead for more than twenty years. He writes letters to his dead grandmother like you'd write letters to a living person. It's as though he doesn't believe she's dead. Does everyone on this island do that, or just doctors?"

Cyan laughed nervously. "Why you ain't go back home, though?"

"Home? To America, you mean? That's not really home. I was born there, but I never felt at home. I feel more at home here."

"I can't understand that. I couldn't call no other place home. Even though the people in my village hate me, to me is still home."

"So are you glad I convinced you to come here tonight?"

"Oh, yes. I enjoying meself very much. But you can't blame me for being skeptical. The way these hotel people does look at you when you pass through just to get to the beach, I ain't expect them would let black people come in here to dance."

"Your money is as good as anybody's, so don't be afraid to go anywhere you want to go."

"It ain't that I frighten. Is that it hard enough living amongst people that make you feel like you ain't belong there. I don't want to feel that way, especially when I going out to have fun."

Koko got up from her seat. "Well, you're right to stay in that village, just as you have a right to be here. I'm ready to dance. You?"

They inched their way through the crowd. There was barely enough room for a centipede to crawl. People leaned on posts, against the bar, sat on the seawall; every ounce of space was filled.

Out of the corner of her eye, Cyan saw the blond touristman who'd asked her to dance keeping a close watch on her. Her head swelled big as a breadfruit at the thought of this good-looking white man watching as though he wanted to jump out of his skin into hers.

She danced mashed up against her friend. And when their eyes made four, Koko would smile. Boldly, Cyan put her hands on Koko's hips as if to direct them to the reckless calypso beat. A short time later the young man who'd dragged Koko onto the dance floor broke them apart. He grabbed Koko crudely around the waist and began to juck on her behind. Koko laughed out loud as if somebody had tickled her, and pooched back to give him more of her behind to work up on. Then another man grabbed her waist from the front and started grinding his pelvis into hers. Koko was now sandwiched between the two men. Her skirt had ridden all the way up her thighs. The man behind her now had his hand planted conspicuously on Koko's ass and was grinding on her with jackhammer speed. Cyan could see her friend was getting turned on by this; her body was shaking with laughter, her eyes full of wildness.

Feeling abandoned, Cyan left the dance floor. She walked back the way they'd come, pausing in the indoor garden to look at the Technicolor tiger lilies.

"Got too hot for you in there?"

Recognizing the European-accented voice over her right shoulder as that of the touristman who'd been eyeing her all night, she smiled to herself. This man must really think she was something special to be following her around like this. Pretending not to hear him, she walked on. He caught up with her in the outside garden.

"Hi, I'm Sven," he said. "Remember me? You promised to dance with me."

"It too crowded in there. Besides, I ain't feel like dancing no more for the night."

She saw disappointment spread over his face.

"Would you at least have a drink with me?"

"I had enough to drink."

"How about a walk on the beach?"

She nodded. How'd she manage to cast such a spell on this white man? But she found herself being ensnared in the same web, for she felt so carefree, she almost burst out laughing when he held her hand and led her off toward the beach.

They took a well-used sandy path between the hotel and the small guest house next to it. Strands of laughter reached down from the top floor of the guest-house and tickled her; they felt like the laughter of love. She giggled.

"What is it?" he asked.

"Nothing."

"Are you laughing at me?"

"I ain't laughing at you. I laughing at life. I laughing 'cause I know what you want. And I feel like giving it to you. Ain't that funny? And I feel like giving it to you right now on the beach. Ain't that real funny?"

And she giggled again.

By the time Cyan came back to the hotel two hours later, the crowd in the nightclub had thinned out. Only couples or hoped-to-be couples remained. Koko was gone. So was her young man.

Sven offered to drive Cyan home in his mini-moke. She was still giddy from all that had happened. But grits of sand chafing her thighs and ass reminded her it'd all been too real. She'd just had sex with a touristman on the beach.

Driving home in the open buggy, he tried to tell her about himself. She wanted to listen, but the wind kept talking nonsense to her, interrupting the melody of his voice. As they charged the wind, it kept asking her if she remembered the roar of Breeze's bike at this time of morning. And when she said no, the wind, like the magician it was, conjured it up, and the roar drowned out everything else. She closed her ears until they passed Oistins, and then she knew she'd won.

At her gap Sven handed her an envelope, said good-bye, and drove off before she could say anything. She watched the mini moke's taillights burn out like wasted stars and realized that it was over. The night of magic had come to an end.

She opened the envelope there under the flickering streetlight. Its contents—an American hundred-dollar bill and a piece of paper with telephone and room numbers—caused her to burst out in wild laughter that woke every dog in the village.

What a night!

Lemuel saw her unaware and decided she was the most beautiful woman he'd ever seen. Unable to sleep, he'd gotten up to read his Bible. From his window he'd seen her get out of the mini-moke. He'd avoided looking at her in this way before. But tonight, seeing her standing under the streetlamp laughing as if she owned the night, he couldn't deny it.

"Cyan!" he called out.

She turned to see him leaning out his window.

"Look like you had a night out on the town," he said.

"You could say that."

"You look real beautiful, Cyan."

"You really think so?"

"Sure, I do."

"You really think I beautiful?"

"You's the most beautifullest woman in this whole village. In fact I would have to say you's the most beautifullest woman in the whole world. I see you got a new boyfriend."

"Who? Oh, that man who bring me home. He ain't my boyfriend. He's just somebody I meet tonight. I don't even know if I go see him again."

"What become of your boyfriend with the bike? I don't hear it come through the gap no more. And I must admit I don't miss it, either. That thing used to keep so much noise it made my shack shake."

"You mean Breeze? He gone long 'bout he business."

"Gone where? Overseas?"

"Coulda gone to Mars for all I care. He try to make a fool outta me. I don't care how much you love somebody, you can't let them make a fool outta yuh. Yuh better off taking the pain and moving on. If somebody don't feel you beautiful enough for them you ain't got no chance no matter how much you love them. I love Breeze so bad I can't stand thinking 'bout him. And a day don't go by without me doing that. Sometimes I does be walking on the beach with my valise thinking 'bout him so hard that I does forget to look out for people who might be interested in my clothes. The other day I did sitting down in a shop in St. Lawrence having a soft drink and I hear his bike pull up outside. I did praying he come in the shop, 'cause though I didn't wanna talk to him, I wanted to see him so bad. And when he come in and see me, he look at me and smile and ask me if I need a drop somewhere. I ain't answer. Then he tell me he miss me. I still ain't answer. I did too frighten to open me mouth. I stiffen up my body like a piece of iron. I did frighten that if I relax it, I would fly on him right there in that shop. Then he look at me for a long time and then he leave. Answer me this: How he could miss me when he had me and know how I did feel 'bout him, know I woulda do anything he ask me to do, and still he couldn't resist them tourist-women? Even though he know if I find out, I woulda leave him, he still couldn't resist. The only explanation I got is that Breeze didn't think I beautiful enough for he."

"Don't worry 'bout Breeze. Breeze is a idiot. Breeze ain't no use to you. If he can't see how beautiful you is, he got a problem."

Lemuel knew what she wanted to hear. He also knew that to say it would be foolish. She wanted to hear that Breeze would come to his senses and realize she loved him better than any other woman could. The next time Breeze came around, be it a year, or two years from now, Cyan would let him right back into her bed. That's the kind of woman Cyan was destined to be. One of those women who knew in their heads what was best for them, but would never do it because it was too logical. What Cyan needed was the Lord. Only the Lord could save her from the likes of Breeze.

"Why you don't come to church with me tomorrow morning?"

"Church?" She laughed.

"If you had the Lord you wouldn't be worrying 'bout Breeze."

"If I had the Lord I would be worrying 'bout something else. Like how to keep *Him.*"

"How you could make a joke like that, Cyan?"

"Who say I making joke?"

"That is pretty close to blasphemy," Lemuel chided.

"I guess speaking the truth is blasphemy, then. You'd rather I tell you a lie?"

"No. Telling the truth is sacred. But making fun of the Lord is blasphemous. You can't talk 'bout God like how you does talk 'bout other people. Like God is your lover."

"Well, God suppose to love everybody, ain't He?"

"You know what I mean. God love everybody, but He ain't nobody lover."

"I ain't got time to argue with you now. I too tired. I got a feeling I go sleep late late tomorrow."

"Want me to come and wake you up for church?"

"No. Not tomorrow. Maybe some other time."

"That's a promise?"

"That's a promise. Come for me Christmas morning."

She laughed and headed down the gap.

He watched her from his window until he saw the light go on in her house.

Chapter Sixteen

The night smelled like sweet green fruit, like mango and mammy-apple. A sweetness that slinked through the young canes of March like a mongoose, through new grass on the edge of valleys, marched across dry ponds, and rose ponderously like new bread to hang in the clear gloss of pink streetlights along the West Coast, hovering under coconut trees emptied of their fruit by persevering young men and women. The stench of North America's rich mixing their new money with the old of Europe was all but lost in the sweet green-fruit night of this tropical paradise.

It was a smell common to all tropical paradises in this part of the world. The once-colonized were free and willing to be colonized again by the burnt smell of suntan lotion, by the sight of broiling white flesh oozing green in the midday sun. Along this strip blood trickled from imported beef. "Make mine rare!" "Extra rare for me!" shouted the businessmen and women, lonely housewives, school-teachers, and policemen turned pleasure-seekers. They brought with them a sense of ownership, of the world belonging to them. And why not? The world spun on the edge of the American dollar.

Everyone on this island knew it. They yearned for it as they yearned for a future.

On this busy stretch, cars, taxis, and buses slammed into the tropical breeze with frantic regularity and sailed past young men too bored to think about their future, too tired to argue about their past, too horny to see their mothers going home from hotel jobs that payed just enough to keep them alive; for there, in reach of their eyes was a touristwoman walking alone. Her whiteness resuscitated them. Was she horny, too? Was she rich? Would she stop to ask directions?

Before she reached them, she turned into the pink portals of a pristine castle, the one their mothers cleaned, the one they were not allowed to enter because the guard at the gate had been told by the white manager not to let black men enter, that they came only to harass the guests; black women could enter, however, because it's okay for touristmen to fuck them. After the beautiful touristwoman disappeared, they sat on the sidewalk counting cars, trying to numb their minds back to reality.

A mile away a young mother fought off her lover whom she hadn't seen in a week. Now he was back for pussy. She didn't know where he'd been and said so with the venom of deprivation. He tried to force her legs open, but they were welded together with the steel will of a spurned woman. She'd been looking for him to get money to feed the baby. Perhaps if he'd come yesterday, he would've gotten what he wanted. He was a day late and plenty dollars short. It didn't matter what he told her now. Couldn't find work? Too bad. She pushed him out the door. The baby was crying for a father it would never get to know.

Friday night. Time to go to work. The sweet smell of green fruit sailed over his head. The wind blew softly into his eyes, teased his ears with the moistness of a woman's lips. It lifted him up, made him hungry. It also made him mad. Why him? Why did he have to toss in the night like a rudderless ship? Where was his future?

He passed a group of boys too young and too hungry to leave their mothers' bosoms. He remembered when he was green like them, counting cars by the sidewalk. That was a long time ago.

"Going dancing tonight, Sailor?" a young pup sang out.

Sailor didn't answer. He was broke. He spoke to pups only when he had money in his pockets.

On the main road to Speightstown a car stopped to give him a ride. He didn't even have to hail it. Drivers knew him by the way he dressed, by the hoppity-skip of his walk. Only the Sailor out looking for his ship walked like that.

He rode in silence with the two men in the Daihatsu down the strip lined with palm trees and lurking mahogany trees, which met to form a canopy blocking out the stars over the road. It was like driving through a paved jungle. Behind the wall of trees were hotels of varying sizes and tastes. This was the West Coast, the gold coast of the hotel industry. The most expensive and exclusive hotels loomed behind walls along this coast waiting for the perfect guest. Deep pockets and no imagination. Up and down the coast these hotels were almost interchangeable, offering the same features: rum punch parties, limbo-dancing, fire-eating, and lithe young girls in skimpy skirts dancing too close to fire. Get drunk and enjoy our simple culture.

At Sandy Lane, Sailor disembarked.

"You going in the Rhino tonight, Sailor?"

Without answering, he slammed the door and walked away.

Sailor crossed the road and slipped behind trees guarding the castle down to the beach where only the rich are allowed to play. But he didn't give a rass about the rich and famous. He dared any man to tell him he couldn't walk on this beach.

The sea was blank and hungry. It was churning up foam and sewage. Sailor hated the smell of the sea. Too raw. He didn't swim in it because he knew the hotels dumped shit into it. The smell got to him. He spat in the sand.

The warm sand welcomed him like a long-lost friend. He felt his feet sink into it. He searched his pockets for cigarettes. Empty. Shit! The night had offered him nothing so far. But he'd make something of it, he always did.

Action. Sailor's cat-eyes picked out two approaching figures: woman and a man holding hands. Black woman, white man. He saw this much too often for his liking. There was a time when a black Bajan woman wouldn't have been caught dead holding hands with a touristman in the open like this. Not that that stopped touristmen from getting their taste of Bajan women. He knew better. He was a product of such a union. His father, a British sailor on a weekend visit, spent one night with his prostitute mother in a tiny room on Nelson Street without ever holding hands. He inherited his father's red hair, now down to his neck in dreadlocks. That was all he ever got from his father.

The couple passed within a few feet of him. He peered closely. The girl looked familiar. Yes, no doubt about it, he knew her.

He let them by without hindrance. The man now had his arms around her waist. She was hugging him back. They stood almost shoulder to shoulder. He was a big man, well dressed in a white jacket. She was tall, slender, dressed well, too. Looked like they might've been out for a fancy dinner.

Several minutes later a solitary figure. A touristwoman, singing. He knew the song, didn't like it; never could stand the Bee Gees. The woman was so close, he could smell her perfume. He knew the type: fat, wearing sexy perfume, and singing stupid words. Her Bajan lover was probably waiting somewhere down the beach.

He stepped from behind the wall. Too quick for her untrained eyes. He grabbed her purse and knocked her down. He heard her scream and laughed. The night was beautiful. Sailor was king again. King for a night.

Cyan listens to the sea's light breathing and smells its raw, early-morning breath. The seaside window is open, and the soft crescendo is the kind of music she loves to wake up to. She's done it many times at

Breeze's house. Her eyes are still closed. She does not want to open them because she wants to hold on to her dream.

The very rich hide with their lovers in this, one of the most lavish and expensive hotels on the island. The American next to her is rich and married. Soon he'll wake up horny. He seems to have an insatiable desire for her body. She is not hungry for him, however.

She met him on the beach three days ago. Sold him two African print dresses and a wrap around skirt for his wife that day. If only she could meet people like him every day. She'd be rich in no time. He'd offered her five times their worth and then invited her to dinner. How the rass Breeze managed to make so much money selling on the beach, she'd like to know. This was hard, unrewarding work. Some days you don't sell anything, some days barely enough to buy cloth. This, after the hours spent late into the night cutting, sewing, and ironing. She'd tried to sell her creations to the shops on Broad Street, but they practically laughed her out of their stores. She'll show all of them. One day she'll have her own store.

That night they ate at La Traviata, an expensive Italian restaurant in Hastings. Later, over drinks, he offered her five hundred dollars a day to be his nightly companion.

She gets offers like this all the time, though not of nearly this much money. Some she accepts, some she laughs at. It still amuses her to see the way touristmen react when they see her naked body. She knows none of them will fall in love with her, and accepts their money without regret, but she goes out with only those she likes, those who stir something in her, and if they do not please her, she will not go out with them again. Sometimes she is tempted to look past that, for otherwise they treat her very well. They take her to the fanciest restaurants, clubs, dancing. She likes the money, but she also likes the freedom to choose her lovers.

She turns over and stares at the American's face, plump and purple from too much sun. Alfred Peachtree is his name. He has already given her one thousand dollars. Last night, after dinner, they walked along the beach holding hands. She's never been treated so special in her life.

Sunlight fights the blinds. The sea serves up a stirring breeze, which parts them, and the sun quietly insinuates itself into the coziness of the secluded room. The way the window curves toward the sea and away from the leeward side, the room gathers little of the sun's direct heat. A shuffle of feet under the window signals the arrival of the hotel employees who, before the guests are ready to play, must return the beach to paradisial perfection by scraping away leaves and other debris left by an indifferent sea or careless carousers during the night.

She lies back and closes her eyes again. She wonders if Breeze went looking for her at home last night. But she knows he didn't. She wonders anyway. She wonders every night, even when she sleeps in her own bed and knows for sure. The wondering comes from a place she does not understand. The same place that told her on the first day they met that he'd be her man. She knows too that if he'd come and she had been there, she would've sent him away again. She loves him, wants him, but could never take him back.

She has seen him only once since she woke up in the middle of the night and found herself with a knife at his throat. He didn't believe her when she told him it was all because of a dream she was having. She was being raped by an angel, only to look into his eyes and see her father. Convinced she tried to kill him over the touristwoman she'd seen on his bike the day before, he'd gotten dressed and left. That was a year and a half ago.

She gets up and treads across the pink carpet to the bathroom. Two slugs on the wall greet her with their daggerlike antennas pointed at her heart. Shit! I thought slugs come only to poor people's houses, she thinks with a smile. The room is damp, but the warm lights in the low ceiling send the slugs crawling slowly in search of darkness. How did slugs get into this fancy hotel?

She is fascinated by their movement. In the methodical way they gather themselves for each solemn thrust down the pink wall away from the light, leaving a thin film of slime, they seem to be refuting the linear passing of time. With each hunch of their sleek form, time seems to stop, waiting for the uncoiling, the release.

It reminds her of the dream she had of the angel who came to her with his swinging horse cock trying to penetrate her, to assault her at that vulnerable moment when the worlds of the subconscious and conscious collide, freezing time; when you're neither awake nor asleep. And in that split second the angel is real. Can you take such a huge thing inside you? Then time begins again, and the angel is a devil with the loving eyes of your father. You can feel the blood course through you with the deliberateness of midnight. Senses are so heightened, you can hear the blood. It's the sea laughing in the morning. It is then you shoot out of bed with a glazed look, but unafraid. Fear immobilizes. You will never be immobilized. You find a knife and are ready for battle. Except it is not a devil but Breeze whose throat you are about to slice

A luminous moment passes—one in which she wonders if slugs have guardian angels—before she begins to mash them into the wall like thick paint, watching their guts ooze out pink and delicious. She's ripping open time's belly, laying it bare for the fluorescent lights of the pristine bathroom, and the joke is that time is nothing but pink shit. Time can be killed.

She wants to laugh at the folly, at the ugliness of white light shining gloriously on pink shit, at time pasted on a pastel wall. The lights are hot. She begins to sweat.

The sound of movement from the bedroom wrenches her attention from the dead slugs. She wonders why she has killed them. Does that make her a murderer? She laughs at the thought. Alfred calls to her from the bedroom.

"What's so funny in there?"

"Oh, just some pink shit."

"Some what?"

"Nothing."

"Do you want me to order up some breakfast?"

"I ain't staying for breakfast. I leaving soon's I take a bath."

"You said you're leaving?"

"Yep. I got things to go home and do."

"What sort of things?"

"Things."

"Can't you postpone them?"

"No."

His purple face appears at the bathroom door. His eyes are puffy and bulging like they're about to leap across the room and bludgeon her. Then he smiles a smile carved out of time, out of pink shit, out of the effortless greeting of strangers in strange hotel rooms, a smile she suspects he never gives his wife in their island-sized home in Connecticut.

He has told her of his wonderful home: the swimming pool recently remodeled in the shape of a circle to symbolize the globe-trotting he and his wife, both investment bankers, have been doing; their son's room—a cornucopia of world cultures, filled with objects from their travels; the three cars that no one but the nanny has time to drive. When she tells him she has no idea what an investment banker is, he laughs out loud and says it isn't something you'd find in Barbados. He seems to like the idea that she knows nothing.

His wife is very beautiful. The picture he displayed over dinner wasn't a good one, but the woman's smile lights up her face. During dessert she wondered why a man with so perfect a wife would be after her, a skinny black girl who knows nothing.

"You're quite something," he tells her later. This is after he's done everything imaginable to turn her on, making love to her with an attention she never got from Breeze. Still, strangely, she is left untouched. His patience annoys her. His lovemaking is too careful for her impatient, combustible mood. She wishes they'd made love on the beach instead of in the hotel room, or in the parking lot in the car under the yellow lights. Or that he'd pinned her legs against her chest forcefully the way Breeze did when she caught this mood. She wishes he'd whispered her name when he came. But he is patient and tender and silent.

"You're quite something. Quite a woman. So beautiful. You know, in the dark, your skin shines. It lights up, almost like fireflies. Did you know that? It's very strange. I've never seen anything like it. And your cunt is like fire. It's so hot inside you, I think if I didn't come fast, my prick would melt." He laughs but she does not see the humor. Touristmen say the strangest things.

"I'd really love it if you'd stay for breakfast. There's something I want to talk to you about. I want to take you to America. Have you ever been to America? I would set you up in a wonderful apartment. Buy you everything you want. You wouldn't have to do anything. Just be there for me when I want you."

She's already in the shower and barely hears what he has said.

"What that you say?"

"I said. . . Never mind."

He closes the bathroom door.

When she comes out, he's standing by the window smoking. He's still naked, and she finds herself being stirred by his long muscular legs. She is feeling more relaxed now. Maybe. . . Maybe she'd be more receptive now. She moves toward him, checks herself in the large gilded mirror over the bed next to a picture of a fisherman plucking one flying fish from an otherwise empty net. How ironic. Her father, in this expensive hotel, still practically empty-handed.

The room is caught in the weird play of sunlight broken up by roving bands of clouds; her image in the mirror suffers. Her legs look elongated and flat in the surreal light. The man by the window, on the other hand, is gold-flecked in front of the thin yellow blinds, a mammoth man, hands akimbo, with his legs wide apart as if straddling the world.

The money is spread out on the bed. Five hundred-dollar bills. The light catches the eyes of the dead presidents and she sees them sparkle. She sparkles a smile of her own—not for the presidents, whose deaths she had not heard about; not for the man by the window, whose death she would not care about. Her smile is for the man on the wall with the single flying fish, whose death she cannot forget.

He turns around as she gathers the money in a small heap, folds it, and slips it into her bag hanging over the arm of the couch.

"What time should I pick you up?"

"I don't know." She reaches for her panties.

"How about five-thirty?" he asks in a casual, confident voice.

In his voice she hears history's laughter. There is something mocking about his confidence, as if he is sure she, a mere pawn in paradise, has nothing else to do but be the object of his fantasy—a black woman who keeps her lava pussy boiling for him. "We need tourist dollars," she remembers hearing the minister of tourism proclaim on television. "We must do whatever we can, especially the little things, to make our guests feel at home." The whole world can come here and feel comfortable, but not those who're born here. This man who arrived white as alabaster from the gloom of winter three days ago knows it, expects it. Now black-and-blue from frolicking in his paradise, he stands ready to claim one more night of pleasure, one more plunge into the well of fantasy. Who would dare deny him?

"Tonight? I not sure I can make it tonight," Cyan says.

"You're not sure. . . what do you mean you're not sure?"

She wants to ignore the mocking tone of his voice. From across the room she can smell his breath, stink with contempt. She begins to get dressed in the silence that follows as he fritters away the last seconds of his money.

"What do you mean, you're not sure you can make it?" he asks again, this time with the authority of a man certain of his power. "Why didn't you tell me this before. I could've gotten somebody else, you know."

She is almost fully dressed now; just her shoes to put on, and the night will be behind her.

"Are you listening to me?" He is ready to let his anger take over, and she is ready to release him from his agony.

"But you ain't want just anybody, do you, John? You want me."

"Damn it, yes. I'm paying you good money. Why can't you drop everything for a week?"

"I didn't promise you I'd be yours for a week, did I?"

"No. . . but. . ."

"Then be happy with what you get. I got a idea. Why you don't try somebody else tonight? Sample another one of our lava pussy women."

"You don't mean that."

"I mean every word of it, John."

"Why're you calling me John? You know that is not my name. My name is Alfred, you know that. Why're you calling me John? I don't understand you."

"Who cares if your name is John or Paul or Alfred? It don't make no difference to me."

"I've never seen you so aroused. I like it."

Laughing, he walks toward her. The ruddiness of his cheeks makes her think of pomegranates. He sees himself in the mirror and stops. She leaves him staring at himself in the mirror, which is too small to hold his image.

She buys pomegranates from a woman selling fruits and vegetables under a tamarind tree a few feet away from the bus stop. As she waits for the bus, she cracks the purple husks and pumps seeds into her mouth by the fistful. Her tongue responds to the pink sweetness, and the morning suddenly feels wonderful. Her eyes take in the sedate, stately surroundings. Tall casuarinas and hibiscuses behind wrought-iron fences shelter the homes of the wealthy from traffic and riffraff. Peppered with red and yellow flowers, the hibiscuses stretch into the air in majestic silent arches that seem to beckon her. But she knows behind those trees are dogs trained to attack intruders and maids trained to turn away the weary.

A bus packed with Saturday-morning shoppers and workers bound for department-store jobs in Bridgetown screams past. There was a time when she envied those girls with easy respectable jobs in town. Some girls, like her sister, were even given dreams of being a doctor or lawyer. She was never allowed to dream such dreams. She wasn't smart enough. But she had dreams. Now she can't remember what they were.

Chapter Seventeen

*I*n the club, music pulsates, vibrates. Bodies angled just the right way kiss with the frenzy of sexual heat not yet ready to be released. The door jams, slams shut. The crowded place stinks with sweat and perfume, but nobody is thinking of leaving. They wait for the hottest band in the island to begin playing.

Breeze sits and waits in his corner booth. The same one he sits in every night. He hasn't paid for it but he owns it nonetheless. Nobody sits there even when he's not in the club.

The band starts up. Calypso crackles and ignites overheated bodies. People emerge from cracks, from bathrooms, from nowhere. Black, white, brown, they crowd the dance floor, spilling into passageways. They grind each other to glass. Legs get twisted, backs get hurt, sprained joints get hard. This joint is jumping past the twinkling eyes of Sailor, who whistles through the door without paying. He doesn't have to pay because the doorman is his sister's lover. Sailor used to be the doorman here not too long ago. Then he met a Canadian woman in the club and. . . Ah, it's the same tired old story A man gets caught doing the wrong thing at the wrong time and loses his job. It's the best thing that ever happened to him.

Breeze sees Sailor and a sudden tenseness invades him. He doesn't like Sailor's cockiness. Sailor saunters over trying to look relaxed. The song the woman was singing last night comes into his head and he begins to whistle it. *Night Fever* describes how he feels. In his pocket the three hundred dollars feel like a million.

"Say, what's the good word, Breeze?" Sailor sings out confidently.

"You're here, that's more than I expected." replies Breeze. He whips out a yellow bandanna and swats sweat from his brow. "Did you bring it?"

"All of it. And more."

"I ain't interested in no more than what belongs to me."

"I got yours, man."

"You better got it."

"I got it."

"Where is it?"

"Got it right here."

"I ain't got time to fuck around, Sailor."

"Relax, Breeze. I got it. Leh we have a drink, man."

"I gotta be moving, man. Open your pockets, let me step on 'bout my business."

"How 'bout a game?"

"A game? Look, Sailor, I ain't got time for that game or this game. Just gimme what belong to me and let me get moving. I got places to go, people to see."

"I ain't seen you with that chick lately, man. Whatever become of she?"

"What chick?"

"The black skinny sparrow with the aching horse eyes. Man, I don't see why you woulda ever mess wid a chick like that. First time I see you with that chick, it puzzle me. Still don't get you hanging with a chick like that."

"If you were to get me, Sailor, I'd be in a lotta trouble. Mankind would be in a lotta trouble."

Breeze gets up from his corner. Sailor knows this definitely means no game tonight. No chance of winning back the two hundred dollars he lost to Breeze at backgammon a month ago.

"Let me get my money, man," Breeze says.

"You won't believe where I saw that chick last night," says Sailor hoping to put a hot stake up Breeze's rass with his story. With no hope of redeeming his losses, he would leave Breeze with his blood boiling. He's seen the way Breeze looked at that chick. Breezed loved her. Perhaps he still does.

"I don't really care, Sailor."

"You would if you'da seen her. Check this out. I'm on the beach, yunno, behind the Grand Paradise, just checking the flow of things. It's dark, yunno, but the lights from the hotel giving off enough light to see by. The breeze is nice, so I just taking it easy. And who should float past me hugging up this white man like he is her long-lost daddy?" He pauses for dramatic effect. "Your chick. The sparrow. An' she chirping, man. Sweet, sweet. Like she just done get feed."

Breeze wants to hit Sailor. Wants to hit him somewhere between his eyes and his balls. To see his tongue flop to one side of his mouth the way a frog that's just been squashed by a car has its tongue pulled out of its head by the force of the blow. He looks Sailor dead in the eye and asks for his money again as politely as he can, but with a coldness that leaves no doubt how he feels about Sailor flicking this tale in his face.

Sailor hands over the money. His hands are shaking. The look Breeze just flashed reminds him that this man has a temper like a coiled chain. A year ago he watched Breeze unmake a hotel guard who tried to stop him from entering the hotel to visit a touristwoman. When the guard threatened to call the police, Breeze broke his nose.

"So how you so sure is Night?"

"That's the bitch's name, man? Night?" Sailor starts a laugh, then tries to break it off when he sees the punch coming. Too late. He knows his jaw is broken before he hits the ground.

• • •

Breeze throws the Kawasaki into high gear before he is out of the parking lot. He enters the street without paying attention to oncoming traffic and almost smashes into a bus. He rounds the corner by the supermarket and passes traffic going more than fifty up the hill. He slices through the wind blowing across the St. George valley and reaches Christ Church before the moon can twitch.

He is thinking he should've let Sailor keep the money. Two hundred dollars was nothing to him. In one day he could make that without breaking sweat. If he'd let Sailor keep the money, Sailor wouldn't have had any reason to try to humiliate him.

What is it about this long-legged woman that has so captivated him? He hasn't seen her in over a year but he thinks about her almost every day. He remembers the smell of her freshly washed hair, the sound of her laughter like a downpour in the morning. He hears her voice singing in the evening as she fries chicken for him; he sees the roguish smile in her eyes as she steadies herself on top of him with the masterful determination of a wavetrain.

He cuts the engine at the top of the gap and coasts the rest of the way. There's a party going on somewhere in the neighborhood. Reggae music mingles with the whistling of frogs and the bored howl of guard dogs with nothing to guard.

All is quiet around the house. Muted by blue blinds, the house lights give off a hazy glow. He parks the bike on the grass, knocks and waits. The door opens and Cyan is standing there looking radiant and beautiful, an exclamation mark at the end of a sensuous poem. He's never seen her more lovely. Just as he begins to wonder if she'll invite him in she turns and walks away leaving the door open. That's his invitation. He'd better not expect anything more.

He follows her to the kitchen where she is making Ovaltine. Waiting for her to speak he leans against the fridge, watchful. He cannot speak. Jealousy is wrapped too tightly around his throat.

He looks at her and can't believe she'd sleep with a touristman. He knew girls who did that, and he didn't think Cyan was that type. But what else could she be doing with a touristman late at night on the beach?

The last time he'd been here was not a happy time. They'd argued about the touristwoman on his bike. He woke up later that night with a knife at his throat. Smelled like it'd been dug up from under a pile of fish bones. Must've been one of her mother's rusty fish knives. The smell alone nearly killed him. He was sure she would've killed him had he not woken up just then. In the dark room that night he saw a coldness in Cyan's eyes that reminded him of his father, whose eyes had no life in them whatsoever.

As a man, he'd have to admit he deserved the look, if not the near-death experience. He held out promises to Cyan he knew he could not keep. No explanation for it. He loved her. Wanted to love her. But in reality he couldn't afford to love her. Nice going, Breeze, his friends would say to him. You couldn't screw her without falling in love? You've had better-looking women than she, what made you fall in love with she? She thinner than rope, man.

They wouldn't say that if they'd ever felt that rope wrap around them.

Tension like a whip. She's too stubborn to speak first. He must overcome his jealousy and take up the chase.

"So, how things going?" he says.

"I real sleepy, man. What you want?"

"A cup o' Ovaltine would be nice."

"You don't drink Ovaltine, man. You say Ovaltine for children, remember?"

"Maybe I feel like a child tonight. Long time no see."

"Long time no see, long time no hear, long time no screw. Anything else we ain't do in a long time that we trying to forget?"

"I can't forget you, Cyan. I miss you."

"I miss my mother, but who cares?"

"How is she? Your mother?"

"Dead."

"When?"

"Who cares?"

"Why do you talk like that? I don't understand it. One would think you didn't care 'bout the woman."

"Who say I do?"

"You ain't gotta say it. I know it. My biggest sister got two teenage daughters, yunno. Them always fighting wid their mother, but let somebody attack she, and see how Denise and Femi jump to she defense. Girl children always fighting wid them mother. That's because one is the same as the other. Like sulfur on a match. Them tie so tight in a bond, them can't escape without catching fire."

"Where you study all this mother-and-daughter shite? At Beachbum University?"

"It don't take no lotta brains to figure that out. That is why wunna had so much trouble getting along."

"Who tell you we had trouble getting along? Look, Breeze, whatever you come here for, I ain't got time for it. And I especially ain't got time for you telling me no shite 'bout why me and my mother didn't get along. You don't know nutten 'bout the two o' we. All you know is what I tell you, and for all you know, I coulda been telling you lies."

This is his opening. Her mother. It's her most vulnerable spot. A certain softness creeps into her eyes whenever she talks about her mother, which isn't often. She'd much prefer to talk about her father. She's happier there, not as vulnerable. He senses that she's lying about her mother. Had her mother died, it would've affected her deeper than this. But he decides to play her game.

"Where you mother buried?" he asks.

"In St. Lucia."

"You went to the funeral?"

"No."

"Why not?"

"Who you think you is, asking me all these blasted questions?"

"I don't believe you, Night."

"Don't call me that."

"You never mind before."

"I mind now. I mind everything now. Like you being here for one. I mind that. I mind it so much I want to know why you come here waking me up, stopping me from getting my sleep. I got things to do tomorrow, yuh know."

"You dress like you just come in."

"What's it to you if I coming or going?"

"Why you lie 'bout your mother like that?"

"It ain't none o' your business, anyway."

"Sailor say he see you last night."

"Who's Sailor?"

"You know Sailor. Short, very light skin with 'locks. You seen him with me sometimes."

"I don't remember him."

"Well, he say he see you last night."

"So, he see me. I glad his eyes working good."

"He say you was on the beach with a man. A white man. A tourist."

"And. . ."

Breeze realizes he is already defeated. That Cyan makes no attempt to deny his accusation shows it up as the flimsy excuse to see her that it is. His charge defused with one little word. . . *And*. And nothing. What else could he say to that?

In trying to understand the power of such a tiny word he sees Cyan's hold over him. Her all consuming will to survive hardly ever shows behind her smile. It is easy to take her for granted. But do it, and you've made a big mistake.

He should've known better. It had taken only a short time for her to go from a frightened girl to a woman in charge of her own affairs, making her way with creativity and perseverance. He remembers how she dragged him to every tie-dye artist and to all the tiny stores in Swan Street looking for cloth, how she made him buy a sewing machine for his house (he'd already bought one for her house) so she could still work when she spent time there.

She reminds him of himself. And perhaps this is why he can't forget her. But he doesn't just want to love her, he wants to be her lord. He wants to possess her like he's never possessed anything. And she will not let him. Not now.

He wants desperately to hold her. To smell her. Would she come willingly to his arms? He grabs her roughly. Surprised, she gasps, guttural and loud, like a dog's angry growl. She pulls away violently.

"Don't touch me, yuh hear!"

He can't stop himself now. He lunges at her again and she slaps him. His dry skin sings out. A sharp pinging sound—the sound of blood rushing to his head.

"Who the rass you think you is, Breeze? Get away from me! Get outta me blasted house!"

"You think you's a bad woman, ah?"

"You's the body that think you's a Guinea-Gog, but I ain't frighten for you. I ain't invite you here. I don't know why you come troubling me."

"Girl, you don't know how I feel 'bout you."

"Don't make me laugh, Breeze. You ain't got no feelings beside how fat you' wallet feel 'gainst you backside. I can't put no money in you' wallet. And even if I could, I won't, so I have nothing to offer you."

"I want you back, Night. I swear I go do things different. We could get married."

"Things ain't go be different 'cause I ain't want you back."

"How you could be such a hard woman, though? You can't forgive a man one mistake?"

"That is what wunna men does always say. One mistake. 'I mek a mistake. Is only one mistake.' If only I could believe it did only one mistake. But I can't believe it, Breeze. I can't believe in you no more. I wish I could, but I can't. You don't know how much faith I had in you, Breeze. I had all my faith in you. But I won't put my faith in you again. What go happen when you hurt me again? I want to keep my sanity, Breeze. I would really kill you next time. I would rather cut out me own heart than put faith in you again, you don't understand that. I tell you before, I would never take you back if you leave me."

"How you could say I leave you? I thought you was going kill me that night. I look in you eyes and I ain't see nothing but death running 'bout."

"You leave me when you pass me with that touristwoman stick on behind you. You did done leave me. All you did waiting for was the excuse to run and I give it to you. How you think it feel like, expecting to get the whole world and end up with nothing? That is how I feel 'bout you, Breeze. That's how you make me feel."

"I swear, Night, I ain't touch a touristwoman since. I swear."

"I ain't care, Breeze. You don't understand I ain't care what you do."

"I swear. On my mother's grave."

"What I look like to you, Breeze? A fool? What you does think when you look at me? That this monkey so backward, it can't climb? That somehow 'cause I born like you on this rock that God gone 'long and ain't look back at that I ain't worth the spit you use to polish you' shoe? What you does see when you look at me, Breeze, or when you look at any women born here? What the shite you does see? You don't see youself? You don't see you' mother? You' grandmother? What the rass you does see? What make them touristwomen more precious than we?"

He wants to take her into his arms and let her tears wash his stinging cheeks, to tell her that yes, he sees himself in her, he sees his grandmother, but that he also sees the ghosts that made their lives so hard. He is afraid of these ghosts. He has stared them down many a morning riding home from the club or from the sunburnt arms of a touristwoman. The past like a great pond yawns in his sleep.

Squashed by a runaway tractor in a cane-piece a week after giving birth to him, his mother did not live to see her thirty-fifth birthday. His grandmother raised him and six other siblings because his father never got over seeing his woman run down. He became a drunk, hardly worked after that day, and spent the rest of his life cursing God for his misfortune, declaring before his family his willingness to follow the Devil, for at least the Devil allowed him the dignity to choose his own death: drowning in alcohol. And every time Breeze saw him in the street, (that's the only place Breeze saw him), he'd just stare. Frozen by the white bitterness in his father's eyes, he would pee himself from fright. In the days before his death his father reneged on his pact with the Devil and was saved in the Pentecostal church in St. Davids in a desperate bid to deny the Devil his soul. Many people felt the Devil gave up on his father's soul long before his death—knowing that an alcohol-soaked soul was useless—to concentrate on his youngest son, Breeze.

Some of his brothers and sisters went on to become schoolteachers, nurses. No one could understand what happened to him. He couldn't, either, but he consoled himself with the knowledge that none of them made as much money as he. Perhaps his behavior could be traced to the discovery, at an early age, that the plantation had refused to compensate them for the life of the mother he never got to know, and that unbeknownst to his family, the lawyer they hired, who found every way possible to bungle the case, was a distant cousin of the plantation manager. In any event, he grew up with no interest in going to school to learn how to take orders or how to defer to his so-called betters or how to become a productive member of a society where politics and privilege were incestuous twins, where political rivals squared off in Parliament over passing a bill to raise the price of gas, then went to pass gas in bed with the same whore. The place was small, too small for daydreams. So he took to the night. When most boys his age were pinned down under kerosene lamps memorizing their times tables or tussling with hard-to-spell words, he was roaming the night with older boys, stealing mangoes, golden apples, and corn, or sitting around a fire that crackled with corn and crab, cursing his father for being a drunken idiot. In the nighttime, dreams were made, dreams were lived. Perhaps it was his love for the night that led him to the work he did, to the soft breezes drifting through the window off the sea seeking his soul, to the presence of this young girl, who until tonight didn't mind being called Night.

At fifteen he fell in with Tall-Boy, who'd since married a Canadian and left the island. Tall-Boy taught him how to make a living from nothing, first by diving for coins off the wharf and later by selling jewelry to tourists. For five years he lived with Tall-Boy in a house in Nelson Street, where he became friends with the whores and drunks. He learned to ignore the stench of the streets, the hungry unwashed children who begged him for money and who were often caught stealing from the stores in the Broad Street; the sweaty young girls who winked at him as he went by, whose mothers were whores and who had no prospects themselves other than to follow their mothers into the profession; the constant fights between whores and their boyfriends, which often spilled into the streets and alleyways. Alleyways led into backyards where children played in filth, where drunks slept with dogs. At night hungry dogs roamed the streets pissing on drunks who slept in doorways of bars, where whores and tourists sought each other. Tall-Boy taught him how to make love to touristwomen in ways they never allowed their husbands.

Tall-Boy didn't teach him about loving a woman like Cyan. There is no way out for him now, hopelessly in love. She'd never believe him.

Never take him back. It is time for him to do like Tall-Boy. Time to learn to fly.

"When a man don't have nothing else, when he can't have what he want, he still want his pride. You think you perfect, Night. Nobody ain't perfect. Not even you. I hope you never make a mistake."

Chapter Eighteen

Lemuel wonders why she decided to stay in the village. The young man her father killed lived in a village only a few miles away and had many friends in Bottom Rock. How many times had he overheard someone commenting on what a "wuffless man" her father was? Or standing outside Lord's rum shop as Cyan passed, he'd hear some fool remark, "If that boy did family to me, I woulda burn down that house already." Most people would've left the village long ago. Is it bravery or just plain stubbornness that keeps Cyan around?

He sees her often now late at night coming home from wherever she goes. He never asks. She seems happy to talk to him, even at that hour. He's the only friend she has in the village.

Last week he went with her to put flowers on the grave of her father and sister. She goes every month.

Roses for her sister and gardenias for her father. The roses she grows and tends herself in her garden, which has the most beautiful roses in the village. The gardenias she buys from a nursery somewhere in the hotel district. Money is of no consequence to Cyan, it seems. He wonders if she really makes all that money selling clothes and jewelry to tourists or if, according to rumor, she's selling herself. Rumors don't seem to bother her. Morality is not a stick she fears. She does what she does, and to hell with anyone else.

Can she ever be saved? There is something sad and gloomy about her sometimes. He notices it when she talks about her father but even more so when she talks about her mother. Obe's name brings on a depression in her that touches even him when he looks at her face, and for a long time after he can do nothing but sit and think about her. He prays for her all the time.

Early morning. The sun just blinked for the first time, dousing the sleeping village in soft light. A group of them are walking from church. He and Cyan trail the group. Ahead the women are singing *Silent Night*.

He wants to hold her hand. That thought and the incipient desire that accompanies it fill him with guilt and shame. No sooner has he stepped out of the Lord's house than he is longing for her. Prayer can't seem to remove such ungodly thoughts from his mind.

She waits when he falls behind. He is ashamed of the way he walks. Why doesn't she walk on and leave him? She must find him repulsive, he thinks.

"I walking too fast?" she asks.

"A little."

"Sorry."

"You ain't tell me if you enjoy the service."

"It was nice. I like the singing. I always like church songs. Especially this time of year. Them make me feel good. Joyful and sometimes sad. But it's a good feeling overall."

"You should come more often."

"I don't have time."

"You have to make time for God, Cyan."

"I have to make time for myself. God got all the time in the world for Heself. I have to make time for Cyan."

"You don't know how it does hurt me to hear you talk like that."

"Then don't make me talk like that."

He's afraid to pursue the matter. It was a miracle that she came to church this morning; he doesn't want to alienate her now. She might never come back.

"You wanna come over and eat today?" she asks. "I cooking black-eyed peas and stew pork. And I bake a ham and some sweetbread."

"Actually, today I going be next door to you with the Baptiste sisters. We meeting for a laying of the hands for Sister Baptiste."

"Which one?"

"Augusta. She been sick now this is two weeks."

"I hope she dead."

"Cyan, that's a nasty thing to say. And you just leave church too."

"I only went 'cause is Christmas and I like to sing Christmas songs. Church don't mean nothing. Look at them two dry-up lizards you going to see. Them does be in church every week an' still the same way. Still gypsy, gypsy like blackbirds. Everybody business is them business. Them is the two wickedest people I know. Why church don't change them?"

"Them ain't that bad, Cyan. Them don't have nothing better to do. Them ain't got no children, no grandchildren. Them only got one another and what else them got to do but talk 'bout but what go on round the place. You know them harmless."

"Harmless to you. Words ain't harmless. Words could kill. You don't know them like me."

"When you was a little girl, you used to spend a lot of time with them sisters. What happen between wunna?"

"You going there today, you ask them. And to think that my father used to give them free pot fish or flying fish when it was in season. And that's another thing. All the mouth the people in this village got now my father dead, half them still owe him for fish that they conveniently didn't have no money to pay for. Still, none of them don't have a good word to say 'bout my father. None of them don't speak to me

Them does pass me like I invisible. I wonder what they would say if I went to them and demand the money them owe my father."

"The problem is that your father never say he was sorry for killing that young man. And on top of that, you tell people the boy shoulda known better than to be pulling at your mother. That he shoulda known 'bout Steel temper. Talk like that does turn people 'gainst you. The young man have nuff friends 'bout here. His mother is a hard-working woman, a nurse at the clinic in Oistins, she help deliver a lot o' these children 'bout here. It was hard for people to be in Steel's corner, especially after he ain't tell the police where he hide the billfish beak. Had the police digging up everybody backyard and house. Is like he make the whole village a suspect in that murder. The people ain't forgive he for that. And them ain't go forgive you neither with talk like that."

"These people is hypocrites, and you know it. Them don't deserve nothing but scorn from me."

"Then don't expect nothing else from them. Look, when I did young, I did very wild. I used to swear, drink, and gamble a lot. Never care 'bout a job except in crop season. When I get sick, all these people join together to help me get better. Who ain't feed me, come by to encourage me; who ain't pray for me, throw down a grog in me name. If you want to win these people sympathy, if you want them on you side, you need to let it be known that you sorry for what you' father do. You need to let them know you ain't like him."

"I don't want to win nobody sympathy. As long as them don't bother me, I won't bother them."

They are standing now in front of Cyan's house.

"Merry Christmas, Cyan."

"Merry Christmas."

From under the almond tree he watches her unlock her door. Cyan's rejection of the village concerns him. The giddiness of youth can cause that, he knows. But life can be funny. When you feel most invincible is when lighting will strike. It caught up to him the night he challenged

God once too often. He'd been gambling with Steel, Percy Small and a few others, and winning. To escape with his loot, he'd made up a story about having to go see his sister who was having a baby. Percy Small, who always walked with a Bible, challenged him to swear on it. He'd placed his hand on the Bible and sworn that if he was lying, God should make him lame, deaf, and blind. God spared him deafness and blindness, but next morning he woke up with his left side dead. The people of Bottom Rock saved him with their prayers.

This is a small community. No space for loners. Sooner or later a person will need help. And what then? As a true friend to Cyan, he will have to save her from herself, from becoming an Ishmaelite. He has to get the village back on her side. What better place to start than with the Baptiste sisters?

The sisters practically raised Cyan. They'd watched her play with Celine in the soursop tree that kissed both houses; they'd helped her as best they could with her times tables and sums. Some mornings they'd give her sugarcakes or ten cents to buy taffy as she set off to school. They'd fed her when the parents had to stay late at the market and had watched her fight her way up and down the gap, beating older boys at sports and laughing at those who tried to corner her smile. She was an unruly child, but that was because her father treated her like a boy, teaching her to play cricket and letting her climb the plum tree by the standpipe with the boys on Saturday mornings.

Remarkably, the trajectory of Trinidad Baptiste's early life had also followed that unruly arc associated with rebels until her indiscretions so scandalized her aunt, who'd become her guardian after her mother died, that an arrangement was made to send Trinidad, then nineteen, to work for a retired English army colonel in the Navy Gardens. Her aunt, who took care of the colonel's aging mother, hoped being among white people, seeing how civilized and cultured they were, would settle her niece down.

Trinidad herself wanted to get away from the uncouthness of her surroundings, from the married men always trying to lure her into a humid patch of bush or centipede-infested cane field with offers of money or clothes for fifteen minutes of their grunting, which always left her sore, sometimes bleeding, and on the brink of tears. Yet she was unable to resist their advances or those of the younger boys content with fondling her breasts under a dim moon or one quick silent thrust in the dark, resulting in the thick discharge that signaled it was time for them to run and tell their friends. There was so much more she wanted to give them. Why were they all so afraid to take what she was really offering? Why were they all so willing to settle for inches when she wanted to give them miles? As if in the minutiae of their existence they could think of nothing grander, nothing bigger, than a life of unfaithful dreams. It was different in the world outside, she imagined, the world that lay beyond her village, the world of white people: big houses, big dreams, big streets with lights, cars instead of bicycles, and slow-moving time. Time to do whatever you wished. Time to get up in the morning and savor the scent of dew hanging on roses, or the hum of the hummingbird's wings outside your window, time to have breakfast of eggs and bacon instead of a cup of tea and two biscuits, time to feel the sun's warmth and not be afraid it will make you too black and ugly, time to experience joy. In the world outside, time did not have wings but was a contented old woman, with nothing on her mind except fulfillment of dreams.

She found the world outside no better for her than her village's world of walled-in expectations, however. The Colonel used her as his sexual thing almost from the start, which she wouldn't have minded had she been allowed to touch that other world. His world of fine speeches and the queen's English spoken with the caress of perfection, which she heard coming from the living room when he entertained or dined with friends. His world of sweet airy music sung with style and grace, which flowed through the house anytime guests were around but would be confined to his bedroom when they were alone. His world of leather-bound books, which he'd sit and read all day, smiling to himself as if rediscovering the forgotten magic of sensuality. She tried to infiltrate this world when he left her alone in the house, to find the key to that superiority, but without a guide she was a saltwater fish in a pond. She practiced their speech, she put on airs and never dispensed with them, even as her fainthearted friends in the village accused her of pretending to be white, of wanting to be "more than them," and abandoned her like the crew of a sinking ship.

By the time she left the colonel's employ after three humiliating years, displaced by her younger sister, Augusta, she had decided that sex was joyless, and there was infinitely more pleasure in the art of giving fine speeches. For a while she advertised herself as the best mistress of ceremonies around and made many appearances at services-of-song and weddings. She married a mason, left him after three years for a man ten years younger, and left him six months later after he came home drunk and heard her practicing her speech one night, asked her if she thought she was from England, and hit her upside the head, knocking her unconscious. Love was not worth the headache. She moved in with her sister, who promptly got her saved and a job with a seamstress, and she'd been happy to reserve herself for the Lord ever since. Then one day, sitting next to Percy Small in church, she felt his hand brush her ankle as he reached down to pick up his Bible, which had dropped at her feet. His hand, it seemed, lingered for longer than was necessary. She said nothing, did nothing, for she was suddenly thrown back in time; she was seventeen again and the burning had returned. They exchanged knowing glances. She looked around, but no one else had noticed.

Now, at the age of fifty-five, she had finally experienced the patient joy of making love to a man whose touch was lingering and who allowed her to unwrap her desire slowly, a man who, when he settled into the folds of her now-buxom body, was in no hurry to depart. Unfortunately, Percy was married and had to sneak into the house after Augusta had gone to bed to save them both from embarrassment.

Augusta, at fifty, had never entertained a man. And proud of it. There was that one time with the colonel, which she'd convinced herself didn't count. In her mind she was still as pure as the Virgin Mary. Until six years ago, only she and God and the colonel—who died shortly after—had seen the one drop of blood that told the tale of her trial, when God put her to the test, then came and got her like Daniel out of the lion's den.

Trinidad had warned her about the colonel. She'd laughed. She was nothing like her sister. Augusta had seen how sexual desire had ruined her sister's reputation in the village. This inconsolable burning like a cane fire caught in high wind, as her sister once described it, had never touched her, and wouldn't. God would see to that. She could not be seduced.

She was unprepared for the colonel's charm, his confidence, and his good humor. Old enough to be her father, he'd kept in good shape. He was slim and muscular, with hair the color of his tanned skin, though gray at the temples, and small cowled eyes that pinched together when he laughed. He spoke so well, it was music to her ears. And when he played Beethoven's breathtaking Ninth and spoke of his travels around the world guarding the many jewels in the British crown, her imagination soared and she herself became a jewel which soon shone with the brilliance of a small fire when he began to remark on her beauty with the carelessness of a natural seducer.

Each evening as she walked along the esplanade to get the bus home, she would reflect on the stirring, the burning she experienced whenever the colonel spoke of her beauty, and fearful of falling into the cavern of desire, she would silently vow not to return. But each day she would return, eager to hear him speak, hungry for the music, anxious for a chance to shine, revivified through prayer, sure that she was strong enough to overcome temptation. Then one day he played that stirring music and held her so close to him, she could see the tiny blood vessels in his eyes. He told her she was the most beautiful woman in the world, more beautiful than the queen of England. The burning swept over her before she had time to temper it. The next thing she knew, she was naked on the bed.

Then God reached out for her. But not before the colonel had managed to draw blood. That blood, while it weighed heavy on her heart all these years, had also produced the savings on which she now lived. In an act of penitence, the colonel, so undone by her screaming when she saw her blood on his penis and on the sheet, had offered her a thousand pounds to keep the matter quiet (though he must've known the police would not have listened to her had she gone to them).

That night she fell on her knees and thanked God for delivering her. In His glory He came to her and told her to take the sheet as a reminder of His power.

The next day she waited in the street until she saw the colonel leave and then used her keys to get in. She found the sheet in the dirty laundry, with the dark red spot the size of a crown, and took it home.

As she approached her village that evening with the sheet stuffed in a crocus bag, the air boiled with madness. Ash from the Soufrière volcano in St. Lucia blacked out the sky. Heat trapped underneath sent people scampering for their Bibles, afraid that Judgment Day had come. Angered that Sir Lancelot had closed his rum shop and grocery to pray with his family, someone had set it on fire.

Augusta saw a swarm of people running from the burning shop with bottles of rum under their arms, their pockets stuffed with tins of sardines and corned beef. A little boy was standing in the street crying while his mother fought over a bag of rice. She stopped, gazing in amazement as her father jumped through a window of the burning shop with a bottle of rum. She called out to him, but he kept on down the street and was soon lost in a billow of dust.

That night she prayed for God to forgive her father and the colonel.

Over the years she'd used some of the money to acquire land, where she built two houses, now rented out, bringing her steady income.

She kept the sheet hidden under her bed, never to be touched by anyone but herself until the day Cyan soaked it in bleach, removing her one true symbol of God's amazing power. It was after that incident with her goddaughter that her troubles started.

"Describe the dream to me," Dr. Mayhem requested.

Augusta sat across from the youthful doctor in his small, neat office. It was a bright, friendly room with two large French windows and yellow drapes pulled back to expose the sunlight. The cushiony brown couch, pictures on the wall of fishermen hauling their nets and women working in cane fields, and plants with green shiny leaves behind the doctor's chair, all blended to give the room a homely air.

This was her first visit; she'd canceled two appointments already and almost canceled this one too.

She'd been counting on prayer to heal her troubled mind. But no amount of prayer had been able to ward off the bad dreams that had troubled her sleep for five years. Finally, at the urging of Dr. Ward, her physician, she made another appointment, but only after he'd persuaded her that seeing a psychotherapist didn't mean she was going mad.

What forced her to reconsider seeing Dr. Mayhem was the dream she'd woken from two weeks ago in such a fright that she started having palpitations. Her heart was beating so fast, she was afraid it'd fly out if she opened her mouth. By midday her body was burning up. Intermittent sweats and chills made her feel like she was caught on a hill somewhere between rain and sunshine. Every time she tried to get out of bed, her head would turn into the earth, large and spinning. The next day she went to Dr. Ward, who'd patiently borne her complaints about the bad dreams for five years. He told her the problem was all in her mind, adding that he wouldn't treat her anymore unless she saw Dr. Mayhem.

Now she held the cup of tea the secretary had given her close to her bosom, her eyes fixed on the beige liquid, which had been too dark at first but now ·was just the right color because she'd asked for more milk. At home she used condensed milk, which sweetened as well as flavored, but she knew big people like doctors didn't use condensed milk.

Hands folded across his chest, the doctor was quietly waiting for her to begin speaking. When she did, her voice was weak and nervous.

"I did standing on my mother's grave, burning. The fire did so bright you could read by it. The earth round me did scorch up black, black, still the air did sweet like molasses, like if the smoke from my burning body did mix up with herbs and spices. I didn't feel no pain, though, none at all. Not even a tingle. It like the fire was water and I was just taking a bath in it. And the fire was shooting up so pretty. All different colors. Blue, purple, yellow. All the colors of the rainbow. It make me think of Guy Fawkes night. I couldn't believe my body was burning, it look so pretty. And then it would just stop. Disappear. And I would jump outta sleep in chills and sweats."

"Your mother, I take it, is not alive."

"No."

"How long ago did she pass on?"

"Long, long ago."

"How long, approximately? How old were you?"

"Six or seven."

"Do you remember anything about her?"

"No. Not really. All I can remember was thinking how come she gone and ain't coming back. I remember asking people, my aunt, my father, where she gone and them telling me she in Heaven with God. And I remember wanting to see this God so bad."

She lifted her eyes and caught the full glint of the doctor's, focused squarely on her. Embarrassed, she dropped hers back to the cup. She sipped nervously. Still too hot and not sweet enough. She wanted so badly to ask the doctor to call his secretary so she could ask her if she had condensed milk.

"You live alone?" asked the doctor.

"No. I live with my sister, Trinidad."

"How do you get along?"

"Good. We get along very good. We been living together since she divorce, this is years now. We ain't got no problem."

"Do you talk about your mother much? With each other?"

"Not much, no. Trinidad remember her a little better than me. She was strict, Trinidad say. I don't remember her beating me, but Trinidad say she used to beat her all the time."

"Do you remember how she died?"

"No. I don't remember. Them say she was sick. But she didn't suffer. It wasn't a long sickness. Nobody ain't really know what it was."

"Any children?"

"No. . .Well, not really. Not my own."

Pause.

Augusta looked up from the cup and for the first time let her eyes linger on the doctor's face. She liked his face; it was small, intense, but friendly.

"There's this girl, our goddaughter, really, we used to mind her from small. Sometimes I used to forget she wasn't mine. I used to see her, the way she fight for everything she get, never giving up, and it used to make me feel so proud. I used to give her anything. She was like my own. We used to take her to Sunday school, she sing in the junior choir. But then. . ."

Augusta clenched the cup tightly. How did she get to talking about Cyan? She was here to talk about the dreams and the sweats and the chills.

"Do I have to talk about her?"

"Not if you don't want to right now," the doctor replied.

Pause.

"How do you feel about her now?" he asked.

She hesitated. "It was such a disappointment to see the way she turn out. You don't know how it does bother me and Trinidad every day to see the way she turn out. Everything we had we was gonna leave for she. It ain't much, but it's more than some people got. But she do something. . . she do something that hurt me, she interfere with something very important to me."

"What did she do?"

The pause was long and fragile. A look of panic crept into Augusta's eyes. She'd just made a wrong step and was about to fall headlong into a deep ravine if she didn't turn back. Then she put her hands to her face and began to cry.

Chapter Nineteen

The letters form an unbroken chain along the back of the dresser. They stand two to a heap, edge to edge, the scribbling of her mother's hand dragged across the envelopes that have never been opened. She will not read the letters, not ever. But she keeps them all. All twenty. Then one day they stopped coming.

She dreams of her mother writing one last letter with the ink of her blood. It's a dream that should frighten her, but she wakes up laughing. Her mother has no blood. Then her spirits trip over, she feels pathetic and small. She wants to cry but fights the pitiful melancholy that rises like smoke from a spent fire. The truth confronts her at every turn: When she goes into the yard to pick up eggs, she sees Obe under the clammy-cherry tree; at the sewing machine she feels Obe's breath on her neck; the wind chimes the bamboo curtain at the kitchen window, and she hears Obe's voice. She doesn't want to face it. But it's there. She misses her mother.

The letters sit, gather dust, hatch the eggs of cockroaches. A few weeks ago she even saw a lizard's egg sitting on top of the letters. The morning it hatches, she wakes up just in time to catch the tiny pink thing struggling free of the cracked shell. There is no one to welcome it, no one to warn that danger lurks beyond the stained edge of the dresser.

Patience and perseverance are hatched in the same moment as the lizard. From the same gray egg. Unhurried, it waits with sunny disposition for life to ready itself. Its wrinkled skin begins to strengthen, to harden, its legs take a solemn stance, it raises its head as if to say, *I'm here. Where are you, Mother? Where are you, Father?* It makes its first baby steps to the light coming through the open window.

Suddenly a blackbird swoops through the window, dismisses Cyan's angry glare with a choreographed twirl of its long tail, and slurps the baby lizard through its glossy beak. With noiseless speed it vanishes through the window again.

Cyan gets up and goes to the window, letting her eyes sweep the yard once. Nothing. Must've been a dream. Dead calm sits before her, the sun half-baked, the world drowsy still.

She turns and looks at the letters again, at the edges curled backward like wilted flowers. The envelopes are all the same pale green color, the kind of envelopes young lovers send postcards in with their broken hearts enclosed. She has never sent such a postcard or such an envelope but her heart has been broken. Too many times. Too many times.

Next to one of the envelopes is the broken skin of the lizard's shell. It's so tiny, like an innocent pebble from an island of innocent pebbles, the kind of pebble young lovers toss to one another on the beach. She has tossed pebbles on the beach back and forth with Breeze, the only man she has ever loved, the only man she would ever love. But for her, breaking hard for twenty-one, love is dead. It died the day she saw the touristwoman latched onto Breeze's back. She feels no remorse at the hasty jettisoning of love from her life. It had its chance.

Gently she picks up the cracked shell, trying to preserve its history. Crumble, crumble. It is dust. She thinks of Lemuel. Were he here he would say: *Dust to dust, ashes to ashes,* or something just as solemn. Lemuel is a preacher; words are important to him, not so much for their meaning as for the comfort that comes with the sounding. With loud mooing a calf claims its mother who is only yards away; so a preacher reclaims himself with repetition of words and stories that have long lost their glory.

Lemuel is coming to eat tonight. He lives alone and spends so much time ministering and praying for others, he hardly has time to cook. He eats where he can, wherever there is food: corned beef and biscuits under the hog-plum tree with the rum drinkers, fish-head soup next to the infirm waiting for God to send a miracle. Members of his congregation take turns cooking for him, leaving the food wrapped carefully on the rickety table in his tiny house, where the door is always open.

She knows he had had one great love. Beside God. Test cricket. She believes he still fantasizes about playing test cricket—the highest form of cricket there is. He denies it, though. Honesty. Can someone who's afraid to acknowledge what's inside him teach about God?

Dinner will be macaroni and cheese with baked ham. She knows he does not like greens, but she'll cook up some spicy spinach with tomatoes and okra anyway. She likes them.

A sweet ham-smell tilts the air. She has finished cooking and is sitting in the front window, letting the pungent aroma make her hungry. The window sill buckles slightly under her weight, and closer examination reveals that it is beginning to rot. She'll have to remember to get it replaced. It is a warm evening, the humidity not at all affected by the presence of a thin breeze. The air is hard and heavy as darkness falls.

Shifting stars of fireflies erupt before her eyes. Goosebumps, one for every firefly, spring out on her body. This has got to be the most beautiful sight in the entire world. What is the Empire State Building compared to this? Or that other tall structure she has seen in Koko's books, the Eiffel Tower?

Lemuel arrives promptly at six-fifteen with flowers. She is overwhelmed. She realizes she does not even know how to accept flowers. No one has ever given her flowers. Not Breeze, not the touristmen who claim her black lips are sweeter than chocolate. She wants to cry. Control. She must keep control.

Throughout the meal she glances at the flowers, which are now in a vase, and smiles. The birds of paradise look ready to fly. The lilies are ready to float away.

He rumbles through the plate like a getaway horse. After the first plate he wants more. He likes her cooking so much, he even eats the greens.

"I didn't know I was so hungry." He laughs.

"I thought you didn't like greens," she jokes after he's wiped the plate clean and licked his fingers for the hundredth time.

"Them was greens?" he asks with a mocking smile. "I couldn't tell what color them was. Them ain't taste like greens, I can tell yuh that."

He wipes the plate one more time as if to make sure he hasn't missed anything. A fleck of ham, thinner than a wisp of hair, hangs on the edge. He captures and devours it.

"If you lick yuh fingers any more, yuh go lick off the skin, yuh hear."

Rubbing his belly, which is beginning to extend beyond his belt, he leans back in the chair and laughs again. Being in Cyan's presence is comforting. She has a way of laughing, a way of making him laugh, a way of making him forget the things that weigh him down: young girls who start out so well in church only to be seduced away from God by lawless youths who spend too much time drinking, older men who drink because it's the only way left for them to prove their manhood. He knows his quest to turn them away from the rum shop to God has failed so far. He knows they laugh at him, at the way he walks; he knows they joke among themselves that he has given his life to God because he can no longer attract a woman. He knows them well, their stories, their fears. Sometimes out of earshot of the others, one of them would reveal his true heart. Farley Bradshaw's wife has lost all respect for him since he lost his job at the factory, and she is having an affair. She has brought her brothers to live with them, and he is powerless to confront her in their own house. Mad-Donkey has nightmares about his boat sinking on a moonlight night; that's why he never goes fishing when the moon is out. Jewl Bright has had two miscarriages in the past year and a half, and though she already has five children, her husband beat her last month because she decided to get her tubes tied without telling him. And though she suffers blackouts when she drinks, she goes to Lord's shop to get drunk, to drum up the nerve to leave. He has advised her to come to church and the Lord would fix her marriage, but she has yet to come.

Tonight he is not concerned about any of that. His thoughts are packed with Cyan's smile. She would never suspect how he feels about her, that he loves her. When he looks at her, it is hard not to be reminded of the days when his body was straight and steady as a casuarina, when his smile was as persuasive as a hummingbird's whispering wings, when he was as feared for his fast bowling on the cricket field as for his ability to steal other men's wives, a time when he was strong enough to work fifteen hours a day in the crop-season with enough energy left to spend his paycheck in one night of *spreeing.*

Perhaps God is testing him. What would be a more appropriate trial for a man who has not seen a naked woman in fifteen years than a young girl blooming with sexuality?

• • •

They have come outside to sit in the gallery after Cyan put the dirty dishes in the kitchen sink, which was installed just last week along with a new gas stove, new fridge and cupboards paid for with money she got from touristmen and proceeds from her business. She sits leaning her head curiously in his direction. He rests on the cement steps.

Fireflies have gathered in a still pond of light. The breeze is gentle. The stillness reminds him of that moment just before the sun comes up when darkness slinks slowly away like an overstuffed mongoose. And like a unified army bringing freedom from darkness, golden light ascends the sky. God's power is so manifest in that moment.

"Do you really think you going to Heaven?" she asks.

"That's a strange question."

"How so?"

"I don't know. Why you asking me that? You know I believe in God."

"I wanna know if you really believe in Heaven."

"What you getting at, girl? If I didn't believe in Heaven why would I try so hard to live by God's laws? I believe in Heaven. And we all got a chance to get there if we do the right things."

"You ever think 'bout screwing me?"

His blood quickens and pulses, he feels a sudden thump at his temples, and his eyes flash a look of feverish agony. The throb races and intensifies down his neck. He suddenly feels faint.

The look on Cyan's face reminds him of his sister. Following his release from the hospital after his stroke, he'd gone to convalesce at her house in Lodge Road. At night the sound of lovemaking from her room punched through the thin wall that separated them. He'd felt ashamed for listening to the pounding and screaming, knowing not only that it was sister in the next room, but that he would never experience such joy again. Then one night a throbbing and his first welcomed erection since the apoplectic episode alerted him to the prospect of full recovery. Excited, he unconsciously began to stroke his penis to the rhythm of his sister's cries. In his agitation he tumbled off the bed, calling out his sister's name so loud that she came running naked into his room.

Cyan's smirk reminds him of his sister's laughter as he lay struggling on the floor like a baby swaddled in sheets and pillows, trying desperately to hide his deflating penis. He has not set eyes on a naked woman since.

Why is Cyan playing with him? To be laughed at by the one you desire—how could love be so humiliating?

He pretends he did not hear her question.

"I would bet your sister Celine's soul in Heaven right now," he says.

"How you know that? God send a messenger to you and tell you that?"

"Faith, Cyan. Faith. You have to believe the spirit will rise from the flesh and be united with He who giveth life."

She bends her head to her knees and pulls on her dreadlocks as if trying to wring from them the truth about the existence of God.

"Most of the time I don't. But sometimes I do. Sometimes I wonder. Is it all worth it in the end? The sufferation and botheration we gotta go through. Is it worth it? The black holes in life that seem to come round and round just when you think you done see the last one. When you finally don't have to face the black holes no more, what's there waiting? Anything? Light? Real light? Peace? Happiness? Nothing? What? Tell me. Where is my father and my sister? Do you really know? And I don't wanna hear that shite you tell the people in church, tell me the truth. Tell me the truth. What you really believe go happen to we when we die?"

"You too cynical, Cyan, that's your problem. Why you think that what I say in church ain't what I really believe?"

"'Cause I know you wanna screw me. And you pretend you don't. You pretend you just wanna be my friend. I ain't meet no man yet that just want to be my friend. If you lie 'bout that, why you wouldn't lie 'bout other things?"

She laughs at his silent confession.

"What if I was to say it okay? What if I was to give you some? What'd you do? Would you do it and then go to church and pray for forgiveness? Would you be man enough to get up and go home and leave it, knowing it's yours to take?"

"I don't know how you could talk to me like this, Cyan. I is one of the few people in this village that don't talk bad 'bout you, that don't abuse you' name behind you' back. I is one of the few people that does stand up for you when I hear people saying how you drive you mother outta she own house."

"So, why do you do all them things for me?"

"'Cause I love you."

The words burst from his mouth like an exorcised demon. As the demon floats away, as his words settle on Night's startled ears, he cannot believe his own utterance.

She recovers quickly. It is almost as if she expected to hear those words, is happy that she heard them but is unwilling to accept responsibility for soliciting them. She gets up and goes into the house.

He is left to ponder his predicament. He finds himself smiling. It is sweet, this feeling, sweeter than the sweet feeling he used to get as a boy swishing his muddy feet in rainwater gathered still cloud-warm in the hoofprints left by Joe Morris's mule at the back of his house, sweeter in fact than being in the pulpit with warm sweat trickling down his armpits while his entire congregation sways to the surge of his voice in the hot air as they catch the spirit that will lift them out of themselves, away from their troubles for an hour.

He is a happy man now. And a free man. Truth does indeed make you free. He gets up, goes into the house to tell her he is leaving.

• • •

That night she comes to him in his room. She is a *godhorse*. There is a strength to her posture that is not merely angelic; it transcends feeling, it transcends thought. She is a glorious naked vision, so long, so lean. A light from Heaven. He wakes up giddy. Drunk. Feeling as though his body had wandered off without him. It is an extraordinary feeling.

Chapter Twenty

Augusta Baptiste's ripe mango complexion contrasted so perfectly with her green dress that Easter morning when she stepped through her door for church that Cyan, looking out her window, could not help but gaze in wonder. As her neighbor stepped onto the stones with the awkwardness of a newborn lamb, Cyan nearly laughed out. The dress was flawless; the new shoes too tight. But, it was the brilliance of the blood red rose, pinned to Augusta's dress just below her collar-bone, as the sunlight clipped it that left Cyan's mouth agape.

That rose humming on Augusta's breast to the beat of sunlight came from Cyan's garden. No doubt about it. Cyan was prepared to go before a judge and swear to it. And it was picked last night. She could tell by the saucy way it opened in the sunlight.

The impulse to rush out and confront Augusta passed quickly; the church-going woman simply looked too beautiful to be accosted in the street. Not over a pilfered rose that she would've been glad to give to anyone who asked. Even Augusta. Well. . . perhaps not.

Minutes later Trinidad emerged, decked out as regally as her sister in a bright yellow dress that contained her plumpness stylishly, with matching shoes and bag. And like her sister she had pinned to her breastbone one of Cyan's roses. Yellow.

Cyan wasn't angry at all, which surprised her; she found it flattering, in fact. Whatever else they might say about her, the people in the village knew she grew the best-looking roses around, most of which ended up on her father's grave. They looked just as resplendent on the bosoms of the two women this bright Easter morning. She saw no harm in letting them keep the roses. After all, she used to love these two women. How many hours had she spent at their feet hearing about the old days, when begging your neighbor for a cup of sugar wasn't cause for embarrassment, when the village gathered under the flamboyant tree at night to share stories and riddles, when people used bush tea to cure all ailments from colds to colic and went to the doctor only when they saw death approaching? These women had taught her more about the history of her island than any teacher had. History could take you only so far in the world, it's true; the present, unpleasant as it could be, still had to be dealt with. Today, however, she'd let history hold sway. She'd choose to think of the sisters as they used to be and let them enjoy their stolen flowers.

Augusta took a camera from her purse. She and Trinidad took pictures of each other, then stood erect in the mounting sun, waiting for someone to photograph them together in front of their newly painted house. Five minutes passed. Only a ten-year-old boy walking gloomily behind a cow whose chain rattled noisily on the stones came by.

"Want me to come and take wunna picture?" Cyan sang out from her window. She didn't expect the sisters to respond, but while they were wearing her roses, she could have a little fun with them, couldn't she?

Faces drawn with surprise, the sisters turned in her direction, then quickly returned their eyes to the street. Five minutes later still only the ten-year-old had passed, returning home.

Cyan repeated her offer more mischievously now. What would the sisters do if nobody else happened by?

"Would you, dear?" Augusta spoke up.

Stunned for a second, Cyan didn't know what to do. Her offer had been just for mock sport. But sport was sport. Play or bow out.

Barefoot and in her nightgown, Cyan emerged and took the camera from Augusta, whose eyes scraped the ground during the exchange. It was a cheap camera, so old the name had been scratched off, the type that took serviceable if ordinary pictures.

"Smile," Cyan said, aiming.

The sisters closed their eyes, hugged each other, and smiled. Cyan laughed. They looked like two children off to play outside for the first time.

"My roses smell good, nuh?" asked Cyan after she'd snapped the last one, with them smiling at each other as they sniffed the roses they had unpinned from their bosoms.

"Yes, they do," they said together, smiling. "Thank you very much."

Cyan could not believe their audacity.

"But yuh know, wunna coulda ask me instead of stealing them."

The sisters looked at her with surprise as they put the roses back in place on their breasts.

"Steal them? What in God's name?" Trinidad said.

"Wunna just admit them is me roses, now wunna go deny stealing them?"

"Oh, we ain't denying them is you roses. Not at all," said Augusta. "But Pastor Armstrong bring them and say you send them."

"Lemuel give you them roses?" asked Cyan in amazement. Her instincts told her the sisters were lying; the look of consternation on their faces didn't convince her one bit. Old people were masters at hiding their true feelings.

"He say you send them, and we believe him," said Trinidad. "We thought you did trying to make back friends with we. That's what the pastor lead we to believe. That's why when you offer to take our picture just now, we let you."

"Why would I wanna make back friends with wunna? Wunna is the ones that tell my mother a lie. If anything, is wunna who should be trying to make back friends, not me."

"If we did know you didn't send these roses, we wouldn'ta take them," said Trinidad, calmly.

Trinidad removed the rose from her breast and offered it to Cyan with a pitying look, like a stranger offering a bone to a stranded dog. Augusta did the same.

"Wunna can keep the roses. What I go do with them? Them done pick already. I can't put them back on the tree."

"Here, take your rose," Augusta said in a stern, maternal voice.

Mechanically, Cyan stretched out her hand. When the roses touched her finger tips she saw them tremble. She closed her hand and felt the roses crumble as she squeezed out the scent. She still held the camera in her right hand. In an instant she would fling it at them.

"Can we have our camera back, please?" Augusta said, curtly.

"I good enough to take wunna pictures, but my roses ain't good enough for wunna. I don't know what the hell I ever do you, Augusta. To this day I don't know what the hell I do you. Wanna see what my mother do because of you?"

She stretched out her right hand to display her scarred fingers.

"I would really like to know what make you tell my mother such a nasty lie? You is the biggest hypocrite ever to come out a womb. God shoulda stifle you before he let you draw breath."

Then she dropped the camera and the crushed roses at their feet and ran back to her house.

She busied herself feeding her newly hatched chickens and sweeping the yard. The urge to cry pressed heavily at her throat; she smothered it with anger. How could she let those two get under her skin? They meant nothing to her. She'd been a fool to open herself to them. And her roses had looked so lovely on them. It was all Lemuel's fault. What was he doing cutting her roses and giving them away without her say-so? He knew how she felt about them.

She dropped the green bush broom and returned to the house. From

behind the bed she fished out a bottle half full of white rum left by her
mother. She choked down a mouthful, coughed some back up, took
another. Then another and another. The clear spirits ran along the sides
of her mouth, down her neck, and evaporated. How could Lemuel
betray her like that? How could he? What kind of friend would do that?
What was he trying to do? Why did he leave her to be humiliated like
this?

Only one way to make him pay. Get him where it really hurts. In his
blasted church. She edged toward drunkenness. Revenge urged her to
get dressed, and she did.

She arrives at the church as Lemuel is beginning his sermon. Freshly
painted in bright yellow, the tiny wooden church is festooned with
flowers, fruits, and vegetables. Above each door and behind the altar
are sugarcanes woven into an archway. Down the aisles, at the doors
and along the back of the church, a harvest of yams, potatoes, breadfruit, and pumpkin in baskets. Flowers on the altar. Sugar apples and
soursop flaunt their aroma above the stale sweat evaporating in the hot
church. Children crying. Faces glistening.

She reeks of rum, but couldn't care less. She walks down the center
aisle, her eyes fixed on Lemuel, and sits in the front pew. It would be
impossible for him not to notice the venom in her stare. She sees his
eyes dissolve in panic because she has the look of someone possessed
by fury.

Leaking sweat, the large woman next to her is fanning herself nonstop. Before long, Cyan begins to sweat. The sun sitting on the
low-slung galvanized-tin ceiling is set at boil. Windows in a row facing the road are flung wide, but the breeze is hiding. Men dressed in
suits, women in polyester and fake pearls—fanning and wiping.
Nothing to cool them. As the sermon heats up, shoulders droop.
Heads drop.

"I see a lot of you in here today dress-up like you just step off a plane from America. I know is only to show off your fancy clothes that bring a whole lotta you in here. If this church could be this full every Sunday the Lord would be happy. All them fancy suits and beautiful dresses might make you the envy of your neighbor, but it ain't go make a bit of difference with God. Hundred-dollar suits don't impress God. Expensive hairdo's and pearls and rings ain't go get you a step closer to the Kingdom of God. If you covet your neighbor's wife, fancy clothes ain't go help you on Judgment Day. Say Amen! If you take the Lord's name in vain, fancy dresses ain't go get you past the pearly gates. Amen! If you lie and cheat, pearls ain't go buy you a seat on that bus heading for glory! If you're a fornicator, gold and silver ain't go help you. Today, as we celebrate the resurrection of Jesus Christ, I want you to think about resurrecting your life from evil. Take yourself out of the Devil's pit, out of the Devil's tomb of suffering, and repent your sins, ask God to have mercy on you, to pity the poor sinner you are, to lift you up with Him to His holy kingdom. All of you who've yet to take God into your heart, who've yet to ask him to forgive you, who've yet to kneel down before Him and ask His mercy, now is the time. Now is the time to get right with God. He's calling you, He's calling all the sinners. Come on, let God into your life. Those of you who've sinned this week and want to renew your vows to God, come to the altar now. Let the light of God guide you, shine upon you. Only He can save you."

Drooping shoulders spring to life. This is the part of the sermon they've been waiting for. It means their torture is almost over. They are hoping no sinners are in church today. Sunday dinner of peas and rice with baked pork and pudding on the side because it is Easter is calling them.

Cyan rises and approaches the altar. She's the only sinner in church today.

The church buzzes with an insistent mechanical murmur as Lemuel steps down from the pulpit to the blue velvet-cushioned altar where Cyan is now kneeling. He gives Cyan a woeful look, his dark eyes watery and shining.

As Lemuel raises his right hand to place it paternally on her head, Cyan quickly slips the straps of the green dress off her shoulders and lets it drop to the edge of the altar. She is naked underneath.

The collective gasp of the congregation must've been heard as far away as Bridgetown.

"You wanna save me or you wanna screw me again like you did on the floor of my house? Make up your mind. Let God and the whole world know what a deceitful man you is."

Lemuel gasps and stumbles, falling to his knees. His face contorts. He tries to get up, but panic nails him to the floor.

Pandemonium breaks out. Worshippers rush to his aid with fans and smelling salts. Water! Water! The pitcher on the pulpit is empty. Someone rushes outside to get water.

Cyan slips her dress on. She rises from the altar. Women glare at her menacingly. One woman spits on her as she goes by. The men stare in awe.

She leaves the church through the door facing the sea. A breeze hits her face, drying the sweat and spit instantly.

Behind her she hears Lemuel saying "I forgive you, Cyan. I forgive you."

She sees the rain coming and hurries home.

For weeks people came and stared at the church. The incident was the topic of conversation under flamboyant trees throughout the island, in the fish market and the rum shops.

"You hear what happen in that church up in Bottom Rock?"

"If I hear? The whole country hear."

'That girl is something, though, nuh?"

"I would like to know who she think mek she? Gone in the people church and strip nekked is she born. She ain't even frighten the Lord strike she deaf, dumb, and blind."

"That girl ain't 'fraid a soul, though, nuh. But I hear she father kill a man and get hang."

"You lie!"

"Yes, man. I hear nobody 'bout that village don't take she on. She so wicked, the mother try to burn off she fingers. Then she run she mother out she own house. That girl got the Devil in she is sure is I know you go buy the next bottle of rum."

"Who me? My woman carry 'way all me money last night. I ain't got a red cent to save me life."

"Man, why you so cheap, nuh?"

A commentator in *The Advocate* wrote about it. Men got drunk and stood outside the church, expecting Cyan to come out naked. Women said she should be ashamed to show her face in the village again.

Cyan went about her business as though the incident never happened. Men whistled as she passed. Little boys threw stones on her roof while she slept. Women cut their eyes at her and *truppsed* up their mouths. She looked them square in the face, unflinching.

With sand still in her shoes and hair, she got off the bus around six o'clock every evening at the stop a few yards from Lord's shop. Lifting her brown vinyl suitcase onto her head, she walked past clammy-cherry and dunce trees where Percy Small tied his donkey to graze, and turned the corner into the gap to her house.

Sometimes Lemuel—since removed as pastor of the church—would be sitting in his window. He'd try to speak to her, but she never stopped. Girls playing jacks and pick-ups or jumping rope in front of their houses would smile if their mothers were looking the other way. She'd stoop to retrieve a wayward ball or stop long enough to watch them jump rope to a few bars of the latest calypso by the Mighty Gabby.

Jack don't want me to bath on my beach.

Jack tell them to kick me outta reach.

Jack tell them I will never make the grade.

Strength and security, build barricade

That can't happen here, in this country.

That can't happen here

Cause that beach belong to we.

Jewl Bright's little girls were always out playing that time of day, and Cyan often brought them Cadbury. Jewl was one of the few people who didn't admonish her children, at least not publicly, for speaking to her. And sometimes she did get the impression, in the way Jewl looked at her, in the way her eyes hinted at a friendly smile, that Jewl wanted to break sympathy with the village and establish at least a speaking relationship, but Cyan did nothing to encourage it.

One Friday evening, a month after the church incident, she got off the bus with an aching back. Soaking herself in a tub of hot water and some Epsom salts for an hour was the only thing on her mind. She wouldn't even bother cooking. As the bus pulled away and she was about to raise her suitcase onto her head, she noticed two fire trucks blocking the gap. A tide of black smoke streamed down the gap. She had to step into the trench to get around the trucks. That was when she saw the crowd of people in front of her house.

Instinct sent her running toward them. A line of people stretched from Augusta's house to hers, transporting buckets of water. Her paling lay flat on the ground like a hurricane had hit it. Firemen scampered back and forth across her backyard, laboring under huge gray hoses that rained on her house. Her yard was a wasteland. Clothes from her broken line were strewn on the ground. The chicken run had been toppled. Chicks lay drowning in pools of black water. Lemuel stood in her garden wetting down the front part of the house with a thin green garden hose.

She ran around the house in disbelief as if trying to make sure she had not turned into the wrong gap and stopped at the wrong house.

Then she ran to the back. A fireman held her from going inside.

"We got it under control. Stay back, woman."

He was right. There were no visible flames, just smoke. The fire had been caught and confined to the rear of the house.

Cyan retreated to the street. Pressed tightly together, members of the crowd viewed the proceedings with no sign of emotion. She began to scream at them.

"Which one of you do this? Which one of you nasty bitches try to burn down me house?"

Someone from the crowd shouted back, "Girl, why you don't shut yuh rasshole mouth and thank God the damn house ain't get burn down? Yuh go only make a fool outta yuhself."

"Why you don't come and shut it up for me?"

A man stepped from the crowd. Stocky and bearded, he held two big rocks in his hands. It was Percy Small.

"You think people 'bout here frighten for you, nuh. Yuh father think he was a bad man, and see what happen to he. I ain't forget what he do to my little boy Isaac, yuh know. Isaac still got the scars on his back from that beating Steel give him. I owe your father. And if we meet in Hell, I go pay he back. If you wanna take these two big rocks for he, you could come along."

Lemuel dropped the hose and rushed forward. He went directly to Percy Small and took the rockstones out of his hands. Percy Small took two steps back.

"Alright, Percy. Don't bring yuhself in no trouble. Go 'long home, man. Go 'long home," Lemuel cautioned.

"She think she bad, man. She think she bad. It ain't me. I minding me own business!" Percy shouted.

"Yes, yuh better go 'long home 'fore I tell yuh wife where yuh does be at night when yuh suppose to be working," Cyan said.

Percy stepped forward to make a rejoinder, but holding him firmly by the shoulder, Lemuel pointed him in the opposite direction and walked him down the gap.

Two hours later the fire trucks rolled away from the mouth of the gap. The fire inspector remained behind, conferring with police under the almond tree. Only the smell of smoke, the sound of water dripping from rafters, and a few stooped stragglers remained of the incident.

Cyan walked through the house. Lemuel watched from the wide-open front door. The kitchen was a charred jungle of broken glass, splintered wood, and twisted utensils. The front-house had not been touched by the fire, but water and smoke had destroyed all her cloth. The police had said that her electricity would be cut off and that an electrician would have to run a check on the wiring before it could be turned back on.

"You can't stay here tonight," Lemuel said when he saw her standing in the front door in tears.

"Where else I go stay?"

"You could spend the night at my place."

"I staying right here. I ain't going nowhere. I know is these nasty people 'bout here that do this. I just wish I did here. It woulda been me and them."

"The police and the fire chief don't know what cause it, so don't go blaming people. It coulda been a bad electric wire or something."

"Ain't no damn electric wire. Is these nasty people 'bout here. I know it."

"Have it your own way, Cyan. I going home. You know my door always open if you change your mind."

She tried to sleep in the house. The smoke and the smell of charred wood made her throat itch, and she couldn't stop coughing. Round ten o'clock she knocked on Lemuel's unlatched door and walked in.

Lemuel was sitting on the bed in pajamas. He got up when she entered and moved to the only chair in the house. A kerosene lamp on a table near the bed cast a pale orange shadow across the room. An open Bible lay on the bed.

"You can sleep in the bed," he said. "I'll take the floor."

She closed the Bible, put it on the table, and then sat on the bed facing him. He fidgeted and stared blankly back at her. The bare mildewed walls looked black in the scant light, and the room had a sweaty smell of unwashed clothes. She wasn't sure this was any better than her smoke-filled house.

"How come you never make the church build you a better house?" she asked.

"What you mean?"

"You mean you couldn't get them to join together and build you something better? You been living like this since Adam was a lad."

He smiled. "What wrong with this house. It don't leak. High winds don't shake it from it foundation. What more can a house do for me?"

"I woulda make them give me a better house if I was pastor."

"Well, I ain't the pastor no more, anyway."

"After what I do to you. After that lie I tell on you that make you lose you church and everything, I surprise you even want to talk to me, far less let me come here to sleep."

"It wasn't really a lie. I wanted to do it. I did it in my mind that very night I tell you I love you. You come to me right here in this house, and you was the most beautiful vision I ever had. So it ain't really a lie."

"But I say you do it on the floor of me house, which is a lie."

He laughed. "Maybe you do me a favor. I don't need a building to do the Lord's work, just like I don't need a big house to be happy. I can preach anywhere, I can sleep anywhere. I can take the message of Jesus anywhere my feet can take me. I see this as my big opportunity. I decide to take on the country as my congregation. I spend the whole of last week in St. Philip. The people accept me better than I expect. Them listen. Them give me a place to sleep and them feed me. I tell them to keep going to church, but remember that going to church alone don't make you a Christian. I believe you got good in you' heart, too, Cyan. You just frighten to let it out."

"I got good for people who got good to me. These people 'bout here ain't do nothing but persecute me. But you watch. I go build back my house. I go build it back bigger. I go build a wall house right there on that spot. I will show them. My father buy that land and build a house on it with his own hands. Not a soul ain't go run me from that spot."

Chapter Twenty-one

The day of the fire Augusta was in such rush to get out of the house before her sister could ask her where she was going that she forgot to put powder on her face. And because she never went anywhere with her face unpowdered, she had to turn back. That piece of forgotten business saved Cyan's house. As Augusta stepped through her front door she saw the smoke and then flames shoot from Cyan's kitchen window.

She hollered inside for Trinidad to get the hose, then rushed back down the gap to the policeman, Martin Prescod's house on the main road, where she begged to use the phone to call the fire brigade. She'd wanted to but hadn't time to call Dr. Mayhem to cancel her appointment for that day.

She'd been seeing him twice a month—that was all she could afford—but until that morning hadn't told Trinidad about the visits. She had run out of excuses for leaving home at nine o'clock every second and fourth Monday of the month, but the fire changed everything. That night she broke down and told her secret to Trinidad, who in turn told her about sneaking Percy into the house at night.

She walked into the doctor's office half an hour late two weeks afterward, ready to face up to what had been troubling her all these years. She'd led the doctor around by the ear talking about her mother, her father, her childhood, her devotion to God, but had ignored his gentle yet persistent prodding to talk about Cyan. Today she was ready. Why now and not before, she didn't know.

Though the room was cool, she began to sweat profusely. She'd slept badly the night before and was feeling irritable. The green taffeta dress with elbow-length sleeves was a bit tight around the neck. She pulled on the collar to get more air as she settled in to wait for the doctor. She took her Bible from her bag, opened it in her lap, and began to read about the virtuous woman in Proverbs.

The door opened and Dr. Mayhem ambled in smiling. He apologized for being late, put his briefcase on the desk, and settled into his leather chair with an exasperated sigh. Dressed in brown gabardine pants and white shirt with a yellow tie, he looked older today. But maybe it was her eyes.

He picked up his fancy ivory-colored phone to call his secretary. The tall dark woman wearing a blue dress that was too tight across her behind opened the door and came in.

"Would you like some tea, Ms. Baptiste?" the doctor asked.

"No, thank you," said Augusta.

"Just a glass of water, then, Minty. Thank you," Dr. Mayhem said.

The secretary left and the therapist pushed his chair away from his desk, sighed again, and leaned back, resting his head in his palms.

"It's time this government started paying more attention to how people use the roads these days. Everywhere you go there's an accident. I don't know how some of these people get licenses." He paused. "Forgive me," he said, "it's just that this country seems to be getting less and less civilized every day. Someone almost ran into the back of my car, and when I got out to tell him he should drive more carefully, he proceeded to swear at me."

Then, with a smile, he rose from behind the desk and came

around to sit in the chair opposite her. "How're you feeling today, Augusta?"

"I feeling somewhat poorly, but I struggling on."

"Well, we can't have you feeling poorly, can we? That's not good. What happened to make you miss your appointment last time? Family problem?"

"Oh, no. There was a fire. Next door. At the girl I was telling you 'bout. My goddaughter. She house nearly get burn down, yuh know. Lucky for she, I see it in time. I know people does pray for bad things to happen to she, but she is still me goddaughter and I wouldn't want to see nothing bad happen. I wish sometimes. . ."

"Go on. Tell me about your goddaughter. What is it you wish?"

"That me and she coulda still talk. That things didn't happen the way it happen."

"What things?"

"You know. Things that happen to people. Things you say that you don't mean, that you wish you could take back."

"What is it you said to her that you'd like to take back?"

There was a pause. Augusta looked squarely at the doctor, letting her eyes linger on his.

"You have to trust yourself," he said. "Trust yourself to find the source of what's troubling you. I can help you search for it, but you have to find it yourself. You have to complete the journey into your heart, into your mind. Trust yourself that what you'll find will help you feel better."

Tears broke from the well in Augusta's eyes.

"I did something bad to her. Something bad bad. I don't think God ready to forgive me yet."

"It's just as important right now that you think about forgiving yourself. It doesn't look like you've done that yet. Perhaps it's time you deal with that. That's why you're here. Take your time and tell me about it."

Augusta opened her Bible. Head down as if searching for the words in the Scriptures, she began. "I tell a lie. I lie on her so bad I don't

know how I live with myself. I didn't mean to lie on her. And I did-
n't mean for her mother to do her so bad because of what I say. After
I hear what her mother do, I was too ashamed to go and tell her I say
what I say out of vexness. 'Cause Cyan make me so vex that day, I
couldn't think straight. I see the sheet in her hand soak in bleach, and
my head get turn round. Right away, I know what had happen. It
come to me like I was there. Like I see she and the boy together. I
remember seeing the boy turn out from we gate that day as me and
Trinidad was turning in the gap. And he didn't even shame to speak
to we. I remember he did smiling bold, bold as a mongoose and asking we how the sun treating we. And when I get home and see Cyan
washing the sheet, it just flash in front me what went on. I get so
angry I couldn't speak. That sheet I didn't let nobody touch, not even
my sister. I had that sheet in a valise under my bed for many, many
years. And not a soul ever touch it but me. And when I come home
and see her washing that sheet, it did like somebody hit me in me
chest with a rockstone. L love Cyan like a daughter, but if she did put
a match to me house I wouldn'ta feel so bad. I did feel lost. I hit she
and chase she home and tell she not to come back. And when she
mother ask me why I hit she, I could only think 'bout what I just lost.
I didn't see the consequences. So I tell her mother she steal money
from me."

"Why was that sheet so important to you?"

"That sheet. . . that sheet was important 'cause God use it to teach
me a lesson. That I ain't nothing without Him. Every time I look at that
sheet it remind me that the Devil does come to you like a wolf in
sheep's clothing, and it take a watchful God to keep you from harm. I
did never never believe I would give in to the temptations of the flesh.
I see what it do to my sister, and I laugh at she. I believe I did too
strong for it to happen to me. But temptation come my way, and I was
weak. I was ready to let that man have his way with me. And just as
he start, God come to me and give me the strength to get away. And
then He tell me to take that sheet which had one drop of my blood on

it and keep it to remind me how powerful He is. And truth be told, every time I unfold that sheet, I use to feel God come to me. As strong as that time I feel him give me the strength to push that man from on top of me, I would feel the spirit come to me. Deeper and stronger than when I get in the spirit at church. Anytime I feel myself getting weak, feel my flesh wanting to betray me, I would go home and unfold the sheet and look at that drop of blood. And God would come to me and give me the strength to fight the Devil. That is why I never wash the sheet. That is why I get so vex with Cyan for washing out that blood."

The doctor sat in silence for a long time, deeply moved by her conviction.·

"Tell me, since then have you felt His spirit come to you the same way? Since Cyan washed the sheet. How do you deal with temptations now?"

Augusta's voice became very soft. "That's the funny thing. I don't get them. Not since Cyan wash the sheet."

"Perhaps that's why you feel so guilty. You have to find a way to forgive yourself. And the only way to do that is to apologize to your goddaughter. Tell her you're sorry. Tell her why you lied to her mother and ask her to forgive you."

"She ain't go forgive me. She hate me like poison now."

"You are poisoning yourself. Is that better?"

Augusta's telling story reverberated in Jonathan Mayhem's mind deep into the afternoon. He found it difficult to concentrate on his other patients and had to apologize to them for not being attentive. One woman stormed out of his office in tears. He wanted to run after her but couldn't seem to get out of his seat. On his way home, his grandmother Reema came to him, and he was not surprised. It was the closing of the circle Augusta had started in his office. That circle that spoke of the power of the human mind to summon up long-held emotions, the way he summoned up Reema. The grandmother who always protected him. From that day when he was four and hid under her skirt to get away from Mad-John, the crazy man who ate children, everybody said, and who lived up the hill from their plot of land where Reema grew beans and corn. And even when he was old enough to know better, he would still try to hide under his grandmother's skirt when he saw Mad-John coming down the hill.

He wasn't sure whether it was religious or sexual ecstasy that sent Augusta back to the sheet. But the primitiveness of it reminded him that every time he hid under Reema's skirt, he could feel the sweat on her legs, inhale the moldy smell of her underwear. And how safe he felt in the darkness there.

That night he lay in bed with a young country girl he'd recently hired, unable to get Augusta off his mind. Then suddenly Reema, Augusta, and Koko were in the room laughing at him with one voice.

The naked girl stared at him bewildered as he jumped from the bed and began to dress.

"I have to go out," he said abruptly. "Get dressed."

Quietly she obeyed.

He dropped the girl off in her village and continued on to Koko's house. When he got there it was nearly ten. The house was closed down; her car was also gone. He parked on the street opposite the house under a broken streetlamp and settled into the bucket seat of the Peugeot to wait with the windows up and the air conditioner on.

Koko came home shortly after midnight. His heart breathed a glad sigh when he saw her step out of the Triumph alone. He didn't know what he would've done had she brought company.

He watched her lock the car, kick the right front tire in disgust, and then turn to climb the steps of the modest wooden house stuck between two larger stucco brick houses as if it had been dropped there inadvertently. She'd reached the top step before he got out of his car and drew attention to himself by calling out her name. At the sound of his voice she turned, surprised, with a skeptical smile.

"Jonathan, what're you doing here?"

"Waiting for you."

He crossed the dark street. The night was humid. The smell of ripe soursop rolled toward him like a fog. "Can I talk to you inside?" he said, climbing the steps.

She said nothing. When he came abreast, she unlocked the door and stepped through the curtainless doorway, leaving the door open for him. He followed her inside. Deftly she made her way in the dark to the other side of the room where, strangely, the light switch had been placed.

The room was small, but sparse furnishing and the wall-size mirror gave it a spacious air. Most of the paintings on the wall were familiar; there was one new photograph of a little girl holding a butterfly by its wings that he'd never seen before. A bamboo sofa with cream cushions and an elegant European-style lamp on a mahogany table near the window occupied the rest of the room. Koko opened windows. A lazy breeze wafted in.

"Sit down," Koko said. "I'll get you a drink."

He sat on the sofa and watched her flicking on lights on her way to the kitchen. She would return with gin and tonic, to be sure. After ten years of marriage one thing your wife was supposed to know was what you liked to drink. As he waited, he tried to think of what he would say, but all he could think of was how ravishing she looked. She'd put on some weight. The tight black slacks she had on displayed her figure far more prominently than he remembered. He thought of the first time he saw her naked. It was in her tiny apartment in Harlem one bitter cold night in winter. A suckling wind outside trumpeted the arrival of winter's first snowstorm. And they'd lain together through the night in the unheated room—having met only hours before—feeding on each other's bodies, and by the time morning arrived in a fluffy white shroud, they'd become inseparable.

"What're you dreaming about?"

He jumped. "Aw, nothing."

He took the drink—gin and tonic—then straightened his shoulders and watched her move to stand by the window.

"Aren't you going to sit down?" he said.

"I'm tired. I'll be more attentive if I stand."

He sighed, seeing a difficult road ahead. "You look wonderful," he said.

She smiled rapturelessly, thanked him, and sipped from her glass of wine.

"Actually, I was thinking about the first time I saw you naked in your apartment. Remember how cold it was?" he said, then chuckled.

An awkward silence followed.

"I want you to come home, Koko. I miss you."

He saw her flinch.

"Don't you miss me at all?" he continued.

She turned to face him, eyes compressed, mouth quivering slightly.

"After living with you for ten years I can't say I don't miss you some-times. But I like my life the way it is. I closed my eyes to a lot when we were together. Why? I don't know. I know you're going to say you've changed and all that. And it might be true. But the fact is, I've also changed, and I can't go back."

"But you don't understand, Koko. It's not so much that I've changed. It's that I've come to understand myself better. I know, it sounds strange. But it's like crossing a two-way street looking one way all the time thinking it's the only way, and *wham!* You get hit by a car. But you get up and realize you're alright. And you've learned a valuable lesson."

"This has been a valuable lesson for both of us. I've learned that I don't need you. I'm quite happy the way things are."

"Are you saying you're happier running around nightclubs picking up young boys like you're some tourist whore? Do you pay those young boys to fuck you, too?"

Koko stared at him; her lips moved but no sound came. Then she turned and stared out the window.

"I'm sorry. I didn't mean that," he muttered.

"I think you should leave," she said, her face turned toward him again.

"Please, Koko, I'm not a man to beg. But can't you see that I still love you?"

"If you still love me today, you'll still love me tomorrow."

"What's that supposed to mean?"

"It means I'm tired and I want you to go."

"I'm not leaving here without you."

"Do you want me to call the police?"

"No police in this country is going to make me leave here after I tell them who I am. After I let them know you're my wife."

She hurled her glass at his head. He ducked. The glass smashed against the photograph of the little girl with the butterfly's wings, showering his head and back with wine and glass.

"Get out, Jonathan. Get out now! Before you make me do something I will regret."

He got up in disbelief and walked to the door. He stopped there feeling the weight of defeat.

"If you don't come back to me I will make sure that you have to leave this country. I have big friends in the government. I could get them to declare you persona non grata and deport you."

"Your threats are empty. The same people you know in government, I know. Many of them want to fuck me, as you very well know."

"Jesus Christ, Koko, this ain't easy for me. Coming here, begging you like this. You think I like making a fool out of myself? But you're my wife. Give a little. How can you remember that first night we spent in your cold apartment giving life and hope to each other and not want to give our marriage another chance? I've often thought of that night. It was the most intense experience of any kind I've ever had. I'd been drifting through life until then. You needed an anchor and I needed to be anchored. Two people never needed each other like we did. I felt your pain and wanted to carry it for you. I felt your anger and wanted to roll it into the snow so you could love me. Something came alive in me that night. I knew I didn't want to come back to Barbados without you."

"If you felt my pain then, how come you didn't feel it later on? You ruined it, Jonathan, and you know it. There were many other nights that I spent in that big house listening to the angry waves, knowing you were with some young girl."

"Why can't we nurse our love back into existence?"

"Because it's dead, Jonathan. You let love die. You can't just pluck it out of the air because you've *found* yourself again."

He opened the door. Outside was quiet, the darkness full of spirits laughing at him. He stepped among them and heard the door close behind him.

Chapter Twenty-two

Cyan hated the rainy season. Apart from being bad for business, it made life miserable. After a big rain her gap became a mud field, especially if Percy Small happened along with his donkey cart, leaving deep furrows behind. Attempts to make the gap weatherproof by filling in the ruts with stones and gravel had failed. Getting to the main road after a big rain remained an adventure.

With Lemuel's help she'd managed to board up the kitchen. Now when rain fell, that room didn't get flooded. Lemuel had also repaired the paling and the chicken run, and she'd bought another batch of chickens from town.

As she left the doctor's that September morning, Cyan wished it would just pour for as long as it had to, then stop so the sun could shine. The nonstop drizzle they'd had to endure for the past five days made everywhere smell like rotten leaves. A dark, defeated aura had settled on the village. People moved noiselessly about, heads down, faces blank. Flowers drooped, roosters hid, hens laid no eggs. Life had slowed to nothing.

She stopped in Oistins to get fish. Around one o'clock she reached home, and without washing her feet clean of the squished mud that had seeped through her sandals and covered her toes, she fell into bed. When light finally penetrated the drizzle it was *foreday* morning. She'd slept for eighteen hours. Mud had dried to a thin brown cake on her feet and on the sheet.

She fought the rising morning sickness, resolving that only if it ejected Breeze's baby from her womb would she give in to puking. Her stubbornness, however, was no match for nature. She had to scramble to the window to avoid vomiting all over the bed. As her guts spewed slime down the side of the house onto the grass below, she could only wince. This was what she got for carelessness, for not replacing her birth control pills after the fire.

She went back to bed, slept for another two hours before getting up to change the sheets and wash. She ate little and accomplished less that day. She tried not to think of the news the doctor had given her with such jovial sincerity. But each time her stomach lurched, her mind flew back to the last time she saw Breeze, and she cursed out loud.

Round two o'clock she dressed for work, changed her mind, and fell back into bed, enervated by the mere thought of having to haggle with strangers over the price of a dress. She cooked rice with okra, swallowed half a mouthful, and had to spit the rest out. The slimy okra made her nauseous.

She sat down to write her mother a letter. But each time she attempted to tell her mother about her pregnancy, she was filled with dread and ripped the page out of the book. She gave up after the twentieth attempt.

Five-thirty saw her dressed and out of the house in a blue culotte that seemed to elongate her bamboo legs. She got a Bypass bus and half an hour later was walking along her favorite beach behind the Pirate's Cove hotel.

Two lovers emerged spiritlike from the belly of a wide evergreen. She frowned as they floated by. That besotted grin on the girl's face could only have been bestowed by a promise of everlasting love. The girl reminded her of herself. How many times had she had that look on her face after she and Breeze had unplastered themselves from the bark of an evergreen on this very beach, where they'd spend the day rolling around in surf, burying each other in sand, and making love in the water, with only the euphonious whooshing of sea spray for company.

Feeling an urge to tell the girl to "take warning," she turned to follow the lovers; they'd disappeared.

She settled into the arm of a y-shaped branch of the evergreen the spirit-lovers had just vacated and opened her Pandora's box of memories. Trying to keep Breeze out of her thoughts was taking too much energy and, considering what their last meeting had produced, was much like trying to stop the sun from supplanting rain-drained clouds on a hot day. Sure, right now her thoughts were bitter, but a part of her still loved him.

The sun stopped its slow processional across a blanched sky and seemed to wink at her. She smiled, remembering how Breeze used to make her laugh saying that ever since he was a boy, he had an impression the sun would stop while dousing its torch and wink at him.

Suddenly a desperate wind rustled the leaves around her and lifted the veil of love from her smile. As she stared at the shimmering sunset she felt its fire entering her and transforming itself into the desire to get rid of Breeze's baby, even though it was *her* baby, too.

"Best way to get something out your system is to find something to replace it." Her mother had rallied around that adage all the time her father was in jail. But that cliché, she had found out, was more music for the ear than for the soul.

How do you get love out of your system when it was in the air you breathe, inhabited the cells of your lips, the tiny hair follicles on your belly? Worst, how do you get love out of your system when it was breathing and living in your womb? She would like to turn the memories of Breeze into dry dust, to scatter them to the farthest corners of the earth, to cover them with hot volcanic lava, but she didn't know how.

With a conjurer's power she'd all but willed him to her the night she got pregnant. She'd run into him earlier that day at the entrance of the Brown Sugar restaurant. Later she felt herself wanting him. A desire, wild and implausible. It disturbed her because she thought after all this time, that she'd finally gotten over him. Desire turned her into a beast of burden. It rode her hourly. She wanted to feel him at her back, stretching her beyond the limit of consciousness. She felt pathetic and wanted to run, to hide until the desire had passed.

That night, when she heard his bike pull up outside, it took all her determination to keep from running to the door.

"I wanted to talk to you today," he said at the door. There was something intense and ominously sad at the edge of his smile. She knew now it was because he'd come to say good-bye.

She gazed stone-faced on his sad smile for a long time. She had opened the door cautiously as if expecting him to be accompanied by a baku or some other demon to destroy her, but his smile was the only demon he'd ever needed to possess her soul.

As she opened the door, a swarm of flying ants rose like a dust cloud behind him, circling about his head. They smashed against the house; their wings fell off and they floated to the ground, disfigured, dead. He stood there looking a little lost.

"Why you bring them ants at me door for?" she said, turning away, expecting him to follow her. She reached the bedroom door and turned around to see him still in the doorway, still smiling as if wonder-stricken.

"You coming in or you come to borrow sugar?"

He closed the door behind him and leaned against it. He smelled of patchouli. She wanted to laugh. How often had he complained about her wearing patchouli, saying he didn't like the smell; she wore it anyway partly to annoy him—Breeze annoyed was his most attentive—but mostly because nothing pleased her more than the smell of patchouli. When he told her to wash it off, she'd make him do it. He'd pretend he didn't want to, but once he started he got into it very well. She had only to say that she'd put the patchouli in hidden places and if he wanted it off he'd have to wash her all over. She suspected that he secretly yearned to wash her, to bathe her, that this was a fantasy he had about women—she knew he would never admit to it.

"You sure you want me in here?" he asked.

"No. But you here already."

"You want me to leave?"

"I want you to screw me, Breeze, that's what I want."

And, after that night, that was the last she saw of him. She wasn't even surprised when Koko, who'd gone to see a friend off, told her she'd seen him board a plane the next day bound for Germany with a fat blonde.

She still loved Breeze. Yes, she'd screwed with other men, but she'd been *available* to only one man, Breeze. Loved him so much she didn't want to have his child. Couldn't stand to look at his child if he wasn't going to be around. Couldn't kill the baby either. After what happened to her sister, no doctor in the world could perform an abortion on her. What other choice was there but to have this blasted baby?

"You'll change your mind when you see that little face smiling up at you," Koko said to her one afternoon as they sat on her verandah watching a dog play with her six pups in the garden of the house across the street. The pups were an assortment of colors, but the most beautiful was a chubby black with a streak of white down its face. Passersby stopped to stroke the pups, but anytime they tried to lift one off the ground, the mother growled and bared her teeth.

"I ain't wanna change my mind," Cyan said.

"Just wait. You will."

"I don't want no child keeping me back. And bechrist I don't want Breeze child. I don't know what I would do if I look at it one day and see Breeze staring back at me. I might wanna kill it."

"You shouldn't be talking like that."

"Is how I feel. I swear, Koko. I don't really wanna be thinking 'bout him no more than necessary."

"Still, it's your child, too. You shouldn't talk like that. Killing your own child. I can't believe what you're saying. That's not you talking."

"I ain't saying I would do it, I just saying I don't know what I would do. Can I ask you something? You ever had an abortion?"

Koko paused. "Yes. Four, to be exact."

"Four! My God! No wonder you ain't got no children. You' husband let you eat all them children so?"

"None of them were from my husband. One was from Breeze."

For a second, Koko's words seemed to hover in the air over Cyan's head, then like sharp snake's tongues they slowly penetrated her brain. Dazed, she looked at Koko, wondering why her friend had chosen to tell her this now. The hush smothered the verandah like a heavy tarpaulin. It blocked out the world beyond. She couldn't see anything moving in the street. Couldn't hear anything, either. Quiet reigned everywhere. Gradually the paralysis of jealousy began to fade away. The sound of the dog across the street snarling at a stranger who tried to steal one of its pups sneaked through. Cyan wished she could laugh in Koko's face.

"I'm sorry, Cyan. It just came out. I don't know why I told you. I've kept it a secret all this time. I didn't mean to upset you. It was before you fell in love with him. Long before."

"I don't really care anyway. Breeze gone. He don't mean nothin' to me," Cyan mouthed.

"I suppose I wanted to let you know I understand how you feel about him."

"How could you understand how I feel 'bout Breeze?" Cyan let out. "How could anybody understand how I feel 'bout Breeze? Did you love him? Did you feel like killing him when he left? Is that how you feel 'bout Breeze? You don't know how I feel 'bout Breeze. I hate that bitch like poison. If what happen to my sister didn't make me so frighten, I would go and cut this baby outta me right now."

"Have you thought about adoption?"

"Who 'bout here go want to adopt my baby?"

"It doesn't have to be somebody you know. In fact it's better if it's someone you don't know."

"You know somebody that want a baby to adopt?"

"Actually, I do. A friend of mine has been trying to adopt a child for a long time. She lives in Illinois. An old school friend. She's well educated, has a good job, and would be a wonderful mother. But if I were you I'd wait. See what happens. Give it time. I've heard women say that when they feel their child kick for the first time, something takes over, a kind of realization that this is the most important thing to happen to them. Maybe you'll feel that way when it happens to you. Give it time. Don't make any decisions now, especially since you're upset."

"I ain't upset. I look like I upset to you?"

They sat for a long time, silent, as if listening to the minute movements of plants in the wind. Koko studied her friend whose eyes were fixed on the crotons in the garden. Cyan's neck seemed to elongate, as if she was stretching out of Koko's reach. Her oiled dreadlocks settled solemnly at the nape of her neck, gilded by the sun's lavish rays.

How could she have let slip that affair with Breeze now? It was for this very reason she'd hidden it from Cyan. She loved Cyan. Hadn't wanted to hurt her. Cyan was as close to a daughter as she would ever have. Could it be guilt? She realized that what she'd said to the young woman wasn't what she'd really wanted to say. She'd really wanted to tell her to have the baby. To keep the baby. To love her baby. But she didn't feel she had the right to try to influence Cyan that way. Cyan had the right to do what she wanted with her body. But Koko knew that some habits were hard to break. After the first abortion the others became easier. Until you've developed a permanent resistance to the idea of motherhood. Instead of warning Cyan, she'd blurted out that she'd had an affair with Breeze.

When Cyan turned to face her again, she held the reflection of red crotons in her wide tortured eyes. She got up and mumbled something about going home, and left.

The passage of time had no effect on Cyan other than to make her more determined to get as far away as possible from the baby she was carrying. She refused to give in to common cravings brought on by pregnancy. Urges she'd heard women joke and commiserate about: "Girl, I can't help it. Since day before yesterday this baby craving nothing but sugar." At that they'd go out and eat all the coconut bread, ice cream, or sugarcakes they could find. "I don't know what wrong with the baby I carrying. Won't let nothing pass me mouth unless it sour." This sent them scouring the tamarind and gooseberry trees for fruit. When Cyan got the urge to eat something sweet, she drank the bitterest mauby. When the craving for sour struck, she ate raw sugar or stuck a finger down her throat, forcing herself to throw up. The slimy feeling in her mouth would banish any craving for food.

But she found she could do nothing to slow the baby down. Her body began to change. Sinew became round. Stretch marks appeared. One night, as she lay naked in bed watching a fat red-rimmed moon glide across a black sky, the light glancing off the dresser mirror fell seductively on her breasts, whose fullness was the only satisfaction she got from the pregnancy. In a matter of months her tiny breasts had swelled like ripe pawpaws. And just as heavy. A certain giddiness came with the fullness, like she'd received a present she hadn't expected. Flushed with the moon's glow, she felt a sudden movement and then a tender pain in her side. The first kick?

Panic was followed by wonder and amazement. Then quickly a wave of anger swept over her and dropped anchor like a spent ship. She got up and paced the room, hoping her movement would keep the baby still.

A boy? A girl? She pondered a moment the possibility of twins, then, not wanting to dwell on the subject, she opened the window and peeped out. There was nothing out there to draw her thoughts away from the first plea for attention from the child in her womb.

It was past midnight. The world outside was dead, the air still and tight as a tuned steelpan. She strained her ears to hear the melody of quiet. The night calm that covered the village was a shield of glass blocking out the world. No one in Bottom Rock would care what she did with her baby; for that matter, no one outside it. No one outside Bottom Rock knew of its existence. No one cared about them, just as no one outside the island knew or cared about the existence of Barbados—she knew that from the tourists she met. What did they care about the island, its people, its culture; they'd never heard of its musicians, its cricketers, its politicians. They sometimes seemed surprised she spoke English.

Orchestrated by the tick-tock of the clock on the dresser, time played on. What an infernal noise! Each tick reminded her of the stabbing pain that had heralded the baby's first kick. The clock was more than ten years old and no longer told time with a straight face. A piece of the its glass had fallen out and the long hand had shrunk from age; now both hands were the same length. Slow by about twenty minutes, the clock said midnight. She'd never bothered to correct the imbalance and looking at it now she realized there was no way to correct time gone awry. She picked up the clock and threw it out the window. If only she could get the baby out of her that easily.

She dressed and stepped outside. The quiet girdled her. Something about the deep warmth of the night soothed her, and she could feel her skin walk from the sheer pleasure of releasing her soul to fly free through the darkness.

At the end of the gap she saw Jewl with her five children huddled close. The three smaller children were crying; the other two, with heads lowered, were silently inspecting the stones by the road.

"Ma, don't go back in there," the older girl was saying.

"I forget the money. We ain't got no money. We can't get to your grandmother house without money. The bus done running for the night. And she live too far for we to walk. We gotta take a taxi."

"But what if Pa wake and see you?"

"Psst, that you, Night?" Jewl called out.

"What you want, Jewl?" Cyan answered.

"When you pass by me house, you see a light on?"

"No. I ain't see no light."

"You could stay with my children for a minute. I gotta run back to the house."

"Where wunna going this time of night?" asked Cyan.

"I trying to get away from Bandy, man. I tired like shite. I got five children for he, and he still want more. I ain't want no more children. And I ain't letting he get on top of me again thinking I go get with child 'cause I ain't. I tell he I can't have no more children, and he can't seem to get that through his blasted head. And every month my period come he beating me, beating me like I's a jackass."

"What you got to go back for?"

"I rush out the house and ain't realize I ain't had no money. I going by the pay phone in Oistins and see if we can get a taxi to St. George."

"You could use my phone. I just put in a phone last month. You wanna use my phone?"

"No, is alright. I just need to get some money."

"Don't go back in that house. I got some money laying around that I ain't got no uses for right now. Stay here. Lemme get it quick."

"No, you ain't got to do that."

"I know I ain't got to, but it ain't no trouble for me. Just wait here."

Cyan ran back to her house and came back with fifty dollars, which she handed to Jewl.

"Thank you, Night. I go pay you back, yuh hear?"

"I hear. Go long quick 'fore Bandy wake up and realize you gone."

She watched Jewl and her children head off down the street and listened to the dying echo of their bare feet slapping the cool tar road.

• • •

The next day Cyan went to see Koko at the gallery situated in a garden compound along with souvenir stores. Next to the gallery was the clothing store to which Cyan had tried unsuccessfully to sell her tie-dye creations. Outside was hot and hazy. Lizards crept silently along walls. Inside, the gallery was packed with browsers hiding from the sun.

They exchanged greetings and she joined the throng. But she wanted to speak to Koko alone and had to wait more than an hour until the galley closed for lunch.

As they strolled along the beach behind the gallery, Koko offered her half a roti. She wasn't hungry. They climbed a rock hill. From there they watched white shiny yachts sail by, and tourists and Bajans cavorting in the water together.

"Koko, I want you to talk to that friend of yours in the States. Tell her I ready. I make up my mind for sure. If she really want this baby, she can have it."

"You sure, Cyan?"

"Sure as that water blue. You say she got a good job and everything?"

"She's doing all right."

"She marr'd?"

"Divorced."

"But she well-off?"

"She's a teacher. She's got a house in the suburbs and a good pension. The baby'll be fine with her."

"How come she can't get no American baby to adopt?"

"Red tape. Regulations. Agencies tend to discriminate against single women. They prefer couples, families. Amanda doesn't plan to get married again."

"She's a wikka?"

"A wikka?"

"Women that like sex with other women."

Koko laughed. "Does it matter to you?"

"I suppose not. Tell her I go need something for my trouble."

"She's fully prepared to pay you. She'd be so grateful, she'd give you anything you ask. Are you sure you want to do this? It's not as simple as you might think. There's a lot of legal stuff involved. You'll have to sign papers in front of witnesses. Once it's done, it's done. You can't change your mind after you sign the papers. Amanda will probably make you agree not to contact her or the baby once you've given it up. It would be like you never gave birth. Do you really think you can do that?"

"Believe me, Koko, when my mind mek up, it mek up. I don't change it. I don't want no child. I got things to do. I know what I want. I want my freedom."

Chapter Twenty-three

$\mathcal{T}$he tall woman in glasses with cinnamon skin and processed shoulder-length hair looked up from her book after the flight attendant announced they would be landing in half an hour. The last time she'd looked up was to glimpse the misty peak of La Soufrière, the quiet volcano on the island of Martinique, at the pilot's urging.

She'd seen her friend Koko only a few times since her move to Barbados, but they'd kept in touch by letters and by phone. Koko knew all about the problems she'd had with adoption agencies over the years.

Koko met Amanda at the airport, and the ride was lively, full of chat and laughter. During momentary lapses into silence, between questions, replies, counterquestions, and knowing glances, she glimpsed a sea of green rushing past, separated by tiny villages made up of houses inhabited by darkness. She couldn't understand why the houses, so brightly painted outside, seemed so dark on the inside. Thick drapes hung from windows she expected would've been flung wide open on such a bright afternoon. What were they hiding?

"Why do they have such thick drapes at the windows?" she asked Koko.

"Oh, I don't know. Must be something left over from when the British ruled the island."

"Do they do everything like the British? Don't they have their own culture?"

"You'll see for yourself. You'll like these people here. They're very friendly and gentle."

Amanda wasn't as sure as Koko that she would like Barbados. She didn't care much for tropical climes. She'd visited Jamaica once and hated it. Entirely too hot for her. But she did meet her current lover on that trip, so it hadn't been an entire waste.

The only reason she'd decided to come to Barbados after years of urging by Koko was that it held the best chance of getting a child. No nosing around in her past by unfeeling adoption officials, no questions about marital status or sexual preference. A successful American woman wanting to adopt a baby would raise no eyebrows here, Koko had promised her.

"The girl hasn't changed her mind, has she?" asked Amanda looking at Koko. She noted that her friend looked more relaxed than the last time they saw each other, two years ago in Chicago at a reunion of their graduating class. The last person she'd expected to get married and move out of the country was Koko, the young radical.

"Cyan is an upstanding girl," Koko was saying. "Her word is money in the bank. She's had a hard life, but she's honest. I don't think she'll change her mind. But if she does, then you'll just have to accept that."

Amanda wondered how her friend could be so nonchalant. Didn't she understand how much getting this baby meant to her? Didn't she understand how many nights she'd spend staring up at the ceiling, hoping that God had finally answered her prayers? Coming this far but not getting her way was unthinkable.

"Everything's been arranged," Koko continued. "I've retained a lawyer who's drawn up the papers, I've contacted the embassy. Everything's been arranged, I should say, except the money. You'll have to pay the lawyer, and of course you'll have to talk to Cyan."

"Why didn't she want to talk to me on the phone? Why did she insist that I come here before she would even talk to me? How do I know she won't change her mind?"

"I can't answer that. That's just the way she is. But I trust her."

They drove past rusted carcasses of tractors and lorries, which looked like the remains of giant reptiles from another era. The car glided through hushed streets lined with half-grown canes, past pink sandstone plantation great-houses now used as restaurants and tourist attractions. Children going home from school bowed their heads and played hide-and-seek in the grass. Such a quiet, peaceful place, Amanda thought as the car pulled up outside the house in Dayrells Road. How come she felt so uneasy? Something about the tight-lipped houses with their thick drapes and the hushed trees by the roadside made her think she was entering a graveyard.

"Why don't you want your baby?" Amanda asks Night.

"You should be glad I don't want it."

"Yes, I suppose I am. But I'd still like to know. Since we're going to be doing business of sorts."

"You want it or not?"

"Yes, I want the child. But. . ."

"Don't butt about, you may crack yuh skull. And then you know what would happen. You wouldn't be needing no baby. How bad you want a baby?"

"By that, I suppose you mean, how much am I willing to pay for it?"

"Yes."

"How much money do you want?"

"As much as I can get."

"Would two thousand be enough?"

"You must be making sport. No. That ain't enough. That ain't nearly enough. I figure something more like ten thousand dollars, U.S."

Amanda thinks of protesting, then she looks at Cyan's quiet, almost rigid demeanor and realizes she is dealing with a shrewd woman. This is no frightened little girl who doesn't know what to do with her baby. This is why she refused to talk to me by phone, this is why she wanted me here before she discussed money, Amanda thinks. But how foolish it would be to bargain with good fortune! She can already feel this baby's heart pulsing next to her bosom. She can already hear its hungry cry early in the morning. Nothing is going to ruin this chance for her. She would pay a million dollars for this baby if she had to.

The sound of a car coming to a halt breaks the deadlock, and they seal the bargain. Moments later a smiling Koko flashes into the room in an indigo tie-dyed dress she'd bought from Cyan.

"Well, look at this!" she says, standing in the archway.

"Yes," Amanda exclaims, "isn't it wonderful! I think this was predestined. God had a hand in this. I couldn't believe it when I met her on the beach today and she told me who she was. I truly believe God stepped in and said it was time. And what're you so excited about?"

"We'll leave that for later. I'm so happy to see you together. And getting along well, I hope."

"Oh, very well, won't you say, Cyan?"

"Yes," replies Cyan. "We getting on very good."

"Wonderful. So everything is worked out?" Koko asks.

"All worked out," says Amanda, looking at Cyan. "It's settled."

"How do you feel, Cyan?" Koko asks.

Cyan gets up from the chair and says, "I tired. I think I going home."

Amanda's eyes dart between Koko and Cyan. "We can't let her leave," she says.

"And why not?" Cyan glares.

"I'm sorry. . . I didn't mean it like that," Amanda says. "I didn't mean it the way it came out."

She takes Cyan's hand excitedly. "Why don't you stay here with us until it's time. Don't you think that's a good idea, Koko?"

Koko smiles. "Yes, of course. It's a great idea. I should've thought of it myself."

"Well, I don't think so," Cyan says stiffly.

"I would love to see the birth of this baby," begs Amanda. "I sure would. Please won't you let me? You can't say no."

"I would have to think 'bout that," says Cyan. "I don't have no clothes here."

"That's no problem," says Koko. "We could drive you home right now, get whatever you need for the next two or three weeks, and come back. We'll be a family. The three of us."

"Well, you could drive me home now, but I won't be coming back. I like sleeping in me own house."

That evening the two American women dined at La Mar's, a small family-run restaurant, set in a deep alcove of trees and beds of flowers, near the sea in St. Lawrence. The outside of the converted chattel house was painted green, and the warmly lit interior, pink. They sat by a window that had been widened to give a roomier feel. Seven tables filled up the space. Two other couples were in the restaurant. A middle-aged white woman staring into the eyes of a young black man as if they held the secrets of the world, and a German couple acting like newlyweds.

Fireflies floated through the window, hovered about in one corner of the room, then floated out again. From where they sat, they could see them gliding on the wet breeze between the trees' leaves. They each ordered the special: fried kingfish served with steamed breadfruit, fried plantain, and avocado salad. Koko, a regular customer, found the spicy kingfish a tender treat that she thought her friend would enjoy.

Koko knew the owner, a compact middle-aged woman who'd

returned from England to bury her mother five years ago and decided not to go back. When Koko saw her silver head bobbing about in the bar, she went to bring her over to introduce Amanda.

"Corly, this is Amanda, my friend from Illinois. She's staying with me for a while."

"Nice to meet you, Amanda. It is always a joy to see Koko. Any friend of Koko's is a friend of mine," the woman said, smiling.

"Nice to meet you too, Corly," Amanda said.

"So where you been, Koko? Ain't seen you in a long time," Corly said.

"A long time?" Koko exclaimed, mockingly. "I ate lunch here last week."

"You did? I ain't seen you."

"From what I recall, you had your eyes on a handsome young man who was over there in the corner. You probably don't remember who else ate here that day."

"You so bad, Koko. Don't know what to do with you."

"My friend here would like to try some of that wonderful rum punch you make."

"Your friend or you?" Corly laughed.

"Well, I'll have my usual large glass. Make that two large glasses. The first one wouldn't take very long to drink. I'm celebrating tonight."

"What are you celebrating?" Corly asked.

"Life. Seeing my friend. I can't tell you how long I've been trying to get her to come to Barbados. I'm celebrating everything good in the world."

Corly departed and returned shortly with drinks. Food came soon after. During the meal they chatted about their college days, about politics in America, about the possibility of a black man becoming-president. If that happened, Koko said jokingly, she might consider moving back to the States.

"It's not a joke, Koko. Jesse has ignited a lot of hearts," Amanda said.

"But he doesn't have a ghost of a chance," replied Koko.

"Maybe. But we like the way the buzz is sweeping the country. We like the attention he's getting. Everybody's excited. White people are talking about it. The media is talking about him, following him. Even if it's just symbolic, it's important that we have a black man in the spotlight again. Not since Martin have we had a black man who wasn't an athlete or threatening to start a war create such excitement in America."

"Is that what this is all about? Creating excitement?"

"Well, in a way, yes. Black people are in the doldrums right now. This will give us a lift. If we don't move to keep pressuring America, white people will start thinking they can take back what we fought for in the sixties."

"I didn't see you doing too much fighting back then," Koko joked. "You were so afraid your father would stop paying your tuition, you wouldn't even pass out flyers."

"Well, you'd be proud of me now. I help organize fund-raisers for Jesse and other progressive candidates. We have to keep sending the message to America that we're still ready to stand together. To unite. That we can't be taken for granted ever again."

"What makes you think America is interested in listening to any black person who is not a musician or a comedian?"

"Martin made them listen, didn't he? Malcolm got their attention."

"Look what happened to them. We don't need to show America nothing. That kind of thinking creates a groveling mentality. I got tired of waiting for America to recognize me. What's going to happen after Jesse runs and loses, even if millions of black people come out to show they're united behind a symbol? What will it change? Will it stop the police from provoking black men so they can shoot them in the streets? Will it keep drugs out of their neighborhoods?"

"You've been away too long, Koko. This baby is not the only thing I came down here for, you know. Your marriage is over. You were part of history in the sixties. Come and be part of it again. I think it's time for you to come home."

"What home? Whose home? Home is where you feel loved. All America has ever shown me was hate. The hate that has destroyed so many of our great black men. If things have changed that much, why can't you and your white lover adopt a child?"

Amanda stared at her friend with a wry smile, letting herself hope for a second that the gleam in Koko's eyes came from a spark of jealousy.

"That has nothing to do with race; it's because we're both women Two white women would have no better chance than me and Alice."

"I'm sorry. I didn't mean to sound disapproving," Koko said with a laugh. "I only know that if I'd stayed in America I'd be in jail or in an asylum or dead. I get treated with respect here, by everybody. God, do you understand what that means to me? Do you understand? I don't feel that rage here. I don't feel like I have to defend who I am. I got tired of fighting for respect in America. I deserved better than what America was offering."

"If this place is so wonderful, why do so many of these people want to get to America? Why is this young girl so willing to sell her baby?"

"Cyan's got very intense personal reasons for not wanting this baby. I hope you're not assuming that young girls all over this island are selling babies to every American that steps off the plane."

"It wouldn't surprise me. You should see how the beach vendors were lining up to sell to me on the beach the minute they realized I was American. Face it, Koko, you're respected here because you're American. You can't run from that. And I think you're being dishonest with yourself if you don't think it makes a difference."

"I will not let you belittle my life on this island. I think of myself as just another citizen here. I vote. I pay taxes. I contribute to the culture. In fact, my gallery is the biggest in the country."

"How many galleries are there? Look Koko, I don't blame you for feeling important. I'm glad you've gotten a chance to feel so integral to this island's culture. But feeling important here is a little like feeling like a giant in Lilliput, don't you think? And I don't mean any disrespect to these people. But you'd be accomplishing much more if you did these things back home. You're belittling your own life by staying here any longer. We're about to make history in America. What history is ever made in a place like this?"

"*This* is my home. I feel so strongly about it, I've just bought a house overlooking the Atlantic Ocean. I'll close on it in a couple of weeks, in fact. When I saw you and Cyan this afternoon I'd just come from the bank where I learned my loan was approved. I may not make history here, but here history will not destroy me, either. And talking about history, the house I bought is located at a place where the slaves were unloaded. How's that for a bit of history? So there's your answer. I'm never going back."

Chapter Twenty-four

Two weeks later, around midnight, Cyan called Koko in panic. She'd felt contractions. Koko rushed her to the hospital. Six hours later, a bright Sunday morning, the baby was born at the Queen Elizabeth Hospital.

"Do you want to see her? She's beautiful," Amanda said to Cyan as she rested in the private room the American had paid for.

Cyan shook her head. Worn out from labor, she'd fallen asleep as soon as the baby was born. Now she felt sore and weak. Thank goodness they didn't have to cut her. That baby's head must be size of a ripe breadfruit.

She wanted to get up, but her body seemed to weigh more than when she was pregnant. She raised her head from the pillow and looked at a smiling Amanda. Suddenly she had the urge to see the baby, to hold it, curious whether it looked like Breeze or her, or perhaps her father. That would be something. She wanted it to look like her father. And then she remembered: The baby wasn't hers. A week ago they'd signed the adoption papers in the lawyer's office. No big deal. She'd felt important, though, when she arrived late, to find all those people waiting on her. And then Amanda and Koko had gone with her to the Barbados National Bank to watch her deposit the ten thousand dollars, which multiplied to twenty thousand on conversion, to her account. She couldn't wait to start building her new house in Bottom Rock.

"Did you say it was a girl?" Cyan asked. Her cracked whisper was barely audible.

"Yes. Are you sure you don't want to see her?"

"I don't think that would be a good idea."

"She's so beautiful. You have to see her. So healthy-looking. And big too. Eight pounds, six ounces."

"She look like me?"

"Let me bring her."

"No." Cyan's voice, filled with alarm, stopped Amanda dead. "Keep the damn baby away from me. You got what you come down here for, now leave me 'lone."

"But I thought. . ."

"You thought what? That my heart make out of rockstone? Just leave me the shite alone."

"I'm sorry," Amanda muttered, departing after a long look in Cyan's direction, which took in the trees outside the window, the vapid blue sky, and the scalding detachment of her eyes.

Cyan drifted off to sleep again after Amanda left, only to be woken up by the sound of babies crying. When it hit her that one of the babies crying down the hall might be hers, a monstrous desire to rush to her baby almost crushed her. A part of *her* was lying in one of those tiny beds. She'd created something that she would never touch. Couldn't. Just for a minute, perhaps: touch her lips, watch her eyes flutter. No. Couldn't. Wouldn't. She refused to talk to Koko or anyone else that day and complained of womb pains so the doctor would give her something to make her sleep. She slept through the night. Next morning she announced she was going home.

Koko and the doctors wanted her to stay at least another day; she would have none of it. She didn't know what she would do if she was near that baby another day. When she got dressed and picked up her little valise to take to the bus, Koko yielded and offered to drive her home.

"I've never met anyone as stubborn as you," Koko fumed as they left the parking lot.

Slouched in the passenger seat, Cyan kept her silence for the length of the trip. She had nothing to say. No amount of artful prodding by Koko could get her to speak.

"Say something, Cyan. What're you thinking about? Why didn't you look at the baby?"

She wasn't thinking. She couldn't think. All she heard was the sound of babies crying.

She's been away from her house for less than two days yet it no longer feels like home. A musty dead smell seems to have settled in it, as if it has been uninhabited for years.

As she collapses in a chair in the front-house she hears a ghostly echo and is shocked to realize it is herself moaning like a caged animal. The smell of death continues to surge at her, and she is forced to cover her nose. She is sure she hadn't left any food or garbage laying around.

She stumbles to the kitchen and looks around for any telltale signs of decay. Nothing in the open. Behind the fridge. Nothing. Behind the stove. Nothing. Where is it coming from?

Her head is whirling like a merry-go-round. About to lose her balance, she leans against the doorpost. Slowly she inches her way to the bedroom, which is hot and dark. There the smell is even stronger. Down on all fours, she looks under the bed. Too dark to see anything. She gets up and unlatches the window. A gusty wind comes along, slaps the window hard against the side of the house. She hears glass shatter and fall to the ground. Light streaks into the room, bringing life to the blinds, which begin to swing wildly in the wind. On her knees again, she peers under the dresser. The remains of a mouse folded like a knot of cloth rest against the right back leg, too far back for her to reach. She settles on the next best thing: Jeyes fluid, which she finds in the kitchen and sprinkles throughout the house to kill the smell. Then she falls onto dusty sheets and passes out.

Her eyes open onto darkness. What time is it? How long has she been asleep? Then she remembers the dead mouse under the dresser and turns on the light.

Soft raindrops on the roof make her think of birds pitter-pattering above her head in the morning. Apart from that sound, there is an eerie quiet as if some other person whom she cannot see is there.

From the kitchen she takes a dustpan and a broom to rake the mouse from its chosen grave. When she looks under the dresser, she is stupefied. Nothing there. The mouse is gone. She sits and stares at the wall, not sure what to think. She peers under the dresser again, and then under the bed to make sure she has not seen it under there and misremembered. She rises and sits on the bed. Is her mind playing tricks on her?

Suddenly she feels like someone has hit her in the heart with a big rock. She hears herself gasp loudly, a birthing cow's moan. Startled and frightened by the depth of her own loneliness, she can't even cry. Choked up, she becomes dizzy, her eyes blur, and then the terror flies at her with hair-triggered and paralyzing aim.

Tears come. Quietly in the beginning, and then her voice rends the night, a death cry like no other, a call to her father, to her mother, to the spirits, to the village, to the night. A wind comes and bears it far across housetops, across the village. Sleeping dogs wake and pick up the beat. She has not cried for her father, barely cried for her sister, but she can't stop crying for a baby she didn't even want.

Rain stops. Day opens its eye. Birds come pitter-pattering on the roof, hear her wailing, and fly away. As the sun rises above evergreen trees, she lifts herself from the bed to go to the window.

She becomes aware of something dripping down the front of her dress. Wet like sweat but hot. Drip, drip. Stop. Drip, drip. From her breasts. Down her chest. Down her stomach.

Lifting her breasts to examine them, she can't help but love their weightiness. Milk drips onto her fingers. A milk-washed finger lifted to her mouth is pleasing to the taste. Fresh. Not too sweet. Squeezing her breast firmly, she fills a cupped hand and drinks.

Shifting the blinds, she offers herself to the sun hoping to be revitalized by its warmth. But the heat takes away what little strength she has left.

She lets the blinds drop and falls back onto the bed with torpid grace, too exhausted to get to the kitchen to make herself a cup of Ovaltine. Sunlight forces past the blinds, burning through them like paper. There is no place to hide. She covers her head with a pillow as the sun takes dead aim at her eyes.

Birds returning to the housetop have brought with them a companion who knocks at the door.

Go away, she wants to scream. Then the voice sounds.

"Cyan, you in there?"

Low and anxious, the voice is alive with concern. Augusta? What is Augusta doing at her door? Cyan remains still.

"Cyan, is me, Augusta. You alright? I couldn't sleep last night and I thought I heard you crying in the middle of the night. You in there? I know you pregnant and all and I just wanna know if you having problems. If you need anything? You hearing me?"

There is no mistaking the compassion in Augusta's voice. It commands Cyan like a beacon to a lost ship.

Cyan struggles to the door. But she does not open it. She speaks from behind drawn blinds.

"What you want, Augusta?"

"That you, Cyan?"

"Who else you think it could be?"

"I couldn't sleep last night. . . Well, I thought I hear crying coming from here the whole night. I couldn'ta been dreaming 'cause I wasn't sleeping. At first I thought it did a baby, but then it sound too loud and deep to be a baby. I know things between you and me ain't good, but I couldn't help wondering if you alright. How you feeling? I ain't seen you around for a couple of days. That baby should be ready to drop soon."

"What you looking to see if I around for?"

"Well, I. . . I just miss you from 'bout the place. You all right?"

"You miss me? You expect me to believe that?"

"I don't expect you to believe. And I can't blame you. But you want any help with anything? When the baby due?"

"The baby dead if that is what you want to know."

After a long pause Cyan spoke again.

"That is what you come for, ain't it? News to carry."

"No, no, I ain't come 'bout that. I so sorry that I give you cause to think that. Could I come in for a minute? I would like to see you. See if you alright. How you getting on?"

"I alright."

"Okay, then. Can I come in and talk to you? You eating alright?"

"Why? You bring food for me?"

"I could bring you something if you want."

"You want to poison me now?"

"You got a right to be vex. I understand. But if I could come in, I could explain. It ain't go take too long."

"Why you wanna talk to me all of a sudden?"

"That's just it. It ain't all of a sudden. It's just that I couldn't get it out before. It take me all these years to say what I shoulda say the very next day."

"I don't want to hear nothing from you. Leave me 'lone."

"I know you hate me and rightly so. I do you a wrong thing. I just want to say I sorry. I really hope you all right. And I hope one day you could forgive me for what I do to you."

Stunned, Cyan waits. She never thought she'd hear those words from Augusta. Then she hears footsteps falling away from the gallery and wants to rush out to drag the woman back but all she can bring herself to do is peep through the louvers in time to see the old woman disappear inside her house.

As she turns away from the door, another knock freezes her.

"Who that?"

"It's me, Lemuel. Open the door."

Dressed in khaki shorts, and a blue twill shirt, with a dingy white hat flopped on his head, Lemuel is leaning against the verandah rail looking across the street, a small brown bag in his hand. He turns around with a broad smile when he hears the door open. One glance at Cyan's puffy, all-night-crying eyes turns his smile into a scowl.

"Girl, you look like the cat done drag you through the dump heap." And then, noticing her shrunken stomach, he lets out a gleeful laugh.

"But look at you, nuh. Yuh ain't even shame. Gone and had baby in secret. Well, move out the door so I could see this wondrous child you bring into the world."

He pushs past her into the bedroom before she can reply. She follows mechanically.

"So where the baby?"

"I ain't got no baby."

"What you mean you ain't got no baby?"

A long pause follows, in which he searchs her eyes for an answer. Her eyes cast down to her feet tells him something he doesn't want to believe.

"You mean. . . you mean you lost it," he whispers hoarsely, as if trying to stifle the thought.

She says nothing, preferring to let him think that than tell him the truth.

"I so sorry, Cyan. God must know why He take your baby."

He goes to her and hugs her. She wants to push him away, to tell him God had nothing to do with taking her baby, but she lets him hold her, purloining the warmth from his chest. Subdued, she leans into him, his frailness now a strength, for there is a gentleness in him that softens her anguish.

After a while he says, "I bring you some conkies. You hungry?"

She looks at him, manages a weak smile, and says, "I didn't know you could make conkies."

"Oh, I ain't make these. You know Mrs. Browne, that live next to Martin Prescod? Her sister just come back from over in Away. You should see the things she bring back from America. Every machine for the kitchen that you could imagine. Food processor, bread slicer, potato peeler, can opener. Gadgets like you wouldn't believe. And clothes. Anyway, they invite me over there to meet she. Well, we get on so good—she just lost her husband and decide to come back home to live—that I spend the whole day in Mrs. Browne house helping them make conkies. And last night I couldn't sleep, and I was thinking 'bout you, wondering how you was. I musta fall asleep round four in the morning 'cause I dream that you was in here crying you' eyeballs out and now I see it wasn't no dream at all."

They eat on the bed. He tries to get her to talk about the baby, but on that topic she remains silent, dropping her head into cupped hands and staring stiffly at the mirror on the dresser. Lemuel unwraps the last of the raisin-filled cornmeal pastry from its banana leaf and offers it to her.

"The last one," he said.

"Then you have it. I full."

"I go leave it here. I full, too. I eat three before I leave home."

He rewraps the conkie, puts it back in the bag, and gets up to put the bag on the dresser.

"So what you go do now, girl?"

"Sleep. I just feel tired all the time."

"Want me to make you a cup of tea?"

"Would you? Thanks. Some Ovaltine."

He makes the Ovaltine and waits until she has fallen asleep.

He leaves the house shaking his head. As long as he lives he will never understand Cyan. He'd never gotten the impression that she wanted the baby. Now that she's lost it he would have thought she'd be happy. But she hadn't bothered to hide her pain. She was strong-headed and don't-carish at times, but always proud. Today, for the first time, he'd seen defeat in her eyes. He cannot believe it. But Cyan's expression told the tale of her despair clearer than Anansi's sly smile. He'd always thought of her as someone, no matter the conditions, who'd paddle her canoe to shore. Now he isn't so sure.

He reaches the promontory overlooking the cricket field and climbs it. Haphazardly, he aims his gaze into the morning sunlight. She will never accept that he loves her. But that is beside the point now. He doesn't have to prove to anyone, including her, that he loves her or is worthy of her affection. Before he left, he'd copied her mother's address off one of the letters on the dresser. He'd tried to help her before and it had ended in disaster. But, no matter the consequences, he has to try again.

He descends the point and retraces his steps onto the main road. It will take him only half an hour to get to the telegram office in Oistins.

Chapter Twenty-five

For three days Cyan cries until her eyes burn like fire. She feels she cannot live without seeing her child at least once. Just once, she tells herself before setting out for Koko's house. Once would be enough. But she knows once will not be enough. She is going to take her daughter back.

The day before, her breasts had dripped like the leaky pipe in the yard, pulsing with the ache of a knife wound, driving her mad. Cup after cup of milk she squeezed from her breasts; still they dripped. Ignoring the pain she tied her nipples with twine to cut off the flow. In the middle of the night her breasts no longer oozed milk but blood. She panicked. She thought she was going to die. Despair surrounded her, but she was determined to fight, to resist. Never, never will she give herself over to despair. She will emerge from this storm unbowed. But first she has to bring her daughter home.

In the subdued light of a slow-breaking dawn, she dresses deliberately. She wants to look good for her daughter. The blue cotton dress her mother had left behind is perfect. She'd tried it on the day after her mother left. Too big then, it fits fine now. She likes the way her image fills the mirror. The pregnancy has been good for her figure.

The decision to put her father's billfish beak in her bosom takes no more than a second's consideration. The American is a reasonable woman and will see things her way. She hasn't spent any of the money and will give it all back. But she feels secure knowing the weapon is there, cold and sharp next to her weeping breasts.

She steps out of the house. The sky is a violent pink with clouds broken apart as though wild dogs have been tearing them. A brash wind teases her ears, bits of paper rise up in swirls from grassy gutters at the side of the road and as she passes under the hog-plum tree next to the standpipe, the leaves shake noisily. By the time she reaches the bus stop in Oistins, a strange coldness has come over her, increased by the dampness slowly spreading across the front of her dress, where her nipples touch the fabric of the tight brassiere that locks her heavy breasts in place.

She squeezes into a bus and is pushed by other impatient passengers behind her into its cramped hot belly, finally coming to rest squashed against the back of an old man standing over a little boy no more than ten years old who is coughing and crying. The man smells of manure and burnt cane. She tries not to breathe. As the bus pulls away, she sees rain sprinkling trees and wishes someone would open the window to let the rain in.

She curses each time the bus stops along the route. A stalled truck near Hastings delays them for fifteen minutes, and Cyan comes close to tears. A woman standing inches away looks at her in bewilderment. They exchange glances, but Cyan's acid stare turns hers back to the newspaper she'd been reading.

She steps off the bus before it comes to a halt by the Garrison Savannah and does not stop running until she reaches Koko's house. Except for a hummingbird plunging its arrowed beak with dizzying speed again and again into the center of a Pride of Barbados, everything is quiet around the house.

She knocks impatiently. After a few seconds she raps again, bruising her knuckles. No response. She curses and knocks as hard as she can. Finally, Koko appears at the door in a silk Chinese robe.

Without a word Cyan pushes past her and runs to the bedroom where Amanda sleeps. Koko stares after her. She is still frozen at the door with a dazed look when Cyan comes back screaming.

"Where my baby?"

Koko stands silent, mesmerized by the wild, desperate look in Cyan's eyes. Every time she moves, her locks fly about her face like angry snakes coming to life.

"Come and sit down, Cyan," Koko finally says as calmly as she can.

"I ain't come here to sit down. You think I come here to sit down? I come for my baby. Where the rass my baby is?"

She raises her arms above her head emphatically as she speaks. Koko looks up, following the gesture as if expecting to see Cyan pluck her baby out of thin air by the force of her will.

"The baby isn't here, Cyan. She's not even in the country. She's gone."

Koko's mouth feels dirty. She wishes she didn't have to say those words to Cyan, and she wishes also that she'd had a chance to brush her teeth and drink a cup of coffee or to wash out her mouth with some warm water at least. Late-night drinking has left the taste of rum. She wants to spit. Her head aches, and she feels dull and slow.

"What you mean she ain't in the country?"

"What I mean, Cyan, is that the baby is gone. Amanda left the island yesterday with the baby."

"I don't believe you. Them here somewhere. She say she was going stay another month."

"She changed her mind. I guess she sensed that you would come looking for the baby. I tried to get her to stay, but she refused."

"You lie!"

"Why would I lie to you?"

"'Cause she's you friend. She's American like you."

The sour taste in her mouth and the fire in Cyan's eyes is beginning to make Koko's temples throb faster.

"You made a decision, now you're just going to have to live with it, Cyan. I'm sorry, but that's the way it is. You'll be able to have more children. It's not the end of the world. Now, come on, let's sit down. I'll make some coffee and we'll talk. Everything'll be all right."

She reaches out to touch Cyan. A soothing gesture, a gesture that she thinks possesses the power to wipe away the troubled look on her friend's face. But to Cyan it is an attack, an assault that says her pain doesn't matter.

The billfish beak leaps from her bosom, light and brittle as a dry leaf in her hand.

She stabs Koko five times. Then she drops the weapon, and runs from the house in tears. All the way home.

She falls asleep on the floor, with the door staring wide open.

Around five in the afternoon she wakes to cut some roses. Then she sits in the window to wait for the arrival of the fireflies at six-thirty.

The police come and take her away. She is charged with murder.

Night-calm, wind stirs, sifting ashes of earlier conversations, lifting dust off past utterances, turning history on its head. The cell is gray, dark, the lighting dull. She is standing outside of herself, looking at herself. She can see nothing. A voice, Breeze's voice from far away whispers to her: *When a man don't have nothing else, when he can't have what he want, he still want his pride. You think you perfect? Nobody perfect, not even you.*

She sees her mother and wonders why she has come. The urge to scream, to tell Obe to go away, soon passes. And then she feels an almost-celestial ecstasy at seeing her mother, as if somewhere deep in her soul she always knew Obe would come to visit her in a place like this.

She does not remember what her mother says. She knows only that they hold each other and pray and cry.

The night folds itself into a ball over the jail and goes to sleep.